Lecture Notes in Computer Science   8949

Commenced Publication in 1973
Founding and Former Series Editors:
Gerhard Goos, Juris Hartmanis, and Jan van Leeuwen

More information about this series at http://www.springer.com/series/7410

Jooyoung Lee · Jongsung Kim (Eds.)

Information Security and Cryptology – ICISC 2014

17th International Conference
Seoul, Korea, December 3–5, 2014
Revised Selected Papers

 Springer

Editors
Jooyoung Lee
Sejong University
Seoul
Korea

Jongsung Kim
Kookmin University
Seoul
Korea

ISSN 0302-9743   ISSN 1611-3349 (electronic)
Lecture Notes in Computer Science
ISBN 978-3-319-15942-3   ISBN 978-3-319-15943-0 (eBook)
DOI 10.1007/978-3-319-15943-0

Library of Congress Control Number: 2015933494

LNCS Sublibrary: SL4 – Security and Cryptology

Springer Cham Heidelberg New York Dordrecht London

Printed on acid-free paper

Springer International Publishing AG Switzerland is part of Springer Science+Business Media
(www.springer.com)

Preface

ICISC 2014, the 17th International Conference on Information Security and Cryptology, was held in Seoul, Korea, during December 3–5, 2014. This year the conference was hosted by the KIISC (Korea Institute of Information Security and Cryptology) jointly with the NSRI (National Security Research Institute).

The aim of this conference is to provide the international forum with the latest results of research, development, and applications in the field of information security and cryptology. The conference received 91 submissions from more than 20 countries and were able to accept 26 papers from 11 countries, with an acceptance rate of 28.6%. The review and selection processes were carried out by the Program Committee (PC) members, 79 prominent experts worldwide. First, each paper was blind reviewed by at least three PC members. Second, to resolve conflicts in the reviewer's decisions, the individual review reports were open to all PC members, and detailed interactive discussions on each paper ensued. For the LNCS post-proceedings, the authors of selected papers had a few weeks to prepare their final versions based on the comments received from the reviewers. We also recommended that authors should revise their papers based on the comments and recommendations they might receive from attendees upon their presentations at the conference.

We would like to thank all authors who have submitted their papers to ICISC 2014 and all PC members. It was a truly nice experience to work with such talented and hardworking researchers. We also appreciate the external reviewers for assisting the PC members in their particular areas of expertise. Finally, we would like to thank all attendees for their active participation and the organizing members who nicely managed this conference. We look forward to see you again in ICISC 2015.

December 2014

Jooyoung Lee
Jongsung Kim

Organization

General Chairs

Heekuck Oh   Hanyang University, Korea
Kwang Ho Kim   National Security Research Institute, Korea

Organizing Committee

Chair

Young-Ho Park   Sejong Cyber University, Korea

Committee Members

Heuisu Ryu   Gyeongin National University of Education, Korea
Junbeom Hur   Chung-Ang University, Korea
Daesung Kwon   National Security Research Institute, Korea
Dooho Choi   Electronics and Telecommunications Research
                   Institute, Korea
Jin-Soo Lim   Korea Information Security Agency, Korea
Howon Kim   Pusan National University, Korea
Okyeon Yi   Kookmin University, Korea
Soonhak Kwon   Sungkyunkwan University, Korea
Hyobeom Ahn   Kongju National University, Korea

Program Committee

Co-chairs

Jooyoung Lee   Sejong University, Korea
Jongsung Kim   Kookmin University, Korea

Committee Members

Joonsang Baek   Khalifa University, United Arab Emirates
Yoo-Jin Baek   Woosuk University, Korea
Andrey Bogdanov   Technical University of Denmark, Denmark
Zhenfu Cao   Shanghai Jiao Tong University, China
Yongwha Chung   Korea University, Korea
Paolo D'Arco   Università degli Studi di Salerno, Italy
Rafael Dowsley   Karlsruhe Institute of Technology, Germany

Johann Großschädl	University of Luxembourg, Luxembourg
Dong-Guk Han	Kookmin University, Korea
Martin Hell	Lund University, Sweden
Swee-Huay Heng	Multimedia University, Malaysia
Jiankun Hu	University of New South Wales Canberra, Australia
Jung Yeon Hwang	Electronics and Telecommunications Research Institute, Korea
Eul Gyu Im	Hanyang University, Korea
David Jao	University of Waterloo, Canada
Dong Kyue Kim	Hanyang University, Korea
Howon Kim	Pusan National University, Korea
Huy Kang Kim	Korea University, Korea
Jihye Kim	Kookmin University, Korea
So Jeong Kim	The Attached Institute of ETRI, Korea
Shinsaku Kiyomoto	KDDI R&D Laboratories, Japan
Jin Kwak	Soonchunhyang University, Korea
Taekyoung Kwon	Yonsei University, Korea
Hyang-Sook Lee	Ewha Womans University, Korea
Jonghyup Lee	Korea National University of Transportation, Korea
Moon Sung Lee	Seoul National University, Korea
Mun-Kyu Lee	Inha University, Korea
Pil Joong Lee	Pohang University of Science and Technology, Korea
Dongdai Lin	Institute of Information Engineering, Chinese Academy of Sciences, China
Hua-Yi Lin	China University of Technology, Taiwan
Sjouke Mauw	University of Luxembourg, Luxembourg
Florian Mendel	Graz University of Technology, Austria
Atsuko Miyaji	Japan Advanced Institute of Science and Technology, Japan
Yutaka Miyake	KDDI R&D Laboratories, Japan
Aziz Mohaisen	Verisign Labs, USA
DaeHun Nyang	Inha University, Korea
Heekuck Oh	Hanyang University, Korea
Katsuyuki Okeya	Hitachi, Japan
Rolf Oppliger	eSECURITY Technologies, Switzerland
Raphael C.-W. Phan	Multimedia University, Malaysia
Christian Rechberger	DTU Matematik, Denmark
Bimal Roy	Indian Statistical Institute, India
Kouichi Sakurai	Kyushu University, Japan
Nitesh Saxena	University of Alabama at Birmingham, USA
Dongkyoo Shin	Sejong University, Korea
Sang-Uk Shin	Pukyong National University, Korea
Rainer Steinwandt	Florida Atlantic University, USA

Hung-Min Sun	National Tsing Hua University, Taiwan
Willy Susilo	University of Wollongong, Australia
Tsuyoshi Takagi	Kyushu University, Japan
Jorge Villar	Universitat Politècnica de Catalunya, Spain
Hongxia Wang	Southwest Jiaotong University, China
Yongzhuang Wei	Guilin University of Electronic Technology, China
Wenling Wu	Institute of Software, Chinese Academy of Sciences, China
Toshihiro Yamauchi	Okayama University, Japan
Wei-Chuen Yau	Multimedia University, Malaysia
Ching-Hung Yeh	Far East University, Taiwan
Sung-Ming Yen	National Central University, Taiwan
Kazuki Yoneyama	Nippon Telegraph and Telephone Corporation, Japan
Myungkeun Yoon	Kookmin University, Korea
Dae Hyun Yum	Myongji University, Korea
Aaram Yun	Ulsan National Institute of Science and Technology, Korea
Fangguo Zhang	Sun Yat-sen University, China
Changhoon Lee	Seoul National University of Science and Technology, Korea
Taeshik Shon	Ajou University, Korea
Sang-Soo Yeo	Mokwon University, Korea
Jiqiang Lu	Institute for Infocomm Research (I2R), Singapore
Hongjun Wu	Nanyang University, Singapore
Elena Andreeva	Katholieke Universiteit Leuven, Belgium
Lejla Batina	Radboud University Nijmegen, The Netherlands
Donghoon Chang	IIIT-Delhi, India
Mridul Nandi	Indian Statistical Institute, India
Souradyuti Paul	University of Waterloo, Canada and IIT-Gandhinagar, India
Hyung Tae Lee	Nanyang Technological University, Singapore
Blazy Olivier	Ruhr University Bochum, Germany
Seokhie Hong	Korea University, Korea
Marion Videau	Université de Lorraine, France

Contents

Cryptographic Protocol

Side-Channel Attacks

RSA Security

General Bounds for Small Inverse Problems and Its Applications to Multi-Prime RSA

Atsushi Takayasu$^{(\boxtimes)}$ and Noboru Kunihiro

The University of Tokyo, Tokyo, Japan
a-takayasu@it.k.u-tokyo.ac.jp, kunihiro@k.u-tokyo.ac.jp

Abstract. In 1999, Boneh and Durfee introduced *small inverse problems* which solve bivariate modular equations $x(N + y) \equiv 1 \pmod{e}$. Sizes of solutions for x, y are bounded by $X = N^\delta$ and $Y = N^\beta$, respectively. They solved the problems for $\beta = 1/2$ in the context of small secret exponents attacks on RSA. They proposed a polynomial time algorithm which works when $\delta < (7 - 2\sqrt{7})/6 \approx 0.284$, and further improved a bound to $\delta < 1 - 1/\sqrt{2} \approx 0.292$. So far, small inverse problems for arbitrary β have also been considered. Generalizations of Boneh and Durfee's lattices to achieve the stronger bound provide the bound $\delta < 1 - \sqrt{\beta}$. However, the algorithm works only when $\beta \geq 1/4$. When $0 < \beta < 1/4$, there have been several works which claimed the best bounds. In this paper, we revisit the problems for arbitrary β. At first, we summarize the previous results for $0 < \beta < 1/4$. We reveal that there are some results which are not valid and show that Weger's algorithm provide the best bounds. Next, we propose an improved algorithm to solve the problem for $0 < \beta < 1/4$. Our algorithm works when $\delta < 1 - 2(\sqrt{\beta(3 + 4\beta)} - \beta)/3$. Our algorithm construction is based on the combinations of Boneh and Durfee's two forms of lattices. This construction is more natural compared with previous works. In addition, we introduce an application of our result, small secret exponent attacks on Multi-Prime RSA with small primes differences.

Keywords: LLL algorithm · Coppersmith's method · Small inverse problems · Cryptanalysis · Multi-Prime RSA

1 Introduction

1.1 Background

Small Inverse Problems. At Eurocrypt 1999, Boneh and Durfee [6] introduced *small inverse problems* (SIP). Given two distinct large integers N, e, find $\tilde{x}, \tilde{y}$ such that $\tilde{x}$ is an inverse of $N + \tilde{y} \mod e$. Sizes of $\tilde{x}, \tilde{y}$ are small and bounded by $X := N^\delta$ and $Y := N^\beta$, respectively. We can solve the problem by solving modular equations,

$$x(N + y) \equiv 1 \pmod{e},$$

whose solutions are $(x, y) = (\tilde{x}, \tilde{y})$. In this paper, we call the problem (δ, β)-SIP.

© Springer International Publishing Switzerland 2015
J. Lee and J. Kim (Eds.): ICISC 2014, LNCS 8949, pp. 3–17, 2015.
DOI: 10.1007/978-3-319-15943-0_1

One of the typical cryptographic applications of SIP is small secret exponent attacks on RSA. Recall RSA key generation $ed \equiv 1 \pmod{\phi(N)}$ where $\phi(N) = (p-1)(q-1) = N - (p+q) + 1$. We can rewrite the equation, $ed + \ell(N - (p+q) + 1) = 1$ with some integer $\ell < N^\delta$. If we can solve $(\delta, 1/2)$-SIP $x(N+y) \equiv 1 \pmod{e}$ whose solutions are $(x, y) = (\ell, -(p+q)+1)$, we can factor RSA moduli N. When public exponents e are full size, a size of a secret exponent d are $\approx \ell < N^\delta$. Boneh and Durfee [6] proposed lattice-based polynomial time algorithms to solve $(\delta, 1/2)$-SIP. At fist, they proposed an algorithm which works when $\delta < (7 - 2\sqrt{7})/6 = 0.28474\cdots$. This results improve the previous bound $\delta < 1/4 = 0.25$ proposed by Wiener [31]. In addition, Boneh and Durfee further improved the bound to $\delta < 1 - 1/\sqrt{2} = 0.29289\cdots$ in the same work. They extracted sublattices from the previous lattices which provide the weaker bound and achieved the improvement. However, the analysis to compute the determinant of the lattice to obtain the stronger bound is involved since the basis matrix is not triangular.

Boneh and Durfee [6] claimed that their bound may not be optimal. They considered the bound should be improved to $\delta < 1/2$. However, though several papers [4,14,20] have followed the work, no results which improved Boneh and Durfee's bound have been reported. At CaLC 2001, Blömer and May [4] considered different lattice constructions to solve $(\delta, 1/2)$-SIP. Their algorithm works when $\delta < (\sqrt{6} - 1)/5 = 0.28989\cdots$. Though the bound is inferior to Boneh and Durfee's stronger bound, superior to the weaker bound. In addition, dimensions of Blömer and May's lattices are smaller than that of Boneh and Durfee's lattices. However, the analysis to compute the determinant of the lattice is also involved since the basis matrix is not triangular.

At PKC 2010, Herrmann and May [14] revisited Boneh and Durfee's algorithms [6]. They used unravelled linearization [13] and analyzed the determinant of the lattice to obtain the stronger bound. They used linearization $z = -1 + xy$ and transform the basis matrices of the lattices which are not triangular to be triangular. The proof is very simple compared with Boneh and Durfee's original proof [6]. At SAC 2011, Kunihiro, Shinohara and Izu [20] followed the work. They used unravelled linearization and gave the simpler proof for Blömer and May's algorithm [4].

General Bounds for Small Inverse Problems. SIP is an important problem in the context of cryptanalysis of RSA and has analyzed in many papers. Several variants of the problem have been considered, small secret exponent attacks on variants of RSA [11,17,23], partial key exposure attacks [1,5,12,26,29], multiple small secret exponent attacks [2,28] and more. To analyze the problem in detail, generalizations of SIP [18,19] have also been considered. One of the well considered generalizations is (δ, β)-SIP for arbitrary $0 < \beta < 1$, not only $\beta = 1/2$. For the attack, generalizations of lattices for $(\delta, 1/2)$-SIP [4,6] have been analyzed.

Weger [30] studied small secret exponent attacks on RSA when a difference of prime factors is small, that is, $|p - q| < N^\gamma$ with $\gamma \leq 1/2$. In this case, they revealed that RSA moduli can be factored when we solve $(\delta, 2\gamma - 1/2)$-SIP. They extended Boneh and Durfee's lattice constructions and construct algorithms to solve (δ, β)-SIP for arbitrary β. Their algorithms solve (δ, β)-SIP when

$$\delta < 1 - \sqrt{\beta} \quad \text{for } \frac{1}{4} \leq \beta < 1, \tag{1}$$

$$\delta < 1 - \frac{1}{3}\left(2\sqrt{\beta(\beta+3)} - \beta\right). \tag{2}$$

The first and the second bound can be obtained by lattice constructions to achieve Boneh and Durfee's stronger bound and weaker bound, respectively. We also note that Weger [30] extends Wiener's algorithm [31] for the attack. The algorithm works when

$$\delta < \frac{3}{4} - \beta. \tag{3}$$

Though the bound (1) is the best among the three bounds, the algorithm works only when $1/4 \leq \beta < 1$. The bound (2) is better when $0 < \beta < 1/8$ and the bound (3) is better when $1/8 \leq \beta < 1/4$.

Sarkar et al. [27] studied small secret exponent attacks on RSA when attackers know the most significant bits of a prime factor p. They solved (δ, β)-SIP for arbitrary β for the attack. In addition to Weger's results [30], Sarkar et al. extended Blömer and May's lattice constructions. Their algorithm solves (δ, β)-SIP when

$$\delta < \frac{2}{5}\left(\sqrt{4\beta^2 - \beta + 1} - 3\beta + 1\right). \tag{4}$$

The bound is superior to Weger's bound (2) and (3) when $3/35 \leq \beta < 1/4$.

Not just generalizations of lattices for $(\delta, 1/2)$-SIP [4,6], Kunihiro Shinohara and Izu [20] considered a broader class of lattices. To solve (δ, β)-SIP for arbitrary β, Kunihiro et al. analyzed hybrid lattice constructions which include Boneh and Durfee's lattices to achieve the stronger bound [6,30] and Blömer and May's lattices [4,27]. To be precise, Kunihiro et al. considered a broader class of lattices and previous two lattices [27,30] are special cases of the class. Therefore, there may be chances to improve the previous results by making use of the structures of two lattices, simultaneously. However, their result becomes the same as Weger's bound (1) for $1/4 \leq \beta < 1$ and Sarkar et al.'s bound (4) for $0 < \beta < 1/4$.

Small Secret Exponent Attacks on Multi-Prime RSA with Small Prime Differences. Multi-Prime RSA is a variant of RSA whose public modulus $N = \prod_{j=1}^{k} p_j$ are product of k distinct primes $p_1, p_2, \ldots, p_k$. Bit length of all prime factors are the same. Key generations of Multi-Prime RSA are the same as the standard RSA, $ed = 1 \pmod{\phi(N)}$ where $\phi(N) = \prod_{j=1}^{k}(p_j - 1)$.

Multi-Prime RSA becomes efficient for its low cost decryption for larger k. Since the main computation costs are modular exponentiations with $\log N/k$ bits moduli when we use Chinese Remaindering. In addition, most algebraic attacks become less efficient for larger k such as small secret exponent attacks [6,31] and partial key exposure attacks [5,12,29]. As the standard RSA, Multi-Prime RSA becomes insecure when extremely small secret exponents $d < N^\delta$ are used. Ciet et al. [7] extends Wiener's [31] and Boneh and Durfee's attacks [6]. Extensions of Wiener's attacks work when $\delta < 1/2k$. To extend Boneh and Durfee's attacks, they solved $(\delta, 1 - 1/k)$-SIP. The algorithms work when $\delta < 1 - \sqrt{1 - 1/k}$. Both bounds become the same as the previous results [6,31] for $k = 2$.

Recently, Zhang and Takagi [32] analyzed small secret exponent attacks on Multi-Prime RSA with small prime difference[1]. Assume $p_1 > p_2 > \cdots > p_k$ without loss of generality. Zhang and Takagi analyzed the case when $|p_1 - p_k| < N^\gamma, 0 < \gamma \le 1/k$. They revealed that Multi-Prime RSA becomes insecure when we can solve $(\delta, 1 + \gamma - 2/k)$-SIP. After that the same authors [33] gave an improved analysis. Multi-Prime RSA becomes insecure when we can solve $(\delta, 1 + 2\gamma - 3/k)$-SIP. When $\gamma = 1/k$, the results [32,33] becomes the same as that of Ciet et al.'s results [7] which solves $(\delta, 1 - 1/k)$-SIP. In addition, the improved result [33] becomes the same as Weger [30] which solves $(\delta, 2\gamma - 1/2)$-SIP for $k = 2$. To solve the SIP, Zhang and Takagi constructed algorithms which achieves only (1) and (3), though (2) and (4) are better for small $\beta = 1 + 2\gamma - 3/k < 1/4$.

1.2   Our Contributions

In this paper, we study (δ, β)-SIP for arbitrary β. At first, we summarize previous lattice constructions [4,6,20,27,30] to achieve the bound (1) to (4). We reveal that a generalization of Blömer and May's lattices to achieve the bound (4) is not valid for $\beta < 1/4$. Therefore, though Sarkar et al. [27] and Kunihiro et al. [20] claimed that the bound (4) is the best when $3/35 < \beta < 1/4$, the results are incorrect. Among previous results, Weger's bound (2) and (3) is the best for $0 < \beta \le 1/8$ and $1/8 < \beta < 1/4$, respectively.

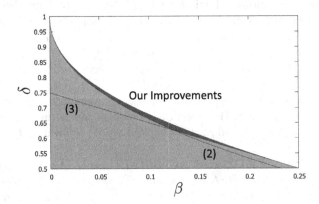

Fig. 1. The comparison of the recoverable sizes of δ for $0 \le \beta \le 1/4$.

Next, we show our improved lattice constructions to solve (δ, β)-SIP for arbitrary β. We consider a broader class of lattices which include Weger's three

---

[1] See also Bahig et al.'s work [3]. They extends Weger's attacks which are based on Wiener's work [31]. The attacks work when $\delta < 1/k - \gamma/2$.

lattices to obtain (1), (2) and (3) [30] for special cases. Therefore, there may be chances to improve the previous results by making use of the structures of previous lattices, simultaneously. When $1/4 \leq \beta < 1$, our lattice provides the same bound as (1). When $0 < \beta < 1/4$, our algorithm works when

$$\delta < 1 - \frac{2}{3}\left(\sqrt{\beta(3+4\beta)} - \beta\right). \tag{5}$$

The bound is superior to the previous bounds. That means our lattice constructions make better use of algebraic structures than previous analysis to solve (δ, β)-SIP [30]. As several previous works [14,20,33], we analyze determinant of lattices using unravelled linearization. Therefore, the proof is rather simple.

Figure 1 compares recoverable sizes of δ for our algorithm and previous ones [27,30] to solve (δ, β)-SIP for $0 \leq \beta \leq 1/4$. When $\beta = 1/4$ and $\beta = 0$, our bound becomes the same as Weger's result $\delta < 0.5$ and $\delta < 1$, respectively. However, our algorithm is better than the two results for $0 < \beta < 1/4$.

As an application of our algorithm, we analyze small secret exponent attacks on Multi-Prime RSA with small prime differences. It is clear that we can improve previous result since our algorithm to solve (δ, β)-SIP is better than that was used in [33].

1.3 Organizations

In Sect. 2, we introduce lattice-based Coppersmith's method to solve modular equations [8,15]. In Sect. 3, we define (δ, β)-SIP and recall previous lattice constructions to solve SIP. In Sect. 4, we propose our lattice constructions to solve SIP for arbitrary β. In Sect. 5, we analyze small secret exponent attacks on Multi-Prime RSA with small prime differences.

2 Preliminaries

In this section, we briefly explain the Coppersmith's method to solve modular equations [8]. We introduce a simpler modification of the method by Howgrave-Graham [15].

2.1 The LLL Algorithm

Given m-dimensional n vectors $\mathbf{b}_1, \ldots, \mathbf{b}_n \in \mathbb{R}^m$, a lattice spanned by the basis vectors are defined as integer linear combinations of the vectors,

$$L(\mathbf{b}_1, \ldots, \mathbf{b}_n) := \{\sum_{j=1}^{n} c_j \mathbf{b}_j | \ c_j \in \mathbb{Z} \text{ for all } j = 1, 2, \ldots, n\}.$$

Matrix representations of bases are also used. Basis matrices of lattices are defined as $n \times m$ matrices each of whose rows are the basis vector $\mathbf{b}_1, \ldots, \mathbf{b}_n$. Lattices spanned by basis matrices B are denoted as $L(B)$. The values n, m

represent a rank and a dimension of a lattice, respectively. When $n = m$, we call lattices full-rank. Parallelpiped of a lattice is defined as $\mathcal{P}(B) := \{\mathbf{c}B : \mathbf{c} \in \mathbb{R}^n, 0 < c_j \leq 1 \text{ for all } j = 1, 2, \ldots, n\}$. The determinant of a lattice $\det(L(B))$ is defined as the n-dimensional volume of the parallelpiped. In general, the determinant can be calculated as $\det(L(B)) = \sqrt{\det(BB^T)}$ where B^T represents the transpose of B. For full-rank lattices, we can compute the determinant as $\det(L(B)) = |\det(B)|$.

Lattices are used in many ways in the context of cryptanalysis. See [9,10, 24,25] for detailed information. One of the cryptanalytic applications which uses lattices is the Coppersmith's method to solve modular equations [8]. To use the method, finding short lattice vectors is essential. In this paper, we introduce the celebrated LLL algorithm [21] as other previous works. In 1982, Lenstra, Lenstra and Lovász proposed a lattice reduction algorithm which finds short lattice vectors in polynomial time.

Proposition 1 (LLL algorithm [21]). *Given m-dimensional basis vectors* $\mathbf{b}_1, \ldots, \mathbf{b}_n$*, the LLL algorithm finds short lattice vectors* $\mathbf{b}'_1, \mathbf{b}'_2$ *that satisfy*

$$\|\mathbf{b}'_1\| \leq 2^{(n-1)/4}(\det(L(B)))^{1/n}, \|\mathbf{b}'_2\| \leq 2^{n/2}(\det(L(B)))^{1/(n-1)},$$

in polynomial time in input length and n, m*.*

2.2 Howgrave-Graham's Lemma

To solve modular equations $h(x, y) = 0 \mod e$ is difficult for the existence of moduli e. Howgrave-Graham [15] revealed that we can find polynomials $h'_1(x, y)$, $h'_2(x, y)$ which have the same roots as $h(x, y) \pmod{e}$ over the integers. For bivariate polynomials $h(x, y) := \sum h_{i,j} x^i y^j$, we define norm of polynomials as $\|h(x, y)\| := \sqrt{\sum h_{i,j}^2}$. Howgrave-Graham showed following lemma which implies the norm of polynomials $h'_1(x, y), h'_2(x, y)$ should be low.

Lemma 1 (Howgrave-Graham's Lemma [15]). *Given integers* X, Y, t*, if a polynomial* $h'(x, y)$ *which has at most n monomials satisfies following two conditions,*

1. $h'(\tilde{x}, \tilde{y}) = 0 \pmod{e^t}$ *where* $|\tilde{x}| < X, |\tilde{y}| < Y$*,*
2. $\|h'(x, y)\| < e^t/\sqrt{n}$*,*

then $h'(\tilde{x}, \tilde{y}) = 0$ *holds over the integers.*

To solve a modular equation $h(x, y) = 0 \pmod{e}$, we can find such low norm polynomials $h'_1(x, y), h'_2(x, y)$ by using the LLL algorithm. We construct a basis matrix B where each basis vector $\mathbf{b}_1, \ldots, \mathbf{b}_n$ consists of a coefficients of a polynomial $h_1(xX, yY), h_2(xX, yY), \ldots, h_n(xX, yY)$. If polynomials $h_1(x, y), h_2(x, y), \ldots, h_n(x, y)$ modulo e^t have roots which are the same as the original solutions of $h(x, y) = 0 \pmod{e}$, all polynomials modulo e^t whose coefficients corresponds to lattice vectors in $L(B)$ have the same roots. Since these polynomials are integer linear combinations of $h_1(x, y), h_2(x, y), \ldots, h_n(x, y)$. Therefore, we can find low norm polynomials $h_1'(x, y), h_2'(x, y)$ whose roots e^t are the same as the original solutions by using the LLL algorithm. If the polynomials $h_1'(x, y), h_2'(x, y)$ satisfy the Howgrave-Graham's Lemma, we can find the roots by finding the roots of the polynomials over the integers. The operation is easy by computing Gröbner bases or resultant of $h_1'(x, y), h_2'(x, y)$. In this paper, we focus on the lattice constructions to solve modular equations as previous works [4,6,14,27].

3   Previous Lattice Constructions to Solve SIP

In this section, we formally define (δ, β)-SIP and summarize previous lattice constructions [4,6,14,20,27,30] to solve the problem.

Definition 1 ($((\delta, \beta)$-SIP). Given distinct integers N, e with the same bit size and real numbers $\delta, \beta \in (0, 1)$, SIP is to find integers $\tilde{x}, \tilde{y}$ which satisfy $|\tilde{x}| < N^\delta, |\tilde{y}| < N^\beta$ and

$$x(N + y) \equiv 1 \pmod{e}.$$

In the rest of the paper, we write upper bounds of the sizes of solutions $\tilde{x}$ and $\tilde{y}$ as $X := N^\delta$ and $Y := N^\beta$, respectively. Though we only consider the case when two integers N, e are the same bit sizes, it is easy to extend to more general cases.

Boneh and Durfee's Lattice I. We introduce Boneh and Durfee's lattices [6] to achieve the weaker bound $\delta < (7 - 2\sqrt{7})/6$ and its generalization by Weger [30] to obtain the bound (2). To solve the modular equation

$$f(x, y) = -1 + x(N + y) = 0 \pmod{e},$$

Boneh and Durfee [6] used two forms of shift-polynomials,

$$g_{[i,u]}^x(x, y) := x^{i-u} f(x, y)^u e^{t-u},$$

$$g_{[u,j]}^y(x, y) := y^j f(x, y)^u e^{t-u}.$$

Each polynomial $g_{[i,u]}^x(x, y)$ and $g_{[u,j]}^y(x, y)$ is called x-shifts and y-shifts, respectively. When all indices i, u, j are non-negative integers, both shifts modulo e^t have roots $(\tilde{x}, \tilde{y})$, that is, $g_{[i,u]}^x(\tilde{x}, \tilde{y}) = 0 \pmod{e^t}$ and $g_{[u,j]}^y(\tilde{x}, \tilde{y}) = 0 \pmod{e^t}$. We select $g_{[i,u]}^x(x, y), g_{[u,j]}^y(x, y)$ and construct a basis matrix B. Note that the selection of shift-polynomials is essential to maximize the solvable root bounds X and Y.

Boneh and Durfee [6] constructed an algorithm which solves $(\delta, 1/2)$-SIP when $\delta < (7 - 2\sqrt{7})/6$. Weger [30] generalize the lattice construction and constructed an algorithm which solves (δ, β)-SIP when the condition (2), $\delta < \frac{1}{3}(\beta + 3 - 2\sqrt{\beta(\beta + 3)})$ holds. We call the lattices Boneh and Durfee's Lattice I.

Boneh and Durfee defined sets of indices,

$$\mathcal{S}_x^{BDI} := \{(i, u)|i = 0, 1, \dots, t, u = 0, 1, \dots, i\},$$

$$\mathcal{S}_y^{BDI} := \{(u, j)|u = 0, 1, \dots, t, j = 1, 2, \dots, \lfloor \eta t \rfloor\},$$

with a parameter $\eta \geq 0$. They selected shift-polynomials $g^x_{[i,u]}(x,y)$ with indices in $\mathcal{S}^{BDI}_x$ and $g^y_{[u,j]}(x,y)$ with indices in $\mathcal{S}^{BDI}_y$. The selections generate triangular basis matrices with diagonals $X^i Y^u e^{t-u}$ for $g^x_{[i,u]}(x,y)$ and $X^u Y^{u+j} e^{t-u}$ for $g^y_{[u,j]}(x,y)$. Ignoring low order terms of t, we can compute the dimension $n = (\frac{1}{2} + \eta)t^2$ and the determinant of the lattices $\det(B) = X^{(\frac{1}{3}+\frac{\eta}{2})t^3} Y^{(\frac{1}{6}+\frac{\eta(1+\eta)}{2})t^3} e^{(\frac{1}{3}+\frac{\eta}{2})t^3}$. The conditions for SIP to be solved $(\det(B))^{1/n} < e^t$ becomes

$$\delta \left(\frac{1}{3} + \frac{\eta}{2} \right) + \beta \left(\frac{1}{6} + \frac{\eta(1+\eta)}{2} \right) + \left(\frac{1}{3} + \frac{\eta}{2} \right) < \frac{1}{2} + \eta,$$

$$\delta < \frac{1 - \beta + 3(1-\beta)\eta - 3\beta\eta^2}{2 + 3\eta}.$$

To maximize the right hand side of the inequality, we set the parameter $\eta = \left(-2\beta + \sqrt{\beta(\beta+3)} \right)/3\beta$ and the condition becomes

$$\delta < \frac{1}{3} \left(\beta + 3 - 2\sqrt{\beta(\beta+3)} \right).$$

Boneh and Durfee's Lattice II. To improve the bound, Boneh and Durfee [6] extracted sublattices from Boneh and Durfee's Lattice I and constructed an algorithm which solves $(\delta, 1/2)$-SIP when $\delta < 1 - 1/\sqrt{2}$. Weger [30] generalize the lattice constructions and constructed an algorithm which solves (δ, β)-SIP when $\delta < 1 - \sqrt{\beta}$. We call the improved lattices Boneh and Durfee's Lattice II.

Boneh and Durfee redefined sets of indices,

$$\mathcal{S}^{BDII}_x := \{(i,u)|i = 0,1,\ldots,t, u = 0,1,\ldots,i\},$$
$$\mathcal{S}^{BDII}_y := \{(u,j)|u = 0,1,\ldots,t, j = 1,2,\ldots,\lfloor \tau u \rfloor\},$$

with a parameter $0 \leq \tau \leq 1$. They selected shift-polynomials $g^x_{[i,u]}(x,y)$ with indices in $\mathcal{S}^{BDII}_x$ and $g^y_{[u,j]}(x,y)$ with indices in $\mathcal{S}^{BDII}_y$. Though the basis matrices generated by the polynomial selections are not triangular, Herrmann and May's analysis [14] revealed that the matrices can be transformed into triangular with linearization $z = -1+xy$. Applying the linearization appropriately and the basis matrices have diagonals $X^{i-u} Z^u e^{t-u}$ for $g^x_{[i,u]}(x,y)$ and $Z^u Y^j e^{t-u}$ for $g^y_{[u,j]}(x,y)$. See [14] for detailed analysis. Ignoring low order terms of t, we can compute the dimension $n = (\frac{1}{2} + \frac{\tau}{2})t^2$ and the determinant of the lattices $\det(B) = X^{\frac{1}{6}t^3} Y^{\frac{\tau^2}{6}t^3} Z^{(\frac{1}{6}+\frac{\tau}{3})t^3} e^{(\frac{1}{3}+\frac{\tau}{6})t^3}$. The conditions for SIP to be solved $(\det(B))^{1/n} < e^t$ becomes

$$\delta \cdot \frac{1}{6} + \beta \cdot \frac{\tau^2}{6} + (\delta + \beta) \left(\frac{1}{6} + \frac{\tau}{3} \right) + \left(\frac{1}{3} + \frac{\tau}{6} \right) < \frac{1}{2} + \frac{\tau}{2},$$

$$\delta < \frac{1 - \beta + 2(1-\beta)\tau - \beta\tau^2}{2 + 2\tau}.$$

To maximize the right hand side of the inequality, we set the parameter $\tau = \sqrt{1/\beta} - 1$ and the condition becomes

$$\delta < 1 - \sqrt{\beta}.$$

Though the bound is the best, the algorithm does not work for arbitrary $0 < \beta < 1$. Since the restriction of the parameter $\tau = \sqrt{1/\beta} - 1 \leq 1$, the algorithm works only when $\beta \geq 1/4$.

Wiener's Lattice. Weger [30] also considered the generalization of Wiener's algorithm [31] and obtain the bound (3).[2] The bound can be obtained by the special case of Boneh and Durfee's Lattice II. We fix the parameter $\tau = 1$ and obtain the bound

$$\delta < \frac{3}{4} - \beta.$$

We call the lattice Wiener's Lattice.

Blömer and May's Lattice. Blömer and May [4] extracted another sublattices from Boneh and Durfee's Lattice I and constructed an algorithm which solves $(\delta, 1/2)$-SIP when $\delta < (\sqrt{6} - 1)/5$. Sarkar et al. [27] generalize the lattice constructions and constructed an algorithm which solves (δ, β)-SIP when $\delta < \frac{2}{5}(\sqrt{4\beta^2 - \beta + 1} - 3\beta + 1)$. We call the improved lattices Blömer and May's Lattice.

Blömer and May defined sets of indices,

$$\mathcal{S}_x^{BM} := \{(i, u) | i = \lfloor(1-\mu)t\rfloor, \lfloor(1-\mu)t\rfloor + 1, \ldots, t, u = 0, 1, \ldots, i\},$$
$$\mathcal{S}_y^{BM} := \{(u, j) | u = \lfloor(1-\mu)t\rfloor, \lfloor(1-\mu)t\rfloor + 1, \ldots, t,$$
$$j = 1, 2, \ldots, \lfloor u - (1-\mu)t\rfloor\},$$

with a parameter $0 \leq \mu < 1$. As Boneh and Durfee's Lattices II, the basis matrices generated by the polynomial selections are not triangular. Following the work of Herrmann and May [14], Kunihiro et al. [20] used linearization $z = -1 + xy$ and transforms the basis matrices to be triangular. Applying the linearization appropriately and the basis matrices have diagonals $X^{i-u}Z^u e^{t-u}$ for $g_{[i,u]}^x(x, y)$ and $Z^u Y^j e^{t-u}$ for $g_{[u,j]}^y(x, y)$. See [20] for detailed analysis. Ignoring low order terms of t, we can compute the dimension $n = \mu t^2$ and the determinant of the lattices $\det(B) = X^{\frac{3\mu - 3\mu^2 + \mu^3}{6}t^3} Y^{\frac{\mu^3}{6}t^3} Z^{\frac{\mu}{2}t^3} e^{\frac{\mu}{2}t^3}$. The conditions for SIP to be solved $(\det(B))^{1/n} < e^t$ becomes

$$\delta \cdot \frac{3\mu - 3\mu^2 + \mu^3}{6} + \beta \cdot \frac{\mu^3}{6} + (\delta + \beta) \cdot \frac{\mu}{2} + \frac{\mu}{2} < \mu,$$
$$\delta < \frac{3 - 3\beta - \beta\mu^2}{6 - 3\mu + \mu^2}.$$

---

[2] In Boneh and Durfee's work [6], they obtain the Wiener's bound $\delta < 1/4$ for $(\delta, 1/2)$-SIP [31]. The bound can be obtained by the special case of Boneh and Durfee's Lattice II with the fixed parameter $\tau = 0$.

To maximize the right hand side of the inequality, we set the parameter $\mu = (1 + \beta - \sqrt{4\beta^2 - \beta + 1})/\beta$ and the condition becomes

$$\delta < \frac{2}{5}\left(\sqrt{4\beta^2 - \beta + 1} - 3\beta + 1\right).$$

Though Sarkar et al. [27] claimed the bound is the best when $3/35 \leq \beta < 1/4$ for (δ, β)-SIP, it is incorrect. Since the restriction of the parameter $\mu = (1 + \beta - \sqrt{4\beta^2 - \beta + 1})/\beta < 1$, the algorithm works only when $\beta > 1/4$.

Kunihiro et al.'s Lattice. Kunihiro et al. [20] considered a broader calss of lattices for (δ, β)-SIP. They defined set of indices,

$$\mathcal{S}_x^{KSI} := \{(i, u)|i = \lfloor(1-\mu)t\rfloor, \lfloor(1-\mu)t\rfloor + 1, \ldots, t, u = 0, 1, \ldots, i\},$$
$$\mathcal{S}_y^{KSI} := \{(u, j)|u = \lfloor(1-\mu)t\rfloor, \lfloor(1-\mu)t\rfloor + 1, \ldots, t,$$
$$j = 1, 2, \ldots, \lfloor\tau(u - (1-\mu)t)\rfloor\},$$

with two parameters $0 \leq \tau \leq 1, 0 \leq \mu < 1$. The sets are hybrid sets with Boneh and Durfee's Lattices II and Blömer and May's Lattice for special cases. We set the parameter $\tau = 1$ and the sets $\mathcal{S}_x^{KSI}, \mathcal{S}_y^{KSI}$ become the same as the sets $\mathcal{S}_x^{BDII}, \mathcal{S}_y^{BDII}$. We set the parameter $\mu = 1$ and the sets $\mathcal{S}_x^{KSI}, \mathcal{S}_y^{KSI}$ become the same as the sets $\mathcal{S}_x^{BM}, \mathcal{S}_y^{BM}$.

As Boneh and Durfee's Lattices II and Blömer and May's Lattice, the basis matrices generated by the polynomial selections are not triangular. Kunihiro et al. [20] used linearization $z = -1 + xy$ and transforms the basis matrices to be triangular. Applying the linearization appropriately and the basis matrices have diagonals $X^{i-u}Z^u e^{t-u}$ for $g_{[i,u]}^x(x, y)$ and $Z^u Y^j e^{t-u}$ for $g_{[u,j]}^y(x, y)$. See [20] for detailed analysis. Ignoring low order terms of t, we can compute the dimension $n = \frac{(2\mu - \mu^2) + \mu^2\tau}{2}t^2$ and the determinant of the lattices $\det(B) = X^{\frac{3\mu - 3\mu^2 + \mu^3}{6}t^3}Y^{\frac{\mu^3\tau^2}{6}t^3}Z^{\frac{(3\mu - 3\mu^2 + \mu^3) + (3\mu^2 - \mu^3)\tau}{6}t^3}e^{\frac{(3\mu - \mu^3) + \mu^3\tau}{6}t^3}$. The conditions for SIP to be solved $(\det(B))^{1/n} < e^t$ becomes

$$\delta \cdot \frac{3\mu - 3\mu^2 + \mu^3}{6} + \beta \cdot \frac{\mu^3\tau^2}{6} + (\delta + \beta) \cdot \frac{(3\mu - 3\mu^2 + \mu^3) + (3\mu^2 - \mu^3)\tau}{6}$$
$$+ \frac{(3\mu - \mu^3) + \mu^3\tau}{6} < \frac{(2\mu - \mu^2) + \mu^2\tau}{2},$$

$$\delta < \frac{(1 - \beta)((3 - 3\mu + \mu^2) + (3\mu - \mu^2)\tau) - \beta\mu^2\tau^2}{2(3 - 3\mu + \mu^2) + (3\mu - \mu^2)\tau}.$$

When $1/4 \leq \beta$, we set the parameter $\mu = 1, \tau = \sqrt{1/\beta} - 1$, and obtain the bound $\delta < 1 - \sqrt{\beta}$ which is the same as Boneh and Durfee's lattice II.

4   New Lattice Constructions to Solve SIP

In this section, we propose a improved algorithm to solve (δ, β)-SIP for arbitrary β.

Theorem 1. *We can solve* (δ, β)*-SIP when*

$$\delta < 1 - \sqrt{\beta} \quad for \;\; 1/4 \leq \beta < 1,$$

$$\delta < 1 - \frac{2}{3} \left(\sqrt{(3 + 4\beta)\beta} - \beta \right) \quad for \;\; 0 < \beta < \frac{1}{4},$$

in polynomial time.

We consider a broader class of lattices which contains Boneh and Durfee's Lattice I, II, and Wiener's Lattice for special cases. The three lattices provide the best results among previous results [20, 27, 30]. Though each lattice is constructed in ad-hoc manner for sizes of β in previous works, we consider the general case regardless of β. When $0 < \beta < 1/4$, we make use of the property of Boneh and Durfee's Lattice I and II, simultaneously and obtain the improved results.

To solve SIP, we define sets of indices

$$S_x := \{(i, u) | i = 0, 1, \ldots, t, u = 0, 1, \ldots, i\},$$

$$S_y := \{(u, j) | u = 0, 1, \ldots, t, j = 1, 2, \ldots, \lfloor \eta t + \tau u \rfloor\},$$

with two parameters $\eta \geq 0, 0 \leq \tau \leq 1$. The sets are hybrid sets with Boneh and Durfee's Lattices I, II, and Wiener's Lattice for special cases. We set the parameter $\tau = 0$ and the sets S_x, S_y become the same as the sets S_x^{BDI}, S_y^{BDI}. We set the parameter $\eta = 0$ and the sets S_x, S_y become the same as the sets S_x^{BDII}, S_y^{BDII}. Since Wiener's Lattice is the special case of Boneh and Durfee's Lattice II, it is the special case of our lattice.

Our selections of polynomials generate basis matrices which are not triangular. However, as Herrmann and May's analysis, we use linearization $z = -1 + xy$ and the matrices can be transformed into triangular with diagonals $X^{i-u} Z^u e^{t-u}$ for $g_{[i,u]}^x(x, y)$ and $Z^u Y^j e^{t-u}$ for $g_{[u,j]}^y(x, y)$. Ignoring low order terms of t, we compute the dimension

$$n = \sum_{i=0}^{t} \sum_{u=0}^{i} 1 + \sum_{u=0}^{t} \sum_{j=1}^{\lfloor \eta t + \tau u \rfloor} 1 = \left(\frac{1}{2} + \eta + \frac{\tau}{2} \right) t^2,$$

and the determinant of the lattices $\det(B) = X^{s_X} Y^{s_Y} Z^{s_Z} e^{s_e}$ where

$$s_X + s_Z = \sum_{i=0}^{t} \sum_{u=0}^{i} i + \sum_{u=0}^{t} \sum_{j=1}^{\lfloor \eta t + \tau u \rfloor} u = \left(\frac{1}{3} + \frac{\eta}{2} + \frac{\tau}{3} \right) t^3,$$

$$s_Y + s_Z = \sum_{i=0}^{t} \sum_{u=0}^{i} u + \sum_{u=0}^{t} \sum_{j=1}^{\lfloor \eta t + \tau u \rfloor} (u + j) = \left(\frac{1}{6} + \frac{\eta}{2} + \frac{\tau}{3} + \frac{\eta^2}{2} + \frac{\tau \eta}{2} + \frac{\tau^2}{6} \right) t^3,$$

$$s_e = \sum_{i=0}^{t} \sum_{u=0}^{i} (m - u) + \sum_{u=0}^{t} \sum_{j=1}^{\lfloor \eta t + \tau u \rfloor} (t - u) = \left(\frac{1}{3} + \frac{\eta}{2} + \frac{\tau}{6} \right) t^3.$$

We can solve SIP when $(\det(B))^{1/n} < e^t$, that is,

$$\delta < \frac{1 - \beta + 3(1 - \beta)\eta + 2(1 - \beta)\tau - 3\beta\eta^2 - 3\beta\tau\eta - \beta\tau^2}{2 + 3\eta + 2\tau}.$$

When $1/4 \le \beta$, we set the parameter $\eta = 0, \tau = \sqrt{1/\beta} - 1$, and obtain the bound

$$\delta < 1 - \sqrt{\beta}$$

which is the same as Boneh and Durfee's lattice II.

When $0 < \beta < 1/4 < 1$, we set the parameter

$$\eta = \frac{-4\beta + \sqrt{\beta(3 + 4\beta)}}{3\beta}, \tau = 1,$$

and obtain the bound

$$\delta < 1 - \frac{2}{3}\left(\sqrt{(3 + 4\beta)\beta} - \beta\right).$$

This bound is the best among all known results [20,27,30] when $0 < \beta < 1/4$.

5   On the Security of Multi-Prime RSA

In this section, we consider the security of Multi-Prime RSA when differences of whose prime factors of Multi-Prime RSA moduli are small. We write Multi-Prime RSA moduli $N = p_1 p_2 \cdots p_k$ and assume $p_1 > p_2 > \cdots > p_k$, $|p_1 - p_k| < N^\gamma$. We write $p'_j = N/p_j$ and

$$\Delta_k = \sum_{j=1}^{k} p'_j - k\left(\prod_{j=1}^{k} p'_j\right)^{1/k}.$$

Note that $k\left(\prod_{j=1}^{k} p'_j\right)^{1/k} = kN^{(k-1)/k}$.

In [32,33], Zhang and Takagi analyzed the security. They revealed that Multi-Prime RSA becomes insecure if we can solve a (δ, β)-SIP.

Lemma 2 (Adapted from Proposition 1 and Theorem 2 of [32]). *Let* $N = p_1 p_2 \cdots p_k$ *with* $p_1 > p_2 > \cdots > p_k$ *be Multi-Prime RSA modulus. All prime factors of* N *are the same bit size and* $p_1 - p_k < N^\gamma$, $0 < \gamma < 1/k$. *Let* e *be a full size public exponent whose corresponding secret exponent* d *is smaller than* N^δ. *Let* $\Delta_k = \sum_{j=1}^{k} p'_j - k\left(\prod_{j=1}^{k} p'_j\right)^{1/k}$ *is smaller than* N^β. *If we can solve* (δ, β)-SIP, *we can factor Multi-Prime RSA modulus* N.

For the attack, to bound the size of β is crucial. Zhang and Takagi [33] proved the following Lemma.[3]

---

[3] In Zhang and Takagi's analysis [33], they do not calculate the factor $2(k-1)$. They bounded $0 < \Delta_k < poly(k) \cdot N^{1+2\gamma-3/k}$ and claimed that $poly(k)$ is too small compared with $N^{1+2\gamma-3/k}$. We give an alternative proof for Lemma 2 and obtain the factor. See the full version of the paper for detailed analysis.

Lemma 3 (Adapted from Proposition 1 of [33]). *Let composite integers* $N = p_1 p_2 \cdots p_k$ *and* Δ_k *as defined in Lemma 2, then*

$$0 < \Delta_k < 2(k-1) \cdot N^{1+2\gamma-3/k}.$$

Since we proposed an improved algorithm for (δ, β)-SIP, we can improve the result for cryptanalysis of Multi-Prime RSA. Combining Lemma 2, Lemma 3 and Theorem 1, we obtain the following result.

Theorem 2. *Let Multi-Prime RSA moduli* N, *public/secret exponent* e, d *as Lemma 2. We can factor Multi-Prime RSA moduli* N *when*

$$\delta < 1 - \sqrt{1 + 2\gamma - 3/k} \quad for \quad \frac{3}{2}\left(\frac{1}{k} - \frac{1}{4}\right) \le \gamma < \frac{1}{k},$$

$$\delta < 1 - \frac{2}{3}\left(\sqrt{(7 + 8\gamma - 12/k)(1 + 2\gamma - 3/k)} - 1 - 2\gamma + 3/k\right)$$

$$for \ 0 < \gamma < \frac{3}{2}\left(\frac{1}{k} - \frac{1}{4}\right).$$

6   Conclusion

In this paper, we studied (δ, β)-SIP for arbitrary β which relates to a security of Multi-Prime RSA. Unlike the results of $(\delta, 1/2)$-SIP [4,6,14], the results for general (δ, β)-SIP are not widely known. It is true that Zhang and Takagi [32,33] reconstruct the algorithm to solve the problem and did not refer some previous works. Therefore, one of the contributions of the paper was to summarize the previous results [4,6,14,20,27,30]. In addition, we revealed that the bound (4) proposed by previous works [20,27] is not valid.

The main contribution of the paper was to provide the improved lattice construction for (δ, β)-SIP for arbitrary β. Our lattice covers broader class and previous results [30] which provides the best bounds among previous works are special cases of our lattice. The lattice make better use of the algebraic structures of modular polynomials and we achieved the improvement.

Based on the improvement, we also showed the improved analysis for the security of Multi-Prime RSA. Our result revealed that Multi-Prime RSA is vulnerable than expected when differences of prime factors are small.

References

1. Aono, Y.: A new lattice construction for partial key exposure attack for RSA. In: Jarecki, S., Tsudik, G. (eds.) PKC 2009. LNCS, vol. 5443, pp. 34–53. Springer, Heidelberg (2009)
2. Aono, Y.: Minkowski sum based lattice construction for multivariate simultaneous coppersmith's technique and applications to RSA. In: Boyd, C., Simpson, L. (eds.) ACISP. LNCS, vol. 7959, pp. 88–103. Springer, Heidelberg (2013)

3. Bahig, H.M., Bhery, A., Nassr, D.I.: Cryptanalysis of multi-prime RSA with small prime difference. In: Chim, T.W., Yuen, T.H. (eds.) ICICS 2012. LNCS, vol. 7618, pp. 33–44. Springer, Heidelberg (2012)

4. Blömer, J., May, A.: Low secret exponent RSA revisited. In: Silverman, J.H. (ed.) CaLC 2001. LNCS, vol. 2146, pp. 4–19. Springer, Heidelberg (2001)

5. Blömer, J., May, A.: New partial key exposure attacks on RSA. In: Boneh, D. (ed.) CRYPTO 2003. LNCS, vol. 2729, pp. 27–43. Springer, Heidelberg (2003)

6. Boneh, D., Durfee, G.: Cryptanalysis of RSA with private key d less than $N^{0.292}$. IEEE Trans. Inf. Theory **46**(4), 1339–1349 (2000)

7. Ciet, M., Koeune, F., Laguillaumie, F., Quisquater, J.-J.: Short private exponent attacks on fast variants of RSA. UCL Crypto Group Technical Report Series CG-2002/4, University Catholique de Louvain (2002)

8. Coppersmith, D.: Finding a small root of a univariate modular equation. In: Maurer, U.M. (ed.) EUROCRYPT 1996. LNCS, vol. 1070, pp. 155–165. Springer, Heidelberg (1996)

9. Coppersmith, D.: Small solutions to polynomial equations, and low exponent RSA vulnerabilities. J. Cryptology **10**(4), 233–260 (1997)

10. Coppersmith, D.: Finding small solutions to small degree polynomials. In: Silverman, J.H. (ed.) CaLC 2001. LNCS, vol. 2146, pp. 20–31. Springer, Heidelberg (2001)

11. Durfee, G., Nguyên, P.Q.: Cryptanalysis of the RSA schemes with short secret exponent from asiacrypt '99. In: Okamoto, T. (ed.) ASIACRYPT 2000. LNCS, vol. 1976, pp. 14–29. Springer, Heidelberg (2000)

12. Ernst, M., Jochemsz, E., May, A., de Weger, B.: Partial key exposure attacks on RSA up to full size exponents. In: Cramer, R. (ed.) EUROCRYPT 2005. LNCS, vol. 3494, pp. 371–386. Springer, Heidelberg (2005)

13. Herrmann, M., May, A.: Attacking power generators using unravelled linearization: when do we output too much? In: Matsui, M. (ed.) ASIACRYPT 2009. LNCS, vol. 5912, pp. 487–504. Springer, Heidelberg (2009)

14. Herrmann, M., May, A.: Maximizing small root bounds by linearization and applications to small secret exponent RSA. In: Nguyen, P.Q., Pointcheval, D. (eds.) PKC 2010. LNCS, vol. 6056, pp. 53–69. Springer, Heidelberg (2010)

15. Howgrave-Graham, N.: Finding small roots of univariate modular equations revisited. In: Darnell, Michael J. (ed.) Cryptography and Coding 1997. LNCS, vol. 1355, pp. 131–142. Springer, Heidelberg (1997)

16. Itoh, K., Kunihiro, N., Kurosawa, K.: Small secret key attack on a variant of RSA (due to Takagi). In: Malkin, T. (ed.) CT-RSA 2008. LNCS, vol. 4964, pp. 387–406. Springer, Heidelberg (2008). See also [17]

17. Itoh, K., Kunihiro, N., Kurosawa, K.: Small secret key attack on a Takagi's variant of RSA. IEICE Trans. Fundam. Electron. Commun. Comput. Sci. **E92–A**(1), 33–41 (2008)

18. Kunihiro, N.: Solving generalized small inverse problems. In: Steinfeld, R., Hawkes, P. (eds.) ACISP 2010. LNCS, vol. 6168, pp. 248–263. Springer, Heidelberg (2010)

19. Kunihiro, N.: On Optimal bounds of small inverse problems and approximate gcd problems with higher degree. In: Gollmann, D., Freiling, F.C. (eds.) ISC 2012. LNCS, vol. 7483, pp. 55–69. Springer, Heidelberg (2012)

20. Kunihiro, N., Shinohara, N., Izu, T.: A unified framework for small secret exponent attack on RSA. In: Miri, A., Vaudenay, S. (eds.) SAC 2011. LNCS, vol. 7118, pp. 260–277. Springer, Heidelberg (2012)

21. Lenstra, A.K., Lenstra Jr., H.W., Lovász, L.: Factoring polynomials with rational coefficients. Mathematische Annalen **261**, 515–534 (1982)

22. May, A.: New RSA Vulnerabilities Using Lattice Reduction Methods. Ph.D. thesis, University of Paderborn (2003)
23. May, A.: Secret exponent attacks on RSA-type schemes with moduli $N = p^r q$. In: Bao, F., Deng, R., Zhou, J. (eds.) PKC 2004. LNCS, vol. 2947, pp. 218–230. Springer, Heidelberg (2004)
24. May, A.: Using LLL-reduction for solving RSA and factorization problems: a survey (2010). http://www.cits.rub.de/permonen/may.html
25. Nguyên, P.Q., Stern, J.: The two faces of lattices in cryptology. In: Silverman, J.H. (ed.) CaLC 2001. LNCS, vol. 2146, p. 146. Springer, Heidelberg (2001)
26. Sarkar, S., Sen Gupta, S., Maitra, S.: Partial key exposure attack on RSA – improvements for limited lattice dimensions. In: Gong, G., Gupta, K.C. (eds.) INDOCRYPT 2010. LNCS, vol. 6498, pp. 2–16. Springer, Heidelberg (2010)
27. Sarkar, S., Maitra, S., Sarkar, S.: RSA Cryptanalysis with Increased Bounds on the Secret Exponent using Less Lattice Dimension. IACR ePrint Archieve: Report 2008/315 (2008)
28. Takayasu, A., Kunihiro, N.: Cryptanalysis of RSA with multiple small secret exponents. In: Susilo, W., Mu, Y. (eds.) ACISP 2014. LNCS, vol. 8544, pp. 176–191. Springer, Heidelberg (2014)
29. Takayasu, A., Kunihiro, N.: Partial key exposure attacks on RSA: achieving the boneh-durfee bound. In: Joux, A., Youssef, A. (eds.) SAC 2014. LNCS, vol. 8781, pp. 345–362. Springer, Heidelberg (2014)
30. de Weger, B.: Cryptanalysis of RSA with small prime difference, applicable algebra in engineering. Commun. Comput. 13, 17–28 (2002)
31. Wiener, M.J.: Cryptanalysis of short RSA secret exponents. IEEE Trans. Inf. Theory 36(3), 553–558 (1990)
32. Zhang, H., Takagi, T.: Attacks on multi-prime RSA with small prime difference. In: Boyd, C., Simpson, L. (eds.) ACISP. LNCS, vol. 7959, pp. 41–56. Springer, Heidelberg (2013)
33. Zhang, H., Takagi, T.: Improved attacks on multi-prime RSA with small prime difference. IEICE Trans. E97−A(7), 1533–1541 (2014)

On the Security of Distributed Multiprime RSA

Ivan Damgård[1], Gert Læssøe Mikkelsen[2]([✉]), and Tue Skeltved[3]

[1] Department of Computer Science, Aarhus University, Aarhus, Denmark
[2] The Alexandra Institute, Aarhus, Denmark
gert.l.mikkelsen@alexandra.dk
[3] Signaturgruppen A/S, Aarhus, Denmark

Abstract. Threshold RSA encryption and signing is a very useful tool to increase the security of the secret keys used. Key generation is, however, either done in a non-threshold way, or computationally inefficient protocols are used. This is not a big problem in a setup where one organization has a few high profile keys to secure, however, this does not scale well to systems with a lot of secret keys, like eID schemes where there exist one key pair per user, especially not if the we want the users' personal devices like smart phones to participate in the threshold setup. In this paper we present novel approaches to distributed RSA key generation which are efficient enough to let smart phones participate. This is done by generating keys consisting of more than two primes instead of generating standard RSA keys.

We present a 2-party protocol based on the ideas of [BH98] which produces a 3-prime modulo. We demonstrate that the protocol is efficient enough to be used in practical scenarios even from a mobile device which has not been demonstrated before. Then we show the first 2-party distributed multiprime RSA key generation protocol that are as efficient as standard centralized key generation, even if security against malicious adversaries is desired. Further, we show that RSA keys based on moduli with more than two prime factors and where part of the factorization is leaked to the adversary are useful in practice by showing that commonly used schemes such as PSS-RSA and OAEP-RSA is secure even if the adversary knows a partial factorization of the multiprime moduli. From all other parties the generated keys cannot be distinguished from standard RSA keys, which is very important as this make these protocols compatible with existing infrastructure and standards.

1 Introduction

Despite the introduction of elliptic curve cryptography and more recently lattice based cryptography, RSA remains one of the the most used public-key schemes. A very large number of e-commerce and net-banking transactions are protected using RSA. In many applications, a user's secret key resides on his own machine,

---

Gert Læssøe Mikkelsen—Supported by the Danish Council of technology and Innovation.

© Springer International Publishing Switzerland 2015
J. Lee and J. Kim (Eds.): ICISC 2014, LNCS 8949, pp. 18–33, 2015.
DOI: 10.1007/978-3-319-15943-0_2

and due to the fact that the security on private PC's is often very poor, keys as well as passwords can be stolen. It is well known that in net-banking, for instance, this has lead to a significant loss of of money.

Countermeasures proposed against this include using extra, special-purpose hardware which is often expensive, or storing secret keys on a central server while implementing some form of conventional access control to the secret keys. While a central server may certainly have better security, this also creates a single point of attack.

One approach that can lead to better solutions is to do *threshold RSA*, i.e., we split the secret key in two or more shares stored in different entities such that signing or decryption requires participation of at least some number of share-holders. The adversary now must break into more than one entity to steal the key. Whether this actually improves security in a real application depends, of course, on the implementation, but the threshold approach certainly creates new possibilities for designing a secure system. For instance, if the design involves a handheld mobile device, it may not be necessary to use a special-purpose high-security device if it will not be storing the entire key. A mobile phone, for instance, may be sufficient.

Threshold RSA is a well studied problem from a theoretical perspective, see for instance [GRJK07,DK01]. In this paper, we focus on the case of two share-holders. For concreteness the reader may think of a mobile device holding one share while the other is held by a server, run by the user himself, or by some organization. This case was studied in [DM09] where a formal model was given for a more realistic scenario where the human user is explicitly modeled as a player. This allows us to take passwords and login credentials into account when proving security. In [DM09] a protocol was given that is secure if the adversary can, at any one time, only corrupt the mobile or the server, but not both. However, this work, like most work on threshold RSA, does not directly consider the problem of generating keys in a distributed fashion, but assumes that shares of the key have been distributed by a trusted party.

To avoid a single point of failure, it is of course desirable to implement the trusted party using a secure protocol executed by the share-holders. Design of such a distributed key generation protocol has been studied in a long line of research. The first reasonably efficient solution to this problem is due to Boneh and Franklin [BF97,BF01]. Except for the work by Algesheimer et al. [ACS02] (which has prohibitively large round complexity), all other works (e.g. [BH98, FMY98,Gil99,DM10,HMRT12]) in this area are more or less variations of the original ideas from [BF97]. In short the idea is to generate a candidate RSA modulus $N = pq$, where p and q are random numbers that are additively shared among the players. They then execute a *distributed biprimality* test to check whether N is the product of two primes. This can be done efficiently because the players have shares of p and q. If N is indeed the product of two primes, then it is output, otherwise the protocol is restarted.

The main problem with this approach is that a candidate N can only be used if both p and q happen to be prime at the same time. This means that the expected number of attempts needed is quadratic in k, were k is the desired length of the modulus, whereas standard centralized key generation is linear in k. This makes the distributed protocol several orders of magnitude slower than standard key generation for realistic values of k.

It was noted already in [BF97] that one can avoid this quadratic slowdown if one is willing to have RSA moduli with several prime factors and leak part of the factorization to the adversary. In particular, [BH98] presents a 3-party protocol secure against one corrupted player that generates a modulus with 3 prime factors. This protocol only requires that the parties have to find and generate a single additive shared prime, but on the other hand the adversary may learn one of the primes of the final modulus.

It is not clear that using such a key in practice is secure. For instance, if the adversary sees public key (N, e) and ciphertext $c = x^e \bmod N$, he can compute a large amount of partial information about x. Say he knows one prime factor p, then he can compute $c^{e^{-1} \bmod (p-1)} \bmod p = x \bmod p$. To the best of our knowledge there has been no previous study of security of RSA based schemes in this scenario, which is perhaps the reason why this idea for key generation has received very little attention so far. In this article we demonstrate that such keys are in fact secure when used with appropriate padding schemes such as PSS-RSA and OAEP-RSA, which are the most widely used padding schemes, and which are an essential part of a secure scheme based on RSA.

1.1   Our Contributions

In this paper, we study the use of multiprime RSA moduli in distributed key generation and for encryption and signatures where the adversary may know part of the factorization. More precisely he may learn (or even get to choose) all but 2 of the prime factors. We concentrate on the 2-party case as this in many cases are a more realistic setup e.g., consiting of a user using a mobile device and a larger organization operating the server side. The 2-party case means that for a malicious adversary, we can only get security with abort: if one player stops prematurely, we cannot complete the protocol.

Our contributions are two-fold; We present two new 2-party distributed RSA key generation protocols and show that multiprime RSA keys used in combination with PSS-RSA or OAEP-RSA is secure even if the adversary knows part of the factorization. It is important to note, that this generalizes to all such keys, not just the ones produced by the protocols presented in this article.

The Protocols. We introduce two 2-party protocols. One is based on ideas from [BH98] which is a 3-party protocol secure against one corrupted player, where two parties generate a prime each locally (say p and q), whereas a random candidate number t is generated in secret-shared form. The players then compute $N = pqt$ securely and do a distributed test to check if N is the product of 3 primes. Since [BH98] assume honest majority, the secure computation needed could be done efficiently based on secret sharing. Here, we adapt the protocol to the two-party case using a homomorphic cryptosystem for two-party distributed computations and we also adapt the primality tests from [BH98] to the 2-party scenario. In our particular implementation the Paillier cryptosystem [Pai99] is used and we demonstrate that this 2-party protocol is efficient enough to be useful even from mobile devices - a result that has not been demonstrated before. As in [BH98], we obtain passive security.

We then introduce a new approach where on the one hand we generate a larger modulus than before, namely with 4 prime factors, but on the other hand the protocol is much more efficient and can easily be made actively secure. The idea is to simply let each party do a normal RSA key generation locally where the only condition is that they agree on the public exponent e. They then exchange the public keys $(N_1, e), (N_2, e)$ and the final public key is $(N_1 N_2, e)$. It follows from the Chinese remainder theorem that the parties can use their locally generated secret exponents to do distributed signing or decryption. This can be made actively secure with very little overhead as long as we enforce that each player must know the factorization of his number, see more details within. It takes only seconds to generate a secure 2048-bit modulus, and thus only seconds to complete the protocol. Note that this system is very easy to build from existing RSA soft- or hardware, since standard key generation and encryption/decryption operations is essentially all that is required. Note also that any two (or even more) users who have the same public exponent can combine their keys in this way, even if they did not anticipate this at key generation time. This is the first 2-party protocol for multiprime RSA key generation that achieves active security while being as efficient as standard RSA key generation.

It is important to understand that this idea is very different from the trivial approach to "threshold" RSA signatures where we just let each shareholder sign with his own key. This would force parties who use or certify the public key to be aware that a certain person is actually "composed" of several entities, thus making practical implementation much more cumbersome. In our approach, we maintain that the public key is simply a standard RSA key (albeit with a longer modulus) and the fact that the key is shared is transparent to other users.

Security of PSS-RSA and OAEP-RSA in the Multiprime Setup. In practice RSA is never used without a secure padding scheme, such as PSS-RSA for signatures or OAEP-RSA for encryption. As show by Bleichenbacher's attack [Ble98] on the PCKS#1 v1.5 standard, provable security of RSA in combination with the padding scheme is very important. We show that both the PSS-RSA and OAEP-RSA padding schemes used with a multi-prime RSA key remain secure even if the adversary knows all but two of the prime factors, and therefore cannot completely factor the modulus but can extract some partial information of the preimage. The security level then corresponds to the security of the RSA modulus formed by the two unknown primes. We can therefore conclude that the keys output by the two key generation protocols presented in this article and similar protocols are indeed useful in application scenarios used today.

2   Preliminaries

Below in Assumption 1 we follow the standard definition of the security of "plain" RSA, by assuming that no efficient algorithm can invert the RSA function without knowledge of the private key.

Definition 1. *Let the algorithm $\mathcal{A}_{RSA}$ be specified as: Given $\{N, e, y\}$ s.t. N is the product of two k-bit primes, $gcd(\varphi(N), e) = 1$, and $y \in \mathbb{Z}_N$, then $\mathcal{A}_{RSA}$ outputs x s.t. $y \equiv x^e \pmod{N}$.*

Assumption 1 (Hardness of RSA). *We assume that no probabilistic polynomial Turing machine (PPT) exists that implements $\mathcal{A}_{RSA}$ for random input, with nonnegligible success rate.*

We now specify an adversary for breaking multiprime RSA (M-RSA), the RSA problem with a modulus consisting of more than two primes, where the adversary have chosen all but two of the prime factors of the modulus. This adversary actually consists of two algorithms, one for generating α the part of the M-RSA modulus known to the adversary and one inverting the RSA function using this modulus. We will see in Lemma 1 that the hardness of RSA implies hardness of M-RSA.

Definition 2. *Let algorithm $\mathcal{A}_{M\text{-}RSA\text{-}Gen}$ be specified as: Given N s.t. N is the product of two k-bit primes, then $\mathcal{A}_{M\text{-}RSA\text{-}Gen}$ outputs $\{\alpha, M, \varphi(\alpha), state\}$, where α is an arbitrary k-bit positive integer, $M = N\alpha$, and state is an arbitrary string.*

Let $\mathcal{A}_{M\text{-}RSA}$ be an algorithm taking as input $\{M, e, y, state\}$ s.t. M and state is the output of $\mathcal{A}_{M\text{-}RSA\text{-}Gen}$, $gcd(\varphi(M), e) = 1$ and $y \in \mathbb{Z}_M$. The output of $\mathcal{A}_{M\text{-}RSA}$ is x s.t. $y \equiv x^e \pmod{M}$.

3   Protocol for Two Players with a Three-Prime Modulus

In this section we present a two-party protocol generating a three-prime RSA modulus. To enable distributed computations between two players the Paillier Cryptosystem [Pai99] is used. The protocol is designed and optimized to run between a mobile device and a server and in particular only the server has to generate a Paillier key pair. The protocol is based on the ideas from [BH98].

To test whether a modulus N is well formed, the parties need an additive sharing of the following two numbers: $\Phi(N) = (p-1)(q-1)(r-1)$ and $\Psi(N) = (p+1)(q+1)(r+1)$, where $N = pqr$, p and q are primes chosen by the two parties respectively and r is a number that is additively shared between them as $r = r_1 + r_2$. The tests ensure that if a N is output, then r is prime except with negligible probability.

In the following, E_k, D_k denotes the Paillier encryption/decryption function with modulus k. Recall that the Paillier scheme uses computation modulo k^2 for the ciphertexts, and is additively homomorphic modulo k. This modulus must be large enough to accommodate without overflow the product of two primes plus room for some added randomness. In the following we denote the two parties S and M for server and mobile device. The Paillier keys are generated by S. We first give a short overview of the main steps in the protocol:

3.1 Protocol Steps

1. **Generate possible candidate N.** The parties jointly generates the public RSA moduli $N = p \cdot q \cdot (r_1 + r_2)$, using primes p, q and random integers r_1, r_2 as input.

2. **Fermat test.** By utilizing Fermat's little theorem, the two parties test if $g^{\phi_a + \phi_b} = 1 \pmod{N}$, for a random element $g \in_R Z_N^*$. Here $\Phi(N) = \phi_a + \phi_b$ denotes the additive shares of $\Phi(N)$ generated by the two parties during the previous step.

3. **Twisted group Fermat test.** The parties perform a Fermat test in the Twisted group T_N, picking a random element $g \in_R T_N$, and testing if $g^{\psi_a + \psi_b} = 1 \pmod{N}$. Here $\Psi(N) = \psi_a + \psi_b$ denotes the additive shares of $\Psi(N)$ generated by the two parties during the first protocol step. For more details on the Twisted Group, see [DMS14].

4. **Check that $N = p^a q^b r^c$, for three distinct primes p, q and r.**

5. **Zero knowledge test that $gcd(N, p + q) = 1$.**

6. **Generate the private key distributed as additive shares.**

3.2 The Protocol

We now give a more detailed account of the first part of the protocol:

i. S generates a random $(n-1)$-bit integer r_2 and sends the encryption $E_k(r_2)$ to M.

ii. M generates a random n-bit prime p, where $p \equiv 3 \pmod{4}$ and a random $(n-1)$-bit integer r_1 and sends $E_k(r \cdot p) = (E_k(r_2) \cdot E_k(r_1))^p \mod k^2$ to S. Note that the randomness in $E_k(r_2)$ will ensure that $E_k(r \cdot p)$ is a random encryption containing $r \cdot p$.

iii. S decrypts $r \cdot p$, optionally runs a trial division test on $r \cdot p$ using small primes and generates a random n-bit prime q, where $q \equiv 3 \pmod{4}$. If the division test fails then S aborts.

iv. $N = r \cdot p \cdot q$ is sent back to M.

The two parties now have a candidate N. To test if N can be used, they need additive shares of $\Phi(N)$ and $\Psi(N)$. As $\Phi(N) = (p-1)(q-1)(r_1 + r_2 - 1)$ they can exploit the fact that:

$$\Phi(N) = N - pr - qr - pq + p + q + r - 1$$

Here we note that $N = p \cdot q \cdot (r_1 + r_2)$, so M has $qr = N/p$ and S has $pr = N/q$. They just need an additive share of pq in order to have all the additive components which they share as follows:

i. S sends $E_k(q)$ to M

ii. M then creates a blinded encryption of $p \cdot q$ by: $E_k(pq + t) = E_k(q)^p \cdot E_k(t) \pmod{k^2}$, where t is a random integer with a maximum bit-length such that $p \cdot q + t$ cannot overflow modulo k

iii. $E_k(pq + t)$ is sent to S

iv. M calculates $qr = N/p$ and then $\phi_a = t - 1 - qr + p + r_1$
v. S calculates $pr = N/q$ and then $\phi_b = N + (-1) \cdot (pq + t) - pr + q + r_2$

Now, $\Phi(N) = \phi_a + \phi_b$. And similar for the sharing of $\Psi(N)$

Due to space limitations, further details of the protocol for doing steps 2–6 above can be found in the full version of this work [DMS14], these steps follow the flow of [BH98], transfered to the two-party setting.

3.3 Passive Security of the Protocol

In the full version of this paper [DMS14], we show that the error probability of our primality tests are as good as the similar tests from [BH98] which implies that the desired probability of N being the product of three large primes can be achieved by repeating the primality tests a certain number of times. Thus correctness is ensured s.t. when the protocol is completed, the two parties have produced a modulus of three large primes except with negligible probability. In [DMS14] we prove that the protocol achieves passive security when the underlying homomorphic cryptosystem is secure.

4 Four-Prime Distributed RSA

This section introduces a new approach for generating a distributed RSA key between two parties constructing a public modulus with four prime factors formed as a product of standard RSA moduli. We use as subprotocol a protocol for proving knowledge of discrete logarithm modulo a composite, this protocol is due to Girault [Gir91] and is essentially the Schnorr protocol [Sch91] done modulo a composite. We note that this protocol can be made non-interactive and zero-knowledge in the random oracle model We denote this protocol the PK-CDL protocol (Proof of Knowledge of Composite DL) in the following.

Key Generation

1. The two parties S and M agree on a public exponent e. They then generate a standard RSA key pair each, denoted by $((N_S, e), (N_S, d_S))$ and $((N_M, e), (N_M, d_M))$, respectively.
2. They exchange the public keys, set $N = N_S N_M$ and the joint public key is defined to be (N, e). S and M store d_S and d_M as their shares of the secret key. N_S, N_M are stored for practical reasons, but are not considered secret.
3. S convinces M that (N_S, e) is well formed as follows:
    (a) M chooses a random $x \in Z_{N_S}^*$ and sends x and $y = x^e$ to S.
    (b) Using the PK-CDL protocol S proofs knowledge of d s.t., $x \equiv y^d \bmod N_S$.
4. The above step is repeated with the roles of M and S interchanged. If any proof fails, the parties abort, otherwise they output the key material defined above.

This idea clearly extends to more than two parties, of course at the expense of having a larger modulus. If only passive security is desired, the last two steps can be omitted. One applies the public key as usual by raising to power e modulo N. In a standard threshold RSA set-up, one would usually secret-share the private exponent additively, we present a protocol for this in [DMS14]. However, in our case it is easier to use the local private exponents that are available anyway. Therefore applying the secret key is done using Chinese remaindering as follows:

Distributed Decryption/Signing

1. On input $y \in Z_N$ to which the secret key should be applied, S and M compute $x_S = y^{d_S} \mod N_S$ respectively $x_M = y^{d_M} \mod N_M$ and exchange these values.
2. Both players use the Chinese Remainder Theorem to compute $x \in Z_N$ such that $x \mod N_S = x_S$, $x \mod N_M = x_M$. They check that $x^e \mod N = y$ and output x if this is the case. Otherwise, they abort.

4.1   Security of Four-Prime Distributed RSA

These protocols are secure for sequential composition, even if one parties are malicious. This is proven via a simulation proof and below we outline the functionality that we prove is implemented by the key generation protocol. We emphasize that we only claim security for sequential composition so that the simulator is allowed to rewind, however, using standard techniques the protocol can be made secure for general composition.

Key Generation Functionality

1. Receive public exponent e as input from the honest party (or parties).
2. If both parties are honest, generate all key material honestly and send it to the parties.
3. If S is corrupt, generate N_M honestly and send N_M, e to the adversary. Receive from the adversary either N_S and the prime factors $p_1, ..., p_t$ in N_S, where e is relatively prime to $\phi(N)$; or "abort". In the first case, output N_S, N_M, d_M to M. In the second case output "abort". If M is corrupt, do the same with S and M interchanged.

Theorem 1. *The* Key Generation Protocol *for* Four-prime Distributed RSA *securely realizes the* Key Generation Functionality *presented above, for sequential composition (allowing rewinding).*

Proof. We assume that S is corrupt. A simulator for the above key generation protocol would then receive N_M, e from the functionality and then execute the protocol with the corrupted S (the adversary). It can simulate M's part of the protocol using N_M, e by simulating the PK-CDL protocol, which is zero-knowledge. When the corrupt S executes the PK-CDL protocol to prove knowledge of d_S, the simulator extracts the witness d_S. If N_S, e was well formed, then the simulator with the knowledge of both e and d_S can easily factor N_S and input these factors to the functionality. In case N_S, e is malformed i.e., $gcd(e, \phi(N_S)) = \alpha \neq 1$, then no inverse d_S of e exists modulo $\phi(N_S)$. Therefore PK-CDL would fail, as the corrupt S cannot know d_S. In this case the simulator input "abort" to the functionality.

As for the protocol for distributed decryption/signing, we can think of it as being executed in a model where the key material has been generated by the functionality we just described. Therefore we know that e is relatively prime to $\phi(N)$ and hence there is a well defined decryption exponent d. First note that if both parties are honest, the result x always equals $y^d \bmod N$. This is because $x \bmod N_S = x_S = y^{d_S} \bmod N_S$ and hence $x^e \bmod N_S = y \bmod N_S$. Similarly we also see that $x^e \bmod N_M = y \bmod N_M$ and hence by the Chinese remainder theorem we have $x^e \bmod N = y$. If one party is corrupt the protocol trivially outputs the correct result or abort, and furthermore, if S is corrupt, it can simulate M's contribution when given the output $x = y^d \bmod N$, simply by computing $x \bmod N_M$.

4.2   Efficiency of Four-Prime Distributed RSA

We now consider the efficiency of this set-up compared to standard RSA with a 2-prime modulus. The Key Generation takes time equivalent to a local key generation plus the time needed for the PK-CDL protocols. The PK-CDL protocol takes time essentially equivalent to 1 exponentiation for both parties. In practice it will actually be less because we can choose e significantly smaller than n_S, and S can optimize her computations using Chinese Remaindering. Note also that the last two steps of the protocol (where S, resp. M plays the role of the prover) can be done in parallel. The local key generation requires a few exponentiations due to the primality tests needed. Therefore we can expect that the full key generation takes time about twice that of standard local key generation.

The time for applying the secret key is clearly equivalent to applying a secret key for a standard modulus, since this is exactly what both parties are doing. The time to apply the public key is larger than in the standard case because the public modulus is twice as long. However, this makes little difference in practice since first, we can use a value of e that is much smaller than the modulus ($e = 2^{16} + 1$ is a standard choice); and second if N_S and N_M are known (which would not hurt security) exponentiation modulo N can be done modulo N_S and N_M using Chinese Remaindering.

5   Implementation Results

In the three-prime protocol one prime has to be found by random trial-and-error computation and a distributed primality test. By the Prime Number Theorem (see [DMS14]) the number of rounds needed on average as well as execution time grow with the target modulus size. In this section we show implementational results from the three-prime protocol presented in this article demonstrating that the protocol is efficient enough to be useful even from a mobile device. Further it demonstrates that computing the needed number of random primes for this and similar protocols is a dominant factor in the overall processing time and thus provides a natural lower bound for this type of protocol.

The following two setups have been used to run the three-prime protocol between a smartphone and a laptop (server):

1. i-7 Q 820 4 x 1.73 GHz, 8 GB RAM and Samsung Galaxy s-II, 2 x 1.2 GHz
2. i7-4712HQ @ 2.3 GHz, 16 GB RAM and HTC ONE Quad-core 1.7 GHz

We present the average running time measured for the protocol to complete between the mobile device and the laptop to illustrate that the protocol is indeed efficient enough to be used in practical scenarios. Then we present results of the protocol being run entirely on the laptop to illustrate that the protocol will finish in just seconds if run between two desktop computers for a 2000 bit key. Further we present the running time of a single thread computing the expected number of random primes needed to complete the protocol. Note that the implementation utilizes all cores available on the devices, so the time needed to generate all the primes for a protocol round on a single thread takes about a quarter when running on a quad core device. Little data is sent between the parties (expected

Table 1. Results from the implementation of the three-prime protocol

Three-prime protocol between phone (no precomputation) and laptop			
Modulus size	Rounds$^\alpha$	First setup$^\beta$	Second setup$^\beta$
1000 bit	117	17 s	7.85 s
2000 bit	234	150 s	75 s
Laptop running both parties without precomputation			
Modulus size	Rounds$^\alpha$	Intel i-7 Q 820	Intel i7-4712HQ
1000 bit	117	3.7 s	1.57 s
2000 bit	234	34.4 s	13.84 s
Laptop running both parties with precomputation			
Modulus size	Rounds$^\alpha$	Intel i-7 Q 820	Intel i7-4712HQ
1000 bit	117	2.26 s	1 s
2000 bit	234	14.32 s	7.6 s
Single thread computational times for all primes, one protocol execution			
Modulus size	Intel i-7 Q 820	Samsung Galaxy SII 1,2Ghz	Intel i7-4712HQ
1000 bit	2.9 s	27 s	1.45 s
2000 bit	30.9 s	222 s	16.5 s

$^\alpha$Expected number of rounds.
$^\beta$Avg. time used on setup.

1 MB for the entire protocol for a 2000 bit key), and the protocol is thus very prone to optimizations using precomputation (computing a set of random primes before execution begins), crypto-hardware etc. We also present results demonstrating the effect of precomputing a large set of the random primes needed in each protocol round (Table 1).

Note that the Samsung smartphone uses 222 s to generate all the expected number of primes needed to complete the protocol for a 2000 bit key on a single thread. Running this on the two cores available on the Samsung device takes an expected 111 s to complete the prime number generation, which accounts of 74 % of the total average time for the protocol to complete. Also note that the time needed on the i7-4712HQ for the generation of a shared key will reduce the expected running time by a factor 2 if two similar computers are running as one of the parties each. The amount of data exchanged in each direction during execution of the three-prime protocol is on average less than 0,5 MB for the 1000 bit modulus and 1 MB for the 2000 bit modulus.

The four-prime protocol. In comparison to the three-prime protocol, the four-prime protocol presented in this article just needs all parties to agree on the public exponent and have each party generate a standard RSA key, which can be done in seconds (or less) - even on mobile devices.

6   Security of the M-RSA Trapdoor Permutation

In this section we will start taking a closer look at the security implications of utilizing multiprime RSA (M-RSA) moduli, generated by our protocols. First, in the lemma below, we look at the security of the general plain M-RSA function in the subsequent sections we analyze the security when M-RSA moduli are used in different specific protocols. It is important to note that the security of these protocols does not follow directly from the lemma below.

Lemma 1 (Security of Plain M-RSA). *Under Assumption 1 (Security of RSA) there does not exist a couple of PPT algorithms implementing $\mathcal{A}_{\text{M-RSA-Gen}}$ and $\mathcal{A}_{\text{M-RSA}}$ with nonnegligible probability of success.*

Proof. Assuming there exist two PPT's implementing $\mathcal{A}_{\text{M-RSA-Gen}}$ and $\mathcal{A}_{\text{M-RSA}}$, we can use these to implement $\mathcal{A}_{\text{RSA}}$ in the following way: Given a two-prime RSA public key $\langle e, N \rangle$ and y, run $\mathcal{A}_{\text{M-RSA-Gen}}$ to obtain α and $\varphi(\alpha)$. We assume $(\alpha, N) = 1$, otherwise factoring N is trivial, then we run $\mathcal{A}_{\text{M-RSA}}(N' = \alpha N, e, y, state)$. If $\mathcal{A}_{\text{M-RSA}}$ returns x' such that $y = (x')^e \mod N'$, then our reduction returns $x = x' \mod N$. Since $y = (x')^e \mod N' = (x')^e \mod \alpha N$ and $y \mod N' = y \mod N$, then $y = x^e \mod N = (x' \mod N)^e \mod N$ Therefore the existence of $\mathcal{A}_{\text{M-RSA-Gen}}$ and $\mathcal{A}_{\text{M-RSA}}$ violates Assumption 1.

It is easy to see that the above reduction is tight, meaning if an adversary can break M-RSA in time t, then we can use this adversary to break RSA in time t plus a little overhead. We will formulate more exact security in the following way: If an algorithm A in time $t(k)$ and with probability $\epsilon(k)$ can break a scheme, for example RSA, we say that A (t, ϵ)-breaks the scheme. If for given functions t and ϵ no algorithm that (t, ϵ)-breaks a scheme exists we call the scheme (t, ϵ)-secure. Regarding to M-RSA the time t describes the running time of both $\mathcal{A}_{\text{M-RSA-Gen}}$ and $\mathcal{A}_{\text{M-RSA}}$. We let k denote the bit-length of the primes in the modulus.

Corollary 1 (Tightness of Plain M-RSA). *If RSA is (t', ϵ')-secure then M-RSA is (t, ϵ)-secure with:*

$$t(k) \geq t'(k) - O(k^2)$$
$$\epsilon(k) \leq \epsilon'(k)$$

Proof. It is easy to see that if $\mathcal{A}_{\text{M-RSA-Gen}}$ and $\mathcal{A}_{\text{M-RSA}}$ break M-RSA then the reduction of Lemma 1 breaks RSA, and therefore $\epsilon(k) \leq \epsilon'(k)$.

The overhead of the reduction of Lemma 1 is the modulo reduction $x = x' \bmod N$, which gives the overhead of $O(k^2)$.

7   Security of Multiprime PSS-RSA Signatures

For various reasons hashing is normally applied to a message before it is signed with the RSA function, this makes RSA signatures semantic secure and in addition it enables signing of messages of arbitrary length. Hashing alone, however, does not give a tight bound on the security of the digital signature scheme, because it cannot be reduced to inverting the RSA function. The same holds for full domain hashing, where hashing is done such that it hits the complete preimage of the RSA function. To get a tighter bound Bellare and Rogaway [BR96] describes a randomized hashing and padding scheme known as PSS-RSA. [BR96] also gave a proof of a tight bound for PSS-RSA in the *Random Oracle* (RO) model.

The PSS-RSA scheme of Bellare and Rogaway has later been augmented and standardized as part of PKCS #1 v2 [RSA02]. This scheme is also known as PSS-RSA. Although the two PSS-RSA schemes have differences, reductions from forging both schemes to inverting plain RSA are analogues. From hereinafter we will concentrate on the PSS-RSA scheme by Bellare and Rogaway, whereas the results will also be valid for the PKCS version.

7.1   Signing with PSS

When signing with PSS-RSA two cryptographic hash functions $h : \{0, 1\}^* \mapsto \{0, 1\}^{k_1}$ and $g : \{0, 1\}^{k_1} \mapsto \{0, 1\}^{k - k_1 - 1}$ are used for hashing and padding the message m. In addition a uniform random value $r \in_R \{0, 1\}^{k_0}$ is used. The uniform randomness of r is crucial for the security proof, even though it is sometimes omitted in real world applications, see [RSA02]. After hashing and padding m, the (private) RSA function f^{-1} is applied to the result, and the output is the signature. Let $\|$ denote bit-wise concatenation.

SignPSS(m)

$$r \xleftarrow{r} \{0,1\}^{k_0}$$
$$w \leftarrow h(m||r)$$
$$y \leftarrow 0||w||(g(w) \oplus (r||0 \ldots 0))$$
$$x \leftarrow f^{-1}(y)$$

To verify m and signature x, the RSA function with the public key is applied s.t. $y \leftarrow f(x)$ is first calculated, afterward r can be reconstructed from y and the hashing and padding of m can be verified. The following theorem, due to [BR96], states the tightness of the PSS-RSA construction, q_{hash} specifies the number of times the adversary is allowed to invoke the hash algorithm (the random oracle) and q_{sig} the number of signed messages he can see before the forgery.

Theorem 2 (From [BR96], Security of PSS-RSA). *In the random oracle (RO) model: If RSA is (t', ϵ')-secure, then for any q_{sig}, q_{hash} the signature scheme PSS-RSA$[k_0, k_1]$ is $(t, q_{sig}, q_{hash}, \epsilon)$-secure, where*

$$t(k) = t'(k) - [q_{sig}(k) + q_{hash}(k) + 1] \cdot k_0 \cdot \Theta(k^3), and \quad (1)$$
$$\epsilon(k) = \epsilon'(k) + [2(q_{sig}(k) + q_{hash}(k))^2 + 1] \cdot (2^{-k_0} + 2^{-k_1}). \quad (2)$$

Proof (short sketch). We assume to have a forger $\mathcal{F}_{\text{PSS-RSA}}$ that has access to an oracle $\mathcal{O}$ that will sign up to q_{sig} messages $m_1, \ldots, m_{q_{sig}}$ and answer up to q_{hash} queries for h or g. Furthermore we assume that $\mathcal{F}_{\text{PSS-RSA}}$ in time less than t and with probability ϵ can output a message m which has not been signed by $\mathcal{O}$.

We will construct an attacker $\mathcal{A}_{\text{RSA}}$ capable of inverting RSA, say given N, e and y can output x s.t. $y = f(x) = x^e \bmod N$. To construct $\mathcal{A}_{\text{RSA}}$, $\mathcal{F}_{\text{PSS-RSA}}$ is instantiated, however, instead of access to $\mathcal{O}$, $\mathcal{A}_{\text{RSA}}$ will answer all queries. A signing request on m_i is answered by randomly selecting $x_i \in_{\text{R}} \mathbb{Z}_N$, calculating $y_i = f(x_i)$ and due to the RO model $\mathcal{A}_{\text{RSA}}$ can specify h and g in a way that makes y_i consistent with m_i. On h or g requests $\mathcal{A}_{\text{RSA}}$ returns a value consistent with $f(x_i)y$ for a random x_i. If $\mathcal{F}_{\text{PSS-RSA}}$ later on makes a forgery s.t. $\tilde{x} = f^{-1}(f(x_i)y)$, then due to the multiplicative homomorphic property of RSA $\tilde{x} = x_i f^{-1}(y)$. Therefore $\mathcal{A}_{\text{RSA}}$ can return $x = \tilde{x} x_i^{-1} = f^{-1}(y)$.

We refer to [BR96] for a full and formal proof.

It is important to note that the proof of Theorem 2 uses the RSA permutation in a blackbox way except for its multiplicative homomorphic property. Therefore the proof will work for PSS used with any multiplicative homomorphic oneway permutation including M-RSA. We can now formulate the security of using M-RSA in connection with PSS-RSA.

Corollary 2 (Security of PSS-M-RSA). *In the RO model: If RSA is (t', ϵ')-secure. Then for any q_{sig}, q_{hash} the signature scheme PSS-M-RSA$[k_0, k_1]$ is $(t, q_{sig}, q_{hash}, \epsilon)$-secure, where*

$$t(k) = t'(k) - [q_{sig}(k) + q_{hash}(k) + 1] \cdot k_0 \cdot \Theta(k^3), and \quad (3)$$
$$\epsilon(k) = \epsilon'(k) + [2(q_{sig}(k) + q_{hash}(k))^2 + 1] \cdot (2^{-k_0} + 2^{-k_1}). \quad (4)$$

Proof. A reduction from PSS-M-RSA to M-RSA follows analogously the reduction from Theorem 2 with the exact same overhead. The overhead of the reduction from M-RSA to RSA (Corollary 1) is dominated by the overhead from PSS-M-RSA to M-RSA.

8   Security of Multi-Prime OAEP-RSA Encryption

In this section we will see how some of the techniques from the previous section also applies to cryptosystems. Lemma 1 and Corollary 1 states the security of plain RSA and therefore also the plain RSA cryptosystem, however, as in the case of digital signatures, and due to some of the same problems plain RSA encryptions are very seldom used in practice. We therefore investigate the security of what is known as OAEP-RSA, a cryptosystem widely in practice.

Bellare and Rogaway [BR94] introduces Optimal Asynchronous Encryption Padding (OAEP) as a way to achieve CCA2 security[1] for RSA in the random oracle model. They proved that OAEP-RSA is plaintext aware 1 (PA1) secure based only on the one wayness of RSA. However, as pointed out and formally proved by Shoup [Sho02] PA1 security does not imply CCA2 security, contrary to this Shoup [Sho02] also proved that if 3 is used as the public exponent then RSA-OAEP is actually CCA2 secure. This result was further extended by Fujisaki et al. [FOPS04] to RSA-OAEP being CCA2 secure regardless of the public exponent. This result is based on additional properties than one wayness, namely that RSA is *Set Partial Domain One Way*.

A permutation is *Partial Domain One Way*, if no adversary is able to extract a certain number of the most significant bits of the preimage, and *Set Partial Domain One Way*, if no adversary is able to compute a set where one of the elements is equal to a certain number of the most significant bits of the preimage.

Definition 3 (Set-Partial-Domain-One-Way). *We define a permutation f as being (ℓ, t, ϵ)-set-partial-domain-one-way if no adversary A outputting a set with ℓ elements and running in time t exists s.t. $Pr(s \in A(f(s\|t)) > \epsilon$, where the length of s is $k - k_0$, with k_0 being defined by the size of the hashing used in OAEP padding.*

To prove the exact security of OAEP-M-RSA we first need to show that M-RSA is *Set Partial Domain One Way*. This is done by taking a lemma which originates from [FOPS04], and states that RSA is *Set Partial Domain One Way*, and see that it also covers M-RSA.

Lemma 2 (Modified [FOPS04, Lemma 4]). *Let A be an algorithm, which in time t and with probability ϵ, is capable of computing a q-set containing $k - k_0$ ($k > 2k_0$) of the most significant bits of the e'th root of its input. Then there exists an algorithms B capable of inverting M-RSA.*

---

[1] Security against adaptively chosen ciphertext attacks.

Proof (short sketch). This proof is analogous to the proof of [FOPS04, Lemma 4]. This proof is based on the self-reducibility of RSA, which is the same for M-RSA. The algorithm B runs A twice to compute two sets containing the a partial preimage of x and $r^e x$, for a random value r. Then B utilizes a special designed lattice version of Gaussian reduction to solve a set of linear modular equations defined by these partially preimages. We refer to [FOPS04] for a full and formal proof.

The theorem bellow, due to [FOPS04], states the tightness of the OAEP-RSA construction. The value q_D specifies the number of times the adversary is allowed to invoke a decryption oracle, and q_H and q_G is the number of allowed invocations to the random oracle simulating the two hash algorithms H and G used in OAEP.

Theorem 3 (Modified [FOPS04, Theorem 2]). *In the RO model, for any q_D, q_G and q_H if there exists an adversary A $(t, q_D, q_G, q_H, \epsilon)$-breaking OAEP-M-RSA (with $k > 2k_0$) then there exists and algorithm B (t', ϵ')-inverting RSA, with:*

$$\epsilon' > \frac{\epsilon^2}{4} - \epsilon \cdot \left(\frac{q_D q_G + q_D + q_G}{2^{k_0}} + \frac{q_D}{2^{k_1}} + \frac{32}{2^{k-2k_0}} \right)$$

$$t' \leq 2t + q_H \cdot (q_H + 2q_G) \cdot O(k^3)$$

Proof. From Fujisaki et al. [FOPS04] we have a Theorem (Theorem 1) stating the security of OAEP used in connection with a *set-partial-one-way* permutation, this in connection with Lemma 2 gives us the above result.

Since the bounds of [FOPS04] (Theorem 1) are less tight compared with the reduction from M-RSA to RSA (Corollary 1), the bound for breaking OAEP-RSA and OAEP-M-RSA is the same. So we achieve the same level of security (bit-length of the individual primes) using M-RSA as using standard RSA.

We note that in addition to the (above) bound equal to Theorem 2 in [FOPS04, FOPS04] also presents a slightly tighter bound in their Theorem 3. This result is also based on the partial domain one-wayness of RSA and therefore proving this bound for OAEP-M-RSA follows analogously from their proof.

References

[ACS02] Algesheimer, J., Camenisch, J.L., Shoup, V.: Efficient computation modulo a shared secret with application to the generation of shared safe-prime products. In: Yung, M. (ed.) CRYPTO 2002. LNCS, vol. 2442, pp. 417–432. Springer, Heidelberg (2002)

[BF97] Boneh, D., Franklin, M.K.: Efficient generation of shared RSA keys. In: Kaliski Jr., B.S. (ed.) CRYPTO 1997. LNCS, vol. 1294, pp. 425–439. Springer, Heidelberg (1997)

[BF01] Boneh, D., Franklin, M.K.: Efficient generation of shared RSA keys. J. ACM **48**(4), 702–722 (2001)

[BH98] Boneh, D., Horwitz, J.: Generating a product of three primes with an unknown factorization. In: Buhler, J.P. (ed.) ANTS 1998. LNCS, vol. 1423, pp. 237–251. Springer, Heidelberg (1998)

[Ble98] Bleichenbacher, D.: Chosen ciphertext attacks against protocols based on the RSA encryption standard PKCS #1. In: Krawczyk, H. (ed.) CRYPTO 1998. LNCS, vol. 1462, p. 1. Springer, Heidelberg (1998)

[BR94]   Bellare, M., Rogaway, P.: Optimal asymmetric encryption. In: De Santis, A. (ed.) EUROCRYPT 1994. LNCS, vol. 950, pp. 92–111. Springer, Heidelberg (1995)

[BR96]   Bellare, M., Rogaway, P.: The exact security of digital signatures - how to sign with RSA and rabin. In: Maurer, U.M. (ed.) EUROCRYPT 1996. LNCS, vol. 1070, pp. 399–416. Springer, Heidelberg (1996)

[DK01]   Damgård, I.B., Koprowski, M.: Practical threshold RSA signatures without a trusted dealer. In: Pfitzmann, B. (ed.) EUROCRYPT 2001. LNCS, vol. 2045, p. 152. Springer, Heidelberg (2001)

[DM09]   Damgård, I., Mikkelsen, G.L.: On the theory and practice of personal digital signatures. In: Jarecki, S., Tsudik, G. (eds.) PKC 2009. LNCS, vol. 5443, pp. 277–296. Springer, Heidelberg (2009)

[DM10]   Damgård, I., Mikkelsen, G.L.: Efficient, robust and constant-round distributed rsa key generation. In: Micciancio, D. (ed.) TCC 2010. LNCS, vol. 5978, pp. 183–200. Springer, Heidelberg (2010)

[DMS14] Damgård, I., Mikkelsen, G.L., Skeltved, T.: On the security of distributed multiprime RSA. IACR ePrint Archive (2014)

[FMY98] Frankel, Y., MacKenzie, P.D., Yung, M.: Robust efficient distributed RSA-key generation. In: Vitter, J.S. (ed.) STOC, pp. 663–672. ACM (1998)

[FOPS04] Fujisaki, E., Okamoto, T., Pointcheval, D., Stern, J.: RSA-OAEP is secure under the RSA assumption. J. Cryptol. 17(2), 81–104 (2004)

[Gil99] Gilboa, N.: Two party RSA key generation. In: Wiener, M. (ed.) CRYPTO 1999. LNCS, vol. 1666, p. 116. Springer, Heidelberg (1999)

[Gir91] Girault, M.: Self-certified public keys. In: Davies, D.W. (ed.) EUROCRYPT 1991. LNCS, vol. 547, pp. 490–497. Springer, Heidelberg (1991)

[GRJK07] Gennaro, R., Rabin, T., Jarecki, S., Krawczyk, H.: Robust and efficient sharing of RSA functions. J. Cryptol. 20(3), 393 (2007)

[HMRT12] Hazay, C., Mikkelsen, G.L., Rabin, T., Toft, T.: Efficient RSA key generation and threshold paillier in the two-party setting. In: Dunkelman, O. (ed.) CT-RSA 2012. LNCS, vol. 7178, pp. 313–331. Springer, Heidelberg (2012)

[Pai99] Paillier, P.: Public-key cryptosystems based on composite degree residuosity classes. In: Stern, J. (ed.) EUROCRYPT 1999. LNCS, vol. 1592, p. 223. Springer, Heidelberg (1999)

[RSA02] RSA Laboratories. PKCS #1 v2.1: RSA cryptography standard. Technical report (2002)

[Sch91] Schnorr, C.-P.: Efficient signature generation by smart cards. J. Cryptol. 4(3), 161–174 (1991)

[Sho02] Shoup, V.: OAEP reconsidered. J. Cryptol. 15(4), 223–249 (2002)

Digital Signature

Formal Modeling of Random Oracle Programmability and Verification of Signature Unforgeability Using Task-PIOAs

Kazuki Yoneyama[✉]

NTT Secure Platform Laboratories,
3-9-11 Midori-cho Musashino-shi, Tokyo 180-8585, Japan
kazuki.yoneyama@gmail.com

Abstract. The task-structured Probabilistic I/O Automata (task-PIOA) framework provides a method to formulate and to prove the computationally-bounded security of non-sequential processing systems in a formal way. Though existing works show security analyses of some classic cryptographic protocols (e.g., the EGL oblivious transfer) against simple adversaries (e.g., honest but curious adversary), there is no case study for fundamental cryptographic primitives (e.g., encryption and signature) against sufficiently strong adversaries (e.g., IND-CCA for encryption and EUF-CMA for signature). In this paper, we propose a formulation of signature against EUF-CMA in the task-PIOA framework. Using the task-PIOA framework allows us to verify security of signature schemes in the non-sequential scheduling manner. We show the validity and usefulness of our formulation by giving a formal security analysis of the FDH signature scheme. In order to prove the security, we also introduce a method to utilize the power of random oracles. As far as we know, this work is the first case study to clarify usefulness of random oracles in this framework.

Keywords: Formal method · Task-PIOA · FDH signature · Random oracle · Programmability

1 Introduction

Analyses of cryptographic protocols are typically complex tasks; and security proofs often contain some error. As a solution, techniques using *formal methods* have been paid attention to. By formulating and verifying some security property of protocols with formal methods, it is easy to define security models and to give rigorous security proofs. Another advantage is that we can analyze protocols automatically or mechanically. The most famous approach is the Dolev-Yao's symbolic model [1]. This approach is mainly interested to verify authentication and confidentiality properties, and has been used to analyses of several practical protocols (e.g., SSL, TLS, Kerberos). However, the basic symbolic analysis does not a priori carry any cryptographic *computational security* guarantees. Computational security means that an adversary is computationally bounded (typically, a polynomial-time in a security parameter).

© Springer International Publishing Switzerland 2015
J. Lee and J. Kim (Eds.): ICISC 2014, LNCS 8949, pp. 37–52, 2015.
DOI: 10.1007/978-3-319-15943-0_3

Thus, after that, several formal analysis frameworks that can grasp computational properties have been studied. One approach is to connect symbolic security and computational security with soundness (e.g., [2–4]). If soundness is guaranteed, a security proof by a symbolic analysis also holds against computational adversaries. For example, Canetti and Herzog proposed a combination of the symbolic model and the universally composable (UC) security framework [5] in order to create a unified framework for proving security of protocols, they named universally composable symbolic analysis (UCSA) [6]. The UCSA framework enables a security analysis that is completely symbolic, and at the same time cryptographically sound with strong composability property. However, since the framework assumes basic cryptographic primitives (e.g., encryption and signature) as symbolic operations, it cannot verify computational security of such primitives. Also, though participants in the protocol are modeled by Interactive Turing Machines (ITMs), a complete analysis of protocols is not abstracted enough because it includes too many low-level machine details. We call this approach *the indirect approach*.

The other approach is to prove computational security directly (e.g., [7–9]). We call this approach *the direct approach*. For example, Canetti et al. [10,11] proposed the task-structured Probabilistic I/O Automata (task-PIOA) framework. Entities in protocols are modeled as variants of PIOAs, not ITMs. By using PIOAs, it is easy to carry out security proofs formally at a high level of abstraction. Each action of entities is classified into input, output or internal actions, and locally controlled actions (i.e., output and internal actions) are combined by an equivalence class (called a *task*). By introducing the notion of tasks, we can manage a sequence of processes with a (non-deterministic and probabilistic) scheduler of tasks. The task-PIOA framework is very suitable to analyze computational security because computational indistinguishability is naturally captured.

The other merit of this framework is to be able to deal with the *non-sequential* scheduling. Sequential activation (or sequential scheduling) means that given a system of processes executed in parallel, multiple processes must not be active simultaneously at any given point in time, and the active process activates the next process by producing and sending some message. Such a sequential scheduling model is commonly adopted by many cryptographic frameworks, e.g., the UC framework [5]. However, in large distributed systems, the sequential scheduling model is not always suitable because the ordering of events cannot be fully controlled by any entity, including adversarial components. For example, since the sequential scheduling model might introduce some constraints in the ordering of events, it might restrict adversaries by hiding characteristics which could be revealed to him in the real world. Practically, even if the specification of a scheme specifies that the protocol must be carried out in a certain ordering manner, unexpected parallel processing may be adopted in implementations of real systems for efficiency. Therefore, to prove the security in the task-PIOA framework guarantees the security in the situation that is closer to the real world than that in previous frameworks.

However, concrete case studies of protocol analyses in the task-PIOA framework are very limited; that is, only on an oblivious transfer protocol [10,11], a key exchange protocol [12], and a zero-knowledge proof [13], and Chaum's Dining Cryptographers Protocol [14]. Furthermore, previous analyses only consider very simple adversaries who behave in the honest but curious manner (i.e., adversaries never attempt any behaviour beyond the honest execution of the protocol). Usually, in the cryptographic community, we suppose strong adversaries which *maliciously* behave. A malicious adversary means that he can access to some adversarial oracle (e.g., a decryption oracle for public-key encryption, and a signing oracle for signature) based on secret information as well as public information. Therefore, it is unclear how to formalize and analyze security against malicious adversaries in the task-PIOA framework.

On the other hand, in the research of cryptography, various proof techniques using *random oracles* (ROs) have been studied. Though there are evidences to show the riskiness of schemes only with security proof in the RO model [15], a proof in the RO model guarantees that the scheme is structurally sound. Indeed, many practical cryptographic primitives (like standardized schemes in ISO/IEC) are proved in the RO model.

Therefore, it was an open problem to clarify the way to treat strong security models and proof techniques with ROs by the task-PIOA framework.

1.1   Our Contribution

Our aim is to formulate and to verify existential forger under adaptively chosen message attacks (EUF-CMA) in the task-PIOA framework as a malicious adversary for signature schemes. We give a security proof of a specific signature scheme against such an adversary to show the validity of our formulation. The proof in the task-PIOA framework can guarantee the security even when each process is executed in the non-sequential scheduling manner. Especially, we choose FDH signature scheme [16] as a case study by the following reason: FDH signature has a very simple structure, and satisfies EUF-CMA. It is desirable that the analyzed protocol is simple because we can concentrate on the difference with previous case studies in the task-PIOA framework. Also, the security proof of FDH signature uses a special property of ROs (i.e., *programmability*) to simulate signing oracle queries. Thus, we show the method to capture such basic techniques to handle ROs in the task-PIOA framework. It can be a useful example when we try to verify other kinds of protocols in the RO model.

1.2   Our Approach

Modeling Random Oracle Programmability. In the hand-written security proof of FDH signature, the simulator embeds a specific value to an output of the hash function before the corresponding message is posed. It can be allowed by programmability of ROs. We apply this technique in the task-PIOA framework. In the security proof, we formulate ROs by two types: one is to generate a hash value from a message by the *honest* computation, and the other is to set a message from an intended hash value by the *programmed* computation (i.e., only for the simulator). We define two types as two task-PIOAs, and we show correspondence of tasks of them and the mapping. Thus, we can show that any environment cannot distinguish two task-PIOAs. This property certainly corresponds to programmability of ROs.

Modeling Unforgeability for Iteration of Identical Action in Single Session. Previous case studies deal with functionalities whose processes are straight line within single sessions. That means, each action occurs only once in a functionality. For example, in the case study for oblivious transfer [10,11], the functionality has two input actions and two output actions, and these actions are executed sequentially on the invocation of the functionality. Conversely, in the case study for signature, we must consider a situation that some actions occur multiple times as follows:

In the EUF-CMA game, a session is initiated to execute the key generation process which generates a pair of a signing key and a verification key. The signature generation process and the signature verification process may be repeated for multiple messages with the common key pair. Also, invocations of these two processes occur with the unordered manner. For example, it is possible to first run two signature generation processes, and then run two signature verification processes. In this case, we must manage states and tasks to synchronize consistency between results of a signature generation and a signature verification. However, it is not easy work to treat a message and a signature in a signature generation process with storing the message and the signature into states, because the scheduling mechanism of the task-PIOA framework is oblivious (i.e., schedulers fix the entire schedule of tasks non-deterministically in advance) and not the perfect-information scheduler (i.e., schedulers have access to local state and history of all components and have unlimited computation power). In the ordinary UC setting with ITMs, such a problem does not occur. To solve this problem, we show a technique to manage such a situation. Specifically, we introduce the notion of message identity which enables messages to correspond to signatures and verification results.

2 Preliminaries

2.1 Task-PIOA Framework

All necessary definitions or notations cannot be shown here due to space limitations. The readers are referred to [11] for them.

Probabilistic I/O Automata. First, we describe the definition of probabilistic I/O automata (PIOA).

A PIOA is defined as a tuple $\mathcal{P} = (Q, \overline{q}, I, O, H, \Delta)$, where each parameter respectively represents a set of states, a start state, a set of input actions, a set of output actions, a set of internal (hidden) actions, and a transition relation that is included in $(Q \times (I \cup O \cup H) \times \mathsf{Disc}(Q))$ where $\mathsf{Disc}(Q)$ is the set of discrete probability measures on Q. We say that an action a is enabled in a state q if $\langle q, a, \mu \rangle \in \Delta$. In particular, $A = I \cup O \cup H$ is called actions of $\mathcal{P}$ and $E = I \cup O$ is called the external actions of $\mathcal{P}$.

The execution of a protocol on PIOA is expressed by sequences such as $\alpha = q_0 a_1 q_1 a_2 \cdots$, where each $q_i \in Q$ and $a_i \in A$ holds. Here, the trace of α denoted by $trace(\alpha)$ is defined as $\{a_i \mid a_i \in \alpha$ and $a_i \in E\}$, i.e., the sequences obtained by removing internal actions from α.

A PIOA can deal with the probabilistic protocol execution, which is described using *probability measures on execution fragments* of PIOA $\mathcal{P}$. By applying this to *trace* of a protocol execution ϵ, the trace distribution of ϵ is defined as $tdist(\epsilon)$, which is an image measure under *trace* of ϵ, and a set of *tdist* of possible probabilistic protocol executions in $\mathcal{P}$ is also defined and denoted as $tdists(\mathcal{P})$, which is used to define indistinguishability in the task-PIOA framework.

One of the other properties on PIOA is, for example, its composability. If two PIOAs $\mathcal{P}_1$ and $\mathcal{P}_2$ satisfy a certain restriction (if they are "compatible"), then the composed PIOA is denoted by $\mathcal{P}_1 || \mathcal{P}_2$. When PIOAs are composed, it is usually necessary to turn some output actions of one composed PIOA into internal actions. For this purpose, there is a hiding operation in the PIOA framework. It turns some output actions of a certain PIOA into internal actions. $hide(\mathcal{P}, S)$ means that output actions S of $\mathcal{P}$ are hidden, i.e., the output actions change to $O' = O \backslash S$ and the internal actions change to $H' = H \cup S$. The actions are assumed to satisfy the following conditions.

- **Input enabling:** For any $q \in Q$ and $a \in I$, a is enabled in q.
- **Transition determinism:** For any $q \in Q$ and $a \in I \cup O \cup H$, there exists at most one $\mu \in \mathsf{Disc}(Q)$ such that $\langle q, a, \mu \rangle \in \Delta$.

Task-PIOAs. Based on the PIOA framework, a task-PIOA is defined as a pair $\mathcal{T} = (\mathcal{P}, R)$, where $\mathcal{P} = (Q, \overline{q}, I, O, H, \Delta)$ is a PIOA and R is an equivalence relation on the locally controlled actions $(O \cup H)$. The equivalence classes by R are called tasks.

The following axiom is imposed on task-PIOAs.

- **Next action determinism:** For any $q \in Q$ and $T \in R$, there exists at most one action $a \in T$ that is enabled in q.

In the task-PIOA framework, the notion of the task scheduler, which chooses the next task to perform, is used. The scheduler simply specifies a sequence of tasks.

As a task-PIOA is defined as a pair of a PIOA and R, composition and hiding can be defined as in the PIOA framework. That is, the composition of task-PIOAs $\mathcal{T}_1 = (\mathcal{P}_1, R_1)$ and $\mathcal{T}_2 = (\mathcal{P}_2, R_2)$ is defined to be $\mathcal{P}_1 || \mathcal{P}_2$ as in the PIOA framework, and $R_1 \cup R_2$ for the relation part. Hiding is also the same as for the PIOA part, and the relation part is not affected by hiding.

Now, the formulation of indistinguishability of the external behavior for a task-PIOA is described using the relation $\leq_0$, which is defined as follows.

Definition 1 (Implementation Relation [11]). *Suppose T_1 and T_2 are task-PIOAs having the same I/O. Then, $T_1 \leq_0 T_2$ if, for every environment Env for both T_1 and T_2, tdists($T_1 \| Env$) $\subseteq$ tdists($T_2 \| Env$). $\leq_0$ is called the implementation relation.*

This definition means that the implementation relation holds if the trace distribution set made in $T_1 \| Env$ is also made in $T_2 \| Env$. Thus, T_2 makes Env unable to distinguish the two protocols. Therefore, to prove the security of a protocol, a real protocol must be constructed using task-PIOAs, and then an ideal protocol must be constructed that is indistinguishable from the real protocol for any environment Env.

We can use another relation called the *simulation relation*, which shows the sufficient conditions for proving the implementation relation. The simulation relation is the equivalence relation on probabilistic executions, which makes it possible to verify whether states in PIOAs are equivalent or not task by task. This method of obtaining proof is favorable to automation. In the security proof, a relation is established and proved to be a simulation relation, and then the next lemma is applied.

Lemma 1 (Theorem 3 in [11]). *Let T_1 and T_2 be two comparable closed action-deterministic task-PIOAs, where the term "comparable" means that T_1 and T_2 have the same I/O, and "closed action-deterministic" means some restriction and assumption on task-PIOAs. If there exists a simulation relation from T_1 to T_2, then tdists($T_1 \| Env$) $\subseteq$ tdists($T_2 \| Env$).*

The task-PIOA framework has the ability to deal with computational issues. This is made possible by considering that each task-PIOA is *time-bounded*. For time-bounded PIOAs, the implementation relation is defined as follows.

Definition 2 (Time-bounded implementation relation [11]). *Let T_1 and T_2 be comparable task-PIOAs, $\epsilon, b \in \mathbb{R}^{\geq 0}$, and $b_1, b_2 \in \mathbb{N}$, where $\mathbb{R}^{\geq 0}$ is the set of real numbers not less than 0 and $\mathbb{N}$ is the set of natural numbers. Then $T_1 \leq_{\epsilon,b,b_1,b_2} T_2$ provided that, for every b-time-bounded environment Env for both T_1 and T_2, and for every b_1-time-bounded task scheduler ρ_1 for $T_1 \| Env$, there is a b_2-time-bounded task scheduler ρ_2 for $T_2 \| Env$ such that $|Paccept(T_1 \| Env, \rho_1) - Paccept(T_2 \| Env, \rho_2)| \leq \epsilon$, where Paccept is the probability that the environment outputs accept.*

When applied to security proofs, $\leq_{\epsilon,b,b_1,b_2}$ is denoted by $\leq_{neg,pt}$ because ϵ is required to be negligible probability and b, b_1, b_2 are required to be probabilistic polynomial-time (PPT). A useful property of this relation is that it is transitive; if $T_1 \leq_{neg,pt} T_2$ and $T_2 \leq_{neg,pt} T_3$, then $T_1 \leq_{neg,pt} T_3$. Thus, a security proof can be done like this: first divide the proof into parts, then prove each part separately, and finally combine them. Though security proofs of large systems are often complex, the task-PIOA framework enables us to carry out of proofs on protocols at a high level of abstraction by modularizing the proof such as by divide and conquer. Other properties such as composition, hiding, and the simulation relation also hold for time-bounded PIOA.

2.2 Security Notion of Signature Schemes

Here, we give the syntax and the security notion for signature schemes.

Definition 3 (Syntax for Signature Schemes). *A single signature scheme consists of following 3-tuple (**gen, sig, ver**):*

- **gen:** *a key generation algorithm which on input 1^k, where k is the security parameter, outputs a pair of keys (vk, sk). vk and sk are called verification key and signing key respectively.*
- **sig:** *a signature generation algorithm which takes as input message m from the signing key sk, outputs a signature σ.*
- **ver:** *a verification algorithm which takes as input a message m, a signature σ and the verification key vk, output a bit 1 or 0.*

Generally, we say that a signature scheme is secure if the scheme satisfies EUF-CMA. The definition of EUF-CMA is as follows.

Definition 4 (EUF-CMA). *A signature scheme is existentially unforgeable under adaptively chosen message attacks (EUF-CMA) if the following property holds for any negligible function $\nu()$ and security parameter k where; For any PPT forger $\mathcal{F}$, $\Pr[(vk, sk) \leftarrow gen(1^k); (m, \sigma) \leftarrow \mathcal{F}^{SO(sk,\cdot)}(vk); 1 \leftarrow ver(m, \sigma, vk)$ and $\mathcal{F}$ never poses the message m to $SO] \leq \nu(k)$. ($\mathcal{F}$ can obtain signatures $\sigma_1, \ldots, \sigma_n$ of $\mathcal{F}$'s own chosen messages $m_1, \ldots, m_n$ from a signing oracle SO, and $\mathcal{F}$ cannot output a new pair of message m and its signature σ, where $m \in \{m_1 \ldots, m_n\}$).*

2.3 Trapdoor One-Way Permutation and FDH Signature

The FDH signature is based on a trapdoor one-way permutation.

Definition 5 (Trapdoor One-way Permutation). *A trapdoor permutation $f : Dom \to Dom$ for the domain Dom and the trapdoor f^{-1} is one-way if the following property holds for any negligible function $\nu()$ and security parameter k where; For any PPT inverter $\mathcal{I}$, $\Pr[x \leftarrow Dom; x' \leftarrow \mathcal{I}(f, f(x)); x = x'] \leq \nu(k)$.*

The protocol of FDH signature is as follows:

gen: For security parameter k, output a signing key $(sk = f^{-1})$ and a verification key $(vk = f)$, where f is a trapdoor one-way permutation with the domain Dom.

sig: For input a message $m \in \{0, 1\}^*$, compute $y = H(m)$ and output a signature $\sigma = f^{-1}(y)$, where $H : \{0, 1\}^* \to Dom$ is a full-domain hash function (i.e., H maps from the message space to the domain and co-domain of the permutation f.).

ver: For inputs a message m and a signature σ, compute $y' = f(\sigma)$ and verify $y' \stackrel{?}{=} H(m)$. If the verification is valid, output 1, otherwise, output 0.

3   Formulation of EUF-CMA for FDH Signature

In this section, we show the construction of a real system and an ideal system of the FDH signature scheme in the task-PIOA framework. The real system represents the execution of the FDH signature protocol in the task-PIOA framework, and the ideal system represents the execution of the ideal process which signature schemes should surely satisfy.

The main difference between our analysis and previous analyses [10,12–14] is how to model iteration of identical process in a single session. In previous analyses, a process is executed only once in a single session because it is unnecessary to consider multiple sessions which include multiple executions of processes for the target primitives (i.e., oblivious transfer, key exchange, zero-knowledge, and dining cryptographer protocol). However, in the case of signature schemes, we must manage multiple pairs of messages and signatures in a single session because a signer can sign multiple messages by the common signing key. In the ideal process of signature schemes, verification results should be determined by binding between a message and the corresponding signature. Here, we show a technique for solving this problem by introducing the notion of the message identity. Our technique is that all entities specify the message identity in the signature generation and the signature verification, and a message and a signature are bound with intermediate of the message identity when the message and the signature are stored in states of a task-PIOA. Thus, messages can correspond to signatures and verification results.

On the other hand, for the modeling of EUF-CMA we have to formulate the interface of the forger and the simulator in order to query to the signing oracle respectively. The corruption model can be formulated with similar modeling as previous analyses which need not consider changes of the corrupted endpoints on the way in the session (i.e., static corruption).

Unfortunately, due to the page limitation we cannot show all formulation in the proceeding version, and just give some intuition. Please see the full version of this paper for details.

3.1   Ideal System IS

An ideal system IS is defined as the specification for the correctness and unforgeability properties which have to be guaranteed in signature schemes. Correctness means that a valid signature according to the protocol description is always accepted by the signature verification.

We define IS as a parameterized task-PIOA with a trapdoor permutation family $\overline{Tdp}$ having domain family $\overline{\mathcal{D}} = \{\mathcal{D}_k\}_{k \in \mathbf{N}}$, where let $Tdpp_k = \{(f_k, f_k^{-1}) : f_k \in Tdp_k\}$ be the set of trapdoor permutation pairs for domain D_k. If $p = (f_k, f_k^{-1}) \in Tdpp_k$, then we refer to the components f_k and f_k^{-1} of p using record notation, as $p.funct$ and $p.inverse$, respectively.

Also, IS is defined as a parameterized task-PIOA, with the following other parameters:

- MID: a set of message identity.
- $\mathcal{M}$: message space.
- $\mathcal{D}$: signature space.
- ψ: a set of corrupted endpoints.

Based on these, we define the following derived sets:

- $\mathcal{M}' = MID \times \mathcal{M}$: a set of message identity and message space pairs. If $m' = (id, m) \in \mathcal{M}'$, then we refer to the components id and m of m' using record notation, as $m'.id$ and $m'.message$, respectively.
- $\mathcal{D}' = MID \times \mathcal{D}$: a set of message identity and signature space pairs. If $\sigma' = (id, \sigma) \in \mathcal{D}'$, then we refer to the components id and σ of σ' using record notation, as $\sigma'.id$ and $\sigma'.signature$, respectively.
- $\mathcal{V}' = MID \times \mathcal{M} \times \mathcal{D} \times Tdp$: a set of message identity, message space, signature space and trapdoor permutation tuple. If $V' = (id, m, \sigma, f) \in \mathcal{V}'$, then we refer to the components id, m, σ and f of V' using record notation, as $V'.id$, $V'.message$, $V'.signature$ and $V'.verkey$, respectively.
- $\mathcal{B}' = MID \times \{0, 1\}$: a set of message identity and verification result space pairs. If $b' = (id, b) \in \mathcal{B}'$, then we refer to the components id and b of b' using record notation, as $b'.id$ and $b'.result$, respectively.

IS consists of two interacting task-PIOAs: the signature functionality $Funct$ and a simulator Sim. We describe the details of these task-PIOAs.

Signature Functionality $Funct$. We define signature functionality in task-PIOA framework as a task-PIOA $Funct$. $Funct$ executes processes of signature schemes (i.e., key generation, signature generation and signature verification) so that correctness and unforgeability are satisfied. Our definition is an interpretation of the signature functionality $\mathcal{F}_{SIG}$ [5] in the UC framework. Thus, correctness and unforgeability are properly captured as $\mathcal{F}_{SIG}$. $Sig \in \psi$ means that the signer is corrupted, and $Ver \in \psi$ means that the verifier is corrupted. Intuitively, $Funct$ operates as follows: For the key generation, $Funct$ receive $reply(f)_{fval}$ from Sim and forwards $out(f)_{fval}$ to Env. For the signature generation, $Funct$ receive $in(m)_{msval}$ from Env, poses $ask(m)_{msval}$ to Sim, receives $reply(\sigma)_{\sigma val}$, and forwards $out(\sigma)_{\sigma val}$ to Env. Also, Sim can pose arbitrary $in(m)_{msval}$ to $Funct$. This situation represents the adaptive chosen message attack. For the signature verification, $Funct$ receive $in(V)_{Vval}$ for $V = (m, \sigma, f')$ from Env, poses $ask(V)_{Vval}$ to Sim, and receives $reply(\theta)_{\theta val}$. If $f' \neq f$, m is previously posed, or either of the signer and the verifier is corrupted, then the verification result is arbitrarily determined by Sim and $Funct$ forwards $out(\phi)_{\phi val}$ for $\phi = \theta$ to Env. Otherwise, θ is ignored and $Funct$ sends the verification result $out(\phi)_{\phi val}$ to Env. Therefore, Sim cannot manage verification results for the valid verification key even while Sim can determine values f and σ. This situation represents existential unforgeability.

Simulator Sim. The simulator Sim is an arbitrary task-PIOA, but there are some constraints to fix the interface.

Complete Ideal System. Complete ideal system IS is the composition of $Funct(MID, \mathcal{M}, \mathcal{D}, Tdp, \psi)$ and $Sim(MID, \mathcal{M}, \mathcal{D}, Tdp, \psi)$. $\{reply(*)\}$, $\{ask(*)\}$, $\{out'(*)\}$ tasks and $\{in(*)\}$ task of Sim are hidden.

An ideal system family $\overline{IS}$ is a family $\{IS_k\}_{k \in \mathbf{N}}$, where for each k, IS_k is an ideal system. An illustration of IS in the case of $\psi = \emptyset$ is given in Fig. 1.

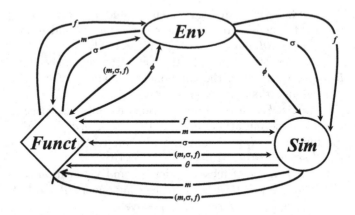

Fig. 1. Ideal system IS (Case of $\psi = \emptyset$)

3.2   Real System RS

A real system RS represents the protocol of the FDH signature.

RS is parameterized by a trapdoor permutation pair $Tdpp$, a trapdoor permutation Tdp, a set of message identity MID, message space $\mathcal{M}$, signature space $\mathcal{D}$ and a set of corrupted endpoints ψ. Based on these parameters, we define the following derived set:

- $\mathcal{H}' = MID \times \mathcal{D}$: a set of message identity and signature space pairs. If $h' = (id, h) \in \mathcal{H}'$, then we refer to the components id and h of h' using record notation, as $h'.id$ and $h'.hashval$, respectively.

We have to capture iteration of identical process in single session and EUF-CMA in RS. Therefore, by introducing message identity as IS, we are able to bind a message and the corresponding signature when multiple signature generations and verifications occur independently. Also, we represent EUF-CMA such that queries to the signing oracle are interpreted as queries to the real signer.

RS consists of four interacting task-PIOAs: signer Sig, verifier Ver, forger $Forge$ and RO with the honest computation ROH. We show the construction of these task-PIOAs. Prior to this, we define a task-PIOA $Src(Dom)$ which is used to pick random values.

Definition 6 (Random Source task-PIOA). *A task-PIOA $Src(Dom)$ chooses a random value uniformly from the designated domain Dom and outputs the value.*

$Src(Dom)$ realizes this functionality with two tasks: $\{choose\text{-}rand\}$ and $\{rand(*)\}$, where $\{choose\text{-}rand\}$ chooses a value (this is an internal task) and $\{rand(*)\}$ outputs the value (this is an output task).

Random Oracle with Honest Computation ROH. ROH is the task-PIOA to generate hash values as the RO with the honest computation. Intuitively, on receiving a message $hash(m)_{msval}$ or $hash(m)_{mvval}$, ROH outputs the corresponding hash value $hashed(h)_{hsval}$ or $hashed(h)_{hvval}$. According to the definition of the RO, if m is not posed yet, then h is randomly chosen with $choose\text{-}rand_{temp}$ and $rand(t)_{temp}$ from $Src(\mathcal{H}')_{temp}$. It means that the RO maps from $\mathcal{M}$ to the domain and co-domain of Tdp (i.e., $\mathcal{D}$).

Signer Sig. Sig is the task-PIOA representing the signer. Intuitively, on receiving a trapdoor permutation pair $rand(p)_{pval}$ for $p = (f, f^{-1}) \in Tdpp$ (generated by $choose\text{-}rand_{pval}$) from $Src(Tdpp)_{pval}$, the signer Sig outputs the verification key $out(f)_{fval}$. After that, on receiving a message $in(m)_{msval}$, Sig poses $hash(m)_{msval}$ to ROH, receives a hash value $hashed(h)_{hsval}$, and computes and outputs the signature $out(\sigma)_{\sigma val}$ for $\sigma = f^{-1}(h) \in \mathcal{D}$.

Verifier Ver. Ver is the task-PIOA representing the verifier. Intuitively, on receiving $out(f)_{fval}$, the verifier Ver sets f as the verification key. After that, on receiving a verification query $in(V)_{Vval}$ for (m, σ, f'), Ver poses $hash(m)_{mvval}$ to ROH and obtains a hash value $hashed(h)_{hvval}$, and outputs the verification result $out(\phi)_{\phi val}$ according to $(h \overset{?}{=} f(\sigma))$.

Forger $Forge$. The forger task-PIOA $Forge$ can obtain the corresponding signature for arbitrary message from Sig and also can pose arbitrary verification request to Ver. In addition, if $\psi \neq \emptyset$ (i.e., there is corrupted endpoint), then $Forge$ can obtain inputs for corrupted endpoints from the environment or other entities. Also, $Forge$ acts for outputs of corrupted endpoints to the environment. $Forge$ may interact with the environment by using arbitrary input and output actions (denote "new" input and "new" output) in addition to explicitly described actions in codes.

Complete Real System. A complete real system RS is the composition of the following five task-PIOAs: Sig, Ver, $Forge$, $Src(Tdpp)_{pval}$, ROH, and $Src(\mathcal{H})_{temp}$, where $\{rand\}$, $\{out'\}$, $\{hash\}$, and $\{hashed\}$ tasks and $\{in\}$ task of $Forge$ are hidden. If $Sig \in \psi$, hide all the $\{reply\}$ task.

A real system family $\overline{RS}$ is a family $\{RS_k\}_{k \in \mathbf{N}}$, where for each k, RS_k is a real system. An illustration of RS in the case of $\psi = \emptyset$ is given in Fig. 2.

4   Security Analysis

In this section, we prove $\overline{RS} \leq_{neg,pt} \overline{IS}$. The proof is divisible by transitiveness of implementation relation. Firstly, we introduce an intermediate system family $\overline{Int}$. Indeed, we divide the proof into $\overline{RS} \leq_{neg,pt} \overline{Int}$ and $\overline{Int} \leq_{neg,pt} \overline{SIS}$ by $\overline{Int}$, where $\overline{SIS}$ is an ideal system family which is concretely constructed by the following simulator. Since it is enough that we show existence of an instance of $\overline{IS}$ such that $\overline{RS} \leq_{neg,pt} \overline{IS}$, the goal of the proof is to show $\overline{RS} \leq_{neg,pt} \overline{SIS}$.

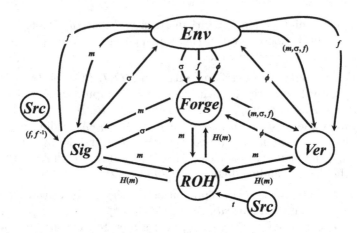

Fig. 2. Real system RS (Case of $\psi = \emptyset$)

4.1   Construction of Simulator $SSim$

For each k, we construct a simulator $SSim_k$ which is parameterized by a trap-door permutation pair $Tdpp$, a trapdoor permutation Tdp, a set of message identity MID, message space $\mathcal{M}$, signature space $\mathcal{D}$ and a set of corrupted endpoints ψ. Based on these parameters, we define a following derived set:

- $\mathcal{S}' = MID \times \mathcal{M} \times \mathcal{D}$: a set of message identity, message space, and signature space tuple. If $s' = (id, m, h) \in \mathcal{S}'$, then we refer to the components id, m and h of s' using record notation, as $s'.id$, $s'.message$ and $s'.hashval$, respectively.

$SSim$ is the composition of following task-PIOAs.

- ROP_k, same as ROH_k except that ROP has additional interfaces to set an intended value in the hash list.
- SV, an abstract combination of Sig and Ver except that SV does not know the signing key f^{-1} if Sig is uncorrupted, and uses ROP to simulate the signature generation.
- $(Src((Tdpp)_k)_{pval})_k$, isomorphic to $Src((Tdpp)_k)_{pval}$.
- $(Src((\mathcal{H}')_k)_{temp})_k$, isomorphic to $Src((\mathcal{H}')_k)_{temp}$.
- $(Src((\mathcal{D}')_k)_{oval})_k$, isomorphic to $Src((\mathcal{D}')_k)_{oval}$.
- $Forge'_k$, isomorphic to the forger $Forge_k$ in RS_k. $Forge'_k$ is same as $Forge_k$ except that its $out'(\sigma)_{oval}$ and $out'(\phi)_{\phi val}$ input actions are renamed to $lout(\sigma)$ and $lout(\phi)_{\phi val}$ respectively.

ROP provides programmability to SV with interface $program(s)_{Sval}$. If $s = (m, f(\sigma))$ is not recorded in a state of ROP, SV can obtain σ from $Src(\mathcal{D})$ embed s as a pair of input and output values though SV only uses f from $Src(Tdpp)$. Note that $Forge'$ cannot use this interface because $Forge'$ does not contain such an interface. SV can simulate executions of Sig and Ver as same as that in the real system for Env without using f^{-1} by the power of programmability. Here, we show the intuitive reason why the simulation is valid.

On receiving $in(m)_{msval}$ and $in(V)_{Vval}$ from Env, $Funct$ poses $ask(m)_{msval}$ and $ask(V)_{Vval}$ to SV, receives $reply(\sigma)_{\sigma val}$ and $reply(\theta)_{\theta val}$ from SV, and returns $out(\sigma)_{\sigma val}$ and $out(\phi)_{\phi val}$ to Env. This interface is same as Sig and Ver in RS. There is the difference between the simulation and the real system in the way to generate signatures. If there is no corrupted endpoint (i.e., $\psi = \emptyset$), SV generates σ by using $program(s)_{Sval}$ with ROP (i.e., without f^{-1}) instead of using f^{-1} and ROH. In this case, the signature generation is still valid because a signature generated with ROP is always accepted as valid by the verification procedure thanks to programmability. Though $Forge$ may ask verification query $Vval$ which is generated by invalid procedures, verification results in two systems are identical except a negligible probability because to generate a signature which is accepted to verification without the valid procedure (without f^{-1}) is difficult by one-wayness of Tdp. Thus, Env cannot distinguish the difference when $\psi = \emptyset$.

If some party is corrupted, hidden interfaces are not same between RS and $SSim$. In the real system, the corrupted endpoints hand final outputs $\{out'(*)\}$ to $Forge_k$, and $Forge_k$ outputs $\{out(*)\}$ instead of the corrupted endpoints. However, in the ideal system, $Funct$ hands final outputs $\{out'(*)\}$ of the corrupted endpoints to $SSim_k$. In order to fit this interface to same one in the real system, SV has an output task $\{lout(*)\}$ as outputs corresponding to $\{out'(*)\}$ in the real system to $Forge'_k$. Therefore, we are able to simulate interactions among Sig, Ver and $Forge_k$ by using SV and $Forge'_k$ since $Forge'_k$ is isomorphic to $Forge_k$ with replacing $\{out'(*)\}$ to $\{lout(*)\}$.

If the signer is corrupted (i.e., $Sig \in \psi$) in RS, then $Forge$ can arbitrarily set the verification key and signatures; that is, verification results are fully controlled. If $Sig \in \psi$ in SIS, then $Funct$ does not provide any guarantee of verification results for verification query $Vval$ which is generated by invalid procedures. $Funct$ simply outputs the verification result $\phi val = \theta val$ where θval is output by SV. Hence, $SSim$ can also control verification results by SV, and Env cannot distinguish the difference when $Sig \in \psi$.

If the verifier is corrupted (i.e., $Ver \in \psi$) in RS, then the verification key used to verify signatures can be different from one generated by the signer. Ver outputs the verification result by using the given verification key from $Forge$ based on fix'_i-ϕval; that is, verification results are fully controlled. If $Ver \in \psi$ in SIS, then $Funct$ simply outputs the verification result $\phi val = \theta val$ for an invalid verification key where θval is output by SV. Hence, $SSim$ can also control verification results by SV, and Env cannot distinguish the difference when $Ver \in \psi$.

The ideal system SIS from $SSim_k$ is defined as $Funct_k \| SSim_k$ with hiding $\{ask\}$, $\{rand\}$, $\{in\}$, $\{out'\}$, $\{lout\}$, $\{program\}$, $\{hash\}$, $\{hashed\}$, $\{ask\}$ and $\{reply\}$ tasks, and $\{in\}$ task of $Forge$. An illustration of SIS in the case of $\psi = \emptyset$ is given in Fig. 3.

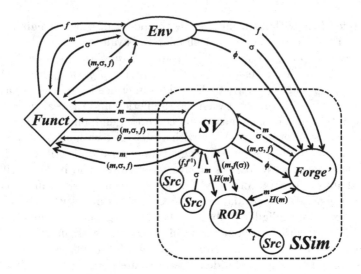

Fig. 3. Simulated ideal system SIS (Case of $\psi = \emptyset$)

4.2 Construction of Intermediate System Int

For each k, we construct an intermediate system Int_k which is parameterized by a trapdoor permutation pair $Tdpp$, a trapdoor permutation Tdp, a set of message identity MID, message space $\mathcal{M}$, signature space $\mathcal{D}$ and a set of corrupted endpoints ψ.

Int is the task-PIOA with replacing SV to SV' in SIS, where the difference between SV and SV' is that SV' generates signatures as the same as the real system. An illustration of Int in the case of $\psi = \emptyset$ is given in Fig. 4.

4.3 Proof of $\overline{RS} \leq_{neg,pt} \overline{Int}$

First, we prove the implementation relation between $\overline{RS}$ and $\overline{Int}$. The difference between two systems is how to decide the verification result ϕval. In $\overline{RS}$, ϕval is decided by whether $hvval(i) = fval(Vval(i).signature)$ holds, while, in $\overline{Int}$, ϕval is decided by whether the message and signature is validly registered or not. The important point is $Forge$ does not have f^{-1} (if Sig is uncorrupted). Thus, $Forge$ cannot obtain $f^{-1}(hsval(i))$ (resp. $f^{-1}(hvval(i))$) for a hash value $hsval(i)$ (resp. $hvval(i)$) without posing the signing query with a non-negligible probability, even if $Forge$ executes any arbitrary new actions. It is ensured from one-wayness of the trapdoor permutation $Tdpp$. Hence, we can show the implementation relation.

For $\overline{RS}$ and $\overline{Int}$, the following theorem holds.

Theorem 1. *If $Tdpp$ is one-way, then $\overline{RS} \leq_{neg,pt} \overline{Int}$.*

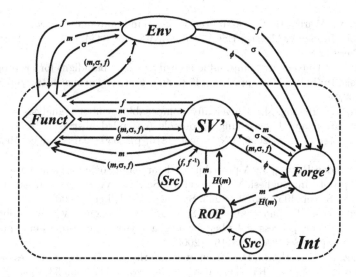

Fig. 4. Intermediate system Int (Case of $\psi = \emptyset$)

4.4 Proof of $\overline{Int} \leq_{neg,pt} \overline{SIS}$

Next, we prove the implementation relation between $\overline{Int}$ and $\overline{SIS}$. The difference between two systems is how to generate signatures. In $\overline{Int}$, σ is generated by using f^{-1} and ROH, while, in $\overline{SIS}$, σ is generated just by using ROP. From the power of programmability, the mapping between these tasks is perfect. More intuition was shown in Sect. 4.1.

For $\overline{Int}$ and $\overline{SIS}$, the following theorem holds.

Theorem 2. $\overline{Int} \leq_{neg,pt} \overline{SIS}$.

4.5 Conclusion of Proof

From transitivity of the implementation relation, $\overline{RS} \leq_{neg,pt} \overline{SIS}$ holds. Therefore, EUF-CMA of the FDH signature is proved in the task-PIOA framework.

References

1. Dolev, D., Yao, A.C.C.: On the security of public key protocols. In: FOCS 1981, pp. 350–357 (1981)
2. Abadi, M., Rogaway, P.: Reconciling two views of cryptography (the computational soundness of formal encryption). In: Watanabe, O., Hagiya, M., Ito, T., van Leeuwen, J., Mosses, P.D. (eds.) TCS 2000. LNCS, vol. 1872, pp. 3–22. Springer, Heidelberg (2000)
3. Micciancio, D., Warinschi, B.: Soundness of formal encryption in the presence of active adversaries. In: Naor, M. (ed.) TCC 2004. LNCS, vol. 2951, pp. 133–151. Springer, Heidelberg (2004)

4. Cortier, V., Warinschi, B.: Computationally sound, automated proofs for security protocols. In: Sagiv, M. (ed.) ESOP 2005. LNCS, vol. 3444, pp. 157–171. Springer, Heidelberg (2005)
5. Canetti, R.: Universally composable security: a new paradigm for cryptographic protocols. In: FOCS 2001, pp. 136–145 (2001). Full version is at http://eprint.iacr.org/2000/067
6. Canetti, R., Herzog, J.: Universally composable symbolic analysis of mutual authentication and key-exchange protocols (extended abstrast). In: Halevi, S., Rabin, T. (eds.) TCC 2006. LNCS, vol. 3876, pp. 380–403. Springer, Heidelberg (2006)
7. Corin, R., den Hartog, J.: A probabilistic hoare-style logic for game-based cryptographic proofs. In: Bugliesi, M., Preneel, B., Sassone, V., Wegener, I. (eds.) ICALP 2006. LNCS, vol. 4052, pp. 252–263. Springer, Heidelberg (2006)
8. Mitchell, J.C., Ramanathan, A., Scedrov, A., Teague, V.: A probabilistic polynomial-time process calculus for the analysis of cryptographic protocols. Theor. Comput. Sci. **353**, 118–164 (2006)
9. Blanchet, B., Pointcheval, D.: Automated security proofs with sequences of games. In: Dwork, C. (ed.) CRYPTO 2006. LNCS, vol. 4117, pp. 537–554. Springer, Heidelberg (2006)
10. Canetti, R., Cheung, L., Kaynar, D.K., Liskov, M., Lynch, N.A., Pereira, O., Segala, R.: Using task-structured probabilistic I/O automata to analyze an oblivious transfer protocol. Technical report, MIT CSAIL-TR-2007-011 (2007)
11. Canetti, R., Cheung, L., Kaynar, D.K., Liskov, M., Lynch, N.A., Pereira, O., Segala, R.: Analyzing security protocols using time-bounded task-PIOAs. Discrete Event Dyn. Syst. **18**(1), 111–159 (2008)
12. Yoneyama, K., Kokubun, Y., Ohta, K.: A security analysis on Diffie-Hellman key exchange against adaptive adversaries using task-structured PIOA. In: FCS-ARSPA 2007, pp. 131–148 (2007)
13. Cheung, L., Mitra, S., Pereira, O.: Verifying statistical zero knowledge with approximate implementations. In: Cryptology ePrint Archive 2007/195 (2007)
14. Jaggard, A.D., Meadows, C., Mislove, M., Segala, R.: Reasoning about probabilistic security using task-PIOAs. In: Armando, A., Lowe, G. (eds.) ARSPA-WITS 2010. LNCS, vol. 6186, pp. 2–22. Springer, Heidelberg (2010)
15. Canetti, R., Goldreich, O., Halevi, S.: The random oracle methodology, revisited (preliminary version). In: STOC 1998, pp. 209–218 (1998)
16. Bellare, M., Rogaway, P.: Random oracles are practical: a paradigm for designing efficient protocols. In: ACM Conference on Computer and Communications Security 1993, pp. 62–73 (1993)

Algebraic Cryptanalysis of Yasuda, Takagi and Sakurai's Signature Scheme

Wenbin Zhang$^{(\boxtimes)}$ and Chik How Tan

Temasek Laboratories, National University of Singapore,
Singapore, Singapore
{tslzw,tsltch}@nus.edu.sg

Abstract. Recently Yasuda, Takagi and Sakurai proposed a new and interesting signature scheme from the classification of quadratic forms over finite fields of odd characteristic published in PQCrypto 2013. In this paper we propose two algebraic attacks to their scheme using only linear algebra. Both attacks are motivated by Kipnis and Shamir's attack to the oil-vinegar signature scheme. Namely we first turn the original problem to a geometric problem and then apply the theory of invariant subspace intensively. We show that Yasuda, Takagi and Sakurai's scheme can be broken by our attacks with complexity $O(m^{\frac{11}{2}} q^d)$ where m is the number of variables and q is the size of the base field. Here d is expected generally to be 1 and is confirmed in our tests. We also compare our attacks with Y. Hashimoto's attack which is just published in PQCrypto 2014.

Keywords: Post-quantum cryptography · Multivariate public key cryptosystem · Quadratic form

1 Introduction

Multivariate public key cryptosystems (MPKCs) are considered as one of the possible candidates that could resist the threat of quantum computer in the future. The public keys of MPKCs are normally constructed as $\bar{F} = L \circ F \circ R :$ $\mathbb{F}_q^n \to \mathbb{F}_q^m$ where the central map $F : \mathbb{F}_q^n \to \mathbb{F}_q^m$ is a polynomial map and $L : \mathbb{F}_q^n \to$ $\mathbb{F}_q^n$, $R : \mathbb{F}_q^m \to \mathbb{F}_q^m$ are invertible affine maps. The security of MPKCs is backed by the NP-hard problem of solving a general system of polynomial equations. This area has been developed fast and many schemes have been proposed since 1980's but most of them have been broken, referring to [WP05b, DGS06, DY09] for an overview.

At PQCrypto 2013, Yasuda, Takagi and Sakurai [YTS13] proposed a new and interesting multivariate scheme using quadratic forms over finite fields of odd characteristic, suitable for signature schemes. The mathematical foundation of their construction is the classification of quadratic forms over finite fields of odd characteristic which classifies all quadratic forms

$$f : \mathbb{F}_q^n \to \mathbb{F}_q, \quad f(x_1, \ldots, x_n) = \sum_{1 \leq i \leq j \leq n} a_{ij} x_i x_j$$

© Springer International Publishing Switzerland 2015
J. Lee and J. Kim (Eds.): ICISC 2014, LNCS 8949, pp. 53–66, 2015.
DOI: 10.1007/978-3-319-15943-0_4

(q odd) into only two equivalence classes, cf. Theorem 3.8 in Chap. 2 of [Sch85]. Each class can be represented by a very simple quadratic form and this classification has a simple matrix representation. Yasuda, Takagi and Sakurai discover that this matrix representation can be used to construct a pair of polynomial maps

$$F_1, F_2 : \mathbb{F}_q^{n^2} \to \mathbb{F}_q^{n(n+1)/2}$$

(q odd) corresponding to the two equivalence classes. Then they use the two maps to construct a multivariate signature scheme. They claim that their scheme is eight to nine times more efficient than the well known Rainbow signature scheme [DS05] in generating a signature. They give a detailed comparison [YTS13] showing that the complexity of inverting the central map (F_1, F_2) of their scheme is $O(n^3)$, while it is $O(n^6)$ for Rainbow. Moreover they claim that their scheme has a security level of 88-bit if $q > 2^{11} = 2048$ and $n = 8$ with public key size of about 154 Kbytes, and of 140-bit if $q > 6781$ and $n = 11$ with public key size of about 990 Kbytes.

However we find that their scheme has very specific algebraic structure and investigate its impact on the security of their scheme. We first find a very simple matrix expression of their public map in terms of the private key, and observe that we may apply here Kipnis and Shamir's idea [KS98, KPG99, CHDY11] of attacking the (unbalanced) oil-vinegar signature scheme [Pat97, KPG99]. Recall that their idea is to first convert the public map of the (unbalanced) oil-vinegar scheme into another form and then the problem of finding an equivalent key [WP05a] becomes a geometric problem, i.e. finding a certain common invariant subspace of a set of linear maps. Motivated by their idea, we convert the problem of finding an equivalent key of Yasuda, Takagi and Sakurai's scheme into a geometric problem: finding a special decomposition of the whole space into certain invariant subspaces and finding appropriate bases for these subspaces. We then propose two methods, using the theory of invariant subspaces [Cla] intensively, to solve this geometric problem and thus recover the private keys of their scheme. Complexity of our two attacks is $O(m^{\frac{11}{2}} q^d)$ where $m = n^2$ and d is expected generally to be 1. This d is in fact always 1 in our dozens of tests. So Yasuda, Takagi and Sakurai's scheme can be broken and should not be used alone. Implementation of our attack is currently in progress and may appear in an extended version of this paper.

We remark that the first version of this paper was submitted to ICISC 2014 in the middle of September and that there is an independent paper of Y. Hashimoto [Has14] published in PQCrypto 2014 just in early October. Hashimoto proposes an attack to Yasuda, Takagi and Sakurai's scheme with complexity $O(m^4)$, and claims that he implements his attack and recovers in several minutes the private key of the scheme with 140-bits security level against the min-rank attacks. Hashimoto's approach and ours are different but also related. We shall give a comparison between the two approaches in this paper.

2   Yasuda, Takagi and Sakurai's Signature Scheme

The topic of quadratic forms is a well studied in mathematics and there is a well known classification of quadratic forms. Yasuda, Takagi and Sakurai discover that this classification can be used to construct a signature scheme. Before giving their scheme, we shall first recall the following classification theorem, c.f. Theorem 3.8 in Chap. 2 of [Sch85].

Theorem 1. *Let q be odd and δ a non-square element in $\mathbb{F}_q$. If $f \in \mathbb{F}_q[x_1, \ldots, x_n]$ is a quadratic form, then f is either equivalent to*

$$x_r^2 + x_{r+1}^2 + \cdots + x_n^2 \tag{1}$$

or

$$x_r^2 + x_{r+1}^2 + \cdots + \delta x_n^2. \tag{2}$$

for a certain unique r, and the above two quadratic forms are not equivalent.

We remark that it does not matter which non-square element is chosen since this classification assures that for any other non-square element ϵ, $x_r^2 + x_{r+1}^2 + \cdots + \epsilon x_n^2$ is equivalent to $x_r^2 + x_{r+1}^2 + \cdots + \delta x_n^2$.

Note that $x_r^2 + x_{r+1}^2 + \cdots + x_n^2$ can be obtained from $y_1^2 + y_2^2 + \cdots + y_n^2$ by applying the transformation $y_i = 0$ for $i < r$ and $y_i = x_i$ for $i \geq r$. The same holds for another one. Thus the above theorem can be restated as follows.

Theorem 2. *Let q be odd and δ a non-square element in $\mathbb{F}_q$. Then any quadratic form $f \in \mathbb{F}_q[x_1, \ldots, x_n]$ can be obtained from*

$$x_1^2 + x_2^2 + \cdots + x_n^2 \tag{3}$$

or

$$x_1^2 + x_2^2 + \cdots + \delta x_n^2. \tag{4}$$

via a certain linear transformation.

This theorem can be expressed in terms of matrices.

Theorem 3. *Let A be an $n \times n$ matrix over $\mathbb{F}_q$, where q is odd, and δ a non-square element in $\mathbb{F}_q$. Then there is an $n \times n$ matrix X over $\mathbb{F}_q$ such that either $A = X^T X$ or $A = X^T I_{n,\delta} X$ where $I_{n,\delta} = \begin{pmatrix} I_{n-1} & \\ & \delta \end{pmatrix}$, and I_{n-1} is the $(n-1) \times (n-1)$ identity matrix.*

It is known in linear algebra how to compute such a matrix X and an algorithm is sketched in [YTS13]. The above result can be applied to construct a signature scheme in the following way following [YTS13].

For $X = (x_{ij})_{n \times n} \in \mathbb{F}_q^{n^2}$ regarded as an $n \times n$ matrix, let

$$F_1(X) = (f_{ij}(X))_{1 \leq i \leq j \leq n}, F_2(X) = (f'_{ij}(X))_{1 \leq i \leq j \leq n} \in \mathbb{F}_q^{n(n+1)/2}$$

be the upper triangular parts of $X^T X$ and $X^T I_{n,\delta} X$ respectively. Then F_1, F_2 are two multivariate quadratic polynomial maps. Neither F_1 nor F_2 is surjective but the union of their images can cover $\mathbb{F}_q^{n(n+1)/2}$. The pair (F_1, F_2) can serve as the central map of a multivariate signature scheme.

Let $R_1, R_2 : \mathbb{F}_q^{n^2} \to \mathbb{F}_q^{n^2}$ and $L : \mathbb{F}_q^{n(n+1)/2} \to \mathbb{F}_q^{n(n+1)/2}$ be three randomly chosen invertible affine transformations and

$$\bar{F}_1 = L \circ F_1 \circ R_1, \quad \bar{F}_2 = L \circ F_2 \circ R_2.$$

Yasuda, Takagi and Sakurai's (YTS' for short) scheme can be described as follows.

Public Key. $\bar{F}_1, \bar{F}_2$.

Private Key. R_1, R_2, L.

Signature Generation. For a message $M = (m_{ij})_{1 \leq i \leq j \leq n} \in \mathbb{F}_q^{n(n+1)/2}$, first compute $M' = (m'_{ij})_{1 \leq i \leq j \leq n} = L^{-1}(M)$, then compute an $n \times n$ matrix X' such that $F_1(X') = M'$ or $F_2(X') = M'$ and finally compute $X = R_1^{-1}(X')$ or $X = R_2^{-1}(X')$ correspondingly.

Verification. A signature X is accepted if $\bar{F}_1(X) = M$ or $\bar{F}_2(X) = M$, otherwise rejected.

It is unnecessary to keep the chosen non-square element δ secret as any non-square element can work equivalently.

3   Our Expression of YTS' Public Map

In this section we shall give a simple and elegant expression of YTS' public map in terms of the private key. This expression is important for our algebraic cryptanalysis. From now on we consider only the first map of the public key

$$\bar{F} = L \circ F \circ R.$$

We remark that if the central map is quadratic homogeneous, then the affine part of R, L can be easily recovered from the linear part of the public key. Such phenomenon is investigated for SFLASH in [GSB01, GS03] and also for YTS' scheme in [Has14]. The method to recover the affine part is indeed just letting the linear part of the public key be zero and then solving the resulted linear system. Hence we simply assume that both L, R are linear in the following.

Write $\bar{F} = (\bar{f}_1, \ldots, \bar{f}_{\frac{1}{2}n(n+1)})$. Since both L, R are assumed linear, $\bar{f}_k$ is homogeneous and can be written as

$$\bar{f}_k(X) = X^T A_k X, \quad X = (x_{11}, \ldots, x_{1n}, x_{21}, \ldots, x_{2n}, \ldots, x_{n1}, \ldots, x_{nn}) \in \mathbb{F}^{n^2}$$

where X is regarded as a column vector and A_k is an $n^2 \times n^2$ matrix publicly known. For $n \times n$ matrix $X' = (x'_{ij})_{n \times n}$,

$$X'^T X' = \begin{pmatrix} x'^2_{11} + \cdots + x'^2_{n1} & x'_{11}x'_{12} + \cdots + x'_{n1}x'_{n2} & \cdots & x'_{11}x'_{1n} + \cdots + x'_{n1}x'_{nn} \\ x'_{11}x'_{12} + \cdots + x'_{n1}x'_{n2} & x'^2_{12} + \cdots + x'^2_{n2} & \cdots & x'_{12}x'_{1n} + \cdots + x'_{n2}x'_{nn} \\ \vdots & \vdots & \ddots & \vdots \\ x'_{11}x'_{1n} + \cdots + x'_{n1}x'_{nn} & x'_{12}x'_{1n} + \cdots + x'_{n2}x'_{nn} & \cdots & x'^2_{1n} + \cdots + x'^2_{nn} \end{pmatrix}$$

thus $F(X') = (f_{ij}(X'))_{1 \le i \le j \le n}$ is given as follows

$$f_{ii} = x_{1i}'^2 + \cdots + x_{ni}'^2, 1 \le i \le n,$$
$$f_{ij} = x_{1i}'x_{1j}' + \cdots + x_{ni}'x_{nj}', 1 \le i < j \le n.$$

Next X' is regarded as the vector $(x_{11}', \ldots, x_{1n}', x_{21}', \ldots, x_{2n}', \ldots, x_{n1}', \ldots, x_{nn}') \in \mathbb{F}^{n^2}$. Write the $\frac{1}{2}n(n+1) \times \frac{1}{2}n(n+1)$ matrix L in the following form

$$L = \begin{pmatrix} l_{1;1,1} & l_{1;1,2} & l_{1;2,2} & \cdots & l_{1;1,n} & \cdots & l_{1;n,n} \\ \vdots & \vdots & \vdots & & \vdots & & \vdots \\ l_{\frac{1}{2}n(n+1);1,1} & l_{\frac{1}{2}n(n+1);1,2} & l_{\frac{1}{2}n(n+1);2,2} & \cdots & l_{\frac{1}{2}n(n+1);1,n} & \cdots & l_{\frac{1}{2}n(n+1);n,n} \end{pmatrix}$$

For each $1 \le k \le \frac{1}{2}n(n+1)$, the kth component of $L \circ F$ is

$$(L \circ F)_k = \sum_{1 \le i \le j \le n} l_{k;i,j} f_{ij} = \sum_{1 \le s \le n} \sum_{1 \le i \le j \le n} l_{k;i,j} x_{si}' x_{sj}'$$

which can be written in the following matrix form

$$(L \circ F)_k(X') = X'^T \begin{pmatrix} L_k & & \\ & \ddots & \\ & & L_k \end{pmatrix} X'$$

where L_k is the following symmetric matrix corresponding to the kth row of L,

$$L_k = \begin{pmatrix} l_{k;1,1} & \frac{1}{2}l_{k;1,2} & \cdots & \frac{1}{2}l_{k;1,n} \\ \frac{1}{2}l_{k;1,2} & l_{k;2,2} & \cdots & \frac{1}{2}l_{k;2,n} \\ \vdots & \vdots & \ddots & \vdots \\ \frac{1}{2}l_{k;1,n} & \frac{1}{2}l_{k;2,n} & \cdots & l_{k;n,n} \end{pmatrix}.$$

Substitute $X' = RX$, then we have the following simple matrix representation for the public map

$$\bar{f}_k(X) = (L \circ F \circ R)_k(X) = X^T R^T \begin{pmatrix} L_k & & \\ & \ddots & \\ & & L_k \end{pmatrix} RX.$$

In particular, the representing matrix A_k of $\bar{f}_k(X) = X^T A_k X$ has the following simple expression

$$A_k = R^T \begin{pmatrix} L_k & & \\ & \ddots & \\ & & L_k \end{pmatrix} R. \tag{5}$$

Based on the above expression, we shall propose two methods to find R and all L_k in the rest of this paper. The starting point of our two methods is motivated by Kipnis and Shamir's idea of attacking the oil-vinegar signature scheme [KS98]. Namely we shall convert the Eq. (5) to another form which has geometric meaning so that the theory of invariant subspaces can be applied here.

4   First Attack

If A_l is invertible (equivalently L_l is invertible), let $A_{lk} = A_l^{-1} A_k$ and $L_{lk} = L_l^{-1} L_k$. Then

$$A_{lk} = R^{-1} \begin{pmatrix} L_l^{-1} \\ & \ddots \\ & & L_l^{-1} \end{pmatrix} R^{-T} R^T \begin{pmatrix} L_k \\ & \ddots \\ & & L_k \end{pmatrix} R = R^{-1} \begin{pmatrix} L_{lk} \\ & \ddots \\ & & L_{lk} \end{pmatrix} R,$$

$$A_{lk} R^{-1} = R^{-1} \begin{pmatrix} L_{lk} \\ & \ddots \\ & & L_{lk} \end{pmatrix}.$$

We observe that this has the following geometric meaning, referring to [Cla] for the theory of invariant subspaces.

Theorem 4. *The linear subspace of* $\mathbb{F}_q^{n^2}$, *denoted* V_s, *spanned by* $R_{(s-1)n+1}, \cdots, R_{sn}$ *where* R_i *the* ith *column vector of* R^{-1}, *is an* n-*dimensional invariant subspace of* A_{lk} *for all possible* l, k, *and*

$$A_{lk}(R_{(s-1)n+1}, \ldots, R_{sn}) = (R_{(s-1)n+1}, \ldots, R_{sn}) L_{lk}.$$

Moreover, $\mathbb{F}_q^{n^2}$ *is a direct sum of these* n *invariant subspaces,*

$$\mathbb{F}_q^{n^2} = \bigoplus_{s=1}^{n} V_s.$$

In addition, we also observe that these invariant subspaces V_s have the following property related to the original A_k. This property will be useful later.

Theorem 5. *For* $\mathbf{u} \in V_s$ *and* $\mathbf{v} \in V_{s'}$ $(s \neq s')$, *we have* $\mathbf{u}^T A_k \mathbf{v} = 0$.

Proof. This is true for $R_{(s-1)n+i}$ and $R_{(s'-1)n+j}$ since

$$(R^{-1})^T A_k R^{-1} = \begin{pmatrix} L_k \\ & \ddots \\ & & L_k \end{pmatrix}.$$

Then the conclusion follows by the definition of V_s.

Based on this observation, our strategy is to first decompose inductively $\mathbb{F}_q^{n^2}$ into a direct sum of smaller linear subspaces,

$$\mathbb{F}_q^{n^2} = U_1 \oplus U_2 \oplus \cdots$$

such that each U_i is invariant under all A_{lk}. If we finally find an invariant decomposition

$$\mathbb{F}_q^{n^2} = \bigoplus_{s=1}^{n} U_s$$

such that each U_s is of dimension n, then compute a basis of U_s such that with respect to this basis, the representing matrix of A_{lk} to U_s is L_{lk}.

4.1   Finding an Invariant Decomposition of $\mathbb{F}_q^{n^2}$

To decompose $\mathbb{F}_q^{n^2}$ into smaller invariant subspaces, we may pick a nonzero vector $\mathbf{u} \in \mathbb{F}_q^{n^2}$, and then compute the invariant subspace, denoted $[\mathbf{u}]$, generated by $\mathbf{u}$ under all possible A_{lk}. There will be two cases: (1) $\dim[\mathbf{u}] = n^2$, i.e. $[\mathbf{u}] = \mathbb{F}_q^{n^2}$, and (2) $\dim[\mathbf{u}] < n^2$. In the second case we shall call $\mathbf{u}$ a proper vector. If it is the first case, then we pick another nonzero vector and repeat this process until a proper invariant subspace is obtained.

For the chance to get a proper vector, we have the following estimation.

Proposition 1. *The probability that a random vector being proper is no less than* $1 - (1 - q^{-n})^n$, *and*

$$q^{-n} < 1 - (1 - q^{-n})^n < nq^{-n}.$$

Proof. Given an invariant decomposition $\mathbb{F}_q^{n^2} = V_1 \oplus \cdots \oplus V_n$ with $\dim V_i = n$, picking randomly a vector $\mathbf{v} \in \mathbb{F}_q^{n^2}$ is equivalently to picking randomly n vectors $\mathbf{v}_i \in V_i$. If there is one $\mathbf{v}_i = 0$, then $\mathbf{v}$ is proper. The probability that at least one $\mathbf{v}_i = 0$ is $1 - (1 - q^{-n})^n$. Thus the probability that a random vector being proper is no less than $1 - (1 - q^{-n})^n$. The claimed inequality comes from the following one

$$q^{-n} < 1 - (1 - q^{-n})^n = q^{-n}[1 + (1 - q^{-n}) + \cdots + (1 - q^{-n})^{n-1}] < nq^{-n}.$$

We remark that even if there is no $\mathbf{v}_i = 0$ for a decomposition $\mathbb{F}_q^{n^2} = V_1 \oplus \cdots \oplus V_n$, there can be other such decomposition having it. Hence the probability that a random vector being proper is expected to be higher than $1 - (1 - q^{-n})^n$.

However, the probability $1 - (1 - q^{-n})^n$ may be too small if q^n is still too large. To increase the chance of getting proper vectors, we shall use the following method to reduce the searching range significantly. From the theory of invariant subspaces, cf. [Cla], invariant subspaces are essentially related with the minimum polynomial of a linear map. From the form of A_{lk}, A_{lk} and L_{lk} share the same minimum polynomial, denoted ϕ_{lk}, and the characteristic polynomial of A_{lk} is the nth power of the one of L_{lk}. For each irreducible factor ψ of ϕ_{lk}, $\ker \psi(A_{lk})$ is a special linear subspace of $\mathbb{F}_q^{n^2}$ with the property that any nonzero vector of it has the irreducible ψ as its minimum polynomial, and

$$\ker \psi(A_{lk}) = \bigoplus_{s=1}^{n} (V_s \cap \ker \psi(A_{lk}))$$

and all $V_s \cap \ker \psi(A_{lk})$ have the same dimension thus $n \mid \dim \ker \psi(A_{lk})$. As $\ker \psi(A_{lk})$ is much smaller than $\mathbb{F}_q^{n^2}$, it is a better space to search for proper vectors. Among all $\ker \psi(A_{lk})$ for all l, k and irreducible factors, we can choose one of them which is of minimum dimension and denote it V_0. Since $n \mid \dim V_0$, write $\dim V_0 = dn$. It is expected that d is generally only 1. Using V_0 to search for proper vectors, the chance of getting a proper vector increases to no less than $1 - (1 - q^{-d})^n$ which satisfies

$$q^{-d} < 1 - (1 - q^{-d})^n < nq^{-d}.$$

We start from picking randomly a nonzero vector $\mathbf{u}_1 \in V_0$. To compute the invariant subspace $[\mathbf{u}_1]$, generated by $\mathbf{u}_1$ under all possible A_{lk}, we may compute the linear subspace spanned by $\mathbf{u}_1$, $A_{lk}\mathbf{u}_1$, ..., $A_{lk}^{n^2}\mathbf{u}_1$ for some l and all k. If n divides its dimension then it is very likely to be $[\mathbf{u}_1]$. If no then extend this subspace by adding more vectors of this form $A_{l'k'}^i A_{lk}^j \mathbf{u}_1$ etc. The probability that $\mathbf{u}_1$ is proper is no less than $1 - (1 - q^{-d})^n > q^{-d}$. If $\dim[\mathbf{u}_1] = \dim V_0 = n^2$, i.e. $[\mathbf{u}_1]$ is the whole space, then try another vector which is linearly independent of $\mathbf{u}_1$. After at most q^d trials, a proper vector can be obtained with probability almost 1.

After getting a proper vector $\mathbf{u}_1 \in V_0$, let $U_1 = [\mathbf{u}_1]$. We next find another proper vector in V_0. Theorem 5 can be used here to significantly reduce the searching range. Namely we search for a proper vector $\mathbf{u}_2 \in V_0 - U_1$ which additionally satisfies $\mathbf{u}_2^T A_k \mathbf{v} = 0$ for all $\mathbf{v} \in U_1$. Then let $U_2 = [\mathbf{u}_2]$ and we have a bigger subspace $U_1 \oplus U_2$.

Continuing this process we can get an invariant decomposition of $\mathbb{F}_q^{n^2} = U_1 \oplus \cdots \oplus U_t$. Some of these factors may have dimension greater than n. For each such factor, we decompose it further using the same method. Finally we can obtain an invariant decomposition $\mathbb{F}_q^{n^2} = V_1 \oplus \cdots \oplus V_n$ with each V_i of dimension n.

4.2   Finding the Desired Bases

After finding such a desired invariant decomposition $\mathbb{F}_q^{n^2} = V_1 \oplus \cdots \oplus V_n$ and a basis $\mathbf{v}_{i1}, \ldots, \mathbf{v}_{in}$ for each V_i, these bases give the following $n^2 \times n^2$ matrix

$$S = (\mathbf{v}_{11}, \ldots, \mathbf{v}_{1n}, \ldots, \mathbf{v}_{n1}, \ldots, \mathbf{v}_{nn})$$

which has the following property

$$S^{-1}A_{lk}S = \begin{pmatrix} L_{lk1} & & \\ & \ddots & \\ & & L_{lkn} \end{pmatrix}, \quad \text{i.e.} \quad A_{lk}S = S\begin{pmatrix} L_{lk1} & & \\ & \ddots & \\ & & L_{lkn} \end{pmatrix},$$

where each L_{lki} is an $n \times n$ matrix. So

$$A_{lk}(\mathbf{v}_{i1}, \ldots, \mathbf{v}_{in}) = (\mathbf{v}_{i1}, \ldots, \mathbf{v}_{in})L_{lki}.$$

Let $(R_1, \ldots, R_n) = (\mathbf{v}_{11}, \ldots, \mathbf{v}_{1n})$. Then $L_{lk} = L_{lk1}$. We want to find $n \times n$ matrices T_i such that

$$(R_{(i-1)n+1}, \ldots, R_{in}) = (\mathbf{v}_{i1}, \ldots, \mathbf{v}_{in})T_i.$$

These T_i satisfy

$$L_{lk} = T_i^{-1} L_{lki} T_i, \quad \text{i.e.} \quad T_i L_{lk} = L_{lki} T_i, \quad \text{for } i > 1.$$

So each T_i can be solved from the following linear equations:

$$T_i L_{lk} - L_{lki} T_i = 0, \quad \text{for all possible } l, k.$$

After computing all T_i, we then obtain R^{-1} and R as well. Thus L_k can be obtained by computing $(R^{-1})^T A_k R^{-1}$. So L is also obtained.

4.3   Our First Algorithm

To summarize, our first algorithm for finding an equivalent key (R, L) is given as follows:

1. Find some invertible A_l among all A_k and compute $A_{lk} = A_l^{-1} A_k$.
2. Compute all the primary factors of the minimum polynomial, or equivalently of the characteristic polynomial of A_{lk}.
3. For each A_{lk} and each primary factor ψ computed in Step 2, compute $\psi(A_{lk})$, then compare the dimension of ker $\psi(A_{lk})$. Among all these ker $\psi(A_{lk})$, pick the one, denoted V_0, with least dimension dn where d is expected generally to be 1.
4. Pick a nonzero vector $\mathbf{u}_1 \in V_0$ and compute the invariant subspace $[\mathbf{u}_1]$ by computing the linear subspace spanned by $\mathbf{u}_1, A_{lk}\mathbf{u}_1, \ldots, A_{lk}^{n^2}\mathbf{u}_1$ for some l and all k — if necessary then add more vectors of this form $A_{l'k'}^i A_{lk}^j \mathbf{u}_1$ etc. If $\dim[\mathbf{u}_1] = \dim V_0 = n^2$, then try another vector which is linearly independent of $\mathbf{u}_1$. A proper vector is expected to be obtained within q^d trials.
5. Search for a proper vector $\mathbf{u}_2 \in V_0 - [\mathbf{u}_1]$ which additionally satisfies $\mathbf{u}_2^T A_k \mathbf{v} = 0$ for all $\mathbf{v} \in [\mathbf{u}_1]$. Continuing this process until we get $\mathbb{F}_q^{n^2} = [\mathbf{u}_1] \oplus \cdots \oplus [\mathbf{u}_t]$.
6. If $\dim[\mathbf{u}_i] > n$, then decompose it using the above method until we get $\mathbb{F}_q^{n^2} = V_1 \oplus \cdots \oplus V_n$ with $\dim V_i = n$ and a basis $\mathbf{v}_{i1}, \ldots, \mathbf{v}_{in}$ for each V_i.
7. Compute $S^{-1} A_{lk} S$ to get L_{lki} and $L_{lk} = L_{lk1}$.
8. Solve linear equations $T_i L_{lk} - L_{lki} T_i = 0$ for all possible l, k to get T_i.
9. Compute $(R_{(i-1)n+1}, \ldots, R_{in}) = (\mathbf{v}_{i1}, \ldots, \mathbf{v}_{in}) T_i$. Then R^{-1} and thus R is found.
10. Compute $(R^{-1})^T A_k R^{-1}$ to find L_k for all k. Thus L is found.

We estimate the complexity of this algorithm in terms of $GF(q)$ operations in the following.

Proposition 2. *The complexity of this algorithm is $O(m^{\frac{11}{2}} q^d)$ where $m = n^2$ is the number of variables of YTS' scheme and d is expected generally to be 1.*

It should be mentioned that this d is in fact always 1 in our dozens of tests of the two parameter sets (1) $q = p = 2053$, $n = 8$, $m = 64$ and (2) $q = p = 6781$, $n = 11$, $m = 121$ in YTS' scheme [YTS13]. So the complexity drops to $O(m^{\frac{11}{2}} q)$.

Proof. Step 1 requires $O(n^8)$ $\mathbb{F}_q$ operations. In Step 2, the primary factors can be computed using Berlekamp's algorithm [Ber67, Ber70, vzGP01] or recent faster algorithms of Kedlaya and Umans whose complexity is $O(n^{1.5+o(1)} \log^{1+o(1)} q + n^{1+o(1)} \log^{2+o(1)} q)$ [KU11], so the complexity of this step is $O((n^2 + n)(n^{1.5+o(1)} \log^{1+o(1)} q + n^{1+o(1)} \log^{2+o(1)} q))$. Step 3 needs $O(n^9)$ $\mathbb{F}_q$ operations, Steps 4–6 require $O(n^{11}q^d)$, and Steps 7–10 needs $O(n^8)$. So the total complexity of this algorithm is $O(n^{11}q^d)$. Since $n = \sqrt{m}$, we have the claimed estimation $O(m^{\frac{11}{2}} q^d)$.

The success probability is expected to be high whose accurate estimation requires further work. Computer implementation of this algorithm also needs to be done in the future.

5   Second Attack

In this section we propose another attack which may be more efficient than the first one. We shall first use the classification of quadratic forms to reduce the searching range of possible equivalent keys, and then apply the first attack with some modification.

Among L_k, $1 \leq k \leq \frac{1}{2}n(n+1)$, we pick an invertible one. The probability is close to 1. Assume L_1 is invertible. Then L_1 has decomposition $L_1 = M^T M$ or $L_1 = M^T I_{n,\delta} M$ where M is invertible, and the probability of any of them is $\frac{1}{2}$. If $L_1 = M^T M$, then

$$A_1 = R^T \begin{pmatrix} M & & \\ & \ddots & \\ & & M \end{pmatrix}^T \begin{pmatrix} M & & \\ & \ddots & \\ & & M \end{pmatrix} R,$$

and $\det A_1$ is a square. If $L_1 = M^T I_{n,\delta} M$, then

$$A_1 = R^T \begin{pmatrix} M & & \\ & \ddots & \\ & & M \end{pmatrix}^T \begin{pmatrix} I_{n,\delta} & & \\ & \ddots & \\ & & I_{n,\delta} \end{pmatrix} \begin{pmatrix} M & & \\ & \ddots & \\ & & M \end{pmatrix} R,$$

and $\det A_1$ is a product of a square and δ^n which implies that $\det A_1$ is a square if n is even and non-square if n is odd. In any case let

$$\bar{R} = \begin{pmatrix} M & & \\ & \ddots & \\ & & M \end{pmatrix} R$$

then

$$A_1 = \bar{R}^T \bar{R}, \quad \text{or} \quad A_1 = \bar{R}^T \begin{pmatrix} I_{n,\delta} & & \\ & \ddots & \\ & & I_{n,\delta} \end{pmatrix} \bar{R},$$

and

$$A_k = \bar{R}^T \begin{pmatrix} M^{-T} L_k M^{-1} & & \\ & \ddots & \\ & & M^{-T} L_k M^{-1} \end{pmatrix} \bar{R},$$

for $k > 1$. This means that $\bar{R}$ and $M^{-T} L_k M^{-1}$ is equivalent to R and L_k, i.e. they are equivalent keys. In other words, L_1 can be simplified as I_n or $I_{n,\delta}$. Or conversely, one may simplify the left upper $n \times n$ submatrix of R as I_n as it can be absorbed into L_1 provided that it is invertible.

On the other hand, we compute decomposition

$$A_1 = P^T P, \quad \text{and/or} \quad A_1 = P'^T \begin{pmatrix} I_{n,\delta} & & \\ & \ddots & \\ & & I_{n,\delta} \end{pmatrix} P'.$$

Any of the two cases can happen, so we should try both of them. For simplicity, we consider only the first case in the following.

After having $A_1 = P^T P$, there is an equivalent key (R, L) with $R = Q^{-1} P$ for a certain $n^2 \times n^2$ orthogonal matrix Q, i.e. $Q^T Q = I_{n^2}$, from the above discussion. The number of all $n^2 \times n^2$ orthogonal matrices is greater than $O(q^{n^2})$ which is too huge so that it is infeasible to check one by one to find a right one. Anyhow we can apply our first attack to find a right orthogonal matrix.

$$R^{-T} A_k R^{-1} = Q^{-1} P^{-T} A_k P^{-1} Q = \begin{pmatrix} L_k & & \\ & \ddots & \\ & & L_k \end{pmatrix}.$$

Let $\bar{A}_k = P^{-T} A_k P^{-1}$, then we have

$$\bar{A}_k Q = Q \begin{pmatrix} L_k & & \\ & \ddots & \\ & & L_k \end{pmatrix}.$$

This has the following geometric meaning: the columns of Q is an orthonormal basis for $\mathbb{F}_q^{n^2}$ since $Q^T Q = I_{n^2}$, and they are divided into n groups in order such that the subspace spanned by each group of vectors is an n dimensional invariant subspace of all $\bar{A}_k$.

Hence we want to find an *orthogonal* invariant decomposition $\mathbb{F}_q^{n^2} = V_1 \oplus \cdots \oplus V_n$ such that $\dim V_i = n$ and each V_i is invariant under all $\bar{A}_k$, i.e. $\bar{A}_k(V_i) \leq V_i$. The rest of this attack is then almost the same as the first attack, but using orthogonality in appropriate places.

Complexity of the second attack is at the same level as the first attack but expected to be more efficient because an additional condition, i.e. the orthogonality used here can reduce the complexity.

6   Comparison with Y. Hashimoto's Attack

In PQCrypto 2014, Y. Hashimoto [Has14] proposes an attack to YTS' scheme in polynomial time. In this section we shall compare our attacks and Hashimoto's using our notations.

The starting difference is the labeling of the variables which results in different expression of the public map. Namely, we label the variables as

$$X = (x_{11}, \ldots, x_{1n}, x_{21}, \ldots, x_{2n}, \ldots, x_{n1}, \ldots, x_{nn})$$

in Sect. 3, while Hashimoto labels them as

$$X = (x_{11}, \ldots, x_{n1}, x_{12}, \ldots, x_{n2}, \ldots, x_{1n}, \ldots, x_{nn}).$$

Corresponding to the two ways of labeling, the first part of the public map has the following expressions respectively,

$$A_k = R^T \begin{pmatrix} L_k & & \\ & \ddots & \\ & & L_k \end{pmatrix} R \quad \text{and} \quad A_k = R^T (L_k \otimes I_n) R.$$

Here $A \otimes B$ is the Kronecker product of two $n \times n$ matrices $A = (a_{ij})_{nn}$ and B defined as

$$A \otimes B = \begin{pmatrix} a_{11}B & \cdots & a_{1n}B \\ \vdots & & \vdots \\ a_{n1}B & \cdots & a_{nn}B \end{pmatrix}$$

Although this seems negligible, it leads to different approaches. Namely the first one has very clear geometric meaning after converting to

$$(A_l^{-1} A_k) R^{-1} = R^{-1} \begin{pmatrix} L_{lk} & & \\ & \ddots & \\ & & L_{lk} \end{pmatrix},$$

and reveals the hidden structures of YTS' scheme. This leads us to a geometric approach to recover the private key by applying the theory of invariant subspaces. However, the second one does not have such geometric interpretation. Hashimoto deals with it in a purely algebraic approach. He first observes that the private key can be recovered if R is of the following special form

$$R = (Q \otimes I_n) \begin{pmatrix} N_1 & & \\ & \ddots & \\ & & N_n \end{pmatrix},$$

where $Q, N_1, \ldots, N_n$ are $n \times n$ matrices, and then for general R, he develops algorithms to find an invertible P such that RP is of this form and thus recovers the private key for the general case.

Despite the above difference, both of the two approaches have some parts influenced by Kipnis and Shamir's attack to the oil-vinegar signature scheme [KS98]. In our approach, we are motivated to convert $A_k = R^T(\cdots)R$ into $A_l^{-1}A_k = R^{-1}(\cdots)R$ so that the problem can be converted into a geometric problem and be solved by the theory of invariant subspaces. In Hashimoto's attack, the method of finding the P is also analogous, to some extent, to Kipnis and Shamir's method.

In addition, the complexity of our attack and Hashimoto's is comparable. Ours is $O(n^{11}q^d)$ with d expected to be 1 generally, while Hashimoto's is $O(n^8)$. It should be noted that here n^2 is the number of variables. Hence Hashimoto's attack is a bit more efficient than ours.

7   Conclusion

Yasuda, Takagi and Sakurai's signature scheme is very efficient due to its special structure. However, we find that this structure has very strong algebraic and geometric property making their scheme very weak on security. Especially finding its private key is equivalent to finding a certain decomposition of the whole space into some invariant subspaces and bases for these subspaces. We propose two methods to solve this geometric problem by applying intensively the theory of invariant subspace. Our methods use only linear algebra and their complexity is $O(m^{\frac{11}{2}}q^d)$ where m is the number of variables and d is expected generally to be 1 as confirmed in our tests. Therefore we give two efficient attacks to break Yasuda, Takagi and Sakurai's signature scheme. Computer implementation is currently in progress and may appear in an extended version of the present paper.

Acknowledgment. The authors would like to thank the anonymous reviewers for their helpful comments on improving this paper.

References

[Ber67]   Berlekamp, E.R.: Factoring polynomials over finite fields. Bell Syst. Tech. J. **46**, 1853–1859 (1967)

[Ber70]   Berlekamp, E.R.: Factoring polynomials over large finite fields. Math. Comput. **24**, 713–735 (1970)

[CHDY11] Cao, W., Hu, L., Ding, J., Yin, Z.: Kipnis-Shamir attack on unbalanced oil-vinegar scheme. In: Bao, F., Weng, J. (eds.) ISPEC 2011. LNCS, vol. 6672, pp. 168–180. Springer, Heidelberg (2011)

[Cla]   Clark, P.L.: Linear algebra: Invariant subspaces. http://math.uga.edu/ ~pete/invariant_subspaces.pdf

[DGS06] Ding, J., Gower, J.E., Schmidt, D.S.: Multivariate Public Key Cryptosystems. Advances in Information Security, vol. 25. Springer, Heidelberg (2006)

[DS05]   Ding, J., Schmidt, D.: Rainbow, a new multivariable polynomial signature scheme. In: Ioannidis, J., Keromytis, A.D., Yung, M. (eds.) ACNS 2005. LNCS, vol. 3531, pp. 164–175. Springer, Heidelberg (2005)

[DY09] Ding, J., Yang, B.-Y.: Multivariate public key cryptography. In: Bernstein, D.J., Buchmann, J., Dahmen, E. (eds.) Post-Quantum Cryptography, pp. 193–241. Springer, Heidelberg (2009)

[GS03] Geiselmann, W., Steinwandt, R.: A short comment on the affine parts of SFLASH^{v3}. Cryptology ePrint Archive, Report 2003/220 (2003). http://eprint.iacr.org/

[GSB01] Geiselmann, W., Steinwandt, R., Beth, T.: Attacking the affine parts of SFLASH. In: Honary, B. (ed.) Cryptography and Coding 2001. LNCS, vol. 2260, pp. 355–359. Springer, Heidelberg (2001)

[Has14] Hashimoto, Y.: Cryptanalysis of the multivariate signature scheme proposed in PQCrypto 2013. In: Mosca, M. (ed.) PQCrypto 2014. LNCS, vol. 8772, pp. 108–125. Springer, Heidelberg (2014)

[KPG99] Kipnis, A., Patarin, J., Goubin, L.: Unbalanced oil and vinegar signature schemes. In: Stern, J. (ed.) EUROCRYPT 1999. LNCS, vol. 1592, pp. 206–222. Springer, Heidelberg (1999)

[KS98] Kipnis, A., Shamir, A.: Cryptanalysis of the oil and vinegar signature scheme. In: Krawczyk, H. (ed.) CRYPTO 1998. LNCS, vol. 1462, pp. 257–267. Springer, Heidelberg (1998)

[KU11] Kedlay, K.S., Umans, C.: Fast polynomial factorization and modular composition. SIAM J. Comput. 40(6), 1767–1802 (2011)

[Pat97] Patarin, J.: The oil and vinegar signature scheme. Presented at the Dagstuhl Workshop on Cryptography, September 1997

[Sch85] Scharlau, W.: Quadratic and Hermitian Forms. Springer, Heidelberg (1985)

[vzGP01] von zur Gathen, J., Panario, D.: Factoring polynomials over finite fields: a survey. J. Symbol. Comput. 31, 3–17 (2001)

[WP05a] Wolf, C., Preneel, B.: Equivalent keys in HFE, C*, and variations. In: Dawson, E., Vaudenay, S. (eds.) Mycrypt 2005. LNCS, vol. 3715, pp. 33–49. Springer, Heidelberg (2005)

[WP05b] Wolf, C., Preneel, B.: Taxonomy of public key schemes based on the problem of multivariate quadratic equations. Cryptology ePrint Archive, Report 2005/077 (2005). http://eprint.iacr.org/2005/077/

[YTS13] Yasuda, T., Takagi, T., Sakurai, K.: Multivariate signature scheme using quadratic forms. In: Gaborit, P. (ed.) PQCrypto 2013. LNCS, vol. 7932, pp. 243–258. Springer, Heidelberg (2013)

Public Key Cryptography

Discrete Logarithms for Torsion Points on Elliptic Curve of Embedding Degree 1

Yasuyuki Nogami[1]([⊠]) and Hwajeong Seo[2]

[1] Graduate School of Natural Science and Technology, Okayama University,
3-1-1, Tsushima-naka, Okayama, Okayama 700-8530, Japan
yasuyuki.nogami@okayama-u.ac.jp
[2] Pusan National University, San-30, Jangjeon-dong, GeumJeong-Gu,
Busan 609-735, Republic of Korea
hwajeong@pusan.ac.kr

Abstract. Recent efficient pairings such as Ate pairing use two efficient subgroups of rational point such that $\pi(P) = P$ and $\pi(Q) = [p]Q$, where π, p, P, and Q are the Frobenius map for rational point, the characteristic of definition field, and torsion points for *pairing*, respectively. This relation accelerates not only *pairing* but also pairing–related operations such as scalar multiplications. It holds in the case that the embedding degree k divides $r - 1$, where r is the order of torsion rational points. Thus, such a case has been well studied. Alternatively, this paper focuses on the case that the degree divides $r + 1$ but not $r - 1$. First, this paper shows a transitive representation for r–torsion points based on the fact that the characteristic polynomial $f(\pi)$ becomes irreducible over $\mathbb{F}_r$ for which π also plays a role of variable. In other words, this paper proposes an elliptic curve discrete logarithm on such a torsion group. After that, together with some example parameters, it is shown how to prepare such pairing–friendly elliptic curves.

Keywords: Pairing–friendly curve · Torsion point · Group structure

1 Introduction

Pairing–based cryptographies have attracted many researchers in these years since it realizes some innovative cryptographic applications such as ID–based cryptography [21] and group signature authentication [18]. Pairing is a bilinear map between two rational point groups on a certain *pairing–friendly* curve and a multiplicative group in a certain finite field, for which rational points need to form a *torsion* group structure of rank 2 [7]. Since it takes a lot of calculation time compared to other operations such as a scalar multiplication for rational point, Ate pairing [19], for example, applies two special rational point subgroups for accelerating *pairing*. The two *special* rational point groups are identified by the factorization of the characteristic polynomial of pairing–friendly curve. In detail, let $E(\mathbb{F}_p)$ be a pairing–friendly curve over prime field $\mathbb{F}_p$ of embedding degree k and thus $E(\mathbb{F}_{p^k})$ has a torsion group structure, where p is the characteristic.

© Springer International Publishing Switzerland 2015
J. Lee and J. Kim (Eds.): ICISC 2014, LNCS 8949, pp. 69–83, 2015.
DOI: 10.1007/978-3-319-15943-0_5

Then, let t be the Frobenius trace of $E(\mathbb{F}_p)$ and r be the order of one cyclic group in the torsion group, the characteristic polynomial $f(\pi)$ is given by and factorized over $\mathbb{F}_r$ as

$$f(\pi) = \pi^2 - t\pi + p$$
$$\equiv (\pi - 1)(\pi - p) \mod r, \tag{1}$$

where π is Frobenius map for rational points in $E(\mathbb{F}_{p^k})$ with respect to $\mathbb{F}_p$. Ate pairing applies the kernels of the maps $(\pi - 1)$ and $(\pi - p)$. Then, several efficient techniques are available not only for accelerating *pairing* [19] but also scalar multiplications [9,22]. Thus, these special groups of r–torsion points have play important roles and been well researched. For those efficiencies, the embedding degree k and the group order r need to satisfy $k \mid (r - 1)$ and implicitly $k > 1$. In what follows, let r be a prime, $E(\mathbb{F}_{p^k})[r]$ denotes the torsion group of which every rational point has the order r.

This paper alternatively deals with *ordinary*, in other words *non–supersingular*, pairing–friendly elliptic curve $E(\mathbb{F}_{p^n})$ such that $n \nmid (r - 1)$ especially with the *minimal embedding field* $\mathbb{F}_{p^l}$, $l = 1, 2$ [12]. The motivation of this research comes from the fact that it has not been well researched [20,23] and thus there are some *unclear* properties especially for its torsion group structure. In addition, recent homomorphic encryptions often need symmetric pairing of large composite order such as RSA cryptography [2,5], where embedding degree becomes 1 or 2. For such pairing friendly elliptic curves, this paper proposes an elliptic curve discrete logarithm problem together with a fully transitive representation of rational point. Though this paper mainly deals with the case that r is a prime number, it is applicable for the case of composite order. First, this paper reviews that the characteristic polynomial $f(\pi)$ becomes an irreducible polynomial over $\mathbb{F}_r$ with respect to π. In other words, $f(\pi)$ cannot be factorized to the form of Eq. (1) with some scalars modulo r for which π also plays a role of *variable*. Then, using $f(\pi)$ as the modular polynomial, this paper gives a fully transitive representation of every r–torsion point for which two cases of definition field $\mathbb{F}_p$ and $\mathbb{F}_{p^n}$ are considered, where n is a certain prime number. In detail for the former case, *skew* Frobenius map $\hat{\pi}_d$ with *twist* technique of degree $d = 3, 4$, and 6 is applied [22] in which the *twisted* characteristic polynomial $f_d(\hat{\pi}_d)$ is used as the modular polynomial. Then, every r–torsion point is able to be represented in the same manner of elements in the quadratic extension field $\mathbb{F}_{r^2}$ such as $([a_0] + [a_1]\pi)P$, $P \in E(\mathbb{F}_{p^n})[r] - \{\mathcal{O}\}$, where $E(\mathbb{F}_{p^n})[r]$ denotes the set of r–torsion points, $a_0, a_1 \in \mathbb{F}_r$, and $\mathcal{O}$ is the infinity point. Thus, the set of rational points in $E(\mathbb{F}_{p^n})[r]$ satisfies the closure with respect to not only an elliptic curve addition but also a *multiplicative operation* defined as

$$P_{\mathcal{A}} = [\mathcal{A}]P = ([a_0] + [a_1]\pi)P, \tag{2a}$$
$$P_{\mathcal{B}} = [\mathcal{B}]P = ([b_0] + [b_1]\pi)P, \tag{2b}$$
$$P_{\mathcal{C}} = [\mathcal{C}]P = [\mathcal{A} \cdot \mathcal{B}]P, \tag{2c}$$

where $a_0, a_1, b_0, b_1 \in \mathbb{F}_r$, $\mathcal{C} \equiv \mathcal{A} \cdot \mathcal{B}$ modulo $f(\pi)$. It is induced from *complex numbers*. Then, this paper shows some properties and how to prepare such pairing–friendly elliptic curves. Thus, the proposed representation enables that the torsion points are fully transitive to each other and accordingly this paper proposes a new elliptic curve discrete logarithm based on the representation.

There are several proposals and discussions around applying pairing–friendly curves of embedding degree 1 to cryptographic applications together with sufficient secure group order r [15,16]. On the other hand, the results of this paper will give some theoretic viewpoints of r–torsion structures regardless of their contributions to cryptographic applications or attacks. Thus, it needs to have an attention. It is partially related to *vector decomposition problem* [24].

2 Fundamentals

This section briefly reviews elliptic curve, twist, Frobenius map π, *skew* Frobenius map $\hat{\pi}_d$, pairing–friendly elliptic curve, characteristic polynomials $f(\pi)$ and $f_d(\hat{\pi}_d)$, minimal embedding field, and some conventional researches.

2.1 Elliptic Curve, Its Order, and Frobenius Map

Let E be an elliptic curve defined over $\mathbb{F}_p$ as

$$E \ : \ y^2 = x^3 + ax + b, \ a, b \in \mathbb{F}_p. \tag{3}$$

The set of rational points including the *infinity point* $\mathcal{O}$ on the curve forms an additive Abelian group denoted by $E(\mathbb{F}_p)$. When the definition field is its extension field $\mathbb{F}_{p^n}$, rational points on the curve E also forms an additive Abelian group denoted by $E(\mathbb{F}_{p^n})$. If the extension degree $n > 1$, $E(\mathbb{F}_{p^n})$ is especially called *subfield* elliptic curve since the coefficient field $\mathbb{F}_p$ of the elliptic curve E is a proper subfield of the definition field $\mathbb{F}_{p^n}$.

For rational points $R(x_R, y_R) \in E(\mathbb{F}_{p^n})$, where x_R, y_R are elements in $\mathbb{F}_{p^n}$, consider Frobenius map π with respect to the coefficient field $\mathbb{F}_p$. In detail, π becomes an endomorphism defined by

$$\pi \ : \ E(\mathbb{F}_{p^n}) \to E(\mathbb{F}_{p^n})$$
$$(x_R, y_R) \mapsto (x_R^p, y_R^p). \tag{4}$$

Thus, $\pi^n = 1$ because of the extension degree n. On the other hand, it is well known that every rational point R in $E(\mathbb{F}_{p^n})$ satisfies

$$(\pi^2 - [t]\pi + [p])R = \mathcal{O}, \tag{5}$$

and the order $\#E(\mathbb{F}_p)$ is written by

$$\#E(\mathbb{F}_p) = p + 1 - t, \tag{6}$$

where t denotes the Frobenius trace of $E(\mathbb{F}_p)$. Then, consider a polynomial $f(\pi)$ with respect to the preceding Frobenius map π as follows.

$$f(\pi) = \pi^2 - t\pi + p, \tag{7}$$

it is often called *characteristic polynomial*. Since p is a prime number and $|t| \leq 2\sqrt{p}$ [7], $f(\pi)$ is obviously irreducible over integers. Then, according to the Weil's theorem [7], the order $\#E(\mathbb{F}_{p^n})$ is given by

$$\#E(\mathbb{F}_{p^n}) = p^n + 1 - t_n, \tag{8}$$

where $t_n = \alpha^n + \beta^n$. α and β are *conjugate* complex numbers such that

$$f(\alpha) = f(\beta) = 0. \tag{9}$$

Using Dickson's polynomial [8], t_n is recursively determined with $p = \alpha\beta$ and $t_1 = \alpha + \beta$. In addition, it is found that $\#E(\mathbb{F}_p)$ divides $\#E(\mathbb{F}_{p^n})$. It ensures that $E(\mathbb{F}_p)$ is a subgroup of $E(\mathbb{F}_{p^n})$. If the extension degree n is a prime, the period of Frobenius map π for rational points becomes 1 or n. The former period corresponds to the rational points in $E(\mathbb{F}_p)$.

In what follows, let the extension degree n be a prime number in order to make the discussions simple. The following remark becomes important.

Remark 1. Let r be a prime number such that $r \mid \#E(\mathbb{F}_{p^n})$ and $r^2 \nmid \#E(\mathbb{F}_{p^n})$, then the subgroup of rational points of order r, that is denoted by $E(\mathbb{F}_{p^n})[r]$, exists in $E(\mathbb{F}_{p^n})$ as a cyclic group. If $r \nmid E(\mathbb{F}_p)$, it is found that the extension degree n divides $r - 1$ because n is the period of Frobenius map [11]. □

2.2   Twists and *Skew* Frobenius map

Let d be the twist degree for elliptic curve such as 2, 3, 4, and 6, it is known that its twisted curve defined over the extension field $\mathbb{F}_{p^d}$ has its isomorphic subgroup [19], where $d \mid (p - 1)$. In what follows, let E_d and E'_d be the base curve and its twisted curve of twist degree d. Let ψ_d be the isomorphic map from $E_d(\mathbb{F}_p)$ to the isomorphic subgroup of order $\#E_d(\mathbb{F}_p)$ in $E'_d(\mathbb{F}_{p^d})$ [19], then *skew* Frobenius map $\hat{\pi}_d$ for rational points in $E_d(\mathbb{F}_p)$ is defined by [22]

$$\hat{\pi}_d = \psi_d^{-1} \pi \psi_d. \tag{10}$$

Thus, *skew* Frobenius map satisfies $\hat{\pi}_d^d = 1$. Since $\hat{\pi}_2$ is just the *negation* map [11], this paper focuses on only the cases that $d = 3, 4,$ and 6. These twists are available for some special forms of curve as

$$d = 4 : y^2 = x^3 + ax, \tag{11}$$
$$d = 3, 6 : y^2 = x^3 + b, \tag{12}$$

where $a, b \in \mathbb{F}_p$. For example, in the case that the twist degree d is equal to 3, the twisted curve E'_3 and the skew Frobenius map $\hat{\pi}_3$ is given as follows [22].

$$E'_3 \; : \; y^2 = x^3 + bv, \tag{13}$$

where v is a certain cubic non residue in $\mathbb{F}_p$. Then, the skew Frobenius map $\hat{\pi}_3$ for $R \in E_3(\mathbb{F}_p)$ is given by

$$\hat{\pi}_3 \; : \quad E_3(\mathbb{F}_p) \rightarrow E_3(\mathbb{F}_p)$$
$$(x_R, y_R) \mapsto (\epsilon x_R, y_R), \tag{14}$$

where ϵ is a primitive cubic root of unity that belongs to $\mathbb{F}_p$ under $3 \mid (p - 1)$.

Consider a prime number r such that $r \mid \#E_d(\mathbb{F}_p)$ and $d \mid (r - 1)$. Let t_d and λ_d be the Frobenius trace of its twisted curve $E_d(\mathbb{F}_p)$ and a primitive d–th root of unity modulo r, respectively. The *twisted* characteristic polynomial $f_d(\hat{\pi}_d)$ of $E_d(\mathbb{F}_p)$ is given by and factorized as

$$f_d(\hat{\pi}_d) = \hat{\pi}_d^2 - t_d\hat{\pi}_d + p \tag{15a}$$

$$\equiv (\hat{\pi}_d - \lambda_d)(\hat{\pi}_d - \lambda_d^{-1}) \pmod{r}. \tag{15b}$$

It is summarized as follows.

Remark 2. When $d \mid (r - 1)$, the twisted characteristic polynomial $f_d(\hat{\pi}_d)$ is reducible modulo r. □

Then, since $^{\forall}R \in E_d(\mathbb{F}_p)$ satisfies

$$(\hat{\pi}_d^d - [1])R = f_d(\hat{\pi}_d)R = \mathcal{O}, \tag{16}$$

the factorization Eq. (15b) is also found as the greatest common divisor of $\hat{\pi}_d^d - 1$ and $f_d(\hat{\pi}d)$ modulo r^1. If $E_d(\mathbb{F}_p)[r]$ is a cyclic group of order r, in other words rank 1, an arbitrary rational point P in $E_d(\mathbb{F}_p)[r]$ satisfies

$$(\hat{\pi}_d - \lambda_d)P = \mathcal{O} \text{ or } (\hat{\pi}_d - \lambda_d^{-1})P = \mathcal{O}, \tag{17}$$

where it is uniquely determined by the isomorphic map ψ_d [14].

On the other hand, if $E_d(\mathbb{F}_p)[r]$ consists of torsion points of order r with rank 2, in the same of Sect. 2.3, Eq. (17) shows the existence of the following cyclic subgroups among the $r + 1$ cyclic groups of order r in $E_d(\mathbb{F}_p)[r]$.

$$\text{Ker}(\hat{\pi}_d - [\lambda_d]) \cap E_d(\mathbb{F}_p)[r], \tag{18a}$$

$$\text{Ker}(\hat{\pi}_d - [\lambda_d^{-1}]) \cap E_d(\mathbb{F}_p)[r]. \tag{18b}$$

In these subgroups, it is known that some pairing–related calculations such as scalar multiplication are carried out efficiently [22].

2.3 Pairing–Friendly Elliptic Curve of Embedding Degree $k > 1$

Let r be a prime number such that $r \mid \#E(\mathbb{F}_p)$. In general, the smallest positive integer k such that r divides $p^k - 1$ is called *embedding degree*. When the degree k is larger than 1, it is well–known that $E(\mathbb{F}_{p^k})[r]$ consists of r–*torsion* points of order r under $r^2 \mid E(\mathbb{F}_{p^k})$ [7]. In detail,

- there are $r^2 - 1$ points of order r,
- $E(\mathbb{F}_{p^k})[r]$ forms a rank 2 group structure, that is r–torsion group,
- there are $r + 1$ cyclic groups order r in $E(\mathbb{F}_{p^k})[r]$,
- one of the $r + 1$ groups is a subgroup of order r in $E(\mathbb{F}_p)$.

---

[1] It is noted that *skew* Frobenius map such as $\hat{\pi}d$ is available for both $E(\mathbb{F}_p)$ and $E_d(\mathbb{F}_p)$ because they are twisted to and from each other.

In addition, since $\#E(\mathbb{F}_p) \equiv p+1-t \equiv 0 \pmod{r}$, the characteristic polynomial Eq. (7) modulo r becomes reducible as

$$f(\pi) \equiv (\pi - 1)(\pi - p) \pmod{r}. \tag{19}$$

For the $r + 1$ cyclic groups of order r in $E(\mathbb{F}_{p^k})[r]$, Eq. (19) implicitly shows the existence of a cyclic subgroup $\mathrm{Ker}(\pi - [p]) \cap E(\mathbb{F}_{p^k})[r]$ [7]. It is found that $\mathrm{Ker}(\pi - [p]) \cap E(\mathbb{F}_{p^k})[r] \not\subset E(\mathbb{F}_p)$. Alternatively, this paper deals with some cases that the characteristic polynomial becomes irreducible modulo r.

This paper focuses on the case of embedding degree $k = 1$ with *ordinary* pairing–friendly curves. In this case, there are some *unclear* properties [23] though some researchers have studied [6] and there are some pairing–based applications such as homomorphic encryptions [2,5] that uses composite order pairing–friendly curves of embedding degree $k = 1$ [3].

2.4   Conventional Researches

As introduced in *Remarks* 1 and 2, it is important that the twist degree d or the extension degree n divides $r - 1$ whichever the group of rational points of order r has a rank 1 or 2 group structure. Then, the calculation costs of some pairing–related operations are substantially reduced [9,19]. On the other hand, the other cases such that $d \nmid (r - 1)$ or $n \nmid (r - 1)$ are briefly introduced [6,23] of which some properties have been unsolved as

- the relation of n, d, r, π, and $\hat{\pi}_d$,
- how to obtain such pairing–friendly curves [20],
- properties on self–pairings [23].

This paper considers a multiplicative extension for representing the group structure that gives a new viewpoints for discrete logarithms on torsion groups in the cases of $d \nmid (r - 1)$ and $n \nmid (r - 1)$. In order to make the discussions clear, this paper introduces *minimal embedding degree* [12] as follows.

Minimal Embedding Field [12]. The calculation result of a pairing of group order r becomes a certain non–zero element of the same order r in the multiplicative subgroup of a certain extension field $\mathbb{F}_{p^l}$ such that

$$r \mid (p^l - 1) \text{ but } r \nmid (p^i - 1), \ 0 \le i < l. \tag{20}$$

Let the embedding degree of pairing be k, the extension degree l of $\mathbb{F}_{p^l}$ is equal to k in general. For example, in the case of Barreto–Naehrig curve, $k = l = 12$ [1]. However, l sometimes becomes smaller than k. Thus, Hitt [12] has especially named such an extension field $\mathbb{F}_{p^l}$ *minimal embedding field*. This paper deals with the case that the *minimal embedding field* $\mathbb{F}_{p^l}$ is the prime field $\mathbb{F}_p$ and accordingly $r \mid (p - 1)$.

3   Fully Transitive Representation

Different from usual pairing situations such as *Remarks* 1 and 2, this paper considers the cases that *twist* degree d or *extension* degree n respectively for $E_d(\mathbb{F}_p)[r]$ or $E(\mathbb{F}_{p^n})[r]$ does not divide $r - 1$. In addition, among such cases, this paper focuses on the following two cases[2]:

1. d is equal to 3 and divides $r + 1$,
2. n is an odd prime such that $r \nmid \#E(\mathbb{F}_{p^n})$, $n \neq r$, and $n \mid (r + 1)$.

As shown in Appendix A, such a curve explicitly has a *torsion* group structure, that is a pairing–friendly curve. Then, this paper shows that every r–torsion rational point of order r on the curve is able to be represented as and dealt with in the same manner of an element in $\mathbb{F}_{r^2}$. In the same manner of the vector representation of $\mathbb{F}_{r^2}$, this paper gives a fully transitive representation for r–torsion points on such a pairing–friendly curve.

3.1   Variants of r–torsion Groups

When the embedding degree $k > 1$, it is found that d divides $r(r - 1)$. Thus, when r is a large prime number for ensuring cryptographic security, $d \mid (r - 1)$ will be satisfied as introduced in *Remark* 2. Such a case has been well researched as introduced in Sect. 2.3.

Alternatively, there are other cases such that d divides $r^2 - 1$. Thus, this paper deals with the case that d divides $r + 1$. Then, as shown in Appendix B, the order r satisfies that $r \mid (p^l - 1)$, where $l = 1$ or 2. Since r is a prime number,

$$p \equiv \begin{cases} 1 & l = 1 \\ -1 & l = 2 \end{cases} \pmod{r}, \tag{21}$$

In brief, $p \equiv \pm 1 \pmod{r}$. Note here that $l = 1$ and $p \equiv 1 \pmod{r}$ when $d = 3$ or n is an odd prime (*see* Appendix B). Then, there are the following two cases:

1. $E_d(\mathbb{F}_p)[r]$ is an r–torsion group of rank 2,
2. $E(\mathbb{F}_{p^n})[r]$ is an r–torsion group of rank 2 such that $r \nmid \#E(\mathbb{F}_p)$.

They are the *target* cases of this research. Note that the embedding degree k is equal to 1 since $p \equiv 1 \pmod{r}$. Especially for the latter case, the technical term *minimal embedding field* [12] is needed for discussion. In detail, $E(\mathbb{F}_{p^n})$ is defined over $\mathbb{F}_{p^n}$ but its minimal embedding field is $\mathbb{F}_p$. In brief, both of the above two cases under $d \mid (r + 1)$ and $n \mid (r + 1)$ have the minimal embedding field $\mathbb{F}_p$, respectively.

Note that d and r are the periods of *skew* Frobenius map $\hat{\pi}_d$ and Frobenius map π, respectively. Thus, they are closely related to whether or not $d \mid (r - 1)$ or $n \mid (r - 1)$. In what follows, the case of $E_d(\mathbb{F}_p)$ is mainly dealt with. In what follows, for the simplicity of notations, the case of $E_d(\mathbb{F}_p)$ with twist degree d is mainly discussed. Just replacing d, $\hat{\pi}_d$, and $f_d(\hat{\pi}_d)$ to n, π, and $f(\pi)$, respectively, the same result for the case of $E(\mathbb{F}_{p^n})$ is obtained.

---

[2] There will be some other cases such that $n = r$.

3.2   Irreducibility of $f_d(\hat{\pi}_d)$

In the case that d does not divide $r - 1$, $\hat{\pi}_d$ does not correspond to any scalar multiplications. It is because any primitive d–th roots of unity does not exist in $\mathbb{F}_r^*$. Thus, it is easily found that the *twisted* characteristic polynomial $f_d(\hat{\pi}_d)$ becomes an irreducible polynomial of degree 2 with respect to $\hat{\pi}_d$ over $\mathbb{F}_r$ for which $\hat{\pi}_d$ also plays a role of a *variable*.

It is also understood from the viewpoint of cyclotomic polynomials. In detail, let $d = 3$ for $f_d(\hat{\pi}_d)$ given by Eq. (15a), substitute $p \equiv 1$ (mod r) and $t_d \equiv -1$ (mod r) [14], where the former is introduced in Sect. 3.1 and the latter is obtained as Appendix C. Then, $f_d(\hat{\pi}_d)$ in the case of $d = 3$ is given by

$$f_d(\hat{\pi}_d) = f_3(\hat{\pi}_3) = \hat{\pi}_3^2 + \hat{\pi}_3 + 1 \equiv 0 \quad (\text{mod } r). \tag{22}$$

It is the cyclotomic polynomial of period 3 with respect to $\hat{\pi}_3$. Since $3 \nmid (r-1)$, it does not correspond to any scalar multiplications such as Eq. (17) and thus it is shown that $f_3(\hat{\pi}_3)$ becomes irreducible over $\mathbb{F}_r$. In what follows, this paper briefly uses the notation d such as $f_d(\hat{\pi}_d)$.

Using $f_d(\hat{\pi}_d)$ as the modular polynomial enables to construct the quadratic extension field $\mathbb{F}_{r^2}$. An arbitrary element $\mathcal{A} \in \mathbb{F}_{r^2}$ is represented as

$$\mathcal{A} = a_0 + a_1 \hat{\pi}_d, \ a_0, a_1 \in \mathbb{F}_r. \tag{23}$$

The above representation is *polynomial* representation with the polynomial basis $\{1, \hat{\pi}_d\}$. Thus, all of r–torsion rational points in $E_d(\mathbb{F}_p)[r]$ are able to be represented in the same manner of elements $\mathbb{F}_{r^2}$.

Let $\mathcal{G} = g_0 + g_1 \hat{\pi}_d$, $g_0, g_1 \in \mathbb{F}_r$ be a generator of the multiplicative *cyclic* group $\mathbb{F}_{r^2}^*$, every element in $\mathbb{F}_{r^2}^*$ is represented as a certain power $\mathcal{G}^i$, where $1 \leq i \leq r^2 - 1$. Accordingly, let $\mathcal{G}^i = g_{i_0} + g_{i_1} \hat{\pi}_d, g_{i_0}, g_{i_1} \in \mathbb{F}_r$, every r–torsion points in $E_d(\mathbb{F}_p)[r]$ are represented as

$$\begin{aligned}[\mathcal{G}^i]P &= ([g_{i_0}] + [g_{i_1}]\hat{\pi}_d) P \\ &= [g_{i_0}]P + [g_{i_1}]\hat{\pi}_d(P),\end{aligned} \tag{24}$$

where P is an arbitrary r–torsion point in $E_d(\mathbb{F}_p)[r] - \{\mathcal{O}\}$. It enables *multiplicative* representations for r–torsion points. The property that every r–torsion point is represented as Eq. (24) corresponds to the fact that the *skew* Frobenius map $\hat{\pi}_d$ is not congruent to any scalar multiplications in $E_d(\mathbb{F}_p)[r]$ when $d \nmid (r + 1)$. Thus, each cyclic subgroup of rational points of order r corresponds to the prime field $\mathbb{F}_r$. Thus, the proposal of this paper gives a fully transitive representation of r–torsion points in $E_d(\mathbb{F}_p)[r]$. In what follows, such a special torsion group as the above $E_d(\mathbb{F}_p)[r]$ is called *fully transitive torsion group*.

3.3   Arithmetic Operations

As introduced above, the basis $\{1, \hat{\pi}_d\}$ and the modular polynomial $f_d(\hat{\pi}_d)$ enables arithmetics such as multiplication and inversion in $\mathbb{F}_{r^2}$ as follows.

Let $\mathcal{A}$ and $\mathcal{B}$ be given by

$$\mathcal{A} = a_0 + a_1\hat{\pi}_d, \tag{25a}$$
$$\mathcal{B} = b_0 + b_1\hat{\pi}_d, \tag{25b}$$

where a_0, a_1, b_0, and b_1 are in $\mathbb{F}_r$. Then, a multiplication $\mathcal{C} \equiv \mathcal{A} \cdot \mathcal{B}$ modulo $f_d(\hat{\pi}_d)$ is given as follows.

$$\begin{aligned}
\mathcal{C} &= (a_0 + a_1\hat{\pi}_d)(b_0 + b_1\hat{\pi}_d) \\
&= a_0 b_0 + (a_1 b_0 + a_0 b_1)\hat{\pi}_d + a_1 b_1 \hat{\pi}_d^2 \\
&= (a_0 b_0 - a_1 b_1) + (a_1 b_0 + a_0 b_1 - a_1 b_1)\hat{\pi}_d,
\end{aligned} \tag{26}$$

where note that $f_d(\hat{\pi}_d) = 0$ is given by Eq. (22).

On the other hand, the multiplicative inverse for a division is obtained as follows. According to Itoh–Tsujii inversion algorithm [13] with Eq. (26), the inverse $\mathcal{B}^{-1}$ in the case of $d = 3$, for example, is given by

$$\begin{aligned}
\mathcal{B}^{-1} &= \mathcal{B}^r \cdot (\mathcal{B} \cdot \mathcal{B}^r)^{-1} \\
&= (b_0 + b_1\hat{\pi}_3^r) \cdot \{(b_0 + b_1\hat{\pi}_3) \cdot (b_0 + b_1\hat{\pi}_3^r))\}^{-1} \\
&= (b_0 + b_1\hat{\pi}_3^{-1}) \cdot \{(b_0 + b_1\hat{\pi}_3) \cdot (b_0 + b_1\hat{\pi}_3^{-1}))\}^{-1} \\
&= \{(b_0 - b_1) - b_1\hat{\pi}_3\} \cdot (b_0^2 + b_1^2 - b_0 b_1)^{-1} \\
&= w \cdot (b_0 - b_1) - (w \cdot b_1)\hat{\pi}_3,
\end{aligned} \tag{27}$$

where $w = (b_0^2 + b_1^2 - b_0 b_1)^{-1} \bmod r$ and $\hat{\pi}_3^r = \hat{\pi}_3^{-1}$ modulo $f_3(\hat{\pi}_3) = 0$. Thus, *division* is also available with the same manner of that of $\mathbb{F}_{r^2}$.

3.4 A Proposal of Discrete Logarithm on the Torsion Group

Together with the above *multiplicative law* for r–torsion points, let $\mathcal{G}$, P, and $+$ be a generator of $\mathbb{F}_{p^2}^*$, a non–zero r–torsion point, and the usual elliptic curve addition for rational points, respectively, $\langle \{[\mathcal{G}^i]P, \mathcal{O}\}, +, \cdot \rangle$ under a certain condition described in Sect. 3.1 forms a fully transitive torsion group isomorphic to $\mathbb{F}_{r^2}$. In the case that the twist degree d is equal to 3, the isomorphic relation is easily understood.

Consider an ECDLP in the fully transitive torsion group $E_d(\mathbb{F}_p)[r]$.

Definition 1. (ECDLP in the fully transitive torsion group $E_d(\mathbb{F}_p)[r]$)

Let $E_d(\mathbb{F}_p)[r]$ be a fully transitive torsion group. Consider $P \in E_d(\mathbb{F}_p)[r]$ of order r and $P_\mathcal{X} \in E_d(\mathbb{F}_p)[r]$. Then, find $\mathcal{X} = x_0 + x_1\hat{\pi}_d$ such that

$$P_\mathcal{X} = [\mathcal{X}]P = ([x_0] + [x_1]\hat{\pi}_d)\, P, \tag{28}$$

where $0 \leq x_0, x_1, < r$. □

The difficulty is basically evaluated as follows. Consider a non–zero r–torsion point P in $E_d(\mathbb{F}_p)[r]$. Using Weil pairing $e(,)$, for example, determine $e(P, \hat{\pi}_d(P))$ that is a certain element in the multiplicative subgroup of order r in $\mathbb{F}_p$, where note that $r \mid (p-1)$. Let $\mathcal{X}$ be $x_0 + x_1 \hat{\pi}_d$, where $x_0, x_1 \in \mathbb{F}_r$, consider an r–torsion point $P_\mathcal{X} = [\mathcal{X}]P$. In detail,

$$P_\mathcal{X} = [\mathcal{X}]P = [x_0]P + [x_1]\hat{\pi}_d(P). \tag{29}$$

According to the properties of Weil pairing,

$$e(P, P) = e(\hat{\pi}_d(P), \hat{\pi}_d(P)) = 1. \tag{30}$$

Thus, since the following relations hold,

$$
\begin{aligned}
e(\hat{\pi}_d(P), P_\mathcal{X}) &= e(\hat{\pi}_d(P), [x_0]P + [x_1]\hat{\pi}_d(P)) \\
&= e(\hat{\pi}_d(P), [x_0]P) \cdot e(\hat{\pi}_d(P), [x_1]\hat{\pi}_d(P)) \\
&= e(\hat{\pi}_d(P), P)^{x_0}, \\
e(P, P_\mathcal{X}) &= e(P, [x_0]P + [x_1]\hat{\pi}_d(P)) \\
&= e(P, [x_0]P) \cdot e(P, [x_1]\hat{\pi}_d(P)) \\
&= e(P, \hat{\pi}_d(P))^{x_1},
\end{aligned}
$$

(31a)

(31b)

the coefficients x_0 and x_1 of $\mathcal{X}$ are given as

$$x_0 = \log_{e(\hat{\pi}_d(P), P)} e(\hat{\pi}_d(P), P_\mathcal{X}), \tag{32a}$$

$$x_1 = \log_{e(P, \hat{\pi}_d(P))} e(P, P_\mathcal{X}). \tag{32b}$$

As shown above, if P and $P_\mathcal{X}$ are known, the coefficients x_0 and x_1 of $\mathcal{X}$ are uniquely determined. In the same of pairing–based cryptographies, it is thus reduced to the simple discrete logarithm problem in $\mathbb{F}_p^*$.

Let us remember that the *minimal* embedding field in this paper is $\mathbb{F}_p$. For the security of pairing–based cryptographies, for example, the size of p needs to be more than 1024 bits in which the above logarithms will not be practically computed. Thus, as introduced in Sect. 1, the above and below considerations will just give some theoretic properties of a fully transitive torsion group regardless of its contributions to cryptographic applications or attacks.

4   How to Construct a Fully Transitive Torsion Group

As a previous work, Shiota et al. [20] have introduced some algorithms for generating pairing–friendly curves including the case that embedding degree k is equal to 1. Most of such related works focus on the case that d or n divides $r - 1$ and the algorithms are based on Cocks–Pinch (CP) method [4]. Corresponding to the cases of $E_d(\mathbb{F}_p)$ and $E(\mathbb{F}_{p^n})$ introduced in Sect. 3.1, this section respectively shows some approaches for generating pairing–friendly curves of *minimal* embedding field $\mathbb{F}_p$ under d or n divides $r + 1$.

4.1   Case of $E_d(\mathbb{F}_p)[r]$

Figure 1 shows the CP–based algorithm for generating an objective pairing–friendly curve when $p \equiv 1 \pmod{r}$. Then, note here that $t \equiv 2 \pmod{r}$ because r divides $\#E_d(\mathbb{F}_p) = p + 1 - t$. Equations (33) shows an example of pairing–friendly curve of twist degree $d = 3$. Generating the curve took $1.7\,$s on the computer environment shown in Table 1.

Input :   bit size b of the prime order r, twist degree $d = \{3, 4, 6\}$,
         CM discriminant $D = 1, 3$ corresponding to the twist degree d
Output : parameters (p, r, t) with an objective pairing–friendly curve E_d

---

1. Generate b–bit prime number r such that $d \mid (r + 1)$.
2. Set $t = 2 + ir$ and $s = jr$ as $i = 1, 2, 3, \cdots$ and $j = 1, 2, 3, \cdots$, respectively.
3. Calculate $p = (t^2 + Ds^2)/4$. If p is a prime number, output p, r, t. Otherwise return to **Step 2** or Step 1.
4. Determine the curve E_d as $y^2 = x^3 + ax$ $(d = 4)$ or $y^2 = x^3 + b$ $(d = 3, 6)$.

Fig. 1. Algorithm for generating pairing–friendly curve of prime order r such that $d \mid (r + 1)$ and $p \equiv 1 \pmod{r}$

Table 1. Computational environment

CPU	Core 2 Duo [a,b] $3\,$GHz
Cash size	4096 KB
OS	Linux(R)[b] 2.6.30.10
Language	C
Compiler	gcc 4.1.2
Library	GNU MP 4.1.4 [10]

[a] Core 2 Duo is a registered trademark of Intel Corporation.
[b] Only single core is used though it has two cores.

As introduced in Sect. 2.2, it is just isomorphic to the subgroup of order $\#E_3(\mathbb{F}_p)$ in the twisted curve $E_3'(\mathbb{F}_{p^3})$. Note that r^2 divides $\#E_3(\mathbb{F}_p)$ and $\#E_3'(\mathbb{F}_{p^3})$. In detail, for the pairing–friendly curve defined by Eq.(33), not only $E_3(\mathbb{F}_p)[r]$ but also its twisted curve $E_3'(\mathbb{F}_{p^3})[r]$ have the rank 2 *torsion* structure.

5   Conclusion and Future Works

This paper proposed a fully transitive representation of r–torsion rational points in the same manner of elemenets in the quadratic extension field $\mathbb{F}_{r^2}$, where the

$$E_3 \; : \; y^2 = x^3 + 7, \tag{33a}$$

$$\begin{aligned}
p = {} & 23753272528686305021605342686821476999442444448 \\
& 77614841079750614536974771558017901020561509 58 \\
& 3535249381425652448582877732361492224835403432 \\
& 2350294302878657636 59 (527\text{-bit}), \tag{33b}
\end{aligned}$$

$$\begin{aligned}
\#E_3(\mathbb{F}_p) = {} & 23753272528686305021605342686821476999442444448 \\
& 77614841079750614536974771558017884578084837 88 \\
& 463549923434578121489996256802366970387530 9829 \\
& 25810030662345685000 4 (527\text{-bit}), \tag{33c}
\end{aligned}$$

$$\begin{aligned}
r = {} & 1157920892373161954235709850086879078532699846 \\
& 6564056403945758400791312964023 7 (257\text{-bit}). \tag{33d}
\end{aligned}$$

Fig. 2. An example of pairing–friendly curve of *minimal* embedding field $\mathbb{F}_p$ such that $r + 1$ is divisible by $d = 3$, where the order r is 257–bit

twist degree d or the extension degree n divides $r + 1$. Then, it was shown that all of r–torsion points except for the infinity $\mathcal{O}$ form a cyclic group in the same of the multiplicative group $\mathbb{F}_{r^2}^*$. In addition, an elliptic curve discrete logarithm problem in such a torsion group was proposed. As a future work, some cryptographic applications or attacks together with *pairing* will be given (Figs. 2 and 3).

Input :   bit size b of the prime order r, extension degree n,
Output : parameters (p, r, t) with an objective pairing–friendly curve E

1. Generate b–bit prime number r such that $n \mid (r + 1)$.
2. Generate p such that $p \equiv \pm 1 \pmod{r}$.
3. Solve $f_n(1, t) - 2 \equiv 0 \pmod{r}$ such that $r \nmid (p + 1 - t)$.
   If t is found in F_r, output p, r, t. Otherwise return to **Step 2** or Step 1.
4. Determine $E \; : \; y^2 = x^3 + ax + b$ by CM method with p, t, r.

Fig. 3. Algorithm for generating pairing–friendly curve of prime order r such that $n \mid (r + 1)$

Acknowledgment. This work was partially supported by JSPS KAKENHI Grant Number 25280047.

A   Torsion Structure When $n \mid (r + 1)$

As introduced in this paper, when d or n divides $r + 1$, the characteristic polynomial $f_d(\hat{\pi}_d)$ or $f(\pi)$ becomes irreducible over $\mathbb{F}_r$. Thus, π does not correspond to any scalar multiplications in $E(\mathbb{F}_{p^n})[r]$. In other words, let P be a rational point of order r that belongs to a cyclic group p in $E(\mathbb{F}_{p^n})[r]$, then $\pi(P)$ has the same order r but it does not belong to p. Thus, $\pi(P)$ needs to belong to another cyclic group $\pi(P) \neq p$ and accordingly $E(\mathbb{F}_{p^n})[r]$ needs to have a torsion structure of rank 2. In the case of $E_d(\mathbb{F}_p)$ with twist degree d, it is shown in the same way.

B $r \mid (p^l - 1)$, $l = 1$ or 2

Let l be the minimal positive integer such that

$$r \mid (p^l - 1). \tag{34}$$

According to Fermat's little theorem, $l \mid (r - 1)$. According to the property of pairing, $r \mid (p^d - 1)$. Thus,

$$l \mid d. \tag{35}$$

On the other hand, d needs to satisfy $d \mid (r + 1)$ in this paper. Therefore,

$$l \mid \gcd(r - 1, r + 1). \tag{36}$$

If r is an odd prime number, $\gcd(r - 1, r + 1) = 2$ and thus it is shown that l is equal to 1 or 2. Moreover, if d is odd such as 3, $l = 1$ from Eq. (35). It is found that l corresponds to the extension degree of the minimal embedding field $\mathbb{F}_{p^l}$. In the case of $E(\mathbb{F}_{p^n})$ with extension degree n, it is shown in the same way. Note here that $l = 1$ in the same when n is odd.

C   Proof of $t_d \equiv -1 \pmod{r}$

According to Morain's report [17], in the case of $d = 3$, t_d that is the Frobenius trace of $E_d(\mathbb{F}_p)$ is given as

$$t_d = (\pm 3v - t)/2, \quad t^2 - 4p = -3v^2. \tag{37}$$

Since $p \equiv 1 \pmod{r}$ and $t \equiv 2 \pmod{r}$ in this paper, the following relation is obtained.

$$t_d \equiv -1 \pmod{r}. \tag{38}$$

References

1. Barreto, P.S.L.M., Naehrig, M.: Pairing-friendly elliptic curves of prime order. In: Preneel, B., Tavares, S. (eds.) SAC 2005. LNCS, vol. 3897, pp. 319–331. Springer, Heidelberg (2006)
2. Boneh, D., Goh, E.-J., Nissim, K.: Evaluating 2-DNF formulas on ciphertexts. In: Kilian, J. (ed.) TCC 2005. LNCS, vol. 3378, pp. 325–341. Springer, Heidelberg (2005)

3. Boneh, D., Sahai, A., Waters, B.: Fully collusion resistant traitor tracing with short ciphertexts and private keys. In: Vaudenay, S. (ed.) EUROCRYPT 2006. LNCS, vol. 4004, pp. 573–592. Springer, Heidelberg (2006)
4. Boneh, D., Rabin, K., Silverberg, A.: Finding composite order ordinary elliptic curves using the cocks-pinch method. In: Cryptology ePrint Archive, Report 2009/533 (2009)
5. Castagnos, G., Laguillaumie, F.: Homomorphic encryption for multiplications and pairing evaluation. In: Visconti, I., De Prisco, R. (eds.) SCN 2012. LNCS, vol. 7485, pp. 374–392. Springer, Heidelberg (2012)
6. Charles, D.: On the existence of distortion maps on ordinary elliptic curves. In: Cryptology ePrint Archive, Report 2006/128 (2006)
7. Cohen, H., Frey, G.: Handbook of Elliptic and Hyperelliptic Curve Cryptography. Discrete Mathematics and Its Applications. Chapman & Hall CRC, Boca Raton (2005)
8. Dickson, L.E.: The analytic representation of substitutions on a power of a prime number of letters with a discussion of the linear group. Ann. Math. **11**, 161–183 (1897)
9. Galbraith, S.D., Scott, M.: Exponentiation in pairing-friendly groups using homomorphisms. In: Galbraith, S.D., Paterson, K.G. (eds.) Pairing 2008. LNCS, vol. 5209, pp. 211–224. Springer, Heidelberg (2008)
10. GNU MP. http://gmplib.org/
11. Hankerson, D., Vanstone, S., Menezes, A.: Guide to Elliptic Curves Cryptography. Springer, New York (2004)
12. Hitt, L.: On the minimal embedding field. In: Cryptology ePrint Archive, Report 2006/415 (2006)
13. Itoh, T., Tsujii, S.: A fast algorithm for computing multiplicative inverses in $GF(2^m)$ using normal bases. Inf. Comp. **78**, 171–177 (1988)
14. Izuta, T., Takeuchi, S., Nishii, K., Nogami, Y., Morikawa, Y.: GLV subgroups on non-supersingular pairing-friendly curves of embedding degree 1. In: Computer Security Symposium 2010, pp. 249–254 (2010)
15. Joux, A.: A one round protocol for tripartite diffie-hellman. J. Cryptol. **17**(4), 263–276 (2004)
16. Koblitz, N., Menezes, A.: Pairing-based cryptography at high security levels. In: Smart, N.P. (ed.) Cryptography and Coding 2005. LNCS, vol. 3796, pp. 13–36. Springer, Heidelberg (2005)
17. Morain, F.: Primality proving using elliptic curves: an update. In: Buhler, J.P. (ed.) ANTS 1998. LNCS, vol. 1423, pp. 111–127. Springer, Heidelberg (1998)
18. Nakanishi, T., Funabiki, N.: Verifier-local revocation group signature schemes with backward unlinkability from bilinear maps. In: Roy, B. (ed.) ASIACRYPT 2005. LNCS, vol. 3788, pp. 533–548. Springer, Heidelberg (2005)
19. Nogami, Y., Akane, M., Sakemi, Y., Kato, H., Morikawa, Y.: Integer variable χ–based ate pairing. In: Galbraith, S.D., Paterson, K.G. (eds.) Pairing 2008. LNCS, vol. 5209, pp. 178–191. Springer, Heidelberg (2008)
20. Ohta, K., Shiota, K.: Construction of CM Curves Suitable for Cryptosystem from the Weil Pairing. Memoirs of the Faculty of Science, Kochi Univ., Vol. 27, No. 1 (2007)
21. Sakai, R., Ohgishi, K., Kasahara, M.: Cryptosystems based on pairing. In: SCIS 2000 (2000)

22. Sakemi, Y., Nogami, Y., Okeya, K., Kato, H., Morikawa, Y.: Skew frobenius map and efficient scalar multiplication for pairing–based cryptography. In: Franklin, M.K., Hui, L.C.K., Wong, D.S. (eds.) CANS 2008. LNCS, vol. 5339, pp. 226–239. Springer, Heidelberg (2008)
23. Smart, N., Blake, I.F., Seroussi, G.: Elliptic Curves in Cryptography. LMS Lecture Note Series. Cambridge University Press, New York (1999)
24. Yoshida, M., Mitsunari, S., Fujiwara, T.: The vector decomposition problem. IEICE Trans. Fundamentals **E93–A**(1), 188–193 (2010)

Efficient Key Dependent Message Security Amplification Against Chosen Ciphertext Attacks

Fuyuki Kitagawa[1,2]([✉]), Takahiro Matsuda[2], Goichiro Hanaoka[2],
and Keisuke Tanaka[1]

[1] Tokyo Institute of Technology, Tokyo, Japan
{kitagaw1,keisuke}@is.titech.ac.jp
[2] National Institute of Advanced Industrial Science and Technology (AIST),
Ibaraki, Japan
{t-matsuda,hanaoka-goichiro}@aist.go.jp

Abstract. Applebaum (EUROCRYPT 2011) showed how to convert a public key encryption (PKE) scheme which is key dependent message (KDM) secure with respect to projection functions (also called *projection-KDM secure*) to a scheme which is KDM secure with respect to functions computable by polynomially bounded-size circuits (also called *bounded-KDM secure*). This result holds in both of the chosen plaintext attack (CPA) setting and the chosen ciphertext attack (CCA) setting. Bellare et al. (CCS 2012) later showed another conversion from a projection-KDM secure scheme to a bounded-KDM secure one, which is more efficient than Applebaum's, but works only in the CPA setting. In this work, we show an efficient conversion from a projection-KDM-*CCA* secure PKE scheme to a bounded-KDM-*CCA* secure PKE scheme. To see that our conversion leads to more efficient bounded-KDM-CCA secure schemes than Applebaum's, we show that by combining our result with several known results, we can obtain currently the most efficient bounded-KDM-CCA secure PKE scheme based on the symmetric external Diffie-Hellman (SXDH) assumption.

Keywords: Public key encryption · Key dependent message security · Chosen ciphertext security · Garbling scheme

1 Introduction

Background and motivation. *Key dependent message (KDM) security*, which is a security notion for an encryption scheme formalized by Black, Rogaway, and Shrimpton [10] and independently by Camenisch and Lysyanskaya [17], captures confidentiality in the situation of encrypting secret keys. Encrypting secret keys is often useful and therefore we need KDM security especially in case we use an encryption scheme as a part of other cryptographic protocols or practical systems like anonymous credential systems [17] and hard disk encryption systems

© Springer International Publishing Switzerland 2015
J. Lee and J. Kim (Eds.): ICISC 2014, LNCS 8949, pp. 84–100, 2015.
DOI: 10.1007/978-3-319-15943-0_6

(e.g., BitLocker [10]). Moreover, KDM security is theoretically important because it can be used to show that computational security and axiomatic security are equivalent [1,2]. KDM security is defined in both of the chosen plaintext attack (CPA) setting and the chosen ciphertext attack (CCA) setting. In order to take adversaries who mount active attacks like tampering of ciphertexts into consideration, in many applications, it is desirable that encryption schemes satisfy CCA security. In addition, since CCA security implies non-malleability, it is considered as a sufficiently strong notion. In this paper, we focus on KDM security under CCA (KDM-CCA security) for public key encryption (PKE) schemes.

Let $\mathcal{F}$ be a function family and $sk_1, \cdots, sk_t$ be secret keys. Informally, a encryption scheme is $\mathcal{F}$-KDM secure if confidentiality of messages is protected even when an adversary can get an encryption of $f(sk_1 \| \cdots \| sk_t)$ under j-th public key, for any $f \in \mathcal{F}$ and $j \in \{1, \cdots, t\}$. In order to guarantee security under various situations, it is desirable to construct schemes which are KDM secure with respect to rich function families.

Today, several works have studied how to construct a $\mathcal{F}_1$-KDM secure scheme using a $\mathcal{F}_2$-KDM secure scheme as a building blocks, where $\mathcal{F}_1$ and $\mathcal{F}_2$ are function families such that $\mathcal{F}_1$ is richer than $\mathcal{F}_2$. Applebaum [4] called this procedure *KDM amplification* and succeeded in achieving a "large" amplification gap. Specifically, he constructed a PKE scheme which is KDM secure with respect to functions which can be computed in some fixed polynomial time (*bounded-KDM secure* [7], for short), from a PKE scheme which is KDM secure with respect to projection functions (*projection-KDM* secure, for short), where a projection function is a function in which each output bit depends on at most a single bit of the input. He noticed that the family of projection functions is almost the simplest function family and bounded-KDM security is strong enough for many applications. Moreover, if the underlying scheme is projection-KDM-CCA secure, then the amplified scheme is also bounded-KDM-CCA secure.

Applebaum's result is very strong in the sense that it achieves a large KDM amplification gap. However, Bellare, Hoang, and Rogaway [8,9] pointed out that schemes obtained by Applebaum's result are inefficient, and showed a much efficient KDM amplification method that achieves the same gap as Applebaum's. (We explain more technical details of these works in the paragraph "Idea for proposed KDM amplification method" below.) Here we notice that Bellare et al. improved efficiency, but their scheme does not satisfy CCA security even if an underlying scheme satisfies CCA security.

In this paper, we try to achieve a KDM amplification method which enjoys efficiency in the same spirit as Bellare et al.'s result [8,9], while achieving the same KDM amplification gap as Applebaum's result [4] in the CCA setting.

Our results. In this paper, we propose an efficient KDM amplification method which achieves the same amplification gap as Applebaum's result in the CCA setting. More specifically, using a projection-KDM-CCA secure PKE scheme, a garbled circuit [8,24], and a universal one-way hash function [22], we construct a bounded-KDM-CCA secure PKE scheme whose efficiency (in particular, ciphertext size) is much better than a scheme obtained by Applebaum's method [3,4].

Our proposed KDM amplification leads to the currently most efficient bounded-KDM-CCA secure PKE scheme. In order to concretely see this, in Sect. 4, we show how to obtain it under the symmetric external Diffie-Hellman (SXDH) assumption by applying our proposed KDM amplification method to a projection-KDM-CCA secure scheme that is derived from the known results [3, 12, 16]. A high-level idea for our proposed amplification method is explained below.

Idea for proposed KDM amplification method. Recall that Applebaum's KDM amplification method [3, 4] converts a projection-KDM secure PKE scheme to a bounded-KDM secure scheme. His method not only succeeds in achieving a large gap, but also has generality. That is, his result holds for any combination of the public key/shared key, CPA/CCA setting, and in the presence of any number of keys. Bellare et al. [8, 9] pointed out that Applebaum's KDM amplification method is inefficient because of its usage of a building block randomized encoding scheme [6] which is in turn based on garbled circuits [24].

More specifically, in the encryption algorithm of an amplified scheme via Applebaum's method, the randomized encoding algorithm is first applied to a plaintext, and then the result is encrypted by the underlying projection-KDM-CPA secure scheme, and the resulting ciphertext is used as a ciphertext of the amplified scheme. We can construct the randomized encoding algorithm from the garbling scheme of Bellare et al. [8, 9]. Then an output of the randomized encoding algorithm consists of a garbled function F of the identity function, an encode X (garbled input) of a plaintext, and decoding information d. Since a garbled function F is extremely large, a bounded-KDM-CPA secure scheme obtained via Applebaum's method is inefficient.

Bellare et al. observes that the resulting scheme remains bounded-KDM-CPA secure even if we send a garbled function and decoding information without encrypting them. Therefore, the main idea of Bellare et al.'s KDM amplification is "not" to encrypt a garbled function and decoding information, and directly uses them as a part of a ciphertext to improve the efficiency of Applebaum's method. However, a scheme obtained via Bellare et al. method does not in general satisfy CCA security because a garbled function is malleable and appears in the clear in a ciphertext.

In this paper, we overcome the problem of malleability of garbled functions in the amplified scheme via Bellare et al.'s approach by (1) encrypting not only the garbled input of a plaintext but also a hash value of a garbled function (and decoding information) by the underlying projection-KDM-CCA secure scheme, and (2) making the decryption algorithm of the amplified scheme check the consistency between a garbled function (and decoding information) that appears in the clear in the amplified scheme and its hash value that is encrypted inside the underlying scheme. Note that the size of hash values is independent of the size of a garbled circuit (and in the case of a universal one-way hash function, it can be as small as a security parameter), and thus the number of bits that need to be encrypted by the underlying projection-KDM-CCA secure scheme increases only by the size of a hash value. Furthermore, attaching a hash value to the plaintext of the underlying scheme is so simple that it does not widen a function family with respect to which the underlying scheme needs to be KDM-CCA secure.

The reasons why this simple idea of using a hash value solves the problem of malleability are roughly explained as follows: suppose, for simplicity, there is only a single KDM query in the security game, and thus the resulting ciphertext can be seen as the challenge ciphertext for an adversary attacking the bounded-KDM-CCA security of a scheme obtained via our amplification method.

Informally, the challenge ciphertext consists of a garbled function F, decoding information d, and the underlying scheme's ciphertext ct which encrypts an encode X (garbled input) of a plaintext and a hash value of $F\|d$. Since the underlying PKE scheme is assumed to be projection-KDM-CCA secure, an adversary cannot gain any useful information from decryption oracle queries by modifying the third component (i.e. the underlying scheme's ciphertext) of the challenge ciphertext. Furthermore, if the used hash function is a universal one-way hash function, any modification of the first and second components F, d leads to a hash value that is different from that of $F\|d$, which means that such a ciphertext is invalid. For more details, see Sect. 3.

Related work. Boneh, Halevi, Hamburg, and Ostrovsky [12] constructed the first KDM secure PKE scheme in the standard model based on the decisional Diffie-Hellman (DDH) assumption (and more generally, K-linear assumption for any $K \geq 1$). Their scheme is KDM secure relative to the family of affine functions (*affine-KDM secure*, for short) which is a comparatively simple function family. Also affine-KDM secure schemes were later constructed under the learning with errors (LWE) [5], quadratic residuosity (QR) [13], decisional composite residuosity (DCR) [13,21], and learning parity with noise (LPN) [5] assumptions.

Boneh et al.'s scheme is KDM secure only in the CPA setting, and thus how to construct a KDM-CCA secure scheme remained open. Camenisch, Chandran, and Shoup [15] later showed how to construct a $\mathcal{F}$-KDM-CCA secure scheme using a $\mathcal{F}$-KDM-CPA secure scheme and a non-interactive zero-knowledge (NIZK) proof system for NP languages as building blocks, where $\mathcal{F}$ is a function family. Recently, in addition, Hofheinz [20] showed the first construction of a circular-CCA secure scheme whose security can be directly proved based on number theoretic assumptions.

Barak, Haitner, Hofheinz, and Ishai [7], and Brakerski, Goldwasser, and Kalai [14] showed how to amplify KDM security. Both constructions succeed in achieving large amplification gaps, but they require some additional property for a building KDM secure scheme. Furthermore, unlike Applebaum's result [4], these KDM amplification methods are not known to work for KDM-CCA security.

2   Preliminaries

In this section we define some mathematical notions.

Notations. In this paper, $x \xleftarrow{r} X$ denotes selecting an element from a finite set X uniformly at random, and $y \leftarrow \mathsf{A}(x)$ denotes assigning y to the output of an algorithm A on an input x. For strings x and y, $x\|y$ denotes the concatenation of x and y. λ denotes a security parameter. $\mathsf{poly}(\lambda)$ denotes a polynomial of λ.

A function $f(\lambda)$ is a negligible function if $f(\lambda)$ tends to 0 faster than $\frac{1}{\lambda^c}$ for every constant $c > 0$. We write $f(\lambda) = \mathsf{negl}(\lambda)$ to denote $f(\lambda)$ being a negligible function. PPT stands for probabilistic polynomial time. $[t]$ denotes the set of integers $\{1, \cdots, t\}$. ϕ denotes an empty set. For a string $x' = x'_1 \cdots x'_n$ and $1 \leq s \leq n$, $x'[1:s]$ denotes $x'_1 \cdots x'_s$.

2.1 Public Key Encryption

Usually a PKE scheme is defined as a three tuple consisting of the key generation, the encryption, and the decryption algorithms. However, KDM security considers situations where there are many users of a scheme and hence many keys, so we define it as a four tuple consisting of the above three algorithms and the setup algorithm.

Let $\mathcal{M}$ be a message space. Formally, we define a PKE scheme Π as a four tuple $(\mathcal{S}, \mathcal{K}, \mathcal{E}, \mathcal{D})$ of PPT algorithms. The *setup* algorithm $\mathcal{S}$, given a security parameter 1^λ, outputs a public parameter pp. The *key generation* algorithm $\mathcal{K}$, given a public parameter pp, outputs a public key pk and a secret key sk. The *encryption* algorithm $\mathcal{E}$, given a public parameter pp, a public key pk and a message $m \in \mathcal{M}$, outputs a ciphertext c. The *decryption* algorithm $\mathcal{D}$, given a public parameter pp, a secret key sk and a ciphertext c, outputs a message $\tilde{m} \in \{\bot\} \cup \mathcal{M}$. For a PKE scheme, we require $\mathcal{D}(pp, sk, \mathcal{E}(pp, pk, m)) = m$ for every $m \in \mathcal{M}$, $pp \leftarrow \mathcal{S}(1^\lambda)$, and $(pk, sk) \leftarrow \mathcal{K}(pp)$.

Next, we define KDM-CCA security.

Definition 1 (KDM-CCA security). *Let $\Pi = (\mathcal{S}, \mathcal{K}, \mathcal{E}, \mathcal{D})$ be a PKE scheme whose message space is $\{0,1\}^s$, and let $\mathcal{F}$ be a function family. We define the $\mathcal{F}$-KDM-CCA game between a challenger and an adversary $\mathcal{A}$ as follows, where t is the number of keys.*

Initialization: *First, the challenger selects a challenge bit $b \xleftarrow{r} \{0,1\}$. Next the challenger computes $pp \leftarrow \mathcal{S}(1^\lambda)$ and $(pk_1, sk_1), \cdots, (pk_t, sk_t) \leftarrow \mathcal{K}(pp)$, and then sends $(pp, pk_1, \cdots, pk_t)$ to $\mathcal{A}$. Finally, the challenger prepares the KDM query list L_{kdm} into which pairs of the form (j, c) will be stored, where $j \in [t]$ is the index of a key and c is a ciphertext, and which is initially empty.*

$\mathcal{A}$ may adaptively make polynomially many queries of the following two types.

KDM queries: *$(j, f) \in [t] \times \mathcal{F}$. The challenger responds with $c \leftarrow \mathcal{E}(pp, pk_j, f(\mathbf{sk}))$ if $b = 1$, and $c \leftarrow \mathcal{E}(pp, pk_j, 0^s)$ if $b = 0$, where $\mathbf{sk} = sk_1\| \cdots \|sk_t$. Finally, the challenger adds (j, c) to L_{kdm}.*

Decryption queries: *(j^*, c^*), where $j^* \in [t]$, and c^* is a ciphertext. The challenger responds with $\bot$ if $(j^*, c^*) \in L_{kdm}$. Otherwise the challenger responds with $m' \leftarrow \mathcal{D}(pp, sk_{j^*}, c^*)$.*

Final phase: *$\mathcal{A}$ outputs $b' \in \{0,1\}$.*

In this game, we define the advantage of the adversary $\mathcal{A}$ as follows:

$$\mathsf{Adv}^{kdm}_{\Pi,\mathcal{A}}(\lambda) = |\Pr[\mathcal{A} \text{ outputs } 1 | b = 0] - \Pr[\mathcal{A} \text{ outputs } 1 | b = 1]|.$$

Π is said to be $\mathcal{F}$-KDM-CCA secure if for any PPT adversary $\mathcal{A}$, we have $\mathsf{Adv}^{kdm}_{\Pi,\mathcal{A}}(\lambda) = \mathsf{negl}(\lambda)$.

In this paper, for simplicity, the number of keys which exist in the security game is fixed in advance. We notice that, like the schemes in [4,7,9], our main scheme is also secure as long as the arity of functions which an adversary can query is bounded by some fixed polynomial but there exists an unbounded number of keys in the security game.

As we can see, KDM security is defined with respect to function families. In this paper, we concretely consider the following two function families.

Projection functions: A projection function is a function in which each output bit depends on at most a single bit of an input. Let f be a function and $y = y_1 \cdots y_m$ be the output on an input $x = x_1 \cdots x_n$, that is $f(x) = y$. Formally, we say that f is a projection function if it satisfies the following property: $\forall j \in \{1, \cdots, m\}, \exists i \in \{1, \cdots, n\} : y_j \in \{0, 1, x_i, 1 - x_i\}$. Let $\mathcal{P}_u^v = \{f | f : \{0,1\}^u \to \{0,1\}^v \text{ is a projection function}\}$.

Functions computable by circuits with polynomial size: Let f be a function and q be a polynomial. We say that f is a function computable by circuits with size q if there exists a circuit C_f such that $C_f(x) = f(x)$ for every x and the number of gates is at most $q(k)$, where k is the number of input wires. Let $\mathcal{B}_{u,q}^v = \{f | f : \{0,1\}^u \to \{0,1\}^v \text{ is a function computable by circuits with size } q.\}$.

2.2 Garbling Scheme

Bellare et al. formalized a garbling scheme for a circuit [8,9]. In this subsection, we review their definition. A garbling scheme $\mathcal{G}$ is a five tuple $(\mathsf{Gb}, \mathsf{En}, \mathsf{De}, \mathsf{Ev}, \mathsf{ev})$ of PPT algorithms. The *garbling* algorithm Gb, given a security parameter 1^λ and a circuit f, outputs (F, e, d), where F is a garbled function, e is encoding information, and d is decoding information. The *garbled encoding* algorithm En, given encoding information e and $x \in \{0,1\}^n$, outputs a garbled input X. The *garbled evaluation* algorithm Ev, given a garbled function F and a garbled input X, outputs a garbled output Y. The *garbled decoding* algorithm De, given decoding information d and a garbled output Y, outputs $y \in \{0,1\}^m$. The *evaluation* algorithm ev, given a circuit f and $x \in \{0,1\}^n$, outputs $y \in \{0,1\}^m$. It is required that $\mathsf{De}(d, \mathsf{Ev}(F, \mathsf{En}(e, x))) = \mathsf{ev}(f, x)$ for every circuit f, $x \in \{0,1\}^n$, and $(F, e, d) \leftarrow \mathsf{Gb}(1^\lambda, f)$.

Projective garbling scheme. A garbling scheme $\mathcal{G} = (\mathsf{Gb}, \mathsf{En}, \mathsf{De}, \mathsf{Ev}, \mathsf{ev})$ is said to be a *projective* garbling scheme if $\mathsf{En}(e, \cdot)$ is a projection function for any $\lambda \in \mathbb{N}$, any circuit f, and any (F, e, d) output by $\mathsf{Gb}(1^\lambda, f)$.

Security definition. Following [8], we introduce a *side-information function* which we use for defining security of garbling schemes. Intuitively, a side-information function models partial information of a circuit being garbled that is not hidden by garbling. Specifically, a side-information function $\phi(\cdot)$, given a circuit f, outputs side-information $\phi = \phi(f)$. In this paper, we use ϕ_{size} which outputs $\phi_{\text{size}}(f) = (n, m, q)$ as partial information, where n, m, and q are the number of input wires, output wires, and gates of the circuit f, respectively.

Then, we define prv.ind security for garbling schemes [8,9]. Briefly, prv.ind security guarantees that an adversary cannot gain any information except for a value $\mathsf{ev}(f, x)$ and $\phi(f)$ from a garbled function F, a garbled input X, and decoding information d.

Definition 2 (Prv.ind security [8]). *Let $\mathcal{G} = (\mathsf{Gb}, \mathsf{En}, \mathsf{De}, \mathsf{Ev}, \mathsf{ev})$ be a garbling scheme and ϕ be a side-information function. We define the prv.ind game between a challenger and an adversary $\mathcal{A}$ as follows.*

Initialization: *The challenger selects a challenge bit $b \xleftarrow{r} \{0, 1\}$ and sends a security parameter 1^λ to $\mathcal{A}$.*
  $\mathcal{A}$ may make the following query only once.
Garble query: *$((f_0, x_0), (f_1, x_1))$, where f_0, f_1 are circuits, and x_0 and x_1 belong to the domain of $\mathsf{ev}(f_0, \cdot)$ and $\mathsf{ev}(f_1, \cdot)$, respectively. The challenger responds with $\perp$ if $\phi(f_0) \neq \phi(f_1)$ or $\mathsf{ev}(f_0, x_0) \neq \mathsf{ev}(f_1, x_1)$. Otherwise, the challenger computes $(F, e, d) \leftarrow \mathsf{Gb}(1^\lambda, f_b)$ and $X \leftarrow \mathsf{En}(e, x_b)$, and then sends (F, X, d) to $\mathcal{A}$.*
Final phase: *$\mathcal{A}$ outputs $b' \in \{0, 1\}$.*

In this game, we define the advantage of the adversary $\mathcal{A}$ as follows:

$$\mathsf{Adv}_{\mathcal{G}, \mathcal{A}}^{prv}(\lambda) = |\Pr[\mathcal{A} \text{ outputs } 1 | b = 0] - \Pr[\mathcal{A} \text{ outputs } 1 | b = 1]|.$$

$\mathcal{G}$ is said to be prv.ind secure relative to ϕ if for any PPT adversary $\mathcal{A}$, we have $\mathsf{Adv}_{\mathcal{G}, \mathcal{A}}^{prv}(\lambda) = \mathsf{negl}(\lambda)$.

This prv.ind security takes care of the situation in which an adversary may make a garble query only once. However, for our purpose, it is useful to consider the following multi-query prv.ind security which captures security against adversaries that may make multiple garble queries.

Definition 3 (Multi-query prv.ind security). *Let $\mathcal{G} = (\mathsf{Gb}, \mathsf{En}, \mathsf{De}, \mathsf{Ev}, \mathsf{ev})$ be a garbling scheme, and ϕ be a side-information function. We define the multi-query prv.ind game between a challenger and an adversary $\mathcal{A}$ in the same way as the prv.ind game except that $\mathcal{A}$ is allowed to adaptively make multiple garble queries. In this game, we also define the advantage $\mathsf{Adv}_{\mathcal{G}, \mathcal{A}}^{multi}(\lambda)$ of the adversary $\mathcal{A}$ analogously to that in the prv.ind game. Then, $\mathcal{G}$ is said to be multi-query prv.ind secure relative to ϕ if for any PPT adversary $\mathcal{A}$, we have $\mathsf{Adv}_{\mathcal{G}, \mathcal{A}}^{multi}(\lambda) = \mathsf{negl}(\lambda)$.*

A prv.ind secure garbling scheme $\mathcal{G} = (\mathsf{Gb}, \mathsf{En}, \mathsf{De}, \mathsf{Ev}, \mathsf{ev})$ is also multi-query prv.ind secure. Formally, the following lemma holds. We can prove this lemma by a standard "query-by-query" hybrid argument, and thus the proof is omitted due to lack of space.

Lemma 1. *Let $\mathcal{G} = (\mathsf{Gb}, \mathsf{En}, \mathsf{De}, \mathsf{Ev}, \mathsf{ev})$ be a garbling scheme which is prv.ind secure relative to ϕ. Then $\mathcal{G}$ is also multi-query prv.ind secure relative to ϕ.*

2.3   Universal One-Way Hash Function

A keyed hash function $\mathcal{H}$ is a two tuple $(\mathsf{G}_h, \mathsf{H})$ of PPT algorithms. The *hash key generation* algorithm G_h, given a security parameter 1^λ, outputs a hash key hk. The *hash* algorithm H, given a hash key hk and a string $x \in \{0,1\}^*$, outputs a hash value $h \in \{0,1\}^\ell$.

Definition 4 (Universal one-wayness [22]). *We define the universal one-wayness game between a challenger and an adversary $\mathcal{A}$ as follows. Initially, the challenger sends a security parameter 1^λ to $\mathcal{A}$. Then, $\mathcal{A}$ sends $x \in \{0,1\}^*$ to the challenger. Then, the challenger generates a hash key $hk \leftarrow \mathsf{G}_h(1^\lambda)$ and sends it to $\mathcal{A}$. Finally, $\mathcal{A}$ outputs $x' \in \{0,1\}^*$. In this game, we define the advantage of the adversery $\mathcal{A}$ as follows:*

$$\mathsf{Adv}^{uow}_{\mathcal{H},\mathcal{A}}(\lambda) = \Pr[x \neq x' \wedge \mathsf{H}(hk, x) = \mathsf{H}(hk, x')].$$

$\mathcal{H}$ is said to be a universal one-way hash function if for any PPT adversary $\mathcal{A}$, we have $\mathsf{Adv}^{uow}_{\mathcal{H},\mathcal{A}}(\lambda) = \mathsf{negl}(\lambda)$.

3   KDM Amplification for Chosen Ciphertext Security

In this section, we describe our bounded-KDM-CCA secure PKE scheme.

The construction is as follows. Let $\mathcal{G} = (\mathsf{Gb}, \mathsf{En}, \mathsf{De}, \mathsf{Ev}, \mathsf{ev})$ be a projective garbling scheme, $\Pi = (\mathcal{S}, \mathcal{K}, \mathcal{E}, \mathcal{D})$ be a PKE scheme, and $\mathcal{H} = (\mathsf{G}_h, \mathsf{H})$ be a universal one-way hash function. We assume that k is the output length of En which depends on the input length of En and a security parameter λ, and ℓ is the output length of H which depends on a security parameter. We require that the message space of Π is $\{0,1\}^{k+\ell}$. We also assume that the secret key space of Π is $\{0,1\}^p$. Furthermore, let t and q be some fixed polynomials of λ, and let $n = \max\{pt, s\}$. Let ID be the circuit that computes the identity function the number of whose wires, that of whose output wires, and that of whose gates are n, n, and $q + n$, respectively.[1] Then, we construct the PKE

$\mathcal{S}'(1^\lambda):$	$\mathcal{E}'(pp', pk, m):$	$\mathcal{D}'(pp', sk, z):$
$pp \leftarrow \mathcal{S}(1^\lambda)$	$(pp, hk, \mathrm{ID}) \leftarrow pp'$	$(pp, hk, \mathrm{ID}) \leftarrow pp'$
$hk \leftarrow \mathsf{G}_h(1^\lambda)$	$x \leftarrow m\|0^{n-s}$	$(F, d, ct) \leftarrow z$
$pp' \leftarrow (pp, hk, \mathrm{ID})$	$(F, e, d) \leftarrow \mathsf{Gb}(1^\lambda, \mathrm{ID})$	$X\|h$ or $\perp \leftarrow \mathcal{D}(pp, sk, ct)$
return pp'	$X \leftarrow \mathsf{En}(e, x)$	if $\mathcal{D}$ outputs $\perp$ or $\mathsf{H}(hk, F\|d) \neq h$
$\mathcal{K}'(pp'):$	$h \leftarrow \mathsf{H}(hk, F\|d)$	then return $\perp$
$(pp, hk, \mathrm{ID}) \leftarrow pp'$	$ct \leftarrow \mathcal{E}(pp, pk, X\|h)$	$Y \leftarrow \mathsf{Ev}(F, X)$
$(pk, sk) \leftarrow \mathcal{K}(pp)$	$z \leftarrow (F, d, ct)$	$x \leftarrow \mathsf{De}(d, Y)$
return (pk, sk)	return z	$m \leftarrow x[1:s]$
		return m

Fig. 1. The proposed construction.

---

[1] See [8,9] for a concrete method for constructing ID.

scheme $\Pi' = (\mathcal{S}', \mathcal{K}', \mathcal{E}', \mathcal{D}')$ as described in Fig. 1. We note that the message space of Π' is $\{0,1\}^s$.

As our main result, we show the following theorem.

Theorem 1. *Let $\mathcal{G}$ be a projective garbling scheme that is prv.ind secure relative to ϕ_{size} and Π be a $\mathcal{P}_n^{k+\ell}$-KDM-CCA secure PKE scheme. Fix any polynomials t and q. Then Π' is $\mathcal{B}_{pt,q}^s$-KDM-CCA secure.*

Proof. We prove this theorem via a sequence of games. Fix any polynomials t and q. Let $\mathcal{A}$ be an adversary that attacks the $\mathcal{B}_{pt,q}^s$-KDM-CCA security of our scheme Π', and makes at most Q KDM queries (for some polynomial Q). Let C_f be the circuit of n inputs, n outputs, $q+n$ gates, such that $C_f(\mathbf{sk}) = \text{ev}(f, sk_1\|\cdots\|sk_t)\|0^{n-s}$, where $f \in \mathcal{B}_{pt,q}^s$ and $\mathbf{sk} = sk_1\|\cdots\|sk_t\|0^{n-pt}$. We consider the following sequence of games.

Game 0: This is the $\mathcal{B}_{pt,q}^s$-KDM-CCA game in case the challenge bit $b = 1$.

Here, we define the notion of a *bad decryption query* as follows.

Bad decryption query: A decryption query $(j^*, z^*) = (j^*, (F^*, d^*, ct^*))$ such that there exists an entry $(j, z) = (j, (F, d, ct)) \in L_{kdm}$ satisfying the following four conditions: **(a)** $\mathcal{D}(pp, sk_{j^*}, ct^*) = X^*\|h^* \neq \bot$; **(b)** $(j^*, ct^*) = (j, ct)$; **(c)** $F^*\|d^* \neq F\|d$; **(d)** $\mathsf{H}(hk, F^*\|d^*) = h^*$. Furthermore, if the entry (j, z) satisfying these conditions was generated and added to L_{kdm} by the challenger when responding to the i-th KDM query, we say that the decryption query (j^*, z^*) is a *bad decryption query for the i-th KDM query*.

Game 1: Same as Game 0 except that if $\mathcal{A}$ makes a bad decryption query, then the challenger returns $\bot$.

Game 2: Same as Game 1 except that if $\mathcal{A}$ makes a KDM query (j, f), then (F, e, d) and X are computed by $(F, e, d) \leftarrow \mathsf{Gb}(1^\lambda, C_f)$ and $X \leftarrow \mathsf{En}(e, \mathbf{sk})$, respectively.

Game 3: Same as Game 2 except that if $\mathcal{A}$ makes a KDM query (j, f), then ct is computed by $ct \leftarrow \mathcal{E}(pp, pk_j, 0^{k+\ell})$.

Game 4: Same as Game 3 except that if $\mathcal{A}$ makes a KDM query (j, f), then (F, e, d) is computed by $(F, e, d) \leftarrow \mathsf{Gb}(1^\lambda, \mathrm{ID})$.

Game 5: Same as Game 4 except that if $\mathcal{A}$ makes a KDM query (j, f), then X and ct are computed by $X \leftarrow \mathsf{En}(e, 0^n)$ and $ct \leftarrow \mathcal{E}(pp, pk_j, X\|h)$, respectively.

Game 6: Same as Game 5 except that if $\mathcal{A}$ makes a bad decryption query, then the challenger responds in exactly the same way as Game 0.

Let $\Pr[T_i]$ be the probability that $\mathcal{A}$ outputs 1 in Game i. Game 6 is the same game as the $\mathcal{B}_{pt,q}^s$-KDM-CCA game in case the challenge bit $b = 0$. Hence we have $\mathsf{Adv}_{\Pi',\mathcal{A}}^{kdm}(\lambda) = |\Pr[T_0] - \Pr[T_6]|$. Then we can estimate $\mathsf{Adv}_{\Pi',\mathcal{A}}^{kdm}(\lambda)$ as follows:

$$\mathsf{Adv}_{\Pi',\mathcal{A}}^{kdm}(\lambda) = |\Pr[T_0] - \Pr[T_6]| \leq \sum_{i=0}^{5} |\Pr[T_i] - \Pr[T_{i+1}]|. \tag{1}$$

Below, we show that each term of the right hand side of the inequality (1) is negligible.

Lemma 2. *Let $\mathcal{H}$ be a universal one-way hash function. Then* $|\Pr[T_0] - \Pr[T_1]| = \mathsf{negl}(\lambda)$.

Proof. For $i_1 \in \{0,1\}$ and $i_2 \in [Q]$, we define the following events.

B_{i_1}: In Game i_1, $\mathcal{A}$ makes at least one bad decryption query.
$B_{i_1}^{i_2}$: In Game i_1, $\mathcal{A}$ makes at least one bad decryption query for the i_2-th KDM query.

Note that Game 0 and Game 1 are identical unless the event B_0 or B_1 occurs in the corresponding games. More specifically, such a query is normally answered in Game 0 while it is answered with $\perp$ in Game 1. Therefore, we have $|\Pr[T_0] - \Pr[T_1]| \le \Pr[B_0] = \Pr[B_1]$. Then, using the adversary $\mathcal{A}$ that attacks Π', we construct the following adversary $\mathcal{A}'$ that attacks the universal one-wayness of $\mathcal{H}$.

Initialization: On input 1^λ, $\mathcal{A}'$ computes $(F_i, e_i, d_i) \leftarrow \mathsf{Gb}(1^\lambda, \mathrm{ID})(i = 1, \cdots, Q)$, and selects $r \xleftarrow{r} [Q]$. Then $\mathcal{A}'$ sends $F_r \| d_r$ to the challenger and receives a hash key hk. Next, $\mathcal{A}'$ computes $pp \leftarrow \mathcal{S}(1^\lambda)$, $(pk_j, sk_j) \leftarrow \mathcal{K}(pp)(j = 1, \cdots, t)$, and $pp' \leftarrow (pp, hk, \mathrm{ID})$, and then sends $(pp', pk_1, \cdots, pk_t)$ to $\mathcal{A}$. Finally, $\mathcal{A}'$ sets $L_{kdm} = \phi$.
KDM queries: For the i-th KDM query $(j_i, f) \in [t] \times \mathcal{B}_{pt,q}^s$ which $\mathcal{A}$ makes, $\mathcal{A}'$ computes $X_i \leftarrow \mathsf{En}(e_i, \mathsf{C}_f(\mathbf{sk}))$, $h_i \leftarrow \mathsf{H}(hk, F_i \| d_i)$, and $ct_i \leftarrow \mathcal{E}(pp, pk_{j_i}, X_i \| h_i)$, and then returns $z = (F_i, d_i, ct_i)$ to $\mathcal{A}$. Finally, $\mathcal{A}'$ adds (j_i, z) to L_{kdm}.
Decryption queries: If $\mathcal{A}$ makes a decryption query $(j^*, z^* = (F^*, d^*, ct^*))$, $\mathcal{A}'$ responds as the challenger in Game 1 does, using sk_{j^*}.
Final phase: When $\mathcal{A}$ terminates, $\mathcal{A}'$ checks whether $\mathcal{A}$ made a bad decryption query $(j^*, (F^*, d^*, ct^*))$ for the r-th KDM query. If this is the case, then $\mathcal{A}'$ outputs $F^* \| d^*$. Otherwise, $\mathcal{A}'$ outputs $\perp$.

$\mathcal{A}'$ simulates Game 1 perfectly for $\mathcal{A}$. Therefore $\mathcal{A}'$ succeeds in finding a collision for $\mathcal{H}$ if r is chosen and B_1^r happens. Note that the choice of r is information-theoretically hidden from $\mathcal{A}$'s view and thus does not affect $\mathcal{A}$'s behavior, and hence we see that $\mathsf{Adv}_{\mathcal{H},\mathcal{A}'}^{uow}(\lambda) = \sum_{i=1}^{Q} \Pr[r = i \wedge B_1^i] = \frac{1}{Q} \cdot \sum_{i=1}^{Q} \Pr[B_1^r]$. $\mathcal{H}$ is a universal one-way hash function, and thus we get $|\Pr[T_0] - \Pr[T_1]| \le \Pr[B_1] \le \sum_{i=1}^{Q} \Pr[B_1^i] = Q \cdot \mathsf{Adv}_{\mathcal{H},\mathcal{A}'}^{uow}(\lambda) = \mathsf{negl}(\lambda)$. $\quad\square$ **(Lemma 2)**

Lemma 3. *Let $\mathcal{G}$ be prv.ind secure with respect to ϕ_{size}. Then* $|\Pr[T_1] - \Pr[T_2]| = \mathsf{negl}(\lambda)$.

Proof. From Lemma 1, $\mathcal{G}$ is multi-query prv.ind secure with respect to ϕ_{size}. Using the adversary $\mathcal{A}$ that attacks Π', we construct the following adversary $\mathcal{A}'$ that attacks the multi-query prv.ind security of $\mathcal{G}$.

Initialization: On input 1^λ, $\mathcal{A}'$ computes $pp \leftarrow \mathcal{S}(1^\lambda)$, $hk \leftarrow \mathsf{G}_h(1^\lambda)$, $(pk_j, sk_j) \leftarrow \mathcal{K}(pp)(j = 1, \cdots, t)$, and $pp' \leftarrow (pp, hk, \mathrm{ID})$, and sends $(pp', pk_1, \cdots, pk_t)$ to $\mathcal{A}$. Finally, $\mathcal{A}'$ sets $L_{kdm} = \phi$.

KDM queries: If $\mathcal{A}$ makes a KDM query (j, f), $\mathcal{A}'$ queries $((\mathrm{ID}, \mathsf{C}_f(\mathbf{sk}))$, $(\mathsf{C}_f, \mathbf{sk}))$ to the challenger and receives (F, X, d). Then, $\mathcal{A}'$ computes $h \leftarrow \mathsf{H}(hk, F \| d)$ and $ct \leftarrow \mathcal{E}(pp, pk_j, X \| h)$, and returns $z = (F, d, ct)$ to $\mathcal{A}$. Finally, $\mathcal{A}'$ adds (j, z) to L_{kdm}.

Decryption queries: If $\mathcal{A}$ makes a decryption query (j^*, z^*), $\mathcal{A}'$ responds as the challenger in Game 2 does, using sk_{j^*}.

Final phase: When A terminates with output $b' \in \{0, 1\}$, $\mathcal{A}'$ outputs this b'.

Let β be a challenge bit in the game between a challenger and $\mathcal{A}'$. Then $\mathcal{A}'$ perfectly simulates Game 1 for $\mathcal{A}$ if $\beta = 0$, and perfectly simulates Game 2 for $\mathcal{A}$ if $\beta = 1$. Therefore, we have $|\Pr[T_1] - \Pr[T_2]| = |\Pr[b' = 1 | \beta = 0] - \Pr[b' = 1|$ $\beta = 1]|$. Since $\mathcal{G}$ is multi-query prv.ind secure, we have $\mathsf{Adv}_{\mathcal{G}, \mathcal{A}'}^{multi}(\lambda) = |\Pr[b' = 1 | \beta = 0] - \Pr[b' = 1 | \beta = 1]| = \mathsf{negl}(\lambda)$, and we see that $|\Pr[T_1] - \Pr[T_2]| = \mathsf{negl}(\lambda)$.

$\square$ **(Lemma 3)**

Lemma 4. *Let Π be $\mathcal{P}_n^{k+\ell}$-KDM-CCA secure. Then $|\Pr[T_2] - \Pr[T_3]| = \mathsf{negl}(\lambda)$.*

Proof. Using the adversary $\mathcal{A}$ that attacks Π', we construct the following adversary $\mathcal{A}'$ that attacks the $\mathcal{P}_n^{k+\ell}$-KDM-CCA security of Π.

Initialization: On input $(pp, pk_1, \cdots, pk_t)$, $\mathcal{A}'$ computes $hk \leftarrow \mathsf{G}_h(1^\lambda)$ and sets $pp' \leftarrow (pp, hk, \mathrm{ID})$. Then $\mathcal{A}'$ sends $(pp', pk_1, \cdots, pk_t)$ to $\mathcal{A}$. Finally, $\mathcal{A}'$ sets $L_{kdm} = \phi$.

KDM queries: If $\mathcal{A}$ makes a KDM query (j, f), $\mathcal{A}'$ responds as follows. First, $\mathcal{A}'$ computes $(F, e, d) \leftarrow \mathsf{Gb}(1^\lambda, \mathsf{C}_f)$ and $h \leftarrow \mathsf{H}(hk, F \| d)$. Next, $\mathcal{A}'$ computes a function g such that $g(\cdot) = \mathsf{En}(e, \cdot) \| h$ and makes a KDM query (j, g) to the challenger to get the answer ct. Finally, $\mathcal{A}'$ returns $z = (F, d, ct)$ to $\mathcal{A}$ and adds (j, z) to L_{kdm}. Recall that $\mathcal{G}$ is a projective garbling scheme, and thus $\mathsf{En}(e, \cdot)$ is a projection function. Hence $g(\cdot) = \mathsf{En}(e, \cdot) \| h$ is also a projection function.

Decryption queries: If $\mathcal{A}$ makes a decryption query $(j^*, z^* = (F^*, d^*, ct^*))$, $\mathcal{A}'$ responds as follows. If $(j^*, ct^*) = (j, ct)$ holds for some entry $(j, (F, d, ct)) \in L_{kdm}$, then $\mathcal{A}'$ returns $\perp$. Otherwise, $\mathcal{A}'$ sends a decryption query (j^*, ct^*) to the challenger to receives the result $X^* \| h^*$. If the result is $\perp$ or $\mathsf{H}(hk, F^* \| d^*) \neq h^*$, then $\mathcal{A}'$ returns $\perp$. Otherwise, $\mathcal{A}'$ computes $Y^* \leftarrow \mathsf{Ev}(F^*, X^*)$ and $x^* \leftarrow \mathsf{De}(d^*, Y^*)$, and returns $x^*[1:s]$ to $\mathcal{A}$.

Final phase: When $\mathcal{A}$ terminates with output $b' \in \{0, 1\}$, $\mathcal{A}'$ outputs this b'.

Let β be a challenge bit in the game between $\mathcal{A}'$ and a challenger. Then $\mathcal{A}'$ perfectly simulates Game 2 for $\mathcal{A}$ if $\beta = 1$, and $\mathcal{A}'$ perfectly simulates Game 3 for $\mathcal{A}$ if $\beta = 0$. Therefore we have $|\Pr[T_2] - \Pr[T_3]| = |\Pr[b' = 1 | \beta = 1] - \Pr[b' = 1 | \beta = 0]|$. Since Π is $\mathcal{P}_n^{k+\ell}$-KDM-CCA secure, $\mathsf{Adv}_{\Pi, \mathcal{A}'}^{kdm}(\lambda) = |\Pr[b' = 1 | \beta = 1] - \Pr[b' = 1 | \beta = 0]| = \mathsf{negl}(\lambda)$, and we see that $|\Pr[T_2] - \Pr[T_3]| = \mathsf{negl}(\lambda)$.

$\square$**(Lemma 4)**

Lemma 5. *Let $\mathcal{G}$ be prv.ind secure with respect to ϕ_{size}. Then $|\Pr[T_3] - \Pr[T_4]| = \mathsf{negl}(\lambda)$.*

The proof is almost the same as that of Lemma 3, and thus omitted.

Lemma 6. *Let Π be $\mathcal{P}_n^{k+\ell}$-KDM-CCA secure. Then $|\Pr[T_4] - \Pr[T_5]| = \mathsf{negl}(\lambda)$.*

Proof. Using the adversary $\mathcal{A}$ that attacks Π', we construct the following adversary $\mathcal{A}'$ that attacks the $\mathcal{P}_n^{k+\ell}$-KDM-CCA security of Π.

Initialization: On input $(pp, pk_1, \cdots, pk_t)$, $\mathcal{A}'$ computes $hk \leftarrow \mathsf{G}_h(1^\lambda)$ and $pp' \leftarrow (pp, hk, \mathsf{ID})$. Then $\mathcal{A}'$ sends $(pp', pk_1, \cdots, pk_t)$ to $\mathcal{A}$. Finally, $\mathcal{A}'$ sets $L_{kdm} = \phi$.

KDM queries: If $\mathcal{A}$ makes a KDM query (j, f), $\mathcal{A}'$ responds as follows. First, $\mathcal{A}'$ computes $(F, e, d) \leftarrow \mathsf{Gb}(1^\lambda, \mathsf{ID})$ and $h \leftarrow \mathsf{H}(k, F\|d)$. Next, $\mathcal{A}'$ computes a function g such that $g(x) = \mathsf{En}(e, 0^n)\|h$ and makes a KDM query (j, g) to the challenger to get the answer ct. Finally, $\mathcal{A}'$ returns $z = (F, d, ct)$ to $\mathcal{A}$ and adds (j, z) to L_{kdm}. Notice that the function g is a constant function, and thus g is also a projection function.

Decryption queries: $\mathcal{A}'$ responds in exactly the same way as in the proof of Lemma 4.

Final phase: When $\mathcal{A}$ terminates with output $b' \in \{0, 1\}$, $\mathcal{A}'$ outputs this b'.

Let β be a challenge bit in the game between $\mathcal{A}'$ and a challenger. Then $\mathcal{A}'$ perfectly simulates Game 4 for $\mathcal{A}$ if $\beta = 0$, and $\mathcal{A}'$ perfectly simulates Game 5 for $\mathcal{A}$ if $\beta = 1$. Therefore, we have $|\Pr[T_4] - \Pr[T_5]| = |\Pr[b' = 1|\beta = 0] - \Pr[b' = 1|\beta = 1]|$, and Π is $\mathcal{P}_n^{k+\ell}$-KDM-CCA secure, and thus $\mathsf{Adv}_{\Pi, \mathcal{A}'}^{kdm}(\lambda) = |\Pr[b' = 1|\beta = 0] - \Pr[b' = 1|\beta = 1]| = \mathsf{negl}(\lambda)$. From the above, $|\Pr[T_4] - \Pr[T_5]| = \mathsf{negl}(\lambda)$. $\square$ **(Lemma 6)**

We note that since $\mathcal{A}'$ only needs to use constant functions $g(x) = \mathsf{En}(e, 0^n)\|h$ (i.e. functions whose output is independent of an input) for KDM queries, we only need ordinary (non-KDM-)CCA security to show Lemma 6.

Lemma 7. *Let $\mathcal{H}$ be a universal one-way hash function. Then $|\Pr[T_5] - \Pr[T_6]| = \mathsf{negl}(\lambda)$.*

The proof is almost the same as that of Lemma 2, and thus omitted.

From the inequality (1) and Lemmas 2 to 7, we see that $\mathsf{Adv}_{\Pi', \mathcal{A}}^{kdm}(\lambda) = \mathsf{negl}(\lambda)$. Therefore, Π' is $\mathcal{B}_{pt,q}^s$-KDM-CCA secure. $\square$ **(Theorem 1)**

Remarks 1: the shared key setting. In this work, we construct a $\mathcal{B}_{pt,q}^s$-KDM-CCA secure encryption scheme from a $\mathcal{P}_n^{k+\ell}$-KDM-CCA secure encryption scheme in the public key setting. We notice that we get the same result in the shared key setting by allowing a shared key encryption scheme to have the setup algorithm that generates a hash key of a universal one-way hash function.

Remarks 2: on the plaintext space and the output length of KDM functions. Let $\mathcal{B}_{pt,q}^* = \{f | f : \{0, 1\}^{pt} \to \{0, 1\}^*$ is a function computable by circuits with size $q.\}$. Although we have shown that our scheme is $\mathcal{B}_{pt,q}^s$-KDM-CCA secure, it is not clear whether our scheme can be shown $\mathcal{B}_{pt,q}^*$-KDM-CCA secure. This is because the underlying scheme which we use is only $\mathcal{P}_n^{k+\ell}$-KDM-CCA secure, and thus it is not clear how our reduction algorithm can deal with a KDM query (j, f) such that f has unbounded output length. However, by assuming that the underlying scheme satisfies $\mathcal{P}_n^*$-KDM-CCA security, where $\mathcal{P}_n^* = \{f | f : \{0, 1\}^n \to \{0, 1\}^*$ is a projection function.$\}$, we can show that our scheme achieves $\mathcal{B}_{pt,q}^*$-KDM-CCA security. We note that Applebaum's KDM amplification method [4] has a similar property.

4   Comparison

In this section, we show a comparison on the efficiency of PKE schemes that are KDM-CCA secure with respect to functions computable by polynomially bounded-size circuits (bounded-KDM-CCA security). Specifically, if we start from projection-KDM-CPA secure schemes which can be obtained from affine-KDM-CPA secure schemes (e.g. [12]) via the method of [3, Appendix A], there are mainly two approaches for obtaining bounded-KDM-CCA secure schemes:

- **"KDM-amplification-first" approach:** First apply the KDM amplification methods for KDM-CPA security (Barak et al. [7], Applebaum [4], or Bellare et al.'s [8,9]) based on garbled circuit-based techniques to obtain a bounded-KDM-CPA secure scheme, and then apply the "CPA-to-CCA" conversion for KDM security based on NIZK by Camenisch et al. [16] to finally obtain a bounded-KDM-CCA secure scheme.
- **"CPA-to-CCA-first" approach:** First apply the "CPA-to-CCA" conversion for KDM security based on NIZK by Camenisch et al. [16] to obtain a projection-KDM-CCA secure scheme, and then apply the KDM amplification methods for KDM-CCA security (Applebaum [4] or ours[2]) to finally obtain a bounded-KDM-CCA secure scheme.

We note that even if we start from a projection-KDM-CPA secure scheme that is realizable using (bilinear-)groups (and thus is compatible with the Groth-Sahai proofs [19] which provide quite practical NIZK proofs for bilinear-group-based languages) such as the scheme of Boneh, Halevi, Hamburg, and Ostrovsky (we call it BHHO scheme) [12], the "KDM-amplification-first" approach in general requires a general NIZK proof (i.e. NIZK proofs for general NP languages) in the "CPA-to-CCA" conversion step because the resulting bounded-KDM-CPA scheme internally uses garbling schemes which will no longer be "Groth-Sahai"-compatible. Therefore, this approach is prohibitively impractical.

On the other hand, in the "CPA-to-CCA-first" approach, if we use the BHHO scheme [12] as the underlying projection-KDM-CPA secure scheme, and if we furthermore use the Groth-Sahai proofs [19] together with some efficient (non-KDM-)CCA secure PKE scheme such as the Cramer-Shoup scheme [18] which is needed in the CPA-to-CCA conversion of [16], then we can obtain a reasonably efficient projection-KDM-CCA secure scheme. More concretely, suppose we consider asymmetric bilinear groups in which the symmetric external Diffie-Hellman

---

[2] It is not known if the KDM amplification method by Barak et al. [7] can be used in the KDM-CCA setting, and thus we do not consider their amplification here.

(SXDH) assumption [11] holds, and assume that the sizes of group elements in the bilinear groups are all $O(\lambda)$, and then, we can construct a projection-KDM-CCA secure scheme with n'-bit plaintext space, so that the key size is $p = O(\lambda)$ bits and the ciphertext size is $O(n'\lambda^2)$ bits, where λ is a security parameter. (We explain more details on how such a projection-KDM-CCA scheme is obtained from [12,18,19] in Appendix A.)

Using this projection-KDM-CCA secure scheme as the underlying scheme, in Table 1, we compare the efficiency of bounded-KDM-CCA secure schemes obtained from the Applebaum's and our amplification methods, in terms of the number of bits needed to be encrypted by the underlying projection-KDM-CCA scheme, and the total ciphertext size. In the table, we assume that the output size of the underlying universal one-way hash function is λ, and that for the underlying garbling scheme of our scheme, Garble1 in [8,9] is used, enhancing it to prv.ind secure with respect to ϕ_{size} by using a universal circuit [23] (which changes the size q of circuits being garbled to $O(q \log q)$). We also assume that for the randomized encoding [6] (which is the building block of Applebaum's amplification method), Garble1 of [8,9] together with a universal circuit is used (how randomized encodings can be obtained from garbling schemes is explained in details in [8,9]). We note that in both Applebaum [4] and our constructions, the circuit that needs to be garbled can be made to be asymptotically the same size, and thus unlike in [8,9], we do not compare the computation costs of garbling.

As mentioned above, the underlying projection-KDM-CCA secure scheme (obtained from [12,16]) that can encrypt n'-bit plaintexts has ciphertext size $O(n'\lambda^2)$. Therefore, the smaller the size of plaintexts that need to be encrypted is, the smaller the ciphertext size of the bounded-KDM-CCA secure scheme becomes. In our scheme, the underlying scheme does not need to encrypt the "garbled function" F, whose size is $O(\lambda r \log r)$ if we use Garble1 of [8,9] (and the conversion using a universal circuit of [23]), and thus our scheme has (asymptotically) much smaller ciphertext size than that of Applebaum's.

Table 1. A comparison of our scheme and Applebaum. In the table, λ is a security parameter. Furthermore, we let $r = q + \max\{p \cdot t, s\}$, where q is the number of gates with respect to which we consider bounded-KDM-CCA security of the resulting scheme, s is the length of plaintexts that can be encrypted by the resulting scheme, $p = O(\lambda)$ is the secret key size of the underlying projection-KDM-CCA secure scheme obtained from [12,16], and t is the number of keys in the presence of which we consider the KDM-CCA security game.

Scheme	Bits encrypted by the projection-KDM-CCA scheme	Ciphertext size
Applebaum [4]	$O(\lambda r \log r)$	$O(\lambda^3 r \log r)$
Ours	$\lambda \cdot \max\{p \cdot t, s\} + \lambda$	$O(\lambda^4 t) + O(\lambda r \log r)$

A   How to Obtain a Projection-KDM-CCA Secure Scheme

In Sect. 4, we consider a projection-KDM-CCA secure scheme obtained from [12,16] for the underlying scheme to which our KDM amplification method and that of Applebaum are applied. Here, we explain how this scheme is obtained in more details.

Recall that the BHHO scheme [12] is shown to be affine-KDM-CPA secure based on the decisional Diffie-Hellman (DDH) assumption. Let us write $\mathbb{G}$ to denote its underlying prime order group. We assume that $|\mathbb{G}| = O(\lambda)$, and that an element of $\mathbb{G}$ has size $O(\lambda)$ bits where λ is a security parameter. Then, the plaintext space of this scheme is $\mathbb{G}$, and the secret key length is $p = 3\log|\mathbb{G}| = O(\lambda)$. Moreover, since a ciphertext of the scheme consists of $(p+1)$ elements of $\mathbb{G}$, its size (for encrypting an element in $\mathbb{G}$) is $(p+1) \cdot O(\lambda) = O(\lambda^2)$ bits.

Applebaum [3] showed how to obtain a projection-KDM-CPA secure scheme from the BHHO scheme: To the best of our knowledge, in Applebaum's method, we have to "encode" each bit of a secret key as an element of $\mathbb{G}$. Furthermore, the BHHO scheme by itself can encrypt one group element, and thus if we use the encoding of a secret key, we only obtain a "single-bit output" projection-KDM-CPA secure scheme. Fortunately, he also showed how to construct a "n-bit output" projection-KDM-CPA secure scheme (with n-bit plaintext space) from a single-bit output projection-KDM-CPA secure scheme by just encrypting each bit of a plaintext and concatenating the resulting ciphertexts. Thus, in summary, from the BHHO scheme one can obtain a projection-KDM-CPA secure scheme with n-bit plaintext space whose ciphertext size is $O(n\lambda^2)$ bits.

Camenisch, Chandran, and Shoup [15,16] showed how to enhance a KDM-CPA secure scheme into a KDM-CCA secure scheme, using NIZK proofs. More precisely, they showed two approaches. The first approach obtains a KDM-CCA secure scheme from a KDM-CPA secure scheme, (non-KDM-)CCA secure scheme, a one-time signature scheme, and NIZK proofs (satisfying soundness and zero-knowledge). The second approach obtains a KDM-CCA secure scheme from a KDM-CPA secure scheme, (non-KDM-)CPA secure scheme, and *simulation-sound* NIZK proofs (also satisfying soundness and zero-knowledge).

We consider the KDM-CCA secure scheme obtained from the second approach. This is because in the first approach we have to use a (non-KDM-)CCA secure scheme that has the same plaintext space as the above mentioned BHHO-based projection-KDM-CPA secure scheme (i.e. $\mathbb{G}^n$ for n-bit plaintexts). However, it is not so easy to obtain a CCA secure scheme (that is compatible with the BHHO-based projection-KDM-CPA secure scheme) whose plaintext space can be flexibly chosen, independently of its public keys. (For example, the Cramer-Shoup scheme [18] has a disadvantage that its plaintext space is fixed once a public/secret key pair is generated.)

Fortunately, [15] showed how to convert the Groth-Sahai proof [19] so that it supports simulation soundness. More specifically, [15] showed how to convert the Groth-Sahai proof into the simulation-sound version by using a (non-simulation-sound) Groth-Sahai proof, (non-KDM-)CCA secure PKE scheme, and a one-time signature scheme. Although this conversion also requires a (non-KDM-)CCA secure scheme, it only needs to encrypt one group element. Therefore, it does not need to support a large plaintext space, and thus we can use the Cramer-Shoup scheme. According to [15], assuming the SXDH assumption in asymmetric bilinear groups, and assuming that the one-time signature scheme shown in [15] under the SXDH assumption is used, if we want to prove the membership of the "linear subspace" language, described by a system of x linear equations with y variables using the simulation-sound version of the Groth-Sahai proof, then the proof size becomes $O(x + y) \cdot O(\lambda) = O((x + y)\lambda)$.

Now, we can construct a projection-KDM-CCA secure scheme that can encrypt n-bit plaintexts via the second method in [15] as follows: A plaintext is encrypted twice, by the KDM-CPA secure scheme and a (non-KDM-)CPA secure scheme (we use the ElGamal scheme), and then attach a "simulation-sound" Groth-Sahai NIZK proof that proves that the two ciphertexts encrypt a same plaintext. Note that the ciphertext size of the projection-KDM-CPA secure scheme is $O(n\lambda^2)$ bits, and the ElGamal scheme (for encrypting n group elements) has ciphertext size $O(n\lambda)$ bits. Furthermore, the equality of the plaintext by n-bit version of BHHO-based projection-KDM-CPA scheme and the plaintext of the ElGamal scheme, can be checked by $O(n\lambda)$ linear equations with $O(n)$ variables, and thus the proof size is $O(n\lambda^2)$ bits. Therefore, in total, the resulting projection-KDM-CCA secure scheme for n-bit plaintexts, which is based on the SXDH assumption, has cipher-text size $O(n\lambda^2)$.

References

1. Abadi, M., Rogaway, P.: Reconciling two views of cryptography (the computational soundness of formal encryption). J. Cryptol. **20**(3), 395 (2007)
2. Adão, P., Bana, G., Herzog, J., Scedrov, A.: Soundness and completeness of formal encryption: the cases of key cycles and partial information leakage. J. Comput. Secur. **17**(5), 737–797 (2009)
3. Applebaum, B.: Key-dependent message security: generic amplification and completeness. J. Cryptol. **27**(3), 429–451 (2014)
4. Applebaum, B.: Key-dependent message security: generic amplification and completeness. In: Paterson, K.G. (ed.) EUROCRYPT 2011. LNCS, vol. 6632, pp. 527–546. Springer, Heidelberg (2011)
5. Applebaum, B., Cash, D., Peikert, C., Sahai, A.: Fast cryptographic primitives and circular-secure encryption based on hard learning problems. In: Halevi, S. (ed.) CRYPTO 2009. LNCS, vol. 5677, pp. 595–618. Springer, Heidelberg (2009)
6. Applebaum, B., Ishai, Y., Kushilevitz, E.: Computationally private randomizing polynomials and their applications. In: CCC 2005, pp. 260–274. IEEE Computer Society (2005)
7. Barak, B., Haitner, I., Hofheinz, D., Ishai, Y.: Bounded key-dependent message security. In: Gilbert, H. (ed.) EUROCRYPT 2010. LNCS, vol. 6110, pp. 423–444. Springer, Heidelberg (2010)
8. Bellare, M., Hoang, V., Rogaway, P.: Foundations of garbled circuits. In: CCS 2012, pp. 784–796. ACM (2012)
9. Bellare, M., Hoang, V., Rogaway, P.: Foundations of garbled circuits. IACR Cryptol. ePrint Arch. **2012**, 265 (2012)

10. Black, J., Rogaway, P., Shrimpton, T.: Encryption-scheme security in the presence of key-dependent messages. In: Nyberg, K., Heys, H.M. (eds.) SAC 2002. LNCS, vol. 2595, pp. 62–75. Springer, Heidelberg (2003)
11. Boneh, D., Boyen, X., Shacham, H.: Short group signatures. In: Franklin, M. (ed.) CRYPTO 2004. LNCS, vol. 3152, pp. 41–55. Springer, Heidelberg (2004)
12. Boneh, D., Halevi, S., Hamburg, M., Ostrovsky, R.: Circular-secure encryption from decision Diffie-Hellman. In: Wagner, D. (ed.) CRYPTO 2008. LNCS, vol. 5157, pp. 108–125. Springer, Heidelberg (2008)
13. Brakerski, Z., Goldwasser, S.: Circular and leakage resilient public-key encryption under subgroup indistinguishability. In: Rabin, T. (ed.) CRYPTO 2010. LNCS, vol. 6223, pp. 1–20. Springer, Heidelberg (2010)
14. Brakerski, Z., Goldwasser, S., Kalai, Y.T.: Black-box circular-secure encryption beyond affine functions. In: Ishai, Y. (ed.) TCC 2011. LNCS, vol. 6597, pp. 201–218. Springer, Heidelberg (2011)
15. Camenisch, J., Chandran, N., Shoup, V.: A public key encryption scheme secure against key dependent chosen plaintext and adaptive chosen ciphertext attacks. IACR Cryptol. ePrint Arch. 2008, 375 (2008)
16. Camenisch, J., Chandran, N., Shoup, V.: A public key encryption scheme secure against key dependent chosen plaintext and adaptive chosen ciphertext attacks. In: Joux, A. (ed.) EUROCRYPT 2009. LNCS, vol. 5479, pp. 351–368. Springer, Heidelberg (2009)
17. Camenisch, J.L., Lysyanskaya, A.: An efficient system for non-transferable anonymous credentials with optional anonymity revocation. In: Pfitzmann, B. (ed.) EUROCRYPT 2001. LNCS, vol. 2045, pp. 93–118. Springer, Heidelberg (2001)
18. Cramer, R., Shoup, V.: A practical public key cryptosystem provably secure against adaptive chosen ciphertext attack. In: Krawczyk, H. (ed.) CRYPTO 1998. LNCS, vol. 1462, pp. 13–25. Springer, Heidelberg (1998)
19. Groth, J., Sahai, A.: Efficient noninteractive proof systems for bilinear groups. SIAM J. Comput. 41(5), 1193–1232 (2012)
20. Hofheinz, D.: Circular chosen-ciphertext security with compact ciphertexts. In: Johansson, T., Nguyen, P.Q. (eds.) EUROCRYPT 2013. LNCS, vol. 7881, pp. 520–536. Springer, Heidelberg (2013)
21. Malkin, T., Teranishi, I., Yung, M.: Efficient circuit-size independent public key encryption with KDM security. In: Paterson, K.G. (ed.) EUROCRYPT 2011. LNCS, vol. 6632, pp. 507–526. Springer, Heidelberg (2011)
22. Naor, M., Yung, M.: Universal one-way hash functions and their cryptographic applications. In: STOC 1989, pp. 33–43. ACM (1989)
23. Valiant, L.: Universal circuits (preliminary report). In: STOC 1976, pp. 196–203. ACM (1976)
24. Yao, A.: How to generate and exchange secrets (extended abstract). In: FOCS 1986, pp. 162–167. IEEE Computer Society (1986)

A Fast Phase-based Enumeration Algorithm for SVP Challenge Through y-Sparse Representations of Short Lattice Vectors

Dan Ding[1]([✉]), Guizhen Zhu[2], Yang Yu[1], and Zhongxiang Zheng[1]

[1] Department of Computer Science and Technology, Tsinghua University,
Beijing 100084, People's Republic of China
`dingd09@mails.tsinghua.edu.cn`
[2] Data Communication Science and Technology Research Institute,
Beijing 100191, People's Republic of China

Abstract. In this paper, we propose a new phase-based enumeration algorithm based on two interesting and useful observations for y-sparse representations of short lattice vectors in lattices from SVP challenge benchmarks [24]. Experimental results show that the phase-based algorithm greatly outperforms other famous enumeration algorithms in running time and achieves higher dimensions, like the Kannan-Helfrich enumeration algorithm. Therefore, the phase-based algorithm is a practically excellent solver for the shortest vector problem (SVP).

Keywords: Lattice-based cryptography · Shortest vector problem(SVP) · y-Sparse representation · Phase-based enumeration algorithm

1 Introduction

Lattice is a set of regularly arranged points in a Euclidean space, and it is widely used in both cryptanalysis and cryptography in recent years. As a promising candidate for the post-quantum cryptography, the lattice-based cryptography [19] attracts much attention from the cryptology community. The seminal paper in 1982 by A.K. Lenstra, H.W. Lenstra and L. Lavász [15] proposes the famous **LLL** algorithm for finding a short lattice basis. In the past 30 years after LLL algorithm, a variety of one-way functions are proposed based on the worst-case hardness of variants of lattice problems [1,17,18], and some new public-key cryptography [3,8,23] are put forward based on the hardness of lattice problems.

Therefore, the lattice problems are of prime importance to cryptography because the security of the lattice-based cryptography is based on the hardness of them. The two famous lattice problems are, the shortest vector problem (SVP), which is to, given a lattice basis, find the shortest nonzero vector in the lattice,

Supported by 973 Program (Grant No. 2013CB834205) and the National Natural Science Foundation of China (Grant No. 61133013).
Supported by the National Development Foundation for Cryptological Research (No. MMJJ201401003).

J. Lee and J. Kim (Eds.): ICISC 2014, LNCS 8949, pp. 101–113, 2015.
DOI: 10.1007/978-3-319-15943-0_7

and the closest vector problem (CVP), which is to, given a lattice basis and a target vector, find the lattice vector closest to the target vector.

The CVP has long been proved to be NP-hard by P. van Emde Baos in 1981 through classical Cook/Karp reduction [27], and the proof is refined by D. Miccancio et al. [16], while, at the same time, the hardness of other lattice problem SVP remains an open problem until SVP is proved to be NP-hard under a randomized reduction by M. Ajtai in 1998 [2]. Therefore, both CVP and SVP are hard enough to afford the security of lattice-based cryptography.

Since the hardness of both lattice problems, the algorithms to solve the two of them attracts interests of more and more researchers in cryptology community recently. In the last 30 years, a variety of algorithms have been proposed for both lattice problems, or, more specifically, for SVP. The SVP algorithms are of the following two categories: the theoretically sound algorithms, and the practically sound ones. The sieve algorithm for SVP [4, 22, 28] is proved to find the shortest vector within $2^{O(n)}$ time complexity with an exponential space complexity, which defies implementation, or, is not practical, especially for lattices of high dimensions. The algorithm based on Voronoi-cell computation [20] is a deterministic SVP algorithm, which is proved to be of $2^{2n+o(n)}$ time complexity, and not practical with an exponential space complexity. The blockwise Korkin-Zolotarev algorithm, or, **BKZ** algorithm [5, 25], falls into the second category, and the **BKZ** algorithm is a basis reduction algorithm and is to find lattice basis with excellent properties (which will be discussed in Sect. 2), which is also, practically, good at finding short vectors. The SVP algorithm is amenable for implementing with polynomial space, but it is still unknown whether the **BKZ** algorithm will terminate within finite steps, though the basis is good enough after finite iterations [9, 10] (not theoretically sound). A genetic algorithm for SVP is proposed [6] based on the y-sparse representation of short lattice vectors, with polynomial space complexity and excellent experimental results, but it is still an open problem to estimate its time complexity.

The enumeration algorithm is sound both practically (of polynomial space complexity) and theoretically (with delicate theoretical analysis). The most famous Kannan-Helfrich enumeration algorithm is proposed by R. Kannan [13] and B. Helfrich [12], which is theoretically analyzed as of $2^{O(n \log n)}$ time complexity [11, 14]. Some further improved enumeration algorithms [7] are proposed afterwards obtaining good experimental results.

The contributions of this paper are twofold. First, we propose some interesting observations for the y-sparse representations of the short lattice vectors: dividing the vector **y** corresponding to the shortest vector in a lattice evenly into phases, the second half of the **y** takes on an ascending order in their ℓ_1-norm of each phases, and sparse as whole; second, based on the observations, we propose a new phase-based enumeration algorithm, and the results show that the algorithm dramatically reduces the running time compared to other famous enumeration algorithms, like the Kannan-Helfrich algorithm, without missing the shortest vector.

The rest of the paper is organized as follows: Sect. 2 presents some necessary preliminaries on lattices and y-sparse representations of short lattice vectors;

Sect. 3 introduces the concept of "phase" to the y-sparse representations of short lattice vectors, and proposes some interesting observations for the short vectors of SVP challenge benchmarks; based on phases, we put forward a fast phase-based enumeration algorithm in Sect. 4; experimental results are reported in Sect. 5, and the conclusion is drawn in the following Sect. 6 and future work in Sect. 7.

2   Preliminaries

Let n be an integer, and let $\mathbb{R}^n$ be the n-dimensional Euclidean space. The Euclidean norm, ℓ_2-norm, of a vector $\mathbf{v}$ is defined as $\|\mathbf{v}\| = \sqrt{\sum_{i=1}^{n} v_i^2}$, and the ℓ_1-norm of $\mathbf{v}$ as $\|\mathbf{v}\|_1 = \sum_{i=1}^{n} |v_i|$, in which $\mathbf{v} = (v_1, \ldots, v_n) \in \mathbb{R}^n$. The linear space spanned by a set of vectors is denoted by span($\cdot$) and its orthogonal complement span($\cdot$)$^\perp$, and $\mathbf{B}^T$ is the transpose of a matrix $\mathbf{B}$. We denote $\lfloor \cdot \rfloor$ as the closest integer less than or equal to a real number, and $\lceil \cdot \rceil$ the upper closest integer. The closed sphere in $\mathbb{R}^n$ is denoted as $\mathcal{B}_n(\mathbf{O}, r)$ with $\mathbf{O}$ as its origin and r its radius. Finally, we denote the inf($\cdot$) as the infimum of the sequence, min($\cdot, \cdot$) as the smaller of the two parameters, and dim($\cdot$) the dimension of the spanned space.

2.1   Lattices

A *lattice* $\mathcal{L}$ is an additive subgroup of the Euclidean space $\mathbb{R}^n$. The lattice can be defined as set of all the integral combinations of n linearly independent vectors $\mathbf{b}_1, \ldots, \mathbf{b}_n$. If all the vectors are of dimensional n, the lattice is called *full-rank*. All the lattices considered in this paper are full-rank if not specified otherwise.

The basis $\mathbf{B}$ of a lattice $\mathcal{L}$ is the matrix $\mathbf{B} = [\mathbf{b}_1, \ldots, \mathbf{b}_n] \in \mathbb{R}^{n \times n}$ with the n vectors $\mathbf{b}_1, \mathbf{b}_2, \ldots, \mathbf{b}_n$ as its columns. Then the lattice can be represented as

$$\mathcal{L}(\mathbf{B}) = \{\mathbf{B}\mathbf{x} | \mathbf{x} \in \mathbb{Z}^n\} = \{\mathbf{v} \in \mathbb{R}^n \, | \mathbf{v} = \sum_{i=1}^{n} \mathbf{b}_i x_i, x_i \in \mathbb{Z}\}.$$

The ith *successive minimum* $\lambda_i(\mathcal{L})$ (for $i = 1, \ldots, n$) of a lattice $\mathcal{L}$ is defined as the smallest radium of a sphere within which there are i linearly independent lattice points, i.e.,

$$\lambda_i(\mathcal{L}) = \inf\{r \in \mathbb{R}^n | \dim\{\mathrm{span}(\mathcal{L} \cap \mathcal{B}_n(\mathbf{O}, r))\} = i\}.$$

Then, the first successive minima $\lambda_1(\mathcal{L})$ is the Euclidean norm, or length, of the shortest nonzero vector in the lattice $\mathcal{L}$. For a basis $\mathbf{B} = [\mathbf{b}_1, \ldots, \mathbf{b}_n]$ of a lattice $\mathcal{L}(\mathbf{B}) \in \mathbb{R}^{n \times n}$, its *Gram-Schmidt Orthogonalization* $\mathbf{B}^* = [\mathbf{b}_1^*, \ldots, \mathbf{b}_n^*]$ is defined as,

$$\mathbf{b}_i^* = \mathbf{b}_i - \sum_{j=1}^{i-1} \mu_{ij} \mathbf{b}_j^*,$$

where

$$\mu_{ij} = \frac{\langle \mathbf{b}_i, \mathbf{b}_j^* \rangle}{\langle \mathbf{b}_j^*, \mathbf{b}_j^* \rangle}, \text{ for } 1 \leq j \leq i \leq n.$$

and the factor matrix $\mu = \{\mu_{ij}\}_{1 \leq i,j \leq n}$ in which $\mu_{ij} = 0$ for $i < j$.

We define $\pi_i : \mathbb{R}^n \mapsto \text{span}(\mathbf{b}_1, \ldots, \mathbf{b}_{i-1})^{\perp}$ as the projection on the orthogonal complement of the span of the first $i - 1$ bases of $\mathbf{B}$, for all $i \in \{1, 2, \ldots, n\}$. $\pi_i(\mathbf{b}_j)$ is expressed as

$$\pi_i(\mathbf{b}_j) = \mathbf{b}_j^* + \sum_{k=i}^{j-1} \mu_{jk} \mathbf{b}_k^*, \quad \text{if} \quad i < j.$$

And, we define $\mathcal{L}_i^{(k)}$ as the lattice of rank k generated by the basis $[\pi_i(\mathbf{b}_i), \ldots, \pi_i(\mathbf{b}_{i+k-1})]$ in which $i + k \leq n + 1$. Clearly, it is true that $\mathcal{L}_i^{(n-i+1)} = \pi_i(\mathcal{L})$, which implies the lattice of rank $n - i + 1$ generated by basis $[\pi_i(\mathbf{b}_i), \ldots, \pi_i(\mathbf{b}_n)]$.

Thereby, we define a basis $\mathbf{B} = [\mathbf{b}_1, \ldots, \mathbf{b}_n]$ as a β-blockwise Korkin-Zolotarev basis, or **BKZ**-reduced basis, if the following conditions hold:

1. Its $|\mu_{ij}| \leq 1/2$, for $1 \leq j < i \leq n$;
2. and $\pi_i(\mathbf{b}_i)$ is the shortest vector of the lattice $\mathcal{L}_i^{(\min(\beta, n-i+1))}$ under the Euclidean norm, or length, for $1 \leq i \leq n$.

You can refer to [16] for details of lattices.

2.2 y-Sparse Representations of Short Lattice Vectors

As defined above, a lattice vector $\mathbf{v} \in \mathcal{L}(\mathbf{B})$ can be represented as $\mathbf{v} = \mathbf{B}\mathbf{x}$, in which $\mathbf{x}$ is an integer vector. Then $\mathbf{x}$ can corresponds to a specific lattice vector $\mathbf{v}$ under a basis $\mathbf{B}$. The y-sparse representation is to regards the lattice $\mathbf{v}$ from another point of view, which is endowed with some excellent properties.

Given a lattice basis $\mathbf{B} = [\mathbf{b}_1, \ldots, \mathbf{b}_n]$ and its Gram-Schmidt orthogonalization $\mathbf{B}^* = [\mathbf{b}_1^*, \ldots, \mathbf{b}_n^*]$ with its factor matrix $\mu = \{\mu_{ij}\}_{1 \leq i,j \leq n} \in \mathbb{R}^{n \times n}$ such that $\mathbf{B} = \mathbf{B}^* \mu^T$, for any vector $\mathbf{v} \in \mathcal{L}(\mathbf{B})$, or $\mathbf{v} = \mathbf{B}\mathbf{x}$, in which $\mathbf{x} = [x_1, \ldots, x_n] \in \mathbb{Z}^n$, we define another vector $\mathbf{t} = [t_1, \ldots, t_n] \in \mathbb{R}^n$ as, for $1 \leq i \leq n$,

$$t_i = \begin{cases} 0 & \text{for } i = n, \\ \sum_{j=i+1}^n \mu_{ji} x_j & \text{for } i < n. \end{cases}$$

and another vector $\mathbf{y} = (y_1, y_2, \ldots, y_n) \in \mathbb{Z}^n$ as, for $1 \leq i \leq n$,

$$y_i = \lfloor x_i + t_i \rceil.$$

Thereby, the definition establishes a one-to-one correspondence between a lattice vector $\mathbf{v}$ and its $\mathbf{y}$ as below:

$$\mathbf{y} \xleftarrow{\mathbf{y} = \mathbf{x} + \lfloor \mathbf{t} \rceil} \mathbf{x} \xleftarrow{\mathbf{v} = \mathbf{B}\mathbf{x}} \mathbf{v},$$

We call $\mathbf{v}$ is correspondent to $\mathbf{y}$, or, $\mathbf{v} \sim \mathbf{y}$.

We call such a representation as sparse because most of the elements in **y** corresponding to short lattice vectors under a **BKZ**-reduced basis are zero's. For example, the shortest vector of the 40-dimensional lattice (generated by $seed = 0$) in SVP challenge **v** is (−398 −305 −268 125 96 214 284 −108 37 −2 402 228 −243 −33 −76 −265 −3 558 323 552 −419 −408 217 2 440 375 −153 108 79 80 −299 −81 385 −80 −53 −294 −170 380 164 172), (and $\|\mathbf{v}\| = 1702$), and its corresponding **y** under its 5-**BKZ** reduced basis is (0 0 0 0 0 0 0 0 0 0 0 0 0 0 0 0 0 0 1 0 0 0 0 0 0 0 0 0 0 −1 −1 0 0 0 1). We can see that only 4 nonzero elements in **y** and they are all distributed in the second half with absolute value of 1.

Actually, most y-sparse representations of the short vectors in the lattice under a **BKZ**-reduced basis shares this excellent property. Therefore, for an integer vector $\mathbf{y} = (y_1, y_2, \ldots, y_n)$ corresponding to a short vector in a lattice under a **BKZ**-reduced basis, we have the following two heuristics as follows:

1. The first half integer elements $y_1, \ldots, y_{\lfloor n/2 \rfloor}$ in **y** are all zero's;
2. The absolute value $y_{\lfloor n/2 \rfloor +1}, \ldots, y_n$ of the second half integers in **y** is bounded by $\sqrt{\frac{\lambda_1}{\|\mathbf{b}_i^*\|}}$ instead of $\frac{\lambda_1}{\|\mathbf{b}_i^*\|}$ as stated in the theorem in [6], for $\lfloor n/2 \rfloor + 1 \leq i \leq n$;

For a more rigorous treatment of y-sparse representation, refer to [6].

3 y-Phase: Some Interesting Observations

In this section, we discuss the phase of the y-sparse representation of short lattice vectors and some interesting and useful observations.

As discussed in Sect. 2, the y that is correspondent to a short vector **v** is sparse, i.e., only a fraction of the elements of **y** is nonzero, and, more precisely, the absolute value of the nonzero elements are small, say 1, 2, or 3, and most nonzero elements fall into the second half of vector **y**. Like the y corresponding to the shortest vector of the random lattice of dimension 40 of SVP challenge, under a **BKZ**-reduced basis, as shown in Fig. 1, only 4 elements are nonzero (of absolute value 1), and they are all distributed in the second half (of index 21–40) of **y**.

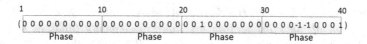

Fig. 1. The y-Phases of the 40-dimensional random lattice of SVP challenge

If we consider the y corresponding more deeply, we can see that nonzero elements are not distributed evenly in the last half elements: the last ten elements includes 3 nonzero elements while only 1 nonzero element falls between index 21 and 30 (the first half of the last 20 elements in **y**). Therefore, we can divide the 40 elements of **y** evenly into 4 *phases*, each of which contains 10 elements. As in Fig. 1, the first two phases are all 0's, and the third phase has 1 nonzero element while the last phase obtains 3. We can notate the first phase as $y_{1,\ldots,10}$, and $y_{11,\ldots,20}, y_{21,\ldots,30}$, and $y_{31,\ldots,40}$ as the following 3 phases, or $y_{l,\ldots,l+9}$ for the low index $l = 1, 11, 21, 31$. On the phases, we can define the ℓ_1-norm of the phases, like $\|y_{l,\ldots,l+9}\|_1$, as a measure for the number of nonzero elements in the phase. Therefore, the ℓ_1-norm of the 4 phases of y corresponding the shortest vector of dimension 40 takes on an ascending order as $(0, 0, 1, 3)$ (Table 2).

Table 1. y-Phases of the random lattice of dimension 95 ($\|v\| = 2584$)

Phases	$y_{l\ldots\min(l+10,n)}$	ℓ_1-norm of the Phases
$y_1, \ldots, y_{10}$	(0 0 0 0 0 0 0 0 0 0	0
$y_{11}, \ldots, y_{20}$	0 0 0 0 0 0 0 0 0 0	0
$y_{21}, \ldots, y_{30}$	0 0 0 0 0 0 0 0 0 0	0
$y_{31}, \ldots, y_{40}$	0 0 0 0 0 0 0 0 0 0	0
$y_{41}, \ldots, y_{50}$	0 0 0 0 0 0 0 0 0 0	0
$y_{51}, \ldots, y_{60}$	0 0 0 0 0 0 0 0 0 0	0
$y_{61}, \ldots, y_{70}$	1 0 0 0 0 0 0 0 0 0	1
$y_{71}, \ldots, y_{80}$	0 0 0 0 1 −1 0 0 0 0	2
$y_{81}, \ldots, y_{90}$	0 0 0 1 0 0 −1 0 0 −1	3
$y_{91}, \ldots, y_{95}$	1 0 0 1 −2)	4

Let us take a look at two more examples. As shown in Table 1, the y corresponding to the short vector of 95-dimensional random lattice, under a **BKZ**-reduced basis, is divided into 10 phases (with each consecutive 10 elements as a phase). We can see that the first 6 phases are of ℓ_1-norm 0, and that the ℓ_1-norm of the last 4 phases are 1, 2, 3, 4 (an ascending order). Similarly, Fig. 2 shows that the y corresponding to the shortest vector v of the 134-dimensional random lattice takes on an ascending order of the ℓ_1-norms of its 14 phases. The ℓ_1-norm of the phases are $(0, 0, 0, 0, 0, 0, 0, 1, 1, 1, 3, 5, 6, 7)$. Actually, most of y corresponding to the short vectors in random lattices of SVP challenges obtains the same property as we observe above, Therefore, we concludes the two useful observations as follows:

Observation 1. *Under a **BKZ**-reduced basis, only a fraction of the y-representation of the short vectors are nonzero elements (only $\frac{1}{10} \sim \frac{1}{6}$). And as stated in [6], the nonzero elements almost all fall into the second half of its y-representation with small absolute value of the nonzero elements. In other words, the ℓ_1-norm of the whole y is approximately between $\frac{n}{10}$ and $\frac{n}{6}$.*

Observation 2. *Divided into phases of length 10, the y-representation of the short vectors of random lattices in SVP challenge, under a **BKZ**-reduced basis, is of an ascending order under ℓ_1-norm.*

The two observations are useful in designing fast enumeration algorithm for SVP challenge as in the next section.

Table 2. y-Phases of the random lattice of dimension 134 ($\|\mathbf{v}\| = 2976$)

Phases	$\mathbf{y}_{l\ldots\min(l+10,n)}$	ℓ_1-norm of the Phases
$y_1, \ldots, y_{10}$	(0 0 0 0 0 0 0 0 0 0	0
$y_{11}, \ldots, y_{20}$	0 0 0 0 0 0 0 0 0 0	0
$y_{21}, \ldots, y_{30}$	0 0 0 0 0 0 0 0 0 0	0
$y_{31}, \ldots, y_{40}$	0 0 0 0 0 0 0 0 0 0	0
$y_{41}, \ldots, y_{50}$	0 0 0 0 0 0 0 0 0 0	0
$y_{51}, \ldots, y_{60}$	0 0 0 0 0 0 0 0 0 0	0
$y_{61}, \ldots, y_{70}$	0 0 0 0 0 0 0 0 0 0	0
$y_{71}, \ldots, y_{80}$	0 0 0 1 0 0 0 0 0 0	1
$y_{81}, \ldots, y_{90}$	0 0 0 0 0 0 0 1 0 0	1
$y_{91}, \ldots, y_{100}$	0 0 0 0 0 1 0 0 0 0	1
$y_{101}, \ldots, y_{110}$	0 −1 0 0 1 0 0 1 0 0	3
$y_{111}, \ldots, y_{120}$	0 0 1 −1 0 0 2 1 0 0	5
$y_{121}, \ldots, y_{130}$	0 0 0 2 −1 0 −1 0 −1 1	6
$y_{131}, \ldots, y_{134}$	3 2 −1 −1)	7

4   A Phase-Based Enumeration Algorithm for SVP Challenge

In this section, we discuss in detail our phase-based enumeration algorithm, which applies the two useful observations in the last section.

4.1   Overview

The low ℓ_1-norm of y-representation of short vectors as in Observation 1 shows us that we need not waste time enumerating all the feasible lattice vectors, and that all we need to do is to enumerate all the $\mathbf{y}$ such that the ℓ_1-norm of the last half of $\mathbf{y}$ is $\frac{n}{10}$ to $\frac{n}{6}$, i.e., $\left\|\mathbf{y}_{\lfloor\frac{n}{2}\rfloor,\ldots,n}\right\|_1 \in [\frac{n}{10}, \frac{n}{6}]$. Moreover, Observation 2

Table 3. The phase-based enumeration algorithm for SVP

Input: A β-**BKZ** reduced basis $\mathbf{B} = [\mathbf{b}_1, \ldots, \mathbf{b}_n]$ of a lattice $\mathcal{L}$.
Output: The Shortest Nonzero Vector $\mathbf{v}'$ in the lattice $\mathcal{L}(\mathbf{B})$
1. Compute $\mathbf{B}$'s Gram-Schmidt Orthogonalizations $\mathbf{B}^* = [\mathbf{b}_1^*, \ldots, \mathbf{b}_n^*]$ and its factor matrix $\mu = \{\mu_{ij}\}_{1 \le i,j \le n}$;
2. Estimate the first minima λ_1 by Gaussian Heuristic;
3. Initialize $\alpha = (\alpha_1, \ldots, \alpha_n)$ as $\alpha_i \leftarrow 0$, for $1 \le i < \lfloor\frac{n}{2}\rfloor$, and $\alpha_i \leftarrow \sqrt{\frac{\lambda_1}{\|\mathbf{b}_i^*\|}}$, for $\lfloor\frac{n}{2}\rfloor \le i \le n$;
4. Let $\mathbf{y} \leftarrow (0, 0, \ldots, 0)$, and $\mathbf{v}' \leftarrow \mathbf{b}_1$;
5. Let $m \leftarrow \lceil\frac{n}{2}/10\rceil$; $\mathbf{d} \leftarrow \{d_1, d_2, \ldots, d_m\}$; //max ℓ_1-norms of phases
6. PHASEENUMERATION$(0, \lfloor\frac{n}{2}\rfloor, \min(\lfloor\frac{n}{2}\rfloor + 10, n), \mathbf{y}, \mathbf{v}')$;
7. **Return** $\mathbf{v}'$;

reveals that the nonzero elements are distributed unevenly among the phases in the last half of $\mathbf{y}$, and, more precisely, the ℓ_1-norm of the phases in the second half takes on an ascending order. Then, we can enumerate phase by phase the $\mathbf{y}$ with ascending ℓ_1-norms for phases in the second half, which highlights the main idea of our phase-based enumeration algorithm.

Our phase-based enumeration predefines an integer sequence $\mathbf{d} = (d_1, \ldots, d_m)$ (m is the number of phases) of the maximum ℓ_1-norm for each phases (the sum of all the ℓ_1-norm are only $\frac{n}{10}$ to $\frac{n}{6}$), and it is clear that the sequence is in an ascending order. Then, the algorithm enumerates $\mathbf{y}$ recursively phase-after-phase with the ith phase of ℓ_1-norm less than d_i. Finally, the algorithm returns the shortest lattice vector. Clearly, the enumeration procedure based on phase searches much less lattice vectors than the common enumeration algorithm which runs over all the lattice vectors, and the two observations in the last section ensure that the shortest vector will not be omitted in such phase-based method.

Table 3 shows the pseudo-codes of the main procedure of our phase-based enumeration algorithm. As in the table, given a lattice basis $\mathbf{B} = [\mathbf{b}_1, \ldots, \mathbf{b}_n]$ (which is BKZ-reduced), the procedure first computes the Gram-Schmidt orthogonalzation $\mathbf{B}^*$ and its μ. Estimating the first minima λ_1 of the lattice, the procedure calculates the bounds $\alpha = (\alpha_1, \ldots, \alpha_n)$ of $\mathbf{y}$ as 0 for the first half of the elements and $\sqrt{\frac{\lambda_1}{\|\mathbf{b}_i^*\|}}$ for the second half, based on theorem and heuristics in [6]. Then, the procedure initialize the integer vector $\mathbf{y}$ as all-zero and the shortest vector $\mathbf{v}'$ as the first vector $\mathbf{b}_1$ of the basis $\mathbf{B}$. Note that we only take the phases in the second half into consideration, and, so, the number of phases m is set as $\lceil \frac{n}{2}/10 \rceil$. After predefining the integer sequence $\mathbf{d} = (d_1, \ldots, d_m)$ in an ascending order with $\sum_{i=1}^{m}(d_i) \leq \frac{n}{6}$, we starts to enumerates all the $\mathbf{y}$ such that the ℓ_1-norm of the ith phase is less than d_i using the subroutine PHASEENUMERATION(), which will be described in the following subsection.

4.2   PHASEENUMERATION() and PHASEENUMERATIONBOTTOM()

In this subsection, we discuss two subroutines PHASEENUMERATION() and PHASEENUMERATIONBOTTOM(), which constitute the main body of our phase-base enumeration algorithm.

Table 4 shows that pseudo-codes of PHASEENUMERATION(). As shown in the table, it is an enumeration procedure using "recursion". Given the parameters of phase number p, the low index of l, the high index h, and the current $\mathbf{y}$, which has been set before the low index l, the procedure searches the current phase such that the ℓ_1-norm of current phase is less than the predefined d_p, i.e., $\|\mathbf{y}_{l,\ldots,h-1}\|_1 \leq d_p - \|\mathbf{y}_{h-10,\ldots,l-1}\|_1$, and, then, it invokes itself or the bottom procedure PHASEENUMERATIONBOTTOM() to search the next phase.

Entering the procedure PHASEENUMERATION(), it invokes the bottom subroutine PHASEENUMERATIONBOTTOM() if the high index h is larger than the lattice rank n. If not, the procedure has not arrived at the last phase, and (at Line 2) it searches all the index between l and h. If the variable i grabs the high index h, the procedure has enters the phase that follows, and, then, it calls itself

Table 4. PhaseEnumeration()

Input: the phase p, low index l, high index h, an integer vector
  $\mathbf{y} = (y_1, \ldots, y_n)$ and a lattice vector $\mathbf{v}'$;
Output: The shortest nonzero vector $\mathbf{v}' = (v_1', \ldots, v_n')$.

---

1. **If** $h \geq n$ **then** PHASEENUMERATIONBOTTOM(l, $\mathbf{y}$, $\mathbf{v}'$, l);
//Enter the bottom procedure
2. **else for** $i \in \{l, \ldots, h\}$ **do**
   (a) **if** $i = h$ **then** PHASEENUMERATION($p + 1$, h, $\min(h + 10, n)$,
      $\mathbf{y}$, $\mathbf{v}'$); //Enter the next phase
   (b) **else for** $j \in \{-\alpha_i, \ldots, \alpha_i\}$ **do**
      (i) **if** $\|\mathbf{y}_{h-10,\ldots,i-1}\|_1 + |j| \leq d_p$ **then**
        (1) Let $y_i \leftarrow j$;
        (2) **if** $\|\mathbf{y}_{h-10,\ldots,i}\|_1 = d_p$ **then** //enter the next phase
          PHASEENUMERATION($p + 1$, h, $\min(h + 10, n)$, $\mathbf{y}$, $\mathbf{v}'$);
        (3) **else** //continue with the current phase
          PHASEENUMERATION(p, $i + 1$, h, $\mathbf{y}$, $\mathbf{v}'$);
        (4) Let $y_i \leftarrow 0$;
3. **Return** $\mathbf{v}'$.

---

with parameters of $p + 1, h, h + 10$. If i grabs an index less than h, the procedure chooses a j as the nonzero value for y_i within bounds $[-\alpha_i, \alpha_i]$. If the newly chosen has not made the ℓ_1-norm of the current phase larger than d_p, y_i is set as j, and the procedure either enters another phase if the ℓ_1-norm of the current phase is equal to d_p, or, otherwise, continues with current phase by invoking itself with the low index l replaced by $i + 1$ (searches between index $i + 1$ and h). Thereby, the procedure searches all the $\mathbf{y}$ that satisfies the requirements of the predefined maximum ℓ_1-norm $\mathbf{d}$.

Table 5. PhaseEnumerationBottom()

Input: the low index l, an integer vector $\mathbf{y} = (y_1, \ldots, y_n)$, a lattice vector $\mathbf{v}'$,
  and the low index l' of the last phase;
Output: The shortest nonzero vector $\mathbf{v}' = (v_1', \ldots, v_n')$.

---

1. **for** $i \in \{l, \ldots, n\}$ **do**
   (a) **for** $j \in \{-\alpha_i, \ldots, \alpha_i\}$ **do**
      (i) **if** $\|\mathbf{y}_{l',\ldots,i}\|_1 + |j| \leq d_m$ **then**
        (1) Let $y_i \leftarrow j$;
        (2) Compute $\mathbf{v} \sim \mathbf{y}$ using $\mathbf{B}^*$ and μ;
        (3) **if** $\|\mathbf{v}\| < \|\mathbf{v}'\|$ **then** $\mathbf{v}' \leftarrow \mathbf{v}$;
        (4) **if** $\|\mathbf{y}_{l',\ldots,i}\|_1 < d_m$ **then**
          PHASEENUMERATIONBOTTOM($i + 1$, $\mathbf{y}$, $\mathbf{v}'$, l');
        (5) Let $y_i \leftarrow 0$.
2. **Return** $\mathbf{v}'$.

Table 5 shows the bottom procedure of our phase-based enumeration algorithm. Given the low index l, the bottom procedure searches all the index between l and the lattice rank n, and updates the shortest vector $\mathbf{v}'$ if it finds shorter vectors. Entering the bottom procedure, the index i runs over $[l, \ldots, n]$

and j chooses all the value between $-\alpha_i$ and α_i for y_i. If the newly-generated nonzero element does not make the ℓ_1-norm of the current phase go beyond d_m, the y_i is set as j and we go on with updating the shortest vector $\mathbf{v}'$ if better solution comes to light. After that, if the ℓ_1-norm of the current phase is still less than d_m, or, in other words, the current phase can still contain more nonzero elements, the procedure continues with the phase by invoking itself with a new low index $i + 1$.

The two subroutines recursively searches all the $\mathbf{y} = (y_1, \ldots, y_n)$ which satisfies that the ℓ_1-norm of each phases is less than a predefined maximum ℓ_1-norm sequence $\mathbf{d} = (d_1, \ldots, d_n)$, thereby finding the shortest vector in the lattice by searching relatively few lattice vectors.

5   Experimental Results

In this section, we compare the running times of our phase-based enumeration algorithm with the seminal Kannan-Helfrich Enumeration algorithm [14] and ℓ_1-norm based enumeration algorithm, and all the three algorithms are implemented using C++ with Victor Shoup's Number Theory Library (NTL) version 6.0.0 [26]. Experiments are performed on a workstation with 16 Intel Xeon 2.4Ghz CPUs and 16G RAM under a Red Hat Linux Server release 5.4. All the experiments are run on the SVP challenge benchmarks [24] of dimension 20–95, and all the random bases are generated using their random lattice generator with random $seed = 0$. All the bases are preprocessed by a **BKZ** subroutine with their block size $\beta < \frac{n}{4}$ (n is their rank of the lattices). The Kannan-Helfrich enumeration algorithm is, actually, to search all the feasible lattice vectors in the hypersphere of $\sum_{i=1}^{n} y_i^2 \|\mathbf{b}_i^*\|^2 \le \lambda_1$, which has been deeply researched into in the recent years [11,12,21], and the ℓ_1-norm based enumeration algorithm is to search $\mathbf{y}$ with the last half of ℓ_1-norm less than $\frac{n}{10} \sim \frac{n}{6}$ (based on Observation 1), or, in other words, the 1-phase enumeration algorithm. Our phase-based enumeration algorithm runs with the predefined maximum ℓ_1-norm for the second half phases $\mathbf{d}$ as $(1, 2, \ldots, m)$.

Table 6. Running time comparison of enumeration algorithms under dimension-40 random lattices

Running time	Enumeration algorithms
3017.3270 s	The Kannan-Helfrich Enumeration Algorithm
12.0048 s	The ℓ_1-Norm Based Enumeration Algorithm
1.47209 s	The Phase-Based Enumeration Algorithm

The three algorithms are run under the random lattice basis of dimension 40 (with a preprocessing of 5-BKZ reduction), the running time of the three are compared in Table 6. As shown in the table, the Kannan-Helfrich enumeration algorithm find the shortest vector (of Euclidean norm 1702) with over 3000 s, and the ℓ_1-norm based enumeration algorithm uses approximately 12 s, and our phase-enumeration algorithm only 1.4 s, which is over 3000 faster than Kannan-Helfrich algorithm and 10 times faster than ℓ_1-norm based algorithm.

We continue to run the three algorithms on the random lattices of dimension 20–95 and the running time comparison is given in Fig. 2. As shown in the figure, the Kannan-Helfrich enumeration algorithm consumes the most running time: it consumes over hundreds of seconds under lattice basis of dimension 20, and it only runs up to lattice basis of dimension 70 with unbearably long time. The ℓ_1-norm enumeration algorithm runs faster: nearly 1.3 s for lattice of dimension 20, and runs up to the 80-dimensional lattice. The second algorithm runs over some lattices of dimension 20–80 and approximately tens or hundreds of times faster than Kannan-Helfrich algorithm. Finally, our phase-based enumeration algorithm outperforms the other two enumeration algorithms: it runs less than 1 s for lattice of dimension 20, and runs through most lattices of dimension 20–95, and it enjoys a thousands of times speedup over Kannan-Helfrich algorithm, and also much better than the 1-phase enumeration. It is clear that the running time of our phase-based algorithm depends heavily on the predefined integer sequence $\mathbf{d}$ of the maximum ℓ_1-norm for phases, and we believe that an improvement can be achieved by choosing a better $\mathbf{d}$.

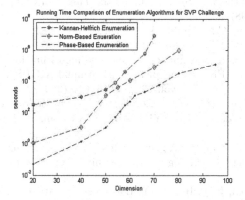

Fig. 2. Running time comparison of the enumeration algorithms for SVP Challenge

The experimental results imply that the phase-based enumeration algorithm gains a great advantage over the other two enumeration algorithm in running time, and it never misses any optimum solution though searching only a fraction of the feasible lattice vectors.

6 Conclusion

In this paper, we propose a novel phase-based enumeration algorithm for shortest vector problems based on the two interesting and useful observations for the short lattice vectors. The experimental results show that the phase-based enumeration greatly outperforms the other famous enumeration algorithms in time complexity under the most random lattice bases in SVP challenge benchmarks [24]. In conclusion, it is practically an excellent algorithm for SVP challenge.

7   Future Work

In the future, we will attempt to give a theoretical and quantitative analysis of time complexity of our phase-based enumeration algorithm compared to Kannan-Helfrich algorithm, and, at the same time, we will run our phase-based enumeration algorithm under the lattices of much higher dimensions, like of dimension 136, with more delicately-chosen predefined maximum phase-wise ℓ_1-norms.

References

1. Ajtai, M.: Generating hard instances of lattice problems (extended abstract). In: STOC, pp. 99–108 (1996)
2. Ajtai, M.: The shortest vector problem in ℓ_2 is np-hard for randomized reductions. In: Proceeding of the 30th Symposium on the Theory of Computing (STOC 1998), pp. 284–406 (1998)
3. Ajtai, M., Dwork, C.: A public-key cryptosystem with worst-case/average-case equivalence. In: STOC, pp. 284–293 (1997)
4. Ajtai, M., Kumar, R., Sivaumar, D.: A sieve algorithm for the shortest lattice vector problem. In: Proceedings of the 33th Annual ACM Symposium on Theory of Computing (STOC 2001), vol. 33, pp. 601–610 (2001)
5. Chen, Y., Nguyen, P.Q.: BKZ 2.0: better lattice security estimates. In: Lee, D.H., Wang, X. (eds.) ASIACRYPT 2011. LNCS, vol. 7073, pp. 1–20. Springer, Heidelberg (2011)
6. Ding, D., Zhu, G., Wang, X.: A genetic algorithm for searching shortest lattice vector of svp challenge. Cryptology ePrint Archive, Report 2014/489 (2014). http://eprint.iacr.org/
7. Gama, N., Nguyen, P.Q., Regev, O.: Lattice enumeration using extreme pruning. In: Gilbert, H. (ed.) EUROCRYPT 2010. LNCS, vol. 6110, pp. 257–278. Springer, Heidelberg (2010)
8. Goldreich, O., Goldwasser, S., Halevi, S.: Public-key cryptosystems from lattice reduction problems. In: Kaliski Jr, B.S. (ed.) CRYPTO 1997. LNCS, vol. 1294, pp. 112–131. Springer, Heidelberg (1997)
9. Hanrot, G., Pujol, X., Stehlé, D.: Analyzing blockwise lattice algorithms using dynamical systems. In: Rogaway, P. (ed.) CRYPTO 2011. LNCS, vol. 6841, pp. 447–464. Springer, Heidelberg (2011)
10. Hanrot, G., Stehlé, D.: improved analysis of kannan's shortest lattice vector algorithm. In: Menezes, A. (ed.) CRypto 2007. LNCS, vol. 4622, pp. 170–186. Springer, Heidelberg (2007)
11. Hanrot, G., Stehlé, D.: Improved analysis of Kannan's shortest lattice vector algorithm. In: Menezes, A. (ed.) CRYPTO 2007. LNCS, vol. 4622, pp. 170–186. Springer, Heidelberg (2007)

12. Helfrich, B.: Algorithms to construct minkowski reduced and hermit reduced bases. Theor. Comput. Sci. **41**, 125–139 (1985)
13. Kannan, R.: Improved algorithms for integer programming and related lattice problems. In: Proceedings of the 15th Symposium on the Theory of Computing (STOC1983), vol. 15, pp. 99–108 (1983)
14. Kannan, R.: Minkowski's convex body theorem and integer programming. Math. Oper. Res. **12**, 415–440 (1987)
15. Lenstra, A.K., Lenstra, H.W., Lavász, L.: Factoring polynomials with rational coefficients. Math. Ann. **261**, 513–534 (1982)
16. Micciancio, D., Goldwasser, S.: Complexity of Lattice Problems: A Cryptographic Perspective. Kluwer Academic Publishers, Boston (2002)
17. Micciancio, D., Regev, O.: Worst-case to average-case reductions based on Gaussian measure. In: Proceedings of the 45th Annual Symposium on Foundations of Computer Science - FOCS 2004, pp. 371–381. IEEE, Rome, October 2004. (Journal verion in SIAM Journal on Computing)
18. Micciancio, D., Regev, O.: Worst-case to average-case reductions based on Gaussian measure. SIAM J. Comput. **37**(1), 267–302 (2007). Preliminary version in FOCS 2004
19. Micciancio, D., Regev, O.: Lattice-based cryptography. In: Bernstein, D.J., Buchmann, J., Dahmen, E. (eds.) Proceeding of the Post-Quantum Cryptography (PQC 2009), pp. 147–191. Springer, Heidelberg (2009)
20. Micciancio, D., Voulgaris, P.: A deterministic single exponential time algorithm for most lattice problems based on voronoi cell computations. In: Proceedings of the 42th Annual ACM Symposium on Theory of Computing (STOC 2010), vol. 42, pp. 351–358 (2010)
21. Micciancio, D., Walter, M.: Fast lattice point enumeration with minimal overhead. Cryptology ePrint Archive, Report 2014/569 (2014). http://eprint.iacr.org/
22. Nguyen, P.Q., Vidick, T.: Sieve algorithms for the shortest vector problem are practical. J. Math. Crypt. **2**(2), 181–207 (2008)
23. Regev, O.: New lattice-based cryptographic constructions. J. ACM **51**(6), 899–942 (2004)
24. Schneider, M., Gamma, N.: SVP challenge (2010). http://www.latticechallenge. org/svp-challenge/
25. Schnorr, C.P.: A hierarchy of polynomial lattice basis reduction algorithms. Theor. Comput. Sci. **53**, 201–224 (1987)
26. Shoup, V.: Number theory C++ library (NTL) vesion 6.0.0 (2010). http://www. shoup.net/ntl/
27. van Emde Boas, P.: Another np-complete partition problem and the complexity of computing short vectors in a lattice, pp. 81–04. Technical report, Mathematisch Instituut, Universiteit van Amsterdam (1981)
28. Wang, X., Liu, M., Tian, C., Bi, J.: Improved Nguyen-Vidick heuristic sieve algorithm for shortest vector problem. In: Proceedings of the 6th ACM Symposium on Information, Computer and Communications Security, pp. 1–9. ACM (2011)

Block Ciphers

How Much Can Complexity of Linear Cryptanalysis Be Reduced?

Sho Sakikoyama[1]([⊠]), Yosuke Todo[2], Kazumaro Aoki[2], and Masakatu Morii[1]

[1] Kobe University, Kobe, Japan
sakikoyama@stu.kobe-u.ac.jp, mmorii@kobe-u.ac.jp
[2] NTT Secure Platform Laboratories, Tokyo, Japan
{todo.yosuke,aoki.kazumaro}@lab.ntt.co.jp

Abstract. The linear cryptanalysis proposed by Matsui is one of the most effective attacks on block ciphers, and he demonstrated an experimental cryptanalysis against DES at CRYPTO 1994. In this paper, we show how to optimize the linear cryptanalysis on modern microprocessors. Nowadays, there are two methods of implementing the linear cryptanalysis. Method 1 reduces the time complexity by reducing the number of computations of round functions, and Method 2 applies the fast Fourier transform (FFT). We implement both methods optimized for modern microprocessors and compare them in terms of computation time so as to discover which method is more appropriate for practical cryptanalysis. From the results of comparative experiments, we show that the fastest implementation depends on the number of given known plaintexts (KPs) and that of guessed key bits. These results clarify the criteria for selecting the method to implement the linear cryptanalysis. Taking the experimental results into account, we implement the linear cryptanalysis on FEAL-8X. In 2014, Biham and Carmeli showed an implementation of linear cryptanalysis that was able to recover the secret key with 2^{14} KPs. Our implementation breaks FEAL-8X with 2^{12} KPs and is the best attack on FEAL-8X in terms of data complexity.

Keywords: Linear cryptanalysis · FFT · Multiple linear cryptanalysis · FEAL-8X

1 Introduction

The linear cryptanalysis introduced by Matsui [8] is one of the most effective attacks on block ciphers. He implemented the cryptanalysis and showed that the secret key of full 16-round DES can be recovered in practical time [9]. Some improvement techniques to reduce the computational complexity have been developed, *e.g.*, key recovery with FFT proposed by Collard *et al.* in 2007 [4]. These techniques are evaluated by using the computational complexity, which is generally estimated by an asymptotic analysis. However, when we consider optimizing the data complexity and implementing practical cryptanalysis, the asymptotic analysis does not provide useful information. If we are to determine

© Springer International Publishing Switzerland 2015
J. Lee and J. Kim (Eds.): ICISC 2014, LNCS 8949, pp. 117–131, 2015.
DOI: 10.1007/978-3-319-15943-0_8

which implementation of linear cryptanalysis is most appropriate, we need to implement their techniques and compare them from the perspective of computation time.

In this paper, we consider two methods for implementing Matsui's Algorithm 2 [8]. Method 1 performs Matsui's Algorithm 2 efficiently by reducing the number of round function computations. If the linear approximation is expressed as the computation of Exclusive OR (XOR) between a value calculated from plaintext and one calculated from ciphertext, we can prevent redundant computations by using memory space. This method is used in the implementation of the linear attack shown by Biham and Carmeli [2]. Method 2 is the technique proposed by Collard, et al. [4], which reduces the computational complexity of Matsui's Algorithm 2. They found that the computation of Matsui's Algorithm 2 is expressed in a multiplication of a circulant matrix and that the computational complexity of such multiplication is reduced with FFT. The key recovery technique with FFT was recently applied to several cryptanalyses, e.g., a multidimensional linear attack [5,13,14], a zero correlation attack [3], and an integral attack [15]. We implement the two methods and optimize them on modern microprocessors, in particular, an Intel CPU, and limited memory. In both implementations, we exploit useful instructions available for a recent Intel CPU. We compare computation times of both methods in experiments, and we show the appropriate implementation depending on the numbers of given KPs and bits of guessed key.

We investigate reducing the data complexity of the attack on FEAL-8X. Matsui announced the FEAL 25th-year prize problem at CRYPTO 2012 [10]. The problem involved recovering the secret key of FEAL-8X with as few KPs as possible. In this prize problem, Biham and Carmeli demonstrated the best attack of FEAL-8X in terms of data complexity. They recovered the secret key in practical time with 2^{14} KPs [2]. We implement a linear attack on FEAL-8X with the two methods. We compare computation time of both methods and adopt faster method. Moreover, our method uses multiple linear cryptanalysis (MLC), which was proposed by Kaliski and Robshaw [6,7]. We show that FEAL-8X is breakable by MLC with 2^{12} KPs with a probability of almost 1 and with 2^{11} KPs with non-negligible probability. As a result, we can recover the secret key of the FEAL 25th-year challenge with 2^{12} KPs.

2   Preliminaries

2.1   Matsui's Algorithm 2

The linear cryptanalysis proposed by Matsui is a kind of known plaintext attack. We focus on the implementation of Matsui's Algorithm 2. In Matsui's Algorithm 2 [8], a linear approximation is used to guess subkeys. Let us consider recovering the rth subkey K_r of the r-round block cipher. The linear approximation of $r-1$ rounds is described as

$$g(K_r, P, C) = \langle \Gamma_P, P \rangle \oplus \langle \Gamma_C, f^{-1}(K_r, C) \rangle, \tag{1}$$

where P and C denote a plaintext and a corresponding ciphertext, respectively. Let f and f^{-1} be the round function of the block cipher and the inverse function of f, respectively. Let $a \oplus b$ be XOR between a and b. Let $\langle a, b \rangle$ be the dot product between a and b. Γ_P and Γ_C denote a mask to extract particular bits. We assume that the computed result of the linear approximation gives 0 or 1 uniformly if the guessed subkey is wrong. If the guessed subkey is correct, the computed result is biased to 0 or 1. Let N be the number of KPs. Matsui's Algorithm 2 is shown in the following.

Step 1. For all given KPs, compute the linear approximation with guessed K_r.
Step 2. Calculate the sum of the computed results of the linear approximation.
Step 3. Save the difference between the sum and $N/2$.
Step 4. Repeat Steps 1–3 for all candidates of K_r.
Step 5. Return the K_r having the maximum difference.

We call the difference of each candidate of K_r in Step 3 as *key deviation*. Let *effective key bits* be K_r's bits that are necessary to compute the linear approximation. Let k be the number of bits of the effective key bits. There are 2^k candidates of K_r. Then, the computational complexity of Matsui's Algorithm 2 is $N \cdot 2^k$. Let p be the probability that the linear approximation computed with correct K_r gives 0. We call $\epsilon = |p - \frac{1}{2}|$ the *bias* of the linear approximation. The higher the bias is, the easier it is to distinguish the correct subkey.

Let us consider the case that the round function can be determined only by an XORed value between K_r and C. Then the linear approximation is given by

$$g(K_r, P, C) = \langle \Gamma_P, P \rangle \oplus \langle \Gamma_C, f^{-1}(K_r \oplus C) \rangle. \tag{2}$$

Let *effective text bits* be C's bits that are necessary to compute the linear approximation. In Eq.(2), the bit position of the effective text bits is the same as one of effective key bits. If the values of effective text bits taken from different ciphertexts are the same, these ciphertexts will give the same result in computation of the linear approximations. All given KPs are classified into 2^k groups indexed by the value of effective text bits. If $N > 2^k$ holds, considering the effective text bits, we can prevent redundant computation of the round function in Matsui's Algorithm 2. Then the computational complexity of Matsui's Algorithm 2 is reduced from $N \cdot 2^k$ to $2^k \cdot 2^k$ round function computation.

2.2 Computation with FFT

Collard, et al. [4] transformed the computation of Matsui's Algorithm 2 into the matrix multiplication as follows:

$$\sigma = M \cdot x. \tag{3}$$

In Eq.(3), let $A \cdot B$ be a matrix multiplication between A and B. Let σ be a column vector having 2^k elements that denote key deviations of each subkey candidate. Let x be a column vector having 2^k elements that denote counters for ciphertexts indexed by the value of effective text bits. Let M be a matrix of size $2^k \times 2^k$, and the ith row and jth column element is defined by

$$M(i,j) = (-1)^{\langle \Gamma_C, f^{-1}(i \oplus j) \rangle}. \tag{4}$$

We regard i $(0, 1, \ldots, 2^k - 1)$ and j $(0, 1, \ldots, 2^k - 1)$ as the value of effective key bits and that of effective text bits, respectively. Key deviations of each subkey candidate are computed with Eq.(3).

Matrix M has a particular structure called a circulant matrix. Therefore, computation of Eq.(3) can be transformed by applying FFT as follows:

$$\sigma = IFFT(FFT(m) * FFT(x)), \tag{5}$$

where the FFT and $IFFT$ function denote FFT and inverse FFT, respectively. Element-wise multiplication called an Hadamard product between A and B is expressed as $A * B$. Column vector m is the transposition of the top row of M. Key deviations are computed with Eq.(5) in place of Eq.(3). The computational complexity of Eq.(5) is $3 \cdot k \cdot 2^k$. For more information, see Collard, et al. [4].

3 Optimization of Implementation of Linear Cryptanalysis

In this section, we consider the optimal implementation of Matsui's Algorithm 2 under the assumption that the number of guessed key candidates is larger than one of KPs, i.e., $2^k > N$ holds. In this case, improved Matsui's Algorithm 2 mentioned in Sect. 2.1 is worthless for reducing the computational complexity. Therefore, we only focus on two methods, one is the optimized implementation of Matsui's algorithm 2 [2] and another is the key recovery using FFT. Hereafter, we implement both methods and compare the computation time of them with different numbers of the guessed key bits and KPs. Moreover, we ignore the success rate of the attack to discuss the computation time for simplicity. In this section, we show both methods that use an $(r-2)$-round linear approximation. We also explain their computational complexity, and how to optimize them. We finally compare them, and show a criteria to determine which implementation is more appropriate.

3.1 Attack with $(r-2)$-round Linear Approximation

We consider $(r-2)$-round linear approximation defined by

$$g(K_P, K_C, P, C) = \langle \Gamma_P, f(K_P \oplus P) \rangle \oplus \langle \Gamma_C, f^{-1}(K_C \oplus C) \rangle \tag{6}$$

because Method 1 is effective only when we utilize it. Let K_P and K_C be the subkeys of the first and last round, respectively. Equation (6) has higher bias than $(r-1)$-round linear approximation defined by Eq.(2), which includes only the last (first) round function. Therefore, we can reduce the data complexity of

---

Algorithm 1. Method 1 - Vectorized Computation of Matsui's Algorithm 2

Input: P_j, C_j $(j = 0, 1, \ldots, N - 1)$
Output: $\mathrm{K_P}$, $\mathrm{K_C}$

Prepare integer vector $dev[2^{k_C}][2^{k_P}]$ and initialize it to $-N/2$.
Prepare bit-string vector $x[2^{k_P}]$ and initialize it to zero.

for $i = 0$ to $2^{k_P} - 1$ **do**
  for $j = 0$ to $N - 1$ **do**
    $x[i] \leftarrow x[i] \oplus (b_P(K_{Pi}, P_j)^{\ll j})$
  end for
end for

for $i = 0$ to $2^{k_C} - 1$ **do**
  $y \leftarrow 0$
  for $j = 0$ to $N - 1$ **do**
    $y \leftarrow y \oplus (b_C(K_{Ci}, C_j)^{\ll j})$
  end for
  for $j = 0$ to $2^{k_P} - 1$ **do**
    $dev[i][j] \leftarrow dev[i][j] + \mathrm{HW}(x[j] \oplus y)$
  end for
end for

Return $\mathrm{K_P}$ and $\mathrm{K_C}$ having the maximum deviation.

---

attacking the block cipher by using Eq.(6) in place of Eq.(2). Let k_P and k_C be the number of effective key bits of K_P and K_C, respectively, where $k_C \geq k_P$ holds. In Matsui's Algorithm 2, it is necessary to compute f and f^{-1} for each of the $2^{k_P+k_C}$ combinations and all given KPs. Then, the computational complexity can be written as $N \cdot 2^{k_P+k_C+1}$. Assuming that k_P and k_C are fixed to several tens, the straightforward implementation of the attack becomes infeasible because of the high computational complexity. The two methods described later can reduce the computation time of the attack to a practical amount of time.

3.2 Method 1 - Vectorized Computation of Matsui's Algorithm 2

Method 1 transforms Matsui's Algorithm 2 to bitwise operations [2]. It is possible if we can independently compute the value calculated from plaintext and one calculated from ciphertext. In that case, we can rewrite Eq.(6) to

$$g = b_P(K_P, P) \oplus b_C(K_C, C), \tag{7}$$

where the b_P function denotes $\langle \Gamma_P, f(K_P \oplus P) \rangle$, and the b_C function denotes $\langle \Gamma_C, f^{-1}(K_C \oplus C) \rangle$. Then, the number of round function computations is reduced from $N \cdot 2^{k_P+k_C+1}$ to $N \cdot 2^{k_P} + N \cdot 2^{k_C}$ by utilizing the memory. The detailed procedure of Method 1 is shown as Algorithm 1. In Algorithm 1, the elements of

Algorithm 2. Method 2 - Computation with FWHT

Input: P_j, C_j $(j = 0, 1, \ldots, N-1)$
Output: K_P, K_C

Prepare integer vectors $m[2^{k_C}]$, $x[2^{k_C}]$, and $dev[2^{k_P}][2^{k_C}]$.

for $i = 0$ to $2^{k_C} - 1$ **do**
  $m[i] \leftarrow (-1)^{\langle \Gamma_C, f^{-1}(i) \rangle}$
end for
$m \leftarrow FWHT(m, 2^{k_C})$

for $i = 0$ to $2^{k_P} - 1$ **do**
  for $j = 0$ to $2^{k_C} - 1$ **do**
    $x[j] \leftarrow 0$
  end for
  for $j = 0$ to $N - 1$ **do**
    if $\langle \Gamma_P, f(i \oplus e_P(P_j)) \rangle = 1$ **then**
      Decrement $x[e_C(C_j)]$ by one
    else
      Increment $x[e_C(C_j)]$ by one
    end if
  end for
  $x \leftarrow FWHT(x, 2^{k_C})$
  for $j = 0$ to $2^{k_C} - 1$ **do**
    $x[j] \leftarrow m[j] \times x[j]$ /* Hadamard Product */
  end for
  $x \leftarrow FWHT(x, 2^{k_C})$
  for $j = 0$ to $2^{k_C} - 1$ **do**
    $dev[i][j] \leftarrow |x[j]|^{\gg k_C}$ /* Multiplication by the normalization factor */
  end for
end for

Return K_P and K_C having the maximum deviation.

vector x and variable y are both N-bit strings. The operator of $\ll$ indicates a left bit-shift operation. The HW function denotes a Hamming weight function.

The dominant computations of Method 1 are XOR, the HW function, and addition iterated for $2^{k_P + k_C}$ times. In a practical implementation, an N-bit string is implemented with an array that has N/w elements, where w denotes the word size of the computer. In this case, XOR, the HW function, and addition are iterated for $\frac{N}{w} \cdot 2^{k_P + k_C}$ times. Let the unit of computation be XOR + HW + ADD, and then the computational complexity can be written as $\frac{N}{w} \cdot 2^{k_P + k_C}$. We can calculate this iterated operation more efficiently than the round function. As for the HW function, we can use the popcnt instruction available in Intel processors supporting SSE4.2.

Algorithm 3. Procedure $FWHT(\boldsymbol{x}, y)$.

Input: $\boldsymbol{x}$, y
Output: $\boldsymbol{x}$
$y \leftarrow y^{\gg 1}$
for $i = 0$ to $y - 1$ **do**
  $temp1 \leftarrow x[i]$
  $temp2 \leftarrow x[i + y]$
  $x[i] \leftarrow temp1 + temp2$
  $x[i + y] \leftarrow temp1 - temp2$
end for
Let $\boldsymbol{v}$ and $\boldsymbol{w}$ be the first half of $\boldsymbol{x}$ and the second half of $\boldsymbol{x}$, respectively
if $y > 1$ **then**
  Substitute the output of $FWHT(\boldsymbol{v}, y)$ for the first half of $\boldsymbol{x}$
  Substitute the output of $FWHT(\boldsymbol{w}, y)$ for the second half of $\boldsymbol{x}$
end if

3.3 Method 2 - Computation with FWHT

Method 2 involves to optimizing the computation with FFT, as proposed by Collard, *et al.* We utilize fast Walsh Hadamard transform (FWHT) in place of FFT since FWHT plays the same role as FFT in computing Eq.(5). FWHT has an advantage in computation time over FFT because FWHT is calculated by addition and subtraction of integers. An attack with FWHT requires memory space for preparing the two vectors mentioned in Sect. 2.2. If we apply FWHT to guessing both K_P and K_C, the required memory will become $2^{k_P + k_C + 1}$ for two vectors that have $2^{k_P + k_C}$ elements. Depending on the number of $k_P + k_C$, it goes beyond the available memory space, *i.e.*, required memory will be over 16GB if $k_P + k_C$ is over 31. For this reason, we apply FWHT to only guessing K_C and we iterate guessing K_C for all candidates of K_P. We show the details of Method 2 as Algorithm 2. Let e_P and e_C be functions to extract the value of effective key bits from the plaintext and from the ciphertext, respectively. Since inverse FWHT has the same procedure as FWHT except for the multiplication of the normalization factor, we utilize the *FWHT* function as inverse FWHT in Algorithm 2. The computation of the k_C-bit shift denotes the multiplication of normalization factor. The detailed algorithm of the *FWHT* function is described in Algorithm 3. Let $\boldsymbol{x}$ be an input vector. Let y be the number of elements of $\boldsymbol{x}$. *FWHT* function performs the butterfly computation by recursive processing.

Let us consider the computational complexity of Method 2. We ignore computation to prepare vector $\boldsymbol{m}$ because it can be done in advance of guessing the subkeys. Computation of the round function is iterated for $N \cdot 2^{k_P}$ times to compute $\langle \Gamma_P, f(i \oplus e_P(P_j)) \rangle$. It is the dominant computation of Method 2 when N is far bigger than $k_C \cdot 2^{k_C}$. When a small number of KPs is given, the computation of the *FWHT* function computed for $2^{k_P + 1}$ times dominates the computation time. In computing FWHT in Method 2, addition and subtraction are iterated for $k_C \cdot 2^{k_C - 1}$ times. Therefore, the computational complexity of Method 2 with a small number of KPs is $k_C \cdot 2^{k_C + k_P}$. Let SUB be one subtraction. The unit of the computation is denoted as ADD + SUB.

3.4   Comparison of the Two Methods

Table 1 shows the computational complexity of each algorithm. First, let us consider the case that $N \gg k_C \cdot 2^{k_C}$ holds. The dominant computation of Method 2 becomes the computation of the round function iterated for $N \cdot 2^{k_P}$ times. Since Method 1 includes this iteration and the other calculations in Method 1 also have a great impact on the computation time, we can say that Method 2 is the superior algorithm.

Table 1. Computational Complexity of Matsui's Algorithm 2 and Methods 1 and 2

Algorithm	Matsui's Alg.2	Method 1	Method 2
#round function computations	$N \cdot 2^{k_P + k_C + 1}$	$N \cdot 2^{k_P} + N \cdot 2^{k_C}$	$N \cdot 2^{k_P} + 2^{k_C}$
computational complexity	$N \cdot 2^{k_P + k_C + 1}$	$\frac{N}{w} \cdot 2^{k_P + k_C}$	$k_C \cdot 2^{k_P + k_C}$
unit of computation	Round Function	XOR + HW + ADD	ADD + SUB

Next, let us clarify which method is superior when a small number of KPs is available. We implemented the two methods and examined their computation time by using an Intel Core i7 4771 quad-core processor @ 3.50GHz and 16GB memory. We performed the comparative experiments with the round function of FEAL. Figure 1 shows the experimental results performed with each number of KPs under the condition $k_P = 15$, $k_C = 15, 16, \ldots, 20$. We can see from Fig. 1 that appropriate implementation changes according to the value of N and k_C. In Fig. 1, both methods need almost the same computation time when $k_C = 20$, $N = 2^{12}$. Therefore, $\frac{2^{12}}{64} \cdot 2^{15} \cdot 2^{20}(\text{XOR} + \text{HW} + \text{ADD}) \approx 20 \cdot 2^{15} \cdot 2^{20}(\text{ADD} + \text{SUB})$, i.e., $3(\text{XOR} + \text{HW} + \text{ADD}) \approx (\text{ADD} + \text{SUB})$ holds. We can estimate the computation time of both methods and select the appropriate implementation of the attack by considering the number of guessed key bits, one of given KPs and this result. We can also see from Fig. 1 that the round function dominates the computation time of Method 2 only when the number of KPs is large and that computation time of the round function do not effect on the threshold to select optimal method. Similar results are expected to appear when we perform the same experiments with the round function of other block cipher because the computation time of the round function is not much different according to the block cipher. Therefore, this result is effective when applying the two methods to general block ciphers.

4   Reducing Data Complexity of Attack on FEAL-8X

In this section, we consider how to reduce the data complexity of the attack on FEAL-8X taking the success rate into account. We apply multiple linear cryptanalysis (MLC) to the attack in order to reduce the data complexity. We first

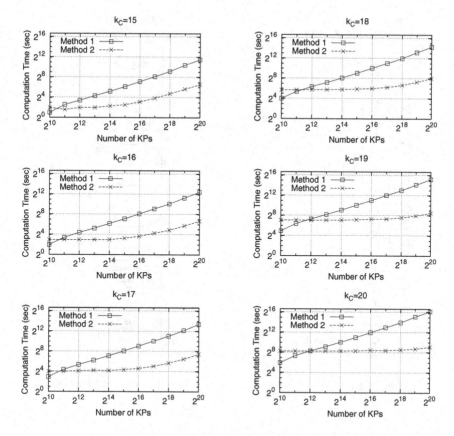

Fig. 1. Computation Time of Method 1 and Method 2

describe the specifications of FEAL-8X. Then, we explain the six-round linear approximation and the basic attack on FEAL-8X using it. Then, we describe how to apply MLC to the attack. After that, we show from experimental results that MLC allows us to obtain the secret key of FEAL-8X with 2^{11} KPs.

4.1   FEAL-8X

FEAL-8X is a block cipher with a 128-bit secret key [12]. The block size of FEAL-8X is 64 bits. The key scheduling algorithm generates sixteen 16-bit subkeys K_i ($i = 1, 2, \ldots, 16$) from the secret key. Plaintexts are encrypted to ciphertexts with the encryption algorithm. Figure 2 illustrates the encryption algorithm of FEAL-8X. Let $a \| b$ be a concatenation of a and b, as a consists of higher bits. Let F be the round function of FEAL. Let P_H and C_H be the higher 32 bits of plaintext and ciphertext, respectively. Similarly, we define P_L and C_L as the lower 32 bits of them, respectively.

The encryption algorithm of FEAL-8X is equivalently transformed into the modified FEAL-8X defined by Matsui and Yamagishi in [11]. We analyze the

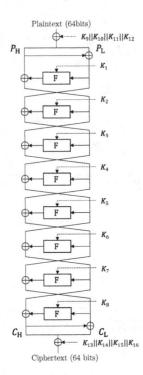

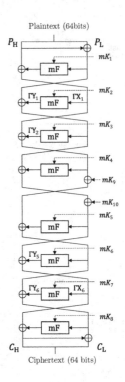

Fig. 2. FEAL-8X   **Fig. 3.** Modified FEAL-8X

modified FEAL-8X illustrated in Fig. 3 because it is easier to analyze than the original. Figure 4 shows the modified F function (mF function). In the definition of the S-boxes in Fig. 4, let i be the index of each S-box. Modified FEAL-8X performs encryption and decryption with 32-bit mK_i $(i = 1, 2, \ldots, 10)$ in place of 16-bit K_i $(i = 1, 2, \ldots, 16)$. Let K_i^H and K_i^L be the higher 8 bits of K_i and the lower 8 bits of K_i, respectively. The relation between K_i and mK_i is as follows:

$$mK_1 = K_1^{\lll 8} \oplus (K_9 || K_{10}) \oplus (K_{11} || K_{12}) \oplus ((K_9^H || K_{10}^L) \oplus (K_{11}^H || K_{12}^L))^{\lll 8}$$
$$mK_2 = K_2^{\lll 8} \oplus (K_9 || K_{10}) \oplus (K_9^H || K_{10}^L)^{\lll 8}$$
$$mK_3 = K_3^{\lll 8} \oplus (K_9 || K_{10}) \oplus (K_{11} || K_{12}) \oplus ((K_9^H || K_{10}^L) \oplus (K_{11}^H || K_{12}^L))^{\lll 8}$$
$$mK_4 = K_4^{\lll 8} \oplus (K_9 || K_{10}) \oplus (K_9^H || K_{10}^L)^{\lll 8}$$
$$mK_5 = K_5^{\lll 8} \oplus (K_{13} || K_{14}) \oplus (K_{13}^H || K_{14}^L)^{\lll 8}$$
$$mK_6 = K_6^{\lll 8} \oplus (K_{13} || K_{14}) \oplus (K_{15}^H || K_{16}^L) \oplus ((K_{13}^H || K_{14}^L) \oplus (K_{15} || K_{16}))^{\lll 8}$$
$$mK_7 = K_7^{\lll 8} \oplus (K_{13} || K_{14}) \oplus (K_{13}^H || K_{14}^L)^{\lll 8}$$
$$mK_8 = K_8^{\lll 8} \oplus (K_{13} || K_{14}) \oplus (K_{15}^H || K_{16}^L) \oplus ((K_{13}^H || K_{14}^L) \oplus (K_{15} || K_{16}))^{\lll 8}$$
$$mK_9 = (K_9 || K_{10}) \oplus (K_{13} || K_{14}) \oplus (K_{15} || K_{16})$$
$$mK_{10} = (K_9 || K_{10}) \oplus (K_{11} || K_{12}) \oplus (K_{13} || K_{14}).$$

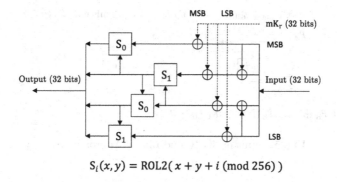

$$S_i(x, y) = \text{ROL2}(\, x + y + i \,(\text{mod } 256)\,)$$

Fig. 4. Modified F function

4.2 Attack Outline

The attack on FEAL-8X consists of three steps. First, we guess mK_1 and mK_8 with the six-round approximation. Then, we recover the rest of the subkeys. Lastly, we derive the secret key of FEAL-8X from the recovered subkeys with negligible complexity. If the correct mK_1 and mK_8 are recovered in the first step, the secret key will be recovered correctly with the second step and the last step. The two steps are iterated until the correct subkeys are detected from the candidates saved in the first step. Let R be the number of candidates saved in the first step according to the value of the key deviation. If the correct mK_1 and mK_8 are ranked within Rth, we can say that we succeeded in breaking FEAL-8X. Therefore, the data complexity of the attack depends on the accuracy of the first step. We apply MLC [6,7] to the first step, which increases the success probability of the attack.

4.3 Attack with Six-Round Linear Approximation

Six-Round Linear Approximation for FEAL-8X. A six-round linear approximation for FEAL-8X can be written by

$$g = \langle \Gamma X_1 \oplus \Gamma Y_2, P_H \oplus mF(mK_1, P_H \oplus P_L) \rangle \oplus \langle \Gamma Y_1, P_H \oplus P_L \rangle$$
$$\oplus \langle \Gamma X_6 \oplus \Gamma Y_5, C_H \oplus mF(mK_8, C_H \oplus C_L) \rangle \oplus \langle \Gamma Y_6, C_H \oplus C_L \rangle. \quad (8)$$

The input of Eq.(8) is illustrated in Fig. 5. The six-round linear approximation covers the middle six rounds of FEAL-8X. The computed result of the six-round linear approximation depends on the partially encrypted data and the partially decrypted data. We first recover subkeys of FEAL-8X with Approximation 1 denoted in Appendix A, whose effective key bits are the 15 bits of mK_1 and the 22 bits of mK_8. Since Approximation 1 has many effective key bits, we implement the attack with the method shown in Sect. 3 to reduce the computation time. To reduce the data complexity, the accuracy of the attack needs to be improved.

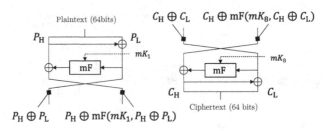

Fig. 5. Input of Six-Round Linear Approximation

Multiple Linear Cryptanalysis. We apply MLC to recover subkeys with the six-round linear approximation to improve the accuracy of the attack. We implement MLC with eight six-round approximations denoted in Appendix A. MLC is possible if every approximation used for the attack has the same effective key bits. Let $dev_1[i][j]$ be a key deviation corresponding to mK_{1i} and mK_{8j} computed with Approximation 1. Similarly, $dev_2[i][j]$, $dev_3[i][j]$, ..., $dev_8[i][j]$ are computed. We define multiple key deviation as

$$m\text{-}dev[i][j] = \epsilon_1 dev_1[i][j] + \epsilon_2 dev_2[i][j] + \cdots + \epsilon_8 dev_8[i][j]. \tag{9}$$

Let ϵ_i $(i = 1, 2, \ldots, 8)$ denotes the bias of each linear approximations. The accuracy of the attack is improved by using multiple key deviation in place of the original key deviation. Computation of the key deviation of each approximation is iterated to compute $m\text{-}dev$. Consequently, the MLC computation time with eight six-round approximations becomes eight times as long as one six-round approximation.

4.4   Recovery of the Remaining Subkeys

The 15 bits of mK_1 and 22 bits of mK_8 that are guessed are confirmed to be the correct key by recovering the rest of the subkeys. We implemented an algorithm to recover the rest of the subkeys correctly. It takes 0.2 s to confirm one candidate with our machine. We briefly describe the algorithm in this subsection.

Five-Round Linear Approximation. We guess the remaining bits of mK_8 and 15 bits of mK_7 by using Approximation 1 as a five-round linear approximation. These subkeys are recovered correctly because the five-round linear approximation has high enough bias to recover subkeys even with 2^{10} KPs. We implemented this process by Method 2.

Three-Round Linear Equation. Matsui and Yamagishi mentioned four three-round linear equations of FEAL, which holds with a probability of 1 [11]. We can recover subkeys correctly by examining whether the equations hold for all KPs. We recover all subkeys except for mK_4, mK_5, mK_9, and mK_{10} with the three-round linear equations.

Simultaneous Equations. We recover mK_4, mK_5, mK_9, and mK_{10} by algebraically solving the simultaneous equations that hold between the partially encrypted data and the partially decrypted data. All subkeys are confirmed

Table 2. Accuracy of the Attack with One Linear Approximation

Number of KPs	Frequency of the Correct Key Rank				Number of Trials
	$[1, 2^8)$	$[2^8, 2^{19})$	$[2^{19}, 2^{24})$	$[2^{24}, 2^{37}]$	
2^{15}	49	1	0	0	50
2^{14}	30	17	3	0	
2^{13}	1	16	16	17	
2^{12}	0	2	7	41	

Table 3. Accuracy of the Attack with MLC

Number of KPs	Frequency of the Correct Key Rank				Number of Trials
	$[1, 2^8)$	$[2^8, 2^{19})$	$[2^{19}, 2^{24})$	$[2^{24}, 2^{37}]$	
2^{14}	50	0	0	0	50
2^{13}	50	0	0	0	
2^{12}	35	13	1	1	
2^{11}	6	15	14	15	
2^{10}	0	1	3	46	

as the correct key by examining whether the encrypted plaintext corresponds with the ciphertext.

4.5 Experimental Results

We implemented MLC taking the results in Sect. 3 into account. We examined the accuracy of MLC and one of the attack with one six-round approximation with each quantity of KPs. Tables 2 and 3 show the experimental results, which denote the counts in which the correct key was ranked within the given range. In each table, let $[A, B)$ be integers between A and B including A but excluding B. Let $[A, B]$ be integers between A and B including A and B. We set the value of R that is the number of saved candidates of mK_1 and mK_8 as 2^{24}. The computation time for searching the rest of the subkeys was 0.2 s as mentioned in Sect. 4.4. Consequently, it took about one minute to search for a correct key from the candidate ranked at the top to the 2^8th candidate with a machine. Similarly, it took about one day to search to the 2^{19}th candidate and about one month to search to the 2^{24}th candidate. We can see from Table 2 that the attack with one linear approximation did not have sufficient accuracy to recover subkeys with less than 2^{14} KPs. By contrast, Table 3 indicates that MLC enables us to attack with less than 2^{14} KPs. If 2^{12} KPs are given, we can recover the subkeys and the secret key in a practical time limit with MLC with a probability of almost 1. If 2^{11} KPs are given, we can recover them with a probability of about 70 %. MLC allows us to recover the secret key of the FEAL 25th-year prize problem with less than 2^{14} KPs. We recovered the secret key of the problem using 2^{13} KPs. The answer is 0x14141c848b6024ce0cacd887a242e30e. We also solved the problem using

2^{12} KPs. The answer is 0x75d647e6a73172c423cb3aecee66d3ed. In solving each problem, the computation time to recover the secret key was about four hours.

5   Conclusion

We focused on two methods of implementing Matsui's Algorithm 2 with $(r-2)$-round linear approximation. We examined the computational complexity of both methods and compared them. We showed from our examination of computational complexity and comparative experiments that the number of KPs and that of the effective key bits determine which method is appropriate. This result clarified the criteria for selecting the method to implement Matsui's Algorithm 2 on a general block cipher. It allows us to select appropriate implementation of the attack without another comparative experiment by considering the condition of the given KPs and the effective key bits. We also investigated reducing the data complexity of the attack on FEAL-8X. We showed that FEAL-8X is breakable with 2^{12} KPs with non-negligible probability by using MLC. This is the best attack on FEAL-8X.

A   Six-Round Linear Approximations

We utilize eight six-round linear approximations to attack FEAL-8X (see Fig. 6). Figure 6 shows the linear approximations, where $\Gamma X_3 = \Gamma Y_3 = 0x00000000$, $\Gamma Y_2 = \Gamma Y_4$, $\Gamma Y_1 = \Gamma Y_5$, $\Gamma X_2 = \Gamma X_4$, and $\Gamma X_1 = \Gamma X_5$ hold. Let ΓX_i ($i = 1, 2, \ldots, 6$) and ΓY_i ($i = 1, 2, \ldots, 6$) be an input mask and an output mask of ith round, respectively. These approximations are found by Aoki, *et al.* in [1].

Approximation1, $\epsilon = 97 \times 2^{-12}$
$\Gamma Y_4 = 0x04031104, \Gamma X_4 = 0x00010504$
$\Gamma Y_5 = 0x00010504, \Gamma X_5 = 0x00000100$
$\Gamma Y_6 = 0x04031004, \Gamma X_6 = 0x10117d7c$

Approximation5, $\epsilon = 97 \times 2^{-12}$
$\Gamma Y_4 = 0x04011904, \Gamma X_4 = 0x00010504$
$\Gamma Y_5 = 0x00010504, \Gamma X_5 = 0x00000100$
$\Gamma Y_6 = 0x04011804, \Gamma X_6 = 0x10117d7c$

Approximation2, $\epsilon = 65 \times 2^{-12}$
$\Gamma Y_4 = 0x04031104, \Gamma X_4 = 0x00010504$
$\Gamma Y_5 = 0x00010504, \Gamma X_5 = 0x00000100$
$\Gamma Y_6 = 0x04031004, \Gamma X_6 = 0x18197574$

Approximation6, $\epsilon = 65 \times 2^{-12}$
$\Gamma Y_4 = 0x04011904, \Gamma X_4 = 0x00010504$
$\Gamma Y_5 = 0x00010504, \Gamma X_5 = 0x00000100$
$\Gamma Y_6 = 0x04011804, \Gamma X_6 = 0x18197574$

Approximation3, $\epsilon = 97 \times 2^{-12}$
$\Gamma Y_4 = 0x04031104, \Gamma X_4 = 0x00010504$
$\Gamma Y_5 = 0x00010504, \Gamma X_5 = 0x00000100$
$\Gamma Y_6 = 0x04031004, \Gamma X_6 = 0x18195d5c$

Approximation7, $\epsilon = 97 \times 2^{-12}$
$\Gamma Y_4 = 0x04011904, \Gamma X_4 = 0x00010504$
$\Gamma Y_5 = 0x00010504, \Gamma X_5 = 0x00000100$
$\Gamma Y_6 = 0x04011804, \Gamma X_6 = 0x18195d5c$

Approximation4, $\epsilon = 65 \times 2^{-12}$
$\Gamma Y_4 = 0x04031104, \Gamma X_4 = 0x00010504$
$\Gamma Y_5 = 0x00010504, \Gamma X_5 = 0x00000100$
$\Gamma Y_6 = 0x04031004, \Gamma X_6 = 0x10115554$

Approximation8, $\epsilon = 65 \times 2^{-12}$
$\Gamma Y_4 = 0x04011904, \Gamma X_4 = 0x00010504$
$\Gamma Y_5 = 0x00010504, \Gamma X_5 = 0x00000100$
$\Gamma Y_6 = 0x04011804, \Gamma X_6 = 0x10115554$

Fig. 6. Eight Six-Round Linear Approximation

Every approximation has the same effective key bits, which are 14 bits (0x007F7F 00) of mK_1, XORed value of the 2 bits (0x00808000) of mK_1, and 22 bits (0x03FFFF0F) of mK_8.

References

1. Aoki, K., Ohta, K., Araki, S., Mitsuru, M.: Linear Cryptanalysis of FEAL-8 (Experimentation Report). Technical Report, ISEC 94-6 (1994-05), IEICE (1994)
2. Biham, E., Carmeli, Y.: An improvement of linear cryptanalysis with addition operations with applications to FEAL-8X. In: Joux, A., Youssef, A. (eds.) SAC 2014. LNCS, pp. 59-76. Springer, Heidelberg (2014)
3. Bogdanov, A., Geng, H., Wang, M., Wen, L., Collard, B.: Zero-correlation linear cryptanalysis with FFT and improved attacks on ISO standards Camellia and CLEFIA. In: Lange, T., Lauter, K., Lisoněk, P. (eds.) SAC 2013. LNCS, vol. 8282, pp. 306-323. Springer, Heidelberg (2014)
4. Collard, B., Standaert, F.-X., Quisquater, J.-J.: Improving the time complexity of matsui's linear cryptanalysis. In: Nam, K.-H., Rhee, G. (eds.) ICISC 2007. LNCS, vol. 4817, pp. 77-88. Springer, Heidelberg (2007)
5. Hermelin, M., Nyberg, K.: Dependent linear approximations: the algorithm of Biryukov and others revisited. In: Pieprzyk, J. (ed.) CT-RSA 2010. LNCS, vol. 5985, pp. 318-333. Springer, Heidelberg (2010)
6. Kaliski Jr., B.S., Robshaw, M.: Linear cryptanalysis using multiple approximations. In: Desmedt, Y.G. (ed.) CRYPTO 1994. LNCS, vol. 839, pp. 26-39. Springer, Heidelberg (1994)
7. Kaliski Jr., B.S., Robshaw, M.J.B.: Linear cryptanalysis using multiple approximations and FEAL. In: Preneel, B. (ed.) Fast Software Encryption. LNCS, vol. 1008, pp. 249-264. Springer, Heidelberg (1995)
8. Matsui, M.: Linear cryptanalysis method for DES cipher. In: Helleseth, T. (ed.) EUROCRYPT 1993. LNCS, vol. 765, pp. 386-397. Springer, Heidelberg (1994)
9. Matsui, M.: The first experimental cryptanalysis of the data encryption standard. In: Desmedt, Y.G. (ed.) CRYPTO 1994. LNCS, vol. 839, pp. 1-11. Springer, Heidelberg (1994)
10. Matsui, M.: Celebrating the 25th year of FEAL - A New Prize Problem - (2012), CRYPTO 2012 Rump Session (2012). http://crypto.2012.rump.cr.yp.to/ 19997d5a295baee62c05ba73534745ef.pdf
11. Matsui, M., Yamagishi, A.: A new method for known plaintext attack of FEAL cipher. In: Rueppel, R.A. (ed.) EUROCRYPT 1992. LNCS, vol. 658, pp. 81-91. Springer, Heidelberg (1993)
12. Miyaguchi, S.: The FEAL cipher family. In: Menezes, A., Vanstone, S.A. (eds.) CRYPTO 1990. LNCS, vol. 537, pp. 627-637. Springer, Heidelberg (1991)
13. Nguyen, P.H., Wei, L., Wang, H., Ling, S.: On multidimensional linear cryptanalysis. In: Steinfeld, R., Hawkes, P. (eds.) ACISP 2010. LNCS, vol. 6168, pp. 37-52. Springer, Heidelberg (2010)
14. Nguyen, P.H., Wu, H., Wang, H.: Improving the algorithm 2 in multidimensional linear cryptanalysis. In: Parampalli, U., Hawkes, P. (eds.) ACISP 2011. LNCS, vol. 6812, pp. 61-74. Springer, Heidelberg (2011)
15. Todo, Y., Aoki, K.: FFT key recovery for integral attack. In: Gritzalis, D., Kiayias, A., Askoxylakis, I. (eds.) Cryptology and Network Security. LNCS, vol. 8813, pp. 64-81. Springer, Heidelberg (2014)

Format-Preserving Encryption Algorithms Using Families of Tweakable Blockciphers

Jung-Keun Lee$^{(\boxtimes)}$, Bonwook Koo, Dongyoung Roh,
Woo-Hwan Kim, and Daesung Kwon

The Attached Institute of ETRI, Daejeon, Korea
{jklee,bwkoo,dyrohnsri,whkim5,ds_kwon}@ensec.re.kr

Abstract. We present two new algorithms, FEA-1 and FEA-2, for secure and efficient format-preserving encryption. Each algorithm is built from a family of dedicated tweakable blockciphers supporting various block bit-lengths. The tweakable blockciphers in the same family have similar structures and are based on common building blocks, enabling security analyses in the same frameworks. Their security follows largely from the structures, the round functions, and the tweak schedules. Their structures are new tweakable Feistel schemes, which are shown to be indistinguishable from tweakable random permutations against adaptive chosen tweak, plaintext, and ciphertext attacks. Their building blocks are shown to have cryptographically strong properties. The proposed algorithms outperform existing ones. They are several times faster than FF1-AES on test platforms.

Keywords: Tweakable blockcipher · Format-preserving encryption · Tweakable Feistel scheme

1 Introduction

1.1 Format-Preserving Encryption

Motivation. Recently, massive leakage of private information such as credit card numbers and social security numbers has been frequently reported. This has increased the importance of format-preserving encryption (FPE) that is more suitable for protection of private information stored in databases than traditional mechanisms using symmetric encryption algorithms such as blockciphers or stream ciphers. Though there are methods currently available for FPE, their performances are quite low compared to the mechanisms mentioned above. But there are applications where encryption performance is critical. For example, when the migration of a large database occurs, the data to be encrypted are massive and encryption has to be performed as fast as possible to minimize unavailability of services. With this in mind, we designed new methods of FPE that are secure and perform much better than existing ones.

© Springer International Publishing Switzerland 2015
J. Lee and J. Kim (Eds.): ICISC 2014, LNCS 8949, pp. 132–159, 2015.
DOI: 10.1007/978-3-319-15943-0_9

Concept. Format-preserving encryption is an encryption mechanism such that the "format" of ciphertext is the same as that of plaintext. Examples of formats are "string of 10 English alphabets", "string of 16 digits", and "string of 12 ASCII characters". We call the set of the plaintexts or ciphertexts the domain of the FPE. Then FPE can also be regarded as "domain-preserving encryption". In most cases, the domain, or message space, of an FPE can be easily mapped bijectively onto a set $\mathbb{Z}_N$ of integers. So we confine ourselves to FPE algorithms having $\mathbb{Z}_N$ as their domain for some integer N. Since most applications of FPE have domains of small size, we concentrate on the cases when the domain size is not larger than 2^{128}. When the domain size is larger, we can apply length-preserving modes of operation using blockciphers, as mentioned in [3].

1.2 Our Work

We present two algorithms, FEA-1 and FEA-2, for format-preserving encryption. For each algorithm, we constructed a family of tweakable blockciphers supporting block bit-lengths in [8..128] and applied the cycle-walking when necessary. The first family consists of tweakable blockciphers supporting key bit-lengths 128, 192, and 256. The tweak bit-length is $128 - n$ when the block bit-length is n. The tweakable blockciphers in the second family support the same key bit-lengths and block bit-lengths but tweak bit-lengths are always fixed to 128. The second algorithm is slightly less efficient than the first one, but makes more resilient application possible by supporting longer tweaks. Each tweakable blockcipher is shown to be secure. Firstly, it resists known attacks against *tweakable* blockciphers including differential and linear cryptanalysis and has a considerable security margin. Secondly, each of the two tweakable Feistel schemes that the tweakable blockciphers are modeled on is secure. We then present performance figures showing that the proposed methods outperform existing ones.

1.3 Our Contribution

We designed families of dedicated tweakable blockciphers such that each tweakable blockcipher provides security claim and shows performance comparable to ordinary blockciphers. Such families are unprecedented and the approach of constructing FPE algorithms using dedicated tweakable blockciphers has not been adopted before, largely due to the absence of methodology to design and analyze the security of dedicated *tweakable* blockciphers. But we have established such an approach by designing and utilizing new tweakable Feistel schemes together with appropriate tweak schedules and cryptographically strong round functions that provide both provable security and security against conventional attacks. We proved that the tweakable Feistel schemes are secure against adaptive chosen tweak, plaintext, and ciphertext attacks. We were also able to examine the resistance of the tweakable block ciphers against known attacks such as differential and linear attacks considering tweak controls. We also proved good bounds on the differential probability of truncated two-round SPN functions in case the diffusion layer is maximum-distance-separable. Using such families of tweakable blockciphers, we presented efficient FPE algorithms.

1.4 Related Works

Format-Preserving Encryption. There are several methods of format-preserving encryption in the literature. Prefix ciphers [7] can be applied only when the domain size is very small and, thus, have severe limitations for general use. Mechanisms based on card shuffles, such as the Thorp shuffle [23], the swap-or-not shuffle [16], the mix-and-cut shuffle [27], and the sometimes-recurse shuffle [22], provide tight security proofs, but are not so practical. VFPE [30], based on the counter mode of block ciphers, is too vulnerable to forgery attack. Some FPE modes of operations such as FFSEM [31], FF1, FF2, and FF3 [12] have their own security claims and show efficiency suitable for most applications, though they show quite low performance compared to most blockciphers, mainly because they require many blockcipher calls per data. NIST is in the process of publishing SP 800-38G that will specify modes of operations for format-preserving encryption.

Tweakable Blockciphers. The concept of the tweakable blockcipher was formalized in [21]. Tweakable blockciphers usually fit into certain modes of operation providing simple security proofs. But instances of tweakable blockciphers go back to hasty pudding ciphers [29], though their security is not considered to be recognized. Mercy cipher [10] is a tweakable blockcipher with large block size and is targeted for disk encryption. The Threefish blockciphers [13] were designed as the building blocks of the hash function family Skein, but they do not support block bit-lengths except 256, 512, and 1024. David Goldenberg et al. studied provably secure tweakable Feistel schemes using pseudorandom functions [14]. They analyzed the security of various ways of inserting tweaks into the ordinary Feistel schemes and presented secure ones. Their results can be interpreted as providing tweakable Feistel structures that are secure against generic attacks not using specific properties of round functions. However, they do not provide specific tweakable blockciphers whose performance is comparable to efficient blockciphers.

1.5 Organization

In Sect. 2, we specify two FPE algorithms. Then we explain the design rationale in Sect. 3 and present results regarding the security and performance of the algorithms in Sects. 4 and 5, respectively. We give conclusive remarks and discuss future works in Sect. 6.

2 Specification

In this section, we specify FEA-1 and FEA-2 supporting domain size in $[2^8 .. 2^{128}]$ and key bit-lengths 128, 192, and 256. When the domain is $\mathbb{Z}_N$ with $2^{n-1} < N \leq 2^n$, each algorithm performs the cycle-walking using a tweakable blockcipher with block bit-length n. So we only have to describe two families $\{\mathsf{TBC}_n^1 : 8 \leq n \leq 128\}$ and $\{\mathsf{TBC}_n^2 : 8 \leq n \leq 128\}$ of tweakable blockciphers to specify FEA-1 and FEA-2 respectively, where each TBC supports key bit-lengths 128, 192, and 256. Tweakable blockciphers in the first and second family are called *type 1* and *type 2 TBCs*, respectively.

2.1   Notations, Abbreviations, and Terminology

We will use the following notations throughout this paper.

- $|x|$: bit-length of the bit string x, or the number of elements of a set x
- $x_{[i:j]}$: substring $x_i\|x_{i+1}\|\cdots\|x_j$ of the string $x = x_0\|x_1\|\cdots\|x_{l-1}$ for $0 \leq i \leq j < l$.

The little-endian convention is used for bit string, i.e., an l-bit string x is expressed as $x = x_0\|x_1\|\cdots\|x_{l-1}$ for $x_i \in \{0,1\}$. We will use the following abbreviations.

- FPE: format-preserving encryption
- TBC: tweakable blockcipher
- MDS: maximum-distance-separable
- MDP/MLP: maximal differential/linear probability
- KTPCA: known tweak, plaintext, and ciphertext attack
- CTPCA-2: adaptive chosen tweak, plaintext, and ciphertext attack

We define a KSP function by a composition of round key addition layer K, substitution layer S, and diffusion layer P, which has round keys as auxiliary parameters. KSP-KS and KSP-KSP functions are similarly defined. We define Tw-KSP-Tr function by a composition of round tweak insertion Tw, KSP function, and truncation Tr, which has round keys and round tweaks as auxiliary parameters. Tw-KSP-KS-Tr and Tw-KSP-KSP-Tr functions are similarly defined. We will denote the type 1 and type 2 TBC with block bit-length n and key bit-length k as $\mathsf{TBC}_n^1[k]$ and $\mathsf{TBC}_n^2[k]$, respectively. When there is no need to specify the key bit-length, we denote them by TBC_n^1 and TBC_n^2, respectively. TBC_n will denote either of them. In this section, n will denote the block bit-length of the TBC. Also, $n_1 = \lceil n/2 \rceil$ and $n_2 = \lfloor n/2 \rfloor$. Cycle-walking is a kind of mode of operations invoking underlying cipher iteratively until encryption yields a ciphertext lying in a pre-defined domain from a plaintext lying in the domain.

2.2   The Structure of TBCs

Overall structure of TBC_n is as follows:

- Feistel structure with tweaks
- Bit-lengths

- Blocks: n $(8 \leq n \leq 128)$
- Keys: 128, 192, or 256
- Tweaks: $128 - n$ (type 1) or 128 (type 2)
- Number of rounds: defined according to the key bit-lengths and TBC types as in Table 1.

For each $n \in [8..128]$, TBC_n encrypts n-bit plaintexts, and two Feistel rounds $\Phi_{n,o}$ and $\Phi_{n,e}$ are applied alternately. $\Phi_{n,o}$ and $\Phi_{n,e}$ of TBC_n are described in Fig. 1 and defined as follows:

$$\Phi_{n,o} : \mathbb{Z}_2^{n_1} \times \mathbb{Z}_2^{n_2} \times \mathbb{Z}_2^{64} \times \mathbb{Z}_2^{64} \times \mathbb{Z}_2^{n_2} \times \mathbb{Z}_2^{64-n_2} \longrightarrow \mathbb{Z}_2^{n_2} \times \mathbb{Z}_2^{n_1}$$
$$(X_a, X_b, RK_a, RK_b, T_a, T_b) \mapsto (Y_a, Y_b),$$

and

$$\Phi_{n,e} : \mathbb{Z}_2^{n_2} \times \mathbb{Z}_2^{n_1} \times \mathbb{Z}_2^{64} \times \mathbb{Z}_2^{64} \times \mathbb{Z}_2^{n_1} \times \mathbb{Z}_2^{64-n_1} \longrightarrow \mathbb{Z}_2^{n_1} \times \mathbb{Z}_2^{n_2}$$
$$(X_a, X_b, RK_a, RK_b, T_a, T_b) \mapsto (Y_a, Y_b),$$

where Y_a and Y_b are determined by the relations

- $Y_a = X_b$ and
- $Y_b = F(X_b \oplus T_a, RK_a, RK_b, T_b) \oplus X_a,$

where the round function F is described in the subsection below. Let r be the number of rounds. Let the round keys and round tweaks be $RK_a^i \| RK_b^i$ and $T_a^i \| T_b^i$, respectively ($i = 1, \cdots, r$). Then the encryption E_n^r and decryption D_n^r are defined as follows: If r is odd, then

$$E_n^r = \mathsf{cat} \circ \mathsf{swap} \circ \Phi_{n,o}^{(r)} \circ \Phi_{n,e}^{(r-1)} \circ \cdots \circ \Phi_{n,o}^{(2)} \circ \Phi_{n,o}^{(1)} \circ \mathsf{split},$$
$$D_n^r = \mathsf{cat} \circ \mathsf{swap} \circ \phi_{n,o}^{(1)} \circ \phi_{n,e}^{(2)} \circ \cdots \circ \phi_{n,e}^{(r-1)} \circ \phi_{n,o}^{(r)} \circ \mathsf{split},$$

and otherwise (if r is even),

$$E_n^r = \mathsf{cat} \circ \mathsf{swap} \circ \phi_{n,e}^{(r)} \circ \phi_{n,o}^{(r-1)} \circ \cdots \circ \phi_{n,e}^{(2)} \circ \phi_{n,o}^{(1)} \circ \mathsf{split},$$
$$D_n^r = \mathsf{cat} \circ \mathsf{swap} \circ \phi_{n,o}^{(1)} \circ \phi_{n,e}^{(2)} \circ \cdots \circ \phi_{n,o}^{(r-1)} \circ \phi_{n,e}^{(r)} \circ \mathsf{split}.$$

Here,

$$\phi_{n,o}^{(i)}(X_a, X_b) := \Phi_{n,o}(X_a, X_b, RK_a^i, RK_b^i, T_a^i, T_b^i),$$

and

$$\phi_{n,e}^{(i)}(X_a, X_b) := \Phi_{n,e}(X_a, X_b, RK_a^i, RK_b^i, T_a^i, T_b^i),$$

for each $i = 1, \cdots, r$, and cat and split are suitable concatenation and splitting maps for bit strings, respectively. swap denotes the Feistel swapping.

Table 1. Numbers of rounds according to the key bit-lengths and TBC types

Key length	Type 1	Type 2
128 bits	12	18
192 bits	14	21
256 bits	16	24

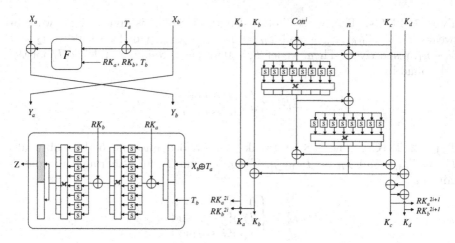

Fig. 1. Feistel round $\Phi_{*,*}$ (left top), the round function F (left bottom), and a round of the key schedule (right)

2.3   Round Function F

The round functions are Tw-KSP-KSP-Tr functions supporting input bit-length in [4..64]. The substitution layer is defined as the eight same 8-bit S-boxes acting in parallel. The diffusion layer is defined as multiplication with an 8×8 MDS matrix $\mathcal{M}$ defined over the field $\mathrm{GF}(2^8)$. The 8-bit S-box S used in the substitution layer is specified in Table 6 and the MDS matrix $\mathcal{M}$ is specified in Sect. D of the Appendix. The round function is depicted in Fig. 1.

2.4   Key Schedule

The key schedule has a k-bit secret key K and the block bit-length n as input, and outputs r 128-bit round keys. It iterates the procedure described in Fig. 1 for $\lceil r/2 \rceil$ times and at each iteration, two 128-bit round keys for two consecutive rounds are generated with a round constant as an auxiliary input. Each round constant $RC_{type,|K|,i}$ is determined by the TBC type, the key bit-length, and the iteration index, as given in Table 7 of the Appendix. The 64-bit values K_a, K_b, K_c and K_d are initialized by the relation $K_a\|K_b\|K_c\|K_d = K\|0^{256-|K|}$. The S-box S and the matrix $\mathcal{M}$ are the same as those used in the round functions of the TBCs.

2.5   Tweak Schedule

Here we specify the tweak schedule for each type, key bit-length, and block bit-length of the TBC.

Type 1 TBCs. The tweak T of bit-length $(128 - n)$ is divided into two sub-tweaks $T_L = T_{[0:64-n_2-1]}$ and $T_R = T_{[64-n_2:128-n-1]}$ of length $64 - n_2$ and $64 - n_1$, respectively. Then, we let $T_a^i = 0$ for every round, and define T_b^i for the i-th round by

$$T_b^i = \begin{cases} T_L & \text{if } i \text{ is odd,} \\ T_R & \text{if } i \text{ is even.} \end{cases}$$

Type 2 TBCs. The 128-bit tweak T is divided into two 64-bit subtweaks $T_L = T_{[0:63]}$ and $T_R = T_{[64:127]}$. Then, T_a and T_b for i-th round are determined as

$$T_a^i \| T_b^i = \begin{cases} 0 & \text{if } i \equiv 1 \bmod 3, \\ T_L & \text{if } i \equiv 2 \bmod 3, \\ T_R & \text{if } i \equiv 0 \bmod 3. \end{cases}$$

3 Design Rationale

In this section, we describe the design rationale we had in determining the structure and components of the algorithms.

3.1 Design Based on Dedicated Tweakable Blockciphers

We started from constructing dedicated TBCs, not resorting to modes of operation, to get FPE algorithms with considerably higher performance than before.

3.2 Tweakable Blockciphers of Variable Block-Lengths

In *rank-then-encipher* frameworks [2], the ranking function converts a plaintext space to $\mathbb{Z}_N$ for some N, which is regarded as a subset of the set of all n-bit strings, where $n = \lceil \log_2 N \rceil$. Then, we can use a single 128-bit blockcipher and encrypt an n-bit string iteratively until the ciphertext falls into $\mathbb{Z}_N$, but the expected number of iterations increases exponentially as n decreases. Thus, we came to design families of blockciphers for each block size n to minimize the number of iterations. In this respect, FFSEM shares similar ideas with the current design. But it works by performing cycle-walking using ordinary blockciphers with even block bit-lengths, not supporting tweaks, and the blockciphers are again obtained from a mode of operation using another blockcipher. Thus it does not show good performance since the blockciphers are not efficient and it requires not a few iterations in the cycle-walking. The maximal bit-length was chosen to be 128, since, for most applications, the domain size will be not larger than 2^{128}, and if the domain size is larger, we can apply length-preserving blockcipher modes of operation. We think that the tweak bit-length of $128 - n$ is sufficiently long for TBCs of block bit-length n in most applications (as in type 1 TBCs), since the main purpose of using tweaks is to prevent codebook attacks. But to serve more general applications, we also designed type 2 TBCs that support 128-bit tweaks regardless of the block bit-length.

3.3 Tweakable Feistel Scheme

Designing (tweakable) blockciphers based on (tweakable) Feistel schemes has several advantages.

- There are many results showing that they are secure if the round function is close to random. Moreover, there are also results showing the security of tweakable blockciphers based on certain tweakable Feistel schemes [14].
- As in our case, it is quite simple to design tweakable blockciphers of various block bit-lengths based on a common building block (a KSP-KSP function) by inserting tweaks and applying truncation. The round functions need not be bijective.
- We do not need inverse circuits of round functions when we implement decryption. This can not only reduce resources required in implementation, but facilitate implementation.

The security of the tweakable Feistel schemes that our type 1 TBCs are based on is guaranteed similarly to ordinary Feistel schemes. Type 2 TBCs are based on new tweakable Feistel schemes that are different from those introduced in [14]. But the schemes are also shown to be provably secure and provide security against conventional attacks more effectively than those in [14] in that they resist known attacks in smaller rounds when our round functions are applied.

3.4 Round Functions

As the structure of the round functions, we chose the substitution-permutation network since such structure can have good cryptographic properties with a small number of rounds. Then, we considered three types of round function structures - KSP, KSP-KS, and KSP-KSP - as candidates and concluded that KSP-KSP structures give simple and strong ciphers. KSP structures are not simple to analyze as the block bit-length varies. KSP and KSP-KS functions have some weaknesses coming from the existence of equivalent tweaks, especially when the block bit-length is small (See Sect. A of the Appendix). In implementation aspects, KSP-KS and KSP-KSP functions have similar efficiency on 32-bit and 64-bit platforms so that there are few advantages to choosing KSP-KS functions in terms of either security or efficiency. In KSP-KSP functions, the S-box was chosen as one with the good algebraic, differential, and linear properties as in the blockcipher Rijndael [11], and the diffusion layer was chosen as the one with the maximal diffusion property. One could consider using an 8×8 binary matrix instead as in the blockcipher Camellia [1], but it would only require more rounds and degrade performance in software implementations. Our MDS matrix was chosen among circulant 8×8 matrices over a $GF(2^8)$ to reduce required resources in 32-bit implementations.

3.5 Tweak Schedule

The tweak schedules influence the security of the tweakable blockciphers critically. They not only enable simple security analyses, but also reflect the structures of the tweakable Feistel schemes we designed. That is, they enable us to analyze the differential and linear properties of the TBCs easily, and prove the security of the tweakable Feistel schemes coming from the tweak schedules. For type 2 TBCs, we also considered applying the subtweaks in different orders. But the current way proved to be the best one according to our analysis. Applying them in the order T_L-T_R-T_L-T_R-$\cdots$, for example, proved not secure due to the existence of differential characteristics of probability 1 regardless of the number of rounds. Applying them in other orders is less efficient by requiring more rounds to achieve similar security level. In the implementation aspects, the tweak schedules incur little overhead regardless of the type or block bit-length, since all the round tweaks are substring of the tweak.

3.6   Key Schedule

We used the same S-box and MDS matrix as encryption round functions for key schedule in order to reduce the required resources for implementation. Then, to remove the similarity to the encryption body, we adopted the Lai-Massey structure [32]. In the round function of the Lai-Massey scheme, we applied SP functions twice to give large non-linearity and diffusion effect. The orthomorphism was chosen as a simple linear map for efficiency. The Lai-Massey structure guarantees that there is little chance of equivalent keys since recovering secret key requires recovering the i-th and $(i + 1)$-th round keys, for every odd i. We also removed possible weaknesses caused by similarity of structures for different cipher types, key bit-lengths, or block bit-lengths by using the block bit-length as a parameter for the key schedule and using different round constants for different types and key bit-lengths. These designs influence the security against attacks using the properties of key schedules, such as the related-key attacks, the slide attack, and the biclique attack.

4   Security

We consider the security of FEA. Note that each of the algorithms is constructed from a family of TBCs using cycle-walking. In [20], it was shown that the cycle-walking does not degrade the security of the underlying cipher. So we mainly consider the security of each TBC in either family. We evaluate the security of each cipher against conventional attacks and claim that it resists known attacks on *tweakable* blockciphers with a considerable security margin. We also show the provable security of the tweakable Feistel scheme to show its structural robustness, or the appropriateness of the way tweaks are inserted into the Feistel schemes to claim additional strength of the design. For simplicity, we assume in this section that the block bit-length is even. The case of odd block bit-lengths can be treated in a similar way.

4.1   Security Against Conventional Attacks

We consider the security of the TBCs in either family against known attacks and claim that each one is secure with a considerable security margin. In the analysis,

Table 2. Numbers of rounds resisting attacks (key = 128 bits)

Attacks	Type 1	Type 2
Differential attack [6]	8	12
Linear attack [15]	8	11
Impossible differential attack [4]	6	9
Truncated differential attack [18]	8	12
Integral attack [19]	6	6
Boomerang/rectangle attack [5,33]	6	9
Higher order differential attack [18]	6	6

we apply the usual methodology used in analyzing ordinary blockciphers, while having in mind that tweaks are also available to the attacker. So, for example, we allow for tweak differences in the differential cryptanaysis. Using the tweaks, we can get longer characteristics in the differential cryptanalysis, linear cryptanalysis, boomerang attacks, and rectangle attacks. Note that adding 3 or more rounds to distinguishing characteristics that are useful for an attack incapacitates key recovery attack using the characteristics mainly due to the property of the round function that most of the 128 round key bits influence each output bit. Similarly, when the key bit-length is 192 or 256, 4 or more rounds should be added to do so. Table 2 summarizes the numbers of rounds that are sufficient to provide resistance against known attacks when the key bit-length is 128.

Differential Cryptanalysis. We claim that there do not exist distinguishing differential characteristics of 6 and 10 rounds for type 1 and type 2 TBCs, respectively, regardless of the block bit-length. The claim implies that type 1 and type 2 TBCs resist differential attack when the numbers of rounds are at least 8 and 12, respectively. We confirm the claim by proving and using a theorem bounding the maximal differential probability (MDP) for the *differentials* of round functions of the TBCs. Compared with usual methods of bounding differential probability for blockciphers using *differential paths* for the round functions, the current result can be considered to be providing more conservative bounds on the MDP for differential paths of the round-reduced TBCs. For a function $f : \mathbb{Z}_2^{l_1} \to \mathbb{Z}_2^{l_2}$, $\Delta x \in \mathbb{Z}_2^{l_1}$, and $\Delta y \in \mathbb{Z}_2^{l_2}$, we denote the differential probability of f with input difference Δx and output difference Δy by $\mathrm{DP}^f(\Delta x \to \Delta y)$. We assume that the round function is a truncated KSP-KSP function that has the same m-bit S-boxes acting in parallel as the substitution layer and a $d \times d$ MDS matrix D over $\mathrm{GF}(2^m)$ as the representation of the diffusion layer. For positive integers d, s, and k such that $d > s$, we say that a collection $\mathcal{S}$ of subsets of $[0..(d-1)]$ *satisfies the condition* $C[d, s, k]$ if each $U \in \mathcal{S}$ has k elements, and for any $U, U' \in \mathcal{S}$ with $U \neq U'$, $|U \cap U'| < d - s$. Then we define $M[d, s, k]$ by $\max\{|\mathcal{S}| : \mathcal{S} \text{ satisfies } C[d, s, k]\}$. For example, $M[d, d-1, k] = \lfloor \frac{d}{k} \rfloor$ for positive integers k and d. Let p be the MDP of the S-box. Then we have Theorems 1 and 2 whose proof is provided in Sect. B of the Appendix.

Table 3. Bounds on MDPs of KSP-KSP truncated to s bytes, upper bounds for $\log_2 \rho^S(b)$, and $\log_2 B(s)$ when $s = i$ or $b = i$

i	0	1	2	3	4	5	6	7
$\log_2 \mathrm{MDP}_s, s = i$		-5.82	-11.82	-17.82	-23.82	-29.82	-35.82	-41.62
$\log_2 \rho^S(b), b = i$		-0.36	-0.98	-1.96	-2.91	-3.83	-4.68	-5.42
$\log_2 B(s), s = i$	0.18	-5.82	-11.82	-17.82	-23.82	-29.82	-35.18	-37.68

Theorem 1. *Assume that the round keys are independent and uniformly random. Then the KSP-KSP function truncated to the s most significant m-bit words has MDP bounded by*

$$p^s \sum_{k=0}^{d-s} \binom{d}{k} p^k + p^d \sum_{k=d-s+1}^{d-1} M[d, s, k]$$

when $0 < s < d$.

For each integer b such that $0 < b < m$, let us define $\rho^S(b)$ as the maximum of $\sum_{j=1}^{2^{m-b}} \mathrm{DP}^S(\Delta\alpha \to \Delta\beta^j)$ when $\Delta\alpha$ and $\{\Delta\beta^j : j = 1, \cdots, 2^{m-b}\}$ run through the followings.

- $\Delta\alpha$ is a nonzero m-bit input difference for S.
- There are $(m - b)$ integers $i_1, \cdots, i_{m-b}$ such that $0 \le i_1 < \cdots < i_{m-b} < m$ and the set of $(m - b)$-bit values $\{\Delta\beta_{i_1}^j \| \cdots \| \Delta\beta_{i_{m-b}}^j : j = 1, \cdots, 2^{m-b}\}$ is the whole set of $(m - b)$-bit values.

Theorem 2. *With the same assumption as in Theorem 1, the KSP-KSP function truncated to the $sm + b$ most significant bits has MDP bounded by*

$$\rho^S(b) \left(p^s \sum_{k=0}^{d-s-1} \binom{d}{k} p^k + p^{d-1} \sum_{k=d-s}^{d-1} M[d, s, k] \right)$$

when $0 \le s < d$ and $0 < b < m$.

Now, we return to our TBCs. In our case, $d = m = 8$, and $p = 2^{-6}$. The bound in Theorem 1 is computed as in Table 3. The values $\rho^S(b)$ and $B(s) := (p^s \sum_{k=0}^{d-s-1} \binom{d}{k} p^k + p^{d-1} \sum_{k=d-s}^{h-1} M[d, s, k])$ are given in Table 3. So if every differential path has at least 3 active rounds, there do not exist differential characteristics useful for differential attack. For example, when the block bit-length is 42, the bit-length of each round function input is $21 = 8 \cdot 2 + 5$, and the MDP of a differentially active round is at most $2^{-3.83} \cdot 2^{-11.82} = 2^{-15.65}$. Each differential path of type 1 TBC has at least one differentially active round in every two consecutive rounds:

- If the difference in the tweak is nonzero, the difference in the round tweak is nonzero in at least one round for every two consecutive rounds.

– Otherwise, the difference in the round input is nonzero in at least one round for every two consecutive rounds.

So each differential path of type 1 TBCs has 3 or more active rounds if the number of rounds is greater than or equal to 6. Note that for each type 2 TBC, the tweak is split into the *xored subtweak* $T_a^2 \| T_a^3 = T_a^5 \| T_a^6 = \cdots$ and the *padded subtweak* $T_b^2 \| T_b^3 = T_b^5 \| T_b^6 = \cdots$. Then the following holds:

– If the difference in the padded subtweak is nonzero, each differential path has at least one active round in every three consecutive rounds.
– Otherwise,
  • if the difference in the xored subtweak is also zero, then the difference in the whole tweak is zero, and each differential path has at least one active round in every two consecutive rounds;
  • otherwise, each differential path has at least one active round in every four consecutive rounds and at least two active rounds in every six consecutive rounds.

So each differential path of type 2 TBCs has 3 or more active rounds in 10 or more rounds.

Linear Cryptanalysis. We claim that there do not exist distinguishing linear characteristics of 6 and 9 rounds for type 1 and type 2 TBCs, respectively, regardless of the block bit-length. The claim implies that type 1 and type 2 TBCs resist linear attack when the numbers of rounds are at least 8 and 11, respectively. The claim is confirmed by using a theorem [17] bounding the maximal linear probability (MLP) of *linear hulls* for the round functions of the TBCs. Consider the truncated KSP-KSP functions described in the differential cryptanalysis. For a KSP-KS function with the same substitution and diffusion layer, the MLP was shown to be bounded by p_L^d when p_L is the MLP of the S-box [17]. The MLP of a KSP-KSP function is the same as that of a KSP-KS function since the additional linear map does not affect MLP. Truncation also does not increase the MLP. Thus MLP of KSP-KSP-Tr function is also bounded by p_L^d, and in our case the bound is 2^{-48}. Note that a linear characteristic with linear probability greater than $2^{-(t+n)}$ may be utilized in a linear attack when n and t are the bit-lengths of the blocks and tweaks, respectively, since pairs of tweaks and inputs can be used as data for the linear attack. For type 1 TBCs, $2^{-(t+n)}$ is always 2^{-128} and for type 2 TBCs, $2^{-(t+n)} = 2^{-(128+n)} \geq 2^{-256}$. So if every linear characteristic has at least 3 and 6 linearly active rounds, there will not exist useful distinguishing linear characteristics for type 1 and type 2, respectively. Since each linear characteristic of our TBCs have at least 2 linearly active rounds in every 3 consecutive rounds, there are no useful linear characteristics when the number of rounds is at least 6 and 9 for type 1 and type 2 TBCs, respectively.

Other Attacks

Impossible Differential Attack. For round-reduced type 1 and type 2 TBCs, there are impossible differential characteristics when the numbers of rounds are

3 and 6, respectively, for some block bit-lengths. But there seem to be no such characteristics when the numbers of rounds are greater than 3 and 6, respectively.

Truncated Differential Attack. Truncated differential attacks (TDCs) considering zero-or-not byte differences could be effective to certain degree if the diffusion layer had been represented by an 8×8 binary matrix. But the MDS diffusion baffles such TDCs and there seem to be no effective TDCs other than the ordinary differential attack.

Boomerang/Rectangle Attack. Considering the analysis results on differential characteristics stated above, we see that there are no 4-round and 7-round boomerang or rectangle characteristics for type 1 and type 2 TBCs, respectively. So round-reduced type 1 and type 2 TBCs are secure if the numbers of rounds are greater than 6 and 9, respectively.

Integral Attack. Integral attacks are not effective against the TBCs since the KSP-KSP function with MDS diffusion layers do not admit good integral characteristics. There are 3-round integral characteristics for our TBCs for some block bit-lengths. But there do not seem to exist useful characteristics when the number of rounds is greater than 4.

Higher Order Differential Attack. Since the output bits of the S-boxes have algebraic degree 7 and have many nonlinear terms with respect to the input bits, and the MDS propagates the influence of each input bit well, the output bits of the round functions have algebraic degree 49. Thus we can expect that there are no higher order differential characteristics useful for attacking round-reduced TBCs if the number of rounds is greater than 4.

Biclique and Zero-Correlation Attack. Biclique attack [8] is not effective against the TBCs since the key schedule of each TBC prevents the existence of bicliques for 3 or more rounds and the round functions have good diffusion effect. Zero-correlation attack [9] is also not effective since the KSP-KSP round functions do not seem to have linear hulls with correlation zero.

Related Key Attacks. There seem to be no effective related key attacks since the Lai-Massey structure of the key schedule prevents the existence of round key differentials with high probability and the structure of the encryption body and the key schedule is quite different.

4.2 Provable Security

In this section, we assume that *the block bit-length of the tweakable blockcipher is $2n$, not n*, for some integer n, following the convention usually adopted in the security consideration of Feistel schemes. We consider the indistinguishability between tweakable Feistel schemes we describe below and tweakable random permutations [21]. Proofs are provided in Sect. C of the Appendix.

Type 1 TBCs. Type 1 TBCs can be considered to be based on the tweakable Feistel schemes such that each round function is a tweakable PRF and tweaks are applied alternately. It is not hard to prove the security of the schemes.

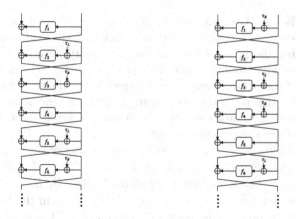

Fig. 2. Tweakable Feistel schemes $\hat{\Psi}^r$ and $\overline{\Psi}^r$

Type 2 TBCs. For each positive integer r, let $\hat{\Psi}^r$ be the r-round tweakable Feistel scheme with $2n$-bit inputs and tweaks defined as follows: Let F_n be the set of all functions $\mathbb{Z}_2^n \to \mathbb{Z}_2^n$. For each $f \in F_n$, $i \in \mathbb{Z}$ and $\tau_L, \tau_R \in \mathbb{Z}_2^n$, let $\psi_i^{\tau_L \| \tau_R}(f) : \mathbb{Z}_2^{2n} \to \mathbb{Z}_2^{2n}$ be the function such that for each n-bit values x_L and x_R,

$$\psi_i^{\tau_L \| \tau_R}(f)(x_L \| x_R) = \begin{cases} x_R \| (x_L \oplus f(x_R)) & \text{if } i \bmod 3 \equiv 1, \\ x_R \| (x_L \oplus f(\tau_L \oplus x_R)) & \text{if } i \bmod 3 \equiv 2, \\ x_R \| (x_L \oplus f(\tau_R \oplus x_R)) & \text{if } i \bmod 3 \equiv 0. \end{cases}$$

Now let $f_1, \cdots, f_r \in F_n$ and let τ be the $2n$-bit tweak. Then for each $2n$-bit value x,

$$\hat{\Psi}^r(f_1, \cdots, f_r)(\tau; x) := (\psi_r^\tau(f_r) \circ \cdots \circ \psi_1^\tau(f_1))(x).$$

Similarly, we define the tweakable Feistel scheme $\overline{\Psi}^r$ as

$$\overline{\Psi}^r(f_1, \cdots, f_r)(\tau; x) := (\psi_{r-1}^\tau(f_r) \circ \cdots \circ \psi_0^\tau(f_1))(x)$$

for each $r \geq 1$. We will denote $\hat{\Psi}^r(f_1, \cdots, f_r)(\tau_L \| \tau_R; x_L \| x_R)$ by $\hat{\Psi}^r(f_1, \cdots, f_r)$ $(\tau_L, \tau_R; x_L, x_R)$.

In each round of type 2 TBCs, we regard T_b as additional randomizer of round functions so that the r-round type 2 TBCs is modeled on the tweakable Feistel scheme $\hat{\Psi}^r$ or $\overline{\Psi}^r$ with the xored subtweak $T_a^2 \| T_a^3$ having the role of the tweak. The attacker cannot exploit T_b's in constructing a distinguisher if the number of rounds is not very small. In this subsection, we claim that $\overline{\Psi}^r$ is secure against adaptive chosen tweak, plaintext, and ciphertext attack (IND-CTPCA-2) when the number of queries is small compared to the birthday bound $2^{\frac{n}{2}}$, where $2n$ is the block bit-length, when the number of rounds $r \geq 8$. Specifically we show that $\overline{\Psi}^8$ with $2n$-bit inputs and tweaks is indistinguishable from random tweakable scheme with inputs and tweaks of the same bit-lengths when the number of queries is small compared to $2^{\frac{n}{2}}$. For the proof we apply

Patarin's Coefficient H techniques [24–26]. The techniques have been used in proving various results on pseudo-random functions and pseudo-random permutations, including the proof of the indistinguishability between random Feistel schemes and random permutations. The proof uses the fact that if the number of tuples of round functions compatible with the query transcript is close to uniform when the query transcript varies, then the scheme is indistinguishable from random permutations. Similar statement holds for tweakable Feistel schemes: For each sequence of q tuples $[A_i, B_i, L_i, R_i, S_i, T_i]$ of n-bit values, let $H_r([A_i, B_i; L_i, R_i, S_i, T_i]_{i=1,\cdots,q})$ denote the number of tuples $(f_1, \cdots, f_r)$ of functions such that $\hat{\Psi}^r(f_1, \cdots, f_r)(A_i, B_i; L_i, R_i) = (S_i, T_i)$ for all $i = 1, \cdots, q$. Here $A_i \| B_i$ is the $2n$-bit tweak value τ_i for each i. $\overline{H}_r([A_i, B_i; L_i, R_i, S_i, T_i]_{i=1,\cdots,q})$ is defined similarly for $\overline{\Psi}^r$. Proposition 1 can be shown as in the Feistel schemes [26]. The line of the proof is the same as in the proof of Theorem 4 [26]. The difference is that, in the case of random permutations, the number of permutations on $2n$-bit values compatible with the query transcript is the same, regardless of the query transcript, but, in the case of random tweakable permutations, the number of tweakable permutations compatible with the query transcript varies, though the minimum is not smaller than (maximum$*(1 - q(q-1)/2^{2n+1})$). The maximum occurs when all the tweaks appearing in the query transcript are different and the minimum occurs when all the tweaks are the same. This causes the advantage of the attacker to increase by up to $q(q-1)/2^{2n+1}$ compared to the case of distinguishing random permutations, but this is negligible when $q \ll 2^{n/2}$. Now we state

Proposition 1. *If there is some small integer c such that*

$$\overline{H}_r([A_i, B_i; L_i, R_i, S_i, T_i]_{i=1,\cdots,q}) \geq \frac{|F_n|^r}{2^{2qn}}\left(1 - \frac{cq^2}{2^n}\right)$$

for each set of q tuples $[A_i, B_i, L_i, R_i, S_i, T_i]$ such that $[A_i, B_i, L_i, R_i] \neq [A_j, B_j, L_j, R_j]$ and $[A_i, B_i, S_i, T_i] \neq [A_j, B_j, S_j, T_j]$ for $i \neq j$, the r-round tweakable Feistel scheme is secure against CTPCA-2 when the number of queries is small compared to $2^{\frac{n}{2}}$.

Then we show

Theorem 3. *For each set of q tuples $[A_i, B_i, L_i, R_i, S_i, T_i]$ such that $[A_i, B_i, L_i, R_i] \neq [A_j, B_j, L_j, R_j]$ and $[A_i, B_i, S_i, T_i] \neq [A_j, B_j, S_j, T_j]$ whenever $i \neq j$, we have*

$$\overline{H}_8([A_i, B_i; L_i, R_i, S_i, T_i]_{i=1,\cdots,q}) \geq \frac{|F_n|^8}{2^{2qn}}\left(1 - \frac{3q(q-1)}{2^n}\right).$$

Thus, by Proposition 1, Theorem 3 implies that the 8-round tweakable Feistel scheme $\overline{\Psi}^8$ is secure against CTPCA-2 by computationally unbounded adversary when the number of queries is small compared to the birthday bound $2^{\frac{n}{2}}$. We mention that the schemes are not secure when the number of rounds is less than or equal to 6. There is a boomerang characteristic that enables to distinguish

Table 4. Platforms for the experiment

	Platform 1	Platform 2
Processor	Intel® Core™i7-2600 K 3.40 GHz	Intel® Xeon®E3-1275 v3 3.50 GHz
OS	Windows 7	Windows Server 2008
Compiler	Visual Studio 2012	Visual Studio 2012

the 6-round scheme from random with few queries. We checked that the 4-round scheme is secure against known tweak, plaintext, and ciphertext attack (KTPCA) when the number of queries is small compared to $\frac{2^n}{n}$ as in the case of ordinary Feistel schemes. Based on this, we suspect that the scheme is secure against CTPCA-2 when the number of queries is small compared to $\frac{2^n}{n}$ if the number of rounds is 16 or greater (Fig. 2).

4.3 Other Considerations

Each of the two algorithms is constructed from TBCs of various block bit-lengths with similar structures. So we also consider the situations an attacker has access to round-reduced versions of both $\mathsf{TBC}_i^a[k_1]$ and $\mathsf{TBC}_j^b[k_2]$ without knowing the keys. To remove the possible vulnerabilities coming from those situations, we made the block bit-lengths, the type of the TBC, and the key bit-lengths affect the values of round keys.

5   Performance

We implemented FEA and FF1 having AES as the underlying blockcipher on 64-bit platforms and compared their performances. We considered two implementations of AES-based FF1, that is, FF1 based on hardware-accelerated AES and non-accelerated AES that we will refer to as FF1-AESNI and FF1-AES, respectively. They were meant to represent FF1 with hardware-accelerated and non-accelerated blockciphers, respectively. As domains of the FPE algorithms, the sets of bit strings, byte strings, and decimal strings were chosen, since most applications of FPE seem to have such sets as domains. The lengths of the strings were chosen so that the domain sizes do not exceed 2^{128}. We optimized FF1 in such a way that in the intermediate rounds of FF1, conversions between bit strings and integers do not occur in the implementations. We experimented on two platforms, each being meant to represent either clients or servers. They support AES instructions and are specified in Table 4.

Figure 3 shows the performances of above-mentioned algorithms. In the figures, the domains are bit strings, byte strings, and decimal strings from left to right, and the horizontal axes represent the lengths of the strings. The performances were measured in terms of Mbps. When the domain is a set of bit strings or byte strings, FEA-1 is about 4 and 3 times faster than the FF1-AES and FF1-AESNI, respectively, on both platforms. When the domain is a set of

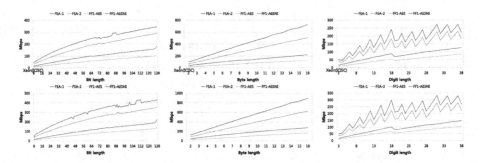

Fig. 3. Experimental results on Platform 1 (top three) and Platform 2 (bottom three)

Table 5. Elapsed time to encrypt 10 million credit card numbers

	FEA-1	FEA-2	FF1-AES	FF1-AESNI
Platform 1	3.432	4.602	10.800	6.443
Platform 2	2.792	3.760	8.533	5.663

decimal strings, FEA-1 is about 3.5 and 2.5 times faster than the FF1-AES and FF1-AESNI, respectively, on the platforms. In this case, FEA-1 and FEA-2 show fluctuations in performances as the length of the strings increases, due to the cycle-walking.

Table 5 shows the elapsed time to encrypt 10 million credit card numbers (16 digits) in seconds. As we can see, FEA-1 is about 3 times faster than the FF1 based on non-accelerated AES, and about twice faster than the FF1 based on hardware-accelerated AES on the platforms.

6   Conclusive Remarks and Future Works

In this paper, we presented two algorithms for secure and efficient format-preserving encryption. They were constructed from families of dedicated tweakable blockciphers having common and simple structures. Each tweakable blockcipher is secure from its structure and cryptographically strong building blocks. It also provides certain provable security in that the tweakable Feistel scheme it is based on is shown to be IND-CTPCA-2 from random tweakable permutations. The algorithm works much faster than existing methods. It is readily applicable in that it is easy to implement and use. As future research, we are considering finding other applications using a family of tweakable blockciphers supporting various block bit-lengths as presented here. For example, we might be able to find a secure method of encoding-and-length-preserving encryption for ASCII or UTF-16 encoded messages using such a family without resorting to the rank-then-encipher frameworks. Proving the IND-CTPCA-2 security of the tweakable schemes presented in this paper beyond the birthday bound is another interesting subject.

A Equivalent Tweak Analysis

In this section, we show that when round functions are Tw-KSP-Tr or Tw-KSP-KS-Tr, the resulting tweakable blockciphers have weaknesses if the block bit-length is small and the number of rounds is not very large. For simplicity, we consider the case where the block bit-length is 16 and the round tweaks are only padded similarly to the type 1 TBCs. In this case, the bit-length of the tweaks, round tweaks, and round inputs are 112, 56, and 8, respectively. Let the secret key K be randomly chosen and let the r-th round key be $RK_0^r \| \cdots \| RK_8^r$ for each r. For the r-th round, let x be the 8-bit input of round function. For each tweak T, let $RT_1^r \| \cdots \| RT_{15}^r$ be the r-th round tweak. Let

$$\eta_{K,T,r} = \sum_{i=1}^{7} M_{0i} S(RT_i^r \oplus RK_i^r)$$

for each key K, tweak T, and round index r. Then the output of Tw-KSP-Tr function is $y = (M_{00} \cdot S(x \oplus RK_0^r)) \oplus \eta_{K,T,r}$ and the output of Tw-KSP-KS-Tr function is $z = S(y \oplus RK_8^r)$. Note that if $\eta_{K,T1,r} = \eta_{K,T2,r}$ for tweaks $T1$ and $T2$, then the round functions coincide for $T1$ and $T2$. Let R be the number of rounds. $\eta_{K,T1,1} = \eta_{K,T2,1}, \eta_{K,T1,2} = \eta_{K,T2,2}, \cdots, \eta_{K,T1,R} = \eta_{K,T2,R}$ implies that $T1$ and $T2$ are equivalent tweaks for the key K. Thus when about 2^{4R} tweaks are applied with the same key, then there exist equivalent tweaks with non-negligible probability. Note that equivalent tweaks are very likely to satisfy the above condition. If we assume this, we can get some direct information useful for recovering the secret key K by the following procedure.

1. Find out equivalent tweaks by encrypting all the 16-bit inputs using 2^{4R} tweaks using the cipher.
2. If such equivalent tweaks are found, we conclude that $\eta_{K,T1,1} = \eta_{K,T2,1}, \eta_{K,T1,2} = \eta_{K,T2,2}, \cdots, \eta_{K,T1,R} = \eta_{K,T2,R}$.

The attack is more effective than exhaustive key search when $16 + 4R$ is smaller than the key bit-length. Thus, when the key bit-length is 128 and the block bit-length is 16, the number of rounds should be at least 28 even if we do not have a security margin.

B Bound of Differential Probability for Truncated KSP-KSP Functions

In [17], the MDP of a KSP-KS function was shown to be bounded by p^d, when the MDP of each S-box is p and P is a diffusion layer represented by a $d \times d$ MDS matrix over $GF(2^m)$. The proof uses Lemma 1 [17].

Lemma 1. *For the linear map $Z_2^{dm} \to Z_2^{dm}$ defined by a $d \times d$ MDS matrix over $GF(2^m)$, d components of input and output, chosen from any d positions among the $2d$ possible ones, determine the remaining d components.*

We now prove Theorem 1 using Lemma 1 as a crucial ingredient.

Proof. We proceed similarly as in [17]. Let D be the $d \times d$ MDS matrix. Let $\pi : \mathbb{Z}_2^{dm} \to \mathbb{Z}_2^{sm}$ be the truncation map outputting the s most significant m-bit words. Let us denote the input value, output value, and the intermediate values by $x, \overline{y}$, and u, v, w, y, respectively. They are related by

$$x \xrightarrow{KS} u \xrightarrow{P} v \xrightarrow{KS} w \xrightarrow{P} y \xrightarrow{\pi} \overline{y}.$$

Each input value and intermediate value has d m-bit components. For example, $x = (x_{(0)}, \cdots, x_{(d-1)})$ with $x_{(i)} \in \mathbb{Z}_2^m$. Now let Δx and $\Delta \overline{y}$ be *fixed* input and output differences. Let h be the number of nonzero components of Δx. We may assume without loss of generality that $\Delta x_{(0)}, \cdots, \Delta x_{(h-1)} \neq 0$. Then we consider differential probability of all paths

$$\Delta x \to \Delta u \to \Delta v \to \Delta w \to \Delta y \to \Delta \overline{y}.$$

Note that we only have to take into consideration Δu's such that $\Delta u_{(h)} = \cdots = \Delta u_{(d-1)} = 0$. Note also that Δu and Δw are determined by Δv and Δy, respectively. For each Δv, we denote

$$\sum_{\Delta w : \pi D(\Delta w) = \Delta \overline{y}} \left(\prod_{i=0}^{d-1} \mathrm{DP}^S(\Delta v_{(i)} \to \Delta w_{(i)}) \right)$$

by $\sigma(\Delta v)$ and

$$\sigma(\Delta v) \prod_{i=0}^{h-1} \mathrm{DP}^S(\Delta x_{(i)} \to \Delta u_{(i)})$$

by $\Theta(\Delta v)$, respectively. For each $j_1, \cdots, j_k$ with $0 \leq j_1 < \cdots < j_k < d$, let

$$\mathsf{V}_{j_1, \cdots, j_k} := \{\Delta v : \Delta v_{(j)} = 0 \text{ iff } j = j_i \text{ for some } i \in \{1, \cdots, k\}\}.$$

Now,

$$\mathrm{DP}^{\mathrm{KSP-KSP-Tr}}(\Delta x \to \Delta \overline{y})$$
$$\leq \sum_{\Delta v} (\prod_{i=0}^{h-1} \mathrm{DP}^S(\Delta x_{(i)} \to \Delta u_{(i)}) \sigma(\Delta v))$$
$$\leq \sum_{k=0}^{d} (\sum_{1 \leq j_1 < \cdots < j_k \leq d} (\sum_{\Delta v \in \mathsf{V}_{j_1, \cdots, j_k}} \Theta(\Delta v))).$$

Note that, by Lemma 1,

$$\sum_{\Delta v \in \mathsf{V}_{j_1, \cdots, j_k}} \left(\prod_{i=0}^{h-1} \mathrm{DP}^S(\Delta x_{(i)} \to \Delta u_{(i)}) \right) \leq p^k$$

for each $j_1, \cdots, j_k$ with $0 \leq j_1 < \cdots < j_k < d$, since $\Delta v \in \mathsf{V}_{j_1, \cdots, j_k}$ forces that $h - k$ nonzero components of Δu (together with $d - h$ zero components of Δu and k zero components of Δv) determine the remaining k nonzero components of Δu.

Then, we consider $\sum_{\Delta v \in \mathsf{V}_{j_1, \cdots, j_k}} \Theta(\Delta v)$ for various k's and $(j_1, \cdots, j_k)$'s.

- If $k \geq h$, then $\sigma(\Delta v) = \Theta(\Delta v) = 0$ for any Δv having at least k zero components.
- If $k \leq d - s$, then for any Δv having k zero components, $\sigma(\Delta v) \leq p^s$, since the corresponding k zero components of Δw, together with the fixed s components of Δy and any $d - s - k$ nonzero components of Δw determine the remaining s components of Δw.
- If $d - s < k < h$, then the number of tuples $(j_1, \cdots, j_k)$ such that $0 \leq j_1 < \cdots < j_k < d$ and $\sum_{\Delta v \in V_{j_1, \cdots, j_k}} \sigma(\Delta v) \neq 0$ is bounded by $M[d, s, k]$: If $\sigma(\Delta v) \neq 0$ and $\sigma(\Delta v') \neq 0$ for some $\Delta v \in V_{j_1, \cdots, j_k}$ and $\Delta v' \in V_{j'_1, \cdots, j'_k}$, then for some $\Delta w \in V_{j_1, \cdots, j_k}$ and $\Delta w' \in V_{j'_1, \cdots, j'_k}$, $P(\Delta w \oplus \Delta w')$ has at least s zero components. Then $\Delta w \oplus \Delta w'$ has at most $d - s - 1$ zero components so that the set $\{j_1, \cdots, j_k\}$ and $\{j'_1, \cdots, j'_k\}$ has at most $d - s - 1$ common elements.

When $d - s < k < h$ and $\Delta v \in V_{j_1, \cdots, j_k}$, we have $\prod_{i=0}^{d-1} \mathrm{DP}^S(\Delta v_{(i)} \to \Delta w_{(i)}) \leq p^{d-k}$ for any Δw. Thus,

$$\sum_{k=0}^{d} \left(\sum_{1 \leq j_1 < \cdots < j_k \leq d} \left(\sum_{\Delta v \in V_{j_1, \cdots, j_k}} \Theta(\Delta v) \right) \right)$$
$$\leq \sum_{k=0}^{d-s} \binom{d}{k} p^{k+s} + p^d \sum_{k=d-s+1}^{h-1} M[d, s, k],$$

which completes the proof.

Lemma 2 follows considering that the row rank and column rank of a matrix are the same and that any block submatrix of an MDS matrix has maximal rank.

Lemma 2. *Let D be a $d \times d$ MDS matrix over $\mathrm{GF}(2^m)$. Let $y = D(w)$, $0 \leq s < d, 1 \leq b < m, 0 \leq j_1 < \cdots < j_s < d, 0 \leq i_1 < \cdots < i_{d-s-1} < d, 1 \leq i, j \leq d, i \notin \{i_1, \cdots, i_{d-s-1}\}$, and $j \notin \{j_1, \cdots, j_s\}$. Then for any b bit positions of w_i, there exists some $m - b$ bit positions of y_j such that the values $w_{(i_1)}, \cdots, w_{(i_{d-s-1})}, y_{(j_1)}, \cdots, y_{(j_s)}$, the b bits of $w_{(i)}$, and the $m - b$ bits of $y_{(j)}$ determine all the other bits of y and w.*

Once Lemma 2 having been proved, Theorem 2 can be proved in the same way as Theorem 1.

C   IND-CTPCA-2 Security of the 8-Round Tweakable Feistel Scheme

In [14], some tweakable Feistel schemes were shown to be secure using the results in [24]. But, we will prove Theorem 3 directly. For the proof, we analyze coefficient H for $\hat{\Psi}^3$ first and prove Lemmas 4, 5, and 6. Using the Lemmas, we will analyze $\hat{\Psi}^6$ and prove Lemma 7, which will easily lead to Theorem 3. Lemma 4 alone provides a proof of the fact that the scheme $\hat{\Psi}^3$ is secure against KTPCA up to near birthday bound. For brevity, we sometimes write $\mathcal{A}, \mathcal{B}, \mathcal{L}, \mathcal{R}, \mathcal{S}$ and $\mathcal{T}$ in places of the sequences $(A_i), (B_i), (L_i), (R_i), (S_i)$ and (T_i) consisting of q n-bit values, respectively. We also write $H_r([\mathcal{A}, \mathcal{B}; \mathcal{L}, \mathcal{R}, \mathcal{S}, \mathcal{T}])$, or shortly H_r, instead of $H_r([A_i, B_i; L_i, R_i, S_i, T_i]_{i=1, \cdots, q})$. We will use Lemma 3 repeatedly.

Lemma 3. *Let $q \leq 2^n$ be an integer and let $\sim$ be an equivalence relation on $[1..q]$. Let $E = q-$(the number of partitions determined by $\sim$). Let $(y_i)_{i=1,\cdots,q}$ and $(z_i)_{i=1,\cdots,q}$ be arbitrary sequences of n-bit values. Then the number of sequences $(x_i)_{i=1,\cdots,q}$ of n-bit values such that*

- $x_i \oplus y_i = x_j \oplus y_j$ *whenever $i \sim j$ and*
- $x_i \oplus z_i \neq x_j \oplus z_j$ *whenever $i \nsim j$*

is at least $2^{n(q-E)}(1 - \frac{q(q-1)}{2^{n+1}})$.

Proof. x_1 can be any n-bit value. Once $x_1, \cdots, x_i$ having been determined to satisfy the condition, determine x_{i+1} as follows. If $i+1 \sim j$ for some $j < i+1$, let $x_{i+1} = y_{i+1} \oplus x_j \oplus y_j$. x_{i+1} is well-defined since $i+1 \sim j_1$ and $i+1 \sim j_2$ implies that $j_1 \sim j_2$ and $x_{j_1} \oplus y_{j_1} = x_{j_2} \oplus y_{j_2}$. If $i+1 \nsim j$ for all $j < i+1$, then choose any x_{i+1} such that $x_{i+1} \notin \{x_j \oplus z_j \oplus z_{i+1} : j < i+1\}$. Thus the number the sequences is at least $2^{n(q-E)}(1 - \frac{1}{2^n})(1 - \frac{2}{2^n}) \cdots (1 - \frac{q-1}{2^n}) \geq 2^{n(q-E)}(1 - \frac{q(q-1)}{2^{n+1}})$.

C.1   3-Round Scheme

We consider the 3-round scheme $\hat{\Psi}^3$ and analyze $H_3([\mathcal{A}, \mathcal{B}; \mathcal{L}, \mathcal{R}, \mathcal{S}, \mathcal{T}])$ for most of sequences $\mathcal{A}, \mathcal{B}, \mathcal{L}, \mathcal{R}, \mathcal{S}, \mathcal{T}$ consisting of q n-bit values. Note that $H_3 \neq 0$ if and only if there exists a sequence $(P_i)_{i=1,\cdots,q}$ of n-bit values satisfying the following conditions CP1, CP2, and CP3:

1. $R_i = R_j \Rightarrow L_i \oplus P_i = L_j \oplus P_j$. (CP1)
2. $S_i \oplus B_i = S_j \oplus B_j \Rightarrow T_i \oplus P_i = T_j \oplus P_j$. (CP2)
3. $P_i \oplus A_i = P_j \oplus A_j \Rightarrow R_i \oplus S_i = R_j \oplus S_j$. (CP3)

When $H_3 \neq 0$, there exist $f_1, f_2,$ and f_3 such that $\hat{\Psi}^3(f_1, f_2, f_3)(A_i, B_i; L_i, R_i) = (S_i, T_i)$ for each i. For such $f_1, f_2,$ and f_3, let $P_i = L_i \oplus f_1(R_i)$ for each i. Then we have $S_i = R_i \oplus f_2(P_i \oplus A_i)$ and $T_i = P_i \oplus f_3(S_i \oplus B_i)$ for each i and the three conditions are satisfied. Conversely, when P_i's satisfy the three conditions, then let f_1 be any functions satisfying $P_i = L_i \oplus f_1(R_i)$ for each i. Such f_1 exists by the first condition. Similarly, there are f_2 and f_3 such that $S_i = R_i \oplus f_2(P_i \oplus A_i)$ and $T_i = P_i \oplus f_3(S_i \oplus B_i)$ for each i. Then we have $\hat{\Psi}^3(f_1, f_2, f_3)(A_i, B_i; L_i, R_i) = (S_i, T_i)$ for all i's so that $H_3 \neq 0$. So it is easily seen that $H_3 \neq 0$ implies the following conditions C1, C2, and C3 are satisfied.

- $(R_i = R_j$ and $L_i \oplus A_i = L_j \oplus A_j) \Rightarrow S_i = S_j$. (C1)
- $(R_i = R_j$ and $S_i \oplus B_i = S_j \oplus B_j) \Rightarrow L_i \oplus T_i = L_j \oplus T_j$. (C2)
- $(S_i \oplus B_i = S_j \oplus B_j$ and $T_i \oplus A_i = T_j \oplus A_j) \Rightarrow R_i \oplus B_i = R_j \oplus B_j$. (C3)

For sequences $\mathcal{A}, \mathcal{B}, \mathcal{L}, \mathcal{R}, \mathcal{S}, \mathcal{T}$ consisting of q n-bit values, we denote by E_1 the number of independent equations $R_i = R_j$. Then $q - E_1$ is the number of different values among R_i's, or the number of partitions determined by the equivalence relation $\sim$ defined on $[1..q]$ such that $i \sim j$ iff $R_i = R_j$. We also denote the numbers of independent equations $(R_i, L_i \oplus A_i) = (R_j, L_j \oplus A_j)$ and $(R_i, L_i \oplus A_i, B_i) = (R_j, L_j \oplus A_j, B_j)$ by E_2 and E_3, respectively.

Forward Direction. Let us assume throughout this subsection that the sequences $\mathcal{A}, \mathcal{B}, \mathcal{L}, \mathcal{R}$ of n-bit values are fixed and consider $H_3(\mathcal{A}, \mathcal{B}; \mathcal{L}, \mathcal{R}, \mathcal{S}, \mathcal{T})$ when $(\mathcal{S}, \mathcal{T})$ varies. The following conditions C4 and C5 are used to filter out *good* pairs of output sequences:

- $R_i \neq R_j \Rightarrow S_i \oplus B_i \neq S_j \oplus B_j$. (C4)
- $(R_i = R_j$ and $L_i \oplus A_i \neq L_j \oplus A_j) \Rightarrow S_i \oplus B_i \neq S_j \oplus B_j$. (C5)

Then we have Lemma 4.

Lemma 4. *If* $(\mathcal{A}, \mathcal{B}, \mathcal{L}, \mathcal{R}, \mathcal{S}, \mathcal{T})$ *satisfies* C1, C2, C3, C4, *and* C5, *then*

$$H_3([\mathcal{A}, \mathcal{B}; \mathcal{L}, \mathcal{R}, \mathcal{S}, \mathcal{T}]) \geq \frac{|F_n|^3}{2^{n(2q - E_2 - E_3)}} \left(1 - \frac{q(q-1)}{2^{n+1}}\right).$$

Proof. Let N_1 be the number of sequences $\mathcal{P} = (P_i)$ such that

- $R_i = R_j \Rightarrow L_i \oplus P_i = L_j \oplus P_j$. (CP1)
- $R_i \neq R_j \Rightarrow P_i \oplus A_i \neq P_j \oplus A_j$. (CP4)
- $(R_i = R_j$ and $L_i \oplus A_i \neq L_j \oplus A_j) \Rightarrow P_i \oplus A_i \neq P_j \oplus A_j$. (CP5)

CP1 and CP4 together force CP5 and $N_1 \geq 2^{n(q - E_1)}(1 - \frac{q(q-1)}{2^{n+1}})$ by Lemma 3. For each $\mathcal{P}$ satisfying the conditions, we have the following.

1. The number of f_1's satisfying $P_i = L_i \oplus f_1(R_i)$ for all i is $\frac{|F_n|}{2^{n(q-E_1)}}$: $R_i = R_j$ implies $L_i \oplus P_i = L_j \oplus P_j$ and the number of different values among R_i's is $q - E_1$.
2. The number of f_2's satisfying $S_i = R_i \oplus f_2(P_i \oplus A_i)$ for all i is $\frac{|F_n|}{2^{(q-E_2)n}}$: $P_i \oplus A_i = P_j \oplus A_j$ implies $R_i = R_j$ and $L_i \oplus A_i = L_j \oplus A_j$, and then $S_i = S_j$ by C1, which again implies $S_i \oplus R_i = S_j \oplus R_j$. The number of different values among $P_i \oplus A_i$'s is equal to the number of different values among $(R_i, L_i \oplus A_i)$'s, which is $q - E_2$.
3. The number of f_3's satisfying $T_i = P_i \oplus f_3(S_i \oplus B_i)$ for all i is $\frac{|F_n|}{2^{(q-E_3)n}}$: $S_i \oplus B_i = S_j \oplus B_j$ implies $R_i = R_j$ (C4) which implies $L_i \oplus P_i = L_j \oplus P_j$, $L_i \oplus A_i = L_j \oplus A_j$ (C5) and $L_i \oplus T_i = L_j \oplus T_j$ (C2) and then $T_i \oplus P_i = T_j \oplus P_j$. The number of different values among $S_i \oplus B_i$'s is equal to the number of different $(R_i, L_i \oplus A_i, B_i)$'s, which is $q - E_3$.

Thus we have $H_3 \geq \frac{|F_n|^3}{2^{n(2q - E_2 - E_3)}}(1 - \frac{q(q-1)}{2^{n+1}})$.

Note that the number of $(\mathcal{S}, \mathcal{T})$'s satisfying C1, C2, C3, C4, and C5 is at least $2^{n(2q - E_2 - E_3)}(1 - \frac{q(q-1)}{2^{n+1}})$. Thus Lemma 4 implies that most nonzero values of $H_3([\mathcal{A}, \mathcal{B}; \mathcal{L}, \mathcal{R}, \mathcal{S}, \mathcal{T}])$ do not deviate much from $\frac{|F_n|^3}{2^{n(2q - E_2 - E_3)}}$.

We also have Lemma 5 whose proof is not hard and omitted.

Lemma 5. *Suppose that* $(\mathcal{A}, \mathcal{B}, \mathcal{L}, \mathcal{R}, \mathcal{S}, \mathcal{T})$ *satisfies* $R_i \neq R_j$ *and* $(S_i \oplus B_i, T_i \oplus A_i) \neq (S_j \oplus B_j, T_j \oplus A_j)$ *whenever* $i \neq j$. *Then*

$$H_3([\mathcal{A}, \mathcal{B}; \mathcal{L}, \mathcal{R}, \mathcal{S}, \mathcal{T}]) \geq \frac{|F_n|^3}{2^{2nq}} \left(1 - \frac{q(q-1)}{2^{n+1}}\right).$$

Backward Direction. Let E_1', E_2' and E_3' denote the numbers of independent equations $S_i \oplus B_i = S_j \oplus B_j, (S_i \oplus B_i, T_i \oplus A_i) = (S_j \oplus B_j, T_j \oplus A_j)$ and $(S_i \oplus B_i, T_i \oplus A_i, B_i) = (S_j \oplus B_j, T_j \oplus A_j, B_j)$, respectively. Let C6 and C7 be the following conditions:

- $S_i \oplus B_i \neq S_j \oplus B_j \Rightarrow R_i \neq R_j$. (C6)
- $(S_i \oplus B_i = S_j \oplus B_j$ and $T_i \oplus A_i \neq T_j \oplus A_j) \Rightarrow R_i \neq R_j$. (C7)

Then similarly to the forward direction, we have Lemma 6.

Lemma 6. *If $(\mathcal{A}, \mathcal{B}, \mathcal{L}, \mathcal{R}, \mathcal{S}, \mathcal{T})$ satisfies C1, C2, C3, C6, and C7, then*

$$H_3([\mathcal{A}, \mathcal{B}; \mathcal{L}, \mathcal{R}, \mathcal{S}, \mathcal{T}]) \geq \frac{|F_n|^3}{2^{n(2q - E_2' - E_3')}} \left(1 - \frac{q(q-1)}{2^{n+1}} \right).$$

C.2   6-Round Scheme

In this subsection, we analyze H_6 using the results on H_3 presented in the preceding subsection. We let $\mathcal{A}, \mathcal{B}, \mathcal{L}, \mathcal{R}, \mathcal{S}, \mathcal{T}$ be sequences consisting of q n-bit values. Let $E_1, E_2, E_3, E_1', E_2',$ and E_3' be as in the case of 3-round scheme. So, for example, $q - E_1$ is the number of different values among R_i's. We consider the cases when the following holds.

- $(R_i, L_i \oplus A_i, B_i) \neq (R_j, L_j \oplus A_j, B_j)$ and $(S_i \oplus B_i, T_i \oplus A_i, B_i) \neq (S_j \oplus B_j, T_j \oplus A_j, B_j)$ whenever $i \neq j$

Note that they cover most of the cases. We will show that

Lemma 7. *In the above cases, we have*

$$H_6([\mathcal{A}, \mathcal{B}; \mathcal{L}, \mathcal{R}, \mathcal{S}, \mathcal{T}]) \geq \frac{|F_n|^6}{2^{2nq}} \left(1 - \frac{2q(q-1)}{2^n} \right).$$

Proof. Let X be the set of sequences (X_i) of n-bit values satisfying the followings.

- $(R_i = R_j$ and $L_i \oplus A_i = L_j \oplus A_j) \Rightarrow X_i = X_j$. (C1X)
- $R_i \neq R_j \Rightarrow X_i \oplus B_i \neq X_j \oplus B_j$. (C4X)
- $(R_i = R_j$ and $L_i \oplus A_i \neq L_j \oplus A_j) \Rightarrow X_i \oplus B_i \neq X_j \oplus B_j$. (C5X)

Then each $\mathcal{X} = (X_i) \in$ X also satisfies the followings.

- $R_i = R_j$ and $X_i \oplus B_i = X_j \oplus B_j$ do not hold simultaneously. (C2X)
- $X_i \oplus B_i \neq X_j \oplus B_j$ whenever $i \neq j$. (C3X)

Thus if $\mathcal{X} \in$ X, then $H_3([\mathcal{A}, \mathcal{B}; \mathcal{L}, \mathcal{R}, \mathcal{X}, \mathcal{Y}]) \geq \frac{|F_n|^3}{2^{n(2q - E_2)}} (1 - \frac{q(q-1)}{2^{n+1}})$ for any sequence $\mathcal{Y}$ of n-bit values by Lemma 4. Note that $|$X$| \geq 2^{n(q - E_2)} (1 - \frac{q(q-1)}{2^{n+1}})$. Similarly, let Y be the set of sequences $\mathcal{Y} = (Y_i)$ of n-bit values such that the followings are satisfied.

- $(S_i \oplus B_i = S_j \oplus B_j$ and $T_i \oplus A_i = T_j \oplus A_j) \Rightarrow Y_i \oplus B_i = Y_j \oplus B_j$. (C3Y)
- $S_i \oplus B_i \neq S_j \oplus B_j \Rightarrow Y_i \neq Y_j$. (C6Y)
- $(S_i \oplus B_i = S_j \oplus B_j$ and $T_i \oplus A_i \neq T_j \oplus A_j) \Rightarrow Y_i \neq Y_j$. (C7Y)

Then $|Y| \geq 2^{n(q-E_2')}(1 - \frac{q(q-1)}{2^{n+1}})$, and $H_3([\mathcal{A}, \mathcal{B}; \mathcal{X}, \mathcal{Y}, \mathcal{S}, \mathcal{T}]) \geq \frac{|F_n|^3}{2^{n(2q-E_2')}}(1 - \frac{q(q-1)}{2^{n+1}})$ for any sequence $\mathcal{X}$ of n-bit values when $\mathcal{Y} \in Y$. Now we have

$$H_6([\mathcal{A}, \mathcal{B}; \mathcal{L}, \mathcal{R}, \mathcal{S}, \mathcal{T}])$$
$$= \sum_{\mathcal{X}, \mathcal{Y}} (H_3([\mathcal{A}, \mathcal{B}; \mathcal{L}, \mathcal{R}, \mathcal{X}, \mathcal{Y}]) H_3([\mathcal{A}, \mathcal{B}; \mathcal{X}, \mathcal{Y}, \mathcal{S}, \mathcal{T}]))$$
$$\geq \sum_{\mathcal{X} \in X, \mathcal{Y} \in Y} (H_3([\mathcal{A}, \mathcal{B}; \mathcal{L}, \mathcal{R}, \mathcal{X}, \mathcal{Y}]) H_3([\mathcal{A}, \mathcal{B}; \mathcal{X}, \mathcal{Y}, \mathcal{S}, \mathcal{T}]))$$
$$\geq \frac{|F_n|^6}{2^{2nq}}(1 - \frac{2q(q-1)}{2^n}),$$

which was to be shown.

C.3 8-Round Scheme

In this subsection, we consider the 8-round scheme $\overline{\Psi}^8$ obtained by adding rounds before and after $\hat{\Psi}^6$, and prove Theorem 3. Let $\mathcal{A}, \mathcal{B}, \mathcal{L}, \mathcal{R}, \mathcal{S}, \mathcal{T}$ be sequences consisting of q n-bit values. Let X be the set of sequences (X_i) satisfying the followings:

- $R_i \oplus B_i = R_j \oplus B_j \Rightarrow L_i \oplus X_i = L_j \oplus X_j$.
- $R_i \oplus B_i \neq R_j \oplus B_j \Rightarrow X_i \neq X_j$.

Then for any $(X_i) \in X, (X_i, R_i \oplus A_i, B_i) \neq (X_j, R_j \oplus A_j, B_j)$ whenever $i \neq j$, since, we would have $(A_i, B_i, L_i, R_i) = (A_j, B_j, L_j, R_j)$ for some $i \neq j$, otherwise. Let Y be the set of sequences $\mathcal{Y} = (Y_i)$ satisfying the followings:

- $S_i = S_j \Rightarrow Y_i \oplus T_i = Y_j \oplus T_j$.
- $S_i \neq S_j \Rightarrow Y_i \oplus B_i \neq Y_j \oplus B_j$.

Then for any $(Y_i) \in Y, (Y_i \oplus B_i, S_i \oplus A_i, B_i) \neq (Y_j \oplus B_j, S_j \oplus A_j, B_j)$ whenever $i \neq j$. Let E_1'' and E_1''' be the numbers of independent equations $R_i \oplus B_i = R_j \oplus B_j$ and $S_i = S_j$, respectively. Then $|X| \geq 2^{n(q-E_1'')}(1 - \frac{q(q-1)}{2^{n+1}})$ and $|Y| \geq 2^{n(q-E_1''')}(1 - \frac{q(q-1)}{2^{n+1}})$. Note that for each $\mathcal{X} \in X$, the number of $f_1 \in F_n$ such that $f_1(R_i \oplus B_i) = L_i \oplus X_i$ for all i is $\frac{|F_n|}{2^{n(q-E1'')}}$ and for each $\mathcal{Y} \in Y$, the number of $f_8 \in F_n$ such that $f_8(S_i) = Y_i \oplus B_i$ for all i is $\frac{|F_n|}{2^{n(q-E1''')}}$. Now, by Lemma 7, we have

$$\overline{H}_8([\mathcal{A}, \mathcal{B}; \mathcal{L}, \mathcal{R}, \mathcal{S}, \mathcal{T}])$$
$$\geq \sum_{\mathcal{X} \in X, \mathcal{Y} \in Y} (\frac{|F_n|}{2^{n(q-E1'')}} \frac{|F_n|}{2^{n(q-E1''')}} H_6([\mathcal{A}, \mathcal{B}; \mathcal{R}, \mathcal{X}, \mathcal{Y}, \mathcal{S}]))$$
$$\geq \frac{|F_n|^8}{2^{2nq}}(1 - \frac{3q(q-1)}{2^n}).$$

Table 6. S-box

	0	1	2	3	4	5	6	7	8	9	a	b	c	d	e	f
00	62	31	70	8e	bc	30	9c	78	e0	5c	ce	bb	42	ac	b8	df
10	29	e7	86	5f	ee	ba	3f	87	c0	36	c3	14	7c	ec	73	da
20	57	72	f6	77	98	3b	c5	c4	4c	52	81	20	15	97	26	fc
30	8b	3c	af	6e	c8	7e	f0	40	24	a1	b1	54	ff	ad	51	bd
40	c1	13	41	b5	6b	94	63	d6	de	6f	89	d2	a9	d4	17	38
50	a5	f2	e3	db	47	66	ed	cb	4e	d5	05	60	8c	06	92	a3
60	be	68	56	a7	80	32	fa	6c	8f	88	d9	50	0a	21	3d	75
70	71	01	e5	7a	c6	b9	82	64	d1	00	7d	2b	a0	1a	5e	f5
80	35	90	2f	2a	83	49	5a	a8	d8	8d	46	96	dc	b0	c9	dd
90	cd	65	44	c7	43	67	55	eb	e1	9d	34	74	b3	4a	ca	d7
a0	79	bf	f7	99	6a	2d	ef	85	e2	5d	fe	11	0f	19	cc	e4
b0	58	09	8a	1b	6d	91	9f	4b	61	2c	2e	cf	27	10	18	b7
c0	1d	0c	9b	39	7f	d3	84	a4	f9	76	33	f4	f3	d0	07	0e
d0	22	1f	fd	25	12	08	1e	4d	b6	b4	53	37	e8	b2	9e	93
e0	02	e9	f1	3a	0b	fb	45	69	ea	f8	c2	1c	04	59	03	48
f0	16	a2	4f	3e	9a	23	aa	ae	5b	e6	95	ab	7b	0d	28	a6

D   S-box Table, Matrix, and Round Constants

The 8-bit S-box used in our TBCs is specified in Table 6. It is defined by an affine transformation following the inversion over the field $\mathrm{GF}(2^8)$ represented by the irreducible polynomial $x^8 + x^4 + x^3 + x^2 + 1$ over $\mathrm{GF}(2)$. The MDS matrix $\mathcal{M}$ is defined by

$$
\mathcal{M} = \begin{pmatrix}
28 & 1a & 7b & 78 & c3 & d0 & 42 & 40 \\
1a & 7b & 78 & c3 & d0 & 42 & 40 & 28 \\
7b & 78 & c3 & d0 & 42 & 40 & 28 & 1a \\
78 & c3 & d0 & 42 & 40 & 28 & 1a & 7b \\
c3 & d0 & 42 & 40 & 28 & 1a & 7b & 78 \\
d0 & 42 & 40 & 28 & 1a & 7b & 78 & c3 \\
42 & 40 & 28 & 1a & 7b & 78 & c3 & d0 \\
40 & 28 & 1a & 7b & 78 & c3 & d0 & 42
\end{pmatrix}
$$

over $\mathrm{GF}(2^8)$ represented by the irreducible polynomial $x^8 + x^6 + x^5 + x^4 + 1$. Table 7 shows the round constants. They are obtained from the fractional parts of $|\cos(k/8) + \sin(k/8)|/\sqrt{2}$ and $\log(k/64)$ with first 64 bits discarded for each key bit-length k, respectively. All the values are represented in hexadecimal forms.

Table 7. Round constants

Type	i	$|K| = 128$	$|K| = 192$	$|K| = 256$
1	1	71366fbd8eef2e7d	d2f928b5c6c08b51	8f1c67da8e609269
	2	9063ff208a85d13f	4cbe190cdcc2962c	9b705f1835e0cddc
	3	fdb54b3c9a86cb08	d0a2a85f772c8a07	6bf524a08a50a621
	4	f2ea772be55e4de0	e3fb1d49f5932802	6b3c821900adab39
	5	7c8814f95b9f8d0b	047117eee8007dfe	1f0eb84f4de6881c
	6	eb21fbffccbb8df5	4390e40073a64c7d	887fba6319cbf504
	7		ee9fab45168ddadc	51547790dd0b8145
	8			ad7c1f118ca88090
2	1	c9e3b39803f2f6af	a4198d55053b7cb5	93c7673007e5ed5e
	2	40f343267298b62d	be1442d9b7e08df0	81e6864ce5316c5b
	3	8a0d175b8baafa2b	3d97eeea5149358c	141a2eb71755f457
	4	e7b876206debac98	aa9782d20cc69850	cf70ec40dbd75930
	5	559552fb4afa1b10	5071f733039a8ed5	ab2aa5f695f43621
	6	ed2eae35c1382144	625c15071ea7bca1	da5d5c6b82704288
	7	27573b291169b825	cf37d8f11024c664	4eae765222d3704a
	8	3e96ca16224ae8c5	86d094e21e74d0a5	7d2d942c4495d18a
	9	1acbda11317c387e	47df6e91fc91754b	3597b42262f870fd
	10		1f0b2f23b88200e7	73d53787626cc076
	11		29816e82b43e6464	4adf41d8ecafee96
	12			e59d0f633aca9195

References

1. Aoki, K., Ichikawa, T., Kanda, M., Matsui, M., Moriai, S., Nakajima, J., Tokita, T.: *Camellia*: a 128-bit block cipher suitable for multiple platforms - design and analysis. In: Stinson, D.R., Tavares, S. (eds.) SAC 2000. LNCS, vol. 2012, pp. 39–56. Springer, Heidelberg (2001)
2. Bellare, M., Ristenpart, T., Rogaway, P., Stegers, T.: Format-preserving encryption. In: Jacobson Jr., M.J., Rijmen, V., Safavi-Naini, R. (eds.) SAC 2009. LNCS, vol. 5867, pp. 295–312. Springer, Heidelberg (2009)
3. Bellare, M., Rogaway, P., Spies, T.: The ffx mode of operation for format-preserving encryption (draft 1.1). NIST submission (2010)
4. Biham, E., Biryukov, A., Shamir, A.: Cryptanalysis of skipjack reduced to 31 rounds using impossible differentials. J. Cryptol. **18**(4), 291–311 (2005)
5. Biham, E., Dunkelman, O., Keller, N.: The rectangle attack - rectangling the serpent. In: Pfitzmann, B. (ed.) EUROCRYPT 2001. LNCS, vol. 2045, pp. 340–357. Springer, Heidelberg (2001)
6. Biham, E., Shamir, A.: Differential Cryptanalysis of the Data Encryption Standard. Springer, Heidelberg (1993)
7. Black, J., Rogaway, P.: Ciphers with arbitrary finite domains. In: Preneel, B. (ed.) CT-RSA 2002. LNCS, vol. 2271, pp. 114–130. Springer, Heidelberg (2002)

8. Bogdanov, A., Khovratovich, D., Rechberger, C.: Biclique cryptanalysis of the full AES. In: Lee, D.H., Wang, X. (eds.) ASIACRYPT 2011. LNCS, vol. 7073, pp. 344–371. Springer, Heidelberg (2011)

9. Bogdanov, A., Rijmen, V.: Linear hulls with correlation zero and linear cryptanalysis of block ciphers. Des. Codes Cryptography **70**(3), 369–383 (2014)

10. Crowley, P.: Mercy: A fast large block cipher for disk sector encryption. In: Schneier [28], pp. 49–63

11. Daemen, J., Rijmen, V.: Rijndael for aes. In: AES Candidate Conference, pp. 343–348 (2000)

12. Dworkin, M.: Recommendation for block cipher modes of operation: methods for formatpreserving encryption. NIST Special Publication 800–38G Draft (2013)

13. Ferguson, N., Lucks, S., Schneier, B., Whiting, D., Bellare, M., Kohno, T., Callas, J., Walker, J.: The skein hash function family (2009)

14. Goldenberg, D., Hohenberger, S., Liskov, M., Schwartz, E.C., Seyalioglu, H.: On tweaking luby-rackoff blockciphers. In: Kurosawa, K. (ed.) ASIACRYPT 2007. LNCS, vol. 4833, pp. 342–356. Springer, Heidelberg (2007)

15. Helleseth, T. (ed.): EUROCRYPT 1993. LNCS, vol. 765. Springer, Heidelberg (1994)

16. Hoang, V.T., Morris, B., Rogaway, P.: An enciphering scheme based on a card shuffle. In: Safavi-Naini, R., Canetti, R. (eds.) CRYPTO 2012. LNCS, vol. 7417, pp. 1–13. Springer, Heidelberg (2012)

17. Hong, S., Lee, S., Lim, J., Sung, J., Cheon, D.H., Cho, I.: Provable security against differential and linear cryptanalysis for the spn structure. In: Schneier [28], pp. 273–283

18. Knudsen, L.R.: Truncated and higher order differentials. In: Preneel, B. (ed.) FSE 1994. LNCS, vol. 1008, pp. 196–211. Springer, Heidelberg (1995)

19. Knudsen, L.R., Wagner, D.: Integral cryptanalysis. In: Daemen, J., Rijmen, V. (eds.) FSE 2002. LNCS, vol. 2365, pp. 112–127. Springer, Heidelberg (2002)

20. Li, J., Jia, C., Liu, Z., Dong, Z.: Cycle-walking revisited: consistency, security, and efficiency. Secu. Commun. Netw. **6**(8), 985–992 (2013)

21. Liskov, M., Rivest, R.L., Wagner, D.: Tweakable block ciphers. J. Cryptol. **24**(3), 588–613 (2011)

22. Morris, B., Rogaway, P.: Sometime-recurse shuffle. In: Nguyen, P.Q., Oswald, E. (eds.) EUROCRYPT 2014. LNCS, vol. 8441, pp. 311–326. Springer, Heidelberg (2014)

23. Morris, B., Rogaway, P., Stegers, T.: How to encipher messages on a small domain. In: Halevi, S. (ed.) CRYPTO 2009. LNCS, vol. 5677, pp. 286–302. Springer, Heidelberg (2009)

24. Patarin, J.: Luby-rackoff: 7 rounds are enough for $2^{n(1-epsilon)}$ security. In: Boneh, D. (ed.) CRYPTO 2003. LNCS, vol. 2729, pp. 513–529. Springer, Heidelberg (2003)

25. Patarin, J.: Security of random feistel schemes with 5 or more rounds. In: Franklin, M. (ed.) CRYPTO 2004. LNCS, vol. 3152, pp. 106–122. Springer, Heidelberg (2004)

26. Patarin, J.: The "Coefficients H" technique. In: Avanzi, R.M., Keliher, L., Sica, F. (eds.) SAC 2008. LNCS, vol. 5381, pp. 328–345. Springer, Heidelberg (2009)

27. Ristenpart, T., Yilek, S.: The mix-and-cut shuffle: small-domain encryption secure against N queries. In: Canetti, R., Garay, J.A. (eds.) CRYPTO 2013, Part I. LNCS, vol. 8042, pp. 392–409. Springer, Heidelberg (2013)

28. Schneier, B. (ed.): FSE 2000. LNCS, vol. 1978. Springer, Heidelberg (2001)

29. Schroeppel, R., Orman, H.: The hasty pudding cipher. AES candidate submitted to NIST (1998)

30. Sheets, J., Wagner, K.R.: Visa format preserving encryption (vfpe). NIST submission (2011)
31. Spies, T.: Feistel finite set encryption mode. Manuscript, posted on NIST's website (2008)
32. Vaudenay, S.: On the lai-massey scheme. In: Lam, K.-Y., Okamoto, E., Xing, C. (eds.) ASIACRYPT 1999. LNCS, vol. 1716, pp. 8–19. Springer, Heidelberg (1999)
33. Wagner, D.: The boomerang attack. In: Knudsen, L.R. (ed.) FSE 1999. LNCS, vol. 1636, pp. 156–170. Springer, Heidelberg (1999)

Bicliques with Minimal Data and Time Complexity for AES

Andrey Bogdanov[1], Donghoon Chang[2], Mohona Ghosh[2(✉)],
and Somitra Kumar Sanadhya[2]

[1] Technical University of Denmark, Copenhagen, Denmark
anbog@dtu.dk
[2] Indraprastha Institute of Information Technology (IIIT-D), Delhi, India
{donghoon,mohonag,somitra}@iiitd.ac.in

Abstract. In this paper, we re-evaluate the security-bound of full round AES against biclique attack. Under some reasonable restrictions, we exhaustively analyze the most promising class of biclique cryptanalysis as applied to AES through a computer-assisted search and find optimal attacks towards lowest computational and data complexities:

- Among the attacks with the minimal data complexity of the unicity distance, the ones with computational complexity $2^{126.67}$ (for AES-128), $2^{190.9}$ (for AES-192) and 2^{255} (for AES-256) are the fastest. Each attack just requires 2 (for AES-128 and AES-192) or 3 (for AES-256) known plaintexts for success probability 1. We obtain these results using the improved biclique attack proposed in Crypto'13.
- Among the attacks with data complexity less than the full codebook, for AES-128, the ones of computational complexity $2^{126.16}$ are fastest. Within these, the one with data complexity 2^{64} requires the smallest amount of data. Thus, the original attack (with data complexity 2^{88}) did not have the optimal data complexity for AES-128. Similar findings are observed for AES-192 as well (data complexity 2^{48} as against 2^{80} in the original attack). For AES-256, we find an attack that has a lower computational complexity of $2^{254.31}$ as compared to the original attack complexity of $2^{254.42}$.
- Among all the attacks covered, the ones of computational complexity $2^{125.56}$ (for AES-128), $2^{189.51}$ (for AES-192) and $2^{253.87}$ (for AES-256) are fastest, though requiring the full codebook. This can be considered as an indication of the limitations of the independent biclique attack approach as applied to AES.

Keywords: Block ciphers · Biclique cryptanalysis · Meet-in-the-middle · Key recovery · Stars · AES-128 · Minimum data complexity

1 Introduction

Today, the most frequently used block cipher is AES (Advanced Encryption Standard) [10] — the current U.S. encryption standard selected by NIST in an

© Springer International Publishing Switzerland 2015
J. Lee and J. Kim (Eds.): ICISC 2014, LNCS 8949, pp. 160–174, 2015.
DOI: 10.1007/978-3-319-15943-0_10

open competition. AES is the only publicly known cipher that is NSA-approved for protecting secret and top secret government information in the U.S. Recently, the theoretical security of AES has been challenged by biclique cryptanalysis [5]. Biclique key recovery attack may be considered as an advancement in the field of symmetric-key cryptography but it has been prepared by a considerable number of works in the area of meet-in-the-middle (MITM) attacks on block ciphers [6,7,9,12] and hash function cryptanalysis [2,3,11] including the introduction of initial structures [15] and bicliques for preimage search in hash functions [14]. The work [5] scrutinizes the notion of initial structures for block ciphers, formalizes it to *bicliques* (complete bipartite graphs) which are efficient to construct and proposes key recovery attacks with computational complexities below brute force for all three variants of the full AES. The original work [5] introducing biclique key recovery leaves several questions unanswered though, which are crucial to judge the real-world security of AES and implications of the biclique cryptanalysis in general:

- *Is there much potential in minimizing the data complexity* of the biclique attacks? In fact, it is low data complexity attacks that are most relevant in practice, especially in the context of efficient implementation of the attacks – the point clearly made in [4]. Actually, the data complexity of the original biclique attack makes any practical implementation of them highly unreasonable since the standard brute force is very likely to be both cheaper and faster in reality (mainly due to the high requirements in terms of storage or oracle access).
- Though the new technique has been coined after bicliques, the initial structures are explicitly limited to balanced bicliques only, i.e.,. complete bipartite graphs in which the two set of vertices have exactly the same cardinality. Canteaut et al. in [8] first suggested construction of unbalanced bicliques where one set of vertices only contain a single element. We call such bicliques - *stars*. Can one take any advantage of using such *unbalanced bicliques* (or stars) as initial structures in AES?
- Finally, no comprehensive investigation of *attack optimality* in terms of computational complexity, data complexity or both has been performed. So it is still not clear if there are *faster biclique attacks*, even in the same class of the attacks as proposed in [5].

In this paper, we aim to bridge these gaps and answer all three questions in the positive for all the variants of AES namely – AES-128, AES-192 and AES-256. In [8], Canteaut et al. also proposed *sieve-in-the-middle* technique which when combined with the biclique method, further reduces the computational complexities. We examine the combination of sieve-in-the middle process alongwith biclique attack procedure in our work and report the new reduced complexities so found.

1.1   Our Contributions

The contributions of this paper are as follows:

- In terms of the attack space exploration for biclique cryptanalysis, we limit ourselves to the most promising class of attacks as applied to AES: Namely, we enumerate all truncated independent balanced bicliques and stars whose key modification trails have upto three active bytes in some state of the expanded key. For the sake of conciseness, we will refer to this class of attacks as based on *tight truncated independent bicliques and stars* (see Sect. 5). This approach to key recovery has resulted in the fastest attack on the full AES-128,192 and 256 so far.

- Using stars as initial structures, we report the first key recovery attack faster than brute force on AES-128, AES-192 and AES-256 with the minimal theoretically possible data complexity.

- Next, we exhaustively enumerate all attacks based on tight truncated independent bicliques and stars for all AES variants which have a data complexity lower than the full codebook. It turns out that for AES-128, the ones of computational complexity $2^{126.16}$ are fastest. Interestingly, this exactly corresponds to the original key recovery on AES-128 [5]. We further investigate the data complexity of these attacks for the biclique dimension $d = 8$ and show that the minimum data complexity is 2^{64} (cf. 2^{88} in the original attack). This implies that the original attack did not have the optimal data complexity. We find similar results for AES-192. The fastest attacks have a computational complexity of $2^{190.16}$ with data complexity being 2^{48} (cf. 2^{80} in the original attack). Interestingly, for AES-256 we find that the fastest attacks under this category have a computational complexity of $2^{254.31}$. This turns out to be lower than $2^{254.42}$ reported in the original attack in [5].

- To investigate the limits of this class of biclique cryptanalysis, we abandon all restrictions on the data complexity and search for the fastest attacks on AES in this class. We find that the ones with computational complexity of $2^{125.56}, 2^{189.51}$ and $2^{253.87}$ for AES-128, AES-192 and AES-256 respectively are the fastest (though requiring the full code book). An interesting outcome of these constructions is that they utilize the longest biclique covered in the full AES attack so far. For AES-128, the longest biclique has length of 3 rounds whereas for AES-192 and AES-256 the longest bicliques cover 5 rounds each.

Using sieve-in-the-middle technique, the above computational complexities can be reduced further. This extension is discussed in Sect. 8. The cryptanalytic results of the paper combined with and without sieve-in-the-middle (SIM) technique are summarized in Table 1.

2   Biclique Key Recovery for AES

Biclique cryptanalysis for ciphers was proposed by [5] in two different paradigms: independent-biclique and long-biclique approaches. It is the independent-biclique technique that has resulted in key recovery for full AES and is the focus of our work.

Table 1. Key recovery with bicliques for full AES. All attacks have success probability 1.

Algorithm	Data	Computations without SIM	Computations with SIM	Biclique length (rounds)	Property shown	Ref
AES-128	2^{88} CC	$2^{126.16}$	-	2.5	-	[5]
	2^4 CP	$2^{126.89}$	-	2	-	[4]
	2^{88} CC	-	$2^{125.69a}$	2.5	-	[8]
AES-128	Unic. dist: 2 KP	$2^{126.67}$	$2^{126.59}$	1	fastest with min. data	Section 4
	2^{64} CC	$2^{126.16}$	$2^{125.98}$	2.5	fastest with $< 2^{128}$ data	Section 6
	2^{128}	$2^{125.56}$	$2^{125.35}$	3	fastest	Section 7
AES-192	2^{80} CC	$2^{190.16}$	-	3.5	-	[5][1]
	2^{48} CC	$2^{190.28}$	-	3.5	-	[1]
AES-192	Unic. dist: 2 KP	$2^{190.9}$	$2^{190.83}$	1.5	fastest with min. data	Section 4
	2^{48} CC	$2^{190.16}$	$2^{190.05}$	3.5	fastest with $< 2^{128}$ data	Section 6
	2^{128}	$2^{189.51}$	$2^{189.31}$	5	fastest	Section 7
AES-256	2^{40} CC	$2^{254.42b}$	-	3.5	-	[5]
	2^{64} CC	$2^{254.53}$	-	3.5	-	[1]
AES-256	Unic. dist: 3 KP	2^{255}	$2^{254.94}$	1.5	fastest with min. data	Section 4
	2^{64} CC	$2^{254.31}$	$2^{254.24}$	3.5	fastest with $< 2^{128}$ data	Section 6
	2^{128}	$2^{253.87}$	$2^{253.82}$	5	fastest	Section 7

[a] Our analysis estimates the cost as $2^{125.98}$.
[b] Our analysis estimates the cost as $2^{254.52}$.

2.1   Description of AES

AES is a block cipher which adopts the classical substitution-permutation network structure. The AES specification defines 3 key sizes - 128 bit, 192 bit and 256 bit with block size limited to a fixed 128 bit size for all the three variants. The number of rounds per full encryption for AES-128, AES-192 and AES-256 are 10, 12 and 14 respectively. Each round consists of 4 steps: SubBytes, ShiftRows, MixColumns and AddRoundKey. AES operates on a state array of 4×4 byte matrix and key array of 4×4, 4×6 and 4×8 byte size respectively. For further information on AES, please refer to [10]. To avoid confusion and facilitate comparison, we follow the same notation as adopted in [5]. Briefly, in a differential path, terms #1, #2 represent the state before SubBytes and after MixColumns for Round 1, terms #3, #4 represent the state before SubBytes and after MixColumns for Round 2 and so on. The 128-bit subkeys are denoted as $0, $1, $2 .... and so on. Bytes are addressed column-wise (0–3#first column), (4–7#second column), (8–11#third column) and (12–15#fourth column). The ith byte in state A is represented as A_i.

2.2 Balanced Bicliques

Biclique attack is a kind of divide-and-conquer approach. To find the unknown secret key, all possible keys are partitioned into a set of groups. Each group of keys has the structure of a *biclique* – a complete bipartite graph. In the standard implementation of independent-biclique cryptanalysis, the biclique consists of two sets S_x and S_y of intermediate cipher states (two disjoint sets of vertices of the biclique), where each set of states has $|S_x| = |S_y| = 2^d$ elements and a set of keys having $|\mathcal{K}| = 2^{2d}$ keys which map each element in one set of states to each element in the other one (edges of the biclique) as shown in Fig. 1. To fix the notation, we denote $S_x = \{x_j\}, S_y = \{y_i\}$, and $\mathcal{K} = \{K[i,j]\}$ with $i, j \in \{0, 2^d - 1\}$. d is called the biclique *dimension*.

Consider two families of related-key differentials over the rounds covered by biclique (from values x_j to y_i): (1) $2^d - 1$ distinct $\Delta - differentials$: $(0, \Delta_i^K) \longmapsto \Delta_i$ with input state difference 0, input key difference Δ_i^K and output state difference Δ_i as well as (2) $2^d - 1$ distinct $\nabla - differentials$: $(\nabla_j, \nabla_j^K) \longmapsto 0$ with input state difference ∇_j, input key difference ∇_j^K and output state difference 0. Now we assume that the Δ- and ∇-differentials do not share any active nonlinear components (S-boxes in the case for AES). Then, it has been shown in [5] that if input x_0, output y_0 and key $K[0,0]$ conforms to both Δ- and ∇-differentials, then the values:

$$x_j = x_0 \oplus \nabla_j,$$
$$y_i = y_0 \oplus \Delta_i,$$
$$K[i,j] = K[0,0] \oplus \nabla_j^K \oplus \Delta_i^K$$

form a balanced biclique of dimension d, with $\Delta_0 = \nabla_0 = \Delta_0^K = \nabla_0^K = 0$. The computation over the biclique rounds from input x_0 to output y_0 with key $K[0,0]$ is called the *base computation*. $K[0,0]$ is called the *base key*.

2.3 Key Recovery

In [5], a meet-in-the-middle key recovery with partial matching (in one intermediate state byte) and splice-and-cut technique (going over the decryption oracle from the generated ciphertexts to the corresponding plaintexts) is applied. The entire space of 2^n keys (where n is the AES key size in bits) is divided into 2^{n-2d} non-overlapping groups (bicliques) of 2^{2d} keys each. In each biclique, the base key is fixed. For each combination of x_j and y_i (corresponding to $K[i,j]$), it is tested if there is a match. For each biclique, the computational cost consists of the complexity $C_{biclique}$ of constructing the biclique, the complexity $C_{precomp}$ of preparing Δ- and ∇-propagations (including preparing the biclique), the complexity C_{recomp} of recomputing states for each key $K[i,j]$, and the complexity $C_{falsepos}$ of checking the key candidates surviving the partial matching:

$$C_{full} = 2^{n-2d}(C_{biclique} + C_{precomp} + C_{recomp} + C_{falsepos}).$$

The computational complexity is dominated by C_{recomp}. The data complexity is determined by the number of state differences Δ_i in all key groups, since the ciphertext of the base computation remains the same in all key groups.

3   Stars

In [8], Canteaut et al. proposed biclique attack where data complexity can be reduced to a single plaintext-ciphertext pair. They suggested construction of bicliques with just one state in one vertex set and 2^{2d} states in the other one: $S_x = \{x\}, S_y = \{y_{i,j}\}, i, j \in \{0, 2^d - 1\}$, where each $y_{i,j}$ is obtained by encrypting x with key $K[i, j]$, covering 2^{2d} keys. We call such unbalanced bicliques which are trees with one node and many leaves as – a *star* of dimension d (as shown in Fig. 2). However, in [8], no application of their improved biclique attack with low data complexity is demonstrated on AES. As such, our work can be considered to be the first attempt towards this direction on all the variants of AES.

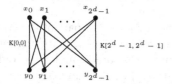
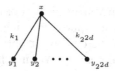

Fig. 1. Balanced biclique of dimension d

Fig. 2. Star: maximally unbalanced biclique of dimension d for the minimum data complexity

If we place the star at the beginning of the cipher, and let x be the *plaintext* (or ciphertext) - the data complexity of the MITM part of the key recovery will be exactly 1. Note that x can be any value and, thus, we deal with a known-plaintext key recovery here. The overall data complexity is solely defined by the unicity distance of the cipher and, therefore, minimal theoretically attainable.

3.1   Stars from Independent Differentials

Similar to balanced bicliques, stars can be constructed efficiently from independent sets of differentials. Unlike balanced bicliques, however, the necessary form of differentials is different. Suppose we have a set of $2^d - 1$ distinct related-key Δ-differentials from x to $y_{i,j}$: $(0, \Delta_i^K) \longmapsto \Delta_i$ and a set of $2^d - 1$ distinct related-key ∇-differentials from over the same part of the cipher: $(0, \nabla_j^K) \longmapsto \nabla_j$.

We assume that the Δ-differentials and ∇-differentials do not share any active nonlinear components. If input x, output $y_{0,0}$ and key $K[0,0]$ conform to both Δ- and ∇-differentials, then the values

$$x,$$
$$y_{i,j} = y_{0,0} \oplus \Delta_i \oplus \nabla_j, \text{ and}$$
$$K[i,j] = K[0,0] \oplus \Delta_i^K \oplus \nabla_j^K$$

form a star of dimension d, with $\Delta_0 = \nabla_0 = \Delta_0^K = \nabla_0^K = 0$.

4   Minimum Data Complexity Key Recovery for AES

In this section, we apply this concept to demonstrate star-based independent-biclique key recoveries for the full AES-128, AES-192 and AES-256.

AES-128. In AES-128, it is possible to construct a star of dimension 8 over the first round. The master key $0, i.e., the first subkey is taken as the base key. The index i is placed in byte 0 whereas index j is placed in byte 1. The base keys are all 16-byte values with two bytes (i.e., bytes 0 and 1) fixed to 0 whereas the remaining 14-bytes take all possible values. Thus, the 128-bit key space is divided into 2^{112} groups with 2^{16} keys in each group. Δ-trail activates byte 0 of key $0 and ∇-trail activates byte 1 of key $0 (shown in Fig. 3(a)). Difference propagation in these differentials over one round is non-overlapping till the end of round 1. In state #3, there is a linear overlap between those and, already in round 2, one has to recompute 2 S-boxes for each key (shown in Fig. 3(a)). Rather surprisingly, even if the length of the star is just one round, the form of its trails is such that this short biclique still allows the adversary to obtain a reasonable computational advantage over brute force.

In the forward direction of matching, starting in round 2, a part of the state has to be recomputed for each key. In the backward direction of matching, one starts with the ciphertext obtained using the encryption oracle under the right key for plaintext x. We match on byte 12 in state #11 of round 5, in which only one S-box needs recomputation. In round 4 and round 6, only 4 S-boxes, respectively, are recomputed. The Δ- and ∇-propagations in the key schedule are such that only 5 bytes of the $10 depend on both Δ and ∇. This means that only 5 S-boxes have to be recomputed in round 10. The S-boxes in the four remaining rounds need to be recomputed completely (another 64 S-boxes). No S-box recomputations are needed in the key schedule.

The whole process yields a recomputation of 80 out of 200 S-boxes (as shown in Fig. 3(b), (c)). Thus, $C_{recomp} \approx 2^{14.67}$ in one key group. About 2^8 keys will be suggested in each key group after the meet-in-the-middle filtering, thus $C_{falsepos} = 2^8$. The complexity of precomputations and star generation is upper-bounded by $C_{precomput} \approx 2^{8.5}$ full AES computations. Thus, $C_{full} \approx 2^{126.67}$. The data complexity exactly corresponds to the unicity distance of AES-128 – the minimal data complexity theoretically attainable. One known plaintext-ciphertext pair can sometimes be enough (with success probability of $1/e \approx 0.3679$). Two known plaintext-ciphertext pairs yield a success probability of practically 1. The memory complexity is upper bounded by 2^8 computations of sub-cipher involved in the precomputation stage [5].

AES-192 and AES-256. In both the cases, we construct a star of dimension 8 over the last 1.5 rounds (the details of these attacks can be found in the full version of the paper to be uploaded on Cryptology eprint archive). The fastest star based attack on AES-192 has a computational complexity of $2^{190.9}$ with two ciphertexts-plaintext pairs being required to carry out the attack with a success probability of 1. In case of AES-256, the fastest star based attack has a computational complexity of 2^{255}. Here, two known plaintext-ciphertext pairs

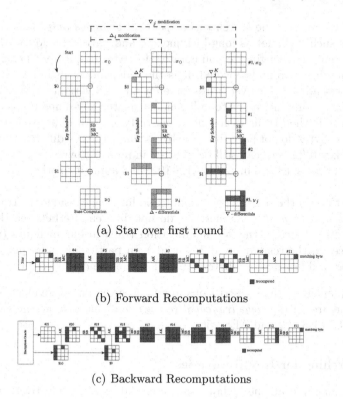

(a) Star over first round

(b) Forward Recomputations

(c) Backward Recomputations

Fig. 3. Fastest biclique attack on AES-128 with minimum data: time $2^{126.67}$ and data 1 or 2 ciphertexts

can sometimes be enough (with success probability of $1/e \approx 0.3679$) whereas three known plaintext-ciphertext pairs yield a success probability of practically 1.

5   A Search Technique for Biclique Attacks on AES

In this section, we describe how we enumerate all biclique key recoveries in a large promising class of biclique attacks.

5.1   Enumerating Bicliques

Clearly, going over all possible initial structures, even without enumerating possibilities for the actual key recovery, would be infeasible for the AES. So we have to confine the search space of attacks by imposing some limitations. We now describe our search strategy along with some justifications for our choices.

– First, we consider bicliques (complete bipartite graphs) as initial structures. We stress that we include *both balanced bicliques and stars* in our search.

- Second, we restrict the search to *independent-bicliques only*. This constraint excludes such bicliques as long-bicliques [5] and narrow-bicliques [13], which are especially challenging to enumerate. However, despite not being optimal in the number of rounds covered, it is the independent-bicliques that attain the highest advantages over brute force for all AES variants so far.
- Third, we confine the search to independent related key-differentials that have a key state in their trails with exactly one or two[1] or three active bytes.[2] Note that these bytes do not have to be the bytes where the key difference is injected and the key difference can still be injected in multiple bytes. We also consider the special rules defined in [5] for AES-192[3] and apply it to other AES variants also.
- Finally, to keep the search space from exploding, we consider the trails of the bicliques in a *truncated* manner: We do not differentiate between the values of the active bytes in the key modification trails in our bicliques (values of differences in the related-key differentials). In particular, it means that once activated, a difference in a byte of a trail cannot be cancelled out.

We implemented these restrictions in a C program and were able to successfully enumerate all the *tight truncated independent balanced bicliques and stars* of AES-128, AES-192 and AES-256.

5.2   Searching for Key Recoveries

Having enumerated all the bicliques as described above exhaustively, we apply meet-in-the-middle (MITM) technique to each of the initial structures obtained to evaluate their time and data complexities. This is done as follows. First of all, we set the opimization goal as *minimizing the time complexity for a given data complexity restriction*. That is, in each search for a key recovery, we fix an upper bound on the data complexity. Then we perform the exhaustive search over all possibilities for matching. In terms of key enumeration, we impose the restriction that the forward and backward key modifications should have at least one state of linear intersection. This enables full key space coverage and success probability of 1. The time complexity is measured as the number of S-box computations that have to be performed per key tested.[4] Depending on the data complexity restriction, the program can find the optimal attack, i.e., the attack with the lowest measured time complexity under the data complexity restriction.

As a second optimization goal, we focus on *minimizing the data complexity for a given time complexity*. This second optimization is applied once the lowest

---

[1] Such trails do not collapse into a single active byte in any of the key states.

[2] Such trails do not collapse into a single active byte or two active bytes in any of the key states.

[3] Here we consider double (i_1, i_2) as well as triple (i_1, i_2, i_3) difference injection in i trail such that all possible (i_1, i_2) / (i_1, i_2, i_3) columns have one zero byte/ two zero bytes respectively, after applying $MixColumns^{-1}$.

[4] One complete evaluation of AES-128, AES-192 and AES-256 corresponds to 200, 224 and 276 S-boxes respectively.

computational complexity for recovering the key has been found in the previous step. At this point, we already know that there are no faster key recoveries in our search space. So we check if the data complexity of the fastest attack identified can be reduced. For this task, we fix the computational complexity to the value that we obtained in the previous step, and then among all the bicliques having that computational complexity, we search for the one that has the lowest data complexity. This task typically requires much less computations.

5.3 Applications to Find Attacks with Minimal Data and Time Complexities

We implemented our program to search for three data complexity restrictions:

- *Minimum data complexity:* The minimum data complexity attacks for AES-128/192/256 were discovered using this program by setting the upper bounds of the data complexity to its theoretical minimum of the unicity distance. So we can claim that this is the fastest biclique key recovery with the minimal data complexity of exactly the unicity distance in the class of bicliques covered by our program.
- *Data complexity strictly lower than the full codebook:* This restriction is a standard line that is informally drawn between interesting attacks – that require less than the full codebook of texts - and less interesting attacks – that can only work with the full codebook. It is found that the fastest biclique key recoveries in the covered class with these restrictions have lower computational complexities (for AES-256) and lower data complexities (for AES-128 and AES-192) as compared to the original attack.
- *No data complexity constraint:* The program finds the fastest biclique key recovery in the entire class of biclique attacks covered when there is no restriction on the amount of data required. This attack provides an important insight into the limits of the independent-biclique approach developed so far.

The fastest key recoveries corresponding to minimum data complexity for AES-128/192/256 are already discussed in Sect. 4. Rest of the above mentioned categories are analyzed for all AES variants and their details are covered in the subsequent sections.

6   Fastest Biclique Key Recovery with Less Than the Full Codebook of Data

AES-128. This attack is based on a balanced biclique of dimension 8 over the last 2.5 rounds of AES-128 (shown in Fig. 4(a)). The key is enumerated in \$9 which is the only key state that is linear in the key modification, both in forward and backward trails. The bytes of key enumeration with i and j differences are non-intersecting. The index i is placed in bytes 0, 4, 8 and 12 while index j is put in bytes 5 and 9. In the MITM stage, in the forward direction $5 + 16 + 4 = 25$ S-boxes and in the backward direction $1 + 4 + 16 + 8 = 29$

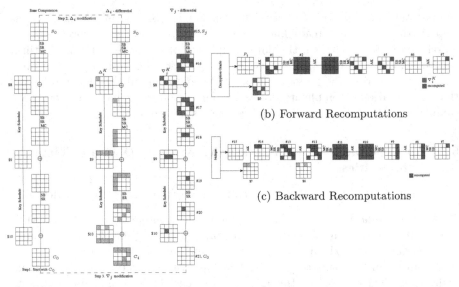

(a) Biclique over last 2.5 rounds

(b) Forward Recomputations

(c) Backward Recomputations

Fig. 4. Fastest biclique attack on AES-128 with less than full codebook: time $2^{126.16}$ and data 2^{64}. Here, v represents the matching byte.

S-boxes are recomputed (as shown in Figs. 4(b), (c) respectively). In total, also counting the necessary recomputations in the key schedule, we arrive at 55 S-boxes that have to be recomputed for each key, resulting in $C_{recomp} \approx 2^{14.14}$. As in the previous attacks, $C_{falsepos} \approx 2^8$ and $C_{precomp} \approx 2^{8.5}$. This yields $C_{full} \approx 2^{126.16}$. Furthermore, since $\Delta_i^K(\$10_3) = \Delta_i^K(\$10_{11}) = \Delta_i^K(\$10_{15})$, the ciphertext bytes C_3, C_{11} and C_{15} are always equal. Hence, the data complexity is 2^{64} chosen ciphertexts. As in all our attacks, the success probability is 1 and memory complexity is 2^8.

AES-192. For AES-192 we could construct a balanced biclique of dimension 8 over the last 3.5 rounds. A total of 62 out of 224 S-boxes are recomputed in the MITM phase (33 S-boxes in the forward direction and 29 S-boxes in the backward direction) yielding a computational complexity of $2^{190.16}$. The ciphertext bytes C_0, C_4 and C_8 are always equal. Hence, the data complexity is 2^{48} chosen ciphertexts.

AES-256. Through our automated program we detected certain discrepancies in the cost calculation in [5]. According to our calculations of the same, the computational complexity should be $2^{254.52}$ (c.f. $2^{254.42}$ in the original attack). For the fastest biclique key recovery attack under this category, we could construct a balanced biclique of dimension 8 over the last 3.5 rounds with lesser number of S-boxes that need to be recomputed. In the matching phase, forward recomputations require 13 S-boxes and backward recomputations require 73 S-boxes yielding a total 86 out of 276 S-boxes recomputations. Thus C_{full} is $\approx 2^{254.31}$. The data complexity does not exceed 2^{64} ciphertexts.

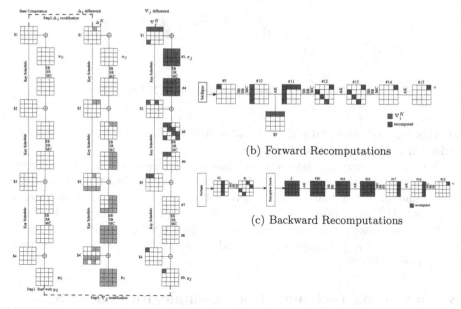

(a) Biclique over 3 rounds in the middle

(b) Forward Recomputations

(c) Backward Recomputations

Fig. 5. Fastest biclique attack on AES-128: time $2^{125.56}$ and data 2^{128}. Here v represents the matching byte.

Due to space restrictions we omit the complete details of the attacks on AES-192 and AES-256 in this version. The complete attack details can be found in the full version of the paper to be uploaded on Cryptology eprint archive.

7   Fastest Biclique Key Recovery in AES with No Restriction on Data Complexity

AES-128. When we drop the constraint of data complexity being below the full codebook, we can construct a balanced biclique of dimension $d = 8$ over 3 full AES-128 rounds and with the minimal recomputation of just one S-box in the fourth round, immediately after the biclique. The biclique is placed in rounds 2–4 which implies the data complexity of 2^{128} for the backward trail (as shown in Fig. 5(a)). In the forward recomputation, 12 S-boxes are recomputed (as shown in Fig. 5(b)) whereas in the backward direction, 25 S-boxes are recomputed (shown in Fig. 5(c)) yielding a total of 37 S-box recomputations. Thus, $C_{full} \approx 2^{125.56}$. The data complexity in this attack is the full codebook. The success probability is again 1 since key coverage is complete. The memory complexity stands at 2^8 memory blocks for precomputation stage.

AES-192 and AES-256. The fastest biclique attacks have a computational complexity of $2^{189.51}$ and $2^{253.87}$ respectively. The bicliques in this case cover 5 rounds each for AES-192 as well as AES-256. The complete attack details

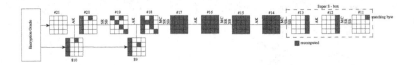

Fig. 6. Backward Recomputations in AES-128 in [5]

of AES-192 and AES-256 can be found in the full version of the paper to be uploaded in Cryptology eprint archive.

This key recovery can be converted into a preimage search for the compression function constituted by AES in Davies-Meyer mode. Here the attack works offline and does not have to make any online queries. This preimage attack requires $2^{125.56}$ operations (for AES-128), $2^{125.51}$ operations (for AES-192) and $2^{125.93}$ operations (for AES-256) and finds a preimage with a probability of about 0.632. The generic preimage search would require 2^{128} time to succeed with a probability of 0.632.

8   Improving Biclique Attack Complexities on AES Through Sieve-in-the-middle Process

Sieve-in-the-middle process (SIM), proposed in Crypto 2013 by Canteaut et al. [8], is a variant of the meet-in-the-middle technique. This technique differs from the traditional meet-in-the-middle process in the sense that it searches for the existence of valid transitions through some middle S-box instead of matching at some intermediate state. Canteaut et al. presented analysis of sieve-in-the-middle process on many block ciphers including AES-128 and showed that for AES-128 there is a diminutive decrease in the total time complexity from $2^{126.1}$ to $2^{125.69}$.[5] The application of this technique essentially involves choosing a set of intermediate states which will form a super S-box (e.g., marked in red rectangle in Fig. 6). A look-up table for that super S-box (say SS), is then constructed where all its possible input-output transitions (i.e., x, y where $y = SS(x)$) are precomputed and stored. For each $(K[i, 0], K[0, j])$ pair, where $K[i, 0]$ forms the forwards key and $K[0, j]$ forms the backwards key, input state x is calculated by forward computation and output state y is computed by backward computation. It is then checked through table lookup if a valid transition from $x \mapsto y$ exists. If not, then the corresponding key pair is discarded and another $(K[i, 0], K[0, j])$ pair is picked up for testing. The process iterates until a valid key pair is obtained. This saves the recomputation of S-boxes involved in the super S-box each time leading to a slight decrease in the overall cost complexity (e.g., 5 S-boxes in case of AES-128 as shown in Fig. 6). However, as pointed out in [8], in case of AES, this attack is faster only in those platforms where lookup in a table of size 2^{32} is faster than five S-box evaluations. The reduced complexities of the attacks for all the cases are described in Table 1.

---

[5] In [8], the attack complexity for AES-128 is mentioned as $2^{125.69}$, however we could not validate it. Our analysis estimates this complexity to be $2^{125.98}$.

9 Conclusions

In this paper, we explore the space of independent bicliques as applied to key recovery for the full AES-128, AES-192 and AES-256 under some reasonable restrictions. The class of bicliques analysed by the tool developed by us looks most promising in terms of cryptanalysis so far. We note that the structure of the biclique is more important for the data complexity of the attack whereas the length of the biclique appears to be correlated with the computational complexity. We demonstrate that our attacks might be considered as an indication of the limits beyond the current approaches to AES key recovery using bicliques.

References

1. Abed, F., Forler, C., List, E., Lucks, S., Wenzel, J.: A framework for automated independent-biclique cryptanalysis. In: Moriai, S. (ed.) FSE 2013. LNCS, vol. 8424, pp. 561–582. Springer, Heidelberg (2014)
2. Aoki, K., Sasaki, Y.: Preimage Attacks on One-Block MD4, 63-Step MD5 and More. In: Avanzi, R.M., Keliher, L., Sica, F. (eds.) SAC 2008. LNCS, vol. 5381, pp. 103–119. Springer, Heidelberg (2009)
3. Aoki, K., Sasaki, Y.: Meet-in-the-middle preimage attacks against reduced SHA-0 and SHA-1. In: Halevi, S. (ed.) CRYPTO 2009. LNCS, vol. 5677, pp. 70–89. Springer, Heidelberg (2009)
4. Bogdanov, A., Kavun, E.B., Paar, C., Rechberger, C., Yalcin, T.: Better than brute-force optimized hardware architecture for effcient biclique attacks on AES-128. In: SHARCS 2012 - Special-Purpose Hardware for Attacking Cryptographic Systems. Washington D.C., USA, March 2012
5. Bogdanov, A., Khovratovich, D., Rechberger, C.: Biclique cryptanalysis of the full AES. In: Lee, D.H., Wang, X. (eds.) ASIACRYPT 2011. LNCS, vol. 7073, pp. 344–371. Springer, Heidelberg (2011)
6. Bogdanov, A., Rechberger, C.: A 3-subset meet-in-the-middle attack: cryptanalysis of the lightweight block cipher KTANTAN. In: Biryukov, A., Gong, G., Stinson, D.R. (eds.) SAC 2010. LNCS, vol. 6544, pp. 229–240. Springer, Heidelberg (2011)
7. Bouillaguet, C., Derbez, P., Fouque, P.-A.: Automatic Search of Attacks on Round-Reduced AES and Applications. In: Rogaway, P. (ed.) CRYPTO 2011. LNCS, vol. 6841, pp. 169–187. Springer, Heidelberg (2011)
8. Canteaut, A., Naya-Plasencia, M., Vayssière, B.: Sieve-in-the-middle: improved MITM attacks (full version). Cryptology ePrint Archive, report 2013/324 (2013). http://eprint.iacr.org/2013/324
9. Chaum, D., Evertse, J.-H.: Crytanalysis of DES with a reduced number of rounds: Sequences of linear factors in block ciphers. In: Williams, H.C. (ed.) Advances in Cryptology - CRYPTO 1985. Lecture Notes in Computer Science, vol. 218, pp. 192–211. Springer, Heidelberg (1985)
10. Daemen, J., Rijmen, V.: The Design of Rijndael: AES - The Advanced Encryption Standard. Information Security and Cryptography. Springer, Heidelberg (2002)
11. Guo, J., Ling, S., Rechberger, C., Wang, H.: Advanced meet-in-the-middle preimage attacks: first results on full tiger, and improved results on MD4 and SHA-2. In: Abe, M. (ed.) ASIACRYPT 2010. LNCS, vol. 6477, pp. 56–75. Springer, Heidelberg (2010)

12. Isobe, T.: A single-key attack on the full GOST block cipher. In: Joux, A. (ed.) FSE 2011. LNCS, vol. 6733, pp. 290–305. Springer, Heidelberg (2011)
13. Khovratovich, D., Leurent, G., Rechberger, C.: Narrow-bicliques: cryptanalysis of full IDEA. In: Pointcheval, D., Johansson, T. (eds.) EUROCRYPT 2012. LNCS, vol. 7237, pp. 392–410. Springer, Heidelberg (2012)
14. Khovratovich, D., Rechberger, C., Savelieva, A.: Bicliques for preimages: attacks on Skein-512 and the SHA-2 family. Cryptology ePrint Archive, report 2011/286 (2011). http://eprint.iacr.org/2011/286
15. Sasaki, Y., Aoki, K.: Finding preimages in full MD5 faster than exhaustive search. In: Joux, A. (ed.) EUROCRYPT 2009. LNCS, vol. 5479, pp. 134–152. Springer, Heidelberg (2009)

Fault Analysis on Simon Family of Lightweight Block Ciphers

Junko Takahashi[1]($\boxtimes$) and Toshinori Fukunaga[2]

[1] NTT Secure Platform Laboratories, NTT Corporation,
3-9-11, Midori-cho, Musashino-shi, Tokyo 180-8585, Japan
takahashi.junko@lab.ntt.co.jp
[2] NTT Technology Planning Department, NTT Corporation, 1-5-1, Otemachi,
Chiyoda-ku, Tokyo 100-8116, Japan
toshi.fukunaga@hco.ntt.co.jp

Abstract. This paper proposes applying differential fault analysis (DFA) to the Simon family of lightweight block ciphers. We perform DFA by examining the characteristics of the AND operation which is a non-linear function of Simon. Then, we evaluate in detail the number of fault injections required to obtain a secret key. To the best of our knowledge, we are the first to show how to extract the entire secret key for all parameters in the Simon family using a practical fault model based on random faults. As an example, for Simon with a 128-bit block size and a 128-bit secret key, we can extract the entire secret key using 7.82 fault injections on average. The results of simulations performed on a PC show that the average number of fault injections required to retrieve a round key agrees with that based on theoretical results. We believe that this study gives new insight into the field of fault analysis because Simon has a property specific to non-linear functions in that it uses the AND operation while not using a substitution box which most block ciphers employ.

Keywords: Fault analysis · Differential fault analysis · Implementation attacks · Lightweight block ciphers · Simon

1 Introduction

Nowadays, lightweight ciphers have been proposed for use in tiny computing environments such as in an RFID devices and microchips for smart phones or vehicles. In these environments, the security of such devices is considered to be very important so that they are not hacked easily. Lightweight ciphers used in resource-constrained devices are developed to maintain a reasonable trade-off between security and performance. Among lightweight block ciphers, the Simon family has recently attracted attention because it exhibits very high performance in terms of both software and hardware compared to other block ciphers such as AES, and because it was proposed by the National Security Agency (NSA) [1]. Up to now, many researchers have published studies on Simon [2–9].

© Springer International Publishing Switzerland 2015
J. Lee and J. Kim (Eds.): ICISC 2014, LNCS 8949, pp. 175–189, 2015.
DOI: 10.1007/978-3-319-15943-0_11

Fault analysis (FA) is an attractive area in the field of cryptographic implementation attacks. This attack deduces the secret key by deliberately inducing faults into the secure device during its cryptographic computation using some fault injection techniques such as employing an optical laser beam [10] or utilizing rapid transient changes in the clock signal [11]. Boneh *et al.* [12] first proposed FA techniques and these techniques were applied to public key cryptosystems such as RSA. Later, Biham and Shamir [13] proposed differential fault analysis (DFA), which is a type of FA, on secret key cryptosystems. Up to now, DFA on block ciphers or lightweight block ciphers have also been proposed [14–17]. Since most block ciphers use a substitution box (S-box) for the non-linear function, the above studies focus on the characteristics of the input and output differences of the S-box.

In 2014, Tupsamudre *et al.* [18,19] were the first to publish DFA on the SIMON and SPECK families. They proposed a basic attack principle to retrieve a round key. In the paper, a one-bit-flip fault model is used for both SIMON and SPECK. Their results showed that the attacker must induce a 1-bit fault $(n/2)$ times for SIMON and $(n/3)$ times for SPECK to extract an n-bit round key. Furthermore, they showed an attack method for SIMON using a random one-byte fault model. The attack principle is almost the same as that for the bit-flip fault model. In this case, their results showed that $(n/8)$ fault injections are needed to extract the n-bit round key in a case where precise control over the fault position is assumed. They proposed only the first simple attempt of DFA and they did not perform a detailed analysis when n bits in the intermediate state are randomly changed by the fault injection. Furthermore, they did not specifically evaluate the number of fault injections to obtain the secret key for all SIMON families.

In this paper, we propose a new DFA on the SIMON family using a practical random fault model in which the fault injection randomly changes the bits in the intermediate state. Investigation of DFA on the SIMON family is valuable because SIMON has a property specific to a non-linear function that uses the AND operation rather than being composed of the S-box that most block ciphers employ. Furthermore, there are only a few studies on DFA techniques that use the property of the AND operation while not using the S-box. We focus on the characteristics of the AND operations and analyze the input and output differences of the operations to obtain the round key. We then examine in detail the average number of fault injections required to obtain the secret key. To the best of our knowledge, we are the first to show in detail how to extract the secret key for all parameters of the SIMON families and show the average number of the fault injections. As an example, based on SIMON with a 128-bit block size and a 128-bit secret key, we can extract the secret key using 7.82 fault injections on average. To verify the proposed attack, we perform an attack simulation on a PC. The simulation results of the average number of fault injections agree with the theoretical results. We believe that the proposed DFA techniques contribute to the study of FA on other cryptographic primitives using AND operations for non-linear functions.

The rest of the paper is organized as follows. Section 2 gives the specifications for the SIMON family. In Sect. 3, we describe the previous DFA study on SIMON.

Analysis on the non-linear function of SIMON and the attack method based on the analysis are shown in Sects. 4 and 5, respectively. In Sect. 6, we present the simulation results of the proposed attack. Finally, we conclude the paper in Sect. 7.

2   Description of SIMON

This section gives the specifications for the SIMON family [1].

SIMON employs the familiar Feistel round function. The algorithm is designed to be extremely small in terms of hardware. SIMON supports the word sizes of $n = 16, 24, 32, 48$ and 64 bits and the block size is $2n$. The key comprises mn-bit words for $m \in \{2, 3, 4\}$, which represents the number of key words and n is the word size. The key length is between 64 and 256 bits. SIMON$2n$ with an mn-bit key is referred to as SIMON$2n/mn$.

SIMON$2n$ encryption and decryption make use of three kinds of operations: bitwise AND, left circular shift on an n-bit word and bitwise XOR. Figure 1 shows the round function of the SIMON family. In the figure, L^r and R^r are the left and right halves of the state after encryption of Round r in the Feistel structure. For $K^r \in \mathrm{GF}(2)^n$, the key-dependent SIMON$2n$ round function is a 2 stage Feistel map defined by

$$L^{r+1} = R^r \oplus F(L^r) \oplus K^r, \quad R^{r+1} = L^r, \tag{1}$$

where $F(L^r) = \{(L^r \lll 1) \& (L^r \lll 8)\} \oplus (L^r \lll 2)$ ($\lll i$ is left circular shift by i bits and $\&$ is a bitwise AND), K^r is the round key and $\oplus$ is a bitwise XOR. SIMON includes no plaintext or ciphertext whitening step. The results of the last round (L^T, R^T), yield a ciphertext where T is the number of rounds, e.g., $T = 68$ in SIMON128/128 [1].

The SIMON key schedule employs a linear feedback shift register (LFSR)-like procedure to generate the total T round keys, $K^0, \cdots, K^{T-1}$. The key schedule requires 3 kinds of procedures depending on the number of the key words, $m \in \{2, 3, 4\}$. As an example, the key schedule procedure for $m = 2$ is described as $K^{r+2} = K^r \oplus (K^{r+1} \ggg 3) \oplus \{(K^{r+1} \ggg 3) \ggg 1\} \oplus c \oplus (z_2)_r$, where $\ggg i$ is right circular shift by i bits, c is a constant value $c = \texttt{0xff}\ldots\texttt{fc}$ and $(z_2)_r$ is the r-th bit of the constant sequence of z_2. At the beginning, the first 2 words, K^0 and K^1, are initialized with the secret key and the remaining round keys K^r ($r = 2, \cdots, T-1$) are generated based on the procedure using the above equation. Interested readers can refer to other cases of $m = 3$ and 4 in [1].

3   Previous Study

This section briefly describes previous DFA techniques applied to SIMON [18,19].

In the attack proposed by Tupsamudre et al. [18,19], it was assumed that the faults are injected into L^{T-2} in the penultimate round, and the attacker induces a 1-bit fault into L^{T-2} and the target bit is flipped. Then, the attacker

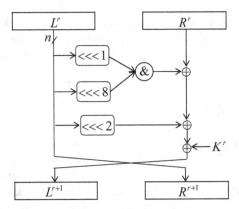

Fig. 1. Simon round function.

deduces the bits in L^{T-2} from the relationship between the two inputs and the output differences in the AND operation. As a result, a 1-bit flip results in obtaining 2 bits in L^{T-2}. Then, the attacker requires $(n/2)$ fault injections to retrieve L^{T-2}. They also showed an attack when a random one-byte fault is injected. The principle to retrieve L^{T-2} is almost the same as that for the bit-flip model. The point of difference is that, when the most and least significant bits of the induced faults are 1, the attacker cannot obtain 2 bits in L^{T-2} at a time and he can only obtain the relationship between them. In other cases, every flipped bit results in obtaining 2 bits in L^{T-2} as is the same with the bit-flip model. Then, the attacker can recover L^{T-2} and the estimated number of required faulty ciphertexts to recover L^{T-2} is $(n/8)$ in a case where precise control over the fault position is assumed. This attack cannot simply be applied to the random fault model, in which each bit in L^{T-2} is randomly flipped, using multiple fault injections. Furthermore, it is difficult to apply this attack simply to evaluate precisely the number of fault injections in the case of the random fault model because the relationships between the bits obtained through multiple fault injections are not considered.

4   Analysis of Non-linear Functions for Simon Family

This section describes our detailed analysis based on the proposed DFA. We analyze the input and output differences in the AND operation when applying random fault injections. Then, we precisely calculate the average number of fault injections to obtain a round key by examining the relationships between the bits obtained through multiple fault injections.

4.1   Characteristics of the AND operation

We focus on the input and output differences of the non-linear function in a round to retrieve the round keys. In the Simon family, the non-linear function

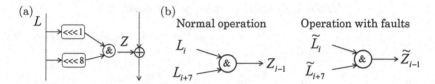

Fig. 2. (a) Operation including a non-linear function in the SIMON structure. We denote L as the input and Z as the output of the non-linear function. (b) The AND operations of the normal operation and operation with injected faults.

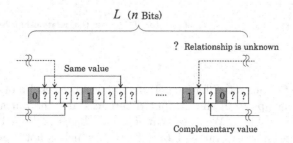

Fig. 3. An image of the obtained values or the relationship between the bits in L from Table 1. Notation "?" means that the value of each bit or the relationship is unknown and gray denotes that the value of each bit is known.

consists of the AND operation as shown in Fig. 2 (a). To obtain a round key in the r-th round, we must deduce n-bit unknown input value L of the non-linear function in the $(r-1)$-th round from the SIMON structure. Then, we consider that we obtain the value of L using the characteristics of the input and output differences of the AND operation.

To obtain the value of L, we examine the relationships among the 2-bit inputs and the 1-bit output of the non-linear function under normal operation and operation with injected faults as shown in Fig. 2(b). In the case of operation with faults, we assume that the bits in the input of the AND operation, L, are randomly changed by a fault injection and the faults are propagated into the output of the AND operation. In the figure, L_i and Z_i denote the i-th bit in L and Z where $i = 0$ denotes the most significant bit. Furthermore, $\widetilde{L}_i$ and $\widetilde{Z}_i$ are faulty values of L_i and Z_i which mean that a bit is randomly flipped with the probability of $1/2$ by the fault injection. The indexes of L and Z in the figure are defined by the left circular shift of the non-linear function. Here, we assume that we know 2 input differences $L_i \oplus \widetilde{L}_i$ and $L_{(i+7)\%n} \oplus \widetilde{L}_{(i+7)\%n}$, and the output difference $Z_{(i-1)\%n} \oplus \widetilde{Z}_{(i-1)\%n}$ where n is the size of L^1. Hereafter, we refer to $L_{(i+7)\%n}$ and $Z_{(i-1)\%n}$ as L_{i+7} and Z_{i-1}, respectively. At this time, we know a part of the value of L_i, L_{i+7} or the relationship between them when we know 2 input

---

[1] In fact, the input differences and the output difference can be known from the correct and faulty ciphertexts when we try to obtain the input of the non-linear function at the penultimate round. A detailed description is given in Sect. 5.2.

Table 1. Calculated values or relationships.

Case	Known Values			Calculated Values or Relationships			Probability
	$L_i \oplus \tilde{L}_i$	$L_{i+7} \oplus \tilde{L}_{i+7}$	$Z_{i-1} \oplus \tilde{Z}_{i-1}$	Value of L_i	Relationship	Value of L_{i+7}	
Case 1	0	0	0	?	?	?	2/8
Case 2	0	1	0	0	?	?	1/8
Case 3	0	1	1	1	?	?	1/8
Case 4	1	0	0	?	?	0	1/8
Case 5	1	0	1	?	?	1	1/8
Case 6	1	1	0	?	$L_i = \neg L_{i+7}$	?	1/8
Case 7	1	1	1	?	$L_i = L_{i+7}$	?	1/8

Notation "?" means that the value of L_i (or L_{i+7}) or the relationship between them is undetermined.

Notation "¬" means bitwise logical NOT.

differences and the output difference. Table 1 shows the results of the obtained bits, the relationships from the 2 input differences and the output difference, and the event probability. We note that if L_i (or L_{i+7}) is flipped by the fault injection, we can know the value of L_{i+7} (or L_i), which is not flipped. In other cases, if both bits L_i and L_{i+7} are flipped, we know the relationships between them. Figure 3 shows an image of the values of the bits and the relationships between the 2 bits from Table 1 when we consider all bits in L. In the figure, each bit represented in gray indicates the known value from the results of Table 1. We also use a double-headed arrow to indicate the relationship of two bits that have the same or complementary values.

4.2 Deducing the Average Number of Fault Injections

Here, we calculate the average number of fault injections, $f_{\mathrm{avg}}(n)$, to obtain n-bit L based on the results in Table 1.

Calculation of the probability that L_i is unknown due to the fault injections. To calculate $f_{\mathrm{avg}}(n)$, we focus on L_i and we calculate the probability that L_i is unknown due to the f fault injections where f is the number of fault injections ($f \geq 1$). We assume that the random faults are induced in L, that is, each bit in L is flipped with the probability of $1/2$. When f random faults are injected into L, the probability that L_i is unknown is calculated by combining the results in Table 1. We note that when $f \geq 2$, the value of the bit (or the relationship among the bits) is obtained if the value (or the relationship) is determined at least one time out of f fault injections. Table 2 shows the results of the combination of the calculated values or relationships due to the f fault injections and the event probability. In the table, the probabilities when $f = 2$ and $f = 3$ are shown as examples. We note that, when $f = 1$, the probability is the same as that in Table 1. Each probability in Table 2 is calculated from the following conditional probability.

- Case A: L_i, L_{i+7}, and the relationship between them are unknown for each fault injection. Then, the probability is $(1/4)^f$ ($= (2/8)^f$) from Table 1.

Table 2. Probability that L_i (or L_{i+7}) is known or relationship between them is known.

Case	Calculated Values or Relationship			Probability		
	L_i	Relationship	L_{i+7}	f Fault Injections	$f = 2$	$f = 3$
Case A	?	?	?	$P_A(f) = (1/4)^f$	1/16	1/64
Case B	?	?	Known	$P_B(f) = (2/4)^f \times \{1 - (1/2)^f\}$	3/16	7/64
Case C	?	Known	?	$P_C(f) = (2/4)^f \times \{1 - (1/2)^f\}$	3/16	7/64
Case D	Known	?	?	$P_D(f) = (2/4)^f \times \{1 - (1/2)^f\}$	3/16	7/64
Case E	Known	?	Known	$P_E(f) = (3/4)^f \times [1 - \{2 \times (2/3)^f - (1/3)^f\}]$	2/16	12/64
Case F	?	Known	Known	$P_F(f) = (3/4)^f \times [1 - \{2 \times (2/3)^f - (1/3)^f\}]$	2/16	12/64
Case G	Known	Known	?	$P_G(f) = (3/4)^f \times [1 - \{2 \times (2/3)^f - (1/3)^f\}]$	2/16	12/64
Case H	Known	Known	Known	$P_H(f) = 1 - (1/4)^f + 3 \times (1/2)^f - 3 \times (3/4)^f$	0/16	6/64

- Case B: Case B-I represents a case in which $(L_i, \text{Relationship}, L_{i+7})$ is (?, ?, Known) and Case B-II represents a case in which $(L_i, \text{Relationship}, L_{i+7})$ is (?, ?, ?). To satisfy Case B, either Case B-I or Case B-II occurs and Case B-I is included at least one time in the f fault injections. Then, the probability is $(2/4)^f \times \{1 - (1/2)^f\}$ where $(2/4)^f$ means that either Case B-I or Case B-II occurs and $\{1 - (1/2)^f\}$ means that Case B-I is included at least one time. In a similar calculation, the probability for Cases C and D is the same as that for Case B.

- Case E: Case E-I represents a case in which $(L_i, \text{Relationship}, L_{i+7})$ is (?, ?, ?), Case E-II represents a case in which $(L_i, \text{Relationship}, L_{i+7})$ is (Known, ?, ?), and Case E-III represents a case in which $(L_i, \text{Relationship}, L_{i+7})$ is (?, ?, Known). For the f fault injections, to satisfy Case E, either Case E-I, Case E-II or Case E-III occurs and Case E-II and Case E-III are included at least one time in the f fault injections. Then, the probability is $(3/4)^f \times [1 - \{2 \times (2/3)^f - (1/3)^f\}]$ where $(3/4)^f$ is the probability that Case E-I, Case E-II or Case E-III occurs and $[1 - \{2 \times (2/3)^f - (1/3)^f\}]$ is the probability that Case E-II and Case E-III occur at least one time. In a similar calculation, the probability for Cases F and G is the same as that for Case E.

- Case H: The probability is calculated as $1 - (1/4)^f + 3 \times (1/2)^f - 3 \times (3/4)^f$.

Here, we consider the situations in which L_i is unknown. If one of the following two conditions is satisfied, L_i is unknown.

1. L_i is unknown, and the relationship between L_i and L_{i-7} and that between L_i and L_{i+7} are unknown.
2. L_i is unknown, the relationship between L_i and other bits is known, and the values of other bits related to L_i are unknown.

Regarding 1, above, two situations to satisfy condition 1 are shown in Fig. 4. One is the case where the combination of (L_{i-7}, L_i, L_{i+7}) is (?, ?, ?). In this case, the probability that L_i and L_{i+7} are unknown is $P_A(f)$ $(= (1/4)^f)$. Under this condition, $\delta_{i-7}(= L_{i-7} \oplus \widetilde{L}_{i-7})$ should be 0 with f times and the probability of $\delta_{i-7} = 0$ with f times is $(1/2)^f$. Then, the probability that L_{i-7}, L_i and L_{i+7} are unknown is $(1/2)^f \times P_A(f)$. The other case is where the combination of the

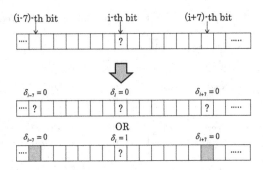

Fig. 4. Situations in which L_i is unknown and the relationship between L_i and L_{i-7}, and that between L_i and L_{i+7} are unknown. Notation "?" denotes the unknown bits, gray denotes the known bits, and $\delta_i = L_i \oplus \tilde{L}_i$.

3-bit values of (L_{i-7}, L_i, L_{i+7}) is (Known, ?, Known). The probability that L_i is unknown and L_{i+7} is known is $P_B(f)$ $(= (2/4)^f \times \{1 - (1/2)^f\})$. Under this condition, δ_{i-7} should be 0 with f times and the probability of $\delta_{i-7} = 0$ with f times is $(1/2)^f$. Then, the probability that the value of L_{i-7} and L_{i+7} are known, and L_i is unknown is $(1/2)^f \times P_B(f)$. Then, the probability that condition 1 is satisfied by the f fault injections, $P_1(f)$, is $P_1(f) = (1/2)^f \times \{P_A(f) + P_B(f)\}$.

Regarding 2, above, the relationships among L_i, L_{i+7}, L_{i+14}, $\ldots$ are known if the relationships between L_i and L_{i+7}, and that between L_{i+7} and L_{i+14}, $\ldots$ are known. Similarly, the relationships among L_i, L_{i-7}, L_{i-14}, $\ldots$ are known if the relationships between L_i and L_{i-7}, and that between L_{i-7} and $L_{i-14} \ldots$ are known. In Fig. 5, we show the situations in which condition 2 is satisfied. We denote the number of sequential connected relationships among L_i and other bits as k $(1 \leq k \leq n - 1)$ where n is the size of L.

When $k = 1$ as shown in Fig. 5, we consider that L_i is in (i) or (ii). Based on the f fault injections, the probability that L_i is unknown and the relationship between L_i and L_{i+7} (or L_{i-7}) is known at least one time out of the f fault injections is $P_C(f)$ in Table 2. Under this condition, δ_{i-7} and δ_{i+14} should be 0 when L_i is in (i) (or δ_{i-14} and δ_{i+7} should be 0 when L_i is in (ii)) and the values of L_{i-7} and L_{i+14} (or L_{i-14} and L_{i+7}) are known as shown in Fig. 5. The probability that $\delta_{i-7} = 0$ and $\delta_{i+14} = 0$ (or $\delta_{i-14} = 0$ and $\delta_{i+7} = 0$) are $(1/2)^{2f}$. Then, the probability that L_i is unknown and the relationship between L_i and other bits is known due to the f fault injections is $2 \times P_C(f) \times (1/2)^{2f}$ where "2" means that L_i is in (i) or (ii). For $k \geq 2$, the situations are the same as that for $k = 1$. As an example, when $k = 2$, L_i is in (i), (ii) or (iii) as shown in Fig. 5. If L_i is in (i), the probability that L_i is unknown and the relationship between L_i and L_{i+7} is known is $P_C(f)$ in Table 2. Under this condition, δ_{i+14} should be 1, and δ_{i-7} and δ_{i+21} should be 0 in order to satisfy the condition of $k = 2$ in Fig. 5. The probability for this is $(1/2)^{3f}$. At this time, the values of L_{i-7} and L_{i+21} are known as shown in Fig. 5. Thus, the probability that L_i is unknown and the relationship between L_i and the other 2 bits is known is $3 \times P_C(f) \times (1/2)^{3f}$ where "3" means that L_i is in (i), (ii) or (iii).

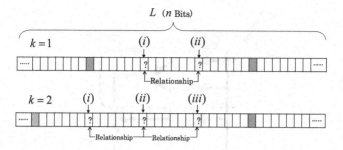

Fig. 5. Situations in which bit L_i is unknown and k relationships among other bits are known due to f fault injections when $k = 1$ and 2. Notation "?" denotes the unknown bits and gray denotes the known bits

Therefore, to satisfy condition 2, the probability that L_i is unknown and the relationships among L_i and k other bits are known is calculated as $P_2(f) = P_C(f)$ $\times \sum_{k=1}^{n-1} \{(k+1) \times (1/2)^{(k+1) \times f}\}$. Then, the probability that L_i is unknown, $P(f, n)$ $(= P_1(f) + P_2(f))$, is

$$P(f, n) = \left(\frac{1}{2}\right)^f \times \{P_A(f) + P_B(f)\} + P_C(f) \times \sum_{k=1}^{n-1} \left\{(k+1) \times \left(\frac{1}{2}\right)^{(k+1) \times f}\right\}.$$
(2)

Calculation of the Average Number of Fault Injections. From Eq. (2), the probability that n-bit L is known is $\{1 - P(f, n)\}^n$ $(= Q(f, n))$ and the probability that at least 1 bit in L is not known is $1 - Q(f, n)$ $(= \overline{Q}(f, n))$. Thus, the probability that n-bit L can be known for the first time at the f-th fault injection is $\overline{Q}(0, n) \times \cdots \times \overline{Q}(f-1, n) \times Q(f, n)$ where $\overline{Q}(f, n) = 1 - Q(f, n)$ and $\overline{Q}(0, n)$ is defined as 1. Then, the average number of fault injections required to obtain n-bit L, $f_{avg}(n)$, is

$$f_{avg}(n) = \sum_{f=1}^{\infty} \left\{f \times \left(\prod_{j=0}^{f-1} \overline{Q}(j, n)\right) \times Q(f, n)\right\}, \quad (\overline{Q}(f, n) = 1 - Q(f, n) \text{ and } \overline{Q}(0, n) = 1).$$
(3)

5   Attack Method

In this section, we describe the attack assumptions and the proposed attack procedures.

5.1   Attack Assumptions

The attack assumptions are as follows.

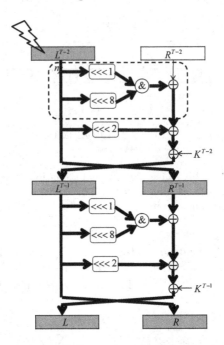

Fig. 6. Fault propagation when L^{T-2} are randomly corrupted. Gray denotes the faulty intermediate states and the heavy lines denote the fault propagations

- We consider transient faults, i.e., we can reset the cryptographic devices to their original state and inject faults into the same devices again during each new execution.
- We know pairs of correct and faulty ciphertexts calculated from the same plaintext and the secret key.
- The left half of the state, L, is randomly corrupted by the fault injection during one encryption calculation. At this time, we do not need to know the induced faulty values that represent the differences between the correct and faulty intermediate states.
- State L^r where we need to induce faults to recover the secret key depends on key word m as follows.

$m = 2$: L^{T-2}, L^{T-3}, $m = 3$: L^{T-2}, L^{T-3}, L^{T-4}, $m = 4$: L^{T-2}, L^{T-3}, L^{T-4}, L^{T-5}.

5.2 Attack Procedures

In order to recover the entire secret key, we need to obtain m round keys based on key word m. That is, we need to obtain K^{T-1} and K^{T-2} for $m = 2$, K^{T-1}, K^{T-2} and K^{T-3} for $m = 3$, and K^{T-1}, K^{T-2}, K^{T-3} and K^{T-4} for $m = 4$. Round key K^{r-1} is calculated as $K^{r-1} = L^r \oplus f(R^r) \oplus L^{r-2}$. If we know L^r, R^r and $L^{r-2}(= R^{r-1})$, we can obtain K^{r-1}. In the last round, we already know

Table 3. Summary of theoretical results of DFA on the SIMON family. All listed attacks use a random fault model.

Block Size	Key Size	Round-Key Size(n)	Key Words(m)	Fault Location	$f_{avg}(n)$	$m \times f_{avg}(n)$
32	64	16	4	$L^{27}, L^{28}, L^{29}, L^{30}$	3.05	12.20
48	72	24	3	L^{32}, L^{33}, L^{34}	3.30	9.91
48	96	24	4	$L^{31}, L^{32}, L^{33}, L^{34}$	3.30	13.22
64	96	32	3	L^{38}, L^{39}, L^{40}	3.48	10.45
64	128	32	4	$L^{39}, L^{40}, L^{41}, L^{42}$	3.48	13.93
96	96	48	2	L^{49}, L^{50}	3.73	7.46
96	144	48	3	L^{50}, L^{51}, L^{52}	3.73	11.19
128	128	64	2	L^{65}, L^{66}	3.91	7.82
128	192	64	3	L^{65}, L^{66}, L^{67}	3.91	11.73
128	256	64	4	$L^{67}, L^{68}, L^{69}, L^{70}$	3.91	15.64

Table 4. Summary of the attack for SIMON128/128.

Attack	Fault Model	$f_{avg}(n)$	$m \times f_{avg}(n)$
[18,19]	One-bit flip in L	32	No description
[18,19]	One-byte fault in L	8	No description
This paper	**Random fault in L**	**3.91**	**7.82**

L^T and R^T because they are ciphertexts, so we can deduce K^{T-1} if we obtain L^{T-2}. We note that we apply the results of the analysis in Sect. 4 to the AND operation at the penultimate round in order to obtain L^{T-2}.

Step 1. Induce Faults. We calculate a correct ciphertext and faulty ciphertexts by inducing faults. At this time, the correct and faulty ciphertexts are calculated from the same plaintext. We induce random faults into L^{T-2} in which the bits are randomly changed. Figure 6 shows the fault propagation in this case.

Step 2. Deduce Faulty Values. Faulty value Δ^{T-2} where $\Delta^{T-2} = L^{T-2} \oplus \widetilde{L}^{T-2} (= R^{T-1} \oplus \widetilde{R}^{T-1})$ is calculated from the correct and faulty ciphertexts as $\Delta^{T-2} = L^T \oplus \widetilde{L}^T \oplus f(R^T) \oplus f(\widetilde{R}^T)$. Since we know $L^T, \widetilde{L}^T, R^T$ and $\widetilde{R}^T$, we can obtain the value of Δ^{T-2}.

Step 3. Deduce L^{T-2}. We know input differences Δ^{T-2}, the output differences of the AND operation calculated from the value of $L^{T-1} (= R^T)$, and Δ^{T-2} as indicated by the dashed rectangle in Fig. 6. Then, we can obtain some bits or the relationship between the bits in L^{T-2} from Table 1 in Sect. 4.

We repeat the random fault injections and obtain some bits until all bits in L are known. At this time, we consider the relationships between the bits obtained by multiple fault injections to deduce more bits in L^{T-2}. Based on the analysis

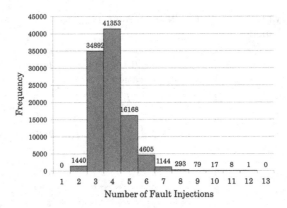

Fig. 7. Histogram of the number of fault injections to obtain 64 bits of L for SIMON128/128. The number of samples is 100,000. Frequency is represented on the vertical axis and the number of fault injections is represented on the horizontal axis. Each numerical value over the bar represents the frequency.

in Sect. 4, the average number of fault injections to obtain all bits in L is $f_{avg}(n)$ in Eq. (3). When we obtain all bits in L^{T-2}, we can obtain all bits of round key K^{T-1}.

Step 4. Deduce m Round Keys. To obtain the secret key, we need to obtain m round keys based on the key word size m. Then, we repeat the fault injections and the analysis on the key extractions from Steps 1 to 3, changing the rounds for the fault injections. As a result, we require $m \times f_{avg}(n)$ fault injections on average to obtain m round keys based on $f_{avg}(n)$ in Eq. (3).

Step 5. Obtain the Secret Key. Based on key expansion, we can calculate the round keys one after another from the m round keys deduced from Step 4. As an example, when $m = 2$, we deduce K^{T-2} and K^{T-1} from Steps 1 to 3, and then, we can calculate K^{T-3} from K^{T-2} and K^{T-1} as $K^{T-3} = K^{T-1} \oplus c \oplus (z_2)_{T-3} \oplus (K^{T-2} \ggg 3) \oplus \{(K^{T-2} \ggg 3) \ggg 1\}$. By repeating the above calculation, we can obtain the initial state in the key expansion, that is, the secret key. Then, we can determine the mn-bit secret key.

Table 3 gives a summary of the DFA applied to the SIMON family. The total number of fault injections to obtain the mn-bit secret key is calculated as $m \times f_{avg}(n)$ where $f_{avg}(n)$ is the average number of fault injections to obtain a round key. In Table 4, we also show a comparison between this study and previous work [18,19] when applying DFA to SIMON128/128, as an example.

6   Simulation Results for SIMON 128/128

This section presents the simulation results. As an example, we consider the results of SIMON with a 128-bit block size and a 128-bit secret key in the SIMON family.

In order to verify the proposed attack and evaluate the average number of fault injections, we implement the attack in C++ code and execute it on an Intel Core i7 2.6 GHz processor with the Windows 7 (64 bits) OS. We use Microsoft Visual C++ 2013 to compile the source code. In the simulation, we assume that L^r is randomly corrupted and the plaintexts and the secret key are randomly chosen. As an example, Fig. 7 shows a histogram of the number of fault injections to obtain all bits in L when $n = 64$. The number of samples is 100,000 in the figure. From the results, the average number of fault injections to obtain 64 bits of L is 3.93. Therefore, the simulation results agree with the theoretical results where the average number of the fault injection, $f_{avg}(64)$, to obtain 64 bits in L is 3.91. The calculation time to obtain n bits of L is within a second.

7   Conclusions

This paper proposed applying DFA to the SIMON family based on a practical random fault model. To apply DFA, we used the relationship among the differences in the two-bit inputs and the one-bit output of the non-linear function. We evaluated the average number of fault injections to obtain a round key in detail by examining the calculated bits and the relationships using multiple fault injections. We first showed how to extract the secret key using a random fault model for all parameters in the SIMON family. As an example, for SIMON with a 128-bit block size and a 128-bit secret key, we extracted the entire secret key using 7.82 fault injections on average. The results of simulations on a PC showed that the average number of fault injections required to obtain a round key in the simulation agreed with theoretically estimated values. We believe that the proposed DFA contributes to the study of FA on other cryptographic primitives using the AND operation for a non-linear function.

In the future, we will investigate a method to reduce the number of fault injections. In the attack steps described earlier, we uniquely determine all bits of K^r in round r and try to deduce K^{r-1} in round $(r - 1)$ using the obtained K^r. At this time, it is possible to try to deduce K^{r-1} using K^r of which some bits remain unknown. However, the unknown bits of K^r increase due to the left circular shift of the non-linear function when we obtain K^{r-1}. In accordance with the unknown bits of K^r, the candidate space of K^{r-1} increases and it is not calculated within a practical amount of time. We need to investigate the increase in the number of unknown bits due to the left circular shift and the degree to which the number of bits of K^r can be reduced using the inconsistency of input and output differences in the AND operation at round $(r - 1)$ even when some bits of K^r remain unknown. Furthermore, how the proposed attack works in the experiments using actual hardware devices and evaluating the DFA when the key schedule is corrupted are topics for future work.

References

1. Beaulieu, R., Shors, D., Smith, J., Treatman-Clark, S., Weeks, B., Wingers L.: The shape SIMON and shape speck families of lightweight block ciphers, cryptology ePrint Archive: Report 2013/404, (2013). http://eprint.iacr.org/
2. Alizadeh, J., Bagheri, N., Gauravaram, P., Kumar, A., Sanadhya, S. K.: Linear cryptanalysis of round reduced SIMON, cryptology ePrint Archive: Report 2013/663, (2013). http://eprint.iacr.org/
3. Abed, F., List, E., Lucks, S., Wenzel, J.: Differential and linear cryptanalysis of reduced-round shape SIMON. Cryptology ePrint Archive: Report 2013/526, (2013). http://eprint.iacr.org/
4. Alkhzaimi, H.A., Lauridsen, M.M.: Cryptanalysis of the SIMON Family of block ciphers. Cryptology ePrint Archive: Report 2013/543, (2013). http://eprint.iacr.org/
5. Alizadeh, J., Alkhzaimi, H.A., Aref, M.R., Bagheri, N., Gauravaram, P., Lauridsen, M.M.: Improved Linear cryptanalysis of round reduced SIMON. Cryptology ePrint Archive: Report 2014/681, (2014). http://eprint.iacr.org/
6. Biryukov, A., Roy, A., Velichkov, V.: Differential analysis of block ciphers SIMON and SPECK. In: Fast Software Encryption (FSE, 2014) (2014)
7. Abed, F., List, E., Lucks, S., Wenzel, J.: Differential cryptanalysis of round-reduced shape SIMON and shape speck. In: FSE 2014 (2014)
8. Bhasin, S., Graba, T., Danger, J.-L., Najm, Z.: A Look into SIMON from a side-channel perspective. In: 2014 IEEE International Symposium on Hardware-Oriented Security and Trust (Host, 2014), pp. 56–59. IEEE-CS (2014)
9. Shanmugam, D., Selvam, R., Annadurai, S.: Differential power analysis attack on SIMON and LED block ciphers. In: Chakraborty, R.S., Matyas, V., Schaumont, P. (eds.) SPACE 2014. LNCS, vol. 8804, pp. 110–125. Springer, Heidelberg (2014)
10. Skorobogatov, S.P., Anderson, R.J.: Optical fault induction attacks. In: Kaliski, B.S., Koç, çK, Paar, C. (eds.) CHES 2002. LNCS, vol. 2523, pp. 2–12. Springer, Heidelberg (2003)
11. Joye, M., Tunstall, M. (eds.): Fault Analysis in Cryptography. ISC. Springer, Heidelberg (2012). In Part V Implementing Fault Attacks
12. Boneh, D., Demillo, R.A., Lipton, R.J.: On the importance of eliminating errors in cryptographic computations. J. Cryptol. **14**, 101–119 (2001). Earlier version was published in EUROCRYPT 1997
13. Biham, E., Shamir, A.: Differential fault analysis of secret key cryptosystems. In: Kaliski Jr, B.S. (ed.) CRYPTO 1997. LNCS, vol. 1294, pp. 513–525. Springer, Heidelberg (1997)
14. Hemme, L.: A Differential fault attack against early rounds of (Triple-)DES. In: Joye, M., Quisquater, J.-J. (eds.) CHES 2004. LNCS, vol. 3156, pp. 254–267. Springer, Heidelberg (2004)
15. Piret, G., Quisquater, J.-J.: A differential fault attack technique against SPN structures, with application to the AES and KHAZAD. In: Walter, C.D., Koç, Ç.K., Paar, C. (eds.) CHES 2003. LNCS, vol. 2779, pp. 77–88. Springer, Heidelberg (2003)
16. Chen, H., Wu, W., Feng, D.: Differential fault analysis on CLEFIA. In: Qing, S., Imai, H., Wang, G. (eds.) ICICS 2007. LNCS, vol. 4861, pp. 284–295. Springer, Heidelberg (2007)
17. Wang, G., Wang, S.: Differential fault analysis on PRESENT key schedule. In: Proceedings of 2010 International Conference on Computational Intelligence and, Security (CIS, 2010), pp. 362–366. IEEE-CS (2010)

18. Tupsamudre, H., Bisht, S., Mukhopadhyay, D.: Differential Fault Analysis on the Families of SIMON and SPECK Ciphers. Cryptology ePrint Archive: Report 2014/267, (2014). http://eprint.iacr.org/ (2014)
19. Tupsamudre, H., Bisht, S., Mukhopadhyay, D.: Differential fault analysis on the families of SIMON and SPECK ciphers. In: Workshop on Fault Diagnosis and Tolerance in Cryptography (FDTC 2014), pp. 40–48. IEEE-CS (2014)

Network Security

A Clustering Approach for Privacy-Preserving in Social Networks

Rong Wang[1,3]($\boxtimes$), Min Zhang[1,2], Dengguo Feng[1], and Yanyan Fu[1]

[1] Trusted Computing and Information Assurance Laboratory, Institute of Software,
Chinese Academy of Sciences, Beijing, China
{wangrong,mzhang,feng,fuyy}@tca.iscas.ac.cn
[2] State Key Laboratory of Computer Science, Institute of Software, Chinese
Academy of Sciences, Beijing, China
[3] University of Chinese Academy of Sciences, Beijing, China

Abstract. Social networks, in which huge numbers of people spread massive information, are developing quite rapidly. Here people can obtain interesting information much more quickly and conveniently. However, people's privacies leak easily here too. A lot of works have been done to deal with this problem. Most of them focused on either attribute information or structure information. It is insufficient, because both attributes and structures, including sensitive attributes, are important in social networks, and we need to protect both of them. In this paper, we introduce a novel approach for privacy-preserving considering both attribute and structure information. In particular, sensitive attributes are considered to resist re-identification attacks. Moreover, we define the entropy to measure capability of preserving sensitive attributes.

Keywords: Privacy-preserving · Social networks · k-anonymity · l-diversity

1 Introduction

Social networks are developing quite rapidly, in which massive information, such as videos, documents, etc., is spread. Here people's personal information, including ages, genders, addresses, and friendships, is also visible. Researchers can take advantage of these valuable information in many areas, for example, recommendation systems. However, there also exists a significant threat to individual privacies. People can re-identify a real person, predict online relationships, and discover sensitive personal information, such as salaries and religious beliefs [1–4]. Malicious users can easily get these privacy information and launch further attacks.

So far, privacies have been preserved mostly in two ways: descriptive information protection and structure information protection. Descriptive information represents individual attributes, such as ages, genders, and home addresses. Some of them, like salaries, are sensitive, and others, which are named quasi-identifier

© Springer International Publishing Switzerland 2015
J. Lee and J. Kim (Eds.): ICISC 2014, LNCS 8949, pp. 193–204, 2015.
DOI: 10.1007/978-3-319-15943-0_12

Table 1. Initial tuples [11]

Node	Age	Zip	Gender	Salary
x^1	25	41076	Male	8000
x^2	25	41075	Male	8000
x^3	27	41076	Male	8000
x^4	35	41099	Male	7000
x^5	38	48201	Female	7000
x^6	36	41075	Female	5000
x^7	30	41099	Male	7000
x^8	28	41099	Male	7000
x^9	33	41075	Female	6000

Table 2. Generalized tuples

Node	Age	Zip	Gender	Salary
x^1	25–27	410**	Male	8000
x^2	25–27	410**	Male	8000
x^3	25–27	410**	Male	8000
x^4	35–38	*****	*	7000
x^5	35–38	*****	*	7000
x^6	35–38	*****	*	5000
x^7	28–33	410**	*	7000
x^8	28–33	410**	*	7000
x^9	28–33	410**	*	6000

attributes, are insensitive. However, multiple insensitive attributes can be combined to identify a person. Structure information represents online friendships.

In 2002, L.Sweeney et al. proposed the k-anonymity model [5], in which every node was indistinguishable with other (at least) $k - 1$ nodes. In 2007, Machanavajhala et al. extended the model and proposed the l-diversity model [6]. They considered not only quasi-identifier attributes but also sensitive attributes. Based on the methods above, Ford and Sun et al. introduced the p-sensitive k-anonymity, p^+-sensitive k-anonymity, and (p, α)-sensitive k-anonymity [7,8]. Most structure-preserving methods are based on k-anonymity. Liu and Terzi et al. defined and implemented the k-degree-anonymous model on network structure [9] to resist degree attacks. Zhou and Pei et al. discussed the k-neighborhood-anonymous model [10], in which for every node, there exist other (at least) $k - 1$ nodes sharing the same neighborhoods.

In a social network, adversaries can take advantage of many kinds of information to launch re-identification attacks. Obviously, protecting either descriptive information or structure information without considering both cannot preserve users' privacies sufficiently. Campan and Truta proposed SaNGreeA (Social Network Greedy Anonymization) [11], which protected quasi-identifier attributes and structure information from re-identification attacks, without consideration of sensitive attributes. Assuming that a company publishes the attribute information (Table 1) and social relationships (Fig. 1(a)) of the employees, we can get generalized data (Table 2 and Fig. 1(b)) by running SaNGreeA, which does not explicitly indicate the names of the employees. However, if an adversary has some background knowledge, for example, he knows some employee's age is 26, he can easily discover that the employee's salary is 8000, which is sensitive to the individual. Yuan proposed the KDLD sequence [12] to resist degree attacks. He claimed that sensitive attributes should satisfy the l-diversity. However, his method didn't consider insensitive attributes.

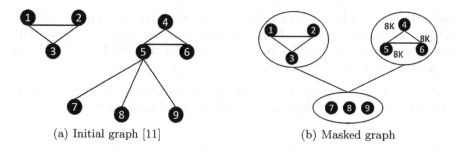

(a) Initial graph [11]   (b) Masked graph

Fig. 1. Social network graph

In this paper, we present a new generalization approach for social networks. Using a clustering method taking into account both k-anonymity and l-diversity, we can protect not only quasi-identifier attributes and structure information (social relations), but also sensitive attributes. The clustering is designed to generating as small information loss as possible. We define an entropy measure that evaluates protection ability of sensitive attributes, and use information loss defined by [11] to measure the total information loss.

The remainder of this paper is structured as follows: Sect. 2 introduces the social network privacy model; SaNGreeA and its information loss measures are briefly introduced in Sect. 3; Sect. 4 starts by presenting our algorithm MASN (Masking Algorithm for Social Networks), and follows by defining the measure of preserving of sensitive attributes; In Sect. 5, there are comparisons between SaNGreeA and MASN; Finally, the paper ends with conclusions and future work in Sect. 6.

2   Social Network Privacy Model

In this paper, a social network is modeled as an undirected graph. Each user is represented by a vertex and described by a tuple including sensitive attributes and quasi-identifier attributes. Quasi-identifier attributes includes numerical ones and categorical ones. The latter are often described as hierarchies, for example, the "Zip" attribute in Table 1 can be represented by:

$$\{*****\} \leftarrow \{\{410**\}, \{482**\}\} \leftarrow \{\{41075\}, \{41076\}, \{41099\}, \{48201\}\}$$

Relations between the users are represented by edges.

Definition 1 (Social Network): A social network SN is defined as a triple $G(V, E, A)$, where:

- V is a set of vertices, and each vertex represents an individual;
- $E \subseteq V \times V$ is the set of the edges between vertices;
- A is the set of corresponding tuples of the vertices, containing sensitive attributes and quasi-identifier attributes.

Definition 2 (Masked Social Network): Given an initial social network SN, SaNGreeA [11] can generate a k-anonymous masked social network MSN with respect to both quasi-identifier attributes and relations. MSN is defined as a triple $MG(MV, ME, MA)$, where:

- $MV = \{cl_1, cl_2, \cdots, cl_m\}$ is a partition of the vertices of SN, including m clusters, generated by SaNGreeA: each cluster contains at least k vertices, $cl_i \cap cl_j = \varnothing (i \neq j)$, and $\bigcup_{i=1}^{m} cl_i = V$;
- ME is the set of the edges between the clusters: $(cl_i, cl_j) \in ME(i \neq j)$, iff $\exists v_p \in cl_i, v_q \in cl_j$, s.t. $(v_p, v_q) \in E$;
- MA is the set of corresponding tuples of the clusters' vertices, including sensitive attributes and generalized quasi-identifier attributes.

Definition 3 (Further Masked Social Network): Given an initial social network SN, MASN, performing SaNGreeA and a further masking successively, can generate a masked social network $FMSN$ fulfilling both k-anonymity and l-diversity. $FMSN$ is defined as $FMG(FMV, FME, FMA)$, where:

- $FMV = \{cl_1', cl_2', \cdots, cl_n'\}$ is a partition of the vertices of SN, including n clusters, generated by MASN: each cluster contains at least k vertices, $cl_i' \cap cl_j' = \varnothing (i \neq j)$, and $\bigcup_{i=1}^{n} cl_i' = V$;
- FME is the set of the edges between the clusters: $(cl_i', cl_j') \in FME(i \neq j)$, iff $\exists v_p \in cl_i', v_q \in cl_j'$, s.t. $(v_p, v_q) \in E$;
- FMA is the set of corresponding tuples of the clusters' vertices, including sensitive attributes and generalized quasi-identifier attributes: each cluster contains at least l distinct sensitive attribute values.

In a further masked social network $FMSN$, we can ensure:

(1) The probability of correctly re-identifying an user is no more than $\frac{1}{k}$.
(2) If an adversary can discover which cluster his target (a vertex) belongs to, the probability of inferring its sensitive attribute value is at most $\frac{1}{l}$.

3   SaNGreeA

SaNGreeA [11], discussed in this section, is a greedy clustering algorithm, which masks an initial social network to generate a k-anonymous one, including generalization of both quasi-identifier attributes and relations. It partitions all the vertices of the initial social network into several clusters greedily, according to the information loss measures. Each cluster of the masked social network should contain at least k vertices.

The generalization of quasi-identifier attributes and relations reduces data quality. Every time, SaNGreeA chooses the vertex that generates minimal information loss, and adds it into the current cluster. Once the cluster satisfies k-anonymity, a new one will be created, until the whole network is masked.

Definition 4 (Generalization Information Loss): Let cl be a cluster, and its quasi-identifier attributes $QID = \{N_1, \cdots, N_p, C_1, \cdots, C_q\}$, where $N_i (i \in [1, p])$ is a numerical attribute and $C_j (j \in [1, q])$ is a categorical attribute. The generalization information loss about cl caused by generalizing QID is:

$$GIL(cl) = |cl| \cdot \left(\sum_{i=1}^{p} \frac{\max\limits_{T \in A_{cl}}(T[N_i]) - \min\limits_{T \in A_{cl}}(T[N_i])}{\max\limits_{T \in A}(T[N_i]) - \min\limits_{T \in A}(T[N_i])} + \sum_{i=1}^{q} \frac{h(H_{cl}[C_i])}{h(H[C_i])} \right) \quad (1)$$

where:

- T is a tuple;
- A is the set of tuples in the initial graph and A_{cl} is that in cl;
- H is the set of hierarchies of categorical attribute values in the initial graph and H_{cl} is that in cl;
- h is the height of a hierarchy.

Definition 5 (Normalized Generalization Information Loss): When masking a graph G based on the partition $S = \{cl_1, \cdots, cl_n\}$, the normalized generalization information loss is:

$$NGIL(G, S) = \frac{\sum\limits_{i=1}^{n} GIL(cl_i)}{|V| \cdot (p + q)} \quad (2)$$

Definition 6 (Distance): The distance between a vertex v and a cluster cl is:

$$D(v, cl) = \frac{\sum\limits_{v^* \in cl} \left| \{v_x | v_x \in V, v_x \neq v, v_x \neq v^*, R(v_x, v) \neq R(v_x, v^*)\} \right|}{|cl| \cdot (|V| - 2)} \quad (3)$$

where $R(v_1, v_2)$ indicates whether v_1 and v_2 are friends.

Definition 7 (Intra-cluster Structural Information Loss): Given a cluster cl, E_{cl} denotes the set of edges that exist in cl. The intra-cluster information loss is quantified as the probability of wrongly identifying an edge between two vertices:

$$intraSIL(cl) = 2 \cdot |E_{cl}| \cdot \left(1 - \frac{|E_{cl}|}{C_{|cl|}^2} \right) \quad (4)$$

Definition 8 (Inter-cluster Structural Information Loss): Given two clusters, cl_1 and cl_2, $E_{1,2}$ denotes the set of edges between them. The inter-cluster information loss is quantified as the probability of wrongly identifying an edge between two clusters:

$$interSIL(cl_1, cl_2) = 2 \cdot |E_{1,2}| \cdot \left(1 - \frac{|E_{1,2}|}{|cl_1| \cdot |cl_2|} \right) \quad (5)$$

Definition 9 (Normalized Structural Information Loss): When masking a graph G based on the partition $S = \{cl_1, \cdots, cl_n\}$, the normalized structural information loss is:

$$NSIL(G, S) = \frac{4}{|V|(|V| - 1)} \cdot \left(\sum_{i=1}^{n} intraSIL(cl_i) + \sum_{1 \leq i \neq j \leq n} interSIL(cl_i, cl_j) \right) \tag{6}$$

Definition 10 (Information Loss): When masking a graph G based on the partition $S = \{cl_1, \cdots, cl_n\}$, the information loss IL is:

$$IL = \alpha \cdot NGIL(G, S) + \beta \cdot D(v, cl) \tag{7}$$

$$IL' = \alpha \cdot NGIL(G, S) + \beta \cdot NSIL(G, S) \tag{8}$$

where α and β ($\alpha + \beta = 1$) are user-defined weights, IL is the information loss measure used during SaNGreeA procedure. $intraSIL, interSIL$, and $NSIL$ are used to evaluate the information loss after the masking is done.

4   MASN

SaNGreeA can effectively protect quasi-identifier attributes and relations, without consideration of sensitive attributes. In this section, MASN, which consists of SaNGreeA and a further masking considering l-diversity, is introduced, including the algorithm and corresponding measures of protection of sensitive attributes.

Algorithm 1. MASN

Input:
    $G(V, E, A)$;
    k as in k-anonymity;
    l as in l-diversity;
    User-defined weight parameters, α and β ($\alpha + \beta = 1$);
Output:
    $FMG(FMV, FME, FMA)$;
1: $MG(MV, ME, MA) \leftarrow SaNGreeA(G, k, \alpha, \beta)$;
2: $FMV \leftarrow \{cl | cl \in MV$, and cl satisfies l-diversity$\}$;
3: $NFMV \leftarrow MV - FMV$;
4: WHILE $NFMV \neq \varnothing$
5:     Get $cl_{e1} \in NFMV$, s.t. $\forall cl \in NFMV(cl \neq cl_{e1})$ $Div(cl_{e1}) \geq Div(cl)$;
6:     $NFMV \leftarrow NFMV - \{cl_{e1}\}$;
7:     WHILE $Div(cl_{e1}) < l$
8:         $(cl_{e2}, v_{e1} \in cl_{e1}, v_{e2} \in cl_{e2}) \leftarrow FindBestCl(cl_{e1}, FMV, NFMV)$;
9:         IF $cl_{e2} \neq \varnothing$ THEN Swap v_{e1} with v_{e2};
10:        ELSE $Disperse(cl_{e1}, FMV, NFMV)$, and GOTO STEP 4;
11:     $FMV \leftarrow FMV \cup \{cl_{e1}\} \cup \{cl | cl \in NFMV, Div(cl) \geq l\}$;
12:     $NFMV \leftarrow NFMV - \{cl | cl \in NFMV, Div(cl) \geq l\}$;
13: Generate FME and FMA according to FMV;
14: **return** FMG;

4.1   The Algorithm

MASN protects sensitive attributes, quasi-identifier attributes, and relation information. Moreover, it is designed to ensure that the information loss after masking is in an acceptable range. Therefore, we put vertices that are as similar as possible together in a cluster.

SaNGreeA is a greedy algorithm, and measures its real-time information loss with IL during its execution. However, IL' is a better measure to evaluate its final information loss. Because our algorithm is based on the result of SaNGreeA, IL' instead of IL is used in our algorithm.

MASN increases the diversity $(Div())$ of a cluster cl_{e1} that doesn't satisfy l-diversity through vertex-swapping, which fulfills the following requirements after swapping:

- $Div(cl_{e1})$ increases;
- Clusters in FMV are still here;
- The information loss is minimal.

Algorithm 2. FindBestCl

Input:
> A cluster cl_{e1};
> FMV, a set whose elements are clusters that satisfy l-diversity;
> $NFMV$, a set whose elements are clusters that don't satisfy l-diversity;

Output:
> $(cl_{e2}, v_{e1}, v_{e2})$, where cl_{e2} is a cluster, $v_{e1} \in cl_{e1}$, and $v_{e2} \in cl_{e2}$;

1: $V_e \leftarrow \{v | v \in cl, \text{ where } cl \in FMV \cup NFMV\}$;
2: $VP \leftarrow cl_{e1} \times V_e$;
3: $(cl_{e2}, v_{e1}, v_{e2}) \leftarrow (\varnothing, NULL, NULL)$;
4: **WHILE** $VP \neq \varnothing$ and $cl_{e2} = \varnothing$
5:    $(v_1^*, v_2^*) \leftarrow \underset{(v_1, v_2) \in VP}{\arg\min} (IL'^*(G, FMV \cup NFMV \cup \{cl_{e1}\}))$;

   $\backslash\backslash IL'^*$ is the information loss after swapping v_1 with v_2.
6:    **IF** $Div(cl_{e1} \cup \{v_2^*\} - \{v_1^*\}) \leq Div(cl_{e1})$ **THEN** $VP \leftarrow VP - \{(v_1^*, v_2^*)\}$;
7:    **ELSE IF** $v_2^* \in cl(cl \in FMV)$, and $Div(cl \cup \{v_1^*\} - \{v_2^*\}) < l$
8:       **THEN** $VP \leftarrow VP - \{(v_1^*, v_2^*)\}$;
9:    **ELSE** $v_{e1} \leftarrow v_1^*, v_{e2} \leftarrow v_2^*$, and $cle2 \leftarrow cl(v_{e2} \in cl)$;
10: **return** $(cl_{e2}, v_{e1}, v_{e2})$;

Given an initial social network as shown in Fig.1 (a) and Table 1, by running MASN, we can get a further masked social network as shown in Fig.2 and Table 3. The information losses are measured in Table 4.

In a further masked social network, an adversary cannot re-identify a user through generalized quasi-identifier attributes because of k-anonymity, and hidden relations. Even if he knows which cluster a user belongs to, he cannot obtain the corresponding sensitive attributes.

Algorithm 3. Disperse

Input:

A cluster cl_{e1};

FMV, a set whose elements are clusters that satisfy l-diversity;

$NFMV$, a set whose elements are clusters that do not satisfy l-diversity;

1: FOREACH v in cl_{e1}

2:      $cl^* \leftarrow \underset{cl \in FMV \cup NFMV}{\arg\min} \ (IL'^*(G, FMV \cup NFMV))$;

     $\backslash\backslash$ IL'^* is the information loss after moving v into cl.

3:      $cl^* \leftarrow cl^* \cup \{v\}$, and $cl_{e1} \leftarrow cl_{e1} - \{v\}$;

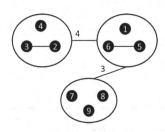

Fig. 2. Further masked graph

Table 3. Further generalized tuples

Node	Age	Zip	Gender	Salary
x^4	25–35	410**	Male	7000
x^2	25–35	410**	Male	8000
x^3	25–35	410**	Male	8000
x^1	28–38	*****	*	8000
x^5	28–38	*****	*	7000
x^6	28–38	*****	*	5000
x^7	28–33	410**	*	7000
x^8	28–33	410**	*	7000
x^9	28–33	410**	*	6000

Table 4. Information loss values

Clusters	GIL/NGIL	intraSIL	interSIL	SIL/NSIL
$cl_1 = \{x^4, x^2, x^3\}$	$GIL = 3*(\frac{10}{13} + \frac{13}{13} + \frac{5}{13}$	$intraSIL(cl_1) = \frac{4}{3}$	$interSIL(cl_1, cl_2) = \frac{40}{9}$	$SIL = 11.11$
$cl_2 = \{x^1, x^5, x^6\}$	$+\frac{1}{2} + \frac{2}{2} + \frac{1}{2}$	$intraSIL(cl_2) = \frac{4}{3}$	$interSIL(cl_1, cl_3) = 0$	$NSIL = 0.617$
$cl_3 = \{x^7, x^8, x^9\}$	$+\frac{0}{1} + \frac{1}{1} + \frac{1}{1}) = 18.46$	$intraSIL(cl_3) = 0$	$interSIL(cl_2, cl_3) = \frac{36}{9}$	
	$NGIL = 0.68$			

4.2 Measure of Preserving Sensitive Attributes

Entropy, used to evaluate the capability of preserving sensitive attributes, is introduced in this section.

Definition 11 (Cluster Entropy): Given a cluster cl, $SA = \{s_1, \cdots, s_n\}$ is the set of its distinct sensitive values. $T = \{t_1, \cdots, t_n\}$, where t_i indicates how many times s_i appears in cl. The cluster entropy is:

$$ClE(cl) = -\sum_{i=1}^{n} \frac{t_i}{|cl|} \cdot \log \frac{t_i}{|cl|} \qquad (9)$$

Given a cluster cl, which is the cluster cl_{e1} in MASN, where:

- $Div(cl) < l;$
- $SA = \{s_1, \cdots, s_i, \cdots, s_n\}, T_1 = \{t_1, \cdots, t_i, \cdots, t_n\};$
- v is the vertex which will be swapped, and s_i is its sensitive attribute value;
- The entropy of a cluster cl before and after swapping are represented by $ClE_1(cl)$ and $ClE_2(cl)$ respectively.

we can find that:

- $t_i \geq 2$, because the diversity of cl increases after swapping;
- $ClE_1(cl) = - \sum\limits_{p=1}^{n} \frac{t_p}{|cl|} \cdot \log \frac{t_p}{|cl|};$
- $ClE_2(cl) = - \sum\limits_{p \neq i} \frac{t_p}{|cl|} \cdot \log \frac{t_p}{|cl|} - \frac{t_i - 1}{|cl|} \cdot \log \frac{t_i - 1}{|cl|} - \frac{1}{|cl|} \cdot \log \frac{1}{|cl|}.$

$$ClE_2(cl) - ClE_1(cl) = - \frac{t_i - 1}{|cl|} \cdot \log \frac{t_i - 1}{|cl|} - \frac{1}{|cl|} \cdot \log \frac{1}{|cl|} + \frac{t_i}{|cl|} \cdot \log \frac{t_i}{|cl|}$$

$$= \frac{1}{|cl|} \cdot [t_i \cdot \log t_i - (t_i - 1) \cdot \log(t_i - 1)]$$

The function $x \cdot \log x$ increases monotonically when $x \geq 1$, and therefore, $ClE_2(cl) - ClE_1(cl) \geq 0$, that is, $ClE_2(cl) \geq ClE_1(cl)$.

The larger the entropy is, the more information an adversary needs to predict a sensitive value correctly. Through the above analyses, we can conclude that the capability of preserving sensitive attributes of a cluster is improved after vertex-swapping.

Definition 12 (Graph Entropy): Given a masked graph MG based on the partition $S = \{cl_1, \cdots, cl_n\}$, the graph entropy is:

$$GE(MG) = \frac{\sum\limits_{cl \in S} ClE(cl)}{|S|} \tag{10}$$

5   Experiment Results

MASN and SaNGreeA are compared in this section, with respect to the quality of the results they produce. The experiments are performed upon social network data, which contains 500 vertices randomly selected from Sina weibo (http://weibo.com/). The sensitive attribute is *Hometown*, and the quasi-identifier attributes are (*FollowingNumber, FollowerNumber, Age*). In the experiments, $\alpha = 0.5$ and $\beta = 0.5$.

To demonstrate the effectiveness of MASN, we consider the basic structure properties of the social network graph, and mainly measure the following property:

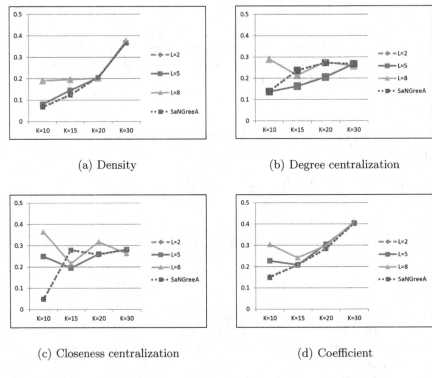

(a) Density

(b) Degree centralization

(c) Closeness centralization

(d) Coefficient

Fig. 3. Comparisons between SaNGreeA and MASN

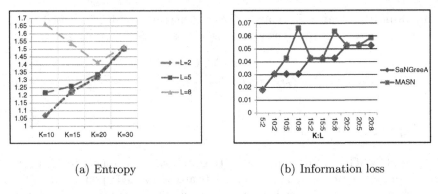

(a) Entropy

(b) Information loss

Fig. 4. Entropy and information loss

- Density, which estimates how many edges actually exist among all possible guesses;
- Degree centralization, which indicates the consistency and integration of a graph;
- Closeness centralization, which measures the closeness between the vertices;
- Cluster coefficient, which is a measure of the aggregation degree of the vertices in a graph.

Figure 3(a–d) depicted the four statistical measurements on MASN and SaN-GreeA with $k = 10, 15, 20, 30$ and $l = 2, 5, 8$. In Fig. 3(a) we can figure out that the density reveals an increasing tendency with k increased, for distinct values of l. To satisfy l-diversity, the number of clusters shows a downward trend and decreases faster than the number of edges. This explanation also applies to the case with the same l but different k. Through Fig. 3(b–d) we can find that the results of SaNGreeA and MASN follow the same trend.

Figure 4 (a) shows that the entropy increases with l increased, and the entropy of MASN is mostly larger than that of SaNGreeA, which indicates that MASN can preserve sensitive attributes more effectively. Figure 4(b) shows that the information loss of MASN is very close to SaNGreeA. In the case that ($k = 10, l = 8$) and ($k = 15, l = 8$), l is very close to k, and therefore, more vertices are swapped, which results in the increment of the information loss. Finally, we discover that MASN can achieve a higher security than SaNGreeA with almost the same utility.

6   Conclusions and Future Work

In this pager, we present MASN for further masking a social network. Compared with SaNGreeA, our method takes into account not only quasi-identifier attributes and relations, but also sensitive attributes. The entropy measure is defined to evaluate protection of sensitive attributes. Through the experiments, we can conclude that MASN can well preserve users' privacies.

In the future, we can extend our model to achieve a stronger privacy protection, which will consider p-sensitive, and t-closeness further.

Acknowledgment. This work was supported by National Natural Science Foundation of China under Grant No.61232005, No.61100237 and No.91118006.

References

1. Ye, M., Yin, P., Lee, W.C., Lee, D.L.: Exploiting geographical influence for collaborative point-of-interest recommendation. In: 34th international ACM SIGIR Conference on Research and development in Information Retrieval, pp. 325–334. ACM, New York (2011)
2. Goel, S., Hofman, J.M., Lahaie, S., et al.: Predicting consumer behavior with web search. Proc. Natl. Acad. Sci. **107**, 17486–17490 (2010)
3. Paul, M.J., Dredze, M.: You are what you tweet: analyzing twitter for public health. In: 5th International AAAI Conference on Weblogs and Social Media, ICWSM, pp. 265–272 (2011)
4. Aramaki, E., Maskawa, S., Morita, M.: Twitter catches the flu: detecting influenza epidemics using twitter. In: The Conference on Empirical Methods in Natural Language Processing, pp. 1568–1576. Association for Computational Linguistics, Stroudsburg (2011)
5. Sweeney, L.: k-anonymity: a model for protecting privacy. Int. J. Uncertainty Fuzziness Knowl. Based Syst. **10**, 557–570 (2002)

6. Machanavajjhala, A., Kifer, D., Gehrke, J., et al.: l-diversity: privacy beyond k-anonymity. ACM Trans. Knowl. Discovey Data (TKDD) **1**, 3 (2007)
7. Ford, R., Truta, T.M., Campan, A.: P-Sensitive K-anonymity for social networks. In: 5th International Conference on Data Mining, pp. 403–409. DMIN, Las Vegas (2009)
8. Sun, X., Sun, L., Wang, H.: Extended k-anonymity models against sensitive attribute disclosure. Comput. Commun. **34**, 526–535 (2011)
9. Liu, K., Terzi, E.: Towards identity anonymization on graph. In: ACM SIGMOD international conference on Management of data, pp. 93–106. ACM, New York (2008)
10. Zhou, B., Pei, J.: Preserving privacy in social networks against neighborhood attacks. In: 24th IEEE International Conference on Data Engineering, pp. 506–515. IEEE Press, New York (2008)
11. Campan, A., Truta, T.M.: A clustering approach for data and structural anonymity in social networks. In: 2nd ACM SIGKDD International Workshop on Privacy, Security, and Trust in KDD, pp. 93–104. ACM, Las Vegas (2008)
12. Yuan, M., Chen, L., Yu, P.S., et al.: Protecting sensitive labels in social network data anonymization. IEEE Trans. Knowl. Data Eng. **25**, 633–647 (2013)

Securely Solving Classical Network Flow Problems

Abdelrahaman Aly$^{(\boxtimes)}$ and Mathieu Van Vyve

Université catholique de Louvain, CORE, Voie du Roman Pays 34,
1348 Louvain-la-Neuve, Belgium
{abdelrahaman.aly,mathieu.vanvyve}@uclouvain.be

Abstract. We investigate how to solve several classical network flow problems using secure multi-party computation. We consider the shortest path problem, the minimum mean cycle problem and the minimum cost flow problem. To the best of our knowledge, this is the first time the two last problems have been addressed in a general multi-party computation setting. Furthermore, our study highlights the complexity gaps between traditional and secure implementations of the solutions, to later test its implementation. It also explores various trade-offs between performance and security. Additionally it provides protocols that can be used as building blocks to solve complex problems. Applications of our work can be found in: communication networks, routing data from rival company hubs; distribution problems, retailer/supplier selection in multi-level supply chains that want to share routes without disclosing sensible information; amongst others.

Keywords: Network Flows · Multi-party computation · Secure collaboration

1 Introduction

Secure Multi-party Computation (MPC), studies the problem where several players want to jointly compute a given function without disclosing their inputs; this problem was first addressed by Yao [1]. Different adversary models can be considered. A semi-honest setting, where corrupted players try to learn only what can be inferred from the information they have been provided with; or an active setting, where they manipulate the data in order to learn from any possible leakage caused. Several cryptographic primitives for secret sharing and homomorphic encryption, e.g. Shamir scheme [2] and Pailler encryption [3], have been proposed to address the problem.

Applications have emerged naturally in different fields, for instance, where all the secret information is sent by the players to a third trusted party who only reveals the final output. For example, in auctions, the auctioneer can be seen as a trusted third party. We study the scenario where no trusted third parties are allowed.

© Springer International Publishing Switzerland 2015
J. Lee and J. Kim (Eds.): ICISC 2014, LNCS 8949, pp. 205–221, 2015.
DOI: 10.1007/978-3-319-15943-0_13

Classical network flow problems arise in real life applications in several areas e.g. project planning, networking, supply chain management, production scheduling. Combinatorial optimization, dynamic programing and mathematical programming have yielded polynomial-time algorithms for many of these problems (a detailed treatment can be found in Ahuja et al. [4]).

Our central objects of study are the shortest path problem on weighted graphs, the Minimum Mean Cycle problem (MMC) and the the Minimum Cost Flow problem (MCF). We present algorithms that address privacy preserving constraints on these problems and solve them in polynomial time. We also empirically test the performance of our implementations. Finally, we show how to use our protocols as building blocks to solve more complex problems. For example, a WLAN network constructed by competing agents that want to securely compute, in a distributed fashion, their routing tables and the network flow configuration that supports its maximum traffic volume at the minimum cost possible. The routing algorithms could use our shortest path protocol to securely define the routing tables. Moreover, a combination of the max flow algorithm [5] with our minimum cost flow protocol could be used to obtain the desired flow distribution securely. Note that for these types of application the number of vertices e.g. routers, is not necessarily very large.

1.1 Our Contributions

We provide algorithmic solutions to three classical network flow problems in a secure, multi-party and distributed setting: the shortest path based on Dijkstra, the minimum mean cycle using Karp's solution and the minimum cost flow using the Minimum Mean Cycle Canceling (MMCC) algorithm. To the best of our knowledge, this is the first time the last two problems have been studied under MPC security constraints. We also introduce a novel technique to hide the vertex selected at each iteration of Dijkstra's algorithm, avoiding the overhead caused by the use of special data structures e.g. oblivious data structures. This is particularly relevant on dense graphs. We refer the reader to Sect. 1.2 for further analysis. Moreover, we show polynomial bounds for all three problems relying only on black box operations. In our configurations, the secret information can be distributed as pleased by the parties. Our work considers all input data to be secret except for a bound on the number of vertices of the graphs.

Security and Correctness. The security of our algorithms comes from the fact that we only use operations from the arithmetic black-box and prevent any information leakage. This implies that the protocols are as secure as the MPC primitives they are implemented over e.g. information-theoretic secure, (see also Sect. 2.1). Furthermore the correctness of our algorithms is essentially inherited from the correctness of the classical algorithms from which they are derived. More specifically, we modify the previously known and correct algorithms to avoid, in general, information leakage, while working on secret data, showing that these modifications do not alter their output.

Table 1. Asymptotic bounds of original and privacy-preserving algorithmic versions

	Advance Impl.	Simple Impl.	Complete Graphs	Privacy Preserving	Secure Comparisons
Dijkstra	$\|E\| + \|V\| \cdot log(\|V\|)$	$\|V\|^2$	$\|V\|^2$	$\|V\|^3$	$\|V\|^2$
MMC	$\|E\| \cdot \|V\|$	$\|E\| \cdot \|V\|$	$\|V\|^3$	$\|V\|^5$	$\|V\|^3$
MMCC	$\|V\|^2 \cdot \|E\|^3 log(\|V\|)$	$\|V\|^2 \cdot \|E\|^3 log(\|V\|)$	$\|V\|^8 \cdot log(\|V\|)$	$\|V\|^{10} \cdot log(\|V\|)$	$\|V\|^8 \cdot log(\|V\|)$

Complexity. We use atomic communication rounds as our main performance unit to determine the complexity (round complexity) of our protocols. Besides, because of the strong differences in performance between comparisons and multiplications we limit the use of comparisons in favor of more arithmetic operations. i.e. additions and multiplications. Table 1 presents the complexity bounds we obtain. In all cases, the number of comparisons matches the complexity of implementations on complete graphs. However, we need to introduce additional multiplications to hide the branchings involved in the algorithms.

1.2 Related Works

Graph Theory Problems. Different alternatives to solve some graph theory problems have been studied by Aly et al. [5], namely the shortest path and maximum flow problems. They provide bounds on the Bellman-Ford and Dijkstra algorithms. Our own bounds are slightly better with our version of Dijkstra's algorithm, using different approaches. Indeed, [5] uses a searching array technique, similar to the one proposed by Launchbury et al. [6], to keep track of a secret shared index. Our proposed Dijkstra implementation does not require the use of this technique, eliminating its overhead. Edmonds-Karp and push-relabel bounds are provided as well for the maximum flow problem. As in our case, their implementations are secure in the *information-theoretic* model relying on the same arithmetic black-box $\mathcal{F}_{ABB}$. Brickell and Shmatikov [7] have addressed the shortest path problem on a two-party case, limited to the honest by curious model. They succeed by revealing at each iteration the new edge of the shortest path added. Our approach attacks the problem in a different fashion by eliminating this requirement. We also address the problem in a multiparty setting and not limited to the two-party case. Moreover, Banton et al. [8] have proposed a data-oblivious alternative for the Breath-First-Search (BFS) algorithm, which is later used to solve the special case of the shortest path problem where all edges have the same weight e.g. all existing edges weight 1 and non-existing 0. We consider instead the more general case with weighted edges. Additionally, they use their BFS algorithm to provide bounds for the Max-Flow problem, where weighted edges with a positive residual capacity are mapped as 1 and its counterparts as 0, extending the definition of an existing edge.

Oblivious data structures over ORAM. Data structures are used to speed-up Dijkstra's algorithm and achieve its optimal complexity. ORAM has been viewed as a suitable mechanism to build oblivious distributed data structures with the corresponding overhead and configuration e.g. The work of Wang et al. [9] designed to work on a client(s)-server configuration. Moreover, secure two-party computation protocols have been developed to take advantage of the recent advances on ORAM e.g. [10,11]. The two-party tool and algorithmic implementations of Liu et al. [12] securely address the shortest path and other combinatorial problems by using these kinds of data structures. More recently, Keller and Scholl [13] show how to use oblivious data structures on a multi-party setting, where none of the players have to fulfill the role of the server. Furthermore, they use their data structures to implement Dijkstra's algorithm. Their experimentation shows how some MPC solutions in the absence of ORAM can perform better for certain kinds of graphs than their proposed counterparts i.e. samples of smaller-to-medium sizes and complete graphs of any size. This is easily explained by the fact that the overhead coming from the ORAM exceeds the asymptotic advantage of the algorithms. Indeed, we address the problem differently, our Dijkstra algorithm is designed to work on plain vectors and matrices and does not require any secure data structure construction, slightly improving the bounds proposed by Aly et al. [5], who's work is later used in Keller and Scholl's analysis. This allows us to avoid any overhead caused by the use of ORAM or static secret sharing arrays. We refer to [13] for details.

1.3 Overview

Section 2 describes the notation we use, as well as the cryptographic primitives. It also serves to introduce "building blocks" i.e. small algorithmic procedures regularly used. In Sect. 3 we present a solution for Dijkstra. Section 4 introduces the minimum mean cycle problem. Section 5 then explains the implementation using MPC primitives. Section 6 gives an overview of the minimum flow problem and the minimum mean cycle-canceling algorithm. In the sections ahead, details on the algorithm are presented. In Sect. 7, we present and discuss our secure algorithmic solution. Section 8 shows the results of our computational experimentation. Lastly, Sect. 9 provides general conclusions.

2   Preliminaries

2.1   Security

We use the terms "securely" and "privacy preserving" indistinctly. We can succinctly formalize their notion as follows: parties $P_1, ..., P_n$ want to jointly and correctly compute the function $y = f(x_1, ..., x_n)$ where x_i is P_i secret input and only y is allowed to be revealed to all parties. In other words, the security constraint is such that each player P_i learns y and what can be inferred from y, but no more. In particular, any information given during the computation process should not allow him to infer information about other secret inputs.

Modulo arithmetic for some M or ring arithmetic allows to simulate secure integer arithmetic. Indeed, several multi-party computation solutions have been designed to work on modulo arithmetic for an appropriate M e.g. a sufficiently big prime number (transforming the ring in a finite field over some M, $\mathbb{Z}_M$), such that no overflow occurs. This is true for secret sharing schemes the likes of Shamir [2] sharing or additive sharing, as well for homomorphic threshold public key encryption.

Primitives like addition between secret shared inputs on secret sharing, as well as additions and multiplications of these by public values, are linear operations and do not require any information transmission between players. When data is communicated between players it is called a communication round or just round. For complexity analysis purposes, we require constant-round protocols for multiplications. By extension, sharing and reconstruction are done in one round as well. There are still local operations involved with all the primitives, but the performance cost is mainly determined by the communication processes, as explained by Maurer [14]. We assume that the execution flavor i.e. sequential and parallel, does not compromise the security of the private data.

The concept of the arithmetic black-box $\mathcal{F}_{ABB}$ [15] embeds this behavior and makes the process transparent for the algorithm designer. It creates an abstraction layer between the protocol construction and functionality specificities, and at the same time it provides the security guarantees desired. Following [5,15] amongst others, we assume the following functionalities are available: storage and retrieval of ring $\mathbb{Z}_M$ elements, additions, multiplications, equality and inequality tests.

On a final note, all our protocols are designed under the *information-theoretic* model in the presence of passive or active adversaries over $\mathcal{F}_{ABB}$. This implies that as long as the parties do not have access to other private data but their own, unbounded computing power would not allow them to obtain any additional information. This means in practice that they will be as secure as the underlying MPC functionality and crypto-primitives they rely on.

2.2 Notation

We use the traditional square brackets e.g. [x], to denote secret shared or encrypted values contained in the $\mathcal{F}_{ABB}$. This notation is commonly used by secure applications e.g. [5]. Sometimes [∞] is used on our algorithms. Given that the $\mathcal{F}_{ABB}$ is limited by the size of M, this value, has to be understood as a sufficiently large constant smaller than M but much bigger than the values of the inputs. On the size of M, it has to be noted that some comparison protocols require a security parameter on the size of M that has to be taken into account when defining its size. We also assume all values analyzed by our protocols, including intermediate data, to be integers bounded to M to avoid overflows. Moreover, secure operations are described using the infix operation e.g. $[z] \leftarrow [x] + [y]$ for secure addition into the $\mathcal{F}_{ABB}$ and $[z] \leftarrow [x] \cdot [y]$ for secure multiplication. The secret result of any secure operation primitive is stored in $[z]$ and onto the $\mathcal{F}_{ABB}$. This notation covers all operations performed with secret values, including those performed between public scalars and secret values. These operations are provided by the $\mathcal{F}_{ABB}$.

We define two repeatedly used subroutines to improve readability and simplify expressions. They only use the primitives available in the $\mathcal{F}_{ABB}$ and work under the same general assumptions.

conditional assignment: Overloaded functionality of the assignment operator represented by $[z] \leftarrow_{[c]} [x] : [y]$. Much like in [5,13], the behavior of the assignment is tied to a secretly shared binary condition $[c]$. If $[c]$ is one, $[x]$ is assigned to $[z]$ or $[y]$ otherwise. The operation can be characterized as follows: $[z] \leftarrow [y] + [c] \cdot ([x] - [y])$. The subroutine can be extended for other mathematical structures i.e. vectors, matrices.

conditional exchange: We define the operator $condexch([c], i, j, [v])$. It exchanges the values held in position i and j of secretly shared vector $[v]$ if a secretly shared binary condition $[c]$ is 1 and leaves the vector unchanged otherwise. We describe the algorithm as Protocol 1. We also extend this operator to work with matrices. In that case both i^{th} and j^{th} rows and columns are swapped.

Protocol 1. condexch: Exchanges the values of 2 different vector positions

---

Input: Any vector $[v]$. Indexes i, j
Output: The vector $[v]$ with values i,j swapped if $[c]$ true.
1 $[a] \leftarrow [c] \cdot ([v]_j - [v]_i)$;
2 $[v]_i \leftarrow [v]_i + [a]$;
3 $[v]_j \leftarrow [v]_j - [a]$;

2.3 On Network Flows and Matrix Representation

The number of vertices in the graph or at least an upper bound on them are assumed to be publicly known with no restrictions on how the information is distributed amongst the players. Following [5,8,13] our protocols assume complete graph representation for their inputs, as a tool to hide the graph structure. That is why an adjacency matrix representation of the graph, using the bound as its size, is preferred. Capacities and/or costs of the edges are represented as elements in matrices. This allows the algorithm designer to decouple the graph representation from its topology. The application designer has to define how information of the topology is actually distributed and what is hidden. For instance, if its known that each player owns at most a single vertex, then, each player has to secretly share a row of a capacity adjacency matrix where he places a [0] at each unconnected vertex position or [∞] if its a cost matrix. We briefly describe some general definitions on graph theory that are often used during the following sections. Ahuja et al. [4] provides more formal notions.

Residual Graph: Is the associated network defined by all edges with positive residual capacities.

Walk: Is a sequence of contiguous edges $(v_1, w_1), ..., (v_k, w_k)$ such that $w_i = v_{i+1}$ for all $1 \leq i \leq n - 1$ and $(v_i, w_i) \in E$ for all $1 \leq i \leq n$.

Path: A path is a walk of G where no vertex is visited more than once. Every path, by definition is a walk, but not all paths are walks.

Cycle: A cycle is a special path $(v_1, w_1)...(v_d, w_d) \in E$ where $v_1 = w_d$. Every cycle by definition is a path, but not all paths are cycles.

3 Dijkstra's Algorithm

The algorithm provides a greedy way to find the shortest path from a source vertex s in a directed connected graph with non-negative capacities. Basically, it selects the vertex with the smallest accumulated distance and then propagates the path forward until all vertices have been explored. This ensures to get the shortest path from a source vertex to all other vertices in the graph. To find the shortest path to a single vertex is also possible. Our secure implementation can be adapted to detect at each iteration whether the target vertex has been reached to stop the algorithm.

Adapting Dijkstra to MPC. The input data in our case is a weighted adjacency matrix $[U]$ where non existing edges are represented by $[\infty]$. Dijkstra's algorithm treats the vertices of the graph in an order that depends on the capacities of the edges. The main challenge is to hide this order. Earlier work [5] has proposed to hide the position of the vertex accessed by using a secretly shared unary vector $[0, 0, ..., 0, 1, 0, ..., 0]$. We introduce a different technique. The basic idea is to exploit the symmetry in the data structure. More precisely, the numbering of the vertices or equivalently, the position of a vertex in the data structure is indifferent for the algorithm. We exploit this by positioning at iteration i, the vertex with the lowest distance in position i. That way we align the vertex exploration of our protocol with the secret data stored in all the structures. This enables us to gain in the number of operations performed because we can avoid considering edges pointing to vertices already explored. The algorithm is detailed as Protocol 2.

Correctness. Because the algorithm constantly reshuffles the positions of the vertices in all matrices and vectors used, we need to (secretly) track the position of the vertices. This is the role of the vector π. Throughout the algorithm π_j holds the node number that is currently in position j.

The loop on lines 5–8 determines the untreated vertex with current minimum distance. This vertex is brought to position i in all data structures. Loop on lines 9–14 scans all edges leaving node in position i to all other untreated vertices (positioned after i). If the edge improves the current best path (Line 11), the current best distances and predecessors are updated (Lines 12–13). The predecessor of node i is recorded as P_j. If the path needs to be kept secret and subsequently used in a parent protocol, then it would be more suitable to record this information in a matrix with $P_{i,j} = 1$ indicating that the predecessor of i is j (and 0 otherwise). It is easy to adapt the algorithm for this case.

Security. Following the correctness analysis, (i) it is easy to check that no intermediate value is revealed. (ii) The execution flow only depends on publicly known

---

Protocol 2. Shortest Path Protocol based on Dijkstra's algorithm

---

Input: A matrix of shared weights $[U]_{i,j}$ for $i, j \in \{1, ..., |V|\}$ and a unit vector $[S]$ encoding the source vertex.

Output: The vector of predecessors $[P]$ and/or the vector of distances $[d]_i$.

1 **for** $i \leftarrow 1$ **to** $|V|$ **do**
2 $\quad | \quad [\pi]_i \leftarrow i; [d]_i \leftarrow_{[S_i]} [0] : [\infty]; [P]_i \leftarrow i[S]_i;$
3 **end**
4 **for** $i \leftarrow 1$ **to** $|V|$ **do**
5 $\quad | \quad$ **for** $j \leftarrow |V|$ **to** $i + 1$ **do**
6 $\quad | \quad | \quad [c] \leftarrow [d]_j < [d]_{j-1};$
7 $\quad | \quad | \quad ([\pi], [P], [d], [U]) \leftarrow condexch([c], j, j - 1, [\pi], [P], [d], [U]);$
8 $\quad | \quad$ **end**
9 $\quad | \quad$ **for** $j \leftarrow i + 1$ **to** $|V|$ **do**
10 $\quad | \quad | \quad [a] \leftarrow [d]_i + [U]_{i,j};$
11 $\quad | \quad | \quad [c] \leftarrow [a] < [d]_j;$
12 $\quad | \quad | \quad [d]_j \leftarrow_{[c]} [a] : [d]_j;$
13 $\quad | \quad | \quad [P]_j \leftarrow_{[c]} [\pi]_i : [P]_j;$
14 $\quad | \quad$ **end**
15 **end**

---

values (the same follows for the execution time memory usage) and (*iii*) all operators on private data is provided by the $\mathcal{F}_{ABB}$.

Complexity. The algorithm performs $|V|^2 + \mathcal{O}(|V|)$ comparisons (at Lines 6 and 11) and $\frac{4 \cdot |V|^3}{3} + \mathcal{O}(|V|^2)$ multiplications, dominated by Line 7 (the 4/3 factor is 4 times the sum of the square of the integers 1 to $|V|$). This distinction is important for small graph instances where the comparison complexity dominates over round complexity. The performance of our privacy preserving version of Dijkstra has an extra factor of $|V|$ when compared with a vanilla implementation. Moreover, it can also be extended to obtain the shortest path between any pair of vertices $(v, w) \in V$.

4   Minimum Mean Cycle Problem

The Minimum Mean Cycle problem (MMC) is to determine on a directed graph $G = (V, E)$ with edge costs C, the cycle W with the minimum averaged cost (total cost divided by the number of edges in W).

Our interest on the MMC problem comes from the fact that it is used as a subroutine to solve the minimum cost flow problem by the minimum mean cycle canceling algorithm [16]. It is also used by other algorithms of the same nature. More details like applications, proofs and algorithms can be found in [4]. The following analysis assumes strong connectivity on G. In case a graph instance does not provide enough edges to fulfill this requirement, edges with a very large cost can be added to the graph.

The solution we study was proposed by Karp [17] and can be divided in two steps: First, we arbitrarily define a vertex s to be the origin of all paths to all vertices in V. Let $d^k(i)$ be the smallest weighted walk from s to the vertex i that contains exactly k edges. The walk obtained might contain one or several cycles. Then, we calculate $d^k(v)$ $\forall v \in V$ with k from 1 to $|V|$. The following shows how to compute this recursively:

$$d^k(j) = \min_{\{i:(i,j)\in E\}} \{d^{k-1}(i) + c_{ij}\}, \tag{1}$$

where $d^0(s) = 0$ and $d^0(v) = \infty$ $\forall v \in \{V - s\}$. Second, we calculate the cost of the minimum mean cycle as follows:

$$\mu^* = \min_{j\in V} \max_{0\leq k\leq |V|-1} \left[\frac{d^{|V|}(j) - d^k(j)}{|V| - k}\right] \tag{2}$$

This expression can be intuitively explained as follows. Let j^* and k^* the indexes achieving μ^*. Then $d^{|V|}(j^*)$ is the cost of a walk containing the cycle W and $d^{k^*}(j^*)$ is the cost of the same walk with the cycle removed e.g. it is a path. The difference between the two yields the cycle cost. Proofs can be found in [17]. A strictly positive or negative μ^* means that at least a positive/negative cycle is present with μ^* as its mean. A case where the answer is 0 might also mean no cycle was found in the graph. The algorithm can be extended to find the cycle W as part of the answer. Overall algorithmic complexity is $\mathcal{O}(|V||E|)$.

5   Privacy-Preserving Minimum Mean Cycle Solution

The privacy-preserving solution we introduce follows the steps provided by the previous section. Moreover, each step and the whole protocol are designed to be used as sub-routines. As usual, our approach assumes all input data is in secret form, including the adjacency matrix of costs $[C]$ (where non-existing edges are represented by $[\infty]$) except the upper bound on the number of vertices. The final goal of the protocol is to obtain not only the mean cost of the minimum cycle, but the cycle itself as well. We use the function *getmincycle* to refer to the protocol.

Correctness. First, we have to replicate the result of Eq. (1). We select node 1 as the source node s. Implementing the recursion is fairly straightforward as the order in which the edges are scanned does not depend on the input. The more difficult task is to encode the walks. To that end, we define the 4-dimensional matrix $[walk]$ where $[walk]_{i,j,k,l}$ is the number of times the edge (i, j) is traversed by the shortest walk of length k from s to l. Also, because of the specific way we want to use our secure version of the MCC algorithm as a sub-routine, we define an additional argument $[b]$ to the protocol. Specifically, $[b]_{i,j} = 1$ indicates that the edge (i, j) is forbidden, i.e. cannot be part of the solution. The algorithm is detailed as Protocol 3.

Loop 5–8 checks whether edge (i, j) improves the walk of length k from s to j. This is done by comparing the best one found so far with cost $[A]_{jk}$ to $[A]_{ik-1}$

Protocol 3. First step of: MMC protocol based on Karp's algorithm

---

Input: A matrix of shared costs $[C]_{i,j}$ for $i, j \in \{1, ..., |V|\}$, a binary matrix on viable edges $[b]_{i,j}$ for $i, j \in \{1, ..., |V|\}$.

Output: A matrix of walk costs $[A]_{i,k}$ for $i \in \{1, ..., |V|\}$ and $k \in \{0, ..., |V|\}$, a walk matrix $walks_{ij}$ for $i, j \in \{1, ..., |V|\}$ encoding these walks.

1 $[A] \leftarrow [\infty]$; $[A]_{00} \leftarrow [0]$; $[C] \leftarrow [C] + [\infty](1 - [b])$;
2 **for** $k \leftarrow 1$ **to** $|V| + 1$ **do**
3   **for** $j \leftarrow 1$ **to** $|V|$ **do**
4   **for** $i \leftarrow 1$ **to** $|V|$ **do**
5              $[c] \leftarrow [A]_{ik-1} + [C]_{ij} < [A]_{jk}$;
6              $[A]_{jk} \leftarrow_{[c]} [A]_{ik-1} + [C]_{ij} : [A]_{jk}$;
7              $[walks]_{..kj} \leftarrow_{[c]} [walks]_{..k-1i} : [walks]_{..kj}$;
8              $[walks]_{ijkj} \leftarrow_{[c]} [walks]_{ijkj} + 1 : [walks]_{ijkj}$;
9   **end**
10   **end**
11 **end**

---

plus the cost of edge (i, j). Depending on the result, the best costs and walks are updated.

Second, we adapt (2) to obtain the value of the minimum mean cycle, as well as the encoding of the cycle. We achieve it by iterating over the matrices $[A]$ and $[walks]$ generated in the *first* step. The only difficulty is to workaround the non-integer division. In place of any costly procedure, we keep track of the numerators and the denominators separately, and compare the cross multiplication instead. The minimum mean cost cycle is encoded as a $|V| \times |V|$ matrix $[min - cycle]$ where $[min - cycle]_{ij} = 1$ if the edge (i, j) is part of the minimum mean cycle. The rest of the algorithm is a straightforward implementation of (2). The details are provided as Protocol 4.

Security. Like with our Dijkstra implementation, no intermediate data is released and the operations are provided by the $\mathcal{F}_{ABB}$, following our definition of security.

Complexity. In total (Protocols 4 and 5), our implementation of MMC requires $\mathcal{O}(|V|^3)$ (Line 5 of Protocol 4) and $\mathcal{O}(|V|^5)$ multiplications or communication rounds (from the conditional assignments of Lines 7 and 8 of Protocol 4). One might ask whether this could not be brought down to $\mathcal{O}(|V|^4)$ by encoding the walks in Protocol 4 as a 3-dimensional matrix holding the predecessor node of each node. However, reconstructing the walks for the operation performed at Line 9 of Protocol 5 would then need $\mathcal{O}(|V|^5)$ conditional assignments instead of the currently $\mathcal{O}(|V|^4)$. So we prefer to stick with our simple and as efficient approach.

6   Minimum Cost Flow Problem

The Minimum-Cost Flow problem (MCF) is of finding a feasible flow in a capacitated directed graph $G = (E, V)$ that minimizes the costs (proportional to the

---

Protocol 4. Second step of: MMC protocol based on Karp's algorithm

---

Input: A matrix of walk costs $[A]_{i,k}$ for $i \in \{1, ..., |V|\}$ and $k \in \{0, ..., |V|\}$, a walk matrix $walks_{ij}$ for $i, j \in \{1, ..., |V|\}$ encoding these walks.

Output: The cost of the minimum mean cycle $[min - cost]$. A matrix with the minimum mean cycle $[\text{min-cycle}]_{i,j}$ for $i, j \in \{1, ..., |V|\}$.

```
1  for j ← 1 to |V| do
2      [max-cycle], [max-cost] ← ∅;
3      for k ← |V| to 1 do
4          [a-num] ← [A]_{j(|V|+1)} − [A]_{jk};
5          [a-den] ← |V| − k;
6          [c] ← [k-num] · [k-den] < [a-num] · [k-den];
7          [k-num] ←_{[c]} [a-num] : [k-num];
8          [k-den] ←_{[c]} [a-den] : [k-den];
9          [max-cycle] ←_{[c]} [walks]_{..|V|j} − [walks]_{..kj} : [max-cycle];
10         [max-cost] ←_{[c]} [A]_{jk} : [max-cost]
11     end
12     [c] ← [j-num] · [k-den] > [k-num] · [j-den];
13     [j-num] ←_{[c]} [k-num] : [j-num];
14     [j-den] ←_{[c]} [k-den] : [j-den];
15     [min-cycle] ←_{[c]} [max-cycle] : [min-cycle];
16     [min-cost] ←_{[c]} [max-cost] : [min-cost]
17 end
```

---

magnitude of the flows). The problem can be modeled as a linear program but there exists more efficient and well known strongly polynomial time combinatorial algorithms, see [4] for details. The more traditional minimum capacitated cost flow problem can be shown to be equivalent to the transshipment and the minimum-cost circulation (MCC) problem.

Formally, the MCC problem is of finding a capacitated flow in a symmetric graph $G = (E, V)$ of minimum cost. The problem can be modeled as follows:

$$\min \qquad \frac{1}{2} \sum_{v,w \in E} C_{v,w} f_{v,w} \qquad\qquad (3)$$

$$\text{subject to} \qquad f_{v,w} \leq U_{v,w} \qquad\qquad \forall (v,w) \in E \qquad (4)$$

$$f_{v,w} = -f_{w,v} \qquad\qquad \forall (v,w) \in E \qquad (5)$$

$$\sum_{v \in \mathbf{E}(w)} f_{v,w} = 0 \qquad\qquad \forall w \in V \qquad (6)$$

Here the graph is assumed to be symmetric, i.e. for every $(v, w) \in E$ there is an edge $(w, v) \in E$. Each edge (v, w) has a maximal capacity $U_{v,w}$ and a cost $C_{v,w}$ per unit of flow. Additionally, all costs are antisymmetric, i.e. $c(v, w) = -c(w, v)$ $\forall (v, w) \in E$. The variable f represents the amount of flow passing through an edge. Using this notation, the residual capacity can be formally defined as $r_{v,w} = U_{v,w} - f_{v,w}$.

Constraints (4) are the capacity constraints. Constraints (5) are the flow antisymmetry constraints. Constraints (6) are the flow conservation constraints at each node. This characterization of the problem is the same used by Goldberg and Tarjan [16] for their description of the MCC problem using the Minimum Mean Cycle-Canceling algorithm (MMCC). It can be seen as a variant of the non-polynomial cycle-canceling algorithm proposed by Klein in [18], but where the next cycle to be canceled is chosen by finding the minimum mean cost cycle. The change makes the algorithm strongly polynomial, i.e. its complexity only depends on $|V|$ and $|E|$ and no other parameter.

The algorithm is based on the finding of Busacker and Saaty [19], which asserts that a circulation with no residual negative cost cycles is of minimal cost. Moreover, the algorithm can be characterized as follows:

1. Initialize the feasible circulation of as 0.
2. Obtain the minimum mean cycle W in the associated residual graph.
3. Set $\delta \leftarrow min\{(v, w) \in Wr_{v,w}\}$.
4. Augment the flow by δ along the cycle W.
5. If there are still negative cycles *goto* 2.

Basically, we compute the cycle with the minimum negative average cost W in the associated residual graph. Then, we augment the flow along this cycle until an edge reaches its capacity. This process is repeated until no negative cycle is found. Its complexity is $O(|V|^2 \cdot |E|^3 \cdot \log |V|)$.

7   Privacy-Preserving Minimum-Cost Flow Problem

The input data are the capacity and cost adjacency matrices $[U]$ and $[C]$, where non-existing edges are represented by $[0]$ on the capacity matrix and by $[\infty]$ on the cost matrix. As usual, all input data is secretly shared, except the bound on the number of vertices. The solution is to be provided as the flow matrix $[F]$ and total cost $[totcost]$. The final composition of $[F]$ might leak some details on the graph's topology depending on the answer. The protocol can be used as a sub-routine for more complex applications in case the final output is kept private. Once the MMF problem is modeled as a MCC problem, it is sufficient to securely solve the minimum circulation problem using a privacy-preserving implementation of the MMCC algorithm to obtain a flow of minimum cost.

Adapting the MMCC algorithm. If one wants to avoid any leakage of information, an important difference between a standard implementation and a secure one is that the augmenting flow process has to be repeated as many times as the worst case analysis guarantees, instead of stopping it as soon as no negative cycle is detected. We call each flow augmentation along the cycle a phase/iteration. We use the bound provided by Goldberg and Tarjan on [16]: $|V||E|^2 \log |V| + |V| \cdot |E|$ flow augmentations at most. Note that this is not an asymptotic bound. Given that we also hide the graph structure, $|E|$ has to be replaced by $|V|^2$ in our capacities estimates. Our secure protocol requires to perform that many iterations to guarantee correctness with no leakage. Possible stopping conditions to reduce the number of iterations are considered later in this section. Protocol 5 shows our privacy-preserving solution for the MMCC algorithm, which is a straightforward translation of the algorithm outlined above.

Protocol 5. Privacy-preserving MMCC

Input: $|V| \times |V|$ matrices of shared capacities $[U]_{i,j}$ and shared costs $[C]_{i,j}$.
Output: The $|V| \times |V|$ matrix of flows $[F]$ and the associated total cost $[totcost]$.

```
 1  [F], [b], [totcost] ← 0 ;
 2  for k ← 1 to |V|^5 log|V| + |V|^3 do
 3  │   [cost], [cycle] ← getmincycle([C], [b]);
 4  │   δ ← [∞];
 5  │   for (i, j) ∈ [U] do
 6  │   │   [r] ← [U]_{ij} − [F]_{ij};
 7  │   │   [c] ← [min − cycle]_{ij} · ([δ] > [r]);
 8  │   │   [δ] ←_c [r] : [δ];
 9  │   end
10  │   [δ] ← [δ] · ([cost] < 0);
11  │   [totcost] ← [totcost] + [δ] · [cost];
12  │   for (i, j) ∈ [F] do
13  │   │   [c] ← [cycle]_{ij};
14  │   │   [F]_{ij} ←_c [F]_{ij} + [δ] : [F]_{ij};
15  │   │   [F]_{ji} ←_c [F]_{ji} − [δ] : [F]_{ji};
16  │   │   [b]_{ij} ← [U]_{ij} − [F]_{ij} > 0;
17  │   end
18  end
```

Correctness. The initial solution is set to zero at Line 1. The body of the main loop is one flow augmentation phase. It starts by calling our secure implementation of the Min Mean Cycle problem, leaving out saturated edges. Loop 5-9 computes the maximum augmentation possible along the cycle identified. If the cycle has non-negative cost, this augmentation is set to zero at Line 10, before updating the cost of the solution. Then, the flow itself is augmented at Loop 12-17.

Security. Following the previous protocols, the current solution does not leak intermediate values and uses $\mathcal{F}_{ABB}$ operations to calculate secret data, respecting our definition of security.

Complexity. The most costly operation during one augmentation phase is the call to *getmincycle* with $\mathcal{O}(|V|^3)$ comparisons and $\mathcal{O}(|V|^5)$ communication rounds. The overall complexity is $\mathcal{O}(|V|^8 \log|V|)$ comparisons and $\mathcal{O}(|V|^{10} \log|V|)$ communicational rounds. As mentioned above, one main difference between our secure MCF algorithm described above and a standard implementation is that, to guarantee no leakage of information, we have to execute as many iterations as in the theoretical worst case. This makes the practical performance of the algorithm much worse than a standard implementation because, in most practical applications, it is expected that the number of iterations needed to find the optimal solution is much smaller than the theoretical upper bound. Of course, one could easily publicly reveal the outcome of the test performed at Line 10 of Protocol 5 and stop the algorithm if the cost of the cycle is non-negative. But some information would be leaked. To limit it, several strategies are possible. One is to open the test every K iterations, with K being a publicly known integer. Another solution is to multiply the result of the test by a random bit (for $= 1$ with probability p) to statistically hide the result. These two would also be combined. In both cases, the parameters (K and/or p) would control the trade-off between performance and information leaked.

8   Computational Experiments

The theoretical bounds only give a rate of increase on the size of the instance. They do not say anything about the actual computing time. Our interest is to determine what is the size of the instances that can be solved in a "reasonable" amount of time. Moreover, we want to determine the impact that the number of players and the size of the graph instances have on CPU time performance. We chose the Virtual Ideal Functionality Framework (VIFF) to run, given its availability (open source) and easy coupling with larger applications, bearing in mind its scalability is an additional concern.

VIFF benefits from passive security under the information theoretic model on the multi-party case. VIFF provides access to Shamir secret sharing and basic arithmetic secure functionality [20]. For comparisons we use the most recent Toft comparison method implemented [21]. Additionally, for our experiments we use randomly generated complete graphs. All results presented are averaged over 20 instances of the same size with 3 and 4 players.

Table 2. CPU time of protocol 2

Number of vertices		4	8	12	16	20
Execution times (in seconds)	3 Players	0.9	5	14	28	48
	4 Players	1	7	17	34	57

All trials used the same workstation, an Intel Xeon CPUs X5550 (2.67GHz) and 42 GB of memory, running Mac OS X 10.7. Additionally, every single process had the same amount of CPU power and memory available.

8.1   Shortest Path Problem

Table 2 shows the results obtained by our shortest path prototype: Additionally, we could run 64-vertex instances, using adjacency matrices, with a total of 4032 edges/matrix entries, taking around 18 minutes. The spike in computing time while working with these big instances follows the fact of the difficulty to manage the memory for large graph instances. Additional experimentation (where we assume the performance cost added by the secure functionalities of our $\mathcal{F}_{ABB}$ to be 0 and implemented on nothing but python) showed that roughly an extra factor of $1.4|V|$ is needed when executing crypto-primitives have 0 cost. Figure 1 also shows the CPU time and the ratios calculated by comparing our Dijkstra prototype against a vanilla implementation of the algorithm:

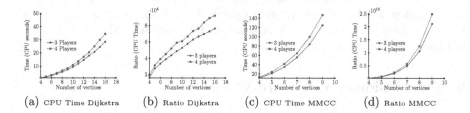

(a) CPU Time Dijkstra   (b) Ratio Dijkstra   (c) CPU Time MMCC   (d) Ratio MMCC

Fig. 1. Dijkstra CPU times and ratio analysis

From our experimentation we can conclude the following: We can solve securely, in reasonable time, shortest path problems on complete graphs of sizes up to 64 vertices over VIFF. As expected, the number of players, have little incidence on the general behavior, given that in VIFF performance cost increases linearly in the number of players [20]. Compared to the standard implementation, roughly a factor of $5000|V|$ is needed to securely solve the Dijkstra algorithm on VIFF. Combining the previous remark and the results obtained by our experimentation, we conclude that out of the $5000|V|$ overhead of our SMC implementation, the factor $|V|$ is explained by algorithmic design, a factor 1.4 is due to non-crypto related VIFF implementation, and the rest (a factor of a few thousands) is due to the crypto-related VIFF implementation.

8.2   Minimum Flow Problem

For the minimum flow problem, we measure the time a single phase (one iteration of Protocol 5) takes to be executed, that is because stopping conditions with some leakage can substantially reduce the number of phases needed e.g. A graph with a single cycle would only take one phase to be completed. To estimate the execution time of the full algorithm, it suffices to multiply this by the known number of phases needed. Our analysis includes the ratio between the time it takes a vanilla implementation to find an answer and the privacy preserving versions full execution time to guarantee correctness with no leakage. The results of these experiments can be found in Table 3 and Fig. 1.

From these we can conclude the following: The fully secure version of our implementation is highly costly in terms of performance even for very small instances. This highlights the necessity of using termination conditions. Once again, the influence of the extra player has little incidence on the overall performance time. The overhead of our secure implementation versus a standard one is

Table 3. Execution times per phase MMCC Algorithm for a complete graph.

Number of vertices		4	5	6	7	8	9
Execution times (in seconds)	MMCC Phase - 3 Players	11	21	35	56	84	125
	MMCC Phase - 4 Players	13	24	42	65	100	147

of the order of $2.5 \cdot 10^8 |V|^2$. Note that both algorithms have different complexity functions and vanilla versions of the algorithm typically converge towards an answer before reaching its worst case complexity. Again, one can observe that the multiplications absorb a larger fraction of the computing time as the size of the instances increases.

9   Conclusions and Future Work

Strongly polynomial-time algorithms are appealing for MPC implementations because, as the worst-case complexity is polynomial, it is possible to obtain fully secure (i.e. no leakage) and theoretically efficient algorithms and implementations. We have demonstrated this for three classical network problems: Shortest Path, Minimum Mean Cycle and Minimum Cost Flow. However, our computational experiments demonstrate that the price to pay for such security is very high for the simplest problem (shortest path) and extremely penalizing for the more complicated ones.

This research raises several questions for further research. A first one is whether theoretically more efficient algorithms can be obtained for these problems. Another one is related to the development of more efficient MPC platforms compared to the one we used for our computational experiments. Also one could consider other classical optimization problems.

Acknowledgements. This research was supported by the WIST Walloon Region project CAMUS and the Belgian IAP Program P7/36 initiated by the Belgian State, Prime Minister's Office, Science Policy Programming. The scientific responsibility is assumed by the authors. The authors are grateful to Edouard Cuvelier, Sophie Mawet, Olivier Pereira and the anonymous reviewers for their feedback.

References

1. Yao, A.C.C.: Protocols for secure computations (extended abstract). In: 23rd Annual Symposium on Foundations of Computer Science, pp. 160–164. IEEE (1982)
2. Shamir, A.: How to share a secret. Commun. ACM **22**(11), 612–613 (1979)
3. Paillier, P.: Public-Key cryptosystems based on composite degree residuosity classes. In: Stern, J. (ed.) EUROCRYPT 1999. LNCS, vol. 1592, p. 223. Springer, Heidelberg (1999)
4. Ahuja, R.K., Magnanti, T.L., Orlin, J.B.: Network Flows: Theory, Algorithms, and Applications. Prentice-Hall Inc., Upper Saddle River (1993)

5. Aly, A., Cuvelier, E., Mawet, S., Pereira, O., Van Vyve, M.: Securely solving simple combinatorial graph problems. In: Sadeghi, A.-R. (ed.) FC 2013. LNCS, vol. 7859, pp. 239–257. Springer, Heidelberg (2013)
6. Launchbury, J., Diatchki, I.S., DuBuisson, T., Adams-Moran, A.:Efficient lookup-table protocol in secure multiparty computation. In: Proceedings of the 17th ACM SIGPLAN International Conference on Functional Programming, ICFP 2012, pp. 189–200. ACM, New York (2012)
7. Brickell, J., Shmatikov, V.: Privacy-preserving graph algorithms in the semi-honest model. In: Roy, B. (ed.) ASIACRYPT 2005. LNCS, vol. 3788, pp. 236–252. Springer, Heidelberg (2005)
8. Blanton, M., Steele, A., Alisagari, M.: Data-oblivious graph algorithms for secure computation and outsourcing. In: Proceedings of the 8th ACM SIGSAC Symposium on Information, Computer and Communications Security, ASIA CCS 2013, pp. 207–218. ACM, New York (2013)
9. Wang, X., Nayak, K., Liu, C., Shi, E., Stefanov, E., Huang, Y.: Oblivious data structures. Cryptology ePrint Archive, Report 2014/185 (2014). http://eprint.iacr.org/
10. Lu, S., Ostrovsky, R.: Distributed oblivious ram for secure two-party computation. Cryptology ePrint Archive, Report 2011/384 (2011). http://eprint.iacr.org/
11. Gordon, S.D., Katz, J., Kolesnikov, V., Krell, F., Malkin, T., Raykova, M., Vahlis, Y.: Secure two-party computation in sublinear (amortized) time. In: Proceedings of the 2012 ACM Conference on Computer and Communications Security, CCS 2012, pp. 513–524. ACM, New York (2012)
12. Liu, C., Huang, Y., Shi, E., Katz, J., Hicks, M.: Automating efficient ram-model secure computation. In: 35th IEEE Symposium on Security and Privacy (2014)
13. Keller, M., Scholl, P.: Efficient, oblivious data structures for mpc. IACR Cryptology ePrint Archive, 137 (2014)
14. Maurer, U.: Secure multi-party computation made simple. Discrete Appl. Math. 154(2), 370–381 (2006). Coding and Cryptography
15. Damgård, I.B., Nielsen, J.B.: Universally composable efficient multiparty computation from threshold homomorphic encryption. In: Boneh, D. (ed.) CRYPTO 2003. LNCS, vol. 2729, pp. 247–264. Springer, Heidelberg (2003)
16. Goldberg, A.V., Tarjan, R.E.: Finding minimum-cost circulations by canceling negative cycles. J. ACM 4, 873–886 (1989)
17. Karp, R.M.: A characterization of the minimum cycle mean in a digraph. Discrete Math. 3, 309–311 (1978)
18. Klein, M.: A primal method for minimal cost flows with applications to the assignment and transportation problems. Manag. Sci. 14(3), 205–220 (1967)
19. Busacker, R., Saaty, T.: Finite Graphs and Networks: An Introduction with Applications. International Series in Pure and Applied Mathematics. McGraw-Hill, New York (1965)
20. Geisler, M.: Cryptographic protocols: theory and implementation. Ph.D. thesis, Aarhus University Denmark, Department of Computer Science (2010)
21. Toft, T.: Primitives and applications for multi-party computation. Ph.D. thesis, Department of Computer Science, Aarhus University (2007)

Remote IP Protection Using Timing Channels

Ariano-Tim Donda[1,2], Peter Samarin[1,2], Jacek Samotyja[1],
Kerstin Lemke-Rust[1(⊠)], and Christof Paar[2(⊠)]

[1] Bonn-Rhein-Sieg University of Applied Sciences, Sankt Augustin, Germany
{peter.samarin,jacek.samotyja,kerstin.lemke-rust}@h-brs.de
[2] Ruhr University Bochum, Bochum, Germany
{ariano-tim.donda,christof.paar}@rub.de

Abstract. We introduce the use of timing channels for digital watermarking of embedded hardware and software components. In addition to previous side channel watermarking schemes, timing analysis offers new perspectives for a remote verification of mobile and embedded products. Timing channels make it possible to detect the presence of a watermark solely by measuring program execution times.

We propose schemes for embedding authorship and fingerprint marks that are built upon conditional timing delays. We provide experimental evidence by protecting an implementation of an image binarization circuit on an FPGA board that is connected over Ethernet to a remote PC. The circuit constantly leaks the watermark over the timing channel by modulating its execution time, which is successfully detected by using an oscilloscope and an EM probe, as well as by using software on a remote PC. Our solution for a remote verification is of special interest for highly performant services as they force an adaptive adversary towards enhanced costs in time, memory, and circuitry when bypassing these schemes.

Keywords: IP protection · Digital watermarking · Timing channel · Timing analysis · Side-channel analysis · Authorship watermark · Fingerprint watermark · FPGA implementation · Embedded systems

1 Introduction

Digital watermarking schemes look back on a long tradition. Basically, a watermark is an identifying information that is embedded in media. It has to fulfill three requirements. First, the watermark shall not impede normal use of the watermarked media, second, the watermark shall become verifiable if it undergoes a specific test, e.g., the paper watermark of a banknote becomes visible in case of exposure to light [9], and third, an unauthorized party should not be able to remove or alter the watermark.

Today, there is a variety of digital watermarking schemes invented for audio, images, video, and software media for many purposes. Due to this diversity and depending on the purpose, different properties of digital watermarking schemes are important. If it shall be a hard problem to remove a watermark from a media,

J. Lee and J. Kim (Eds.): ICISC 2014, LNCS 8949, pp. 222–237, 2015.
DOI: 10.1007/978-3-319-15943-0_14

robustness is needed. Otherwise, if authenticity of a media shall be guaranteed, this calls for fragility of the watermark in case of any modification of the media. In [14] a valuable taxonomy on digital watermarks can be found.

Our security objective is to protect embedded systems against plagiarism. In this paper we introduce watermarks based on conditional timing delays that are deeply embedded into software and hardware components. A watermark becomes verifiable if timing differences such as program execution times or parts thereof are analyzed. Timing analysis for detecting digital watermarks can be done by measuring power consumption or electromagnetic (EM) radiation of a device [11,12], and even remotely without the need for any special equipment.

This paper provides high-level schemes for embedding an authorship mark and a fingerprint mark [14] in the timing side channel in order to protect embedded hardware and software. The schemes and their realizations in the timing channel are presented in Sect. 3. An authorship mark embeds information identifying its author. A fingerprinting mark embeds information identifying the serial number of the purchaser of the component. For both marks, robustness is an important security property.

In Sect. 4, we provide evidence of a successful implementation of these schemes in an image binarization circuit on an FPGA that is connected over Ethernet to a PC. For timing analysis, we tested three different measurement settings: (i) in proximity to the FPGA board using an EM probe, (ii) at the Ethernet cable using a contact-based measurement and an EM probe, and (iii) on a remote PC. The first two settings use an USB oscilloscope, while the third set-up uses only an open-source software library for capturing UDP packets on the PC.

Electromagnetic radiation and power consumption side channels have been used to leak a watermark before [3,4], however, previous work did not consider the timing side channel. The advantage of using the timing side channel is that the watermark can additionally be verified at a remote network device. Exploitation of the timing side channel has been explored by [5,10,15] to infer the secret key of a remote server, however, not to transmit a watermark, as in our approach. Section 2 views our approach in context of other work done in this area.

2   Related Work

The first known use of a timing channel traces back to inter-process communication on a secure operating system using dynamically shared resources in order to bypass information flow models. Such a timing channel can be activated by page faults, CPU demand, segment activation, disk cache loading, and other means [16].

Timing analysis was also the first published side channel based attack [10] that provides a methodology to compromise keys of RSA, DSS and other cryptosystems by measuring the execution time of the overall cryptographic operation. For success, it is required that the execution times of the elementary operations of a modular exponentiation are data dependent. As the secret key is the exponent, successively finding out the sequence of elementary operations reveals the secret key. More recent side channel attacks exploit timing delays on CPUs such as cache attacks [5,15] and branch prediction [1].

Timing measurements are also of high interest for traffic analysis of anonymizing networks such as Tor (The Onion Router), e.g., cf. [13,17]. It was shown that low latency anonymizing networks are susceptible to timing attacks that actively add timing delays to selected packets. In [17] watermarking of packets of a Skype call was done by actively imprinting time delays on packets according to a 24-bit watermark on one communication endpoint and it was shown that the watermark can be revealed after passing through the anonymizing network on the other endpoint.

The idea of combining side-channel analysis and digital watermarking for protecting intellectual property (IP) was first developed in [3,4]. In the earlier work [4], the authors introduced side-channel watermarks for integrated circuits. In the later work [3], an implementation in embedded software was suggested. Their contributions are based on power analysis as introduced by [11]. Power analysis requires tapping a power pin of the device under test and measuring it with an oscilloscope. In [4] the authors present a spread spectrum watermark and an input-modulated watermark. The spread spectrum watermark amplifies the output bit of a pseudo random number generator (PRNG) or, alternatively, a stream cipher with a leakage circuit in each clock cycle. Verification is done by simulating the outcome of the PRNG and correlating it with the power measurements of the leakage. The input-modulated watermark uses a combinatorial function of some input bits that computes one output bit that is sent to the leakage circuit. Verification is done by correlation power analysis. Basically the same scheme is proposed in [3] for embedded software. Herein, it is made more concrete: the authors use a combination function of 32-bit input bits and a 64-bit watermark key to compute one bit that is leaked out over the power consumption.

3   Watermarking Through Timing Channels

3.1   The Adversary Model

In our model, the owner of IP rights aims to protect an embedded product against unauthorized use. For this purpose, the product is watermarked in order to detect fraud due to unauthorized use of copies, plagiarism, and their distribution chain. The owner of the IP rights co-operates with the watermarker $\mathcal{W}$ who embeds digital watermarks based on conditional timing delays, compiles the sources, and distributes the product under copyright.

In this paper we use the term f to denote a function that has been protected by a watermark. Let f' denote a possibly different function with a functionality that is similar to f. Function f' is the object of investigation done by verifier $\mathcal{V}$ in order to decide whether it contains the watermark of $\mathcal{W}$ or not. The function f is assumed to have a data input and a data output channel. Both may be optional under certain conditions that are detailed further in this paper.

Our security objective is twofold:

O_1: Verifier $\mathcal{V}$ detects copyright violations of function f.

O_2: Verifier $\mathcal{V}$ discloses the distribution chain of the illegal copy of f in order to identify the issuer of the illegal copy or plagiarism.

In our model, the adversary is in possession of the compiled machine code of f. The adversary transforms the binary code: $f \rightarrow f'$ and distributes f', eventually as part of another program. Transformations include subtractive, distortive, and additive attacks to the embedded watermark.

In this work, we act on the assumption that a complete reverse engineering of f is a hard problem. Regarding FPGAs this is a reasonable assumption as decoding tools for FPGA bitstreams are not publicly available. Software reverse engineering requires disassembling and debugging tools which are available for many processors, but it is manual work and very time consuming. The resistance of a software implementation against reverse engineering can be significantly enhanced by using anti-debugging and anti-disassembly techniques, obfuscation, secret splitting, and encryption of parts of program code that is decrypted at run-time [2].

3.2   The Timing Channel

The timing channel is realized by using a start and end time of the regular input and output channel of function f. The timing channel can be built on any time difference between two successive observable events within f provided that they can be measured, e.g. network activities of f or special characteristics in a power or EM trace. Hereby, we assume that the start time can be triggered or observed and the end time can be observed. In order to send data over the timing channel, the sender introduces a timing delay into the regular output channel and the receiver can read the data from the timing channel by noting the time difference between input and output.

In practice, the task of the receiver is a signal detection problem. The time difference is considered as a physical observable that implicitly depends on the conditional timing delay besides other deterministic contributions and noise. Depending on the implementation of the timing channel (see Binary Method and Sliding Window Method below) two or more populations with different timing delays arise. Each population is labeled according to its timing delay. A measurement outcome of this observable is denoted by Δ_t. The receiver measures Δ_t and computes the likelihood for observing Δ_t in each population. The receiver decides for the population yielding the maximum likelihood and decodes the information on the timing channel accordingly.

Binary Method. The simplest implementation of the timing channel constitutes a binary method, i.e., there are two populations and a zero bit is encoded without delay and a delay δ_t is added if the bit is one. Assuming that both events are equally likely the following decision rule applies: If Δ_t is longer than the mean time difference $\overline{\Delta_t}$, the output bit b on the physical output channel is decoded to bit one, otherwise it decodes to bit zero.

$$b = \mathrm{decode}(\Delta_t) := \begin{cases} 1 & \text{if } \Delta_t \geq \overline{\Delta_t} \\ 0 & \text{if } \Delta_t < \overline{\Delta_t} \end{cases}$$

Sliding Window Method. An alternative implementation of the timing channel is a sliding window method that can output more than one bit in each Δ_t. More precisely, each zero bit is separately encoded without any timing delay and an l-bit sequence of ones is encoded with a delay of $l\delta_t$, i.e. the delay is proportional to the number of ones in a run given that l is smaller than an implementation specific maximum run length m. The output bits w on the physical output channel are decoded by empirical statistics using probability distributions $P_{i,j,m}$ with $i \in \{0,1\}$, $1 \leq j \leq m$ if $i = 1$ (i.e. a run of bit one) and $j = 1$ if $i = 0$ (i.e. a zero bit). In the simplest case decoding can be done by computing the differences of Δ_t from the means $\mu_{i,j,m}$ of all probability distributions and deciding for that probability distribution that minimizes the difference:

$$(b,l) = \mathrm{decode}(\Delta_t) := \min \arg_{i \in \{0,1\}, 1 \leq j \leq m} |\Delta_t - \mu_{i,j,m}|$$

If l is incorrectly decoded, the sliding window method leads to a desynchronization of sender and receiver and follow-up errors. Because of that, a backtracking algorithm needs to be foreseen to correct such wrong decodings. Alternatively, a reset function of f may be used for re-synchronization.

From perspective of performance, it is desirable to not substantially reduce the overall performance by introducing the timing delay. This requires that the computation of f is decoupled from its output, so that the application does not remain idle while waiting for the delay to run out. This can be accomplished by computing outputs during a delay and storing them in a buffer, so that when the delay is finished, the next output can be sent immediately.

Notation. In the following, we generalize the timing channel by using functions sndTC and rcvTC to indicate the data transmitted and received over the physical channel. $l = \mathrm{sndTC}(c,i)$ encodes the delay corresponding to bitstream c starting at offset i and outputs the number of bits l that are sent. $(b,l) = \mathrm{rcvTC}(\Delta_t)$ decodes an l-bit run of bit b on the receiver side. w denotes a run with bit length l i.e. $w = (b,l)$. The auxiliary function $\mathrm{cmp}(c,i,w)$ checks whether the bits starting at offset i in c are equal to l-bit run w and outputs 'true' or 'false'.

3.3   Authorship Watermarks

In order to detect copyright violations of function f, i.e., our security objective O_1, we propose the use of authorship watermarks. Authorship watermarks are used to identify the owner of IP. We introduce two authorship watermarking schemes: a codeword scheme and a challenge-response scheme.

Codeword Scheme. The codeword scheme cyclically broadcasts a fixed secret n-bit codeword c_{CW} on the timing channel. This scheme does not require any input data channel. Figure 1 shows the protocol for verifying one or a few bits of the codeword. $\mathcal{V}$ checks in each protocol run, whether the decoded bit of the measured execution time corresponds to the expected bit of the codeword. The number of successful authentications suc is counted. Both parties continue to increment the offset i in the codeword for further function calls to f. An extension of this watermarking scheme towards an output sequence of a linear feedback shift register (LFSR) instead of a codeword is an alternative protocol design.

Challenge-Response Scheme. This proposal is based on a common cryptographic challenge-response scheme (cf. [6]). The security aim is that f authenticates to verifier $\mathcal{V}$. This scheme introduces a timing delay depending on the outcome of an encryption algorithm E that is parameterized with a secret key k and initialized with data c that are input to function f. The key is the authorship mark. Therefore, it requires a data input channel for receiving the challenge of $\mathcal{V}$.

At each execution of f, the input c is taken as an input to cipher E. If the cipher is a block cipher, function f computes $E_k(c)$. If the cipher is a stream cipher, then E is initialized with a secret key k and the initialization vector (IV) c. $E_k(c)$ is then transmitted to $\mathcal{V}$ over the timing channel. Verifier $\mathcal{V}$ knows the cipher and its secret key and is able to check the correctness of the result for every input data c. The protocol for verifying one bit is given in Fig. 2.

The protocol design can be optimized for performance if the number of ciphering operations can be reduced for successive invocations to f. This can be achieved with a stream cipher in which the keystream is initialized at the first invocation of f using data input c. Starting with offset 0 of the key stream bits, at further invocations of f the pointer to the key stream is incremented by the number of sent bits until a reset occurs. A similar but limited optimization is possible for block ciphers where successively all bits of an output block are sent on the timing channel before the encryption is executed again.

3.4   Fingerprint Watermarks

Fingerprint marks are intended to be invisible. For this proposal we re-visit the idea of an Easter egg watermark [8]. An Easter egg watermark performs some action if it receives a highly unusual input from the user. This action is assumed to be definitively detectable by the user.

For an Easter egg, timing delays do not slow down the performance of function f in normal use so that a long delay on the timing channel is feasible. We assume that $\mathcal{V}$ possesses a list of secret keys that are allocated by $\mathcal{W}$. In case that the number of distributors and therefore the number of fingerprints is very high, our protocols can be extended with a tree search to speed up the verification process.

Our aim of a challenge-response scheme is to use cryptographic means in order to insert the timing delay only if the verifier $\mathcal{V}$ has been successfully

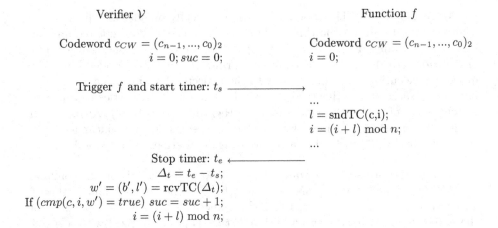

Verifier $\mathcal{V}$ Function f

Codeword $c_{CW} = (c_{n-1}, ..., c_0)_2$ Codeword $c_{CW} = (c_{n-1}, ..., c_0)_2$
$i = 0; suc = 0;$ $i = 0;$

Trigger f and start timer: t_s $\longrightarrow$

                                                    ...
                                                    $l = \text{sndTC(c,i)};$
                                                    $i = (i + l) \bmod n;$
                                                    ...

Stop timer: t_e $\longleftarrow$
$\Delta_t = t_e - t_s;$
$w' = (b', l') = \text{rcvTC}(\Delta_t);$
If $(cmp(c, i, w') = true)\ suc = suc + 1;$
$i = (i + l) \bmod n;$

Fig. 1. Protocol for embedded authorship watermark with a codeword c_{CW}.

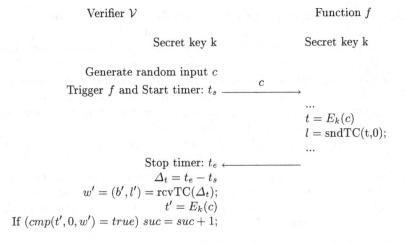

Verifier $\mathcal{V}$ Function f

Secret key k   Secret key k

Generate random input c
Trigger f and Start timer: t_s $\xrightarrow{\quad c \quad}$

                                                    ...
                                                    $t = E_k(c)$
                                                    $l = \text{sndTC(t,0)};$
                                                    ...

Stop timer: t_e $\longleftarrow$
$\Delta_t = t_e - t_s$
$w' = (b', l') = \text{rcvTC}(\Delta_t);$
$t' = E_k(c)$
If $(cmp(t', 0, w') = true)\ suc = suc + 1;$

Fig. 2. Protocol for embedded challenge-response authorship watermark using a block cipher E_k.

authenticated before. Therefore, we use a successful challenge-response authentication as trigger for the visibility of the watermark. If the authentication fails, the watermark remains invisible.

For this scheme shown in Fig. 3, it is necessary that the data input channel and data output channel are available and can be used for the watermarking scheme. The fingerprint watermark protocol requires two runs of f. E is a secure encryption algorithm that is parameterized with a secret key k, which is the fingerprint of the distributor in this scheme. The challenge-response protocol runs as follows. In each protocol run, function f generates a new random output value r, computes $t = E_k(r)$ and stores the result. Verifier $\mathcal{V}$ obtains r from

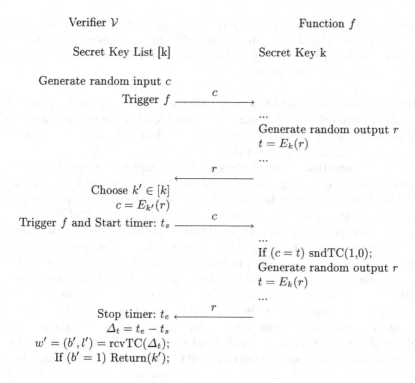

Fig. 3. Protocol for embedded challenge-response fingerprint watermark using a block cipher E_k.

the data output channel, selects one secret key k' from its list of secret keys, computes $c = E_{k'}(r)$, and sends c on the data input channel to function f. If $c = t$ holds, function f causes a long timing delay that signals a successful authentication to $\mathcal{V}$. Thereby, $\mathcal{V}$ reveals the fingerprint key that was originally built in function f.

3.5 Security Analysis and Implementation Considerations

The adversary can try to remove, rearrange and add code parts to f.

Subtraction. The challenge of subtraction is to identify single parts of the binary code containing the timing watermark and to leave the main part of f intact. Identification of such parts may be feasible with reverse engineering, possibly with the help of side channel analysis. Any measure that enhances the robustness of the implementation helps in resistance against subtraction. Further, start-up tests such as known-answer tests for encryption units and timing channel encoding help to detect subtractions. Subtraction attacks are considered to be a relevant threat for software, but much less for hardware implementations.

Distortion. The challenge is to reorder the code of f in order to destroy the timing delay but to leave the main part of f intact. Again, such an attack strongly depends on reverse engineering results and is considered to threaten software and much less hardware.

Addition. The addition attack aims to hide the timing watermark. If the adversary adds random delays this enhances the noise level of the timing channel and the number of queries a remote verifier has to ask to gain a specific confidence level, but it cannot hide the watermark.

One strong addition attack is obvious: If the execution time of f' is set to a constant value the timing channel is blocked for remote verifiers. This addition can be pre-programmed for the codeword scheme and needs to be adjusted in real-time for the challenge-response schemes. The drawback of this attack is that such a wrapper attack slows down overall performance of f' as the constant time difference needs to be set to the maximum time difference of f that can occur. Because of this, the sliding window method is advantageous in pushing the execution time of f' to significantly higher limits which may make such a wrapper attack inefficient for an adversary. Further, the fingerprint mark is rarely affected as the timing delay is long. Besides performance penalty a wrapper attack requires sufficient memory for intermediate storage and possibly additional circuits, thereby imposing additional costs to the adversary. For embedded devices with significant I/O load and tight timing requirements this wrapper attack may lead to data loss. Note that side channel analysis in the near-field may be able to detect the presence of a wrapper attack.

4 Experimental Results with an FPGA Implementation

To demonstrate the feasibility of timing watermarks, the protection scheme has been applied to a simple computer vision task of image binarization implemented on an Altera DE2-70 board. The board has an FPGA with 70 k logic elements that is based on SRAM and needs to be reconfigured with the bitstream at each power-up.

4.1 Image Binarization Circuit

The image binarization circuit converts images with 8 bits per pixel into images with 1 bit per pixel, thus, each pixel is either dark or bright. The decision to convert the pixel to dark or bright pixel is made by comparing the 8-bit pixel values to a user-controlled threshold. The images are obtained from a camera running at 119 frames per second with a resolution of 640 × 480 pixels. The binarized images are split into 60 parts and sent over an Ethernet interface to a fixed IP address using the UDP protocol. Each UDP packet is numbered from 0 to 59 to make it possible for the receiver to properly reassemble the images. Binary images are reconstructed using the packet number and the pixel data.

4.2   Establishing the Timing Channel

We use the binary method to establish a timing channel between the board and a generic receiver that can be an EM probe, a power consumption probe, or a remote PC listening on the network. The timing channel is realized by introducing artificial delays into the packet transmitting circuit on the FPGA board. Thus, presence of a delay denotes a binary "1", and the lack thereof means a binary "0", cf. Sect. 3.2 for the use of the binary method. Since each frame consists of 60 packets, it is possible to send 60 bits of information per image over the timing channel.

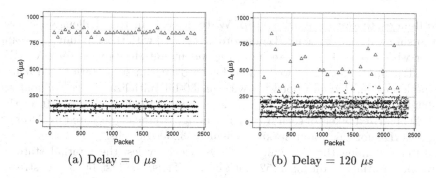

(a) Delay $= 0$ μs (b) Delay $= 120$ μs

Fig. 4. Time differences between consequent packets captured on the PC for different delays. Gray triangles show the timing differences between the first packet of image frame and the last packet of the previous image frame. Black dots show the time differences between packets in the same frame.

The data is captured on the PC by using the libpcap library, which provides elementary procedures for capturing and analyzing network packets. For every two consecutive packets, the time difference is computed by subtracting their respective timestamps. Figure 4 shows the timing channel of a challenge response authorship watermarking scheme of 2400 UDP packets obtained from 20 image frames. Time differences between the last packet of one frame and the first packet of the next frame, as denoted by gray triangles, are much larger than the time differences between packets of the same frame. When no delay is introduced in the timing channel, there is little variance in the time differences. In contrast, a large delay results in high variances in the timing channel. If many delays are introduced in one frame, the time difference between the last frame and the subsequent frame is shorter.

4.3   Circuit Watermarking

The binarization circuit is protected by two proposed authorship watermarking schemes.

Codeword Authorship Watermark. A 60-bit codeword watermark was implemented by using a 60 bits shift register that has a 1-bit output and wraps around upon each shift operation. Again, 60 bits are chosen for convenience, because exactly 60 packets are necessary to transmit one frame. The design overhead measured by Altera's Quartus IDE for this watermarking scheme is 60 logic cells.

Before sending a packet, the output bit of the shift register is consulted. If its value is a binary "1", a delay is introduced, otherwise the packet is sent right away. After sending a packet, the shift register is shifted, and its output is set to the next bit in the bitstring. In this way, a codeword authorship watermark is repeatedly transmitted over the timing channel.

Challenge-Response Authorship Watermark. In the challenge-response authorship watermark the fixed codeword is replaced with the Trivium [7] stream cipher with a fixed key and an input-dependent initialization vector (IV). We chose Trivium because it is well-suited for hardware implementation and it has a simple design. Trivium operates with an 80-bit initialization vector and an 80-bit key. In our system, the IV for the Trivium circuit is obtained from the first 80 binarized pixels of each frame. The design overhead measured by Altera's Quartus IDE for this watermarking scheme is 320 logic cells.

After obtaining the IV, which takes 80 clock cycles, the internal state of Trivium is initialized during 1152 clock cycles. Thus, the first bit of the stream cipher is available after 1232 clock cycles after receiving the first image pixel. However, it will not be used before processing 8 image lines, which takes at least $640 \cdot 8 = 5120$ clock cycles. After sending 60 bits on the timing channel, the Trivium circuit is reset and initialized again. This has the advantage that the verifier can analyze the timing channel already after receiving a single frame.

4.4 Timing Analysis for Watermark Recognition

EM Emanation in Proximity of the FPGA Board. Timing measurements were done (i) in proximity of the FPGA board using an EM probe, (ii) at the Ethernet cable using a contact-based measurement and an EM probe, and (iii) on the remote PC by using the libpcap library. The first two settings used the USB oscilloscope Picoscope 5203 by Picotech while the third set-up uses only the libpcap library on the PC. Our objective is to reveal the timing delay from the measurements without the help of any special triggers from the FPGA board. For illustration purposes, such a trigger indicating the presence of a 10 μs delay is plotted in Fig. 6(a).

This measurement set-up corresponds to a standard EM set-up for side-channel analysis cf. [12]. The positioning of the EM probe RF-U5-2 by Langer EMV is shown in Fig. 5(a). The sampling rate was 1 GHz. Figure 5(b) includes two single measurements, the measurement in the top does not include the delay, whereas the delay is present in the bottom trace. We added a vertical line in Fig. 5(b) to roughly indicate the relevant pattern used for the detection. The time difference is about 40 ns which corresponds to two clock cycles. As a result,

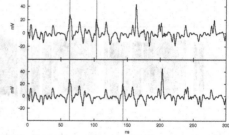

(a) Measurement set-up for the EM emanation in the near field.

(b) Timing analysis at the EM setup. The timing difference is clearly visible in single EM traces

Fig. 5. Results of the EM-Setup in proximity of the FPGA board.

the minimum delay of two clock cycles can be reliably detected so that one single measurement trace is sufficient to read-out more than 60 bits that are transmitted over the timing channel.

Timing Analysis at the Ethernet Cable. In this experiment it is our aim to study to which extent timing analysis can be conducted at the Ethernet connection between the FPGA and the remote PC. In the first experiment, we cut off and directly contacted the Ethernet cable with a passive probe at a sampling rate of 1GHz. Figure 6(b) shows that the minimum delay of two clock cycles is clearly visible in the power trace. We note that reducing the sampling rate is feasible down to about 25 MHz where it still yields a sufficient precision for the timing measurement.

In an alternative experiment, we positioned a near-field probe near the Ethernet cable. Also, these experiments were successful with a precision of down to the minimum delay of two clock cycles. Figure 6(c) shows timing measurements for the EM probe.

Remote Verification Using a PC. The remote verification was done on a PC with a 3.10 GHz quad-core Intel Xeon E3-1220 processor running 64-bit Debian with kernel 3.2.0-4. During remote verification, the presence of an authorship watermark is confirmed by connecting the FPGA board over its regular data channel to the PC. This has the advantage that no additional equipment is needed. The FPGA board and the PC are positioned in two different rooms and are connected to the department network that is used by approximately 50 people. Altogether, there are two routers and three switches that separate the board from the PC. Unlike the measurements done on a USB oscilloscope, remote verification introduces the problem that the libpcap library assigns a timestamp to a packet at the moment when it is transferred from kernel space to user space, and not when it is received by the Ethernet controller of the PC.

In order to find out the dependency between the delay in the timing channel and the confidence of the verifier, several measurements with different delays in

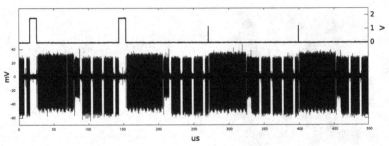

(a) Probe connected to the Ethernet cable and special trigger signal for a delay of 10 μs.

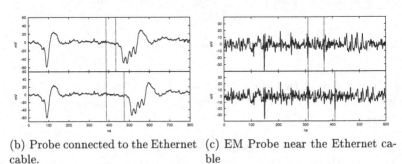

(b) Probe connected to the Ethernet cable.

(c) EM Probe near the Ethernet cable

Fig. 6. Results at the Ethernet connection.

the timing channel have been carried out. The delays varied from 0 to 120 μs, with the step size of 20 μs which resulted in 6 datasets.

The performance of this approach has been evaluated on the captured data by computing the ratio between the incorrectly recognized timing channel bits and the total number of bits sent over the timing channel. Figure 7 shows the distribution of the time differences between the packets of four datasets with different delays. When no additional delay is introduced, no data is sent over the timing channel because the packets are indistinguishable from each other.[1] With delay, the distributions for zeros and ones, as denoted by black and gray, respectively, start drifting away from each other. The distributions separate almost completely when the delay reaches 120 μs.

The delay has only a small impact on the performance of our application— the average packet timestamp difference $\overline{\Delta_t}$ is pushed from 128 μs to 135.7 μs. However, this is only because of the way how our computer vision application is implemented. The binarized images are temporarily stored in a first in first out (FIFO) buffer before they are sent to the PC. This explains the effect observable in Fig. 7—as the delay increases, the average time difference of packets

---

[1] The two peaks in absence of delay in Fig. 7(a) arise from the combination of operating system and the kernel. The peaks can be observed even when the board is directly connected to the PC. However, when using a different operating system, e.g., Ubuntu with a more recent kernel, only one peak emerges in absence of delay.

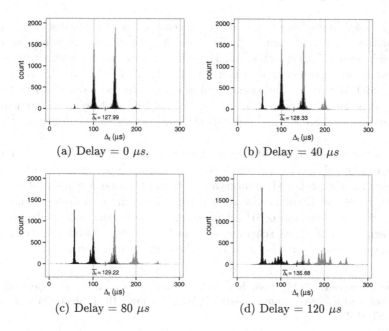

Fig. 7. Distributions of time differences for different delays. Zeros are denoted by black frequency bars, ones are denoted by gray frequency bars. In case of an overlap, the bars stack on top of each other. $\overline{\Delta_t}$ denotes the empirical mean of the time differences. Each graph was computed from 20 k consecutive bits sent from the FPGA board to the PC over the timing channel.

without delay becomes smaller than the overall average, and while the average time of packets with delay becomes larger, the overall average time difference $\overline{\Delta_t}$ increases only by a small amount. Multiple peaks arise because the time differences between two packets become dependent on the delay in preceding packets.

Table 1 shows the error rate for all captured datasets. At higher delays, it is possible to recover the data sent over the timing channel with a higher confidence. The delay can be adjusted depending on desired performance of the application and the desired confidence of the watermark verifier.

Table 1. Error rate depending on the timing delay

Timing delay (µs)	0	20	40	60	80	100	120
Error rate		0.5047	0.3440	0.2682	0.2521	0.0936	0.0953	0.0583

5 Conclusion

In this paper we introduce a new class of IP protection for embedded systems using timing channels. In contrast to previous side channel watermarking schemes [3,4], timing analysis does not necessarily need laboratory equipment and can be conducted remotely. We propose protocol schemes for both: an authorship and a fingerprint mark. Experimental evidence for this proposal is provided by an implementation on an Altera DE2-70 FPGA board. Using single power and EM traces, conditional timing delays can be reduced to two clock cycles. For network measurements a conditional timing delay of $120\,\mu s$ leads to an error rate of 5.83 % while only slightly decreasing the overall performance by $8\,\mu s$.

An adaptive adversary aiming at blocking the timing channel for remote detection is forced towards enhanced costs in time, memory and circuitry. We are confident that the proposed methods are indeed applicable in real-world solutions for protecting the IP of hardware and software components and a first step towards remote detection of IP infringement. Future work will study practical implementations of these schemes in embedded software and their degree of robustness on transformation attacks to the embedded watermark.

Acknowledgement. This work has been supported in parts by the German Federal Ministry of Education and Research (BMBF) through the project DePlagEmSoft, FKZ 03FH015I3.

References

1. Aciicmez, O., Seifert, J.-P., Koc, C.K.: Predicting Secret Keys via Branch Prediction. Cryptology ePrint Archive, Report 2006/288 (2006). http://eprint.iacr.org/
2. Aycock, J.: Computer Viruses and Malware. Springer, New York (2006)
3. Becker, G.T., Burleson, W., Paar, C.: Side-channel watermarks for embedded software. In: 9th IEEE NEWCAS Conference (2011)
4. Becker, G.T., Kasper, M., Moradi, A., Paar, C.: Side-channel based Watermarks for Integrated Circuits. In: Plusquellic, J., Mai, K. (eds.) HOST, pp. 30–35. IEEE Computer Society (2010)
5. Bernstein, D.J.: Cache-timing attacks on AES. Technical report (2005)
6. Boyd, C.: Protocols for Authentication and Key Establishment. Springer, Heidelberg (2003)
7. De Cannière, C.: TRIVIUM: a stream cipher construction inspired by block cipher design principles. In: Katsikas, S.K., López, J., Backes, M., Gritzalis, S., Preneel, B. (eds.) ISC 2006. LNCS, vol. 4176, pp. 171–186. Springer, Heidelberg (2006)
8. Collberg, C.S., Thomborson, C.D.: Software watermarking: models and dynamic embeddings. In: Appel, A.W., Aiken, A. (eds.) POPL, pp. 311–324. ACM (1999)
9. Cox, I.J., Miller, M.L., Bloom, J.A., Fridrich, J., Kalker, T.: Digital watermarking and steganography. Elesevier Inc. (2008)
10. Kocher, P.C.: Timing attacks on implementations of Diffie-Hellman, RSA, DSS, and other systems. In: Koblitz, N. (ed.) CRYPTO 1996. LNCS, vol. 1109, pp. 104–113. Springer, Heidelberg (1996)
11. Kocher, P.C., Jaffe, J., Jun, B.: Differential power analysis. In: Wiener, M. (ed.) CRYPTO 1999. LNCS, vol. 1666, p. 388. Springer, Heidelberg (1999)
12. Mangard, S., Oswald, E., Popp, T.: Power Analysis Attacks. Springer, New York (2007)

13. Murdoch, S.J., Danezis, G.: Low-cost traffic analysis of Tor. In: IEEE Symposium on Security and Privacy, pp. 183–195. IEEE Computer Society (2005)
14. Nagra, J., Thomborson, C.D., Collberg, C.S.: A Functional taxonomy for software watermarking. In: Oudshoorn, M.J. (ed.) ACSC. CRPIT, vol. 4, pp. 177–186. Australian Computer Society (2002)
15. Page, D.: Theoretical Use of Cache Memory as a Cryptanalytic Side-Channel. IACR Cryptology ePrint Archive 2002:169 (2002)
16. Van Vleck, T.: Timing Channels. http://multicians.org/timing-chn.html
17. Wang, X., Chen, S., Jajodia, S.: Tracking anonymous peer-to-peer VoIP calls on the internet. In: Atluri, V., Meadows, C., Juels, A. (eds.) ACM Conference on Computer and Communications Security, pp. 81–91. ACM (2005)

Mobile Security

Detecting Camouflaged Applications on Mobile Application Markets

Su Mon Kywe[1]([✉]), Yingjiu Li[1], Robert H. Deng[1], and Jason Hong[2]

[1] School of Information Systems, Singapore Management University,
Singapore, Singapore
{monkywe.su.2011,yjli,robertdeng}@smu.edu.sg
[2] Human Computer Interaction Institute, Carnegie Mellon University,
Pittsburgh, USA
jasonh@cs.cmu.edu

Abstract. Application plagiarism or application cloning is an emerging threat in mobile application markets. It reduces profits of original developers and sometimes even harms the security and privacy of users. In this paper, we introduce a new concept, called camouflaged applications, where external features of mobile applications, such as icons, screenshots, application names or descriptions, are copied. We then propose a scalable detection framework, which can find these suspiciously similar camouflaged applications. To accomplish this, we apply text-based retrieval methods and content-based image retrieval methods in our framework. Our framework is implemented and tested with 30,625 Android applications from the official Google Play market. The experiment results show that even the official market is comprised of 477 potential camouflaged victims, which cover 1.56 % of tested samples. Our paper highlights that these camouflaged applications not only expose potential security threats but also degrade qualities of mobile application markets. Our paper also analyze the behaviors of detected camouflaged applications and calculate the false alarm rates of the proposed framework.

Keywords: Camouflaged applications · Application plagiarism · Cloning

1 Introduction

With the growing number of third-party applications on mobile market places, it becomes increasingly hard to manage these applications and ensure that they are authentic, secure and of high quality. One of the emerging problems that the market owners encounter is plagiarism or cloning of mobile applications. During cloning, malicious parties copy all or parts of original applications and create similar applications or the clones. Such application plagiarism causes two main problems in mobile application markets. Firstly, it allows malicious parties to siphon revenues from original developers by replacing the advertisement libraries of plagiarised applications or by selling the clones with different prices to users. It has been shown that original developers, who are the victims of plagiarism, lost

© Springer International Publishing Switzerland 2015
J. Lee and J. Kim (Eds.): ICISC 2014, LNCS 8949, pp. 241–254, 2015.
DOI: 10.1007/978-3-319-15943-0_15

14 % of their advertising revenues and 10 % of their user base to the attackers [6]. Secondly, there are cases, where attackers add malicious payloads to the clones of popular applications and threaten the security and privacy of mobile application users. In a recent study by Zheng M. et al. [30], cloning is even regarded as one of the main distribution channels of mobile malwares.

Thus, to hinder application plagiarism, a number of clone detection methods have been proposed in [3,7,13,29]. However, these methods only focuses on repackaged applications, which are the clones created from the reverse-engineered codes of original applications. As such, these methods only search for code similarities among applications, consequently missing out a different set of clones, called camouflaged applications. Hence, in this paper, we introduce the concept of camouflaged applications. Camouflaged applications are applications whose external information, such as application names, icons, user interfaces or application descriptions, are cloned. These clones may or may not have similar codes as original applications but like other clones, they plagiarise and take advantage of other applications without consensus from original developers. They are not only confusing and harmful to the users but also discourage application development by affecting developers' reputation and monetary profits.

Therefore, in this paper, we propose a detection framework for finding camouflaged applications. Our method is based on external features of applications and applies text similarity and image similarity measurements, calculated by information retrieval systems. Although information retrieval systems have been applied to detect phishing web pages, we are the first to apply these technologies to efficiently detect camouflaged applications in mobile platforms. Our detection framework is tested with 30,625 Android applications from Google Play market. The experiment shows that 477 applications (1.56 %) are potential camouflaged applications. We further analyze the behaviors of detected camouflaged applications and inspect the false alarms rate of our detection method. A total of 44 false positives, which is 9.22 % of tested application samples, are identified.

Our paper is organized as follows. Problem definition of camouflaged applications and threat model are provided in Sect. 2. Background information about information retrieval systems and repackaged applications are given in Sect. 3. Our detection framework is proposed in Sect. 4 and our experiment results are shown in Sect. 5. Discussion about our findings, limitations of our method and future direction are provided in Sect. 6. After that, related work on repackaged applications are summarized in Sect. 7 and we conclude the paper in Sect. 8.

2   Problem Definition

Informally, camouflaged applications are defined as "copycat" applications or "confusingly similar" applications. There have been a lot of such applications on both official Google Play store and Apple's iTunes store. Generally, the features being cloned in camouflaged applications are icons, names, screenshots and descriptions. For instance, there are camouflaged applications with very similar names, such as "Irate Birds" for the official "Angry Birds" and "Snip the Rope" for the official "Cute the Rope"[1]. Moreover, some camouflaged applications focus on screenshots to deceive users. For example, fake Pokemon Yellow application used Nintendo's popular Game Boy RPG as its application screenshots. It even managed to rise to top 3 position on iTunes store before being removed [19].

Camouflaged applications may exist on different application markets of the same platforms or across different platforms. According to Zhou et al. [29], 5–13% of the applications from unofficial Android market places are cloned from the official Google Play market. In addition, some clones may also spans across different platforms, such as Android or iOS. For instance, fake versions of popular iOS applications, such as Infinity Blade II[2] and Temple Run[3], appeared on Google Play, even before their official releases in Android version.

Market owners have imposed various developer policies for trademarks, copyrights, and patents of applications. For instance, Google Play has a policy for impersonation, stating (1) not to pretend as another company, (2) not to link to another website to represent itself as another application and (3) not to use another application's branding in title and description [20]. Moreover, Google Play's Trademark Infringement policy suggests to use distinct name, icon and logo and not to use those that are "confusingly similar" to another company's trademark. However, according to Liebergeld et al. [14], there is insufficient market control in Google Play market, because uploaded applications are not checked upfront on whether they indeed follow the policies. The policy enforcement relies heavily on feedbacks from users and developers.

Threat Model: The main goal of attackers is to trick users into installing their camouflaged applications. There are two ways by which users can install applications on their mobile devices. One way is to use default installer applications, such as Play Store or iTune Store, on mobile devices. Another way is to use desktop browsers, download applications from the providers' websites and later synchronize the applications to their mobile devices. In both cases, there are two situations in which user can be tricked to install the camouflaged applications. One is during the search and another is after the user goes to the detailed information page.

– When browsing applications or searching for an application, users can only observe application icons, application names and publishing company names. Some users download applications directly from the search results, instead of going to the detailed pages. Therefore, these three pieces of information play an important role in tricking the users. Although the ranking algorithm used by the Google also plays a role, it is out of scope of our paper.

---

[1] http://arstechnica.com/gaming/2012/08/google-play-cracks-down-on-confusingly-similar-apps/.

[2] http://www.pocketgamer.co.uk/r/Android/Infinity+Blade+II/news.asp?c=43572.

[3] http://m.androidcentral.com/temple-run-android-still-isnt-out-anything-else-just-malware.

– In the detailed information pages, application descriptions and screenshots
  are the main visual elements for users. Thus, they also play a critical role in
  tricking the users by attackers.

There are several ways in which attackers can gain profit for creating camouflaged applications. Table 1 summarizes different attackers' motivations as well
as various possible attacks from camouflaged applications. Attack type may vary
from mild copy-right violation and information theft to severe phishing and malware attacks. From the table, we can see that in addition to users and developers, other third-parties, such as banks and telecom providers, can be adversely
affected by camouflaged applications.

Table 1. Categorizing attacks of camouflaged applications

Attacker motivation	Attack type	Mainly affected parties
Replacing advertise libraries	Copy-right violation	Developers
Creating paid version of free applications	Copy-right violation	Developers
Selling users' information to third parties	Information theft	Users
Stealing users' bank credentials	Phishing	Users and banks
Sending premium SMSes	Malware	Users and telecom providers

3   Background

3.1   Information Retrieval Systems

Information retrieval systems are used for retrieving relevant information from a
collection of information resources. Most information retrieval systems includes
two processes: indexing and retrieving. During indexing, the systems process
documents that are either text documents or image, and extract useful information from them. During retrieving steps, query objects that are also processed,
cleaned and their useful information are extracted. Then, similarity distance are
measured between the query document and a collection of documents by using
their representations. Ranked or sorted results are then returned to the users,
together with the similarity scores.

Information retrieval techniques have also been used to detect phishing websites [24,25]. However, the traditional phishing detection methods cannot be
applied directly on platform providers' websites, such as Google Play Store.
This is because camouflaged applications and original applications can be fea-
tured on the same official website. Thus, meta-data analysis of web contents,
such as hyper-links, web titles, web links, etc., cannot be applied in detecting
camouflaged applications.

3.2   Repackaging and Code-Based Detectors

Cloned applications are often the result of repackaging, which includes recovering source codes of original applications and illegally re-compiling them with

different developers' certificates. Repackaging is common in Android application platform. In Android applications, Java source code are compiled into the Dalvik executable (DEX) format and run in Dalvik virtual machines. Dalvik byte codes can be easily reverse engineered by publicly available online tools, such as dex2jar and jd-gui.

As the repackaged clones are created from source codes of original applications, their source codes are similar to certain extent. Thus, code-based detectors can be used to detect repackaged applications. Generally, there are three types of code similarity detectors: feature-based, structure-based and PDG (Program Dependence Graph)-based. Feature-based detectors extracts features, such as number or size of classes, methods, loops, variables, from the applications and detects their similarities. Structure-based detectors convert applications into a stream of tokens and compare their streams. On the other hand, PDG-based detectors construct PDGs from the applications and compare them to derive the similarity scores. Many other code-based detectors, that have been proposed for repackaged applications, will be discussed more in Sect. 7.

4   A Framework for Detecting Camouflaged Applications

Accuracy and scalability are the key factors, considering the number of third-party applications in mobile markets. Thus, the goal of our paper is to have a lightweight simple detection system, which can efficiently detects the camouflaged applications. The implementation of our framework should allow developers to check their applications before submitting to the application stores. It can also used by Google Play for vetting before or after the application submission.

Our system leverages on the light-weight information retrieval systems, such as text retrieval and content-based image retrieval systems. There are four features with which we try to find camouflaged applications: application name, description, icon and screenshot. Application name and descriptions are handled by text retrieval systems, while application icon and screenshots are handled by image retrieval system. Figure 1 shows the architecture of our detection system. Our detection system includes four main steps: crawling, indexing, querying and detecting.

4.1   Crawling

First, we need a collection of existing applications, with which the potential camouflaged applications are compared. This application collection can be from different markets of different mobile platforms, depending on where we want to detect camouflaged applications. For instance, if we want to detect camouflaged applications, which are uploaded on unofficial Android markets, existing application collection should be crawled from official Google Play market and tested applications should be crawled from unofficial Android markets. However, if we want to detect camouflaged applications on Google Play's Android market, which are copied from iTunes market, the existing application collection

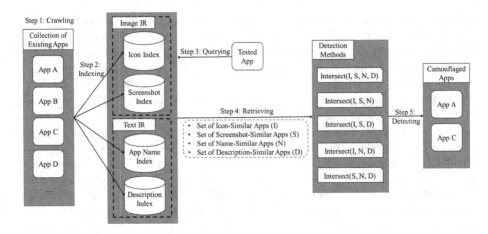

Fig. 1. Framework for detecting camouflaged applications

should be from official Google Play market and tested applications should be from Apple's iTunes market.

Our framework is independent of mobile platform and application market. It can be used on any platforms or markets as long as the market displays application names, icons, screenshots and descriptions. In our experiment, we crawled applications from official Android market and detect camouflaged applications within the same market. We use unofficial Google API to crawl App info, such as id, name, developer, rating as well as application description, icon and screenshots. Total of 30,625 applications are crawled for the experiment.

4.2   Indexing

The second step of most information retrieval systems is indexing. During indexing, a collection of documents are cleaned and processed to get ready for queries. We call both texts and images as "documents". Indexing can be done offline and just one time. Therefore, it is suitable for a large collection of documents. For each application in our 30,625 crawled applications, we create a name index, description index, icon index and screenshot index. Name and description indexes are created by text retrieval engines, while icon and screenshot indexes are handled by image retrieval engine.

Text Indexing. There are many types of text retrieval systems, such as boolean model, vector space model, probabilistic models. Most of them can be plugged and played in our detection framework. However, in our experiment, vector space model is used as it applies similar-word matching instead of exact-word matching algorithm. In the vector space model, each document is represented by a weighted vector in high-dimensional space. The weights from vectors are measured by TF-IDF scheme, which stands for Term Frequency (TF) and Inverse Document

Frequency (IDF). Open-source software, such as Lucene [18], can be used to implement TF-IDF scheme. Tokenizing, stemming and removal of stop words are all handled by Lucene.

Image Indexing. Similar to text retrieval methods, there are also many types of image retrieval methods. They extract visual features from the images and index those features with a pointer to the parent image. The extracted features include colors, color distributions, textures or joint histograms, which involve both color and texture information. Different algorithms have their own advantages and disadvantages on performance and robustness depending on the applied scenarios and types of images. We choose auto color correlogram algorithm [9], which uses the spatial correlation of colors. The algorithm is tested using SIMPLIcity data set [23] and is shown to be both effective and inexpensive in general purpose situations [17]. Note that our framework can also be easily modified to use other visual information retrieval algorithms. We use an open-source software, LIRE [16], to perform the visual information retrieval.

4.3 Querying and Retrieving

The third step is to query the index databases with potential camouflaged applications. In our case, the same 30,625 crawled applications are used as potential camouflaged applications. For each queried application, we retrieved applications, which have similar user interfaces but are from different developers. Information retrieval systems are used to calculate the similarity scores, and developer ID information, obtained from Google Play website, is used to ensure that similar applications are not from the same developer.

For each query, information retrieval systems calculate the cosine similarity score between query document and a set of indexed documents. The cosine similarity score measures the similarity distance between two vector representations of documents. The score ranges from 0 to 1, where similarity score of 0 represents two totally different documents and similarity score of 1 represents two totally similar documents. The retrieved similarity score are then used to rank the documents. In our case, retrieved set of applications is sorted based on the decreasing similarity scores, meaning the most similar ones are on the top of the list. We only use top-ten similar applications in each retrieved set to reduce false positives.

The output of each queried application is four sets of similar applications, namely I, S, N and D, where

- I is a set of applications that have similar icons as queried application,
- S is a set of applications that have similar screenshots as queried application,
- N is a set of applications that have similar names as queried application and
- D is a set of applications that have similar description as queried application.

Each set contains at most ten similar applications and many sets have fewer than ten applications. Note that although we use the same application set for indexing and querying, different application set can also be applied in our architecture if we want to differentiate camouflaged applications across different markets.

4.4 Detecting

The fourth step of our framework is detection. Our detection method is different intersection sets of the four retrieved set I, S, N and D. This step generates the following five different result sets for each potential camouflaged application.

- Intersect(I,S,N,D) is a set of applications that have similar icons, screenshots, names and descriptions as queried application,
- Intersect(I,S,N) is a set of applications that have similar icons, screenshots and names as queried application but are not included in Intersect(I,S,N,D),
- Intersect(I,S,D) is a set of applications that have similar icons, screenshots and descriptions as queried application but are not included in Intersect(I,S,N,D),
- Intersect(I,N,D) is a set of applications that have similar icons, names and descriptions as queried application but are not included in Intersect(I,S,N,D),
- Intersect(S,N,D) is a set of applications that have similar screenshots, names and descriptions as queried application but are not included in Intersect (I,S,N,D).

Since these sets contain very similar applications from different developers, they are considered as camouflaged applications. Nonetheless, there can also be false alarms, where the result set contains non-camouflaged applications. False alarms are created because information retrieval methods cannot differentiate them, although they are obvious to normal users that they are not camouflaged applications.

5   Experiment and Results

Out of 30,625 applications, we find that 477 applications (1.56 %) have 1 to 6 camouflaged applications. Figure 2 shows the exact number of camouflaged

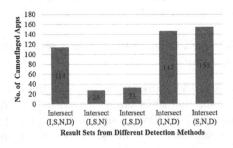

Fig. 2. Number of camouflaged applications for each detection method

Fig. 3. Example of detected camouflaged application

application from each result set. According to the figure, we can see that Intersect(I,S,N,D), Intersect(I,N,D) and Intersect(S,N,D) reports more camouflaged applications than Intersect(I,S,N) and Intersect(I,S,D) methods.

An example of detected camouflaged applications, namely "VTX Mobile Dialer" and "OneSuite Mobile Dialer", is shown in Fig. 3. The two applications have the very similar screenshots, application name and description. Thus, they are reported in Intersect(S,N,D) set. However, they use different developer IDes as well as different contact information. The developer website and email address of "VTX Mobile Dialer" are https://www.vtxtelecom.com/ and *mobileapp@vtxtelecom.com*. On the other hand, the developer website and email address of "VTX Mobile Dialer" are http://www.onesuite.com/ and *mobileapp@ onesuite.com*. Although they claim to be from different companies, their user interfaces are suspiciously similar. Therefore, they are regarded as camouflaged applications.

Determining the False Alarms: Determining the false positives and false negatives for camouflaged applications is a challenge, as we do not have any ground truth samples. Thus, we decide to do manual inspection on the result sets to determine the false positives. Though tedious, expert manual inspection has been a common way to test the efficiencies of information retrieval systems. To our surprise, a lot of the reported camouflaged applications have almost identical user interfaces. This makes our manual inspection easier.

Our manual inspection shows that the result sets contain a total of 44 false positives, which is 9.22 % of reported camouflaged applications. However, false positives exist only in the Intersect(I,N,D) and Intersect(S,N,D). Intersect(I,N,D) contains 21 false positive samples and Intersect(S,N,D) contains

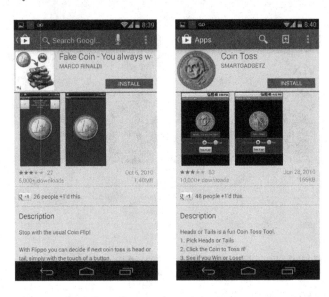

Fig. 4. Example of false-positive camouflaged applications

23 false positive samples. No false positive applications have been identified in Intersect(I,S,N,D), Intersect(I,S,N) and Intersect(I,S,D), which consider the similarity of both icons and screeenshots. This indicates that icons and screenshot similarity measures are great indicators of camouflaged applications.

Figure 4 shows an example of false alarm applications, called "Fake Coin - You always win!" and "Coin Toss". Although their user interfaces are similar, it is quite obvious to the real users that they provide different functions: the former application is for tricking friends and the latter application is for randomly tossing the coin. Therefore, these two applications should not be regarded as camouflaged applications.

6   Discussion

In this section, we will discuss about our findings on camouflaged applications as well as limitations of our method and future work.

Feature Selection in Detection Method: Our detection method is limited to camouflaged applications with at least three similar features. Nonetheless, there can still be camouflaged applications with only one or two similar features. For instance, there are camouflaged applications with only similar icons. Although our method can be easily extended to find applications with one or two similar features, many applications use very simple and easily searchable icons, such as a light bulb. Consequently, there are a lot of false alarms when we use only two features. Thus, it is still a challenge on how to ensure quality control on icons and names of applications in the market.

Applications from Open-Source Projects: Our result shows that there are applications, which are modified from open-source projects, such as e-book readers, music players and map applications. Although they use different contents, such different books or songs, and change the themes, the applications are still highly similar as they use source codes from the same projects. Thus, although they do not copy from each other, they are still considered as camouflaged applications in our framework.

Applications with Different Versions: We find out that some camouflaged applications claim to be different versions from one another. They use version differentiating words, such as "HD" (High Definition), "full", "II" (two), "plus" and "pro". However, many of them do not provide additional functionalities, although they claim to be upgraded versions. It is possible that a malicious attacker tries to attract more customers by claiming to provide upgraded version of the victim application. To solve this problem, application markets should enforce that developers use the same account, when they claim to provide upgraded version of an existing application. Our detection framework for camouflaged applications can serve as an automatic policy enforcement mechanism for these kind of applications.

Internationalized Applications: Another finding of our experiment is that many international companies, such as banks, have different applications developed for different countries and languages. Unfortunately, they also use different developer ID in Google Play to update them. For instance, "Banco Weng Hang, S.A." application uploaded by "Banco Weng Hang, S.A." provides banking services in Chinese, while "Wing Hang Bank" application uploaded by "Wing Hang Bank Ltd" provides the same services in English. This is actually a vulnerability, which allows attackers to impersonate as legitimate applications and launch phishing attacks.

7 Related Work

Studies on the repackaged applications have become popular recently. Zhou et al. [30] studies 1260 Android malwares and finds out that 1083 malwares are repackaged applications. Balanza et al. [1] analyzes a repackaged malware, called DroidDreamLight and states that trojanizing or repackaging is common form of infection in Android market. Jung et al. [11] launches repackaging attack on bank applications. Moreover, Vidas et al. [22] shows that some malwares are even repackaged with the valid certificates from original developers. It also proposes an authentication protocol for market applications which makes it difficult for an attacker to perform repackaging.

Chen et al. [2] also studies the underground economy of Android application plagiarism. Similarly, Gibler et al. [6] studies the impact of repackaged applications and finds out that 14 % of original developers' revenues and 10 % of user based are redirected to the attacker. Zheng et al. [26] presents various obfuscation techniques which allow automatic repackaging of original malwares to different variants. Transformed malwares are then used to test the robustness of Android anti-virus systems. Potharaju et al. [21] uses permission information and estimates that 29.4 % of applications are likely to be plagiarized. They also detect repackaged applications using Deckard [10], which is a tree-based detection algorithm of cloned codes.

DroidMOSS [29] and Juxtapp [7,13] and apply fuzzy hashing on program instruction sequence and derive the similarity score by calculating the edit distance between two generated fingerprints. Crussell et al. [3] proposes DNADroid, which uses Program Dependence Graph(PDG) to determine code similarity. DNADroid is similar to our approach because it filters the applications based on application names, packages, markets, owners and descriptions. However, such filtering is performed only to make the PDG comparison more scalable for determining the similarity between two applications.

AnDarwin [4] applies Locality-Sensitive Hashing (LSH) to detect the repackaged applications. Zhou et al. [28] calls repackaged applications as "piggybacked" applications and proposes linearithmic search algorithm in a metric space to detect them. Desnos et al. [5] proposes an algorithm, which uses Normalized Compression Distance (NCD) to analyze the similarity and differences between two Android applications. Similarly, Lin et al. [15] apply thread-grained system call sequences to detect repackaged applications. Ko et al. [12] extract k-gram based software birthmarks from the dissembled codes and measure the similarity of DEX files.

Huang et al. [8] proposes an evaluation framework for detection algorithms of repackaged application by measuring their resilience to obfuscation methods. Different from other approaches, [27] proposes to use software watermarking to prevent repackaging. In summary, researchers have proposed different ways of detecting repackaged applications by measuring the source code similarity or software watermarking. However, none of them have yet considered camouflaged applications, which have very similar user interfaces, instead of similar source codes.

8   Conclusion

Our paper highlights the existence of camouflaged applications in mobile application markets as well as their exposed risk on application users and developers. Although there have been papers about repackaged applications and their copyright infringement, our paper is the first to introduce the concept of camouflaged applications and consider their user interface similarity. Our paper describes a proper threat model of camouflaged applications, including their attack scenarios and attackers' motivations. Moreover, we propose a simple, yet effective, detection framework, which applies text and image retrieval systems that are accurate and scalable in detecting camouflaged applications. The proposed framework is tested and the experiment result shows that 477 applications are camouflaged. We analyze these camouflaged applications, discuss their behaviors and calculate the false alarm rates. Our paper shows that detecting camouflaged applications is important, not only for maintaining a safe mobile application market but also for controlling the quality of mobile applications.

References

1. Balanza, M., Abendan, O., Alintanahin, K., Dizon, J., Caraig, B.: Droiddreamlight lurks behind legitimate android apps. In: Proceedings of the 2011 6th International Conference on Malicious and Unwanted Software, MALWARE 2011, pp. 73–78. IEEE Computer Society, Washington, DC (2011)
2. Chen, H.: Underground economy of android application plagiarism. In: Proceedings of the First International Workshop on Security in Embedded Systems and Smartphones, SESP 2013, pp. 1–2. ACM, New York (2013)
3. Crussell, J., Gibler, C., Chen, H.: Attack of the clones: detecting cloned applications on android markets. In: Foresti, S., Yung, M., Martinelli, F. (eds.) ESORICS 2012. LNCS, vol. 7459, pp. 37–54. Springer, Heidelberg (2012)
4. Crussell, J., Gibler, C., Chen, H.: Scalable semantics-based detection of similar android applications. In: 18th European Symposium on Research in Computer Security, ESORICS 2013, Egham, U.K. (2013)
5. Desnos, A.: Android: static analysis using similarity distance. In: Proceedings of the 2012 45th Hawaii International Conference on System Sciences, HICSS 2012, pp. 5394–5403. IEEE Computer Society, Washington, DC (2012)
6. Gibler, C., Stevens, R., Crussell, J., Chen, H., Zang, H., Choi, H.: Adrob: Examining the landscape and impact of android application plagiarism. In: Proceedings of 11th International Conference on Mobile Systems, Applications and Services (2013)
7. Hanna, S., Huang, L., Wu, E., Li, S., Chen, C., Song, D.: Juxtapp: a scalable system for detecting code reuse among android applications. In: Flegel, U., Markatos, E., Robertson, W. (eds.) DIMVA 2012. LNCS, vol. 7591, pp. 62–81. Springer, Heidelberg (2013)
8. Huang, H., Zhu, S., Liu, P., Wu, D.: A framework for evaluating mobile app repackaging detection algorithms. In: Huth, M., Asokan, N., Čapkun, S., Flechais, I., Coles-Kemp, L. (eds.) TRUST 2013. LNCS, vol. 7904, pp. 169–186. Springer, Heidelberg (2013)
9. Huang, J., Kumar, S.R., Mitra, M., Zhu, W.-J., Zabih, R.: Image indexing using color correlograms. In: Proceedings of the 1997 Conference on Computer Vision and Pattern Recognition (CVPR 1997), CVPR 1997, pp. 762–768. IEEE Computer Society, Washington, DC (1997)
10. Jiang, L., Misherghi, G., Su, Z., Glondu, S.: Deckard: scalable and accurate tree-based detection of code clones. In: Proceedings of the 29th International Conference on Software Engineering, ICSE 2007, pp. 96–105. IEEE Computer Society, Washington, DC (2007)
11. Jung, J.-H., Kim, J.Y., Lee, H.-C., Yi, J.H.: Repackaging attack on android banking applications and its countermeasures. Wirel. Pers. Commun. 73(4), 1421–1437 (2013)
12. Ko, J., Shim, H., Kim, D., Jeong, Y.-S., Cho, S.-J., Park, M., Han, S., Kim, S.B.: Measuring similarity of android applications via reversing and k-gram birthmarking. In: Proceedings of the 2013 Research in Adaptive and Convergent Systems, RACS 2013, pp. 336–341. ACM, New York (2013)
13. Li, S.: Juxtapp and DStruct: detection of similarity among android applications. Master's thesis, EECS Department, University of California, Berkeley, May 2012
14. Liebergeld, S., Lange, M.: Android security, pitfalls and lessons learned. In: Gelenbe, E., Lent, R. (eds.) Information Sciences and Systems 2013. LNEE, vol. 264, pp. 409–417. Springer, Heidelberg (2013)

15. Lin, Y.-D., Lai, Y.-C., Chen, C.-H., Tsai, H.-C.: Identifying android malicious repackaged applications by thread-grained system call sequences. Comput. Secur. **39**, 340–350 (2013)
16. Lux, M., Chatzichristofis, S.A.: Lire: lucene image retrieval: an extensible java cbir library. In: Proceedings of the 16th ACM International Conference on Multimedia, MM 2008, pp. 1085–1088. ACM, New York (2008)
17. Marques, O., Lux, M.: Visual information retrieval using java and lire. In: Hersh, W.R., Callan, J., Maarek, Y., Sanderson, M. (eds.) SIGIR, p. 1193. ACM (2012)
18. McCandless, M., Hatcher, E., Gospodnetic, O.: Lucene in Action: Covers Apache Lucene 3.0, 2nd edn. Manning Publications Co., Greenwich (2010)
19. Orland, K.: Fake pokemon yellow rises to no. 3 position on itunes app charts (2012)
20. Play, G.: Intellectual property
21. Potharaju, R., Newell, A., Nita-Rotaru, C., Zhang, X.: Plagiarizing smartphone applications: attack strategies and defense techniques. In: Barthe, G., Livshits, B., Scandariato, R. (eds.) ESSoS 2012. LNCS, vol. 7159, pp. 106–120. Springer, Heidelberg (2012)
22. Vidas, T., Christin, N.: Sweetening android lemon markets: measuring and combating malware in application marketplaces. In: Proceedings of the Third ACM Conference on Data and Application Security and Privacy, CODASPY 2013, pp. 197–208. ACM, New York (2013)
23. Wang, J.Z., Li, J., Wiederhold, G.: Simplicity: semantics-sensitive integrated matching for picture libraries. IEEE Trans. Pattern Anal. Mach. Intell. **23**(9), 947–963 (2001)
24. Xiang, G., Hong, J.I.: A hybrid phish detection approach by identity discovery and keywords retrieval. In: Proceedings of the 18th International Conference on World Wide Web, WWW 2009, pp. 571–580. ACM, New York (2009)
25. Zhang, Y., Hong, J.I., Cranor, L.F.: Cantina: a content-based approach to detecting phishing web sites. In: Proceedings of the 16th International Conference on World Wide Web, WWW 2007, pp. 639–648. ACM, New York (2007)
26. Zheng, M., Lee, P.P.C., Lui, J.C.S.: ADAM: an automatic and extensible platform to stress test android anti-virus systems. In: Flegel, U., Markatos, E., Robertson, W. (eds.) DIMVA 2012. LNCS, vol. 7591, pp. 82–101. Springer, Heidelberg (2013)
27. Zhou, W., Zhang, X., Jiang, X.: Appink: watermarking android apps for repackaging deterrence. In: Proceedings of the 8th ACM SIGSAC Symposium on Information, Computer and Communications Security, ASIA CCS 2013, pp. 1–12. ACM, New York (2013)
28. Zhou, W., Zhou, Y., Grace, M., Jiang, X., Zou, S.: Fast, scalable detection of "piggybacked" mobile applications. In: Proceedings of the Third ACM Conference on Data and Application Security and Privacy, CODASPY 2013, pp. 185–196. ACM, New York (2013)
29. Zhou, W., Zhou, Y., Jiang, X., Ning, P.: Detecting repackaged smartphone applications in third-party android marketplaces. In: Proceedings of the Second ACM Conference on Data and Application Security and Privacy, CODASPY 2012, pp. 317–326. ACM, New York (2012)
30. Zhou, Y., Jiang, X.: Dissecting android malware: characterization and evolution. In: IEEE Symposium on Security and Privacy, pp. 95–109. IEEE Computer Society (2012)

WrapDroid: Flexible and Fine-Grained Scheme Towards Regulating Behaviors of Android Apps

Xueqiang Wang[1,2,3], Yuewu Wang[1,2], Limin Liu[1,2(✉)],
Lingguang Lei[1,2], and Jiwu Jing[1,2]

[1] Data Assurance and Communication Security Research Center, CAS,
Beijing, China
[2] Institute of Information Engineering, CAS, Beijing, China
[3] University of Chinese Academy of Sciences, Beijing, China
lmliu@is.ac.cn

Abstract. Accompanying the wide spread of Android mobile devices and the openness feature of Android ecosystem, untrusted Android apps are flooding into user's device and prepared to perform various unwanted operations stealthily. To better manage installed apps and secure mobile devices, Android app behaviour regulating schemes are required. In this paper, we present WrapDroid, a dynamic app behaviour regulating scheme on Android device. Different from other similar approaches, the key components of WrapDroid are implemented based on dynamic memory instrumentation and system call tracing and require no modification to Android system source code. Thus, WrapDroid could be flexibly adopted by Android devices. Moreover, by automatically reconstructing call context of Java or native operations, WrapDroid may provide a full range of control on both java runtime and system call layers of an app. We also develop a WrapDroid prototype and evaluate it on several devices from different mainstream OEMs. Evaluation results show that Wrap-Droid can effectively regulate the behaviors of Android apps according to given policies with negligible performance overhead.

Keywords: Android · App behaviour regulating · Dynamic instrumentation · Flexible · Fine-grained

1 Introduction

Google's Android is undoubtedly the most prevalent mobile platform in the world. In the second quarter of 2014, Android's market share of the global smartphone shipments reached record 84.6 % [1]. Unfortunately Android's growth in popularity and its openness feature of app ecosystem have also raised increasing security concerns. According to the report by Cisco, 99 % of all mobile malwares in 2013 targeted Android platform [2]. These malicious apps perform various harmful operations, such as reading personal information or sending SMS without the user's consent, which may incur privacy leakage or other losses for device user. While anti-virus measures have been adopted, it is still hard to ensure that all malicious code is isolated from user's Android device.

© Springer International Publishing Switzerland 2015
J. Lee and J. Kim (Eds.): ICISC 2014, LNCS 8949, pp. 255–268, 2015.
DOI: 10.1007/978-3-319-15943-0_16

Regulating the behaviors of untrusted Android apps according to given security policies may hold back the attack procedure of malicious code and secure user's device effectively. Android provides permission system to control app's behaviors. However, this permission model is too coarse-grained and only grants an "all-or-nothing" installation option for mobile users to either accept all the permissions an app asks for or simply decline to install the app. In Android 4.3, an experimental feature called App Ops [3] is added to permit mobile users to configure one app's runtime permissions, but this feature has been removed from Android 4.4.2 due to the increasing burden for user configuration and the impacts on advertisement market [4].

Several other works are carried out to exert more fine-grained controls on app's behaviors. These works mainly focused on two major research directions. The first direction is accomplished by modifying Android source code. Several extensions have been introduced into Android permission framework by system customization [5–9]. And some efforts are made to adopt mandatory access control (MAC) to Android [10,11]. However, these approaches require Android source code modification and would suffer from deployment problem. Changes on a general Android branch is hard to be built for devices of different OEMs because of their heterogeneities.

The second one is integrating behavior enforcement module into Android apps with app rewriting before the app is installed on user's device [12–18]. This approach does not require any change to Android source code and easy to deploy. However, it also has several limitations. Firstly, user have to ensure that all installed untrusted apps are correctly wrapped. Thus, this scheme applies only to ordinary apps because those stock apps cannot be replaced easily and the burden on user is greater. Secondly, the scheme, based on rewriting bytecode of an app, can be easily bypassed by dynamically loading native code into app's address space. Finally, the impaction on apps is permanent. For instance, the data associated with the original app will be lost because of different app signature.

In this paper, a flexible and fine-grained scheme called WrapDroid is presented to regulate Android apps' behaviors dynamically. We observed that even through an app may realize an operation through various interfaces, its operation traces will always appear in Dalvik interpreter or go through Linux system calls. By checking these two points, app's behaviours, whether performed by native code or Java reflections, can be examined and supervised completely. Fine-grained policies to constrain behavior of Android apps are supported by our approach because parameter details of each operation are analysed automatically at the check points. To guarantee its flexibility and easy deployment, the enforcement modules are based on dynamic Dalvik instrumentation and system call tracing. The advantages of the dynamic implementation are threefold. Firstly, both ordinary apps and stock apps are under regulation. Secondly, the modules that loaded during run-time are also monitored. Finally, we can launch behavior regularization flexibly by instrumenting app's memory address space and remove its effect by restoring context of the app. In other words, app's running environment are modified temporary, which brings no further impact on original app. This paper mainly focuses on the implementation of behavior regulating, so only an example policy is discussed even through various security policies can be accepted by WrapDroid. Moreover, Java code regulating can also be achieved in ART runtime by *.oat* instrumentation, which makes WrapDroid available to the latest Android version with some amending.

In summary, we make the following contributions in this paper.

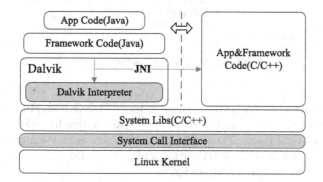

Fig. 1. Android application code structure

- We solved the flexibility problem of regulating behaviors of Android apps. Our approach is based on dynamic Dalvik instrumentation and system call tracing, which requires no modification to Android OS. Moreover, the impact of WrapDroid is minimized because only address space of supervised apps are instrumented temporarily.
- We achieve a complete and fine-grained control on Android apps. Based on monitoring of runtime interpreter and system calls of supervised app, both Java and native code behaviors are put under monitoring. These behavior context accompanying with well-designed policies make our scheme fine-grained.
- We develop a WrapDroid prototype and evaluate its effectiveness and efficiency on several Android devices. The evaluation result show that WrapDroid can effectively regulating behaviors of Android apps and meanwhile incurs an ignorable performance overhead.

The remaining of the paper is organized as follows. Section 2 introduces necessary background knowledge. Section 3 presents WrapDroid system design. A prototype implementation is detailed in Sect. 4. Section 5 discusses the evaluation of WrapDroid. We describe related works in Sect. 6. Finally, we conclude the paper in Sect. 7.

2 Background

2.1 App Code Structure

Android, built on top of Linux Kernel, adopts a unique app architecture that supports both Java code and native (C/C++) code. For one thing, Java code is

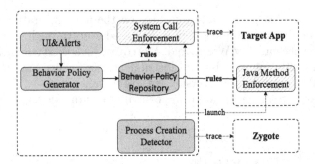

Fig. 2. WrapDroid architecture

compiled into bytecode and runs on register-based Dalvik VM. For another, linux shared objects (.so) are available for apps to reuse native libraries or accelerate performance-critical tasks. These two parts interacts with each other based on Java Native Interface (JNI) specification and reflection. Figure 1 shows in detail the code layers in an app's address space.

App Java code is written based on well-documented Android framework APIs, most of which are implemented in Java. In order to get executed, Java classes are compiled into Dalvik Executable Format (.dex) and transferred to Dalvik VM. The VM is introduced into app's address space as *libdvm.so* and all Java methods are eventually managed in its interpreter. However, part of the Java methods of an app or Android framework are declared as JNI methods and their required operations, like file and socket operations, are completed in native code. The native code relies on lower level system libraries and system calls of Linux kernel.

No matter how complicated an app seems, its code will always appear in Dalvik interpreter or go through related system calls in order to realize its functionalities. This provides a convenient and complete check point at which an app's behaviours can be dynamically examined and supervised.

2.2   App Launching

In Android, app processes are not generated by forking an ordinary process directly as that in Linux. Instead, *zygote* process is created during system booting to serve all process creation request. After we tapped an app icon on the home screen, a trusted system service, named Activity Manager Service would send a process creation request to *zygote* through zygote socket under the hood. The *zygote* is able to fork itself and configure child process properties (e.g. gid, uid) according to the request. Because the child process has inherited loaded libraries, resources and a Dalvik instance from *zygote*, it is prepared to load Java classes of the specific app and get them executed. Therefore, invocations of *fork* system call by *zygote* indicate the very beginning of app processes' life cycle. They work as reliable trigger event at which an app is put under monitor.

3   System Design

As described in Sect. 2.1, by monitoring interpretation of bytecode or invocation of system calls initiated by an app, a complete behavior map of the app can be retrieved and supervised. Our WrapDroid is designed based on the above observation. The WrapDroid is composed of six components that scatter in different processes and cooperate to supervise target apps. Its architecture is shown in Fig. 2.

It is device owner oriented and the *UI&Alerts* accepts behaviour policy items from the owner. These items consist of target apps and a set of regulated behaviour patterns for them. The *Behaviour Policy Generator (BPG)* translates all the items and passes them on to *Behaviour Policy Repository (BPR)*.

When WrapDroid is deployed, the *Process Creation Detector (PCD)* starts tracing *zygote* for newly created processes. The *PCD* maps these child processes to their hosting apps. If a hosting app is designated as a monitoring target, its processes are put under monitor immediately after process creation completes. The *System Call Enforcement (SCE)* implements a system call interposition based on *ptrace* and is responsible to regulate native code operations of target process by enforcing confinement on system calls according to *BPR*. The *Java Method Enforcement (JME)* is injected into target process and works by hijacking entry functions of interpreter. Every time a sensitive method frame is retrieved from interpretation stack, *JME* would determine whether its execution should be confined.

4   Implementation

We have implemented a WrapDroid prototype and the detailed description of each key component is given below.

4.1   Process Creation Detector

As shown in Sect. 2, *zygote* is responsible to fork an app process upon a process creation request from Activity Manager Service. To guarantee that the entire life cycle of the target app is monitored, *PCD* is introduced to detect newly created processes by tracing system calls of *zygote*.

We surveyed several existing system call tracing techniques, but most of them cannot satisfy the flexibility requirement. Some of them require enabling certain Linux kernel features, including *kprobes* [19]. Some others, like *ftrace* [20], is inflexible and weak in system call supervision. In our work, we monitor system calls of target process based on *ptrace*. Because signals are delivered from target process to our tracer at both the entry and exit of system calls, we have to use a history stack to distinguish between *syscall-enter-stop* and *syscall-exit-stop*. Moreover, by analysing and interposing registers and address space of the target process, detailed parameters of system calls are retrieved and their execution controlled.

Because any app identifier hasn't been set for the new process when *fork* returns, we have to relate the process to an app through other ways. In Android, each app package is regarded as a user and assigned a unique *uid*. We observed that the new process will set its *uid* right after *fork* returns from *zygote*. Therefore, identifying parameters of *setuid* helps to map the process to an app. If the hosting app should be monitored, WrapDroid would immediately start *SCE* and inject *JME* component into the process.

However, not all processes that related to an app derive from *zygote*. For example, an app process may launch *Runtime.exec* or directly *fork* its own child process. In this case, it's not complete to trace only *zygote* in *PCD*. To address this problem, the app process tree is traced recursively in *PCD* by means of specifying PTRAC_O_TRACEFORK option for *ptrace*.

4.2 Java Method Enforcement

The *JME* works in target process and is based on code injection. Because Android is built on top of Linux kernel, code injection techniques used in Linux also apply to Android. And *ptrace* offers us an available way. Listing 1.1 shows an overview of code injection procedure. Target process is attached to our tracer by *attchToTarget*. Upon a successful attachment, registers of target process are reserved so as to restore original execution state. Then we can obtain free memory for injected code by initiating a *mmap* function in target process. Because all Android processes share an identical mapping of system libraries including *libc.so* where *mmap* is defined, the *mmap* address in target process is the same as that in the tracer and can be easily obtained. After running *putCodeInTarget* method, the free memory is filled with the injected code. By adjusting registers (*pc, lr, etc.*) of target process, the injected code gets executed before restoring normal code sequence. Now the environment of target process has been changed and we can detach our tracer.

Listing 1.1. Code injection based on *ptrace*

```
1   void codeInjection(pid_t pid,
                        const char* func,
3                       int length,
                        ...){
5       attchToTarget(pid);
        regs = getRegsOfTarget(pid);
7
        //freeMem: where code is injected
9       freeMem = getMemoryOfTarget(pid);

11      //func: address of injected code
        //length: size of the code
13      putCodeInTarget(pid, freeMem,
                        func, length);
15
        manageRegs(&regs);
17      setRegsOfTarget(pid, regs);
        detachTarget(pid);
19  }
```

Every Dalvik thread maintains an interp stack in order to manage Java method and mimicked native method frames. These frames could be consumed by interpreter or by execution of native functions. Figure 3 shows some details inside of the VM. After obtaining a frame from interp stack, the thread would firstly decide whether the frame represents a JNI method. Native code of a JNI method is retrieved from *DalvikBridgeFunc* field of *Method* structure. A Java method frame is dispatched to different entries of interpreter in the light of different interpreter mode. The interpreter in fast/jit mode is coded in assembly language or has adopted Just In Time (jit), and thus relatively faster in bytecode interpretation. The method frame is delivered to an entry function named *dvmMterpStdRun* under this mode. However, for portability consideration, interpreter in portable mode is implemented in C language. Its entry function is *dvmInterpStd*. In our work, interpreter mode is fetched from system property *dalvik.vm.execution-mode*. By inline-hooking of the above entry functions, execution flow can be regulated based on information of current method and thread state. As can be seen in Fig. 3, function *javaMethEnforce* hijacks the interpreter and is responsible to enforce constraints on Java methods.

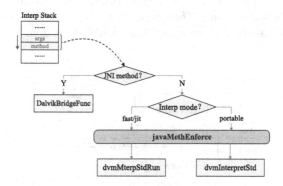

Fig. 3. Java method enforcement implementation

The key step of *javaMethEnforce* is extracting method details. We process parameters by scanning the method signature, where parameter types are designated. Primitive parameters are directly stored in stack and reference ones could be retrieved from Dalvik heap. Some simple reference variables, including *String* and primitive arrays, are parsed directly from heap memory. While the compound ones, like *Intent*, are sophisticated and made up of nested variables. Inside of Dalvik, every reference type is represented by a *ClassObject*. All fields and methods of the type are defined in the *ClassObject*. We automatically analyse compound variables by enumerating its fields and reduce them to simple types. To make our idea clear, a typical method that containing a SMS intent is given in Table 1. Particularly, reflection method can be detected from an object that labelled *Ljava/lang/reflect/Method;*.

Table 1. A typical method resolved in *JME*

Property name	Property value
Package	com.example.android.Msg
Thread	Main
Class	Landroid/app/instrumentation;
Method	checkStartActivityResult(IL)
Argument	Intent[mAction(android.intent.action.SEND), Uri(smsto:10010)]

Java method can be regulated by fabricating input parameters and return values. However, implementation of *JME* depends on interleaved structure and function definitions inside Dalvik. It's tedious to include all the definitions one by one. Hence, we compile *JME* on top of Dalvik part of Android Open Source Project (AOSP). Because no hardware module is involved in Dalvik, the recompiled *JME* applies to devices from different OEMs. Moreover, there exist different definition details through Android versions. For example, interpreter entry of Android 2.3 requires parameter of type *InterpState* pointer, while Android 4.0 or higher version requires *Thread* pointer. To guarantee compatibility, we customize a *JME* module for every existing Android version.

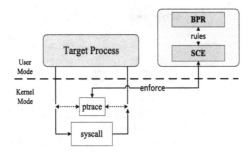

Fig. 4. Workflow of system call enforcement (SCE)

4.3 System Call Enforcement

The *SCE* component implementes the *ptrace* approach described in Sect. 4.1. Figure 4 outlines how *SCE* works. The target process would be suspended at the entry and exit of system calls. And meanwhile, *SCE* would be awakened by signals from the target process. The *SCE* is then able to enforce constraints based on system call details and rules from *BPR*.

For example, *SCE* enforces a series of network rules to regulate how an app accesses network resources. Basically, each app is prohibited from interacting with malicious remote addresses that defined in an IP blacklist. By managing parameters at the entry of socket related system calls, including *connect, sendto* and *recvfrom,* communications between the app and malicious network servers are restricted. Furthermore, to fully regulate an app's network access and meanwhile guarantee its usability, network data that from untrusted IP are forged before handling it to user space app. It is accomplished by modifying return data at the exit of socket calls, like buffer of *recvfrom.*

4.4   Behaviour Policy Definition

In WrapDroid, device user is able to initiate policies for an app with *UI&Alerts* module. The *BPG* is responsible to translate human-readable policies to policy items stored in *BPR.* We have defined WrapDroid policy language on top of policies of FireDroid [21] and the syntax is shown in Listing 1.2. Compared to FireDroid, our system pays more emphasis on high-level Java code regulation and alleviates the tediousness of defining low-level policies.

Listing 1.2. The syntax of the WrapDroid policy language

```
1 Package Operation [param-list]
2 if condition then outcome
```

The *package* works as a unique identification for target processes and is the basic unit for policy enforcement. A *package* requests an *Operation* on a *condition.* The policy would evaluate the *outcome* (allow or deny) for this behaviour. Different from FireDroid, our *condition* clause supports not only related context information but also how this behaviour is performed (e.g., normal Java APIs, Java reflections, native code). To make the syntax clear, we introduce a scenario to regulate SMS behaviours. Listing 1.3 shows how SMS destination, frequency and content are constrained for package *com.android.mms.* Particularly, some malicious apps may send SMS in native code by reflection to evade static analysis. The *isByReflection* clause prevents this kind of behavior.

Listing 1.3. Policy to control SMS

```
1 com.android.mms sendSMS [dst, content, lastSMSTime]
2    if (isByReflection) then deny
3    if (blacklist contains dst) then deny
4    if ((currentTime-lastSMSTime) < 1h) then deny
5    if (content contains 'Y') then deny
6    if (content contains number) then deny
```

5   Performance Evaluation

We evaluate the performance of WrapDroid in three aspects: (I) to demonstrate its effectiveness by enforcing restriction on prevalent apps; (II) to evaluate app performance overhead caused by adoption of WrapDroid; (III) to evaluate the impact on app launching. The experiment results demonstrate that WrapDroid can effectively regulate app's operations with reasonable performance overhead.

5.1 Effectiveness Evaluation

To test effectiveness of WrapDroid, we downloaded top 1050 apps from *wandoujia* [22], one of the most popular Android market of China, as an experiment sample. We evaluate how WrapDroid works to regulate SMS sending behavior of sample apps. By static analysis, 113 out of 1050 apps are found to request SEND_SMS permission in their manifest files. We originally planned to run each of the selected apps with *monkey*, an automatic event generator. However, only a few SMS sending operations are detected for random fuzzing feature of *monkey*. Hence, manual work is merged in our evaluation. Among the 113 apps, 35 apps have actually sent SMS and 40 destination numbers have been detected. In the experiment, we set the policy as "shutting down all the SMS message sending operations" and "restricting all SMS messages sent to "1065*"" separately. According to the bill from SMS service provider, WrapDroid meets our behaviour regulating expectation exactly.

5.2 App Running Efficiency

CaffeineMark 3.0 supports Android platform and runs as an Android app. It's score represents app's running efficiency. We run the benchmark on Nexus S with Android 4.1.2 under normal Android system and when WrapDroid is active. The result is shown in Fig. 5. As can be seen, the overhead of sieve, logic, loop and float tests incurred by WrapDroid is limited to 7 %. The string and method tests suffer from more performance loss of 16 % and 11 % because much more work is done on method and parameter analysis. While the overall overhead of CaffeineMark is 8.5 %, which means no noticeable impact has been brought to user experience.

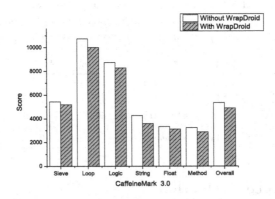

Fig. 5. CaffeineMark result of app running efficiency

Most of the functionality of Android apps are achieved by Framework APIs, which is not the key test factor of the above benchmark. Hence, we experimented on an app that performs a large amount of API invocations. An overhead comparison is made between WrapDroid and Aurasium [15], which is a

Table 2. Comparing WrapDroid with Aurasium

200 API invocations	Without WrapDroid	With WrapDroid	WrapDroid overhead	Aurasium overhead
Get device info	131 ms	145 ms	11 %	35 %
Get last location	71 ms	79 ms	12 %	34 %
Query contact list	132 ms	143 ms	8 %	14 %

policy enforcement scheme based on libc interposition. The evaluation result is shown in Table 2. Our WrapDroid is accomplished in higher Dalvik layer and thus more direct in parsing operations than Aurasium. Correspondingly, API invocation overhead of WrapDroid is much smaller than Aurasium.

5.3 App Launching Efficiency

As described in Sects. 2 and 4, app launching procedure stretches across several processes (e.g., *zygote*, *system_server*). Efficiency of app launching would be affected because these processes are under monitoring of system call tracing and runtime instrumentation. We evaluate it by designing an experimental app. The app initiates a *startService* request, and calculates time consumed when the service succeeds in running *onCreate*. The app is executed 10 times in normal Android and when WrapDroid is active on three devices: Nexus S (Samsung) with Android 2.3.6, Sony LT29i with Android 4.1.2, Meizu MX II with Android 4.2.1 and Samsung Galaxy Note II with Android 4.2.1. The result is shown in Table 3. We notice that the maximal time difference is within 23 ms, which can be ignored given the low frequency of app launching events.

Table 3. App launching efficiency

Device	Without WrapDroid	With WrapDroid	Delay
Nexus S (Samsung)	73 ms	90 ms	17 ms
Sony LT29i	95 ms	112 ms	17 ms
Meizu MX II	98 ms	106 ms	8 ms
Samsung Galaxy Note II	50 ms	73 ms	23 ms

6 Related Work

Researchers have worked on various aspects to regulate behaviors of Android apps and we categorize them into three classes by technical features.

Modifying Android source code. Many approaches based on source code customization have been proposed to regulate behaviors of Android apps. Some of them aim to enforce constraints based on extending permission mechanism. Apex [5] enables user to grant a selected set of permissions and supports user-defined restrictions on apps. CRePE [6] introduces external device context to refine permission policies. The privacy mode of TISSA [7] empowers users to define the kinds of personal information that are accessible to apps. And Comapat [8] restricts permissions of components to mitigate security problems aroused by a third-party component. Another way is accomplished by introducing Security Enhanced Linux (SELinux). References [10,11] implements concepts of SELinux on both Android's middleware and kernel layers to enhance a flexible mandatory access control (MAC). Besides directly regulating behaviors of Android apps, securing privacy data leads to the same destination. Reference [23] replaces private data with dummy data before providing it to apps. However, these approaches require Android source code modification and would suffer from deployment problem because of vendor customization. Our system performs all modification to Android apps by dynamic Dalvik instrumentation and system call tracing and thus can be deployed easily.

App rewriting. To make them portable, many approaches are implemented by integrating behavior regularization modules into Android apps by rewriting. With the rewritten dalvik bytecode, [12] is able to identify and interpose Security Sensitive APIs. Reference [13] uses static and dynamic method interception to retrofit app's behaviors. Reference [14] is an on-the-phone instrumentation scheme and its policies are based on interception of high-level java calls. Nevertheless, security policies of [15] are enforced by interposing low-level *libc.so*. Reference [16] introduces a new module that supports parameterized permissions and requests of sensitive resources from apps are forwarded to this module. App rewriting is an effective way that requires no modification to Android ROM. However, incomplete implementations of bytecode rewriting may result in several potential attacks [17]. It is difficult to assure that all apps installed are rewritten version of the original app. Due to signature difference of repackaging process, all history information of the original app cannot be shared by the rewritten app. In addition, system apps cannot be replaced easily so app rewriting only applies to third-party apps.

7   Conclusions and Future Work

Based on an observation that behaviours of an app can always be monitored completely in Dalvik interpreter or execution of system calls, we propose an app behaviour regulating scheme named WrapDroid based on dynamic instrumentation of Dalvik runtime and system call tracing. WrapDroid is flexible to enforce constraints on Android apps because this dynamic approach requires not any Android source code modification. WrapDroid monitors app's behavior from both Dalvik and system call layer, so operations of Java and native code are regulated completely. Moreover, through automatic recovery of operation context (e.g. parameters or call logs) and a set of policies, we can achieve a fine-grained control on Android apps. The evaluation of WrapDroid prototype demonstrates that our system can effectively regulate apps' behaviors with reasonable overhead.

At Google I/O 2014 conference, Android L was unveiled and the previously experimental Android Runtime (ART) has replaced Dalvik as a default environment. ART compiles byte code into executable ELF only once during app installation. We are now designing a scheme that monitors an app executed on ART by instrumenting compiled *.oat* executable file. WrapDroid would be fully effective on even the newest ART runtime after this future work is merged in.

Acknowledgement. This research was supported by the National Grand Fundamental Research 973 Program of China (Grant No. 2013CB338001 and No. 2014CB340603) and program of Computer Network Information Center of Chinese Academy of Sciences.

References

1. Strategy analytics: 85 % of phones shipped last quarter run android. http://bgr. com/2014/07/31/android-vs-ios-vs-windows-phone-vs-blackberry/
2. Cisco 2014 annual security report. http://www.cisco.com/web/offer/gist_ty2_ asset/Cisco_2014_ASR.pdf
3. App ops: Android 4.3's hidden app permission manager, control permissions for individual apps! http://www.androidpolice.com/2013/07/25/app-ops-android-4-- 3s/hidden-app-permission-manager/-control-permissions-for/-individual-apps/
4. App ops removed by google in android 4.4.2 update. http://www.phonearena.com/ news/App-Ops-removed-by-Google-in-Android-4.4.2-update_id50340/
5. Nauman, M., Khan, S., Zhang, X.: Apex: extending android permission model and enforcement with user-defined runtime constraints. In: Proceedings of the 5th ACM Symposium on Information, Computer and Communications Security (2010)
6. Conti, M., Nguyen, V.T.N., Crispo, B.: CRePE: context-related policy enforcement for android. In: Burmester, M., Tsudik, G., Magliveras, S., Ilić, I. (eds.) ISC 2010. LNCS, vol. 6531, pp. 331–345. Springer, Heidelberg (2011)
7. Zhou, Y., Zhang, X., Jiang, X., Freeh, V.W.: Taming information-stealing smartphone applications (on android). In: McCune, J.M., Balacheff, B., Perrig, A., Sadeghi, A.-R., Sasse, A., Beres, Y. (eds.) Trust 2011. LNCS, vol. 6740, pp. 93–107. Springer, Heidelberg (2011)
8. Wang, Y., Hariharan, S., Zhao, C., Liu, J., Du, W.: Compac: enforce component-level access control in android. In: Proceedings of the 4th ACM Conference on Data and Application Security and Privacy (2014)
9. Ongtang, M., McLaughlin, S., Enck, W., McDaniel, P.: Semantically rich application-centric security in android. In: Annual Computer Security Applications Conference (2009)
10. Bugiel, S., Heuser, S., Sadegh, A.R.: Flexible and fine-grained mandatory access control on android for diverse security and privacy policies. In: 22nd USENIX Security Symposium (USENIX Security 2013) (2013)
11. Smalley, S., Craig, R.: Security enhanced (SE) android: bringing flexible mac to android. In: NDSS (2013)
12. Davis, B., Sanders, B., Khodaverdian, A., Chen, H.: I-arm-droid: a rewriting framework for in-app reference monitors for android applications. In: Proceedings of the Mobile Security Technologies 2012, MOST 2012. IEEE (2012)

13. Davis, B., Chen, H.: RetroSkeleton: retrofitting android apps. In: Proceeding of the 11th Annual International Conference on Mobile Systems, Applications, and Services (2013)

14. Backes, M., Gerling, S., Hammer, C., Maffei, M., von Styp-Rekowsky, P.: AppGuard – enforcing user requirements on android apps. In: Piterman, N., Smolka, S.A. (eds.) TACAS 2013 (ETAPS 2013). LNCS, vol. 7795, pp. 543–548. Springer, Heidelberg (2013)

15. Xu, R., Saïdi, H., Anderson, R.: Aurasium: practical policy enforcement for android applications. In: Proceedings of the 21st USENIX Conference on Security Symposium (2012)

16. Jeon, J., Micinski, K.K., Vaughan, J.A., Fogel, A., Reddy, N., Foster, J.S., Millstein, T.: Dr. Android and Mr. Hide: fine-grained permissions in android applications. In: Proceedings of the Second ACM Workshop on Security and Privacy in Smartphones and Mobile Devices (2012)

17. Hao, H., Singh, V., Du, W.: On the effectiveness of API-level access control using bytecode rewriting in android. In: Proceedings of the 8th ACM SIGSAC Symposium on Information, Computer and Communications Security (2013)

18. Hao, S., Li, D., Halfond, W.G., Govindan, R.: SIF: a selective instrumentation framework for mobile applications. In: Proceeding of the 11th Annual International Conference on Mobile Systems, Applications, and Services (2013)

19. Kernel probes. http://sourceware.org/systemtap/kprobes/

20. Ftrace. http://elinux.org/Ftrace

21. Russello, G., Jimenez, A.B., Naderi, H., van der Mark, W.: FireDroid: hardening security in almost-stock android. In: Proceedings of the 29th Annual Computer Security Applications Conference (2013)

22. Wandoujia. http://www.wandoujia.com/

23. Hornyack, P., Han, S., Jung, J., Schechter, S., Wetherall, D.: These aren't the droids you're looking for: retrofitting android to protect data from imperious applications. In: Proceedings of the 18th ACM Conference on Computer and Communications Security, CCS 2011 (2011)

Hash Functions

A Collision Attack on a Double-Block-Length Compression Function Instantiated with Round-Reduced AES-256

Jiageng Chen[1], Shoichi Hirose[2]([✉]), Hidenori Kuwakado[3], and Atsuko Miyaji[1]

[1] School of Information Science,
Japan Advanced Institute of Science and Technology, Nomi, Japan
[2] Graduate School of Engineering, University of Fukui, Fukui, Japan
hrs_shch@u-fukui.ac.jp
[3] Faculty of Informatics, Kansai University, Suita, Japan

Abstract. This paper presents the first non-trivial collision attack on the double-block-length compression function presented at FSE 2006 instantiated with round-reduced AES-256: $f_0(h_0\|h_1, M)\|f_1(h_0\|h_1, M)$ such that

$$f_0(h_0\|h_1, M) = E_{h_1\|M}(h_0) \oplus h_0 \,,$$
$$f_1(h_0\|h_1, M) = E_{h_1\|M}(h_0 \oplus c) \oplus h_0 \oplus c \,,$$

where $\|$ represents concatenation, E is AES-256 and c is a non-zero constant. The proposed attack is a free-start collision attack. It uses the rebound attack proposed by Mendel et al. It finds a collision with time complexity 2^8, 2^{64} and 2^{120} for the instantiation with 6-round, 8-round and 9-round AES-256, respectively. The space complexity is negligible. The attack is effective against the instantiation with 6-/8-round AES-256 if the 16-byte constant c has a single non-zero byte. It is effective against the instantiation with 9-round AES-256 if the constant c has four non-zero bytes at some specific positions.

Keywords: Double-block-length compression function · Free-start collision attack · Rebound attack · AES-256

1 Introduction

Background. Cryptographic hash functions are very important primitives and used in almost all cryptographic protocols. They are often called hash functions, and we follow this convention.

There are several design strategies of hash functions, and the most popular ones are block-cipher-based and permutation-based. The block-cipher-based approach is much more classical than the permutation-based approach. The permutation-based approach is fairly new, and the SHA-3 Keccak [2] is designed with the approach. Well-known hash functions such as MD5 [33], SHA-1 and

© Springer International Publishing Switzerland 2015
J. Lee and J. Kim (Eds.): ICISC 2014, LNCS 8949, pp. 271–285, 2015.
DOI: 10.1007/978-3-319-15943-0_17

SHA-2 [11] can be regarded as being designed with the block-cipher-based approach using dedicated block ciphers. Hash functions MDC-2 and MDC-4 [6] using DES predate them.

Hash functions using an existing block cipher seem useful for resource-constrained devices such as low-end microcontrollers and RFIDs. Even for high-end devices with AES-NI, hash functions using AES [8,12] may be an option. How to construct secure hash functions using a block cipher has been an important research topic [4,30]. When using existing block ciphers such as AES, one should adopt double-block-length construction [6,14,15,20,27] for sufficient level of collision-resistance.

Our Contribution. This paper presents a non-trivial collision attack on the double-block-length (DBL) compression function [15] instantiated with round-reduced AES-256. As far as the authors know, this is the first collision attack on the DBL compression function instantiated with AES-256. The DBL compression function is defined as $f_0(h_0\|h_1, M)\|f_1(h_0\|h_1, M)$ such that

$$f_0(h_0\|h_1, M) = E_{h_1\|M}(h_0) \oplus h_0\,,$$
$$f_1(h_0\|h_1, M) = E_{h_1\|M}(h_0 \oplus c) \oplus h_0 \oplus c\,,$$

where $\|$ represents concatenation, E is AES-256 and c is a non-zero constant. The proposed collision attack assumes that the final round of round-reduced AES-256 does not have the MixColumns operation. The time complexity of the attack is 2^8, 2^{64}, and 2^{120} for the instantiation with AES-256 of 6 rounds, 8 rounds, and 9 rounds, respectively. The space complexity is negligible.

The proposed collision attack makes use of the following fact: If $(h_0\|h_1, M)$ and $((h_0 \oplus c)\|h_1, M)$ are a colliding pair for f_0, then they are also a colliding pair for f_1. The rebound attack [21] is used to find such a colliding pair for f_0. Thus, it largely depends on the value of c whether the proposed attack works well or not. The attack is effective against the instantiation with 6-/8-round AES-256 if the 16-byte constant c has a single non-zero byte. It is effective against the instantiation with 9-round AES-256 if the constant c has four non-zero bytes at some specific positions.

Related Work. The rebound attack was proposed by Mendel et al. [26], and was applied to the hash functions Whirlpool [31] and Grøstl [18], which have similar structure to AES. The rebound attack on Whirlpool was further improved by Lamberger et al. [21]. The rebound attack was also applied to a few other SHA-3 finalists [9,17,32].

There is some work on cryptanalyses of single-block-length hashing modes of AES. Biryukov, Khovratovich and Nikolić [3] presented a q-multicollision attack on the Davies-Meyer (DM) compression function instantiated with full-round AES-256. It is very powerful and its time complexity is $q \cdot 2^{67}$. The proposed attack does not seem to be able to use their attack since their attack needs some difference on the key input of AES. Mendel et al. [25] presented a collision attack on the DM compression function instantiated with 5-round AES-128 with time complexity 2^{56}. The collision attack on 5.5-round Whirlpool [21] can easily be extended to a collision attack on the DM, Matyas-Meyer-Oseas (MMO), Miyaguchi-Preneel (MP) compression functions instantiated with 6-round AES-128 or the DM compression function instantiated with 6-round AES-192/256. Its time complexity is 2^{56}. Jean, Naya-Plasencia and Peyrin [16] presented a collision attack on the DM compression function instantiated with 6-round AES-128 with time complexity 2^{32}. Sasaki presented preimage and second-preimage attacks on DM, MMO and MP modes of 7-round AES [34].

There is little work on cryptanalyses of instantiations of DBL hashing modes. Ferguson [10] presented a few generic attacks on H-PRESENT-128 [5]. Wei et al. [35] presented collision and preimage attacks on various hashing modes instantiated with the block cipher IDEA [19]. They concluded that IDEA should not be used for hashing. The hashing modes include the DBL modes such as Abreast-DM, Tandem-DM [20], the mode by Hirose [15], the mode by Peyrin et al. [29] and MJH [23]. Our proposed collision attack is unlikely to be applied to them except for the Hirose mode.

The collision resistance and the preimage resistance were provided proofs in the ideal cipher model for Abreast-DM [1,13,22], Tandem-DM [1,24], the Hirose compression function [1,15]. In particular, Abreast-DM and the Hirose compression function were shown to be optimally collision-resistant in the ideal cipher model.

Organization. A brief description of AES is given in Sect. 2. An overview of the proposed collision attack on the DBL compression function is described in Sect. 3. The collision attacks on the compression function instantiated with AES-256 of 6 rounds, 8 rounds and 9 rounds are detailed in Sects. 4, 5 and 6, respectively. A concluding remark is given in Sect. 7.

2   Preliminaries

2.1   AES

This section gives a description of the AES [8,12] together with some properties of its components necessary for the discussions later.

AES is a block cipher with 128-bit block length and 128/192/256-bit key length. The transformations of AES are performed on a (4×4)-byte array called the state. Each byte is regarded as an element in $\mathrm{GF}(2^8)$. Multiplication is performed modulo $x^8 + x^4 + x^3 + x + 1$. The state is initially a plaintext.

The encryption of AES consists of four transformations: SubBytes, ShiftRows, MixColumns and AddRoundKey. It starts with the AddRoundKey transformation followed by iteration of a round function. The round function applies SubBytes, ShiftRows, MixColumns and AddRoundKey transformations in this order to the state. The final round does not have the MixColumns transformation.

The SubBytes transformation is byte-wise application of the nonlinear S-box function. For the S-box S, an input x satisfying the equation $\mathsf{S}(x) \oplus \mathsf{S}(x \oplus \Delta I) = \Delta O$ is called an admissible input for the pair of an input difference ΔI and an output difference ΔO. We will say that an input difference and an output difference are compatible with each other if there exist admissible inputs for the pair.

Table 1 shows the numbers of the pairs of input and output differences which have the specified numbers of admissible inputs. The probability that there exist any admissible inputs for a pair of input and output differences $(\Delta I, \Delta O)$ chosen uniformly at random is about $1/2$. An admissible input of the SubBytes transformation is defined similarly.

Table 1. Correspondence between the number of input-/ouput-difference pairs and the number of their admissible inputs for the AES S-box

The number of admissible inputs	0	2	4	256
The number of difference pairs	33150	32130	255	1

The ShiftRows transformation is byte-wise cyclic transposition of each row. It shifts the i-th row by i-bytes cyclically to left for $0 \leq i \leq 3$.

The MixColumns transformation is linear transformation of each column. It can be represented with a matrix. For a 4-byte column b of a state, it is represented by Mb, where

$$M = \begin{pmatrix} 02\ 03\ 01\ 01 \\ 01\ 02\ 03\ 01 \\ 01\ 01\ 02\ 03 \\ 03\ 01\ 01\ 02 \end{pmatrix} \quad \text{and} \quad M^{-1} = \begin{pmatrix} 0e\ 0b\ 0d\ 09 \\ 09\ 0e\ 0b\ 0d \\ 0d\ 09\ 0e\ 0b \\ 0b\ 0d\ 09\ 0e \end{pmatrix} .$$

The AddRoundKey transformation is bitwise XOR of a round key to a state. The round keys are generated by a key expansion algorithm. The round keys of AES-256 are generated in the following way. Let (4×4)-byte array K_r be the round key of the r-th round for $r \geq 0$, where K_0 is for the initial AddRoundKey transformation. The 256-bit key input is given to K_0 and K_1. Let $K_r[j]$ be the j-th column of K_r for $0 \leq j \leq 3$. For $r \geq 2$, if r is even, then

$$K_r[0] = K_{r-2}[0] \oplus \text{SW}(K_{r-1}[3]^\uparrow) \oplus C_r ,$$
$$K_r[j] = K_{r-2}[j] \oplus K_r[j-1] \quad \text{for } 1 \leq j \leq 3 ,$$

where SW represents byte-wise application of the AES S-box, $K_{r-1}[3]^\uparrow$ represents cyclic 1-byte shift of $K_{r-1}[3]$ to the top, and C_r is a specified constant. If r is odd, then

$$K_r[0] = K_{r-2}[0] \oplus \text{SW}(K_{r-1}[3]) ,$$
$$K_r[j] = K_{r-2}[j] \oplus K_r[j-1] \quad \text{for } 1 \leq j \leq 3 .$$

For simplicity, the SubBytes, ShiftRows, MixColumns and AddRoundKey transformations are denoted by SB, SR, MC and AK, respectively.

The state in the r-th round is denoted by S_r. S_r^{SB}, S_r^{SR}, S_r^{MC} and S_r^{AK} represent the state S_r just after SB, SR, MC and AK transformations, respectively. S_{-1} represents a plaintext input.

For $0 \leq i \leq 3$ and $0 \leq j \leq 3$, $S_r[i][j]$ represents the byte of S_r in the i-th row and the j-th column. $S_r[j]$ represents the j-th column of S_r.

3   Collision Attack on DBL Compression Function Instantiated with Round-Reduced AES-256

This section gives an overview of the proposed free-start collision attack on a DBL compression function [15] instantiated with round-reduced AES-256. The target DBL compression function

$$v_0 \| v_1 = F(h_0 \| h_1, M) = f_0(h_0 \| h_1, M) \| f_1(h_0 \| h_1, M)$$

is defined by

$$f_0(h_0 \| h_1, M) = E_{h_1 \| M}(h_0) \oplus h_0 \ ,$$
$$f_1(h_0 \| h_1, M) = E_{h_1 \| M}(h_0 \oplus c) \oplus h_0 \oplus c \ ,$$

where $\|$ represents concatenation, E is a block cipher and c is a non-zero constant. F is depicted in Fig. 1.

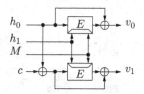

Fig. 1. The target DBL compression function. c is a non-zero constant and E is a block cipher.

The proposed attack uses the following simple fact:

Fact 1. *Suppose that $(h_0 \| h_1, M)$ and $((h_0 \oplus \Delta h_0) \| h_1, M)$ cause a collision for f_0, that is, $f_0(h_0 \| h_1, M) = f_0((h_0 \oplus \Delta h_0) \| h_1, M)$ and that $\Delta h_0 = c$. Then, $(h_0 \| h_1, M)$ and $((h_0 \oplus \Delta h_0) \| h_1, M)$ also cause a collision for f_1.*

The algorithm of the collision attack on F is given below:

1. Find a colliding pair of inputs $(h_0 \| h_1, M)$ and $((h_0 \oplus \Delta h_0) \| h_1, M)$ for f_0.
2. Output $(h_0 \| h_1, M)$ and $((h_0 \oplus \Delta h_0) \| h_1, M)$ if $\Delta h_0 = c$. Otherwise, return to Step 1.

The first step returns a colliding pair of inputs for f_0 such that the non-zero bytes of Δh_0 are located at the same positions as the non-zero bytes of the constant c. Thus, it largely depends on the value of c if the proposed attack is effective or not. The attack is effective against F instantiated with 6-/8-round AES-256 if the 16-byte constant c has a single non-zero byte. It is effective against F instantiated with 9-round AES-256 if the constant c has four non-zero bytes at some specific positions. Sections 4, 5 and 6 present how the collision attack is applied to F instantiated with AES-256 of 6, 8 and 9 rounds, respectively.

4 Collision Attack on F with 6-Round AES-256

This section presents a collision attack on f_0 instantiated with 6-round AES-256. It returns a pair of colliding inputs for any given $\Delta h_0 (= c)$ whose bytes are zero except for the first byte. The time complexity is 2^8, and the space complexity is negligible.[1] Thus, the total time complexity of the collision attack on the compression function F instantiated with 6-round AES-256 is also 2^8.

The collision attack on f_0 is based on the rebound attack on the 5.5-round Whirlpool hash function by Lamberger et al. [21]. Different from the attack by Lamberger et al., it is a free-start collision attack. Its goal is to find a pair of inputs, $(h_0 \| h_1, M)$ and $(h_0' \| h_1, M)$, which follow the differential path given in Fig. 2. Colored bytes in Fig. 2 are non-zero differences.

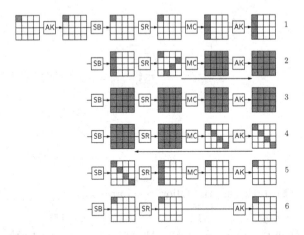

Fig. 2. The differential path used by the collision attack on the compression function f_0 instantiated with 6-round AES-256. Colored bytes are non-zero differences.

A detailed description of the attack is given below. It proceeds in two phases. It first fixes the values of differences on the differential path so that the pair of input and output differences of each SB transformation are compatible, that is,

---

[1] The complexity to compute admissible inputs of the AES S-box is omitted.

they have admissible inputs (Steps 1 to 5). Then, it selects admissible inputs of the SB transformations and connects them using the round keys (Steps 6 to 15).

Input: $\Delta h_0 = \Delta S_{-1}$.

Procedure:

1. Select the difference ΔS_1^{SB} compatible with $\Delta S_0^{AK} = \Delta S_{-1}$. Then, compute $\Delta S_1^{AK} = \Delta S_1^{MC} = \mathsf{MC}(\mathsf{SR}(\Delta S_1^{SB}))$.
2. Select ΔS_2^{SB} compatible with ΔS_1^{AK}. Then, compute ΔS_2^{AK}.
3. Select $\Delta S_5^{AK} = \Delta S_5^{MC}$ compatible with $\Delta S_6^{SB} = \Delta S_6^{AK} = \Delta S_{-1}$. Then, compute $\Delta S_5^{SB} = \mathsf{SR}^{-1}(\mathsf{MC}^{-1}(\Delta S_5^{MC}))$.
4. Select ΔS_4^{AK} compatible with ΔS_5^{SB}. Then, compute ΔS_4^{SB}.
5. Compute ΔS_3^{SB} and ΔS_3^{AK} compatible with ΔS_2^{AK} and ΔS_4^{SB}, respectively, such that $\Delta S_3^{AK} = \mathsf{MC}(\mathsf{SR}(\Delta S_3^{SB}))$. They can be computed column by column, and the expected time complexity is $4 \times 2^4 = 2^6$.
6. Select an admissible input S_2^{AK} for the pair of ΔS_2^{AK} and ΔS_3^{SB}.
7. Select an admissible input S_3^{AK} for the pair of ΔS_3^{AK} and ΔS_4^{SB}.
8. Compute the round key $K_3 = S_3^{MC} \oplus S_3^{AK} = \mathsf{MC}(\mathsf{SR}(\mathsf{SB}(S_2^{AK}))) \oplus S_3^{AK}$.
9. Compute S_4^{MC} from S_3^{AK}.
10. Select the diagonal elements of an admissible input S_4^{AK} for the pair of ΔS_4^{AK} and ΔS_5^{SB}. Then, compute the diagonal elements of K_4: $K_4[i][i] = S_4^{MC}[i][i] \oplus S_4^{AK}[i][i]$ for $0 \leq i \leq 3$.
11. The diagonal elements of S_5^{SB} are fixed by those of S_4^{AK}, and they further fix $S_5^{MC}[0]$.
12. Select an admissible input $S_5^{AK}[0][0]$ for the pair of ΔS_5^{AK} and ΔS_6^{SB}. Then, compute $K_5[0][0] = S_5^{MC}[0][0] \oplus S_5^{AK}[0][0]$.
13. Select an admissible input $S_1^{AK}[0]$ for the pair of ΔS_1^{AK} and ΔS_2^{SB}. $S_1^{AK}[0]$ fixes $S_2^{SB}[0]$. The following condition on the round key K_2 is obtained:

$$S_2^{SB}[0] = \mathsf{SR}^{-1}(\mathsf{MC}^{-1}(S_2^{AK} \oplus K_2))[0]$$
$$= \mathsf{SR}^{-1}(\mathsf{MC}^{-1}(S_2^{AK}))[0] \oplus \mathsf{SR}^{-1}(\mathsf{MC}^{-1}(K_2))[0] \ .$$

14. Select an admissible input $S_0^{AK}[0][0]$ for the pair of ΔS_0^{AK} and ΔS_1^{SB}. $S_0^{AK}[0][0]$ fixes $S_1^{SB}[0][0]$. The following condition on the round key $K_1[0]$ is obtained:

$$S_1^{SB}[0][0] = (0\mathsf{e}, 0\mathsf{b}, 0\mathsf{d}, 09)(S_1^{AK}[0] \oplus K_1[0])$$
$$= (0\mathsf{e}, 0\mathsf{b}, 0\mathsf{d}, 09)S_1^{AK}[0] \oplus (0\mathsf{e}, 0\mathsf{b}, 0\mathsf{d}, 09)K_1[0] \ .$$

15. Compute the round keys satisfying all the conditions obtained so far. The following bytes of the round keys are already fixed: K_3, $K_4[0][0]$, $K_4[1][1]$, $K_4[2][2]$, $K_4[3][3]$ and $K_5[0][0]$. The conditions on the other bytes of round keys can be expressed by equations on K_2. The expected time complexity to compute K_2 is 2^8. Details are given in Sect. 4.1.
16. Compute the input S_{-1} from S_2^{AK} and the round keys. Output $h_0 = S_{-1}$, $h_1 = K_0$ and $M = K_1$.

The time complexity of the collision attack is about 2^8. The space complexity is negligible. An example of collision is given in Appendix A.

The same kind of differential path as the one in Fig. 2 is able to be constructed when given an input difference Δh_0 with a single non-zero byte at any byte position. Due to the asymmetry of the key expansion algorithm, however, a little more analyses are required to confirm whether the same kind of very efficient attack really works or not.

4.1   Conditions on the Round Key K_2

The following five conditions are led from the key expansion algorithm:

$$K_2[0][0] = K_4[0][0] \oplus \mathsf{S}(K_3[1][3]) \oplus RC_2 \tag{1}$$

$$K_2[1][0] \oplus K_2[1][1] = K_4[1][1] \oplus \mathsf{S}(K_3[2][3]) \tag{2}$$

$$K_2[2][0] \oplus K_2[2][1] \oplus K_2[2][2] = K_4[2][2] \oplus \mathsf{S}(K_3[3][3]) \tag{3}$$

$$K_2[3][0] \oplus K_2[3][1] \oplus K_2[3][2] \oplus K_2[3][3] = K_4[3][3] \oplus \mathsf{S}(K_3[0][3]) \tag{4}$$

$$K_2[0][1] \oplus K_2[0][2] \oplus K_2[0][3] = K_4[0][0] \oplus K_4[0][3], \tag{5}$$

where RC_2 is a constant in the key expansion algorithm. $K_4[0][3] = \mathsf{S}^{-1}(K_3[0][0] \oplus K_5[0][0])$. Notice that all the bytes of the round keys on the right side of the equations above are fixed.

The following conditions are mentioned in the step 13 of the algorithm in Sect. 4:

$$(0e, 0b, 0d, 09)K_2[0] = S_2^{\mathsf{SR}}[0][0] \oplus (0e, 0b, 0d, 09)S_2^{\mathsf{AK}}[0] \tag{6}$$

$$(0b, 0d, 09, 0e)K_2[1] = S_2^{\mathsf{SR}}[3][1] \oplus (0b, 0d, 09, 0e)S_2^{\mathsf{AK}}[1] \tag{7}$$

$$(0d, 09, 0e, 0b)K_2[2] = S_2^{\mathsf{SR}}[2][2] \oplus (0d, 09, 0e, 0b)S_2^{\mathsf{AK}}[2] \tag{8}$$

$$(09, 0e, 0b, 0d)K_2[3] = S_2^{\mathsf{SR}}[1][3] \oplus (09, 0e, 0b, 0d)S_2^{\mathsf{AK}}[3]. \tag{9}$$

The following last condition is nonlinear. It is also led from the key expansion algorithm:

$$\mathsf{SW}(K_2[3]) = K_1[0] \oplus K_3[0],$$

where $K_1[0]$ satisfies

$$(0e, 0b, 0d, 09)K_1[0] = S_1^{\mathsf{SB}}[0][0] \oplus (0e, 0b, 0d, 09)S_1^{\mathsf{AK}}[0]. \tag{10}$$

SW represents transformation of each byte with the AES S-box.

We compute K_2 satisfying the conditions above by first computing $K_2[3]$ satisfying the last nonlinear condition. $K_2[3]$ is computed as follows:

1. Choose $K_2[3]$ satisfying Eq. (9) uniformly at random, and compute $K_1[0] = \mathsf{SW}(K_2[3]) \oplus K_3[0]$.
2. Check if $K_1[0]$ satisfies Eq. (10).

In the second step of the procedure, the probability that Eq. (10) holds is 2^{-8}. It is easy to compute the remaining twelve bytes of K_2 satisfying the linear equations from (1) to (9).

5   Collision Attack on F with 8-Round AES-256

This section presents a free-start collision attack on f_0 instantiated with 8-round AES-256. It returns a pair of colliding inputs with difference Δh_0 whose bytes are zero except for one byte at any specified position. The time complexity is 2^{56}, and the space complexity is negligible. The probability that $\Delta h_0 = c$ is 2^{-8} if c has a single non-zero byte at the same position as the non-zero byte of Δh_0. Thus, the total time complexity of the collision attack on F instantiated with 8-round AES-256 is 2^{64}.

The collision attack on f_0 is based on the rebound attack on the 7.5-round Whirlpool compression function by Lamberger et al. [21]. The goal of the attack is to find a pair of inputs, $(h_0\|h_1, M)$ and $(h_0'\|h_1, M)$, which follow the differential path given in Fig. 3.

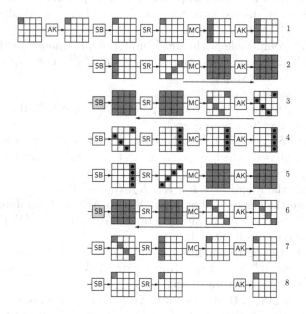

Fig. 3. The differential path used by the collision attack on the compression function f_0 instantiated with 8-round AES-256. Colored bytes are non-zero differences.

The proposed attack uses two inbound phases: The first one is in the second and the third rounds, and the second one is in the fifth and the sixth rounds. The algorithm of the attack is described below. It first selects the values of differences of the two inbounds (Steps 1 and 2) and those between the two inbounds (Step 3). Then, for each pair of an admissible input of SB in the third round and that of SB in the sixth round, it connects them with the round keys (Steps 4a to 4c), and extends the state transformation to the outbounds to check if a colliding pair of inputs are obtained (Steps 4d to 4f).

1. This step looks for a pair of compatible input/output differences of SubBytes of the third round in the following way:
   (a) Select ΔS_2^{SR}, $\Delta S_3^{AK} = \Delta S_3^{MC}$ uniformly at random, and compute

$$\Delta S_2^{AK} = \Delta S_2^{MC} = MC(\Delta S_2^{SR}),$$
$$\Delta S_3^{SB} = SR^{-1}(MC^{-1}(\Delta S_3^{MC})).$$

   (b) If there are no admissible inputs for the pair of ΔS_2^{AK} and ΔS_3^{SB}, then return to Step 1a.
   The expected number of repetitions of this step is 2^{16}. The number of admissible inputs obtained for S_2^{AK} with this step is 2^{16}. Actually, this step can be made more efficient since the trials can be done column by column. However, this speed-up does not change the time complexity of the overall algorithm.

2. This step looks for a pair of compatible input/output differences of SubBytes of the sixth round in the same way as the step 1. 2^{16} admissible inputs are obtained for S_5^{AK} with this step.

3. Select ΔS_3^{SB} compatible with ΔS_3^{AK} uniformly at random until $\Delta S_4^{AK} = \Delta S_4^{MC} = MC(SR(\Delta S_4^{SB}))$ is compatible with ΔS_5^{SB}. The expected number of repetitions of this step is 2^4.

4. Perform the following procedure:
   (a) Select a new pair among the 2^{32} pairs of S_2^{AK} and S_5^{AK}. If there exists no new pair, then return to Step 1.
   (b) Compute $S_3^{SB} = SB(S_2^{AK})$. Then, run the algorithm for connecting two inbound phases, which is given in Sect. 5.1, and obtain the round keys K_3, K_4 and K_5.
   (c) Compute the round keys K_0, K_1, K_2, K_6 and K_7.
   (d) Compute the corresponding input S_{-1} to AES and the difference ΔS_{-1} from S_2^{AK} and ΔS_2^{AK}. If any byte of ΔS_{-1} other than $\Delta S_{-1}[0][0]$ is non-zero, then return to Step 4a.
   (e) Compute the corresponding output S_8^{AK} from AES and the difference ΔS_8^{AK} from S_5^{AK} and ΔS_5^{AK}. If any byte of ΔS_8^{AK} other than $\Delta S_8^{AK}[0][0]$ is non-zero, then return to Step 4a.
   (f) If $\Delta S_{-1} = \Delta S_8^{AK}$, then proceed to Step 5. Otherwise, return to Step 4a.

5. Output the pair of inputs (K, S_{-1}) and $(K, S_{-1} \oplus \Delta S_{-1})$, which are mapped to the same hash value by f_0 instantiated with 8-round AES-256, where $K = K_0 \| K_1$.

For Step 4d in the algorithm above, the probability that only $\Delta S_{-1}[0][0]$ is non-zero (the transition from ΔS_1^{MC} to ΔS_1^{SR} is successful) is 2^{-24}. Similarly, for Step 4e, the probability that only $\Delta S_8^{AK}[0][0]$ is non-zero is 2^{-24}. For Step 4f, the probability that $\Delta S_{-1} = \Delta S_8^{AK}$ is 2^{-8}. Thus, the estimated time complexity of the algorithm above is $2^{24 \times 2 + 8} = 2^{56}$.

The collision attack returns a colliding pair of inputs whose non-zero difference is located at the top-left corner. Owing to the symmetry of AES, the collision attack can easily be extended so that it returns a colliding pair of inputs whose non-zero difference is located at any specified byte position.

5.1   Algorithm to Connect Two Inbound Phases

An algorithm to connect two inbound phases is described in this section. It gives a pair of sequences of state values between SB in the third round and SB in the sixth round whose differences follow the differential path in Fig. 3. The initial and final state values of the sequences are given to the algorithm as input as well as the values of the differences. The algorithm outputs the round keys (K_3, K_4 and K_5) which connect these values. The algorithm pays specific attention to the bytes of states with black circles in Fig. 3. They are given priority simply because they are bytes with non-zero differences.

Input: S_3^{SB}, S_5^{AK}, and ΔS_3^{SB}, ΔS_4^{SB}, ΔS_5^{AK}.

Output: Round keys K_3, K_4 and K_5.

Procedure:

1. Compute ΔS_3^{AK}, ΔS_4^{AK} and ΔS_5^{SB}:

$$\Delta S_3^{AK} = \Delta S_3^{MC} = \mathsf{MC}(\mathsf{SR}(\Delta S_3^{SB}))$$
$$\Delta S_4^{AK} = \Delta S_4^{MC} = \mathsf{MC}(\mathsf{SR}(\Delta S_4^{SB}))$$
$$\Delta S_5^{SB} = \mathsf{SR}^{-1}(\mathsf{MC}^{-1}(\Delta S_5^{MC})), \text{ where} \Delta S_5^{MC} = \Delta S_5^{AK}.$$

2. Select admissible inputs of the S-boxes with non-zero differences of SB in the fourth round: $S_3^{AK}[0][3]$, $S_3^{AK}[1][0]$, $S_3^{AK}[2][1]$ and $S_3^{AK}[3][2]$.
3. Compute $K_3[0][3]$, $K_3[1][0]$, $K_3[2][1]$ and $K_3[3][2]$ from the corresponding bytes of $S_3^{MC} = \mathsf{MC}(\mathsf{SR}(S_3^{SB}))$ and S_3^{AK}.
4. Select admissible inputs of the S-boxes with non-zero differences of SB in the fifth round: $S_4^{AK}[3]$. Then, compute $S_5^{SB}[3]$.
5. $K_4[3] = S_4^{MC}[3] \oplus S_4^{AK}[3]$, where $S_4^{MC}[3]$ can be computed from the corresponding bytes of S_3^{AK}.
6. Compute the round key K_5 satisfying the conditions obtained so far. They can be expressed by 8 linear equations on the bytes of K_5. The equations are given in Sect. 5.2.
7. Compute the remaining bytes of K_3 from K_5 and $K_4[3]$.
8. Compute S_4^{MC} and S_4^{AK} from S_3^{SB} with K_3 and from S_5^{AK} with K_5, respectively. Then, compute $K_4[j] = S_4^{MC}[j] \oplus S_4^{AK}[j]$ for $0 \leq j \leq 2$.

5.2   Conditions on the Round Key K_5

The following four conditions are led from the key expansion algorithm:

$$K_5[1][0] = K_3[1][0] \oplus \mathsf{S}(K_4[1][3])$$
$$K_5[2][0] \oplus K_5[2][1] = K_3[2][1]$$
$$K_5[3][1] \oplus K_5[3][2] = K_3[3][2]$$
$$K_5[0][2] \oplus K_5[0][3] = K_3[0][3].$$

Notice that all the bytes of K_3 and K_4 on the right side are already fixed by the algorithm.

The other condition comes from the fixed bytes of $S_5^{SB}[3]$:

$$SR(S_5^{SB}[3]) = MC^{-1}(S_5^{AK})[3] \oplus MC^{-1}(K_5)[3].$$

Notice that S_5^{AK} is given to the algorithm as input. They can be expanded to the following four equations:

$$(0b, 0d, 09, 0e)K_5[0] = S_5^{SR}[3][0] \oplus (0b, 0d, 09, 0e)S_5^{AK}[0]$$
$$(0d, 09, 0e, 0b)K_5[1] = S_5^{SR}[2][1] \oplus (0d, 09, 0e, 0b)S_5^{AK}[1]$$
$$(09, 0e, 0b, 0d)K_5[2] = S_5^{SR}[1][2] \oplus (09, 0e, 0b, 0d)S_5^{AK}[2]$$
$$(0e, 0b, 0d, 09)K_5[3] = S_5^{SR}[0][3] \oplus (0e, 0b, 0d, 09)S_5^{AK}[3].$$

6   Collision Attack on F with 9-Round AES-256

The collision attack on f_0 instantiated with 8-round AES-256 can be extended to the collision attack on f_0 instantiated with 9-round AES-256 for different choice of the constant c. The differential path used by this attack is presented in Fig. 4. $\Delta h_0 = \Delta S_{-1}$ has four non-zero bytes on its diagonal. The differential path from the third round to the sixth round is equal to the differential path from the second round to the fifth round in Fig. 3. Thus, the algorithm to connect two inbound phases shown in Sect. 5.1 can also be used here.

In the outbound phase of the attack,

- the success probability of the transition from ΔS_2^{MC} to ΔS_2^{SR} is 2^{-24},
- the success probability of the transition from ΔS_8^{SR} to ΔS_8^{MC} is 2^{-32}, and
- the probability that $\Delta S_{-1} = \Delta S_9^{AK}$ is 2^{-32}.

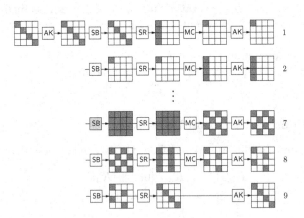

Fig. 4. The differential path used by the collision attack on the compression function f_0 instantiated with 9-round AES-256. Colored bytes are non-zero differences. The differential path from the third round to the sixth round is omitted since it is equal to the differential path from the second round to the fifth round in Fig. 3.

Thus, the estimated time complexity of the attack is $2^{24+32+32} = 2^{88}$. Though it is beyond the complexity of the birthday attack for f_0, it is effective for our purpose.

Due to the symmetry of AES, the attack also works with the same kind of the differential paths with ΔS_{-1} such that the four non-zero bytes of ΔS_{-1} are

- $\Delta S_{-1}[0][1]$, $\Delta S_{-1}[1][2]$, $\Delta S_{-1}[2][3]$, $\Delta S_{-1}[3][0]$,
- $\Delta S_{-1}[0][2]$, $\Delta S_{-1}[1][3]$, $\Delta S_{-1}[2][0]$, $\Delta S_{-1}[3][1]$, or
- $\Delta S_{-1}[0][3]$, $\Delta S_{-1}[1][0]$, $\Delta S_{-1}[2][1]$, $\Delta S_{-1}[3][2]$.

The total time complexity of the collision attack on F is $2^{88+32} = 2^{120}$ since the probability that $\Delta h_0 = c$ is 2^{-32} for constant c which has four non-zero bytes at the same positions as the non-zero bytes of Δh_0.

7   Conclusion

This paper has presented a free-start collision attack on the DBL compression function [15] instantiated with round-reduced AES-256. A drawback of the attack is that it is effective against restricted constants. It is interesting if the restriction is reduced. It is also interesting to apply the attack to instantiations with other block ciphers.

Acknowledgments. The authors would like to thank the anonymous reviewers for their valuable comments. This work was supported by JSPS KAKENHI Grant Numbers 21240001 and 25330150.

A   Example of Collision for f_0 Instantiated with 6-Round AES-256

Table 2 gives an example of collision for f_0 instantiated with 6-round AES-256.

Table 2. An example of collision for f_0 instantiated with 6-round AES-256

Δh_0	ff000000 00000000 00000000 00000000
h_0	5950c89a 7243695a b5561aa0 78899ca7
h_1	e9141904 6ab77163 f77410dc 429d3463
M	f5e6ee51 ac004900 1d47b1e7 8394e656
Output	6ecccd37 579174c9 457e605d f2cdeecb

References

1. Armknecht, F., Fleischmann, E., Krause, M., Lee, J., Stam, M., Steinberger, J.: The preimage security of double-block-length compression functions. In: Lee, D.H., Wang, X. (eds.) ASIACRYPT 2011. LNCS, vol. 7073, pp. 233–251. Springer, Heidelberg (2011)
2. Bertoni, G., Daemen, J., Peeters, M., Van Assche, G.: The Keccak sponge function family (2008). http://keccak.noekeon.org
3. Biryukov, A., Khovratovich, D., Nikolić, I.: Distinguisher and related-key attack on the full AES-256. In: Halevi, S. (ed.) CRYPTO 2009. LNCS, vol. 5677, pp. 231–249. Springer, Heidelberg (2009). An extended version is "Cryptology ePrint Archive: Report 2009/241" at http://eprint.iacr.org/
4. Black, J., Rogaway, P., Shrimpton, T., Stam, M.: An analysis of the blockcipher-based hash functions from PGV. J. Cryptol. **23**(4), 519–545 (2010)
5. Bogdanov, A., Leander, G., Paar, C., Poschmann, A., Robshaw, M.J.B., Seurin, Y.: Hash functions and RFID tags: mind the gap. In: Oswald, E., Rohatgi, P. (eds.) CHES 2008. LNCS, vol. 5154, pp. 283–299. Springer, Heidelberg (2008)
6. Brachtl, B.O., Coppersmith, D., Hyden, M.M., Matyas Jr., S.M., Meyer, C.H.W., Oseas, J., Pilpel, S., Schilling, M.: Data authentication using modification detection codes based on a public one-way encryption function, March 1990. US Patent # 4,908,861
7. Canteaut, A. (ed.): FSE 2012. LNCS, vol. 7549. Springer, Heidelberg (2012)
8. Daemen, J., Rijmen, V.: The Design of Rijndael. Springer, Heidelberg (2002)
9. Duc, A., Guo, J., Peyrin, T., Wei, L.: Unaligned rebound attack: application to Keccak. In: Canteaut [7], pp. 402–421
10. Ferguson, N.: Observations on H-PRESENT-128. CRYPTO 2011 Rump Session (2011). http://www.iacr.org/cryptodb/archive/2011/CRYPTO/video/rump/
11. FIPS PUB 180-4. Secure hash standard (SHS), March 2012
12. FIPS PUB 197. Advanced encryption standard (AES) (2001)
13. Fleischmann, E., Gorski, M., Lucks, S.: Security of cyclic double block length hash functions. In: Parker [28], pp. 153–175
14. Hirose, S.: Provably secure double-block-length hash functions in a black-box model. In: Park, C., Chee, S. (eds.) ICISC 2004. LNCS, vol. 3506, pp. 330–342. Springer, Heidelberg (2005)
15. Hirose, S.: Some plausible constructions of double-block-length hash functions. In: Robshaw, M. (ed.) FSE 2006. LNCS, vol. 4047, pp. 210–225. Springer, Heidelberg (2006)
16. Jean, J., Naya-Plasencia, M., Peyrin, T.: Multiple limited-birthday distinguishers and applications. In: Lange, T., Lauter, K., Lisoněk, P. (eds.) SAC 2013. LNCS, vol. 8282, pp. 533–550. Springer, Heidelberg (2014)
17. Khovratovich, D., Nikolić, I., Rechberger, C.: Rotational rebound attacks on reduced skein. In: Abe, M. (ed.) ASIACRYPT 2010. LNCS, vol. 6477, pp. 1–19. Springer, Heidelberg (2010)
18. Knudsen, L.R., Gauravaram, P., Matusiewicz, K., Mendel, F., Rechberger, C., Schläffer, M., Thomsen, S.S.: Grøstl - a SHA-3 candidate (2008). http://www.groestl.info
19. Lai, X., Massey, J.L.: A proposal for a new block encryption standard. In: Damgård, I.B. (ed.) EUROCRYPT 1990. LNCS, vol. 473, pp. 389–404. Springer, Heidelberg (1991)

20. Lai, X., Massey, J.L.: Hash functions based on block ciphers. In: Rueppel, R.A. (ed.) EUROCRYPT 1992. LNCS, vol. 658, pp. 55–70. Springer, Heidelberg (1993)
21. Lamberger, M., Mendel, F., Rechberger, C., Rijmen, V., Schläffer, M.: The rebound attack and subspace distinguishers: application to Whirlpool. Cryptology ePrint Archive, Report 2010/198 (2010). http://eprint.iacr.org/
22. Lee, J., Kwon, D.: The security of Abreast-DM in the ideal cipher model. IEICE Trans. **94-A**(1), 104–109 (2011)
23. Lee, J., Stam, M.: MJH: a faster alternative to MDC-2. In: Kiayias, A. (ed.) CT-RSA 2011. LNCS, vol. 6558, pp. 213–236. Springer, Heidelberg (2011)
24. Lee, J., Stam, M., Steinberger, J.: The collision security of Tandem-DM in the ideal cipher model. In: Rogaway, P. (ed.) CRYPTO 2011. LNCS, vol. 6841, pp. 561–577. Springer, Heidelberg (2011)
25. Mendel, F., Peyrin, T., Rechberger, C., Schläffer, M.: Improved cryptanalysis of the reduced Grøstl compression function, ECHO permutation and AES block cipher. In: Jacobson Jr, M.J., Rijmen, V., Safavi-Naini, R. (eds.) SAC 2009. LNCS, vol. 5867, pp. 16–35. Springer, Heidelberg (2009)
26. Mendel, F., Rechberger, C., Schläffer, M., Thomsen, S.S.: The rebound attack: cryptanalysis of reduced Whirlpool and Grøstl. In: Dunkelman, O. (ed.) FSE 2009. LNCS, vol. 5665, pp. 260–276. Springer, Heidelberg (2009)
27. Özen, O., Stam, M.: Another glance at double-length hashing. In: Parker [28], pp. 176–201
28. Parker, M.G. (ed.): Cryptography and Coding 2009. LNCS, vol. 5921. Springer, Heidelberg (2009)
29. Peyrin, T., Gilbert, H., Muller, F., Robshaw, M.J.B.: Combining compression functions and block cipher-based hash functions. In: Lai, X., Chen, K. (eds.) ASIACRYPT 2006. LNCS, vol. 4284, pp. 315–331. Springer, Heidelberg (2006)
30. Preneel, B., Govaerts, R., Vandewalle, J.: Hash functions based on block ciphers: a synthetic approach. In: Stinson, D.R. (ed.) CRYPTO 1993. LNCS, vol. 773, pp. 368–378. Springer, Heidelberg (1994)
31. Rijmen, V., Barreto, P.S.L.M.: The Whirlpool hash function (2000). http://www.larc.usp.br/pbarreto/WhirlpoolPage.html
32. Rijmen, V., Toz, D., Varıcı, K.: Rebound attack on reduced-round versions of JH. In: Hong, S., Iwata, T. (eds.) FSE 2010. LNCS, vol. 6147, pp. 286–303. Springer, Heidelberg (2010)
33. Rivest, R.: The MD5 message-digest algorithm. Request for Comments 1321 (RFC 1321), The Internet Engineering Task Force (1992)
34. Sasaki, Y.: Meet-in-the-middle preimage attacks on AES hashing modes and an application to Whirlpool. IEICE Trans. Fundam. **E96-A**(1), 121–130 (2013)
35. Wei, L., Peyrin, T., Sokołowski, P., Ling, S., Pieprzyk, J., Wang, H.: On the (in)security of IDEA in various hashing modes. In: Canteaut [7], pp. 163–179. The full version is "Cryptology ePrint Archive: Report 2012/264" at http://eprint.iacr.org/

LSH: A New Fast Secure Hash Function Family

Dong-Chan Kim, Deukjo Hong$^{(\boxtimes)}$, Jung-Keun Lee, Woo-Hwan Kim,
and Daesung Kwon

The Attached Institute of ETRI, Daejeon, Korea
{dongchan,hongdj,jklee,whkim5,ds_kwon}@ensec.re.kr

Abstract. Since Wang's attacks on the standard hash functions MD5 and SHA-1, design and analysis of hash functions have been studied a lot. NIST selected Keccak as a new hash function standard SHA-3 in 2012 and announced that Keccak was chosen because its design is different from MD5 and SHA-1/2 so that it could be secure against the attacks to them and Keccak's hardware efficiency is quite better than other SHA-3 competition candidates. However, software efficiency of Keccak is somewhat worse than present standards and other candidates. Since software efficiency becomes more important due to increase of kinds and volume of communication/storage data as cloud and big data service spread widely, its software efficiency degradation is not desirable.

In this paper, we present a new fast hash function family LSH, whose software efficiency is above four times faster than SHA-3, and 1.5–2.3 times faster than other SHA-3 finalists. Moreover it is secure against all critical hash function attacks.

Keywords: Hash function · Merkle-Damgård mode · Wide-pipe structure · PGV model · Parallel implementation · SIMD instruction · ARX operations

1 Introduction

1.1 Background and Motivation

As critical attacks were found for dedicated hash functions including MD5 and SHA-1 [50,54,55], doubts on the security have been continuously raised that SHA-2 may be vulnerable to such attacks due to similar design approach to attacked hash functions. For this reason, NIST has prepared a new US standard hash function SHA-3 based on Keccak, the winner of SHA-3 Cryptographic Hash Algorithm Competition (2007–2012) [8]. NIST said that Keccak is chosen because its design is different from MD5 and SHA-1/2 so that it could be secure against the attacks to them and Keccak's hardware efficiency is quite better than other SHA-3 competition candidates. However Keccak shows relatively low software performance compared to other candidates.

Much more and bigger data needs to be hashed in the era of smart devices, cloud and big data, so the faster hash function is strongly required to prevent any

© Springer International Publishing Switzerland 2015
J. Lee and J. Kim (Eds.): ICISC 2014, LNCS 8949, pp. 286–313, 2015.
DOI: 10.1007/978-3-319-15943-0_18

degradation in the performance of cryptographic modules or services. To maximize such performance, implementing cryptographic algorithm at the hardware level would be a good way. However, the hardware implementation won't be able to have the competitive edge in price to the software one without large quantity production. Even when the hardware implementation costs less, the software implementation has many advantages in terms of management: flexibility, portability, ease of use/upgrade, etc. [12]. Upon these, a cryptographic algorithm having good software performance would be more marketable. In accordance with given circumstances and this consideration, we have developed a new hash function family LSH.

1.2 Design Approach

We kept the following two principles in mind when designing the hash function family LSH:

- (Security) Adopt a hash structure which is provably secure and has full security bounds in the ideal setting, and design a compression function which has enough security margin to be defended against critical hash function attack.
- (Implementation) Design a compression function which can be easily implemented using parallel processing instructions SSE, AVX2 and NEON provided by pervading processors at present, such that a high-speed implementation can maximize the operational efficiency on platforms of servers and smart devices, as good as it gets.

1.3 Hash Function Family LSH

This paper presents a new hash function family LSH. Its best feature is that it shows the software performance superior to the other existing hash functions, thanks to the use of parallel processing instructions such as SSE, AVX2 and NEON.

Brief Design Description. The hash function family LSH consists of n-bit hash functions based on w-bit word, $\{\text{LSH-}8w\text{-}n : w = 32 \text{ or } 64, 1 \leq n \leq 8w\}$. The hash structure of LSH-$8w$-n is wide-pipe Merkle-Damgård mode with one-zeros padding. After all message blocks are compressed, LSH-$8w$-n returns n-bit hash value by a finalization function. The compression function is designed on the 17th PGV structure [18]. Bit length of a chaining variable is $16w$ and that of a message block is $32w$. The compression of a message block is proceeded by repeating step function operations. The number of step functions is 26 if $w = 32$, or 28 if $w = 64$. Each step function has three layers: (i) Message addition layer, (ii) Mix layer, (iii) Word-permutation layer. The message addition layer is a mere exclusive-or process between a chaining variable and a sub-message generated from a given message block. In mix layer, every two words are mixed independently. This layer is designed for parallel implementation with ARX (modular Addition, bit-Rotation, eXclusive-or) operations. Word-permutation layer plays the role of diffusion. Section 2 shows the specification of LSH-$8w$-n in detail.

Security. The structure of LSH-$8w$-n which is composed of wide-pipe Merkle-Damgård mode and the compression function designed on the 17th PGV, is essentially proved to have full security under the ideal cipher model proof [18], i.e., the structure has 2^n pre-image and 2nd pre-image resistance, and $2^{n/2}$ collision resistance. We analyzed security of LSH with various cryptanalytic methods, and got the result that LSH-256-256 is secure against all the existing hash function attacks when the number of steps is 13 or more, while LSH-512-512 is secure if the number of steps is 14 or more. Note that the steps which work as security margin are 50 % of the compression function. See Sect. 4.2 for details.

Comparison with SHA-3 Finalists. Keccak does not have good software performance among SHA-3 finalists. The designs of LSH, Blake, and Skein are based on ARX systems, but LSH is 1.5–2.3 times faster than the others. The best known attack on Keccak is the second-preimage attack on 8 rounds [13]. So, one may doubt that the high speed of LSH stems from relatively short steps by considering that the number of attacked rounds of Keccak is just 1/3 of its underlying permutation. However, he is missing the difference between design and attack in the sense that designers should determine a safe guideline for security and any attack result does not exclude possibility of better one in future. Note that we give the safe boundary for number of steps for all the existing attacks and 12 steps of LSH-256-256 and 13 steps of LSH-512-512 have never been broken by any hash function attack.

Performance. The software speed of LSH is measured on various platforms and we compare the speed of LSH-$8w$-n with SHA-2 and SHA-3 competition finalists because they have been matured in terms of security. At the platform based on Haswell architecture CPU, the speed of LSH-256-n is 3.60 cycles/byte and the speed of LSH-512-n is 2.39 cycles/byte. LSH-$8w$-n is the fastest one on this platform. LSH-512-n is about 2.3-times faster than the second best one, Skein-512 of 5.58 cycles/byte. At the platform based on Samsung Exynos 5250 ARM Cortex-A15 CPU, the speed of LSH-256-n and LSH-512-n are 11.17 cycles/byte and 8.94 cycles/byte respectively. LSH-$8w$-n is the fastest one among them as well. Excepting LSH-$8w$-n, the highest speed is 13.46 cycles/byte of Blake-512, and LSH-512-n is about 1.5 times faster than it. See Sect. 5.3.

Contents of the paper. Section 2 introduces the specification of LSH-$8w$-n. Section 3 presents the design rationale of LSH-$8w$-n. Section 4 presents security analysis of LSH-$8w$-n. Sections 5 and 6 show software and hardware implementation. Differential characteristics for collision attacks of LSH-$8w$-n are added at Appendixes A.

2   Specification

The hash function family LSH consists of n-bit hash functions based on w-bit word, $\{$LSH-$8w$-$n : w = 32$ or $64, 1 \leq n \leq 8w\}$.

Table 1. Hex digit representation of a 4-bit string

hex	bit string	hex	bit string	hex	bit string	hex	bit string
0	0000	4	0100	8	1000	c	1100
1	0001	5	0101	9	1001	d	1101
2	0010	6	0110	a	1010	e	1110
3	0011	7	0111	b	1011	f	1111

2.1 Definitions, Notation and Conventions

Glossary of Terms and Acronyms

- Bit: Value of 0 or 1.
- Byte: 8-bit string.
- Word: w-bit string where w is either 32 or 64. In this paper, w is used as bit length of a word.
- Array: Collection of bytes or words.
- $\mathcal{W}^t$: Set of all t-word arrays ($t \geq 1$). In this paper, let $\mathcal{W}$ denote $\mathcal{W}^1$.
- LSH-$8w$-n: The n-bit hash function based on w-bit word ($1 \leq n \leq 8w$).

Bit Strings and Convention. The little-endian convention is used when expressing an l-bit string x, i.e., $x = x_0||x_1||\cdots||x_{l-1}$ for all $x_i \in \{0,1\}$. However, for convenience, the big-endian convention is used when expressing an w-bit word, so that within each word, the most significant bit is stored in the left-most bit position, i.e., a word X is written in a bit string $x_{w-1}||x_{w-2}||\cdots||x_1||x_0$ for all $x_i \in \{0,1\}$. A hex digit is the representation of a 4-bit string as Table 1.

Operations. We define the following operations:

Operations on bit strings. Let x and y be bit strings.

- $x \parallel y$: Concatenation of x and y.
- $x \oplus y$: Bit-wise exclusive-or of x and y.
- $|x|$: Bit length of x.
- $x_{[i:j]} := x_i||x_{i+1}||\cdots||x_j$: Sub-bit string of a l-bit string $x = x_0||x_1||\cdots||x_{l-1}$ for $i \leq j$.

Operations on words. Let $X = x_{w-1}||\cdots||x_0$ and Y be words and $Z = \sum_{l=0}^{w-1} z_l \cdot 2^l$ be an integer where $x_l, z_l \in \{0,1\}$ for all l.

- $X^{\lll i}$: i-bit left rotation of X.
- $X^{\ggg i} := X^{\lll w-i}$: i-bit right rotation of X.
- $\text{WORDTOINT}(X) := \sum_{l=0}^{w-1} x_l \cdot 2^l$.
- $\text{INTTOWORD}(Z) := z_{w-1}||\cdots||z_0$.
- $X \boxplus Y := \text{INTTOWORD}(\text{WORDTOINT}(X) + \text{WORDTOINT}(Y) \bmod 2^w)$.
- $X_{[i:j]} := x_i||x_{i-1}||\cdots||x_j$: Sub-bit string of a word X for $i \geq j$.

Data Array Assignment and Conversion. Let $X = (X[0], \ldots, X[s-1])$ and $Y = (Y[0], \ldots, Y[s-1])$ be s-word arrays, and let $z = (z[0], z[1], \ldots, z[t-1])$ be a t-byte array, where $t = sw/8$. Let $p = w/8$.

- $X \leftarrow Y$: Assign a t-word array Y to X as $X[l] \leftarrow Y[l]$ for all l.
- $X \leftarrow z$: Assign a t-byte array z to a s-word array X as (1).

$$X[l] \leftarrow z[pl + (p-1)] \parallel \cdots \parallel z[pl+1] \parallel z[pl], \text{ for } 0 \le l < s. \qquad (1)$$

- $z \leftarrow X$: Assign a s-word array X to a t-byte array z as (2).

$$z[l] \leftarrow X[\lfloor l/p \rfloor]^{\ggg 8l}{}_{[7:0]}, \text{ for } 0 \le l < t, \qquad (2)$$

where $\lfloor x \rfloor$ is the largest integer not greater than x.

Algorithm Parameters. The parameters used in the specification are as follows:

- n: Bit length of a hash value ($1 \le n \le 8w$).
- N_s: Number of step functions used in a compression function.
- $M^{(i)} := (M^{(i)}[0], \ldots, M^{(i)}[31])$: The i-th 32-word array message block.
- $M_j^{(i)} := (M_j^{(i)}[0], \ldots, M_j^{(i)}[15])$: The j-th 16-word array sub-message generated from the i-th message block $M^{(i)}$.
- $IV := (IV[0], \ldots, IV[15])$: The 16-word array initialization vector.
- $CV^{(i)} := (CV^{(i)}[0], \ldots, CV^{(i)}[15])$: The i-th 16-word array chaining variable.
- $SC_j := (SC_j[0], \ldots, SC_j[7])$: The j-th 8-word array step constant.
- $T := (T[0], \ldots, T[15])$: The 16-word array temporary variable used in a step function.

2.2   Hash Structure

The n-bit hash function based on w-bit word, LSH-$8w$-n has the wide-pipe Merkle-Damgård structure with one-zeros padding. The message hashing process of LSH-$8w$-n consists of the following three stages.

1. *Initialization*:
   - One-zeros padding of a given bit string message.
   - Conversion to 32-word array message blocks from the padded bit string message.
   - Initialization of a chaining variable with the initialization vector.
2. *Compression*:
   - Updating of chaining variables by iteration of a compression function with message blocks.
3. *Finalization*:
   - Generation of an n-bit hash value from the final chaining variable.

Intialization. Let m be a given bit string message. The m is padded by one-zeros, i.e., the bit '1' is appended to the end of m, and the bit '0's are appended until a bit length of a padded message is $32wt$-bit, where $t = \left\lceil \frac{|m|+1}{32w} \right\rceil$ and $\lceil x \rceil$ is the smallest integer not less than x.

Let $m' = m_0\|m_1\|\cdots\|m_{32wt-1}$ be the one-zeros-padded $32wt$-bit string of m. Then m' is considered as a $4wt$-byte array $\mathsf{m} = (m[0], \ldots, m[4wt - 1])$, where $m[l] = m_{8l}\|m_{8l+1}\|\cdots\|m_{8l+7}$ for all l. By (1), the $4wt$-byte array m converts into a $32t$-word array $\mathsf{M} = (M[0], \ldots, M[32t - 1])$. From the word array M, we define the t 32-word array message blocks $\{\mathsf{M}^{(i)}\}_{i=0}^{t-1}$ by (3).

$$\mathsf{M}^{(i)} \leftarrow (M[32i], M[32i + 1], \ldots, M[32i + 31]). \tag{3}$$

The 16-word array chaining variable $\mathsf{CV}^{(0)}$ is initialized to the initialization vector IV of LSH-$8w$-n, shown in Sect. 2.4, i.e., $\mathsf{CV}^{(0)} \leftarrow \mathsf{IV}$.

Compression. In this stage, the t 32-word array message blocks $\{\mathsf{M}^{(i)}\}_{i=0}^{t-1}$, which are generated from a message m, are compressed by iteration of compression functions. The compression function $\mathrm{CF} : \mathcal{W}^{16} \times \mathcal{W}^{32} \to \mathcal{W}^{16}$ has two inputs; the i-th 16-word chaining variable $\mathsf{CV}^{(i)}$ and the i-th 32-word message block $\mathsf{M}^{(i)}$, and returns the $(i+1)$-th 16-word chaining variable $\mathsf{CV}^{(i+1)}$. For the detail process of a compression function CF, see Sect. 2.3.

Finalization. The finalization function FIN_n return n-bit hash value h from the final chaining variable $\mathsf{CV}^{(t)} = (CV^{(t)}[0], \ldots, CV^{(t)}[15])$. Let $\mathsf{h} = (h[0], \ldots, h[w-1])$ be an w-byte array. FIN_n proceeds as (4).

$$\mathsf{h} \leftarrow (CV^{(t)}[0] \oplus CV^{(t)}[8],\ CV^{(t)}[1] \oplus CV^{(t)}[9],\ \ldots, CV^{(t)}[7] \oplus CV^{(t)}[15]),$$
$$h \leftarrow (h[0] \| \cdots \| h[w - 1])_{[0:n-1]}. \tag{4}$$

Algorithm 1 shows the message hashing process of LSH-$8w$-n.

2.3 Compression Function

The i-th 16-word chaining variable $\mathsf{CV}^{(i)}$ and the i-th 32-word message block $\mathsf{M}^{(i)}$ are inputs of a compression function $\mathrm{CF} : \mathcal{W}^{16} \times \mathcal{W}^{32} \to \mathcal{W}^{16}$. The following four functions are used in a compression function:

1. $\mathrm{MSGEXP} : \mathcal{W}^{32} \to \mathcal{W}^{16(\mathrm{N}_s+1)}$ (Message expansion function),
2. $\mathrm{MSGADD} : \mathcal{W}^{16} \times \mathcal{W}^{16} \to \mathcal{W}^{16}$ (Message addition function),
3. $\mathrm{MIX}_j : \mathcal{W}^{16} \to \mathcal{W}^{16}$ (Mix function),
4. $\mathrm{WORDPERM} : \mathcal{W}^{16} \to \mathcal{W}^{16}$ (Word-permutation function),

where the number N_s is defined in (5) and $0 \le j < \mathrm{N}_s$.

$$\mathrm{N}_s := \begin{cases} 26, & \text{if LSH-256-}n, \\ 28, & \text{if LSH-512-}n. \end{cases} \tag{5}$$

Algorithm 1. Hash function LSH-$8w$-n

Input: Bit string message m

Output: n-bit hash value h of m

1. One-zeros padding of m
2. Generation of t message blocks $\{M^{(i)}\}_{i=0}^{t-1}$, where $t = \left\lceil \frac{|m|+1}{32w} \right\rceil$ from the padded bit string
3. $\mathsf{CV}^{(0)} \leftarrow \mathsf{IV}$
4. **for** $i = 0$ to $t - 1$ **do**
5. $\mathsf{CV}^{(i+1)} \leftarrow \mathrm{CF}(\mathsf{CV}^{(i)}, \mathsf{M}^{(i)})$
6. **end for**
7. $h \leftarrow \mathrm{FIN}_n(\mathsf{CV}^{(t)})$
8. **return** h

Here we define the j-th step function $\mathrm{STEP}_j : \mathcal{W}^{16} \times \mathcal{W}^{16} \to \mathcal{W}^{16}$ by (6).

$$\mathrm{STEP}_j := \mathrm{WORDPERM} \circ \mathrm{MIX}_j \circ \mathrm{MSGADD}. \tag{6}$$

In a compression function, the message expansion function MSGEXP generates $\mathrm{N}_s + 1$ 16-word array sub-messages $\{M_j^{(i)}\}_{j=0}^{\mathrm{N}_s}$ from given $\mathsf{M}^{(i)}$. Let $\mathsf{T} = (T[0], \ldots, T[15])$ be a temporary 16-word array set to the i-th chaining variable $\mathsf{CV}^{(i)}$. The j-th step function STEP_j having two inputs T and $\mathsf{M}_j^{(i)}$ updates T, i.e., $\mathsf{T} \leftarrow \mathrm{STEP}_j(\mathsf{T}, \mathsf{M}_j^{(i)})$. All step functions are proceeded in order $j = 0, \ldots, \mathrm{N}_s - 1$. Then one more MSGADD operation by $\mathsf{M}_{\mathrm{N}_s}^{(i)}$ is proceeded, and the $(i+1)$-th chaining variable $\mathsf{CV}^{(i+1)}$ is set to T. Algorithm 2 shows the process of a compression function in detail.

Message Expansion Function. Let $\mathsf{M}^{(i)} = (M^{(i)}[0], \ldots, M^{(i)}[31])$ be the i-th 32-word array message block. The message expansion function MSGEXP generates $\mathrm{N}_s + 1$ 16-word array sub-messages $\{M_j^{(i)}\}_{j=0}^{\mathrm{N}_s}$ from a message block $\mathsf{M}^{(i)}$. The first two sub-messages $\mathsf{M}_0^{(i)} = (M_0^{(i)}[0], \ldots, M_0^{(i)}[15])$ and $\mathsf{M}_1^{(i)} = (M_1^{(i)}[0], \ldots, M_1^{(i)}[15])$ are defined by (7).

$$\mathsf{M}_0^{(i)} \leftarrow (M^{(i)}[0], \ldots, M^{(i)}[15]), \quad \mathsf{M}_1^{(i)} \leftarrow (M^{(i)}[16], \ldots, M^{(i)}[31]). \tag{7}$$

The next sub-messages $\{M_j^{(i)} = (M_j^{(i)}[0], \ldots, M_j^{(i)}[15])\}_{j=2}^{\mathrm{N}_s}$ are generated by (8).

$$\mathsf{M}_j^{(i)}[l] \leftarrow \mathsf{M}_{j-1}^{(i)}[l] \boxplus \mathsf{M}_{j-2}^{(i)}[\tau(l)], \text{ for } 0 \leq l < 16, \tag{8}$$

where τ is the permutation over $\mathbb{Z}_{16}$ defined by Table 3.

Algorithm 2. Compression function CF

Input: The i-th chaining variable $\mathrm{CV}^{(i)}$ and the i-th message block $\mathsf{M}^{(i)}$

Output: The $(i+1)$-th chaining variable $\mathrm{CV}^{(i+1)}$

1. $\{\mathsf{M}_j^{(i)}\}_{j=0}^{\mathrm{N}_s} \leftarrow \mathrm{MSGEXP}(\mathsf{M}^{(i)})$
2. $\mathsf{T} \leftarrow \mathrm{CV}^{(i)}$
3. **for** $j = 0$ to $\mathrm{N}_s - 1$ **do**
4. $\quad \mathsf{T} \leftarrow \mathrm{STEP}_j(\mathsf{T}, \mathsf{M}_j^{(i)}) \begin{cases} \mathsf{T} & \leftarrow \mathrm{MSGADD}(\mathsf{T}, \mathsf{M}_j^{(i)}) \\ \mathsf{T} & \leftarrow \mathrm{MIX}_j(\mathsf{T}) \\ \mathsf{T} & \leftarrow \mathrm{WORDPERM}(\mathsf{T}) \end{cases}$
5. **end for**
6. $\mathrm{CV}^{(i+1)} \leftarrow \mathrm{MSGADD}(\mathsf{T}, \mathsf{M}_{\mathrm{N}_s}^{(i)})$
7. **return** $\mathrm{CV}^{(i+1)}$

Message Addition Function. The message addition function MSGADD : $\mathcal{W}^{16} \times \mathcal{W}^{16} \rightarrow \mathcal{W}^{16}$ is defined by (9): for two 16-word arrays $\mathsf{X} = (X[0], \ldots, X[15])$ and $\mathsf{Y} = (Y[0], \ldots, Y[15])$,

$$\mathrm{MSGADD}(\mathsf{X}, \mathsf{Y}) := (X[0] \oplus Y[0], \ldots, X[15] \oplus Y[15]). \tag{9}$$

Mix Function. The j-th mix function $\mathrm{MIX}_j : \mathcal{W}^{16} \rightarrow \mathcal{W}^{16}$ updates the 16-word array $\mathsf{T} = (T[0], \ldots, T[15])$ by mixing every two-word pair; $T[l]$ and $T[l+8]$ for $0 \leq l < 8$. For $0 \leq j \leq \mathrm{N}_s - 1$, the mix function MIX_j proceeds (10).

$$(T[l], T[l+8]) \leftarrow \mathrm{MIX}_{j,l}(T[l], T[l+8]), \text{ for } 0 \leq l < 8, \tag{10}$$

where $\mathrm{MIX}_{j,l}$ is a two-word mix function. Let X and Y be words. The two-word mix function $\mathrm{MIX}_{j,l} : \mathcal{W}^2 \rightarrow \mathcal{W}^2$ is defined by Fig. 1 and (11). Here the bit rotational amounts $\alpha_j, \beta_j, \gamma_l$ used in $\mathrm{MIX}_{j,l}$ are shown in Table 2.

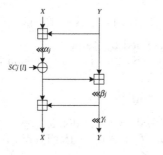

$$\begin{aligned} X &\leftarrow X \boxplus Y, \\ X &\leftarrow X^{\lll \alpha_j}, \\ X &\leftarrow X \oplus SC_j[l], \\ Y &\leftarrow X \boxplus Y, \\ Y &\leftarrow Y^{\lll \beta_j}, \\ X &\leftarrow X \boxplus Y, \\ Y &\leftarrow Y^{\lll \gamma_l}. \end{aligned} \tag{11}$$

Fig. 1. Two-word mix function $\mathrm{MIX}_{j,l}(X, Y)$

Table 2. Bit rotation amounts: α_j, β_j and γ_l

Algorithm	j	α_j	β_j	γ_0	γ_1	γ_2	γ_3	γ_4	γ_5	γ_6	γ_7
LSH-256-n	even	29	1	0	8	16	24	24	16	8	0
	odd	5	17								
LSH-512-n	even	23	59	0	16	32	48	8	24	40	56
	odd	7	3								

The j-th 8-word array constant $\mathsf{SC}_j = (SC_j[0], \ldots, SC_j[7])\}$ used in $\mathrm{MIX}_{j,l}$ for $0 \leq l < 8$, is defined as follows: The initial 8-word array constant $\mathsf{SC}_0 = (SC_0[0], \ldots, SC_0[7])$ of LSH-256-n and LSH-512-n are defined by (12) and (13). Let $\delta = 768372$, where 76, 83, 72 are ASCII codes of 'L,' 'S,' and 'H' respectively.

– LSH-256-n: These are the first 256-bit of the fractional parts of $\sqrt{\delta}$.

$$
\begin{aligned}
SC_0[0] &= \mathtt{917caf90}, & SC_0[1] &= \mathtt{6c1b10a2}, \\
SC_0[2] &= \mathtt{6f352943}, & SC_0[3] &= \mathtt{cf778243}, \\
SC_0[4] &= \mathtt{2ceb7472}, & SC_0[5] &= \mathtt{29e96ff2}, \\
SC_0[6] &= \mathtt{8a9ba428}, & SC_0[7] &= \mathtt{2eeb2642}.
\end{aligned}
\tag{12}
$$

– LSH-512-n: These are the first 512-bit of the fractional parts of $\sqrt[3]{\delta}$.

$$
\begin{aligned}
SC_0[0] &= \mathtt{97884283c938982a}, & SC_0[1] &= \mathtt{ba1fca93533e2355}, \\
SC_0[2] &= \mathtt{c519a2e87aeb1c03}, & SC_0[3] &= \mathtt{9a0fc95462af17b1}, \\
SC_0[4] &= \mathtt{fc3dda8ab019a82b}, & SC_0[5] &= \mathtt{02825d079a895407}, \\
SC_0[6] &= \mathtt{79f2d0a7ee06a6f7}, & SC_0[7] &= \mathtt{d76d15eed9fdf5fe}.
\end{aligned}
\tag{13}
$$

For $1 \leq j \leq N_s - 1$, the j-th constant $\mathsf{SC}_j = (SC_j[0], \ldots, SC_j[7])$ is generated by (14).

$$
SC_j[l] \leftarrow SC_{j-1}[l] \boxplus SC_{j-1}[l]^{\lll 8}, \text{ for } 0 \leq l < 8.
\tag{14}
$$

Word-Permutation Function. Let $\mathsf{X} = (X[0], \ldots, X[15])$ be an 16-word array. The word-permutation function $\mathrm{WORDPERM} : \mathcal{W}^{16} \to \mathcal{W}^{16}$ is defined by (15).

$$
\mathrm{WORDPERM}(\mathsf{X}) := (X[\sigma(0)], \ldots, X[\sigma(15)]),
\tag{15}
$$

where σ is the permutation over $\mathbb{Z}_{16}$ defined by Table 3.

Figure 2 shows the j-th step function STEP_j of a compression function.

2.4   Initialization Vector Generation

The initialization vector $\mathsf{IV} \in \mathcal{W}^{16}$ of LSH-$8w$-n is defined by $\mathrm{CF}(\mathsf{X}, \mathsf{Y})$, where $\mathsf{X} \in \mathcal{W}^{16}$ such that $X[0] = \mathrm{INTTOWORD}(w)$, $X[1] = \mathrm{INTTOWORD}(n)$, and $X[l]$ are all zero words for $2 \leq l \leq 15$, and $\mathsf{Y} \in \mathcal{W}^{32}$ such that all $Y[l]$ are all zero words. The initialization vector of LSH-256-256 and LSH-512-512 are (16) and (17) respectively.

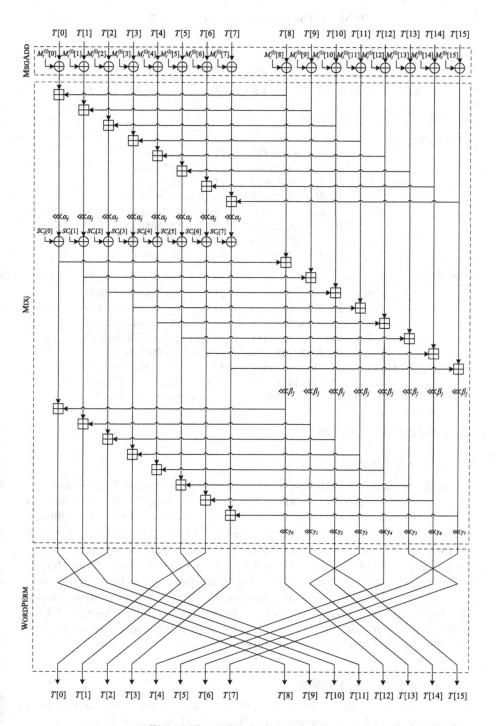

Fig. 2. The j-th step function STEP_j

Table 3. The permutation $\tau, \sigma : \mathbb{Z}_{16} \to \mathbb{Z}_{16}$

l	0	1	2	3	4	5	6	7	8	9	10	11	12	13	14	15
$\tau(l)$	3	2	0	1	7	4	5	6	11	10	8	9	15	12	13	14
$\sigma(l)$	6	4	5	7	12	15	14	13	2	0	1	3	8	11	10	9

– LSH-256-256

$$
\begin{aligned}
IV[0] &= \texttt{46a10f1f}, & IV[1] &= \texttt{fddce486}, \\
IV[2] &= \texttt{b41443a8}, & IV[3] &= \texttt{198e6b9d}, \\
IV[4] &= \texttt{3304388d}, & IV[5] &= \texttt{b0f5a3c7}, \\
IV[6] &= \texttt{b36061c4}, & IV[7] &= \texttt{7adbd553}, \\
IV[8] &= \texttt{105d5378}, & IV[9] &= \texttt{2f74de54}, \\
IV[10] &= \texttt{5c2f2d95}, & IV[11] &= \texttt{f2553fbe}, \\
IV[12] &= \texttt{8051357a}, & IV[13] &= \texttt{138668c8}, \\
IV[14] &= \texttt{47aa4484}, & IV[15] &= \texttt{e01afb41}.
\end{aligned}
\tag{16}
$$

– LSH-512-512

$$
\begin{aligned}
IV[0] &= \texttt{add50f3c7f07094e}, & IV[1] &= \texttt{e3f3cee8f9418a4f}, \\
IV[2] &= \texttt{b527ecde5b3d0ae9}, & IV[3] &= \texttt{2ef6dec68076f501}, \\
IV[4] &= \texttt{8cb994cae5aca216}, & IV[5] &= \texttt{fbb9eae4bba48cc7}, \\
IV[6] &= \texttt{650a526174725fea}, & IV[7] &= \texttt{1f9a61a73f8d8085}, \\
IV[8] &= \texttt{b6607378173b539b}, & IV[9] &= \texttt{1bc99853b0c0b9ed}, \\
IV[10] &= \texttt{df727fc19b182d47}, & IV[11] &= \texttt{dbef360cf893a457}, \\
IV[12] &= \texttt{4981f5e570147e80}, & IV[13] &= \texttt{d00c4490ca7d3e30}, \\
IV[14] &= \texttt{5d73940c0e4ae1ec}, & IV[15] &= \texttt{894085e2edb2d819}.
\end{aligned}
\tag{17}
$$

3 Design Rationale

3.1 Hash Structure

The hash structure of LSH-8w-n is wide-pipe Merkle-Damgård mode, and the compression function is designed on the 17th PGV model [18] which has no feed-forward computation of input. Input feed-forward structure is not efficient in terms of memory use since input value should be reserved till the end of all round or step function computations in a compression function. So we use the memory resource to expand the length of a message block. Even though LSH-8w-n uses the 17th PGV model, it is easily proven that the structure has 2^n preimage and second-preimage resistance, and $2^{n/2}$ collision resistance under the ideal cipher model proof thanks to wide-pipe mode [18,24]. See Sect. 4.1 for details. LSH-8w-n uses one-zeros padding for implementation efficiency because any padding can be applied to wide-pipe mode [22].

3.2 Compression Function

Bit length of a message block of LSH-8w-n is $32w$, whereas $16w$ is that of a chaining variable. The compression function of LSH-8w-n is designed for parallel implementation paying attention to efficient memory resource usage as well as fast software performance, even in short length message case. That is, all functions of a compression function are chosen to implement with 128/256-bit register SIMD (Single Instruction Multiple Data) instructions readily.

Message Expansion. The message expansion function MSGEXP generates the j-th sub-message $\mathsf{M}_j^{(i)}$ with two sub-messages $\mathsf{M}_{j-1}^{(i)}$ and $\mathsf{M}_{j-2}^{(i)}$. This structure is good for efficient memory usage implementation. MSGEXP has every 4-word array updating structure. The permutation τ of MSGEXP is chosen to have efficient implementation using SIMD instructions.

Mix Function. As shown in Fig. 2, the j-th mix function MIX_j of the j-th step function STEP_j is designed by 8-word parallel operations except the γ_l-bit rotations $(0 \leq l < 8)$ operation. In order to strengthen security of LSH-$8w$-n, we needed all different gammas. By the way, all different bit-rotations operation is inefficient in the implementation using SIMD instructions, only except the case that γ_ls are multiples of 8. In that case, the implementation using SIMD instructions get efficient because they support byte shuffle instructions, such as `pshufb` (in SSSE3), `vpshufb` (in AVX2) and `vext.8` (in NEON). Therefore, the γ_ls were searched under the following two conditions:

1. They should be multiples of 8.
2. They should minimize the iterative difference pattern probability derived from the structural issue without reference to α_j and β_j.

After decision of γ_ls satisfying the above, the α_j and β_j are chosen from the group of candidates which minimizes difference probability. See Sect. 4.2 for details. The exclusive-or with a constant is added to have resistance against rotational attack [28,34].

Word-Permutation Function. The word-permutation function WORDPERM is chosen to satisfy the following feature:

1. Easy to implement using SSE/AVX2/NEON-instructions:
   - First, the permutation σ used in WORDPERM permutes every 4-word arrays, and then re-arranges the position of the four 4-word arrays. See Fig. 2. Since word-shuffle instructions are supported in SSE, AVX2 and NEON, WORDPERM can be efficiently implemented with low latency. See Sect. 5.1 for details.
2. The fastest propagation of a word change:
   - Any word value $T[l]$ of the input $\mathsf{T} = (T[0], \dots, T[15])$ of a step function affects all words of T after five step function processes. $T[l]$ acts on all words after four step function operations for $l \in \{0, 1, 4, 5, 8, 9, 12, 13\}$, while the other ls need five step functions.

One More Message Addition. We need the final message addition process in a compression function because there is no input feed-forward computation. If this process does not exist, the last step function is meaningless.

Number of Step Functions. The number of step functions is determined such that the compression function guarantees at least 50 % security margin. More precisely, our security analysis shows that 13 steps of LSH-256-256 and 14 steps of LSH-512-512 are sufficient to defeat all the existing attack methods. As a result, we determined the number of steps as 26 for LSH-256-256 and 28 for LSH-512-512, respectively, by doubling the estimated safe boundaries.

4   Security Analysis

We study the security of LSH. Firstly, we introduce secure bounds of number of queries for LSH structure by referring previous research results in ideal setting. Then, we explain how we analyzed security of LSH against hash function attacks. Finally, we also how to translate the distinguishers used for block cipher attacks.

4.1   Security in the Ideal Cipher Model

The compression function of LSH is a kind of permutation family because it is a permutation on a chaining variable for a fixed message block. So, we can model it as an ideal cipher, i.e., it is uniformly chosen from the set of all block ciphers. For $n = 8w$, we denote LSH-$8w$-n by $\mathcal{H} : \{0,1\}^* \to \{0,1\}^n$ and consider the compression function CF as the 17th PGV scheme which is $\mathrm{CF}(\mathsf{CV}^{(i)}, \mathsf{M}^{(i)}) = E(\mathsf{CV}^{(i)}, \mathsf{M}^{(i)})$, where E is a permutation family. We define Bloc to be the set of all block ciphers with block bit length $2n(= 16w)$ and key bit length $4n(= 32w)$. In the ideal cipher model, we assume that an adversary $\mathcal{A}$ is a probabilistic algorithm which has oracle access to a random cipher $E \xleftarrow{\$} \mathsf{Bloc}$. The advantages of $\mathcal{A}$ finding a collision, a preimage, and a second-preimage are defined as (18)–(20), respectively.

$$\mathcal{A}_{\mathcal{H}}^{\mathrm{coll}}(\mathcal{A}) = \Pr[E \xleftarrow{\$} \mathsf{Bloc}, (M, M') \leftarrow \mathcal{A}^E : M \neq M' \wedge \mathcal{H}(M) = \mathcal{H}(M')], \qquad (18)$$

$$\mathcal{A}_{\mathcal{H}}^{\mathrm{epre}}(\mathcal{A}) = \max_{h \in \{0,1\}^n} \Pr[E \xleftarrow{\$} \mathsf{Bloc}, M \leftarrow \mathcal{A}^E(h) : \mathcal{H}(M) = h], \qquad (19)$$

$$\mathcal{A}_{\mathcal{H}}^{\mathrm{esec}[\lambda]}(\mathcal{A}) = \max_{M \in \{0,1\}^\lambda} \Pr[E \xleftarrow{\$} \mathsf{Bloc}, M' \leftarrow \mathcal{A}^E(M) : M \neq M' \wedge \mathcal{H}(M) = \mathcal{H}(M')], \qquad (20)$$

where λ is the bit length of the target message.

In order to analyze preimage security, we consider the notion of everywhere preimage resistance, which guarantees security on every range point; for the second-preimage security analysis, we consider the notion of everywhere second-preimage resistance, which guarantees security on every domain point [49]. For the above advantages, we define the maximum advantages of any adversary making q queries by $\mathrm{Adv}_{\mathcal{H}}^{\mathrm{coll}}(q)$, $\mathrm{Adv}_{\mathcal{H}}^{\mathrm{epre}}(q)$, and $\mathrm{Adv}_{\mathcal{H}}^{\mathrm{esec}[\lambda]}(q)$, respectively.

chopMD is the Merkle-Damgård hash function with a chop function which returns a hash value by truncating a part of the output of the last compression function [22]. It is easily proved that LSH-$8w$ is as secure as chopMD with the 17th PGV compression function in the ideal cipher model and has full security bounds for collision resistance, preimage resistance, and second-preimage resistance, from the previous results of [18, 24]. Lemma 1 summarizes the security analysis of LSH-$8w$ in the ideal cipher model.

Lemma 1. *Let* $L = \lceil \lambda/4n \rceil$. *Then we have the followings: (i)* $\mathrm{Adv}_{\mathcal{H}}^{\mathrm{coll}} \leq \frac{q(q+1)}{2^n}$, *(ii)* $\mathrm{Adv}_{\mathcal{H}}^{\mathrm{epre}} \leq \frac{q(q+1)}{2^{2n}} + \frac{q}{2^n}$, *(iii)* $\mathrm{Adv}_{\mathcal{H}}^{\mathrm{esec}[\lambda]} \leq \frac{q(q+L)}{2^{2n}} + \frac{q}{2^n}$.

Lemma 1 implies that LSH-$8w$ is collision-resistant for $q < 2^{n/2}$ and preimage-resistant and second-preimage-resistant for $q < 2^n$ in the ideal cipher model. Roughly, it means that LSH-$8w$ has no weakness as long as its internal permutation family is not attacked. By [43], we can also show that LSH-$8w$ is indifferentiable from a random oracle.

4.2 Collision Security

A colliding message pair makes a differential path. Our concern is focused on how difficult any adversary finds good differential paths. We use differential cryptanalysis [16] used for block ciphers assuming all the modular additions are independent.

Framework of Collision Security Analysis. We translate the collision search as finding a message pair making zero output difference for any fixed input difference of the compression function, and extend it to the problem of finding a message pair making an intended and fixed output difference for any fixed input difference of the compression function. So, our concern is moved to high-probability differential characteristics for the compression function. For this, we linearize the compression function by replacing the additions with XORs, search low-weight paths for the linearized structure, and evaluate the probabilities by assuming all additions are independent. Of course, this approach can cause invalid differential characteristics which do not hold, but we prefer finding high-probability characteristics to valid ones.

We consider the threshold of the probability as 2^{-48w}. Note that $48w$ is the bit length of the chaining variable plus the bit length of the message block. The reason why we adopt this threshold is the message-modification paradigm, in which the attacker uses freedom degree of input (chaining variable and message block) for achieving his goal. It is usually applied to collision-finding attack on dedicated hash functions [54, 55]. The basic idea of message modification technique is to control the values of the message blocks instead of choosing a pair of message blocks uniformly at random. A one-bit condition in the differential characteristic can be satisfied probabilistically, or by a message modification which requires at least one bit of a message or a chaining variable to be fixed. Based on this reasoning, we can make an argument that message modification techniques will be hardly successful if the number of conditions in a differential characteristic significantly exceeds the number of input bits. For LSH-$8w$, the number of input bits is $48w(= 16w(\text{chaining variable}) + 32w(\text{message block}))$.

Table 4. Linearized differential characteristics with lowest weights. The probabilities are calculated with Lipmaa-Moriai formula assuming the independency of modular additions.

Number of steps	LSH-256	LSH-512
12	2^{-1340}	2^{-1655}
13	2^{-1858}	2^{-2562}
14	2^{-2396}	2^{-3538}

Differential Characteristic. Considering the message modification technique, the remaining work is to examine the differential characteristics. It is very difficult to find the best differential characteristic for ARX structure or to estimate a tight upper bound of the probabilities of differential characteristics. Alternatively, we simplify the problem by linearizing the compression function of LSH-8w such that every modular addition is replaced with exclusive-or.

We tried various strategies and techniques from coding theory for characteristic search. After linearization, the compression function can be considered as a linear code. We can regard a characteristic yielding a collision as a shortening codeword, and a high-probability characteristic is mostly a low-weight codeword. There are a few probabilistic low-weight codeword searching algorithms [21,48], but it is still difficult to find a good linearized differential path since finding a minimum-weight codeword is known as one of NP-complete problems.

The probabilities of the characteristics are computed with Lipmaa-Moriai formula [42] by assuming that all additions in step functions and message expansion are independent. The hypothesis of the independence between additions can lead to impossible characteristics or misleading probability estimation. Leurent indicated a similar problem for the differential analysis of MD5 and SHA-1/2 and presented the multi-bit constraint technique for improving the differential characteristic search in ARX structures [40]. At the very least, however, a high-weight codeword is seldom a high-probability characteristic, and we are devoted to finding a codeword with as low weight as possible.

The best ones which we found are 12-step characteristic with the probability 2^{-1340} for LSH-256 and 13-step characteristic with the probability 2^{-2562} for LSH-512. Table 4 shows each differential probability of LSH-256 and LSH-512. They are found by starting at low-weight intermediate values of an internal state and sub-messages and computing them in forward and backward directions with the linearized form.

Iterative Characteristic. Our characteristic search methods do not find any iterative patterns. So, we take a different approach for iterative differential characteristics.

Lemma 2. *In the linearized setting, we have the followings:* (i) *The order of* MsgExp *of LSH-8w divides 12.* (ii) *For any positive integer k, $(3k+1)$ or $(3k+2)$-step iterative differential characteristics require zero message difference.*

Lemma 2 implies that 3, 6, 9, or 12 can be considered as the iteration number. Start at the $2j$-th step function. For 3-step iterative differential characteristic, we obtain the following input difference $(\Delta T, \Delta M_{2j} \| \Delta M_{2j+1})$ by making a system of corresponding linear equations and solving it with some conditions:

$$
\begin{aligned}
\Delta T &= (0, 0, 0, 0, 0, 0, 0, 0, 0, 0, 0, 0, 0, 0, 0, 0), \\
\Delta M_{2j} &= (0, 0, 0, 0, A, A, A, A, 0, 0, 0, 0, A, A, A, A), \\
\Delta M_{2j+1} &= (A, A, A, A, A, A, A, A, A, A, A, A, A, A, A, A),
\end{aligned}
$$

where $A \in \mathcal{W}$ such that $A = A^{\lll \alpha_{2j} + \beta_{2j+1}} = A^{\lll \alpha_{2j+1} + \beta_{2j}}$. For convenience, let $(\alpha_{2j}, \beta_{2j}, \alpha_{2j+1}, \beta_{2j+1})$ denote by $(\alpha_0, \beta_0, \alpha_1, \beta_1)$. Since this 3-step iterative differential characteristic starts from zero ΔT and ends with a bilateral-symmetric output difference, it can be straightforwardly used as a collision path on step-reduced LSH-8w. However, its probability for LSH-8w is too low to be available for long steps. The condition for A shows how the rotation amounts $(\alpha_0, \beta_0, \alpha_1, \beta_1)$ affect the iterative differential characteristic. For $g = \gcd(w, \alpha_0 + \beta_1, \alpha_1 + \beta_0)$, A must be composed of w/g repetition of least significant g bits. For example, if $(\alpha_0, \beta_0, \alpha_1, \beta_1) = (5, 23, 25, 19)$, then $\alpha_0 + \beta_1 = 24$ and $\alpha_1 + \beta_0 = 48$, and we could take $A = 80\ldots80$. For the current version of $(\alpha_0, \beta_0, \alpha_1, \beta_1)$, A should equal either aa...aa or 55...55 which produce high-weight codewords. Obviously, the former makes characteristics with much higher probabilities than the latter as well as ones in Table 4.

Differential Characteristic with Zero Message Difference. As mentioned in Sect. 4.2, our main concern for the analysis of collision security is a differential characteristic with non-zero message difference. However, in the sense of algorithm design, it is desirable that differential characteristics with zero message difference should also have low probabilities.

Our characteristic search methods did not find any good zero-message-difference characteristic with significantly high probability. However, we found such one by solving a system of equations for an iterative differential characteristic.

Let $X = (X[0], \ldots, X[15])$ be the difference of the input chaining variable. For 1-step iterative differential characteristic with zero message difference, we obtain the following conditions for X.

$$
\begin{aligned}
&X[l] = X[l]^{\lll \alpha_j}, \quad X[l] = X[l]^{\lll \beta_j} \text{ for all } l \in \{0, 1, ..., 15\}, j \in \{0, 1\}, \\
&X[0] = X[1] = X[2] = X[3] = X[12] = X[13] = X[14] = X[15], \\
&X[8] = X[9] = X[10], \quad X[5] = X[7].
\end{aligned}
$$

Since α_0, α_1, β_0, and β_1 are odd numbers, each $X[l]$ equals either 00...00 or ff...ff. The lowest differential characteristics are constructed by setting one of $X[4]$, $X[6]$, and $X[11]$ to ff...ff and each of the other 15 words to 00...00.

We also considered a pseudo-iterative differential characteristic with zero message difference, and its input difference is as follows.

$$
X[l] = \begin{cases} A^{\lll \gamma_1}, & \text{if } l \in \{3, 7, 11, 15\}, \\ A, & \text{otherwise.} \end{cases}
$$

Table 5. The best probabilities of differential characteristics ϕ and ψ. The probabilities are calculated with Lipmaa-Moriai formula assuming the independency of modular additions.

Number of steps	LSH-256		LSH-512	
	ϕ	ψ	ϕ	ψ
1	2^{-93}	2^{-80}	2^{-189}	2^{-176}
2	2^{-186}	2^{-176}	2^{-378}	2^{-368}
3	2^{-279}	2^{-272}	2^{-567}	2^{-560}
4	2^{-372}	2^{-368}	2^{-756}	2^{-752}
5	2^{-465}	2^{-464}	2^{-945}	2^{-944}
6	2^{-558}	2^{-560}	2^{-1134}	2^{-1136}
7	2^{-651}	2^{-656}	2^{-1323}	2^{-1328}
8	2^{-744}	2^{-744}	2^{-1512}	2^{-1512}
9	2^{-837}	2^{-824}	2^{-1701}	2^{-1688}
10	2^{-930}	2^{-920}	2^{-1890}	2^{-1880}

where $A \in W$ such that $A = A^{\lll \gamma_0} = A^{\lll \gamma_2} = A^{\lll \gamma_1 + \gamma_3}$ and $A^{\lll \gamma_j} = A^{\lll \gamma_{j+4}}$ for $j \in \{0, 1, 2, 3\}$. After k steps, the corresponding output difference Y is computed as $Y[l] = X[l]^{\lll \Sigma_j \beta_j + \gamma_1}$ for $l \in \{3, 7, 11, 15\}$ and $Y[l] = X[l]^{\lll \Sigma_j \beta_j}$ for $l \notin \{3, 7, 11, 15\}$. The condition of A shows how the rotation amounts $(\gamma_0, \gamma_1, \ldots, \gamma_7)$ affect the pseudo-iterative differential characteristic. We define g by $g = \gcd(w, \gamma_0, \gamma_2, \gamma_1 + \gamma_3, \gamma_0 - \gamma_4, \gamma_1 - \gamma_5, \gamma_2 - \gamma_6, \gamma_3 - \gamma_7)$, where w is the bit length of a word. A must be composed of w/g repetition of least significant g bits. For current version of $(\gamma_0, \gamma_1, \ldots, \gamma_7)$, we have $g = 8$.

We denote the 1-step iterative differential characteristic by ϕ and the pseudo-iterative differential characteristic by ψ. Table 5 lists the best probabilities of ϕ and ψ. It shows that for same steps ϕ and ψ have much higher probabilities than the differential characteristics with non-zero message difference in Table 4. However, we note that no technique is known for using them to make a hash function attack for LSH-8w.

Nonlinear Differential Characteristic. We also tried to find nonlinear differential characteristics with higher probabilities than linear ones. We can obtain them by optimizing the linearized differential characteristics. We used various techniques for characteristic optimization. For example, we have used a SAT solver. Recently, Mouha and Preneel presented a proof about the security of Salsa20 against differential cryptanalysis [47]. Since the large internal state of the compression function of LSH-8w greatly complicates SAT-solver-based analysis, we had to need some additional assumptions.

Again, the goal of the analysis is to measure the minimum number of step functions making the compression function of LSH-8w secure against a collision attack. However, in spite of hard works for characteristic optimization, the improvement of the probability is not significant such that there is no effect on the result of the secure steps in Table 4. In [40], Leurent presented the multi-bit constraint technique which is useful for searching more plausible characteristics than linearized ones. In [41], he used it to find differential characteristics for Skein [25]. For LSH-8w, search with the multi-bit constraints finds only the differential characteristics with significantly lower probabilities than ones in Tables 4 and 5.

4.3   (Second-)Preimage Attacks

In the (second-)preimage attack, the adversary has to find a proper message block mapping the fixed input chaining variable to the fixed hash value. Firstly, we check possibility of the meet-in-the-middle attack. It is trivially applied up to two steps. It can be partially applied to eight $\mathrm{MIX}_{j,l}$ functions of three steps (two in the first step; two in the second step; four in the third step), and requires roughly computational complexity of 2^{12w}. The meet-in-the-middle preimage attack requires large complexity close to 2^{16w} for more than three steps, while the complexity of a typical brute force attack is 2^n for LSH-8w-n. Aoki-Sasaki's meet-in-the-middle attack framework [10,50] consists of constructing a pseudo-preimage-finding algorithm and converting it to a preimage-finding algorithm [46, Fact 9.99]. We can not use the framework because we can find trivially a pseudo-preimage of LSH but it is not helpful for finding a preimage at all.

Biclique technique is often used for preimage attack [19,36,37]. We can make a biclique of dimension w for 6 steps. However, we have two problems to apply biclique technique to preimage attack on LSH. One is that existing biclique construction methods do not cause a particular output of the compression function of LSH. We need an advanced technique related to the finalization function FIN_n for a proper biclique construction. The other one is that a biclique-based preimage attack requires large complexity near 2^{16w}.

Kelsey-Schneier's generic attack [33] for finding second-preimages is not applicable to wide-pipe structure of LSH because its complexity is not less than that of brute-force attack. We do not exclude possibility of message-modification technique in second-preimage attacks, within 12 steps of LSH-256 and 13 steps of LSH-512.

4.4   Distinguishers and Other Attacks

We investigated distinguishers for the compression function of LSH, as well as differential characteristics.

- We can construct 16-step and 17-step boomerang distinguishers [53] for LSH-256 and LSH-512, respectively, by combining short differential characteristics. Some advanced combination techniques [17,23] may improve slightly boomerang distinguishers which we found.

- A linear approximation [44] exists up to 7 steps for LSH-256 and 8 steps for LSH-512. We consider the possibility to combine a short differential characteristic and a short linear approximation to construct a differential-linear approximation [15] up to 13 steps for LSH-256 and 15 steps for LSH-512. Multidimensional techniques [30] may slightly improve cryptanalyses based on linear approximations.
- A truncated differential characteristic [38] with the probability 1 exists up to 4 steps in forward direction and 5 steps in backward direction. We can combine them to construct 9-step impossible differential characteristics [14]. We also observe a similar property for linear approximations, and combine 9-step zero-correlation linear approximations [20].
- An integral characteristic [39] exists up to 7.5 steps in forward direction and 8 steps in backward direction. We can combine them to construct a 11-step known-key distinguisher.
- We simulated empirical tests to LSH, which Skein designers did to the block cipher component Threefish of Skein [25]. Specifically, we fix a 1-bit difference and insert it to the same position of the input chaining variable and the first sub-message used in the first step. We observe the biases of the output difference bits by testing 20 to 50 million pairs satisfying this form. The output difference bits with bias > 0.0001 are found up to 6 steps of LSH-256 and LSH-512, while such things are found up to 17 rounds of Threefish.

We can study block cipher attacks for the LSH compression function by regarding the input chaining variable, the output chaining variable, and the message block as the plaintext, the ciphertext, and the key. However, it is not so valuable to discuss high complexity attacks because LSH-8w-n aims to $2^{n/2}$ collision security and 2^n (second-)preimage security. Therefore, we consider only distinguishing and key-recovery attacks which require less than 2^{256} complexity for LSH-256 or 2^{512} complexity for LSH-512, as valid.

In conclusion, any valid distinguishing or key-recovery attacks have not been found for more than 13 steps of LSH-256 and 14 steps of LSH-512. A biclique attack [19] is the only key recovery attack which works for full steps of the compression function of LSH-8w, but it requires a large amount of data and its computational complexity is close to 2^{16w}. We do not think that it causes any weakness. Rotational [34] and rebound [45] cryptanalysis which have been popularly researched during SHA-3 competition are not applicable to LSH. A rotational attack [34] is essentially improper to LSH because of the step constants. So, rotational rebound attack is not applicable, either [35]. A typical rebound attack [45] does not work well because LSH is based on ARX operations instead of S-boxes.

5   Software Implementation

The n-bit hash function based on w-bit word, LSH-8w-n is designed for parallel implementation. SSE and AVX2 are SIMD instruction sets using 128/256-bit register, which are supported on Intel processors [31]. SSE instructions up to SSE4.1are available on Intel CPUs since 2008, and AVX2 can be used on CPUs based on Haswell architecture which are released in June, 2013. XOP is an extension of the SSE instructions in the x86 and AMD64 instruction set for the Bulldozer processor core released on 2011 [7]. NEON is a SIMD instruction set using 128-bit register for the ARM Cortex-A series CPUs [4]. In this section, we present the implementations of LSH-$8w$-n using these SIMD instructions.

5.1 Parallelism

Let r-bit register $\mathcal{X}$ define an s-word array $(X[0], \ldots, X[s-1])$, where $X[l] \in \mathcal{W}$ for $0 \le l \le s-1$, $s = r/w$ and r is either 128 or 256, i.e., $\mathcal{X} := (X[0], \ldots, X[s-1])$.

Operations on registers. Let $\mathcal{X} = (X[0], \ldots, X[s-1])$ and $\mathcal{Y} = (Y[0], \ldots, Y[s-1])$ be r-bit registers, and let ρ be a permutation over $\mathbb{Z}_s$. We define the following operations on registers:

- $\mathcal{X} \oplus \mathcal{Y} := (X[0] \oplus Y[0], \ldots, X[s-1] \oplus Y[s-1])$.
- $\mathcal{X} \boxplus \mathcal{Y} := (X[0] \boxplus Y[0], \ldots, X[s-1] \boxplus Y[s-1])$.
- $\mathcal{X}^{\lll i} := (X[0]^{\lll i}, \ldots, X[s-1]^{\lll i})$.
- $\mathcal{X}^{\lll i_0, i_1, \ldots, i_{s-1}} := (X[0]^{\lll i_0}, \ldots, X[s-1]^{\lll i_{s-1}})$.
- $\rho(\mathcal{X}) := (X[\rho(0)], \ldots, X[\rho(s-1)])$.

Implementation Using SIMD Instructions. SSE, AVX2 and NEON have instructions for word-wise exclusive-or "$\oplus$" and word-wise modular addition "$\boxplus$" of two registers. The word-wise all same bit-rotation " $\lll i$ " is supported only in XOP. The operation should be implemented using two "bit-shifts" and one "or" instructions in SSE, AVX2 and NEON.

NEON has the instruction for the different bit-rotation " $\lll i_0, i_1, \ldots, i_{s-1}$ ", but the others don't. Intel announced that they had a plan to release AVX-512 in 2015 which supports these bit-rotation operations [31]. If the rotational amounts are divided by 8, the operation can be implemented by byte shuffle instructions **pshufb** and **vpshufb** (latency 1 on Haswell) in SSE and AVX2, respectively [2,6], and byte extraction instruction **vext.8** in NEON. Since the rotational amounts $\gamma_0, \ldots, \gamma_7$ used in the mix function MIX_j are multiples of 8, we use these instructions. Note that the instruction **pshufb** is supported in SSSE3 or above which are extensions of SSE3.

For the word-permutation ρ, SSE and AVX2 have more instructions (for example, **pshufd**, **vpshufd**, **vperm2i128**, **vpermq**) than NEON. However, the word-permutations, τ and σ used in LSH-$8w$-n are efficiently implemented by a few number of instructions like **vext.32** and **vrev64.32** and so on.

Mix function. LSH-$8w$-n has a 16-word array chaining variable and a 32-word array message block. Each can be converted into a 2t-register array and a 4t-register array where $t = 8w/r$, respectively. Let $\mathsf{T} = (T[0], \ldots, T[15]) \in \mathcal{W}^{16}$ be the temporary variable used in the function MIX_j of the j-th step function and let $\mathsf{SC}_j = (SC_j[0], \ldots, SC_j[7]) \in \mathcal{W}^8$ be the constant of that. Let $\widehat{\mathcal{T}} = (\mathcal{T}[0], \ldots, \mathcal{T}[2t-1])$ and $\widehat{\mathcal{SC}_j} = (\mathcal{SC}_j[0], \ldots, \mathcal{SC}_j[t-1])$ be register arrays for T and SC_j defined by (21).

$$\mathcal{T}[l] \leftarrow (T[2tl], T[2tl+1], \ldots, T[2t(l+1)-1]), \text{ for } 0 \le l < 2t,$$
$$\mathcal{SC}_j[l] \leftarrow (SC_j[tl], SC_j[tl+1], \ldots, SC_j[t(l+1)-1]), \text{ for } 0 \le l < t. \quad (21)$$

Then, (22) shows the process of the mix function MIX_j, and Fig. 3 is r-bit register representation of MIX_j depending on t. For $0 \le l < t$,

$$\mathcal{T}[l] \leftarrow ((\mathcal{T}[l] \boxplus \mathcal{T}[l+t])^{\lll \alpha_j}) \oplus \mathcal{SC}_j[l],$$
$$\mathcal{T}[l+t] \leftarrow (\mathcal{T}[l] \boxplus \mathcal{T}[l+t])^{\lll \beta_j},$$
$$\mathcal{T}[l] \leftarrow \mathcal{T}[l] \boxplus \mathcal{T}[l+t],$$
$$\mathcal{T}[l+t] \leftarrow \mathcal{T}[l+t]^{\lll \gamma_{tl}, \ldots, \gamma_{t(l+1)-1}}. \quad (22)$$

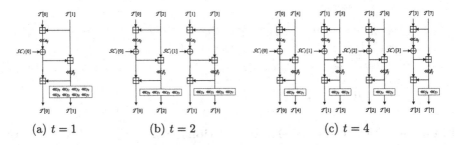

(a) $t = 1$ (b) $t = 2$ (c) $t = 4$

Fig. 3. r-bit register representation of MIX_j

As we mentioned, all operations of MIX_j can be efficiently implemented using NEON, SSE and AVX2 instructions.

5.2 Performance Results on Several Platforms

Intel/AMD Processors. Table 6 shows the speed performance of 1MB message hashing of LSH-8w-n at the platforms based on Intel/AMD CPU. LSH-8w-n on the platform $\Theta 1$ is implemented using AVX2 intrinsics. On the platform $\Theta 2$ and $\Theta 3$, LSH-8w-n is implemented using SSE4.1instrinsic, and LSH-8w-n on the platform $\Theta 4$ is implemented using XOP intrinsic.

Recall that we compare the speed of LSH-8w-n with SHA-2 and SHA-3 competition finalists because they are matured in terms of security. On the platforms $\Theta 1$–$\Theta 4$, LSH-8w-n is the fastest one. The second fastest hash function on the platform $\Theta 1$ is Skein-512 with 5.58 cycles/byte [3]. On the platform $\Theta 2$, Blake-512 is the second fastest with 5.65 cycles/byte [3]. On the platform $\Theta 3$, Blake-256 is the second fastest with 8.48 cycles/byte [3].

Since there is no speed result of other hash functions on the platform $\Theta 4$ in eBash [3], we compare the speed results of LSH-8w-n with that on the platform AMD FX-8150 @ 3.6 GHz. Blake-512 with 6.09 cycles/byte is the second fastest. See Table 7 in detail.

Table 6. 1MB message hashing speed on Intel/AMD/ARM processor (cycles/byte)

Platform	$\Theta 1$	$\Theta 2$	$\Theta 3$	$\Theta 4$	$\Lambda 1$	$\Lambda 2$	$\Lambda 3$	$\Lambda 4$
LSH-256-n	3.60	3.86	5.26	3.89	11.17	15.03	15.28	14.84
LSH-512-n	2.39	5.04	7.76	5.52	8.94	18.76	19.00	18.10

*$\Theta 1$: Intel Core i7-4770K @ 3.5GHz (Haswell), Ubuntu 12.04 64-bit, GCC 4.8.1 with "-m64 -mavx2 -O3"

*$\Theta 2$: Intel Core i7-2600K @ 3.40GHz (Sandy Bridge), Ubuntu 12.04 64-bit, GCC 4.8.1 with "-m64 -msse4 -O3"

*$\Theta 3$: Intel Core 2 Quad Q9550 @ 2.83GHz (Yorkfield), Windows 7 32-bit, Visual studio 2012

*$\Theta 4$: AMD FX-8350 @ 4GHz (Piledriver), Ubuntu 12.04 64-bit, GCC 4.8.1 with "-m64 -mxop -O3"

*$\Lambda 1$: Samsung Exynos 5250 ARM Cortex-A15 @ 1.7GHz dual core (Huins ACHRO 5250), Android 4.1.1

*$\Lambda 2$: Qualcomm Snapdragon 800 Krait 400 @ 2.26GHz quad core (LG G2), Android 4.4.2

*$\Lambda 3$: Qualcomm Snapdragon 800 Krait 400 @ 2.3GHz quad core (Samsung Galaxy S4), Android 4.2.2

*$\Lambda 4$: Qualcomm Snapdragon 400 Krait 300 @ 1.7GHz dual core (Samsung Galaxy S4 mini), Android 4.2.2

Platforms Based on ARM. We measured the speed performance at the platforms based on Cortex-A15 CPU and similar one which are the mainstream of current smart device market. Table 6 shows the speed performance of 1MB ($=2^{20}$bit) message hashing of LSH-$8w$-n on the platforms.

LSH-$8w$-n is implemented using NEON intrinsics, and GCC 4.8.1 is used with option "-mfpu=neon -mfloat-abi=softfp -O3".

On the platform $\Lambda 1$, LSH-512-n (8.94 cycles/byte) is the fastest among them. Blake-512 (13.46 cycles/byte) is the second fastest one. See Table 8. The speed of LSH-$8w$-n is even faster than that of SHA-256 at Apple A7 based on ARMv8-A which has a SHA-2 (SHA-256 only) instruction. The speed of LSH-256-n and LSH-512-n on the platform $\Lambda 1$ corresponds to about 150MB/s and 190MB/s, respectively. In iPhone5S equipped with A7 SoC, the speed of SHA-256 is about 102.2MB/s (single core setting) [51]. Since there is no speed result from other hash functions in eBASH [3], we can not compare the speed to others in $\Lambda 2$, $\Lambda 3$, and $\Lambda 4$.

5.3   Comparison with SHA-2 and the SHA-3 Competition Finalists

Tables 7 and 8 are speed comparisons with SHA-2 and the SHA-3 finalists, reported in eBASH [3]. All values are the first quartile of many speed measurement. Table 7 is the comparison at the platform based on Haswell, LSH-$8w$-n is measured on Intel Core i7-4770k @ 3.5 GHz quad core platform, and others

Table 7. Speed benchmark of LSH, SHA-2 and the SHA-3 finalists at the platform based on Haswell CPU (cycles/byte)

Algorithm	Message byte length					
	long	4,096	1,536	576	64	8
LSH-256-256	3.60	3.71	3.90	4.08	8.19	65.37
Skein-512-256	5.01(?)	5.58	5.86	6.49	13.12	104.50
Blake-256	6.61(?)	7.63	7.87	9.05	16.58	72.50
Grøstl-256	9.48(?)	10.68	12.18	13.71	37.94(?)	227.50(?)
Keccak-256	10.56	10.52	9.90	11.99	23.38	187.50
SHA-256	10.82(?)	11.91(?)	12.26	13.51	24.88	106.62
JH-256	14.70(?)	15.50(?)	15.94	17.06(?)	31.94	257.00
LSH-512-512	2.39	2.54	2.79	3.31	10.81	85.62
Skein-512-512	4.67(?)	5.51(?)	5.80	6.44	13.59	108.25
Blake-512	4.96(?)	6.17(?)	6.82	7.38	14.81	116.50(?)
SHA-512	7.65(?)	8.24	8.69	9.03	17.22	138.25
Grøstl-512	12.78(?)	15.44	17.30	17.99(?)	51.72	417.38
JH-512	14.25(?)	15.66	16.14(?)	17.34	32.69	261.00
Keccak-512	16.36(?)	17.86	18.46(?)	20.35	21.56(?)	171.88(?)

∗ Question marks mean the measurements with large variance [3], so each value should be re-measured.

are measured on Intel Core i5-4570S @ 2.9 GHz quad core platform. Table 8 is measured on Samsung Exynos 5250 ARM Cortex-A15 @ 1.7 GHz dual core platform. In these tables, Keccak-256 and Keccak-512 mean Keccak[r=1088,c=512] and Keccak[r=576,c=1024], respectively.

6 Hardware Implementation

We have implemented LSH with Verilog HDL and synthesized to ASIC. For HDL implementation and verification of our design, we have used Mentor Modelsim 6.5f for RTL simulation and Synopsys Design Compiler Ver. B-2008.09-SP5 for its synthesis. Our RTL level design result of LSH is synthesized to ASIC with the UMC 0.13μm standard cell library and 100 MHz operating frequency.

We compared the hardware implementation results of LSH in the sense of FOM (throughput/area) with SHA-2 and the SHA-3 competition finalists where each throughput is revised for the clock frequency 100 MHz. We did not consider lightweight hash functions because their designs are quite far from FOM optimization. Table 9 shows the comparison. We referred webpages of eHash for it [1]. Except Keccak, LSH has as good as FOM efficiency among the hash functions.

For JH and Keccak, we considered only 256-bit hash since they get slower for 512-bit hash than for 256-bit hash even though these have same size of area. For SHA-512, we could not find a good ASIC implementation result for comparison.

Table 8. Speed benchmark of LSH, SHA-2 and the SHA-3 finalists at the platform based on Exynos 5250 ARM Cortex-A15 CPU (cycles/byte)

Algorithm	Message byte length					
	long	4,096	1,536	576	64	8
LSH-256-256	11.17	11.53	12.16	12.63	24.42	192.68
Skein-512-256	15.64	16.72	18.33	22.68	75.75	609.25
Blake-256	17.94	19.11	20.88	25.44	83.94	542.38
SHA-256	19.91	21.14	23.03	28.13	90.89	578.50
JH-256	34.66	36.06	38.10	43.51	113.92	924.12
Keccak-256	36.03	38.01	40.54	48.13	125.00	1000.62
Grøstl-256	40.70	42.76	46.03	54.94	167.52	1020.62
LSH-512-512	8.94	9.56	10.55	12.28	38.82	307.98
Blake-512	13.46	14.82	16.88	20.98	77.53	623.62
Skein-512-512	15.61	16.73	18.35	22.56	75.59	612.88
JH-512	34.88	36.26	38.36	44.01	116.41	939.38
SHA-512	44.13	46.41	49.97	54.55	135.59	1088.38
Keccak-512	63.31	64.59	67.85	77.21	121.28	968.00
Grøstl-512	131.35	138.49	150.15	166.54	446.53	3518.00

Table 9. Comparison of hardware implementations of LSH and other hash functions

Algorithm	Area (kGEs)	Throughput[a] (Mbps)	Tech. (nm)	Max. Freq. (MHz)	FOM (Mbps/GE)
Keccak-256 [9]	10.5	4,251	90	454.5	0.405
LSH-256-256	26.67	3,793	130	100.0	0.142
LSH-512-512	64.22	7,043	130	100.0	0.110
Skein-512-512 [32]	57.93	5,120	32	631.3	0.088
Blake-256 [11]	58.30	3,318	180	114	0.057
Skein-256-256 [52]	53.87	2,561	180	68.8	0.048
Blake-512 [29]	128.00	5,965	90	298.0	0.047
Grøstl-256 [56]	110.11	5,110	130	188	0.046
SHA-256 [26]	71.9	776	65	179.86	0.041
Grøstl-512 [27]	341.00	7,315	180	85.1	0.021
JH-256 [5]	54.6	1,110	90	763.4	0.020

[a]Throughtput@100MHz

Acknowledgements. We would like to thank research members in Pusan National University and COSIC, KU Leuven including Howon Kim, Donggeon Lee, Vincent Rijmen, and Nicky Mouha for helpful discussion on security and efficiency of hash function designs.

A   Differential Characteristics for Collision Attack

LSH-256-256. The best 12-step differential characteristic with probability 2^{-1340} (2^{-1317} in step functions, 2^{-23} in message expansion) is as follows: Note that this characteristic starts from the step function STEP_1.

– Difference of a chaining variable: ΔT

```
7055c502 2762a531 ecb0207c 59a126ed 7d9ea591 0ce1f4ce a4805bfd
91c2e233 5667e004 ae09ec85 f684c37f 058406d2 da80b205 1e76c9a1
00767204 4adc413a
```

– Difference of sub-messages: $\Delta M_1 \| \Delta M_2$

```
80000004 80000004 00000000 00000000 00000000 00000000 00000000
00000000 80000000 00000000 80000000 80000000 00000000 00000000
00000000 00000000 00000000 80000004 80000004 80000004 00000000
00000000 00000000 00000000 00000000 80000000 00000000 00000000
00000000 00000000 00000000 00000000
```

LSH-512-512. The best 13-step differential characteristic with probability 2^{-2562} (2^{-2535} in step functions, 2^{-27} in message expansion) is as follows: Note that this characteristic starts from the step function STEP_1.

– Difference of a chaining variable: ΔT

```
51102224b4620122 0c29d317cb02ef13 000090414918c242 a046aa4209442500
0c83e503b765044a 13aa3fff2cba2c36 5211940602291c46 7942d68622882342
10100306f1000120 5ca5b115acae2bcd 800091639c90e720 210083200116c000
8082c0829641060e df9637b8ad8f8662 3901976042bed0e3 f42b15854c588246
```

– Difference of sub-messages: $\Delta M_1 \| \Delta M_2$

```
8000010000000000 8000010000000000 0000000000000000 0000000000000000
0000000000000000 0000000000000000 0000000000000000 0000000000000000
8000000000000000 0000000000000000 8000000000000000 8000000000000000
0000000000000000 0000000000000000 0000000000000000 0000000000000000
0000000000000000 8000010000000000 8000010000000000 8000010000000000
0000000000000000 0000000000000000 0000000000000000 0000000000000000
0000000000000000 8000000000000000 0000000000000000 0000000000000000
0000000000000000 0000000000000000 0000000000000000 0000000000000000
```

References

1. ehash webpage - sha-3 hardware implementations. http://ehash.iaik.tugraz.at/wiki/SHA-3_Hardware_Implementations
2. Intel intrinsics guide. http://software.intel.com/sites/landingpage/IntrinsicsGuide
3. Measurements of sha-3 finalists, indexed by machine. http://bench.cr.yp.to/results-sha3.html
4. Neon. http://www.arm.com/products/processors/technologies/neon.php

5. Rcis webpage (other asic implementations). http://staff.aist.go.jp/akashi.satoh/SASEBO/en/sha3/others.html
6. x86, x64 instruction latency, memory latency and cpuid dumps. http://instlatx64.atw.hu
7. Amd64 architecture programmer's manual volume 6: 128-bit and 256-bit xop, fma4 and cvt16 instructions. Technical report, May 2009
8. Sha-3 standard: Permutation-based hash and extendable-output functions, May 2014
9. Akin, A., Aysu, A., Ulusel, O.C., Savaş, E.: Efficient hardware implementations of high throughput sha-3 candidates keccak, luffa and blue midnight wish for single- and multi-message hashing. In: Proceedings of the 3rd International Conference on Security of Information and Networks, SIN 2010, pp. 168–177. ACM, New York (2010)
10. Aoki, K., Sasaki, Y.: Meet-in-the-middle preimage attacks against reduced SHA-0 and SHA-1. In: Halevi, S. (ed.) CRYPTO 2009. LNCS, vol. 5677, pp. 70–89. Springer, Heidelberg (2009)
11. Aumasson, J.-P., Henzen, L., Meier, W., Phan, R.C.-W.: Sha-3 proposal blake. Submission to NIST (Round 3) (2010)
12. Barker, E.B., Barker, W.C., Lee, A.: Guideline for implementing cryptography in the federal government (2005)
13. Bernstein, D.J.: Second preimages for 6 (7? (8??)) rounds of keccak? NIST mailing list (2010)
14. Biham, E., Biryukov, A., Shamir, A.: Cryptanalysis of skipjack reduced to 31 rounds using impossible differentials. In: Stern, J. (ed.) EUROCRYPT 1999. LNCS, vol. 1592, pp. 12–23. Springer, Heidelberg (1999)
15. Biham, E., Dunkelman, O., Keller, N.: Enhancing differential-linear cryptanalysis. In: Zheng, Y. (ed.) ASIACRYPT 2002. LNCS, vol. 2501, pp. 254–266. Springer, Heidelberg (2002)
16. Biham, E., Shamir, A.: Differential Cryptanalysis of the Data Encryption Standard. Springer, London (1993)
17. Biryukov, A., Khovratovich, D.: Related-key cryptanalysis of the full AES-192 and AES-256. In: Matsui, M. (ed.) ASIACRYPT 2009. LNCS, vol. 5912, pp. 1–18. Springer, Heidelberg (2009)
18. Black, J.A., Rogaway, P., Shrimpton, T.: Black-box analysis of the block-cipher-based hash-function constructions from PGV. In: Yung, M. (ed.) CRYPTO 2002. LNCS, vol. 2442, pp. 320–335. Springer, Heidelberg (2002)
19. Bogdanov, A., Khovratovich, D., Rechberger, C.: Biclique cryptanalysis of the full AES. In: Lee, D.H., Wang, X. (eds.) ASIACRYPT 2011. LNCS, vol. 7073, pp. 344–371. Springer, Heidelberg (2011)
20. Bogdanov, A., Wang, M.: Zero correlation linear cryptanalysis with reduced data complexity. In: Canteaut, A. (ed.) FSE 2012. LNCS, vol. 7549, pp. 29–48. Springer, Heidelberg (2012)
21. Canteaut, A., Chabaud, F.: A new algorithm for finding minimum-weight words in a linear code: application to mceliece's cryptosystem and to narrow-sense bch codes of length 511. IEEE Trans. Inform. Theory 44(1), 367–378 (1998)
22. Chang, D., Nandi, M.: Improved indifferentiability security analysis of chopMD hash function. In: Nyberg, K. (ed.) FSE 2008. LNCS, vol. 5086, pp. 429–443. Springer, Heidelberg (2008)
23. Dunkelman, O., Keller, N., Shamir, A.: A practical-time related-key attack on the kasumi cryptosystem used in GSM and 3G telephony. J. Cryptology, 1–26 (2013)

24. Duo, L., Li, C.: Improved collision and preimage resistance bounds on pgv schemes. Cryptology ePrint Archive, Report 2006/462 (2006). http://eprint.iacr.org/

25. Ferguson, N., Lucks, S., Schneier, B., Whiting, D., Bellare, M., Kohno, T., Callas, J., Walker, J.: The skein hash function family. Submission to NIST (Round 3) (2010)

26. Muheim, B., Homsirikamol, E., Keller, C., Rogawski, M., Kaeslin, H., Kaps, J., Gürkaynak, G., Gaj, K.: Lessons learned from designing a 65nm asic for evaluating third round sha-3 candidates. In: Third SHA-3 Candidates Conference (2012). http://csrc.nist/gov/groups/ST/hash/sha-3/Round3/March2012/documents/papers/GURKAYNAK_paper.pdf

27. Gauravaram, P., Knudsen, L.R., Matusiewicz, K., Mendel, F., Rechberger, C., Schlffer, M., Thomsen, S.S.: Grøstl - a sha-3 candidate. Submission to NIST (Round 3) (2011)

28. Guo, J., Karpman, P., Nikolic, I., Wang, L., Wu, S.: Analysis of blake2. Cryptology ePrint Archive, Report 2013/467 (2013). http://eprint.iacr.org/

29. Henzen, L., Aumasson, J.-P., Meier, W., Phan, R.C.-W.: Vlsi characterization of the cryptographic hash function blake. IEEE Trans. Very Large Scale Integration (VLSI) Syst. **19**(10), 1746–1754 (2011)

30. Hermelin, M., Nyberg, K.: Multidimensional linear distinguishing attacks and boolean functions. Crypt. Commun. **4**(1), 47–64 (2012)

31. Intel. Intel architecture instruction set extensions programming reference. 319433-018, February 2014

32. Mathew, S.K., Walker, J., Sheikh, F., Krishnamurthy, R.: A skein-512 hardware implementation. In: Second SHA-3 Candidate Conference (2010). http://csrc.nist/gov/groups/ST/hash/sha-3/Round2/Aug2010/documents/papers/WALKER_skein-intel-hwd.pdf/

33. Kelsey, J., Schneier, B.: Second preimages on n-bit hash functions for much less than 2^n Work. In: Cramer, R. (ed.) EUROCRYPT 2005. LNCS, vol. 3494, pp. 474–490. Springer, Heidelberg (2005)

34. Khovratovich, D., Nikolić, I.: Rotational cryptanalysis of ARX. In: Hong, S., Iwata, T. (eds.) FSE 2010. LNCS, vol. 6147, pp. 333–346. Springer, Heidelberg (2010)

35. Khovratovich, D., Nikolić, I., Rechberger, C.: Rotational rebound attacks on reduced skein. In: Abe, M. (ed.) ASIACRYPT 2010. LNCS, vol. 6477, pp. 1–19. Springer, Heidelberg (2010)

36. Khovratovich, D., Rechberger, C., Savelieva, A.: Bicliques for preimages: attacks on Skein-512 and the SHA-2 family. In: Canteaut, A. (ed.) FSE 2012. LNCS, vol. 7549, pp. 244–263. Springer, Heidelberg (2012)

37. Knellwolf, S., Khovratovich, D.: New preimage attacks against reduced SHA-1. In: Safavi-Naini, R., Canetti, R. (eds.) CRYPTO 2012. LNCS, vol. 7417, pp. 367–383. Springer, Heidelberg (2012)

38. Knudsen, L.R.: Truncated and higher order differentials. In: Preneel, B. (ed.) FSE 1994. LNCS, vol. 1008, pp. 196–211. Springer, Heidelberg (1995)

39. Knudsen, L.R., Wagner, D.: Integral cryptanalysis. In: Daemen, J., Rijmen, V. (eds.) FSE 2002. LNCS, vol. 2365, pp. 112–127. Springer, Heidelberg (2002)

40. Leurent, G.: Analysis of differential attacks in ARX constructions. In: Wang, X., Sako, K. (eds.) ASIACRYPT 2012. LNCS, vol. 7658, pp. 226–243. Springer, Heidelberg (2012)

41. Leurent, G.: Construction of differential characteristics in ARX designs application to skein. In: Canetti, R., Garay, J.A. (eds.) CRYPTO 2013, Part I. LNCS, vol. 8042, pp. 241–258. Springer, Heidelberg (2013)

42. Lipmaa, H., Moriai, S.: Efficient algorithms for computing differential properties of addition. In: Matsui, M. (ed.) FSE 2001. LNCS, vol. 2355, pp. 336–350. Springer, Heidelberg (2002)

43. Luo, Y., Gong, Z., Duan, M., Zhu, B., Lai, X.: Revisiting the indifferentiability of pgv hash functions. Cryptology ePrint Archive, Report 2009/265 (2009). http://eprint.iacr.org/

44. Matsui, M.: Linear cryptanalysis method for DES cipher. In: Helleseth, T. (ed.) EUROCRYPT 1993. LNCS, vol. 765, pp. 386–397. Springer, Heidelberg (1994)

45. Mendel, F., Rechberger, C., Schläffer, M., Thomsen, S.S.: The rebound attack: cryptanalysis of reduced whirlpool and Grøstl. In: Dunkelman, O. (ed.) FSE 2009. LNCS, vol. 5665, pp. 260–276. Springer, Heidelberg (2009)

46. Menezes, A.J., Vanstone, S.A., Van Oorschot, P.C.: Handbook of Applied Cryptography, 1st edn. CRC Press Inc., Boca Raton (1996)

47. Mouha, N., Preneel, B.: Towards finding optimal differential characteristics for arx: application to salsa20. Cryptology ePrint Archive, Report 2013/328 (2013). http://eprint.iacr.org/

48. Nad, T.: The codingtool library (2010). Presentation

49. Rogaway, P., Shrimpton, T.: Cryptographic hash-function basics: definitions, implications, and separations for preimage resistance, second-preimage resistance, and collision resistance. In: Roy, B., Meier, W. (eds.) FSE 2004. LNCS, vol. 3017, pp. 371–388. Springer, Heidelberg (2004)

50. Sasaki, Y., Aoki, K.: Finding preimages in full MD5 faster than exhaustive search. In: Joux, A. (ed.) EUROCRYPT 2009. LNCS, vol. 5479, pp. 134–152. Springer, Heidelberg (2009)

51. Shimpi, A.L.: The iphone 5s. review, 17 September 2013. http://www.anandtech.com/show/7335/the-iphone-5s-review/4

52. Tillich, S.: Hardware implementation of the sha-3 candidate skein. Cryptology ePrint Archive, Report 2009/159 (2009). http://eprint.iacr.org/

53. Wagner, D.: The boomerang attack. In: Knudsen, L.R. (ed.) FSE 1999. LNCS, vol. 1636, pp. 156–170. Springer, Heidelberg (1999)

54. Wang, X., Yin, Y.L., Yu, H.: Finding collisions in the full SHA-1. In: Shoup, V. (ed.) CRYPTO 2005. LNCS, vol. 3621, pp. 17–36. Springer, Heidelberg (2005)

55. Wang, X., Yu, H.: How to break MD5 and other hash functions. In: Cramer, R. (ed.) EUROCRYPT 2005. LNCS, vol. 3494, pp. 19–35. Springer, Heidelberg (2005)

56. Nazhandali, L., Guo, X., Huang, S., Schaumont, P.: Fair and comprehensive performance evaluation of 14 second round sha-3 asic implementations. In: Second SHA-3 Candidate Conference (2010). http://csrc.nist/gov/groups/ST/hash/sha-3/Round2/Aug2010/documents/papers/SCHAUMONT_SHA3.pdf

Information Hiding and Efficiency

Lossless Data Hiding for Binary Document Images Using n-Pairs Pattern

Cheonshik Kim[1]([✉]), Jinsuk Baek[2], and Paul S. Fisher[2]

[1] Department of Digital Media Engineering, Anyang University,
Anyang-si, Gyeonggi-do, Korea
mipsan@paran.com
[2] Department of Computer Science, Winston-Salem State University,
Winston-Salem, NC, USA
{baekj,fisherp}@wssu.edu

Abstract. Lossless data embedding theory has entered a new era for data hiding and information security. In a lossless scheme, the original data and the embedded data should be completely recoverable. Our n-pairs pattern method is a significant advance in lossless data hiding schemes. This paper shows that the proposed n-pairs pattern method can achieve greater embedding capacity while keeping distortion at the same level as the PS-K method (Pattern Substitution by pseudo random number generator to produce a key K). The performance of the n-pairs pattern method is thus shown to be better than the performance of PS-K.

Keywords: Binary document · Data hiding · Lossless · n-Pair pattern

1 Introduction

Data hiding techniques [1–5] can be used in various applications such as annotations, communications, and copyrights [6]. For most images, the modification of the pixel values is not detectable by the human visual system as long as the modification is extremely small. However, a binary image is very sensitive and is easily affected by weak pixel flipping [6–8]. Therefore, many researchers have focused on developing reversible data hiding methods related to binary images [9–15]. While existing methods are efficient, they each have limitations.

Ho et al. [6] propose a reversible data hiding method using pattern substitution that has a reasonable performance. The method uses 4-bit vector patterns as the binary sequences for the difference images. *Tseng et al.* [8] use matrix encoding to hide data in binary images. The input binary image is divided into 3×3 blocks (or larger). The flipping priorities of pixels in a 3×3 block are then computed and those with the lowest scores are changed to embed the data. In *Chen et al.* [10], an input binary image is divided into blocks of 8×8 pixels. The numbers of black and white pixels in each block are then altered by embedding data bits 1 and 0. A data bit 1 is embedded if the percentage of white pixels is

© Springer International Publishing Switzerland 2015
J. Lee and J. Kim (Eds.): ICISC 2014, LNCS 8949, pp. 317–327, 2015.
DOI: 10.1007/978-3-319-15943-0_19

less than a given threshold. This method is robust against noise if the difference between the thresholds for the data bits 1 and 0 is sufficiently large; however, this technique also decreases the quality of the marked document.

In this paper, we propose a lossless data hiding scheme for binary document images using the n-pairs pattern method. Although the proposed scheme is very simple, it has a high embedding capacity and produces an image of reasonable quality. Our new scheme makes it possible to control the embedding capacity and quality of an image, so that the stego-image has a higher quality than those produced by traditional approaches under the same embedding scale.

The remainder of this paper is organized as follows. Section 2 describes the histogram modification method for reversible data hiding. Section 3 presents our new n-pairs pattern method in detail and our proposed data hiding scheme for binary document images. Section 4 discusses our experimental results, and Sect. 5 presents our conclusions.

2   Histogram Modification Method

Many researchers have proposed reversible data hiding schemes that use histogram pairs of gray-scale images. In the histogram we first find a *zero point*, and then a *peak point*. A *zero point* corresponds to the gray-scale value that no pixel in the given image has. A *peak point* corresponds to a gray-scale value that the largest number of pixels in the image has. The purpose of finding a *peak point* is to increase the embedding capacity as much as possible because, as we show below, the number of bits that can be embedded into an image by this algorithm is equal to the number of pixels that are associated with the *peak point*([9]).

In the following discussion we will refer to the maximum and minimum points. For an $M \times N$ image, each pixel has a gray-scale value $x \in [0, 255]$:

Step 1: Generate its histogram $H(x)$.

Step 2: In the histogram $H(x)$, find the maximum point $h(\alpha)$, $\alpha \in [0, 255]$ and the minimum point $h(\beta)$, $\beta \in [0, 255]$.

Step 3: If the minimum point $h(\beta) \geq 0$, then record the coordinates (i, j) of those pixels and the pixel gray-scale value β as overhead bookkeeping information (referred to as *overhead information* for short), and set $h(\beta)$ to 0.

Step 4: Without loss of generality, assume that $\alpha < \beta$. Move the whole part of the histogram $H(x)$ with $x \in (\alpha, \beta)$ to the right by 1 unit. The result is that all of the pixel gray-scale values in the interval (α, β) are incremented by 1.

Step 5: Scan the image until meeting the pixel whose gray-scale value is α; check the to-be-embedded bit. If the to-be-embedded bit is 1, the pixel gray-scale value is changed to $\alpha + 1$. If the bit is 0, the pixel value remains α.

In this way, the actual data embedding capacity, C, is calculated as follows:

$$C = h(\alpha) - O, \tag{1}$$

where O denotes the amount of data used to represent the overhead information. We refer to O as *pure payload* in this paper. Clearly, if the required payload is greater than the actual capacity, more pairs of maximum and minimum points need to be used. The embedding algorithm with multiple pairs of maximum and minimum points is presented in next Section.

3 Our Proposed n-Pair Pattern Scheme

3.1 n-Pair Pattern Basic

Generally, data hiding with reversibility using histogram pairs ([9–12, 14, 15]) has the advantage that the original image is recoverable, but the hiding capacity of this method is restricted. To obtain reversible data hiding with a greater hiding capacity, we propose an n-pair pattern scheme. In the proposed scheme, the relationship between neighboring pixels is explored.

We have two reasons for proposing an n-pair pattern. First, the reversible data hiding method in [9,13] is based on gray-scale images. Thus, these techniques cannot be directly applied to binary images for data hiding. Our proposed n-pair pattern scheme extends histogram pairs for binary data hiding. Second, our proposal for reversible binary data hiding does not require a location map. Because it is possible to remove location map by adjustment number of n-pair pattern. Next, we sketched out our proposed scheme. First of all, each group of n-pixel in an image transform into a decimal number. These decimal numbers represent gray-scale colors such that 0 is black, $2n - 1$ is white, and the values in between are various shades of gray. Based on these decimal numbers, an n-pairs pattern is generated.

Figure 1 shows a histogram generated from decimal numbers of three consecutive bits. Position 0 and 7 are all white and black, so they are not fit to

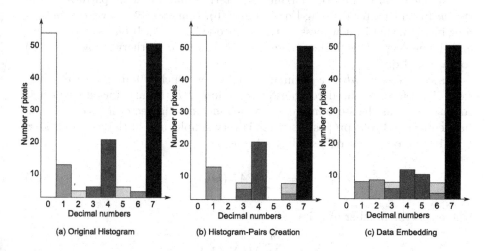

(a) Original Histogram   (b) Histogram-Pairs Creation   (c) Data Embedding

Fig. 1. Concept of data embedding using histogram modification

conceal to data hiding. Note that the number pixels at position 1 is dominating in the range of position 1 and 3. Therefore, the position 2 is emptied. Similarly, the position 5 is cleared. Of course, the position 2 merge with position 3. The position 2 should be marked using the location map.

Similarly, another location map is necessary for the merged position 6. After securing vacant positions, reversible data embedding starts by distributing the numbers in the positions 2 and 5 according to the message to be hidden. The secret message string includes the location map. The decoding procedure is very simple. In the beginning, the location map and the secret message string are recovered from position 2 and 3, 5 and 6. Figure 1(c) is changed to Fig. 1(b) after recovering positions and obtaining the hidden message. Based on the recovered location map, the contents of the merged positions can be exactly split and reconstructed as Fig. 1(a).

$$\delta = h_1, h_2, \ldots, h_n \| m_1, m_2, \ldots, m_n. \tag{2}$$

These procedures are called n-pair pattern methods. We assume that δ is a payload with the included messages $h_1 \ldots h_n$ and the location maps $m_1 \ldots m_n$ in Eq. (2). δ is composed of the bits 0 and 1, as specified in Eq. (3). The variable hh in Eq. (4) is a decimal value that is calculated from the binary bitmap image, where n is the size of payload, p is the size of bitmap pairs and dec is a function that transforms a binary value into a decimal value. We assume that a vector of decimal values is considered to be a discrete gray-scale image hh.

$$\delta_i \in \{0, 1\}, 1 \le i \le n, where \ n = size(payload), \tag{3}$$

$$hh_k^{\frac{(M \times N)}{p}} = \sum_{i=1}^{M \times N} \sum_{j=1}^{M \times N} dec(BI(j : j + p)), \tag{4}$$

To hide data, we find the maximum pattern α and minimum pattern β from the hh (n-pair pattern), using Eqs. (5) and (6). Equation (7) shows the embedding method, that is, how messages are embedded into hh_i. If hh_i is an α pattern and the message bit is 0, then there is no change in hh_i; otherwise, add $(\beta - \alpha)$ to hh_i (see Eq. (7)).

As can be seen, hh is a decimal value vector which is hiding a secret message. Therefore, we need to transform hh into BI (Binary Image), which is reconstructed as the stego image and which includes the secret message. As can be seen in Fig. 1, our proposed scheme is very simple, and in these examples we have introduced a reversible hiding scheme.

$$\alpha = \sum_{i=1}^{n} MAX(hh_i), \tag{5}$$

where n is the number of pairs.

$$\beta = \sum_{i=1}^{n} MIN(hh_i), \tag{6}$$

where n is the number of pair.

$$hh'_i = \begin{cases} hh_i & if \;\; hh_i = \alpha \; and \; \delta_i = 0 \\ hh_i + (\beta - \alpha) & if \;\; hh_i = \alpha \; and \; \delta_i = 1 \end{cases} \tag{7}$$

3.2   Embedding Procedure

The flowchart in Fig. 2 below depicts the procedure of embedding messages into binary document images.

Input. Original binary document image BI of size $M \times N$ (in pixels) and the secret data, $\delta = [h_1, h_2, , h_{size(message)} \;||\; m_1, m_2, , m_n]$, $cnt = |\delta|$.

Output. Stego image SI, the maximum point α, and the minimum point β.

Step 1: Divide BI into a group of n-bits with non-overlap. All of the subgroups are then transformed into one decimal value, x, and these are stored in vector hh. The histogram H is created from the vector hh, where $i \in \{0, 1, \cdots, 2n-1\}$ and n is the number of pixels used to transform a decimal number, i.e., $n = [5, \cdots, 8]$. In H, obtain maximum point α and minimum point β. If the number of point $\beta > 0$, record the coordinate of those pixels and the pixel value as overhead keeping information.

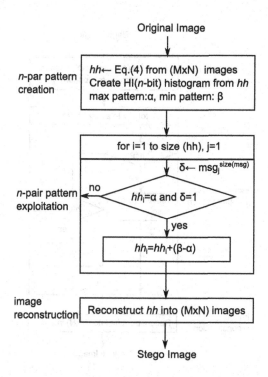

Fig. 2. Flowchart for the embedding algorithm based on an n-pair pair pattern

Step 2: Scan the hh until meeting the pixel whose virtual gray-scale value is α; check the to-be-embedded bit. If the to-be-embedded bit is '1', the virtual pixel gray-scale value is changed to $\alpha + (\beta - \alpha)$. If the bit is '0', the pixel value remains α.

Step 3: Let $cnt = cnt - 1$. if $cnt = 0$ go to Step 4; otherwise, go to Step 2 to continue the embedding processes.

Step 4: When the process of embedding secret messages has been completed, convert hh into an $M \times N$ image SI, which is the stego image.

3.3   Extracting Procedure

Figure 3 below shows the flowchart for extracting messages from binary document images. We first create virtual gray-scale images and then extract messages from these images. The extraction procedure is as follows:

Input. Stego image SI, the maximum point α, the minimum point β, and the length of the payload $cnt = |p|$.

Output. Original binary document image BI and the secret data p.

Step 1: Divide SI into a group of n-bits with non-overlap. All of the sub-groups are then transformed into decimal values, and these are stored in vector hh.

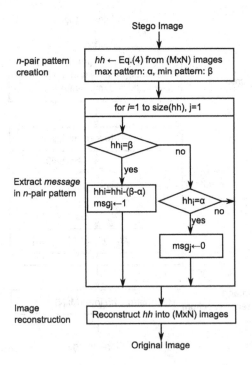

Fig. 3. Flowchart for the extraction algorithm based on the n-pair pattern scheme

Step 2: Scan the decimal values from hh_i in the same order as in the embedding phase. If the scanned value is a β pattern, then a hidden bit can be recognized by 1 in the hh. $\delta = \delta||'1'$. After that, a β pattern in hh_i can be the original pattern as $hh_i = hh_i - (\beta - \alpha)$. If the scanned value is an α pattern, then extract 0 from the virtual image. $\delta = \delta||'0'$.

Step 3: $cnt = cnt - 1$; Repeat Step 2 until $cnt = 0$.

Step 4: Reconstruct the binary image to transform hh into BI.

3.4 Computational Complexity

Our proposed scheme is in the spatial domain. The methods computational complexity is low since it does not need to perform DCT (Discrete Cosine Transform) or DWT (Discrete Wavelet Transform,). The method requires generating the n-pair pattern for a cover image, determining maximum and minimum points α and β based on the n-pair pattern, hiding information, and performing the inverse transformation in the spatial domain. Thus, the execution time needed for the proposed scheme is quite small. Assume that the block size is $P \times Q$ and that there are k blocks in a cover image. Our proposed scheme only needs to scan each block five times during the hiding phase. Hence the computational complexity for the scanning is $O(5PQ)$ and as a result, the overall computational complexity is $O(5PQk)$.

4   Experimental Results

In binary document images, a number of flipped pixels can conceal messages. We need to find an empty pair pattern in the image. In the case of the 4-pair pattern, it is difficult to find the empty pair pattern. As the number n increases, some local peaks become more dominant compared to neighboring pixels. When n is large, there appear to be a large number of empty pixels next to the local peak pixels. By choosing other peaks or increasing the size of the n-pair pattern, we can control the image quality. Additionally, it is possible to increase the embedding capacity by increasing the size of patterns for flipping.

Table 1 shows the number of bits that can be embedded into the English-1 image (Fig. 4(a)). In the 5-pair pattern method, position 1 (00000_b in binary representation) has a population of 2,539 bits, while position 10 (01010_b) has 0. Therefore, the location map has to mark 0 bits. As n increases, the capacity for data hiding in the binary document image will decrease. If there are *high peaks* with relatively high neighboring pixels, a large location map is required. If there are relatively *high peaks* with very low or empty neighboring pixels, the location map size is negligible or zero.

Table 2 compares the data-hiding capacities of PS-K [6] and our proposed scheme, using the 5-bit pair method. PS-K has a case where the location map is relatively large, while the location map for our proposed scheme is no or few (with $n = 5$).

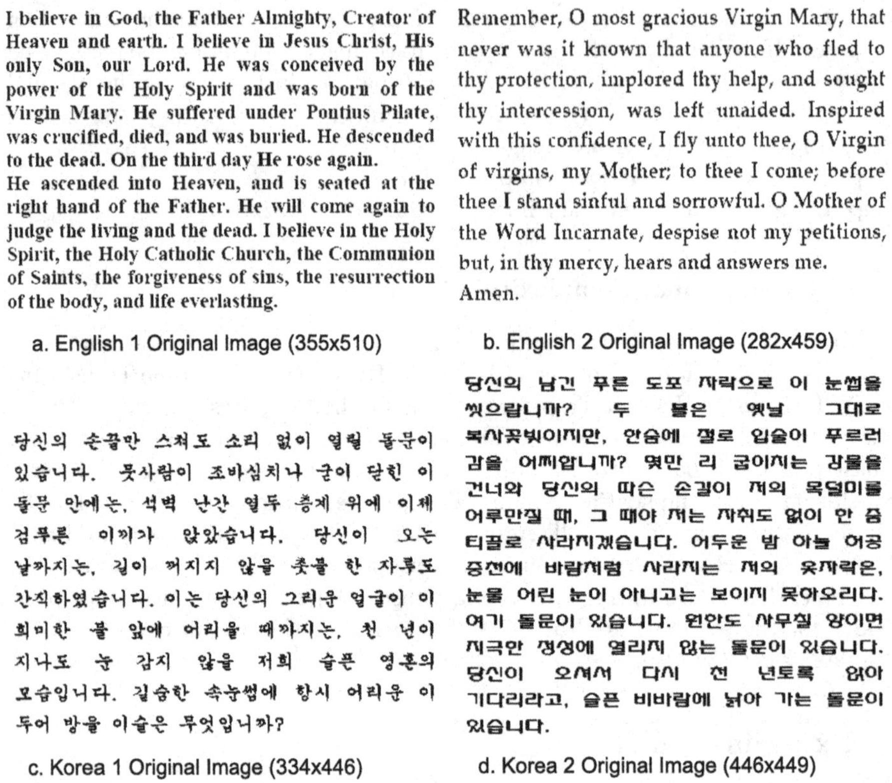

I believe in God, the Father Almighty, Creator of Heaven and earth. I believe in Jesus Christ, His only Son, our Lord. He was conceived by the power of the Holy Spirit and was born of the Virgin Mary. He suffered under Pontius Pilate, was crucified, died, and was buried. He descended to the dead. On the third day He rose again.
He ascended into Heaven, and is seated at the right hand of the Father. He will come again to judge the living and the dead. I believe in the Holy Spirit, the Holy Catholic Church, the Communion of Saints, the forgiveness of sins, the resurrection of the body, and life everlasting.

a. English 1 Original Image (355x510)

Remember, O most gracious Virgin Mary, that never was it known that anyone who fled to thy protection, implored thy help, and sought thy intercession, was left unaided. Inspired with this confidence, I fly unto thee, O Virgin of virgins, my Mother; to thee I come; before thee I stand sinful and sorrowful. O Mother of the Word Incarnate, despise not my petitions, but, in thy mercy, hears and answers me.
Amen.

b. English 2 Original Image (282x459)

당신의 손끝만 스쳐도 소리 없이 열릴 돌문이 있습니다. 뭇사람이 조바심치나 굳이 닫힌 이 돌문 안에는, 석벽 난간 열두 층계 위에 이제 검푸른 이끼가 앉았습니다. 당신이 오는 날까지는, 길이 꺼지지 않을 촛불 한 자루도 간직하였습니다. 이는 당신의 그리운 얼굴이 이 희미한 불 앞에 어리울 때까지는, 천 년이 지나도 눈 감지 않을 저희 슬픈 영혼의 모습입니다. 길숨한 속눈썹에 항시 어리운 이 두어 방울 이슬은 무엇입니까?

c. Korea 1 Original Image (334x446)

당신의 남긴 푸른 도포 자락으로 이 눈썹을 씻으랍니까? 두 볼은 옛날 그대로 복사꽃빛이지만, 안슴에 절로 입술이 푸르러 감을 어찌압니까? 몇만 리 굽이지는 강물을 건너와 당신의 따슨 손길이 저의 목덜미를 어루만질 때, 그 때야 저는 자취도 없이 한 줌 티끌로 사라지겠습니다. 어두운 밤 하늘 어공 중천에 바람처럼 사라지는 저의 옷자락은, 눈물 어린 눈이 아니고는 보이지 못하오리다. 여기 돌문이 있습니다. 왼안도 사무칠 양이면 지극한 정성에 열리지 않는 돌문이 있습니다. 당신이 오셔서 다시 천 년토록 앉아 기다리라고, 슬픈 비바람에 낡아 가는 돌문이 있습니다.

d. Korea 2 Original Image (446x449)

Fig. 4. Original document images used for experiments

When there is no empty pair pattern in an image, we use the minimum pattern for data hiding. In this case, we don't need to record the original minimum pattern in the location map. For the 1-bit payload, 20 bits for location map are required. The set of hidden bits for the proposed method is large compared to the size needed for PS-K.

Table 1. Comparison of hiding capacity and quality in a 355×510 image (Fig. 4(a)) with different size patterns

n-bits	Payload	Location map	Hidden bits
5	2539	0	2539
6	1766	0	1766
7	1228	0	1228
8	882	0	882

Table 2. Comparison of PS-K and our proposed method

Images	PS-K			Proposed Method		
	Payload	Location Map	Hidden Bits	Payload	Location Map	Hidden Bits
English 1 (355 x 510)	2076	13 x 20 bit	1816	2539	0	2539
English 2 (282 x 459)	1160	17 x 20 bit	820	832	0	832
Korea 1 (344 x 446)	1139	22 x 20 bit	699	839	0	839
Korea 2 (446 x 449)	2073	8 x 20 bit	1913	2393	0	2393

I believe in God, the Father Almighty, Creator of Heaven and earth. I believe in Jesus Christ, His only Son, our Lord. He was conceived by the power of the Holy Spirit and was born of the Virgin Mary. He suffered under Pontius Pilate, was crucified, died, and was buried. He descended to the dead. On the third day He rose again. He ascended into Heaven, and is seated at the right hand of the Father. He will come again to judge the living and the dead. I believe in the Holy Spirit, the Holy Catholic Church, the Communion of Saints, the forgiveness of sins, the resurrection of the body, and life everlasting.

a. English 1 Stego Image - 1,000 bits

당신의 손끝만 스쳐도 소리 없이 열릴 돌문이 있습니다. 뭇사람이 조바심치나 굳이 닫힌 이 돌문 안에는, 석벽 난간 염두 총계 위에 이제 검푸른 이끼가 앉았습니다. 당신이 오는 날까지는, 길이 꺼지지 않을 촛불 한 자루도 간직하였습니다. 이는 당신의 그리운 얼굴이 이 희미한 불 앞에 어리울 때까지는, 천 년이 지나도 눈 감지 않을 저희 슬픈 영혼의 모습입니다. 질숨한 속눈썹에 항시 어리운 이 두어 방울 이슬은 무엇입니까?

Remember, O most gracious Virgin Mary, that never was it known that anyone who fled to thy protection, implored thy help, and sought thy intercession, was left unaided. Inspired with this confidence, I fly unto thee, O Virgin of virgins, my Mother; to thee I come; before thee I stand sinful and sorrowful. O Mother of the Word Incarnate, despise not my petitions, but, in thy mercy, hears and answers me. Amen.

b. English 2 Stego Image - 800 bits

당신의 남긴 푸른 도포 자락으로 이 눈썹을 씻으랍니까? 두 불은 옛날 그대로 녹사꽃빛이지만, 언숨에 절로 입술이 푸러러 감을 어찌압니까? 몇만 리 굽이지는 강물을 건너와 당신의 따슨 손결이 저의 목덜미를 어루만질 때, 그 때야 저는 자취도 없이 안 숨 티끌로 사라지겠습니다. 어두운 밤 아늘 어공 증천에 바람처럼 사라지는 저의 웃자락은, 눈물 어린 눈이 아니고는 보이지 못아오리다. 여기 돌문이 있습니다. 왼안도 사무질 양이면 지극한 정성에 열리지 않는 돌문이 있습니다. 당신이 오셔서 다시 천 년토록 앉아 기다리라고, 슬픈 비바람에 낡아 가는 돌문이 있습니다.

c. Korea 1 Stego Image - 800 bits

d. Korea2 Stego Image - 1,000 bits

Fig. 5. Stego document images including secret messages

According to [6], the maximum data hiding capacity (MDHC) can be calculated as:

$$MDHC \leq \frac{(M \times N)}{4}, \tag{8}$$

where M is the width, and N is the height of a binary image. On the other hand, our proposed scheme can be computed as Eq. (9).

$$MDHC \leq \frac{(M \times N)}{n}, \tag{9}$$

where n is $\{3, 4, \ldots, 8\}$. Therefore, n-pair pattern show higher embedding capacity compared to PS-K.

Figure 5 shows the stego document images including secret data as a result of experiments. In fact, it is difficult to find many vestiges from the stego images since our scheme shows a similar level of PSNR with PS-K method. More importantly, it can be possible to completely recover original images from the stego images.

5   Conclusions

In this paper we proposed the n-pair pattern method as a scheme of data hiding for binary document images, and we used this method to annotation or copyright for binary document images. Our proposed data hiding scheme has the advantage of having a high data hiding capacity and reversibility, which is achieved with low deterioration of visual quality. Moreover, the proposed scheme is easy to implement with a simple efficient algorithm. The n-pair pattern method does not require the use of the original cover image to carry out the decoding process. In near future, we will focus on more improving the quality of the binary document images.

Acknowledgements. This research was supported by the Basic Science Research Program Through the National Research Foundation of Korea (NRF) by the Ministry of Education, Science and Technology (20120192).

References

1. Kim, H.J., Kim, C., Choi, Y., Wang, S., Zhang, X.: Improved modification direction methods. Comput. Math. Appl. **60**(2), 319–325 (2010)
2. Kim, C., Shin, D., Shin, D., Zhang, X.: Improved steganographic embedding exploiting modification direction in multimedia communications. Commun. Comput. Inf. Sci. **186**, 130–138 (2011)
3. Kim, C.: Data hiding by an improved exploiting modification direction. Multimedia Tools Appl. **69**(3), 569–584 (2014)
4. Kim, C., Yang, C.N.: Improving data hiding capacity based on hamming code. In: Park, J.J., Zomaya, A., Jeong, H.-Y., Obaidat, M. (eds.) Frontier and Innovation in Future Computing and Communications. LNEE, pp. 697–706. Springer, The Netherlands (2014)

5. Baek, J., Kim, C., Fisher, P., Chao, H.: (N, 1) Steganography approach for secret sharing with digital images. In: Proceedings of 2010 IEEE International Conference on Wireless Communications, Networking and Information Security, pp. 325–329 (2010)
6. Ho, Y.A., Chan, Y.K., Wu, H.C., Chu, Y.P.: High-capacity reversible data hiding in binary images using pattern substitution. Comput. Stand. Interfaces **31**, 787–794 (2009)
7. Tsai, C.L., Chiang, H.F., Fan, K.C., Chung, C.D.: Reversible data hiding and lossless reconstruction of binary images using pair-wise logical computation mechanism. Pattern Recogn. **38**(11), 1993–2006 (2005)
8. Tseng, Y.C., Chen, Y.Y., Pan, H.K.: A secure data hiding scheme for binary images. IEEE Trans. Commun. **50**(8), 1227–1231 (2002)
9. Ni, Z., Shi, Y.Q., Asari, N., Su, W.: Reversible data diding. IEEE Trans. Circuits Syst. Video Technol. **16**(3), 354–362 (2006)
10. Chen, M., Wong, E.K., Memon, N., Adams, S.: Recent developments in document image watermarking and data hiding. In: Proceedings of the SPIE Conference 4518: Multimedia Systems and Applications IV, pp. 166–176 (2001)
11. Lee, S.-K., Suh, Y.-H., Ho, Y.-S.: Lossless data hiding based on histogram modification of difference images. In: Aizawa, K., Nakamura, Y., Satoh, S. (eds.) PCM 2004. LNCS, vol. 3333, pp. 340–347. Springer, Heidelberg (2004)
12. Lin, C.C., Tai, W.L., Chang, C.C.: Multilevel reversible data hiding based on histogram modification of difference images. Pattern Recogn. **41**, 3582–3591 (2008)
13. Tian, J.: Reversible data embedding using a difference expansion. IEEE Trans. Circuits Syst. Video Technol. **13**(8), 890–896 (2003)
14. Tsai, P., Hu, Y.C., Yeh, H.L.: Reversible image hiding scheme using predictive coding and histogram shifting. Signal Process. **89**, 1129–1143 (2009)
15. Xuan, G., Shi, Y.Q., Ni, Z., Chai, P., Cui, X., Tong, X.: Reversible data hiding for JPEG images based on histogram pairs. In: Kamel, M.S., Campilho, A. (eds.) ICIAR 2007. LNCS, vol. 4633, pp. 715–727. Springer, Heidelberg (2007)

Montgomery Modular Multiplication on ARM-NEON Revisited

Hwajeong Seo[1], Zhe Liu[2], Johann Großschädl[2],
Jongseok Choi[1], and Howon Kim[1]($\boxtimes$)

[1] School of Computer Science and Engineering, Pusan National University, San-30,
Jangjeon-Dong, Geumjeong-gu, Busan 609–735, Republic of Korea
{hwajeong,howonkim,jschoi85}@pusan.ac.kr
[2] Laboratory of Algorithmics, Cryptology and Security (LACS),
University of Luxembourg, 6, rue R. Kirchberg,
1359 Luxembourg-Kirchberg, Luxembourg
{zhe.liu,johann.groszschaedl}@uni.lu

Abstract. Montgomery modular multiplication constitutes the "arithmetic foundation" of modern public-key cryptography with applications ranging from RSA, DSA and Diffie-Hellman over elliptic curve schemes to pairing-based cryptosystems. The increased prevalence of SIMD-type instructions in commodity processors (e.g. Intel SSE, ARM NEON) has initiated a massive body of research on vector-parallel implementations of Montgomery modular multiplication. In this paper, we introduce the Cascade Operand Scanning (COS) method to speed up multi-precision multiplication on SIMD architectures. We developed the COS technique with the goal of reducing Read-After-Write (RAW) dependencies in the propagation of carries, which also reduces the number of pipeline stalls (i.e. bubbles). The COS method operates on 32-bit words in a row-wise fashion (similar to the operand-scanning method) and does not require a "non-canonical" representation of operands with a reduced radix. We show that two COS computations can be "coarsely" integrated into an efficient vectorized variant of Montgomery multiplication, which we call Coarsely Integrated Cascade Operand Scanning (CICOS) method. Due to our sophisticated instruction scheduling, the CICOS method reaches record-setting execution times for Montgomery modular multiplication on ARM-NEON platforms. Detailed benchmarking results obtained on an ARM Cortex-A9 and Cortex-A15 processors show that the proposed CICOS method outperforms Bos et al's implementation from SAC 2013 by up to 57 % (A9) and 40 % (A15), respectively.

Keywords: Public-key cryptography · Modular arithmetic · SIMD-level parallelism · Vector instructions · ARM NEON

This work was supported by the ICT R&D program of MSIP/IITP. [10043907, Development of high performance IoT device and Open Platform with Intelligent Software].

© Springer International Publishing Switzerland 2015
J. Lee and J. Kim (Eds.): ICISC 2014, LNCS 8949, pp. 328–342, 2015.
DOI: 10.1007/978-3-319-15943-0_20

1   Introduction

Despite more than three decades of research efforts, public-key cryptography
(PKC) is still considered computation-intensive, especially when executed on
embedded processors. This is mainly because the underlying arithmetic operations (e.g. exponentiation, scalar multiplication) are performed on operands of
a size of several hundreds or even thousands of bits. Multi-precision modular
arithmetic is a performance-critical building block of both traditional public-key
algorithms (e.g. RSA) and elliptic curve cryptosystems. This is in particular
the case for the modular multiplication, which demands careful optimization to
achieve acceptable performance, especially on embedded processors. In order to
reduce the execution time of modular multiplication, cryptographers have developed several efficient reduction algorithms, while software engineers made efforts
to implement them in an optimal way. One of the most important modular reduction techniques is Montgomery's algorithm, which was originally introduced in
1985 [10] and has been widely deployed in real-world applications. Some other
examples for reduction algorithms are the methods of Barrett [1] and Quisquater
[12,13].

In recent years, an increasing number of embedded microprocessors started
to provide Single Instruction Multiple Data (SIMD) instructions to better support multimedia workloads. In order to exploit the parallel computing power of
SIMD instructions, traditional algorithms need to be redesigned and software
needs to be rewritten into a vectorized form. There exist a few papers related
to the implementation of cryptographic algorithms; for example, the authors
of [2,6,7,14] propose ways to speed up cryptography using the NEON instruction set extensions, which is a relatively new SIMD (i.e. vector) architecture
for mobile devices developed by ARM. In particular, to achieve fast public-key
cryptography, it is important to develop optimized SIMD implementations of
multi-precision modular multiplication. In [3], an efficient 128-by-128-bit integer
multiplication using Freescale's SIMD extension is introduced. Various implementations, including [9], adopt a reduced-radix representation with 29 bits per
word for a better handling of the carry propagation. In [4], vector instructions
on the CELL microprocessor are used to perform multiplication on operands
represented with a radix of 2^{16}. More recently, Gueron et al. [8] described an
implementation for the new AVX2 SIMD platform (Intel Haswell architecture)
that uses 256-bit wide vector instructions and a reduced-radix representation for
faster accumulation of partial products. At HPEC 2013, a novel modular reduction method was introduced for the NIST primes P192 and P224 [11], which is
also based on a reduced-radix representation for the operands.

However, a reduced-radix representation (sometimes also called redundant
representation) requires to compute more partial products and, thus, execute
more multiply instructions compared to a canonical (i.e. non-redundant) representation. For example, if we use a radix-2^{24} representation (i.e. 24 bits per
word) for 192-bit operands, the total number of partial products is $8 \times 8 = 64$. On
the other hand, a conventional non-redundant representation based on a radix
of 2^{32} reduces the number of partial products to only $6 \times 6 = 36$. At SAC 2013,

Bos et al. introduced a 2-way Montgomery multiplication for SIMD processors including ARM NEON [5]. Their implementation computes the multiplication and reduction operation simultaneously using a non-redundant representation, which allowed them to exploit the SIMD-level parallelism provided by the NEON engine. However, the performance of their implementation suffers from Read-After-Write (RAW) dependencies in the instruction flow. Such dependencies cause pipeline stalls since the instruction to be executed has to wait until the operands from the source registers are available to be read. For example, the VMULL instruction takes two clock cycles to issue the operation, but the result is only available after (at least) seven clock cycles, which means VMULL has a fairly long latency. If a data conflict occurs, the pipeline is halted for seven clock cycles rather than just two clock cycles.

In this paper, we describe optimizations to further push the performance of multi-precision multiplication and Montgomery multiplication on ARM-NEON processors. We present a non-redundant Cascade Operand Scanning (COS) method for multiplication, which achieves record-setting execution times on ARM Cortex-A9 and Cortex-A15 processors. The COS method processes the partial products in a non-conventional order to reduce the number of data-dependencies in the carry propagation from less to more significant words, which also reduces the number of pipeline stalls. The same strategy can be applied for a two-way NEON-optimized Montgomery multiplication method, called Coarsely Integrated Cascade Operand Scanning (CICOS) method, which essentially consists of two COS computations, whereby one contributes to the multiplication and the second to the Montgomery reduction. Our experimental results show that a Cortex-A15 processor is able to execute a CICOS Montgomery multiplication with 1024-bit operands in only 5600 clock cycles, which is almost 40 % faster than the NEON implementation of Bos et al. (8527 cycles according to [5, Table 3][1]).

The remainder of this paper is organized as follows. In Sect. 2, we recap the previous best results for multiplication and Montgomery multiplication on 32-bit SIMD-based architectures. In Sect. 3, we present novel methods for multi-precision multiplication and Montgomery multiplication on SIMD-based processors, especially ARM-NEON. Thereafter, we will summarize our experimental results in Sect. 4. Finally, in Sect. 5, we conclude the paper.

2   Previous Work

Long integer arithmetic is not straightforward to implement on SIMD-based architectures, mainly due to the propagation of carries from one word to the next, which has to be carried out in addition, multiplication, and other operations. In order to deal with this problem, many recent SIMD implementations adopt a redundant representation with a reduced number of active bits per

---

[1] Note that the timings in the proceedings version of Bos et al's paper differ from the version in the IACR eprint archive at https://eprint.iacr.org/2013/519. We used the faster timings from the eprint version for comparison with our work.

register with the goal of keeping the final result within remaining capacity of a register so that no carry propagations are needed. In [8], by exploiting the AVX2 instruction set extension with redundant representation, the authors showed a performance enhancement of 51 % over the OpenSSL 1.0.1 implementation. In [11], Pabbuleti et al. implemented the NIST-recommended prime-field curve including P192 and P224 on the Snapdragon APQ8060 within 404, 405 clock cycles via applying multiplicand reduction method into SIMD-based machine. Recently, in SAC'13, a different approach to split the Montgomery multiplication into two parts, being computed in parallel, was introduced [5]. They flip the sign of the precomputed Montgomery constant and accumulate the result in two separate intermediate values that are computed concurrently while avoiding a redundant representation. This method is to compute the multiplication and reduction step simultaneously using 2-way SIMD instructions at the cost of some overheads and shows a performance increase of a factor of 1.5 or more than sequential implementation on the Atom platform for 2048-bit modulo. In this paper, we take a different approach computing the multiplication using 2-way SIMD instructions first and subsequently the reduction using 2-way SIMD. The approach uses non-redundant representation and computes the carry propagations using 2-way SIMD instructions

3   Proposed Method

Throughout the paper, we will use the following notations. Let A and B be two operands with a length of m-bit that are represented by multiple-word arrays. Each operand is written as follows: $A = (A[n-1], ..., A[2], A[1], A[0])$ and $B = (B[n-1], ..., B[2], B[1], B[0])$, whereby $n = \lceil m/w \rceil$, and w is the word size. The result of multiplication $C = A \cdot B$ is twice length of A, and represented by $C = (C[2n-1], ..., C[2], C[1], C[0])$. For clarity, we describe the method using a multiplication structure and rhombus form. The multiplication structure describes order of partial products from top to bottom and each point in rhombus form represents a multiplication $A[i] \times B[j]$. The rightmost corner of the rhombus represents the lowest indices $(i, j = 0)$, whereas the leftmost represents corner the highest indices $(i, j = n-1)$. The lowermost side represents result indices $C[k]$, which ranges from the rightmost corner $(k = 0)$ to the leftmost corner $(k = 2n-1)$. Particularly, SIMD architecture computes two 32-bit partial products with single instruction, so we use two multiplication structures to describe SIMD operations. These block structures placed in the row represent two partial products with single instruction.

3.1   Cascade Operand Scanning Multiplication for SIMD

SIMD architecture is able to compute multiple data with single instruction. However, SIMD instruction does not provide carry handling registers and therefore, results in imposing huge overheads on SIMD machine to manage carry propagations. In order to alleviate this problem, many of the previous work adopted the so-called redundant representation which absorbs carry propagations into remaining bits in the destination registers, but this architecture also has performance degradations because redundant representation increases number of partial products. In order to address both drawbacks, we choose non-redundant representation, suggesting an efficient carry handling with simple operand realignments.

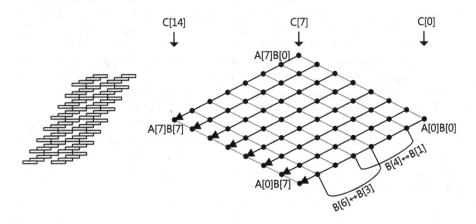

Fig. 1. Cascade operand scanning multiplication for 256-bit operand

In Fig. 1, we designed multi-precision multiplication for SIMD architecture. Taking the 32-bit word with 256-bit multiplication as an example, our method works as follows[2]. Firstly, we re-organized operands by conducting transpose operation, which can efficiently shuffle inner vector by 32-bit wise. Instead of a normal order $((B[0], B[1]), (B[2], B[3]), (B[4], B[5]), (B[6], B[7]))$, we actually classify the operand as groups $((B[0],B[4]), (B[2], B[6]), (B[1], B[5]), (B[3], B[7]))$ for computing multiplication where each operand ranges from 0 to $2^{32} - 1$ (i.e. 0xffff_ffff in hexadecimal form). Secondly, multiplication $A[0]$ with $((B[0], B[4]), (B[2], B[6]), (B[1], B[5]), (B[3], B[7]))$ is computed, generating the partial product pairs including $((C[0], C[4]), (C[2], C[6]), (C[1], C[5]), (C[3], C[7]))$ where the results are located from 0 to $2^{64} - 2^{33} + 1$, namely, 0xffff_fffe_0000_0001 in hexadecimal form. Third, partial products are separated into higher bits $(64 \sim 33)$ and lower bits $(32 \sim 1)$ by using transpose operation with 64-bit initialized registers having 0 value(0x0000_0000_0000_0000), which outputs a pair of 32-bit results ranging from 0 to $2^{32} - 1$ (i.e. 0xffff_ffff). After then the higher bits are added to lower bits of upper intermediate results. For example, higher bits of $((C[0], C[4]), (C[1], C[5]), (C[2], C[6]), (C[3]))$ are added to lower bits of $((C[1], C[5]), (C[2], C[6]), (C[3], C[7]), (C[4]))$. By referring to

---

[2] Operands $A[0 \sim 7]$ and $B[0 \sim 7]$ are stored in 32-bit registers. Intermediate results $C[0 \sim 15]$ are stored in 64-bit registers. We use two packed 32-bit registers in the 64-bit register.

Fig. 2, our method establishes SIMD friendly addition process and the carry values are propagated in grouped cascade way. The proposed method finely rearranges each intermediate result and order of carry propagation to conduct carry handling with only four additions in non-redundant representation and no pipeline stalls. After addition, the least significant word ($C[0]$, lower bits of $B[0] \times A[0]$) is placed within 32-bit in range of $[0,$ 0xffff_ffff$]$ so this is directly saved into temporal registers or memory. On the other hand, remaining intermediate results from $C[1]$ to $C[7]$ are placed within $[0,$ 0x1_ffff_fffe$]^3$, which exceed range of 32-bit in certain cases. Fortunately, the addition of intermediate results ($C[1 \sim 7]$) and 32-bit by 32-bit multiplication in next step are placed into 64-bit registers without overflowing, because addition of maximum multiplication result $2^{64} - 2^{33} + 1$ (i.e. 0xffff_fffe_0000_0001) and intermediate result $2^{33} - 2$ (i.e. 0x1_ffff_fffe) outputs the final results within 64-bit $2^{64} - 1$ (i.e. 0xffff_ffff_ffff_ffff)^4. For this reason, we don't need to propagate 33th carry bit of intermediate results ($C[1 \sim 7]$) in each round but we delay the carry propagations to very end of round and conduct whole carry propagations at once. Before move to next round, lower bits of $C[4]$ and higher bits of $C[7]$ are re-grouped into ($C[4], C[8]$) and then intermediate result pairs are re-shaped in (($C[1], C[5]$), ($C[2], C[6]$), ($C[3], C[7]$), ($C[4], C[8]$)). This process is repeated with remaining operands ($A[1 \sim 7]$) by seven times more to complete the multiplication. After eight rounds of multiplication, the results from $C[0]$ to $C[7]$ are perfectly fit into 32-bit, because the least significant word is outputted in 32-bit in every round. However, remaining intermediate results ($C[8] \sim C[15]$) are not placed within 32-bit so we should process a chain of carry propagations over 32-bit by conducting final alignment. The final alignment executes carry propagation results from $C[8]$ to $C[15]$ with sequential addition and transpose instructions. This process causes pipeline stalls by 8 times, because higher bits of former results are directly added to next intermediate results. Therefore, proposed COS incurs pipeline stalls by the number of n for final alignment. In case of 512-, 1024- and 2048-bit COS multiplications, we should conduct 4, 16 and 64 times of 256-bit COS multiplications because the 256-bit COS multiplication is maximum operand size on NEON processor due to limited number of registers^5. Unlike 256-bit version, intermediate result should be stored and re-loaded, so we assigned temporal memory and stack storages to retain intermediate results.

---

^{3} In the first round, the range is within $[0,$ 0x1_ffff_fffd$]$, because higher bits and lower bits of intermediate results ($C[0 \sim 7]$) are located in range of $[0,$ 0xffff_fffe$]$ and $[0,$ 0xffff_ffff$]$, respectively. From second round, the addition of higher and lower bits are located within $[0,$ 0x1_ffff_fffe$]$, because both higher and lower bits are located in range of $[0,$ 0xffff_ffff$]$.

^{4} In the first round, intermediate results ($C[0 \sim 7]$) are in range of $[0,$ 0x1_ffff_fffd$]$ so multiplication and accumulation results are in range of $[0,$ 0xffff_ffff_ffff_fffe$]$. From second round, the intermediate results are located in $[0,$ 0x1_ffff_fffe$]$ so multiplication and accumulation results are in range of $[0,$ 0xffff_ffff_ffff_ffff$]$.

^{5} NEON engine supports sixteen 128-bit registers. We assigned four registers for operands (A, B), four for intermediate results (C) and four for temporal storages.

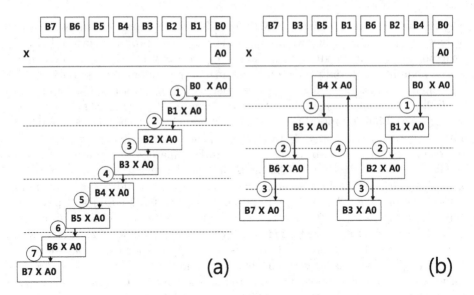

Fig. 2. Carry propagations in non-redundant representation, (a) ordinary operand scanning method, (b) proposed method(operand B is transposed before computations)

Finally, several `load`, `store`, `push` and `pop` instructions are used to establish 512-, 1024- and 2048-bit implementations.

3.2 Coarsely Integrated Cascade Operand Scanning Multiplication for SIMD

In [5], Bos et al. introduced a 2-way Montgomery multiplication for SIMD architecture. However, the proposed 2-way Montgomery multiplication has high data interdependency because they used ordinary operand-scanning method for multiplication and reduction procedures which compute partial products in incremental order and previous partial product results are directly used in next steps. Finally this resource access conflicts results in pipeline stalls. In order to resolve this problem, we rescheduled the order of operations to achieve a latency-hidden design. We implemented the Coarsely Integrated Cascade Operand Scanning (CICOS) algorithm by using COS method since separated version needs to `load` and `store` intermediate results twice more than integrated version, while the finely integrated mode leads to high interdependency between each intermediate result. To describe Montgomery multiplication properly, we grouped two rhombus forms in Fig. 3. Upper rhombus represents multi-precision multiplication and lower rhombus represents Montgomery reduction. In order to distinguish both computations, we painted structure forms of multiplication process in white and reduction process in yellow.

In the following, we will take a 256-bit case (M' has a length of 32-bit) as an examples to further explain our implementation of Montgomery reduction for

Algorithm 1. Calculation of the Montgomery reduction

Require: An odd m-bit modulus M, Montgomery radix $R = 2^m$, an operand T where
$T = A \cdot B$ in the range $[0, 2M-1]$, and pre-computed constant $M' = -M^{-1} \bmod R$
Ensure: Montgomery product $Z = \text{MonRed}(T, R) = T \cdot R^{-1} \bmod M$
1: $Q \leftarrow T \cdot M' \bmod R$
2: $Z \leftarrow (T + Q \cdot M)/R$
3: **if** $Z \geq M$ **then** $Z \leftarrow Z - M$ **end if**
4: **return** Z

Algorithm 1. As shown in Fig. 3, part of the operand Q (i.e. $Q[0 \sim 7]$) is computed by multiplying intermediate results with M'. All partial products with $Q[0]$ and $M[0 \sim 7]$ are executed throughout the row. After then $T + Q \cdot M$ (i.e. Step 2 of Algorithm 1) can be computed using COS method. For Montgomery multiplication on SIMD architecture, we integrated two COS methods[6]. Firstly, we re-organized multiplicands (B) by conducting transpose operation. This process takes $((B[0], B[1]), (B[2], B[3]), (B[4], B[5]), (B[6], B[7]))$ as inputs and generates the new operand groups as $((B[0], B[4]), (B[2], B[6]), (B[1], B[5]), (B[3], B[7]))$ where each operand ranges from 0 to $2^{32} - 1$(0xffff_ffff). Secondly, multiply $A[0]$ with $((B[0], B[4]), (B[2], B[6]), (B[1], B[5]), (B[3], B[7]))$, and generating partial product pairs including $((C[0], C[4]), (C[2], C[6]), (C[1], C[5]), (C[3], C[7]))$ where multiplication results range from 0 to $2^{64} - 2^{33} + 1$ (0xffff_fffe _0000_0001). Third, partial products are separated into higher bits and lower bits by using the transpose operation with initialized registers, which outputs results in range of $[0, \text{0xffff\_ffff}]$. After then the higher bits are added to lower bits of upper intermediate results. For example, higher bits of $(C[0], C[4]), (C[2], C[6]), (C[1], C[5]), (C[3])$ are added to lower bits of $(C[1], C[5])$, $(C[3], C[7]), (C[2], C[6]), (C[4])$. These intermediate results are placed between 0 and $2^{33} - 2$(0x1_ffff_fffe)[7]. The remaining higher bits of $(C[7])$ are copied to $(C[8])$. After then lower bits of $C[0]$ in range of $[0, \text{0xffff\_ffff}]$ is multiplied with operand M' to generate $Q[0]$ in range of $[0, \text{0xffff\_ffff}]$. In case of operand (M), the variables are stored in ordered way like this $((M[0], M[4]), (M[2], M[6]), (M[1], M[5]), (M[3], M[7]))$. Fourthly, multiply $Q[0]$ with $((M[0], M[4]), (M[2], M[6]), (M[1], M[5]), (M[3], M[7]))$ are executed with intermediate results pairs including $((C[0], C[4]), (C[2], C[6]), (C[1], C[5]), (C[3], C[7]))$ where the results range from 0 to $2^{64} - 1$(0xffff_ffff _ffff_ffff). Lastly, partial products are separated into higher bits and lower bits. After then the higher bits of $((C[0], C[4]), (C[1], C[5]), (C[2], C[6])$, and the lower bits of $(C[4]))$ are added to lower bits of $((C[1], C[5]), (C[2], C[6]), (C[3], C[7]))$, and the higher bits of $(C[3]))$,

---

[6] Operands $A[0 \sim 7]$, $B[0 \sim 7]$, $M[0 \sim 7]$, $Q[0 \sim 7]$ and M' are stored in 32-bit registers. Intermediate results $C[0 \sim 15]$ are stored in 64-bit registers.

[7] In the first round, the range is within $[0, \text{0x1\_ffff\_fffd}]$, because higher bits and lower bits of intermediate results $(C[0 \sim 7])$ are located in range of $[0, \text{0xffff\_fffe}]$ and $[0, \text{0xffff\_ffff}]$, respectively. From second round, the addition of higher and lower bits are located within $[0, \text{0x1\_ffff\_fffe}]$, because both higher and lower bits are located in range of $[0, \text{0xffff\_ffff}]$.

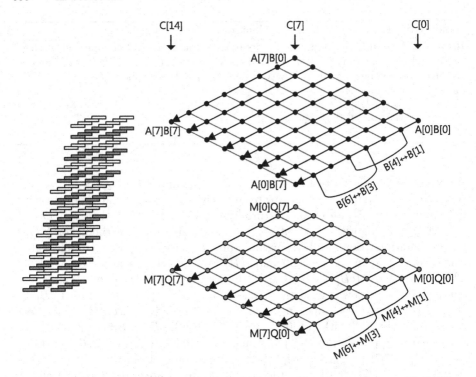

Fig. 3. Coarsely integrated cascade operand scanning for Montgomery multiplication in 256-bit

which output the accumulated results ranging from 0 to $2^{33} - 2(\texttt{0x1\_ffff\_fffe})$. Particularly, higher bits of $(C[7])$ are added to lower bits of $(C[8])$ and then higher bits of $(C[3])$ and lower bits of $(C[8])$ are re-grouped in $(C[4], C[8])$. Finally, the result $C[0]$ is set to zero which is discarded and intermediate results are re-constructed like this $((C[1], C[5]), (C[2], C[6]), (C[3], C[7]), (C[4], C[8]))$. The multiplication and reduction process is repeated with remaining operands $(A[1 \sim 7])$ by seven times more to complete the Montgomery multiplication. After then, final alignment and final subtraction follow. As like COS, maximum operand size of CICOS method is 256-bit. For longer integers such as 512-, 1024- and 2048-bit, we should conduct 4, 16 and 64 times of 256-bit CICOS Montgomery multiplication.

3.3 Requirements for Pipeline

The NEON engine consists of four timing models. Among them, we should carefully concern on both issue and result clock cycles. Issue clock is minimum clock cycles to trigger instruction. After the issue clock cycle, we can issue next instructions in pipelined way. In a contrast, result clock is time to get the final results. If we access to result registers before result clock, we should wait until the data is ready during remaining result clock cycles. For fully pipelined computation, we

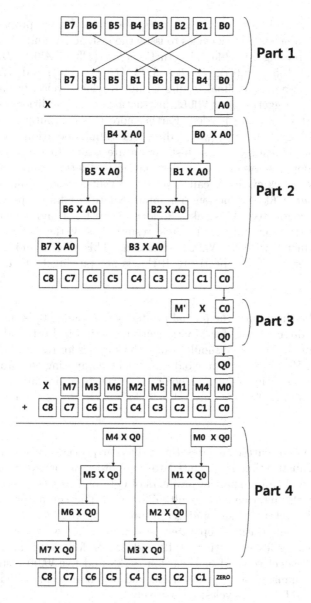

Fig. 4. Structure of coarsely integrated cascade operand scanning Montgomery multiplication

should issue several instructions and then access to certain results which satisfy the result clock cycle. We analyze proposed method by referring Fig. 4.

Part 1. This part starts with operand alignments. Operands B are transposed by conducting the single VTRN instruction on eight 32-bit packed variables. The operation needs 1 clock cycle to issue the instruction and 2 clock cycles take to get the final results.

Part 2. The second part consists of multiplication and carry propagation. The VMULL operation needs 2 clock cycles to issue the instruction and 7 clock cycle for result. By conducting four VMULL instructions for $((B[0] \times A[0]), (B[4] \times A[0]))$, $((B[1] \times A[0]), (B[5] \times A[0]))$, $((B[2] \times A[0]), (B[6] \times A[0]))$ and $((B[3] \times A[0]), (B[7] \times A[0]))$, we can get final results within 13 clock cycles, because 8 (2×4) clock cycles for triggering four VMULL instructions and 5 additional clock cycles to get the last results are needed. Furthermore this computation order satisfies result clock cycle because we conduct four VMULL operations taking 8 clock cycles to issue so results of first instruction are ready. In a contrast, if there is interdependency between former destination and latter source registers, the costs rise to 28 clock cycles, because we should wait for four result clock cycles. After then four VTRN instructions for intermediate results on previous partial products are conducted. This takes 5 clock cycles for 4 and 1 clock cycles to trigger the instruction and wait for final results. Lastly, the five carry propagations are conducted with five VADD instructions. This takes 5 and 2 clock cycles to issue and get results, respectively. If this is not pipelined, the overheads are 15 clock cycles.

Part 3. In the third part, the partial product of M' and $C[0]$ is computed. The result $Q[0]$ is directly used for Montgomery reduction in Part 4. If we conduct this instruction in Part 3, we should wait 7 clock cycles for results to be ready for the next step. However, we can avoid the cost by computing the product during Part 2. After obtaining $C[0]$ and before the transpose operation, we conduct VMULL on M' and $C[0]$. This only takes 2 clock cycles to issue so we can save 5 clock cycles.

Part 4. The last part calculates the reduction process. In contrast to Part 2, the VMLAL instruction is exploited to compute multiplication and addition simultaneously. The four partial products of $Q[0]$ and $M[0 \sim 7]$ are conducted, accumulating the intermediate results $C[0 \sim 7]$. The computation takes only 8 and 5 clock cycles to issue and get results. If we conduct the addition and multiplication computations separately in non-pipelined way, the overheads are up-to 40 clock cycles consisting of 12 and 28 for four VADD and four VMULL instructions, respectively. After then, four VTRN and five VADD instructions are conducted to manage carry propagation and accumulate intermediate results, which take 5 and 7 clock cycles, respectively.

Table 1. Comparison of pipeline stall for Montgomery multiplication

Our CICOS MM		Bos's 2-way MM [5]	
Pipelined	Pipeline stall	Pipelined	Pipeline stall
n^2	$2n$	-	$n^2 + n$

Final Alignment and Subtraction/Addition. The final results from $C[8]$ to $C[15]$ should be aligned to propagate carry bits from least significant word ($C[8]$) to most ($C[15]$). Firstly, higher bits of $C[8]$ are added to $C[9]$ and this is iterated to most significant intermediate result ($C[15]$). Unlike multiplication and reduction process, the final alignment occurs pipeline stalls due to interdependency between former and next variables. After final alignment, final subtraction follows and this also requires to conduct the carry propagation incurring pipeline stalls. Finally, our Montgomery method includes the overheads of pipeline stalls by $2n$ times (n for final alignment and n for final subtraction). In case of pipelined instruction, we conduct n^2 times of carry propagations during multiplication and reduction process. On the other hand, Bos's 2-way Montgomery multiplication has $n^2 + n$ times of pipeline stalls because former multiplication results are directly used in next operations by following ordinary operand scanning. Particularly, Bos's method incurs pipeline stalls during multiplication and reduction process by n^2 times and final subtraction/addition is required to conduct sequential subtraction by n times. The comparison results are drawn in Table 1.

4   Results

In this section, we report the execution time of the proposed methods on 32-bit ARM Cortex-A9 and Cortex-A15 processors and compare our results with the related works.

4.1   Target Platforms

Cortex Series. The ARM Cortex series are full implementation of the ARMv7 architecture including NEON engine. Register sizes are 64-bit and 128-bit for double(D) and quadruple(Q) word registers, respectively. Each register provides short bit size computations such as 8-bit, 16-bit, 32-bit and 64-bit. This feature provides more precise operation and benefits to various word size computations. The Cortex-A9 processor is adopted in several devices including iPad 2, iPhone 4S, Galaxy S2, Galaxy S3, Galaxy Note 2, and Kindle Fire. The Cortex-A15 is used in Chromebook, NEXUS 10, Tegra 4 and Odroid-XU.

4.2   Evaluation

We prototyped our methods for ARM Cortex-A9 and A15 processors, which are equivalent to the target processors used in Bos et al's work [5]. We compared our results with best previous results from proceedings version of Bos et al's paper presented at SAC 2013 [5]. In Table 2, we categorize the timings with respect to the architecture that served as experimental platform. In the case of 1024-bit Montgomery multiplication, we achieve an execution time of 8358 clock cycles on the Cortex-A9 series, while Bos et al's SIMD implementation requires 17464 clock cycles. Furthermore, on a Cortex-A15, we compute a 1024-bit Montgomery multiplication within 5600 clock cycles rather than 8527 clock cycles as specified

Table 2. Results of multiplication and Montgomery multiplication in clock cycle on ARM Cortex-A9/A15 platforms

Bit	Cortex-A9			Cortex-A15		
	Our NEON	NEON [5]	ARM [5]	Our NEON	NEON [5]	ARM [5]
Multiplication						
256	308	n/a	n/a	219	n/a	n/a
512	1050	n/a	n/a	658	n/a	n/a
1024	4298	n/a	n/a	2810	n/a	n/a
2048	17080	n/a	n/a	10672	n/a	n/a
Montgomery Multiplication						
256	658	n/a	n/a	308	n/a	n/a
512	2254	5236	3175	1485	2473	2373
1024	8358	17464	10167	5600	8527	8681
2048	32732	63900	36746	26232	33441	33961

in [5, Table 3]. Thus, our 1024-bit implementation outperforms Bos et al's work by approximately 52 % and 34 % on a Cortex-A9 and Cortex-A15, respectively. The speed-ups are even more significant for 512-bit operands: 57 % on the A9 and 40 % on the A15. Our results show that the NEON instructions improve the execution time by 29 % and 18 % (512 and 1024-bit on Cortex-A9) as well as 37 % and 35 % (512 and 1024-bit on Cortex-A15) over a sequential implementation that does not take advantage of the NEON engine. The case for 2048-bit also shows, our method improves performance by 48.7 % and 21.5 % on A9 and A15, respectively. Compared with the sequential implementations, still our 2048-bit implementations have enhancements by 10.9 % and 22.7 %. The following is reason for the significant speed-up compared to Bos et al's NEON implementation. First, we process the operands in a special order so as to reduce pipeline stalls caused by RAW data dependencies. Second, we perform the carry propagation in an efficient fashion in the NEON engine by adding grouped intermediate results.

5   Conclusions

We presented optimization techniques to improve the performance of multi-precision arithmetic operations (in particular multiplication and Montgomery multiplication) on 2-way SIMD platforms. More specifically, we introduced the COS method for multi-precision multiplication, which processes the words of one of the operands in a non-conventional order so as to reduce pipeline stalls caused by data dependencies. Furthermore, we described the CICOS method for performing Montgomery multiplication by coarsely interleaving COS-based multiplication and Montgomery reduction steps. Thanks to these optimizations, we were able to achieve record-setting execution times for conventional multiplication as well as Montgomery multiplication on ARM NEON platforms.

For example, on an ARM Cortex-A15 processor, our CICOS method performs a 1024-bit Montgomery multiplication only 5600 clock cycles, which is roughly 34 % faster than the NEON implementation of Bos et al. (8527 cycles). On a Cortex-A9, the performance gain is even higher, namely 52 % (8358 vs. 17464 cycles, i.e. we save 9106 cycles). In case of 2048-bit operands, our methods have improved performance by 21.5 % (A15) and 48.7 % (A9). These gaps further increase for 512-bit operands to 40 % (A15) and 57 % (A9). We also outperform Bos et al's non-vectorized implementation (which uses only standard ARM instructions) on the two platforms by between 11 % and 37 %. Based on these results, we can draw the following conclusion. Our re-ordering of operands along with a "coarse" integration of multiplication and reduction is significantly faster than the conventional operand ordering and "fine" integration approach followed by Bos et al. The interesting future work would be asymptotically faster integer multiplication method like Karatsuba multiplication, which trades multiplications for several additions, on SIMD architecture. However, when it comes to non-redundant representation, addition produces a chains of carry propagations which incur high overheads. For practical purposes, we should study further how to employ an efficient addition operation over non-redundant representation.

References

1. Barrett, P.: Implementing the rivest shamir and adleman public key encryption algorithm on a standard digital signal processor. In: Odlyzko, A.M. (ed.) CRYPTO 1986. LNCS, vol. 263, pp. 311–323. Springer, Heidelberg (1987)
2. Bernstein, D.J., Schwabe, P.: NEON crypto. In: Prouff, E., Schaumont, P. (eds.) CHES 2012. LNCS, vol. 7428, pp. 320–339. Springer, Heidelberg (2012)
3. Lin, B.: Solving sequential problems in parallel: An SIMD solution to RSA cryptography, Feb 2006. http://cache.freescale.com/files/32bit/doc/app_note/AN3057.pdf
4. Bos, J.W., Kaihara, M.E.: montgomery multiplication on the cell. In: Wyrzykowski, R., Dongarra, J., Karczewski, K., Wasniewski, J. (eds.) PPAM 2009, Part I. LNCS, vol. 6067, pp. 477–485. Springer, Heidelberg (2010)
5. Bos, J.W., Montgomery, P.L., Shumow, D., Zaverucha, G.M.: Montgomery multiplication using vector instructions. In: Lange, T., Lauter, K., Lisoněk, P. (eds.) SAC 2013. LNCS, vol. 8282, pp. 471–490. Springer, Heidelberg (2014)
6. Câmara, D., Gouvêa, C.P.L., López, J., Dahab, R.: Fast software polynomial multiplication on ARM processors using the NEON engine. In: Cuzzocrea, A., Kittl, C., Simos, D.E., Weippl, E., Xu, L. (eds.) CD-ARES Workshops 2013. LNCS, vol. 8128, pp. 137–154. Springer, Heidelberg (2013)
7. Faz-Hernández, A., Longa, P., Sánchez, A.H.: Efficient and secure algorithms for GLV-based scalar multiplication and their implementation on GLV-GLS curves. In: Benaloh, J. (ed.) CT-RSA 2014. LNCS, vol. 8366, pp. 1–27. Springer, Heidelberg (2014)
8. Gueron, S., Krasnov, V.: Software implementation of modular exponentiation, using advanced vector instructions architectures. In: Özbudak, F., Rodríguez-Henríquez, F. (eds.) WAIFI 2012. LNCS, vol. 7369, pp. 119–135. Springer, Heidelberg (2012)

A Fair and Efficient Mutual Private Set Intersection Protocol from a Two-Way Oblivious Pseudorandom Function

Sumit Kumar Debnath[(✉)] and Ratna Dutta

Department of Mathematics, Indian Institute of Technology Kharagpur,
Kharagpur 721302, India
sd.iitkgp@gmail.com, ratna@maths.iitkgp.ernet.in

Abstract. We present a two-way Oblivious Pseudorandom Function (mOPRF) secure in the malicious model under the Decisional Composite Residuosity (DCR) and Decisional Diffie-Hellman (DDH) assumptions. Using this mOPRF, we construct an optimistic mutual Private Set Intersection (mPSI) protocol preserving fairness. Unlike existing optimistic protocols our mPSI supports semi-trusted arbiter instead of fully-trusted arbiter. Semi-trusted arbiter never get access to the private information of any of the parties while follow the protocol honestly. Our design is the *first* fair mPSI with *linear* communication and computation complexities, and is proven to be secure in the standard model against malicious parties under Decisional q-Diffie-Hellman Inversion (Dq-DHI), DCR and DDH assumptions.

Keywords: PSI · mPSI · OPRF · Semi-honest adversary · Malicious adversary · Fairness · Optimistic

1 Introduction

Private Set Intersection (PSI) protocol is a two party cryptographic protocol, where both the parties engage with their respective private sets and at the end of the protocol, either one of them gets the intersection, yielding–*one-way* PSI, or both of them get the intersection yielding–*mutual* PSI (mPSI). PSI has found several practical privacy preserving applications [8]. For instance, suppose two Facebook account holders want to know their common friends in Facebook, while none of them willing to disclose the whole friend list to the other. mPSI is appropriate in this scenario.

Designing efficient mPSI protocol is not a trivial task and has received considerable attention to the recent research community due to its importance and wide applications. Fairness is a critical issue for an mPSI. *Fairness* ensures that if one party gets the intersection then the other party should also get the intersection. De Cristofaro and Tsudik [7] proposed an mPSI by combining two instantiations of an one-way PSI protocol. However, the scheme does not preserve fairness, as there is no way to prevent a player from prematurely aborting the protocol.

© Springer International Publishing Switzerland 2015
J. Lee and J. Kim (Eds.): ICISC 2014, LNCS 8949, pp. 343–359, 2015.
DOI: 10.1007/978-3-319-15943-0_21

Most prior work on developing fair cryptographic protocols are *optimistic* in the sense that they use an off-line trusted third party, called *arbiter*, to efficiently realize fairness. Arbiter takes part in the protocol to recover the output for the honest party only if a corrupted player prematurely aborts the protocol. In PSI protocol, optimistic fairness is not easy to achieve.

Our Contribution: In this paper, we concentrate mainly on designing *fair optimistic* mPSI protocol in the *malicious* setting with *linear* complexity. The mPSI protocols available in the literature so far are [4,8,12,13], to the best of our knowledge. However, none of them achieve all the above mention objectives simultaneously. We propose a fair Oblivious Pseudorandom Function (OPRF) based mPSI protocol. An OPRF is a two party protocol run between a sender S with a private key k and a receiver R with a private input x, enabling R to construct a pseudorandom function (PRF) [10] $f_k(x)$, while S gets nothing. Our approach in designing an mPSI is as follows:

We first design a two-way OPRF, namely mOPRF, that facilitates both the parties to obtain the pseudorandom function $f_k(x)$ of [11]. The proposed mOPRF is proven to be secure in the malicious model under the DCR and DDH assumptions with a total 176 exponentiations in contrast to the OPRF of [11] that requires only 76 exponentiations. However, the OPRF of [11] is one-way in the sense that only one party (receiver) gets the pseudorandom function $f_k(x)$ after the completion of the protocol. On the other hand, we use an off-line arbiter, which is a semi-trusted third party, in such a way that at the end of the protocol if one party gets the pseudorandom function $f_k(x)$ then the other party should also get $f_k(x)$ and none of them learns more than $f_k(x)$. Arbiter can resolve disputes without knowing the private information of the two parties and has the ability to correctly carry out the instructions. Arbiter can engaged in the protocol and recover the output for the honest party only when a corrupted player prematurely aborts the protocol.

We then compose the proposed mOPRF in parallel to construct a parallel mOPRF, namely pa-mOPRF, which is used to build an efficient mPSI protocol. Achieving fairness in mPSI is a challenging task. Our mPSI is the *first* fair mPSI protocol with *linear* communication and computation complexities. Security is achieved in the standard model against both the malicious parties under the Decisional q-Diffie-Hellman Inversion (q-DHI), DCR and DDH assumptions, where a safe RSA modulus must be pre-generated by a trusted party. Our mPSI protocol is optimistic as we have used an off-line arbiter to achieve fairness. Unlike many optimistic protocols that require fully trusted arbiter, our mPSI requires only semi trusted arbiter, who does not have access to the private information of any of the parties, but follow the protocol honestly. Our mPSI protocol is more efficient than the existing mPSI protocols [4,8,12,13] (see Table 1). The mPSI protocols of [4,8,13] have quadratic computation complexities, whereas that for our mPSI protocol is linear. In [8], the party constructing the polynomial should have more number of inputs than the other party, whereas our protocol is not restricted to this. Besides, the mPSI of [12,13] do not preserve fairness.

Table 1. Comparison of mPSI protocols (w and v are sizes of the input sets)

Protocol	Adversarial model	Security assumption	Comm. cost	Comp. cost	Fairness	Optimistic	Based on
[13]	Malicious		$O(w+v)$	$O(wv)$	No	No	AHE
[4]	Malicious	Strong RSA	$O(w+v)$	$O(wv)$	Yes	Yes	
[12]	Semi-honest		$O(w+v)$	$O(w+v)$	No	No	AHE
[8]	Malicious		$O(w+v)$	$O(wv)$	Yes	Yes	AHE+VE
Our mPSI	Malicious	Dq-DHI, DCR, DDH	$O(w+v)$	$O(w+v)$	Yes	Yes	

AHE: any additively homomorphic encryption and VE: verifiable encryption.

2 Preliminaries

Throughout the paper the notations κ, $r = \lfloor n/4 \rfloor$, $a \leftarrow A$, $x \hookleftarrow X$ and $\mathcal{A} \equiv^c \mathcal{B}$ are used to represent "security parameter", "r is the greatest integer such that $r \leq n/4$" "a is output of the procedure A", "variable x is chosen uniformly at random from set X" and "the output of the process $\mathcal{A}$ is *computationally indistinguishable* from the output of the process $\mathcal{B}$" respectively. Informally, $\mathcal{A} \equiv^c \mathcal{B}$ means $|Pr[\mathcal{A}(1^\kappa) = 1] - Pr[\mathcal{B}(1^\kappa) = 1]|$ is negligible of κ. A function $\epsilon : \mathbb{N} \to \mathbb{R}$ is said to be *negligible function* of κ if for each constant $c > 0$, we have $\epsilon(\kappa) = o(\kappa^{-c})$ for all sufficiently large κ.

Definition 1. Oblivious Pseudorandom Function [9]: *The* Oblivious Pseudorandom Function OPRF *is a two party protocol between a sender S with a private key k and a receiver R with a private input x, enabling R to securely compute a PRF $f_k(x)$ while S learns nothing.*

Definition 2. *A functionality, computed by two parties S and R with inputs X_S and X_R respectively by running a protocol Π, is denoted as $\mathcal{F}_\Pi : X_S \times X_R \to Y_S \times Y_R$, where Y_S and Y_R are the outputs of S and R respectively after completion of the protocol Π between S and R.*

2.1 Cryptographic Assumptions

Definition 3. Factoring Assumption [11]: *Let $\mathcal{RSAGen}$ denotes an algorithm that, on the input 1^κ, generates a safe RSA modulus n, where $n = PQ$, $P = 2p_1 + 1$, $Q = 2q_1 + 1$, $|p_1| = |q_1| = \kappa$, P, Q, p_1, q_1 are all primes. We say that factoring a safe RSA modulus is hard if for every PPT algorithm $\mathcal{A}$, the probability $Pr[\mathcal{A}(n) \in \{P, Q\} | n \leftarrow RSAGen(1^\kappa)]$ is a negligible function of κ.*

Definition 4. Decisional Diffie-Hellman (DDH) Assumption [2]: *Let the algorithm gGen generates a modulus n and a generator g of a multiplicative group $\mathbb{G}$ of order n on the input 1^κ. Suppose $a, b, c \hookleftarrow \mathbb{Z}_n$. Then the DDH assumption states that no PPT algorithm $\mathcal{A}$ can distinguish between the two distributions $\langle g^a, g^b, g^{ab} \rangle$ and $\langle g^a, g^b, g^c \rangle$.*

Definition 5. Decisional q-Diffie-Hellman Inversion (DHI) Assumption
[11]: *Let gGen be an algorithm that, on the input 1^κ, outputs a modulus n and a generator g of a multiplicative group $\mathbb{G}$ of order n. The Decisional q-DHI assumption states that given $n, g, g^\alpha, \ldots, g^{\alpha^q}$, it is hard to distinguish $g^{1/\alpha} \in \mathbb{G}$ from a random element h of $\mathbb{G}$ for every PPT algorithm $\mathcal{A}$, where $\alpha \leftarrow \mathbb{Z}_n^*$ and q is a positive integer.*

Definition 6. Decisional Composite Residuosity (DCR) Assumption
[14]: *On the input 1^κ, let the algorithm $\mathcal{R}Gen$ generates an RSA modulus $n = PQ$, where P and Q are distinct primes. The DCR assumption states that for an RSA modulus n, it is hard to distinguish a random element u of $\mathbb{Z}_{n^2}$ from a random element of the subgroup $\{x^n | x \in \mathbb{Z}_{n^2}^*\}$ of nth-residues modulo n^2 for every PPT algorithm $\mathcal{A}$.*

2.2 Homomorphic Encryption [3]

The semantically secure version of Camenisch-Shoup additively homomorphic encryption $\mathcal{HE} = (\mathsf{Setup}, \mathsf{KGen}, \mathsf{Enc}, \mathsf{Dec})$ works as follows:

Setup. On input 1^κ, a trusted third party outputs public parameter par$=(n, g)$, where $n = PQ$, $P = 2p_1 + 1$, $Q = 2q_1 + 1$, $|p_1| = |q_1| = \kappa$, P, Q, p_1, q_1 are all primes and g is a generator of cyclic subgroup $\mathbb{G}$ of $\mathbb{Z}_{n^2}^*$ of order $\bar{n} = p_1 q_1$.
KGen. Let $h = n + 1$. User chooses $x \leftarrow \mathbb{Z}_{\lfloor n/4 \rfloor}$, computes $y = g^x$, and sets $pk = (n, g, h, y)$ as his public key and retains $sk = x$ as his secret key.
Enc. Encryptor encrypts a message $m \in \mathbb{Z}_n$ using the public key $pk = (n, g, h, y)$ by picking $r \leftarrow \mathbb{Z}_{\lfloor n/4 \rfloor}$ and outputs $C_m = \mathsf{Enc}_{pk}(m) = (u = g^r, e = y^r h^m)$ as the corresponding ciphertext.
Dec. Decryptor has the the secret key $sk = x$. On receiving the ciphertext $C_m = (u = g^r, e = y^r h^m)$, the decryptor computes $\hat{m} = (e/u^x)^2$. If $\hat{m}$ does not belong to $\langle h \rangle$, the subgroup generated by $h = n + 1$ of order n i.e., if n does not divides $\hat{m} - 1$, reject the ciphertext. Otherwise, set $\overline{m} = \frac{\hat{m}-1}{n}$, recover $m = \overline{m}/2 \bmod n = \mathsf{Dec}_{sk}(C_m)$.

Semantic security of the encryption $\mathcal{HE}$ holds under the DCR assumption on $\mathbb{Z}_{n^2}^*$. The encryption scheme $\mathcal{HE}$ is also a verifiable encryption scheme [3].

2.3 Verifiable Encryption [3]

We describe below a CCA2-secure verifiable encryption scheme $\mathcal{VE} = (\mathsf{Setup}, \mathsf{KGen}, \mathsf{Enc}, \mathsf{Dec})$ over composite order group, where DDH problem is hard. This is a variant of Cramer-Shoup cryptosystem [6] over prime order group.

Setup. On input 1^κ, a trusted third party outputs a public parameter parm$=(n, g, \widehat{g}, H)$, where $n = PQ$, $P = 2p_1 + 1$, $Q = 2q_1 + 1$, $|p_1| = |q_1| = \kappa$, P, Q, p_1, q_1 are all primes, $g, \widehat{g}$ are generators of cyclic subgroup $\mathbb{G}$ of $\mathbb{Z}_{n^2}^*$ of order $\bar{n} = p_1 q_1$ and $H : \{0,1\}^* \to \mathbb{Z}_j$ is a cryptographically secure hash function with $j \leq \lfloor n/4 \rfloor$.

KGen. User chooses $u_1, u_2, v_1, v_2, w \hookleftarrow \mathbb{Z}_{\lfloor n/4 \rfloor}$, computes $a = g^{u_1} \widehat{g}^{u_2}, b = g^{v_1} \widehat{g}^{v_2}$, $c = g^{w_1}$, publishes $pk = (n, g, \widehat{g}, a, b, c)$ as his public key and keeps $sk = (u_1, u_2, v_1, v_2, w_1)$ secret to himself.

Enc. To encrypt a message $m \in \mathbb{G}$ using public key $pk = (n, g, \widehat{g}, a, b, c)$, encryptor picks $z \hookleftarrow \mathbb{Z}_{\lfloor n/4 \rfloor}$ and sets $e_1 = g^z, e_2 = \widehat{g}^z, e_3 = c^z m$, constructs a label $L \in \{0,1\}^*$ using information that are available to both encryptor and decryptor, computes $\rho = H(e_1, e_2, e_3, L)$, sets $e_4 = a^z b^{z\rho}$, and sends the ciphertext (e_1, e_2, e_3, e_4).

Dec. On receiving ciphertext (e_1, e_2, e_3, e_4), decryptor computes $\rho = H(e_1, e_2, e_3, L)$ and then verifies $e_1^{u_1} e_2^{u_2} (e_1^{v_1} e_2^{v_2})^\rho = e_4$ using secret key $sk = (u_1, u_2, v_1, v_2, w_1)$. If the verification succeeds, then he recovers the message m by computing $e_3/(e_1^{w_1}) = c^z m/g^{zw_1} = g^{zw_1} m/g^{zw_1} = m$.

2.4 Zero-Knowledge Proof of Knowledge [1]

We describe below a general construction of zero-knowledge proofs of knowledge, denoted by

$$\mathsf{PoK}\{(\alpha_1, \alpha_2, \ldots, \alpha_l) \mid \wedge_{i=1}^m X_i = f_i(\alpha_1, \alpha_2, \ldots, \alpha_l)\}, \tag{1}$$

where the prover wants to prove the knowledge of $(\alpha_1, \alpha_2, \ldots, \alpha_l)$ to the verifier by sending the commitments $X_i = f_i(\alpha_1, \alpha_2, \ldots, \alpha_l), i = 1, 2, \ldots, m$ such that extracting $(\alpha_1, \alpha_2, \ldots, \alpha_l)$ from $X_1, X_2, \ldots, X_m$ is infeasible for anyone. For each $i = 1, 2, \ldots, m$, f_i is publicly computable linear function from $\mathcal{X}^l$ to $\mathcal{Y}$, where $\mathcal{X}$ is additive set and $\mathcal{Y}$ is multiplicative set. The verification of the proof is done by executing the following steps:

1. The prover chooses $v_1, v_2, \ldots, v_l$ and sends the commitments $\overline{X}_i = f_i(v_1, v_2, \ldots, v_l), i = 1, 2, \ldots, m$ to the verifier.
2. The verifier sends a challenge $c \in \mathcal{X}$ to the prover.
3. For each $j = 1, 2, \ldots, l$, prover sets $r_j = v_j + c\alpha_j$ and sends the response $(r_1, r_2, \ldots, r_l)$ to the verifier.
4. The verifier checks whether the relations $f_i(r_1, r_2, \ldots, r_l) = \overline{X}_i X_i^c, i = 1, 2, \ldots, m$ hold or not. If all of them hold, then the verifier accepts it, otherwise rejects it.

3 Protocol

3.1 The mOPRF

Our protocol consists of a **Setup** algorithm, an **mOPRF protocol** and a **Dispute Resolution protocol**. Four parties are involved in the protocol execution – a trusted party, S, R, and an off-line arbiter Ar. The trusted party generates the global parameter by **Setup** algorithm, while S and R engage in mOPRF protocol with their private inputs to compute the following PRF [11]:

$$f_k(x) = \begin{cases} g^{1/(k+x)} & \text{if } gcd(k+x, n) = 1 \\ 1 & \text{otherwise,} \end{cases}$$

where $x \in \{0,1\}^{|q|}$ is the private input of R and $k \in \mathbb{Z}_n^*$ is the private input of S. This PRF is secure under the Decisional q-DHI assumption. The arbiter Ar participates in the protocol only when a corrupted player prematurely aborts the protocol in order to recover the output for the honest party. The arbiter Ar resolves disputes without knowing the private information of the two parties and correctly carries out the instructions. In the following discussion, we use the notation $C_m^{(U)}$ to denote the ciphertext generated from the plaintext m under the public key of user U using encryption scheme $\mathcal{HE}$. Moreover, $(C_{m_1}^{(U)})^{\lambda_1}(C_{m_2}^{(U)})^{\lambda_2} = C_{\lambda_1 m_1 + \lambda_2 m_2}^{(U)}$ for some scalars λ_1, λ_2, since the underlying encryption scheme used to generate the ciphertext is additively homomorphic. We define $u^\lambda = (u_1^\lambda, u_2^\lambda, \ldots, u_l^\lambda)$ for a tuple $u = (u_1, u_2, \ldots, u_l)$.

Setup: Our construction uses the additively homomorphic verifiable encryption scheme $\mathcal{HE}$ and the verifiable encryption scheme $\mathcal{VE}$ described in Sects. 2.2 and 2.3 respectively. The trusted party generates the global parameter

$$\text{parm} = (n, g, \widehat{g}, H) \leftarrow \mathcal{VE}.\text{Setup},$$

where $n = PQ$, $P = 2p_1 + 1$, $Q = 2q_1 + 1$, $|p_1| = |q_1| = \kappa$, P, Q, p_1, q_1 are all primes, $g, \widehat{g}$ are generators of cyclic subgroup $\mathbb{G}$ of $\mathbb{Z}_{n^2}^*$ of order $\bar{n} = p_1 q_1$ and $H : \{0,1\}^* \rightarrow \mathbb{Z}_j$ is a cryptographically secure hash function with $j \leq \lfloor n/4 \rfloor$. The off-line arbiter Ar generates a key pair $(pk_{Ar}, sk_{Ar}) \leftarrow \mathcal{VE}.\text{KGen}$ and reveals the public key $pk_{Ar} = (n, g, \widehat{g}, a, b, c)$ through the trusted third party who works as certifying authority in this case. Ar then keeps the secret key $sk_{Ar} = (u_1, u_2, v_1, v_2, w_1)$ as secret. Both the parties S and R will use the Pedersen commitment [15] to commit their private values. The commitment of an element x is defined as $\text{Com}_x = c^{Z_x} g^x$ for some $Z_x \hookleftarrow \mathbb{Z}_{\lfloor n/4 \rfloor}$, where c is the component of the public key $pk_{Ar} = (n, g, \widehat{g}, a, b, c)$ of the arbiter Ar.

mOPRF Protocol: The parties S and R have the common inputs parm, $\text{Com}_k = c^{Z_k} g^k, \text{Com}_x = c^{Z_x} g^x$, where $Z_x, Z_k \hookleftarrow \mathbb{Z}_{\lfloor n/4 \rfloor}$. In Fig. 1, the communication flow of our mOPRF protocol is given. The interaction between S and R is as follows:

–*Step* 1. The party S generates a key pair (pk_S, sk_S), ciphertext $C_k^{(S)}$ and proof π_1 as follows by selecting $r_1, x_1 \hookleftarrow \mathbb{Z}_{\lfloor n/4 \rfloor}$:

(i) $(pk_S = (n, g, h, y_1 = g^{x_1}), sk_S = x_1) \leftarrow \mathcal{HE}.\text{KGen}$,

(ii) $C_k^{(S)} = \mathcal{HE}.\text{Enc}_{pk_S}(k) = (u_1 = g^{r_1}, e_1 = y_1^{r_1} h^k)$,

(iii) $\pi_1 = \text{PoK}\{(r_1, k, Z_k) | (u_1 = g^{r_1}) \wedge (e_1 = y_1^{r_1} h^k) \wedge (\text{Com}_k = c^{Z_k} g^k)\}$. (2)

S sends $(pk_S, C_k^{(S)}, \pi_1)$ to R.

–*Step* 2. On receiving $(pk_S, C_k^{(S)} = (u_1, e_1), \pi_1)$, R verifies π_1 by interacting with S as explained in Sect. 2.4. If verification fails then R aborts. Otherwise, R generates a key pair (pk_R, sk_R), ciphertexts $C_a^{(R)}, C_x^{(S)}, C_\beta^{(S)}$ and proof π_2 as follows, where $a \hookleftarrow \mathbb{Z}_n^*$, $r_2, r_3, x_2 \hookleftarrow \mathbb{Z}_{\lfloor n/4 \rfloor}$ are selected by R, x is the private input of R and $\beta = a(k + x)$ implicitly:

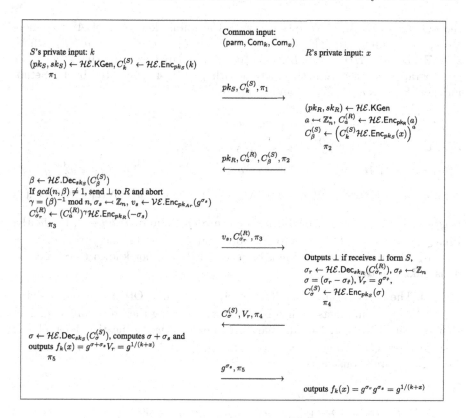

Fig. 1. : Communication flow of our mOPRF

(i) $(pk_R = (n, g, h, y_2 = g^{x_2}), sk_R = x_2) \leftarrow \mathcal{HE}.\mathsf{KGen}$,

(ii) $C_a^{(R)} = \mathcal{HE}.\mathsf{Enc}_{pk_R}(a) = (u_2 = g^{r_2}, e_2 = y_2^{r_2} h^a)$,

(iii) $C_x^{(S)} = \mathcal{HE}.\mathsf{Enc}_{pk_S}(x) = (u_3 = g^{r_3}, e_3 = y_1^{r_3} h^x)$,

(iv) $C_\beta^{(S)} = (C_k^{(S)} C_x^{(S)})^a = (u_4 = (u_1 u_3)^a = u_1^a g^{a r_3}, e_4 = (e_1 e_3)^a = e_1^a y_1^{a r_3} h^{ax})$,

(v) $\pi_2 = \mathsf{PoK}\{(r_2, a, r_3, x, Z_x) | (u_2 = g^{r_2}) \wedge (e_2 = y_2^{r_2} h^a) \wedge (u_4 = u_1^a g^{a r_3})$

$\wedge (e_4 = e_1^a y_1^{a r_3} h^{ax}) \wedge (\mathsf{Com}_x = c^{Z_x} g^x)\}.$ (3)

R sends $(pk_R, C_a^{(R)}, C_\beta^{(S)}, \pi_2)$ to S. Note that $C_\beta^{(S)}$ is an encryption of $\beta = a(k + x)$ generated by R under the public key pk_S of S although β is explicitly not known to R Fig. 1.

–*Step* 3. The party S, on receiving $(pk_R, C_a^{(R)}, C_\beta^{(S)}, \pi_2)$ from R, checks the validity of the proof π_2 in the similar manner as discussed in Sect. 2.4. S aborts if the verification fails, else S decrypts $C_\beta^{(S)}$ to get $\beta = \mathcal{HE}.\mathsf{Dec}_{sk_S}(C_\beta^{(S)})$. S then checks whether $gcd(n, \beta) = 1$ or not. If not, then S sends a null string $\perp$ to R, outputs $\perp$ and aborts. Note that the probability of $gcd(n, \beta) \neq 1$ is negligible under the factoring assumption. Otherwise, S computes $\gamma = \beta^{-1}$ mod n, chooses $\sigma_s \leftarrow \mathbb{Z}_n$ and encrypts g^{σ_s} with the public key pk_{Ar} of Ar to generate $v_s = \mathcal{VE}.\mathsf{Enc}_{pk_{Ar}}(g^{\sigma_s}) = (t_1 = g^z, t_2 = \widehat{g}^z, t_3 = c^z g^{\sigma_s}, t_4 = a^z b^{z\rho})$, where $z \leftarrow \mathbb{Z}_{\lfloor n/4 \rfloor}, \rho = H(t_1, t_2, t_3, L)$, $L \in \{0,1\}^*$ is a label and $H : \{0,1\}^* \to \mathbb{Z}_j$ is cryptographically secure hash function with $j \leq \lfloor n/4 \rfloor$ generated by $\mathcal{VE}.\mathsf{Setup}$. Further, S picks $r_5 \leftarrow \mathbb{Z}_{\lfloor n/4 \rfloor}$ and computes

(i) $C^{(R)}_{-\sigma_s} = \mathcal{HE}.\mathsf{Enc}_{pk_R}(-\sigma_s) = (u_5 = g^{r_5}, e_5 = y_2^{r_5} h^{-\sigma_s})$,

(ii) $C^{(R)}_{\sigma_r} = (C_a^{(R)})^\gamma C^{(R)}_{-\sigma_s} = (u_6 = u_2^\gamma u_5, e_6 = e_2^\gamma e_5)$,

(iii) $\pi_3 = \mathsf{PoK}\{(\beta, x_1, r_5, \sigma_s, z) | (y_1 = g^{x_1}) \wedge (e_4 h^{-\beta} = u_4^{x_1}) \wedge (u_6 = u_2^{\beta^{-1}} g^{r_5}) \wedge$
$(e_6 = e_2^{\beta^{-1}} y_2^{r_5} h^{-\sigma_s}) \wedge (t_1 = g^z) \wedge (t_2 = \widehat{g}^z) \wedge (t_3 = c^z g^{\sigma_s}) \wedge (t_4 = a^z b^{\rho z})\}$,(4)

where x_1 is the secret key of S generated in *Step 1* and $\sigma_r = a\gamma - \sigma_s$ implicitly. Finally S sends $(v_s, C^{(R)}_{\sigma_r}, \pi_3)$ to R. Note that $C^{(R)}_{\sigma_r}$ is the encryption of $\sigma_r = a\gamma - \sigma_s$ under the public key pk_R of R although a is not known to S, thereby σ_r is unknown to S.

–*Step* 4. The party R outputs $\bot$ if he receives $\bot$ form S. Otherwise, on receiving $(v_s, C^{(R)}_{\sigma_r}, \pi_3)$, R interacts with S to verify π_3 following the procedure similar to that described in Sect. 2.4. The party R aborts if the verification fails, else R first decrypts $C^{(R)}_{\sigma_r}$ to get $\sigma_r = \mathcal{HE}.\mathsf{Dec}_{sk_R}(C^{(R)}_{\sigma_r})$. R chooses $\sigma_{\widehat{r}} \leftarrow \mathbb{Z}_n$, selects $r_7 \leftarrow \mathbb{Z}_{\lfloor n/4 \rfloor}$ and constructs

(i) $V_r = g^{\sigma_{\widehat{r}}}, \sigma = \sigma_r - \sigma_{\widehat{r}}$,

(ii) $C^{(S)}_\sigma = \mathcal{HE}.\mathsf{Enc}_{pk_S}(\sigma) = (u_7 = g^{r_7}, e_7 = y_1^{r_7} h^\sigma)$

(iii) $\pi_4 = \mathsf{PoK}\{(x_2, \sigma_r, r_7, \sigma, \sigma_{\widehat{r}}) | (y_2 = g^{x_2}) \wedge (e_6 h^{-\sigma_r} = u_6^{x_2})$
$\wedge (u_7 = g^{r_7}) \wedge (e_7 = y_1^{r_7} h^\sigma) \wedge (v_r = g^{\sigma_{\widehat{r}}})\}$, (5)

where x_2 is the secret key of R generated in the *Step* 2. R sends $(C^{(S)}_\sigma, V_r, \pi_4)$ to S.

–*Step* 5. On receiving $(C^{(S)}_\sigma, V_r, \pi_4)$ from R, S checks the proof π_4 as usual using the similar technique as discussed in Sect. 2.4. If verification fails, S aborts and wait for the response of Ar in dispute resolution protocol, if any. Otherwise, S decrypts $C^{(S)}_\sigma$ to get $\sigma = \mathcal{HE}.\mathsf{Dec}_{sk_S}(C^{(S)}_\sigma)$. Note that $\sigma = \sigma_r - \sigma_{\widehat{r}} = a\gamma - \sigma_s - \sigma_{\widehat{r}} = a\beta^{-1} - \sigma_s - \sigma_{\widehat{r}} = a(a(k+x)^{-1}) - \sigma_s - \sigma_{\widehat{r}} = 1/(k+x) - \sigma_s - \sigma_{\widehat{r}}$. Using σ_s chosen by S in *Step* 3, σ extracted from $C^{(S)}_\sigma$ and the received value V_r from R, S computes

(i) $f_k(x) = g^{\sigma + \sigma_s} V_r = g^{1/(k+x)}$,

(ii) $\pi_5 = \mathsf{PoK}\{z | (t_1 = g^z) \wedge (t_2 = \widehat{g}^z) \wedge (t_3 = c^z g^{\sigma_s}) \wedge (t_4 = a^z (b^\rho)^z)\}$ (6)

and sends (g^{σ_s}, π_5) to R.

The party R on receiving (g^{σ_s}, π_5), first verifies π_5 by interacting with S following the approach in Sect. 2.4. If the verification succeeds, then using σ_r

extracted from $C_{\sigma_r}^{(R)}$ in *Step 4*, R computes $f_k(x) = g^{\sigma_s} g^{\sigma_r} = g^{\sigma_s} g^{a\gamma - \sigma_s} = g^{a\gamma} = g^{a(a(k+x)^{-1})} = g^{1/(k+x)}$. If R does not get g^{σ_s} from S or the verification of π_5 fails, then R can send a dispute resolution request to Ar to raise a dispute.

Dispute Resolution Protocol: On receiving a dispute resolution request from R, the arbiter Ar interacts with S and R as follows:

–Step 1. The party R sends all the messages sent and received in *Steps* 1–3 of the mOPRF protocol to the arbiter Ar, which in turn checks the consistency between messages and the label. If it does not verify or if the transcript ends before the *Step* 3 of the mOPRF protocol then Ar aborts so that none of S and R gets any advantage. Otherwise, continue with the following steps.

–Step 2. As in *Step* 4 of the mOPRF protocol, the party R decrypts $C_{\sigma_r}^{(R)}$ to recover $\sigma_r = \mathcal{HE}.\mathsf{Dec}_{sk_R}(C_{\sigma_r}^{(R)})$ and chooses $\sigma_{\hat{r}}$ randomly from $\mathbb{Z}_n$. R encrypts $\sigma = \sigma_r - \sigma_{\hat{r}}$ as $C_{\sigma}^{(S)} = \mathcal{HE}.\mathsf{Enc}_{pk_S}(\sigma)$ with the public key pk_S of S, sets $V_r = g^{\sigma_{\hat{r}}}$, π_4 as in Eq. 5 and sends $(C_{\sigma}^{(S)}, V_r, \pi_4)$ to Ar.

–Step 3. On receiving $(C_{\sigma}^{(S)}, V_r, \pi_4)$, Ar verifies π_4 by interacting with R using the similar procedure as in Sect. 2.4. If verification fails, Ar aborts so that none of R and S gets any advantage. Otherwise, Ar sends $C_{\sigma}^{(S)}, V_r = g^{\sigma_{\hat{r}}}$ to S who in turns can compute $f_k(x) = g^{1/(k+x)}$ as in *Step* 5 of the mOPRF protocol. Also Ar decrypts $v_s = \mathcal{VE}.\mathsf{Enc}_{pk_{Ar}}(g^{\sigma_s})$ and sends $g^{\sigma_s} = \mathcal{VE}.\mathsf{Dec}_{sk_{Ar}}(v_s)$ to R, thereby R can compute $f_k(x) = g^{1/(k+x)}$ as in *Step* 5 of our mOPRF protocol. Observe that the arbiter Ar should be unable to compute $f_k(x)$ for a secure mOPRF. In this construction g^{σ_r} is unknown to Ar. Consequently, Ar cannot compute $f_k(x)$ following *Step* 5 of our mOPRF even though Ar has the knowledge of g^{σ_s}.

Complexity: Let Exp stands for number of exponentiations, Inv denotes number of inversions, H represents number of hash query and GE counts number of group elements. In mOPRF protocol S requires 71 Exp, 40 GE, 3 Inv, 1 H and R requires 73 Exp, 35 GE, 1 Inv. On the other hand, in dispute resolution protocol S requires 2 Exp, 1 Inv, R requires 12 Exp, 33 GE and Ar requires 18 Exp, 5 GE, 1 Inv, 1 H. Hence, our mOPRF requires at most 176 Exp and communication overhead is 113 GE.

The Parallel mOPRF: The parallel mOPRF protocol, namely pa-mOPRF composes our proposed mOPRF in parallel between two parties – one party holding k as private input and the other party holding the set $X = \{x_1, x_2, \ldots, x_w\}$ ($w < q$) as private input. One execution of the mOPRF enables each party to compute only one PRF $f_k(x)$ for some $x \in X$ in one round. On the contrary, each party is able to compute the entire set of PRFs $\mathbb{X} = \{f_k(x_1), f_k(x_2), \ldots, f_k(x_w)\}$ at a time by a single run of pa-mOPRF.

3.2   The mPSI

Input: The party S has the private input set $X = \{x_1, x_2, \ldots, x_w\}$ and the party R with the private input set $Y = \{y_1, y_2, \ldots, y_v\}$, where $x_i, y_t \in \{0, 1\}^{|q|}$ for all $i = 1, 2, \ldots, w$ and $t = 1, 2, \ldots, v$ with $w, v < q$.

Auxiliary Inputs: Auxiliary input include the security parameter κ, the polynomial q bounding the lengths of all elements in X and Y, v (the size of Y) and w (the size of X).

Utilizing the proposed pa-mOPRF protocol, S and R executes the following steps to get the intersection $X \cap Y$ in our mPSI protocol.

(a) S chooses $k_1 \leftarrow \mathbb{Z}_n$ and sends $\mathsf{Com}_{k_1} = c^{Z_{k_1}} g^{k_1}$ and $\{\mathsf{Com}_{x_i} = c^{Z_{x_i}} g^{x_i}\}_{i=1}^{w}$ to R, where $Z_{k_1}, \{Z_{x_i}\}_{i=1}^{w}$ are randomly chosen from $\mathbb{Z}_{\lfloor n/4 \rfloor}$ and $c = g_1^w$ is a component of the public key $pk = (n, g, \widehat{g}, a, b, c)$ of the arbiter Ar.

(b) R chooses $k_2 \leftarrow \mathbb{Z}_n$ and sends $\mathsf{Com}_{k_2} = c^{Z_{k_2}} g^{k_2}$ and $\{\mathsf{Com}_{y_t} = c^{Z_{y_t}} g^{y_t}\}_{t=1}^{v}$ to S, where $Z_{k_2}, \{Z_{y_t}\}_{t=1}^{v}$ are randomly chosen from $\mathbb{Z}_{\lfloor n/4 \rfloor}$.

(c) The parties S and R involve in a pa-mOPRF protocol with S's input k_1 and R's input $\widehat{Y} = \{k_2 + y_1, k_2 + y_2, \ldots, k_2 + y_v\}$. They generate individually the set $\overline{Y} = \{\bar{y}_1, \bar{y}_2, \ldots, \bar{y}_v\}$, where $\bar{y}_t = g^{1/(k_1 + k_2 + y_t)}, t = 1, 2, \ldots, v$.

(d) The parties S and R again involve in pa-mOPRF protocol with R's input k_2 and S's input $\widehat{X} = \{k_1 + x_1, k_1 + x_2, \ldots, k_1 + x_w\}$ and generate individually the set $\overline{X} = \{\bar{x}_1, \bar{x}_2, \ldots, \bar{x}_w\}$, where $\bar{x}_i = g^{1/(k_1 + k_2 + x_i)}, i = 1, 2, \ldots, w$.

(e) S compares $\overline{X}, \overline{Y}$ for common elements and outputs $\{x_i \in X | \bar{x}_i \in \overline{Y}, i = 1, 2, \ldots, w\} = X \cap Y$. Similarly, R matches the set $\overline{X}$ with $\overline{Y}$ and outputs $\{y_t \in Y | \bar{y}_t \in \overline{X}, t = 1, 2, \ldots, v\} = X \cap Y$.

Correctness of our mPSI protocol follows from the following facts: $x_i \in X \cap Y$ iff $\bar{x}_i \in \overline{Y}$ iff $\bar{x}_i \in \overline{X} \cap \overline{Y}$ and $y_t \in X \cap Y$ iff $\bar{y}_t \in \overline{X}$ iff $\bar{y}_t \in \overline{X} \cap \overline{Y}$.

4   Security

4.1   Security of mOPRF

Theorem 1. *If the encryption schemes $\mathcal{VE}$ and $\mathcal{HE}$ are semantically secure, the associated proof protocols are zero knowledge proof and the hardness of factoring of safe RSA modulus holds, then the protocol mOPRF presented in Sect. 3.1 is a secure computation protocol for functionality $\mathcal{F}_{\mathsf{mOPRF}} : (k, x) \to (f_k(x), f_k(x))$.*

Proof. Let $\mathcal{C}$ be the adversary that breaks the security of our mOPRF protocol among three parties S, R and Ar in the real model and in the ideal process, there be an incorruptible trusted party T, parties $\bar{S}, \bar{R}, \bar{A}r$ and simulator $\mathcal{SIM}$. In real world a trusted party generates the global parameter $\mathsf{parm} = (n, g, \widehat{g}, H)$ and certifies the public key pk_{Ar} of Ar, whereas in ideal model simulator $\mathcal{SIM}$ does those things. The joint output of $S, R, Ar, \mathcal{C}$ in the real world is denoted by $\mathsf{REAL}_{\mathsf{mOPRF}, \mathcal{C}}(k, x)$ and the joint output of $\bar{S}, \bar{R}, \bar{A}r, \mathcal{SIM}$ in the ideal process is denoted by $\mathsf{IDEAL}_{\mathcal{F}_{\mathsf{mOPRF}}, \mathcal{SIM}}(k, x)$.

• **Case I (When the adversary $\mathcal{C}$ corrupts two parties).**
S and Ar are corrupted. Let $\mathcal{Z}$ be a distinguisher that controls $\mathcal{C}$, feeds the input of the honest party R, and also sees the output of R. Now we will show that $\mathcal{Z}$'s view in the real world ($\mathcal{C}$'s view $+R$'s output) and its view in the idea world ($\mathcal{C}$'s view $+ \bar{R}$'s output) are indistinguishable by presenting a series of

games $\mathbf{G_0}, \mathbf{G_1}, \ldots, \mathbf{G_6}$. Each $\mathbf{G_i}$ modifies $\mathbf{G_{i+1}}$ slightly for $i = 0, 1, \ldots, 6$. We argue that $\mathcal{Z}$'s views in consecutive games are indistinguishable. Let $Pr[\mathbf{G_i}]$ denotes the probability that $\mathcal{Z}$ distinguishes the view of $\mathbf{G_i}$ from the view of real protocol. We denote the simulator in $\mathbf{G_i}$ as S_i.

$\mathbf{G_0}$: The $\mathbf{G_0}$ corresponds to the real world protocol, where the simulator S_0 simulates R and interacts with $\mathcal{C}$. Therefore, $Pr[\mathsf{REAL}_{\mathsf{mOPRF},\mathcal{C}}(k,x)] = Pr[\mathbf{G_0}]$.

$\mathbf{G_1}$: $\mathbf{G_1}$ is same as $\mathbf{G_0}$ except that if the verification of the proof π_1 succeeds, then the simulator S_1 runs the extractor algorithm for π_1 with $\mathcal{C}$ to extract the input k of S such that $\mathsf{Com}_k = c^{Z_k} g^k$. As the proof π_1 satisfies the property simulation soundness, $\mathcal{Z}$'s views in $\mathbf{G_0}$ and $\mathbf{G_1}$ are indistinguishable. Therefore, $|Pr[\mathbf{G_1}] - Pr[\mathbf{G_0}]| \leq \epsilon_1(\kappa)$, where $\epsilon_1(\kappa)$ is a negligible function.

$\mathbf{G_2}$: $\mathbf{G_2}$ is same as $\mathbf{G_1}$ except that if the verification of the proof π_3 succeeds, then the simulator S_2 runs the extractor algorithm for π_3 with $\mathcal{C}$ to extract σ_s. By simulation soundness property of the proof π_3, $\mathcal{Z}$'s views in $\mathbf{G_1}$ and $\mathbf{G_2}$ are indistinguishable. Therefore, there exists a negligible function $\epsilon_2(\kappa)$ such that $|Pr[\mathbf{G_2}] - Pr[\mathbf{G_1}]| \leq \epsilon_2(\kappa)$.

$\mathbf{G_3}$: In this game note that the simulator S_3 knows extracted value k in $\mathbf{G_1}$, extracted value σ_s in $\mathbf{G_2}$ and the input x of R. This game is same as $\mathbf{G_2}$ except that

(a) if $gcd(k + x, n) \neq 1$ in the *Step* 4 of mOPRF protocol, then S_3 outputs $\perp$ as the final output of R,
(b) if the verification of the proof π_5 succeeds, then S_3 outputs $f_k(x) = g^{1/(k+x)}$ as the final output of R,
(c) if the verification of the proof π_5 fails or $\mathcal{C}$ aborts in the mOPRF protocol and S_3 receives an element $v \in \mathbb{G}$ from $\mathcal{C}$ in the dispute resolution protocol, then S_3 outputs $vg^{1/(k+x)-\sigma_s}$ as the final output of R,
(d) if $\mathcal{C}$ aborts in the mOPRF protocol or the verification of the proof π_5 fails and $\mathcal{C}$ aborts in the dispute resolution protocol, then S_3 outputs $\perp$ as the final output of R.

Simulation soundness property of the proof π_5 makes $\mathcal{Z}$'s views in $\mathbf{G_2}$ and $\mathbf{G_3}$ indistinguishable. Therefore, $|Pr[\mathbf{G_3}] - Pr[\mathbf{G_2}]| \leq \epsilon_3(\kappa)$, where $\epsilon_3(\kappa)$ is a negligible function.

$\mathbf{G_4}$: $\mathbf{G_4}$ is same as $\mathbf{G_3}$ except that as long as $gcd(k + x, n) = 1$, the simulator S_4 does the following after extracting k:

(a) $(pk_R, sk_R) \leftarrow \mathcal{HE}.\mathsf{KGen}$,
(b) $\beta \leftarrow \mathbb{Z}_n^*$, $C_\beta^{(S)} = \mathcal{HE}.\mathsf{Enc}_{pk_S}(\beta)$,
(c) sets $a = \beta/(k+x)$, $C_a^{(R)} = \mathcal{HE}.\mathsf{Enc}_{pk_R}(a)$.
(d) sends $(pk_R, C_a^{(R)}, C_\beta^{(S)})$ to $\mathcal{C}$ and simulates the proof π_2.

Note that the probability of $gcd(k + x, n) \neq 1$ is negligible under the factoring assumption. If $gcd(k + x, n) = 1$ then the tuple $(pk_R, C_a^{(R)}, C_\beta^{(S)})$ is distributed identically in $\mathbf{G_3}$ and $\mathbf{G_4}$ as the associated encryption scheme $\mathcal{HE}$ is semantically secure. By zero-knowledge (simulatability) of π_2 and indistinguishability of the tuple $(pk_R, C_a^{(R)}, C_\beta^{(S)})$ in $\mathbf{G_3}$ and $\mathbf{G_4}$ the views of $\mathcal{Z}$ in these two games are indistinguishable. Therefore, there exists a negligible function $\epsilon_4(\kappa)$ such that $|Pr[\mathbf{G_4}] - Pr[\mathbf{G_3}]| \leq \epsilon_4(\kappa)$.

$\mathbf{G_5}$: $\mathbf{G_5}$ is same as $\mathbf{G_4}$ except that in the line (c) of $\mathbf{G_4}$, S_5 replaces a by a random $\bar{a} \hookleftarrow \mathbb{Z}_n^*$. By the semantic security of the encryption scheme $\mathcal{HE}$, $\mathcal{Z}$'s view $\mathbf{G_5}$ and $\mathbf{G_4}$ are indistinguishable. Hence $|Pr[\mathbf{G_5}] - Pr[\mathbf{G_4}]| \leq \epsilon_5(\kappa)$, where $\epsilon_5(\kappa)$ is a negligible function.

$\mathbf{G_6}$: $\mathbf{G_6}$ is same as $\mathbf{G_5}$ except that the simulator S_6 does the following after extracting σ_s:

(a) computes $V = f_k(x)$
(b) $\sigma_{\hat{r}} \hookleftarrow \mathbb{Z}_n$, sets $C_\sigma^{(S)} = \mathcal{HE}.\mathsf{Enc}_{pk_S}(\sigma_{\hat{r}} - \sigma_s)$ and $V_r = f_k(x)/g^{\sigma_{\hat{r}}}$,
(c) sends $(C_\sigma^{(S)}, V_r)$ to $\mathcal{C}$ and simulates the proof π_4.

Since the encryption scheme $\mathcal{HE}$ is semantically secure, the pair $(C_\sigma^{(S)}, V_r)$ is identically distributed in $\mathbf{G_5}$ and $\mathbf{G_6}$. By zero-knowledge (simulatability) of the proof π_4 and indistinguishability of the pair $(C_\sigma^{(S)}, V_r)$ in $\mathbf{G_5}$ and $\mathbf{G_6}$, $\mathcal{Z}$'s view in $\mathbf{G_5}$ and $\mathbf{G_6}$ are indistinguishable. Therefore, there exists a negligible function $\epsilon_6(\kappa)$ such that $|Pr[\mathbf{G_6}] - Pr[\mathbf{G_5}]| \leq \epsilon_6(\kappa)$.

Now we construct the ideal world adversary $\mathcal{SIM}$ that has oracle access to $\mathcal{C}$, simulates the honest party R and controls $\bar{S}$, $\bar{A}r$. $\mathcal{SIM}$ incorporates all steps from $\mathbf{G_6}$.

(i) First $\mathcal{SIM}$ plays the role of trusted party by generating the global parameter $\mathsf{parm} = (n, g, \hat{g}, H)$ and working as certifying authority to get public key pk_{Ar} of Ar. $\mathcal{SIM}$ then invokes $\mathcal{C}$.

(ii) On receiving $(pk_S, C_k^{(S)} = (u_1, e_1), \pi_1)$ from $\mathcal{C}$, $\mathcal{SIM}$ verifies π_1 by interacting with $\mathcal{C}$ as explained in Sect. 2.4. If the verification succeeds, then $\mathcal{SIM}$ runs the extractor algorithm for π_1 with $\mathcal{C}$ to extract k such that $\mathsf{Com}_k = c^{Z_k} g^k$. If not then $\mathcal{SIM}$ instructs $\bar{S}$ to send $\bot$ to T and terminates the execution.

(iii) $\mathcal{SIM}$ generates a key pair $(pk_R, sk_R) \leftarrow \mathcal{HE}.\mathsf{KGen}$ and gives the public key to $\mathcal{C}$.

(iv) $\mathcal{SIM}$ chooses $a, \beta \hookleftarrow \mathbb{Z}_n^*$, sends $C_a^{(R)}$, $C_\beta^{(S)}$ to $\mathcal{C}$ and simulates the proof π_2.

(v) If $\mathcal{SIM}$ receives $\bot$ from $\mathcal{C}$, then $\mathcal{SIM}$ instructs $\bar{S}$ to send $\bot$ to T and terminates the execution. Otherwise, on receiving $(v_s, C_{\sigma r}^{(R)}, \pi_3)$, $\mathcal{SIM}$ checks the validity of the proof π_3 in the similar procedure as described in Sect. 2.4. If the verification succeeds, then $\mathcal{SIM}$ runs the extractor algorithm for π_3 with $\mathcal{C}$ to extract σ_s and instructs $\bar{S}$ to send k to T, $\bar{A}r$ to send $b_s = \circ$ to T. $\mathcal{SIM}$ then receives $f_k(x) = g^{1/(k+x)}$ or $f_k(x) = 1$ (if $gcd(k+x, n) \neq 1$) from T. Note that the probability of $gcd(n, k+x) \neq 1$ is negligible under the factoring assumption. Otherwise, if the verification fails, then $\mathcal{SIM}$ instructs $\bar{S}$ to send $\bot$ to T and terminates the execution.

(vi) $\mathcal{SIM}$ chooses $\sigma_{\hat{r}}$ randomly from $\mathbb{Z}_n$, sets $C_\sigma^{(S)} = \mathcal{HE}.\text{Enc}_{pk_S}(\sigma_{\hat{r}} - \sigma_s)$ and $V_r = f_k(x)/g^{\sigma_{\hat{r}}}$, sends $C_\sigma^{(S)}$ and V_r to $\mathcal{C}$ and simulates the proof π_4. $\mathcal{SIM}$ then executes steps according to $\mathcal{C}$'s reply.

(vii) If $\mathcal{C}$ instructs S to send an element v of the group $\mathbb{G}$, then $\mathcal{SIM}$ verifies the proof π_5. If the verification succeeds then $\mathcal{SIM}$ instructs $\bar{Ar}$ to send $b_r = \circ$, else instructs $\bar{Ar}$ to send $b_r = \perp$ to T. Then $\mathcal{SIM}$ outputs whatever $\mathcal{C}$ outputs and terminates.

(viii) If $\mathcal{C}$ instructs both S and Ar to abort, then $\mathcal{SIM}$ instructs $\bar{Ar}$ to send $b_r = \perp$ to T, outputs whatever $\mathcal{C}$ outputs and terminates.

(ix) If $\mathcal{C}$ instructs S to abort and Ar to send an element v of the group $\mathbb{G}$, then $\mathcal{SIM}$ instructs $\bar{Ar}$ to send $b_r = v(f_k(x)/g^{\sigma_s})$ to T. Then $\mathcal{SIM}$ outputs whatever $\mathcal{C}$ outputs and terminates.

Note that $\mathcal{SIM}$ provides $\mathcal{C}$ the same environment as the simulator S_6 does in $\mathbf{G_6}$. Thus $Pr[\text{IDEAL}_{\mathcal{F}_{\text{mOPRF}},\mathcal{SIM}}(k,x)] = Pr[\mathbf{G_6}]$. Now we have,

$$|Pr[\text{IDEAL}_{\mathcal{F}_{\text{mOPRF}},\mathcal{SIM}}(k,x)] - Pr[\text{REAL}_{\text{mOPRF},\mathcal{C}}(k,x)]| = |Pr[\mathbf{G_6}] - Pr[\mathbf{G_0}]|$$

$$\leq |Pr[\mathbf{G_6}] - Pr[\mathbf{G_5}]| + |Pr[\mathbf{G_5}] - Pr[\mathbf{G_4}]| + |Pr[\mathbf{G_4}] - Pr[\mathbf{G_3}]|$$

$$+|Pr[\mathbf{G_3}] - Pr[\mathbf{G_2}]| + |Pr[\mathbf{G_2}] - Pr[\mathbf{G_1}]| + |Pr[\mathbf{G_1}] - Pr[\mathbf{G_0}]|$$

$$\leq \epsilon_6(\kappa) + \epsilon_5(\kappa) + \epsilon_4(\kappa) + \epsilon_3(\kappa) + \epsilon_2(\kappa) + \epsilon_1(\kappa) = \rho(\kappa), \text{ where}$$

$\rho(\kappa)$ is a negligible function. Hence $\text{IDEAL}_{\mathcal{F}_{\text{mOPRF}},\mathcal{SIM}}(k,x) \equiv^c \text{REAL}_{\text{mOPRF},\mathcal{C}}(k,x)$.

R and Ar are corrupted. Consider a distinguisher $\mathcal{Z}$ that controls $\mathcal{C}$, feeds the input of the S, and also sees the output of S. Now we will prove that $\mathcal{Z}$'s view in the real world ($\mathcal{C}$'s view $+S$'s output) and its view in the idea world ($\mathcal{C}$'s view $+ \bar{S}$'s output) are indistinguishable by presenting a series of games $\mathbf{G_0}, \mathbf{G_1}, \ldots, \mathbf{G_5}$, where each $\mathbf{G_{i+1}}$ modifies $\mathbf{G_i}$ slightly for $i = 0, 1, \ldots, 5$. We argue that $\mathcal{Z}$'s views in two consecutive games are indistinguishable. Let us assume that $\mathcal{Z}$ distinguishes his view of $\mathbf{G_i}$ from the view of real protocol with the probability $Pr[\mathbf{G_i}]$ and S_i be the simulator in $Pr[\mathbf{G_i}]$.

$\mathbf{G_0}$: In this game the simulator S_0 simulates S and interacts with $\mathcal{C}$ exactly as in the real world. Therefore, $Pr[\text{REAL}_{\text{mOPRF},\mathcal{C}}(k,x)] = Pr[\mathbf{G_0}]$.

$\mathbf{G_1}$: $\mathbf{G_1}$ is same as $\mathbf{G_0}$ except that instead of proving π_1 as in $\mathbf{G_0}$, the simulator S_1 simulates the proof. By zero-knowledge (simulatability) of the proof π_1, $\mathcal{Z}$'s views in $\mathbf{G_0}$ and $\mathbf{G_1}$ are indistinguishable. Therefore, there exists a negligible function $\epsilon_1(\kappa)$ such that $|Pr[\mathbf{G_1}] - Pr[\mathbf{G_0}]| \leq \epsilon_1(\kappa)$.

$\mathbf{G_2}$: $\mathbf{G_2}$ is same as $\mathbf{G_1}$ except that if the verification of the proof π_2 succeeds, then the simulator S_2 runs the extractor algorithm for π_2 with $\mathcal{C}$ to extract the input x of R such that $\text{Com}_x = c^{Z_x}g^x$. As the proof π_2 satisfies the property simulation soundness, $\mathcal{Z}$'s views in $\mathbf{G_1}$ and $\mathbf{G_2}$ are indistinguishable. Therefore, $|Pr[\mathbf{G_2}] - Pr[\mathbf{G_1}]| \leq \epsilon_2(\kappa)$, where $\epsilon_2(\kappa)$ is a negligible function.

$\mathbf{G_3}$: In this game note that the simulator S_3 knows k and x. $\mathbf{G_3}$ is same as $\mathbf{G_2}$ except that

(a) if $gcd(k + x, n) \neq 1$, in the *Step* 3 of mOPRF protocol S_3 outputs $\bot$ as the final output of S and aborts,

(b) if the verification of the proof π_4 succeeds, then S_3 outputs $f_k(x) = g^{1/(k+x)}$ as the final output of S,

(c) if the verification of the proof π_4 fails or C aborts the mOPRF protocol and S_3 receives a ciphertext $C_\sigma^{(S)}$ an element $v \in \mathbb{G}$ from C in the dispute resolution protocol, then S_3 outputs $g^{\sigma + \sigma_s}v$ as the final output of S,

(e) if C aborts the mOPRF protocol or the verification of the proof π_4 fails and C aborts in the dispute resolution protocol, then S_3 outputs $\bot$ as the final output of S.

By simulation soundness of the proof π_4, $\mathcal{Z}$'s views in $\mathbf{G_2}$ and $\mathbf{G_3}$ are indistinguishable. Therefore, there exists a negligible function $\epsilon_3(\kappa)$ such that $|Pr[\mathbf{G_3}] - Pr[\mathbf{G_2}]| \leq \epsilon_3(\kappa)$.

$\mathbf{G_4}$: This game is same as $\mathbf{G_3}$ except that the simulator S_4 does the following after extracting x:

(a) computes $V = f_k(x)$; if $V = 1$ i.e., if $gcd(n, \beta) \neq 1$ sends $\bot$ to C and abort.

(b) chooses $\sigma_s \hookleftarrow \mathbb{Z}_n$, sets $v_s = \mathcal{VE}.\text{Enc}_{pk_{Ar}}(f_k(x)/g^{\sigma_s})$, $C_{\sigma_r}^{(R)} = \mathcal{HE}.\text{Enc}_{pk_R}(\sigma_s)$.

(c) sends $(v_s, C_{\sigma_r}^{(R)})$ to C and simulates the proof π_3.

Note that the probability of $gcd(k + x, n) \neq 1$ is negligible under the factoring assumption. If $gcd(k+x, n) = 1$ then the pair $(v_s, C_{\sigma_r}^{(R)})$ is distributed identically in $\mathbf{G_3}$ and $\mathbf{G_4}$ as the associated encryption schemes $\mathcal{VE}$, $\mathcal{HE}$ are semantically secure. By zero-knowledge (simulatability) of π_3 and indistinguishability of the pair $(v_s, C_{\sigma_r}^{(R)})$ in $\mathbf{G_3}$ and $\mathbf{G_4}$ the views of $\mathcal{Z}$ in these two games are indistinguishable. Hence $|Pr[\mathbf{G_4}] - Pr[\mathbf{G_3}]| \leq \epsilon_4(\kappa)$, where $\epsilon_4(\kappa)$ is a negligible function.

$\mathbf{G_5}$: $\mathbf{G_5}$ is same as $\mathbf{G_4}$ except that in *Step* 5 of mOPRF protocol the simulator S_5 sends $f_k(x)/g^{\sigma_s}$ as g^{σ_s} to C and simulates the proof π_5. Then $\mathcal{Z}$'s views in $\mathbf{G_5}$ and $\mathbf{G_4}$ are indistinguishable. Therefore, there exists a negligible function $\epsilon_5(\kappa)$ such that $|Pr[\mathbf{G_5}] - Pr[\mathbf{G_4}]| \leq \epsilon_5(\kappa)$.

Let us construct the ideal world adversary $\mathcal{SIM}$ that has oracle access to C, simulates the honest party S, controls $\bar{R}$, $\bar{A}r$ and incorporates all steps from $\mathbf{G_5}$.

(i) First $\mathcal{SIM}$ plays the role of trusted party by generating the global parameter $\text{parm} = (n, g, \hat{g}, H)$ and working as certifying authority to get public key pk_{Ar} of Ar. $\mathcal{SIM}$ then invokes C.

(ii) $\mathcal{SIM}$ generates a key pair $(pk_S, sk_S) \leftarrow \mathcal{HE}.\text{KGen}$, gives the public key to C.

(iii) $\mathcal{SIM}$ chooses $\bar{k}$ randomly from $\mathbb{Z}_n$, sends $\mathcal{HE}.\text{Enc}_{pk_S}(\bar{k})$ as $C_k^{(S)}$ to C and simulates the proof π_1.

(iv) $\mathcal{SIM}$, on receiving $(pk_R, C_a^{(R)}, C_\beta^{(S)}, \pi_2)$ from C, checks the validity of the proof π_2 in the similar manner as discussed in Sect. 2.4, decrypts $C_\beta^{(S)}$ to get $\beta = \mathcal{HE}.\text{Dec}_{sk_S}(C_\beta^{(S)})$. If $gcd(n, \beta) = 1$ and the verification of the proof π_2 succeeds, then $\mathcal{SIM}$ runs the extractor algorithm for π_2 with C

to extract x such that $\mathsf{Com}_x = c^{Z_x} g^x$. $\mathcal{SIM}$ then instructs $\bar{R}$ to send x to T and instructs $\bar{A}r$ to send $b_r = \circ$ to T. $\mathcal{SIM}$ then receives $f_k(x)$. If $f_k(x) = 1$ i.e., $gcd(n, \beta) \neq 1$ or the verification of the proof π_2 fails, then $\mathcal{SIM}$ instructs $\bar{R}$ to send $\perp$ to T and terminates the execution.

(v) $\mathcal{SIM}$ chooses σ_s randomly from $\mathbb{Z}_n$, sets $C^{(R)}_{\sigma_r} = \mathcal{HE}.\mathsf{Enc}_{pk_R}(\sigma_s)$ and $v_s = \mathcal{VE}.\mathsf{Enc}_{pk_{Ar}}(f_k(x)/g^{\sigma_s})$, sends v_s and $C^{(R)}_{\sigma_r}$ to $\mathcal{C}$ and simulates the proof π_3. Then $\mathcal{SIM}$ executes steps according to $\mathcal{C}$'s replay.

(vi) If $\mathcal{C}$ instructs both R and Ar to abort, then $\mathcal{SIM}$ instructs $\bar{A}r$ to send $b_s = \perp$ to T. Then outputs whatever $\mathcal{C}$ outputs and terminates.

(vii) If $\mathcal{C}$ instructs R to send an element v of the group $\mathbb{G}$ and a ciphertext, then $\mathcal{SIM}$ checks that whether the verification of the proof π_4 succeeds or not. If succeeds then $\mathcal{SIM}$ instructs $\bar{A}r$ to send $b_s = \circ$ to T and sends $f_k(x)/g^{\sigma_s}$ as g^{σ_s} to $\mathcal{C}$ and simulates the proof π_5. If verification fails and $\mathcal{C}$ instructs Ar to abort then $\mathcal{SIM}$ instructs $\bar{A}r$ to send $b_s = \perp$ to T. If verification fails and $\mathcal{C}$ instructs Ar to send an element v of the group $\mathbb{G}$ and a ciphertext then $\mathcal{SIM}$ decrypts the ciphertext to get σ and instructs $\bar{A}r$ to send $b_s = g^{\sigma}(f_k(x)/g^{\sigma_s})v$ to T. Then $\mathcal{SIM}$ outputs whatever $\mathcal{C}$ outputs and terminates.

(viii) If $\mathcal{C}$ instructs R to abort and Ar to send an element v of the group $\mathbb{G}$ and a ciphertext then $\mathcal{SIM}$ decrypts the ciphertext to get σ and instructs $\bar{A}r$ to send $b_s = g^{\sigma}(f_k(x)/g^{\sigma_s})v$ to T. Then $\mathcal{SIM}$ outputs whatever $\mathcal{C}$ outputs and terminates.

Hence the ideal world adversary $\mathcal{SIM}$ provides $\mathcal{C}$ the same simulation as the simulator S_5 as in $\mathbf{G_5}$. Therefore $Pr[\mathsf{IDEAL}_{\mathcal{F}_{\mathsf{mOPRF}},\mathcal{SIM}}(k,x)] = Pr[\mathbf{G_5}]$ and

$$|Pr[\mathsf{IDEAL}_{\mathcal{F}_{\mathsf{mOPRF}},\mathcal{SIM}}(k,x)] - Pr[\mathsf{REAL}_{\mathsf{mOPRF},\mathcal{C}}(k,x)]| = |Pr[\mathbf{G_5}] - Pr[\mathbf{G_0}]|$$

$$\leq |Pr[\mathbf{G_5}]-Pr[\mathbf{G_4}]|+|Pr[\mathbf{G_4}]-Pr[\mathbf{G_3}]|+|Pr[\mathbf{G_3}]-Pr[\mathbf{G_2}]|+|Pr[\mathbf{G_2}]-Pr[\mathbf{G_1}]|$$

$$+|Pr[\mathbf{G_1}] - Pr[\mathbf{G_0}]| \leq \epsilon_5(\kappa) + \epsilon_4(\kappa) + \epsilon_3(\kappa) + \epsilon_2(\kappa) + \epsilon_1(\kappa) = \rho(\kappa), \text{ where}$$

$\rho(\kappa)$ is a negligible function. Thus $\mathsf{IDEAL}_{\mathcal{F}_{\mathsf{mOPRF}},\mathcal{SIM}}(k,x) \equiv^c \mathsf{REAL}_{\mathsf{mOPRF},\mathcal{C}}(k,x)$.
S and R are corrupted. In this case $\mathcal{C}$ has full knowledge of k and x. The encryption scheme used by Ar is semantically secure. Therefore a simulator can always be constructed.

• Case II (When the adversary $\mathcal{C}$ corrupts only one party).

In the case that only Ar is corrupted, Ar is not involved in the protocol because S and R are honest, so it is trivial to construct a simulator. If only S is corrupted the simulator can be constructed as steps (i)–(vi) of the case when S and Ar are corrupted. If only R is corrupted the simulator can be constructed as steps (i)–(v) of the case when R and Ar are corrupted. Arbiter $\bar{A}r$ is honest and always sends $\circ$ to T in each of the cases when only S or R is corrupted.

Since the mOPRF protocol is secure, using standard hybrid arguments [5], we have the following theorem that ensures the security of pa-mOPRF. Due to limited space proofs of Theorem 2 and Theorem 3 will appear in the full version.

Theorem 2. *The* mOPRF *scheme can be securely composed in parallel, provided the zero-knowledge proof systems it uses remain zero-knowledge and simulation-sound under parallel composition.*

Theorem 3. *The* mPSI *is a secure computation protocol for the functionality* $\mathcal{F}_{mPSI} : (X, Y) \rightarrow (X \cap Y, X \cap Y)$ *provided the* pa-mOPRF *is secure.*

5   Conclusion

In this paper, we have presented a mOPRF protocol and using that we have constructed a fair mutual private set intersection protocol secure in the malicious model under standard cryptographic assumptions, with linear complexities. Our protocol is optimistic as fairness is obtained by an off-line trusted third party, arbiter who is semi-trusted in the sense that he cannot get access to private informations of the two parties and he has the capability to correctly carry out the instructions. Our mPSI protocol is more efficient than prior works. In particular, our mPSI protocol is the *first* fair mPSI with *linear* complexities.

References

1. Bellare, M., Goldreich, O.: On defining proofs of knowledge. In: Brickell, E.F. (ed.) CRYPTO 1992. LNCS, vol. 740, pp. 390–420. Springer, Heidelberg (1993)
2. Boneh, D.: The decision Diffie-Hellman problem. In: Buhler, J.P. (ed.) ANTS 1998. LNCS, vol. 1423, pp. 48–63. Springer, Heidelberg (1998)
3. Camenisch, J.L., Shoup, V.: Practical verifiable encryption and decryption of discrete logarithms. In: Boneh, D. (ed.) CRYPTO 2003. LNCS, vol. 2729, pp. 126–144. Springer, Heidelberg (2003)
4. Camenisch, J., Zaverucha, G.M.: Private intersection of certified sets. In: Dingledine, R., Golle, P. (eds.) FC 2009. LNCS, vol. 5628, pp. 108–127. Springer, Heidelberg (2009)
5. Canetti, R.: Security and composition of multiparty cryptographic protocols. J. Cryptol. **13**(1), 143–202 (2000)
6. Cramer, R., Shoup, V.: A practical public key cryptosystem provably secure against adaptive chosen ciphertext attack. In: Krawczyk, H. (ed.) CRYPTO 1998. LNCS, vol. 1462, pp. 13–25. Springer, Heidelberg (1998)
7. De Cristofaro, E., Tsudik, G.: Practical private set intersection protocols with linear complexity. In: Sion, R. (ed.) FC 2010. LNCS, vol. 6052, pp. 143–159. Springer, Heidelberg (2010)
8. Dong, C., Chen, L., Camenisch, J., Russello, G.: Fair private set intersection with a semi-trusted arbiter. In: Wang, L., Shafiq, B. (eds.) DBSec 2013. LNCS, vol. 7964, pp. 128–144. Springer, Heidelberg (2013)
9. Freedman, M.J., Ishai, Y., Pinkas, B., Reingold, O.: Keyword search and oblivious pseudorandom functions. In: Kilian, J. (ed.) TCC 2005. LNCS, vol. 3378, pp. 303–324. Springer, Heidelberg (2005)
10. Goldreich, O., Goldwasser, S., Micali, S.: How to construct random functions. J. ACM (JACM) **33**(4), 792–807 (1986)

11. Jarecki, S., Liu, X.: Efficient oblivious pseudorandom function with applications to adaptive OT and secure computation of set intersection. In: Reingold, O. (ed.) TCC 2009. LNCS, vol. 5444, pp. 577–594. Springer, Heidelberg (2009)
12. Kim, M., Lee, H.T., Cheon, J.H.: Mutual private set intersection with linear complexity. In: Jung, S., Yung, M. (eds.) WISA 2011. LNCS, vol. 7115, pp. 219–231. Springer, Heidelberg (2012)
13. Kissner, L., Song, D.: Privacy-preserving set operations. In: Shoup, V. (ed.) CRYPTO 2005. LNCS, vol. 3621, pp. 241–257. Springer, Heidelberg (2005)
14. Paillier, P.: Public-key cryptosystems based on composite degree residuosity classes. In: Stern, J. (ed.) EUROCRYPT 1999. LNCS, vol. 1592, pp. 223–238. Springer, Heidelberg (1999)
15. Pedersen, T.P.: Non-interactive and information-theoretic secure verifiable secret sharing. In: Feigenbaum, J. (ed.) CRYPTO 1991. LNCS, vol. 576, pp. 129–140. Springer, Heidelberg (1992)

Cryptographic Protocol

Security Analysis of Polynomial Interpolation-Based Distributed Oblivious Transfer Protocols

Christian L.F. Corniaux[(✉)] and Hossein Ghodosi

James Cook University, Townsville 4811, Australia
chris.corniaux@my.jcu.edu.au, hossein.ghodosi@jcu.edu.au

Abstract. In an unconditionally secure *Distributed Oblivious Transfer* (DOT) protocol, a receiver contacts at least k servers to obtain one of the n secrets held by a sender. Once the protocol has been executed, the sender does not know which secret was chosen by the receiver and the receiver has not gained information on the secrets she did not choose. In practical applications, the probability distribution of the secrets may not be uniform, e.g., when DOT protocols are used in auctions, some bids may be more probable than others.

In this kind of scenario, we show that the claim "a party cannot obtain more than a linear combination of secrets" is incorrect; depending on the probability distribution of the secrets, some existing polynomial interpolation-based DOT protocols allow a cheating receiver, or a curious server, who has obtained a linear combination of the secrets to determine all the secrets.

Keywords: Cryptographic protocol · Distributed Oblivious Transfer · Linear combination of secrets · Probability distribution · Unconditional security

1 Introduction

Unconditionally secure *Distributed Oblivious Transfer* (DOT) protocols allow a receiver to obtain one of the n secrets held by a sender (see for example [3,8,9]), like *Oblivious Transfer* (OT) protocols. But, unlike in OT protocols, the sender and the receiver do not directly interact with each other; the sender distributes information on his secrets to m servers and the receiver contacts k of them to collect enough data to determine the secret she wishes to obtain.

The security level of a DOT protocol is characterized by the threshold parameter k, corresponding to the minimum number of servers the receiver has to interact with, to obtain the chosen secret. The protocol itself is composed of two phases. In a first phase (the *set-up phase*), the sender distributes parts — called *shares* — of the secrets to the servers and does not intervene in the rest of the protocol. In a second phase (the *transfer phase*), the receiver selects the index of a secret, sends shares of this index to t servers ($k \leq t \leq m$) and receives back t

© Springer International Publishing Switzerland 2015
J. Lee and J. Kim (Eds.): ICISC 2014, LNCS 8949, pp. 363–380, 2015.
DOI: 10.1007/978-3-319-15943-0_22

shares allowing her to reconstruct the chosen secret. The security of a DOT protocol may be assessed thanks to the following informal security conditions based on definitions given by Blundo, D'Arco, De Santis and Stinson [2,3]:

C_1. Correctness – The receiver is able to determine the chosen secret once she has received information from t contacted servers ($t \geq k$).

C_2. Receiver's privacy – A coalition of up to λ_R servers ($1 \leq \lambda_R \leq k-1$) cannot obtain any information on the choice of the receiver.

C_3. Sender's privacy with respect to λ_S servers and the receiver – A coalition of up to λ_S servers ($1 \leq \lambda_S \leq k-1$) with the receiver does not obtain any information about the secrets before the protocol is executed.

C_4. Sender's privacy with respect to a "greedy" receiver – Once the protocol has been executed, a coalition of up to λ_C dishonest servers ($0 \leq \lambda_C \leq k-1$) and the receiver does not obtain any information about secrets which were not chosen by the receiver. This security condition may be decomposed into two parts; Given the transcript of the interaction with t servers ($t \geq k$),

    $C_{4.1}$. The receiver does not obtain any information about secrets she did not choose ($\lambda_C = 0$).

    $C_{4.2}$. A coalition of up to λ_C dishonest servers and the receiver does not obtain any information about secrets which were not chosen by the receiver ($\lambda_C > 0$).

Blundo et al. [3] define a DOT protocol as *private* if the following security conditions are satisfied: C_1, for $t = k$, C_2, for $\lambda_R = k-1$, C_3, for $\lambda_S = k-1$ and $C_{4.1}$. A DOT protocol is defined as *strongly private* if it is private and if condition $C_{4.2}$ is satisfied for $\lambda_C = k-1$. Blundo et al. have shown that one-round polynomial interpolation-based DOT protocols cannot reach strong privacy, i.e., if $t = k$ and $\lambda_R = k-1$, then condition $C_{4.2}$ cannot be satisfied for $\lambda_C = k-1$ (a round is a set of consistent requests/responses exchanged between the receiver and t servers in the transfer phase). More generally, Nikov, Nikova, Preneel and Vandewalle [9] have demonstrated that the relation $\lambda_R + \lambda_C < k$ needs to be satisfied for conditions C_2 and $C_{4.2}$ to be guaranteed.

In their OT protocol allowing a receiver to obtain one of the n secrets held by a sender, Brassard, Crépeau and Robert [4] note that it should be impossible for the receiver to gain joint information on the secrets held by the sender. This remark is the consequence that, in classical cryptography, shifting the letters of an English message thanks to a secret word is not secure. For example, an adversary can break the Vigenère cryptosystem, which basically produces a cryptogram by shifting the letters of a message according to a secret key, in plain English too. The non-uniform repartition of letters in the original message, and in the key for some variants of Vigenère's cryptosystem, allows an adversary to retrieve both the original text and the key from a cryptogram (*index of coincidence* technique [6] and *Kasiski method* [7]). Aware of this weakness, OT and DOT protocols' designers have taken a great care to construct protocols where receivers cannot learn a linear combination of the secrets held by a sender.

In some instances, where the secrets are elements randomly selected in a finite field, the precaution is useless. But when the probability distribution of each secret is not uniform (like for letters in English messages), the control is essential.

In some polynomial interpolation-based DOT protocols, e.g. [3,8], it is claimed that a party "cannot learn more than a linear combination of secrets". In this paper, we show that such claims are incorrect. Overall, the knowledge of a linear combination of secrets combined with the knowledge of the probability distributions of the same secrets may lead to the knowledge of the secrets themselves. In other words, if a curious server obtains a linear combination of secrets, security condition C_3 cannot be satisfied and similarly, if a curious or malicious receiver obtains a linear combination of secrets, security condition $C_{4.1}$ cannot be satisfied. In addition, we demonstrate that in Blundo et al.'s sparse polynomial interpolation-based DOT protocol, the two techniques preventing the servers and the receiver from learning linear combinations of secrets make the protocol insecure (in spite of Blundo et al.'s claim, security condition $C_{4.1}$ is not satisfied); indeed, only one of the two techniques should be applied to guarantee the security of the protocol.

The organization of the paper is as follows. In Sect. 2 we introduce a few notations and show that the combined knowledge of the probability distributions of secrets and of a linear combination of these secrets may lead to the knowledge of all of them. Then, in Sect. 3, we shortly describe the general form of polynomial interpolation-based DOT protocols and show how in these protocols a receiver is able to obtain a linear combination of secrets. Section 4 is devoted to the analysis of some protocols [1,2,8,9] in the light of the previous section. In Sect. 5, we show that even Blundo et al.'s sparse polynomial interpolation-based DOT protocol [3], designed to protect the sender's privacy against a malicious receiver in presence of honest servers, does not satisfy security condition $C_{4.1}$. Our conclusion follows in Sect. 6.

2   Preliminaries

2.1   Notations and Definitions

The settings of the different DOT protocols described in this paper encompass a sender S who owns n secrets $\omega_1, \omega_2, \ldots, \omega_n$ ($n > 1$), a receiver $\mathcal{R}$ who wishes to learn a secret ω_σ, and m servers S_j ($j \in \mathcal{I}_m$ where $\mathcal{I}_m \subset \mathbb{N}$ is a set of $m \geq 2$ indices).

The protocols require the availability of private communication channels between the sender and the servers and between the receiver and the servers. We assume that these communication channels are secure, i.e., any party is unable to eavesdrop on them and they guarantee that communications cannot be tampered with.

All operations are executed in a finite field $\mathbb{K} = \mathbb{F}_p$ (p prime, $p > 2$). We assume that $p > \max(n, \omega_1, \omega_2, \ldots, \omega_n, m)$. By an abuse of language, a polynomial and its corresponding polynomial function will not be differentiated. We denote $\mathbb{K}^*$ the set $\mathbb{K} \setminus \{0\}$, $[n]$ the set of natural numbers (or elements of the prime finite field $\mathbb{K}$) $\{1, 2, \ldots, n\}$, and δ_i^j the Kronecker's symbol, equal to 0 if

$i \neq j$ and to 1 if $i = j$. If $\boldsymbol{u} = (u_1, u_2, \ldots, u_n)$ and $\boldsymbol{v} = (v_1, v_2, \ldots, v_n)$ are two n-tuples of elements of $\mathbb{K}$, we define $\boldsymbol{u} \bullet \boldsymbol{v} = \sum_{i=1}^{n} u_i \times v_i$.

We also formally define a *quasi-random* polynomial.

Definition 1. *If* $(\mathbb{K}[X], +, \times)$ *is the ring of polynomials over* $\mathbb{K}$ *and* $(\mathbb{K}_d[X], +)$ *the additive group of polynomials of degree at most* d *over* $\mathbb{K}$, *we say that a polynomial* $F = \sum_{i=0}^{d} f_i X^i$ *of* $\mathbb{K}_d[X]$ *is* quasi-random, *if the coefficients* f_i $(1 \leq i \leq d)$ *are randomly selected in* $\mathbb{K}$ *and the constant term* $f_0 \in \mathbb{K}$ *has a predefined value.*

In addition, we denote p_ω the probability mass function associated with the secret ω taken in the finite field $\mathbb{K}$.

2.2   Linear Combination of Two Secrets

In some DOT protocols, e.g. [3,8], it is claimed that the receiver cannot learn more than a linear combination of secrets. Actually, the knowledge of a linear combination of secrets combined with the knowledge of the probability distributions of the same secrets may lead to the knowledge of the secrets themselves, as shown in the following basic example.

Example 1. Let ω_1 and ω_2 be two secrets in the prime finite field $\mathbb{K} = \mathbb{F}_{11}$ with the probability distributions:

$$\begin{cases} p_{\omega_1}(0) = 0.5, p_{\omega_1}(1) = 0.5, p_{\omega_1}(i) = 0 \text{ if } i \neq 0 \text{ and } i \neq 1, \\ p_{\omega_2}(0) = 0.5, p_{\omega_2}(3) = 0.5, p_{\omega_2}(i) = 0 \text{ if } i \neq 0 \text{ and } i \neq 3. \end{cases}$$

We assume that a party is able to determine, for instance, the linear combination $\ell = \omega_2 - \omega_1$. From the probability distributions of the secrets, the only possible values of ℓ are:

$$\begin{cases} 0, & \text{if } \omega_1 = 0 \text{ and } \omega_2 = 0, \\ 3, & \text{if } \omega_1 = 0 \text{ and } \omega_2 = 3, \\ 10, & \text{if } \omega_1 = 1 \text{ and } \omega_2 = 0, \text{ and} \\ 2, & \text{if } \omega_1 = 1 \text{ and } \omega_2 = 3. \end{cases}$$

In this scenario where all the potential values of ℓ are different, the party just has to compare ℓ with the values 0, 3, 10 and 2 to determine the secrets ω_1 and ω_2.

2.3   Linear Combination of Secrets

More generally, we have

Lemma 1. *Let* $\omega_1, \omega_2, \ldots, \omega_n$ *be* n *secrets in* $\mathbb{K} = \mathbb{F}_p$ *(p prime) and* s *be the integer such that* $2^s \leq p < 2^{s+1}$. *If* $n \leq s$ *and* $\ell \in \mathcal{V} = \{0, 1, \ldots, 2^n - 1\} \subset \mathbb{K}$, *there exists probability distributions* $p_{\omega_1}, p_{\omega_2}, \ldots, p_{\omega_n}$ *such that one and only one* n-*tuple of secrets satisfies the linear combination* $\ell = \omega_1 + \omega_2 + \ldots + \omega_n$.

Proof. Given an element ℓ of $\mathbb{K}$ such that $0 \leq \ell \leq 2^n - 1$, we just have to exhibit n probability distributions $p_{\omega_1}, p_{\omega_2}, \ldots, p_{\omega_n}$, such that only one n-tuple $(\omega_1, \omega_2, \ldots, \omega_n)$ allows the linear combination $\ell = \omega_1 + \omega_2 + \ldots + \omega_n$ to be satisfied.

We define the probability distribution of the secret ω_i $(1 \leq i \leq n)$ by

$$p_{\omega_i}(j) = \begin{cases} 0.5, & \text{if } j = 0 \\ 0.5, & \text{if } j = 2^{i-1} \\ 0, & \text{otherwise.} \end{cases}$$

If $\ell \in \mathcal{V}$, let $B^\ell = b_{n-1}^\ell b_{n-2}^\ell \ldots b_1^\ell b_0^\ell$ be the unique binary representation of ℓ. The n-tuple $(b_{n-1}^\ell, b_{n-2}^\ell, \ldots, b_1^\ell, b_0^\ell)$ is denoted β^ℓ and the set $\mathcal{U}$ is defined by $\mathcal{U} = \{\beta^0, \beta^1, \ldots, \beta^{2^n - 1}\}$. We also define the function

$$f : \mathcal{V} \longrightarrow \mathcal{U}$$
$$\ell \longmapsto \beta^\ell$$

The sets $\mathcal{U}$ and $\mathcal{V}$ have the same size (2^n elements) and the function f is injective, since every element $\ell \in \mathcal{V}$ has a unique binary representation; therefore f is bijective. We conclude that for any element $\ell \in \mathcal{V}$, there exist a unique n-tuple $(b_{n-1}^\ell, b_{n-2}^\ell, \ldots, b_1^\ell, b_0^\ell)$ where $b_i^{(\ell)} \in \{0, 1\}$ for $i = 0, 1, \ldots, n-1$ such that ℓ is written as a linear combination of the secrets $\omega_1, \omega_2, \ldots, \omega_n$:

$$\ell = b_{n-1}^\ell \times 2^{n-1} + b_{n-2}^\ell \times 2^{n-2} + \ldots + b_1^\ell \times 2^1 + b_0^\ell \times 2^0$$
$$= \omega_n + \omega_{n-1} + \ldots + \omega_2 + \omega_1$$

We conclude that $\omega_i = b_{i-1}^\ell \times 2^{i-1}$ for $i = 1, 2, \ldots, n$. □

Using this basic result, we review in the next section some polynomial interpolation-based DOT protocols and show that their security is weaker than expected.

3   Polynomial Interpolation-Based DOT Protocols

Each of the existing unconditional secure polynomial interpolation-based DOT protocols, for example [1–3,5,8,9], follows the same principle.

– Before the protocol is executed, some details are made public: the number n of secrets, the threshold parameter k, the sender's privacy parameter λ_S, the sender's strong privacy parameter λ_C, the receiver's privacy parameter λ_R, the meaning of each secret ω_i $(1 \leq i \leq n)$, the joint probability $p_{\omega_1, \omega_2, \ldots, \omega_n}$ of the secrets, the encoding parameter e $(e > 0)$, the encoding function E where $E : [n] \longrightarrow \mathbb{K}^e$ encodes the index chosen by the receiver, the hiding parameter N corresponding to the number of monomials of the hiding polynomial Q (see set-up phase below) before reduction and N e-variate polynomials V_i $(1 \leq i \leq N)$ of $\mathbb{K}[Y_1, Y_2, \ldots, Y_e]$. The degree of the multivariate polynomial V_i is v_i; it is the highest degree of the monomials of V_i, assuming that the degree of a monomial is the sum of the degrees of its variables.

- In the set-up phase, the sender $\mathcal{S}$ generates N quasi-random polynomials U_i ($1 \leq i \leq N$) of $\mathbb{K}_{u_i}[X]$ ($u_i \leq k-1$) such that $\sum_{i=1}^{N} U_i(0)V_i(E(j)) = \omega_j$, for $j = 1, 2, \ldots, n$. The free coefficient of U_i is $U_i(0) = a_{i,0} + \sum_{j=1}^{n} a_{i,j}\omega_j$ where the coefficients $a_{i,j}$ ($0 \leq j \leq n$) are randomly selected in $\mathbb{K}$. Then, $\mathcal{S}$ builds an ($e+1$)-variate polynomial:

$$Q(x, y_1, y_2, \ldots, y_e) = \sum_{i=1}^{N} U_i(x) \times V_i(y_1, y_2, \ldots, y_e),$$

and distributes the N-tuple $\boldsymbol{u}_j = (U_1(j), U_2(j), \ldots, U_N(j))$ to the server S_j ($j \in \mathcal{I}_m$).

- In the oblivious transfer phase, the receiver $\mathcal{R}$ who wishes to obtain the secret ω_σ prepares an e-tuple $E(\sigma) = (q_1, q_2, \ldots, q_e)$ as well as e quasi-random polynomial Z_i ($1 \leq i \leq e$) of $\mathbb{K}_{\lambda_R}[X]$ ($\lambda_R \leq k-1$) such that $Z_i(0) = q_i$. Then, $\mathcal{R}$ selects a subset $\mathcal{I}_t \subset \mathcal{I}_m$ of t indices ($k \leq t \leq m$) and sends to each server S_j ($j \in \mathcal{I}_t$) the request $\boldsymbol{z}_j = (Z_1(j), Z_2(j), \ldots, Z_e(j))$. On reception of $\boldsymbol{z}_j$, S_j calculates and returns $\boldsymbol{u}_j \bullet \boldsymbol{v}_j$ to $\mathcal{R}$, where $\boldsymbol{v}_j = (V_1(\boldsymbol{z}_j), V_2(\boldsymbol{z}_j), \ldots, V_N(\boldsymbol{z}_j))$. Because the relation $u_i + \lambda_R \times v_i \leq k-1$ is satisfied for $i = 1, 2, \ldots, N$, the receiver $\mathcal{R}$ is able to interpolate a polynomial $R \in \mathbb{K}_{k-1}[X]$ from the t pairs ($i_j, \boldsymbol{u}_j \bullet \boldsymbol{v}_j$) and to calculate $\omega_\sigma = R(0)$.

The characteristics of the sparse polynomial interpolation-based DOT protocols analysed hereafter ([1–3,8,9]) are described in Annex A.

We note that if the receiver $\mathcal{R}$ does not follow the protocol and prepares, instead of $E(\sigma)$, the e-tuple ($\gamma_1, \gamma_2, \ldots, \gamma_e$) such that $V_i(\gamma_1, \gamma_2, \ldots \gamma_e) = \alpha_i$ ($1 \leq i \leq N$), then she is able to compute

$$\begin{aligned}
R(0) &= \sum_{i=1}^{N} U_i(0)V_i(\gamma_1, \gamma_2, \ldots, \gamma_e) \\
&= \sum_{i=1}^{N} \left(\alpha_i \left(a_{i,0} + \sum_{j=1}^{n} a_{i,j}\omega_j \right) \right) \\
&= \sum_{i=1}^{N} \alpha_i a_{i,0} + \sum_{j=1}^{n} \left(\sum_{i=1}^{N} \alpha_i a_{i,j} \right) \omega_j
\end{aligned}$$

Consequently, if $\mathcal{R}$ is able to determine an e-tuple ($\gamma_1, \gamma_2, \ldots, \gamma_e$) such that $\sum_{i=1}^{N} \alpha_i a_{i,0} = 0$, she obtains a linear combination of the secrets $\omega_1, \omega_2, \ldots, \omega_n$.

In addition, if the values $\alpha_1, \alpha_2, \ldots, \alpha_N$ resulting from the choice of ($\gamma_1, \gamma_2, \ldots, \gamma_e$) are such that $\sum_{i=1}^{N} \alpha_i a_{i,j} = 1$, for $j = 1, 2, \ldots, n$, then $\mathcal{R}$ is able to establish the environment of the scenario of Sect. 2.3.

4 Weaknesses of Some DOT Protocols

4.1 Protocols Insecure Against Curious Servers

In 2000, Naor and Pinkas [8] introduced a sparse polynomial interpolation-based unconditionally secure DOT protocol where the sender $\mathcal{S}$ holds two secrets ω_1

and ω_2. In this protocol, the hiding parameter N described in Sect. 3 is $N = 2$ and the polynomials U_1 and U_2 are:

$$U_1(x) = \omega_1 + \sum_{i=1}^{k-1} a_{1,i} x^i$$

and

$$U_2(x) = \omega_2 - \omega_1$$

where the coefficients $a_{1,i}$ ($1 \leq i \leq k - 1$) are randomly selected in $\mathbb{K}$ (see Annex A.1). It follows that in the set-up phase, each server S_j ($j \in \mathcal{I}_m$) receives a pair $\boldsymbol{u}_j = (U_1(j), U_2(j) = \omega_2 - \omega_1)$ from $\mathcal{S}$. That is, every server receives a linear combination of secrets and may (see Lemma 1) determine both secrets. Consequently, security condition C_3 is not guaranteed.

The sparse polynomial interpolation-based unconditionally secure DOT protocol proposed by Blundo et al. [2] in 2002 is an extension of Naor and Pinkas's protocol to n secrets $\omega_1, \omega_2, \ldots, \omega_n$ where $n \geq 2$. The hiding parameter is $N = n$, the free coefficient of U_1 is $U_1(0) = \omega_1$ and the free coefficient of U_i ($2 \leq i \leq n$) is $U_i(0) = \omega_i - \omega_1$ (see Annex A.2). Each server S_j ($j \in \mathcal{I}_m$) receives an n-tuple $\boldsymbol{u}_j = (U_1(j), \omega_2 - \omega_1, \omega_3 - \omega_1, \ldots, \omega_n - \omega_1)$ in the set-up phase and thus holds linear combinations of the secrets. Again, according to Lemma 1, each server may determine all the secrets of the sender and security condition C_3 is not satisfied.

Another polynomial interpolation-based unconditionally secure DOT protocol was introduced in 2002 by Nikov et al. [9]. In this protocol, like in Blundo et al.'s protocol, the hiding parameter is $N = n$, the free coefficient of U_1 is $U_1(0) = \omega_1$ and the free coefficient of U_i ($2 \leq i \leq n$) is $U_i(0) = \omega_i - \omega_1$. The polynomial U_1 belongs to $\mathbb{K}_{k-1}[X]$ and the polynomials $U_2, U_3, \ldots, U_n$ belong to $\mathbb{K}_{\lambda_C}[X]$ (see Annex A.4). We note that if $\lambda_S = \lambda_C = 0$, which is not allowed with our security model since $\lambda_S \geq 1$ (see security parameters in Sect. 1), each server S_j ($j \in \mathcal{I}_m$) receives an n-tuple $\boldsymbol{u}_j = (U_1(j), \omega_2 - \omega_1, \omega_3 - \omega_1, \ldots, \omega_n - \omega_1)$ in the set-up phase. Again, according to Lemma 1, each server may determine all the secrets of the sender.

Similarly, in the interpolation-based unconditionally secure DOT protocol constructed from a private information retrieval protocol presented by Beimel, Chee, Wang and Zhang [1], each server may determine all the secrets of the sender if $\lambda_S = \lambda_C = 0$. In this case, the hiding parameter is $N = n + 1$, the free coefficient of U_1 is $U_1(0) = a_{1,0}$, a random element of $\mathbb{K}$ and the free coefficient of U_i ($2 \leq i \leq n+1$) is $U_i(0) = \omega_{i-1} - a_{1,0}$. The polynomial U_1 belongs to $\mathbb{K}_{k-1}[X]$ and the polynomials $U_2, U_3, \ldots, U_n$ belong to $\mathbb{K}_{\lambda_C}[X]$ (see Annex A.5). Again, in our security model, security condition C_3 is not guaranteed.

4.2   Protocols Insecure Against a Greedy Receiver

In the sparse polynomial interpolation-based unconditionally secure DOT protocol introduced by Naor and Pinkas [8], the encoding function is $E(\sigma) = \left(1, \delta_\sigma^1\right)$

and the polynomials V_1 and V_2 are $V_1(y_1, y_2) = 1$ and $V_2(y_1, y_2) = y_2$. As mentioned in the previous section, the free coefficient of U_1 is $U_1(0) = \omega_1$. If a cheating receiver sends a request[1] $z_j = (1, 1/2)$ to each server S_j ($j \in \mathcal{I}_t$), it receives back $\sum_{i=1}^{2} U_i(j)V_i(z_j) = U_1(j) + 1/2(\omega_2 - \omega_1)$. Interpolating a polynomial R from $t \geq k$ collected values, the receiver calculates $R(0) = U_1(0) + 1/2(\omega_2 - \omega_1) = 1/2(\omega_2 + \omega_1)$. From this linear combination, the receiver may (see Lemma 1) determine both secrets. Consequently, security condition $C_{4.1}$ is not guaranteed.

The insecurity is the same in Blundo et al.'s protocol [2]; the receiver sends the n-tuple request $z_j = (1, 1/n, 1/n, \ldots, 1/n)$ to each server S_j ($j \in \mathcal{I}_t$). The linear combination determined by the receiver is then $R(0) = 1/n \sum_{i=1}^{n} \omega_i$. Like in Naor and Pinkas's protocol, security condition $C_{4.1}$ is not guaranteed.

In the DOT protocol introduced by Nikov et al. [9], the free coefficient of U_1 is $U_1(0) = \omega_1$ and the free coefficient of U_i ($2 \leq i \leq n$) is $U_i(0) = \omega_i - \omega_1$, exactly like in Blundo et al.'s protocol. Therefore, with the same n-tuple request $z_j = (1, 1/n, 1/n, \ldots, 1/n)$ as above sent to servers S_j ($j \in \mathcal{I}_t$), the receiver determines a linear combination $R(0) = 1/n \sum_{i=1}^{n} \omega_i$ and security condition $C_{4.1}$ is not guaranteed.

The polynomial interpolation-based unconditionally secure DOT protocol designed by Beimel et al. [1] assumes a semi-honest security model: the receiver may be curious but has to follow the protocol. Thus, in this model, security condition $C_{4.1}$ is guaranteed.

5   A More Robust Protocol

In [3], Blundo et al. have ameliorated the protocol presented in [2] to prevent (1) the servers and (2) the receiver from learning a linear combination of secrets. We show below that in spite of three different improvements, the protocol is still insecure regarding a greedy receiver.

5.1   First Improvement

To prevent servers from receiving a linear combination of secrets (see Sect. 4.1), each secret ω_i ($2 \leq i \leq n$) is multiplicatively masked by an element r_i randomly selected in $\mathbb{K}$. More precisely, in the set-up phase, the sender S randomly selects $n - 1$ masks $r_2, r_3, \ldots, r_n$ in $\mathbb{K}$ and generates an $(n + 1)$-variate polynomial

$$Q(x, y_1, y_2, \ldots, y_n) = \sum_{i=1}^{n} U_i(x) \times V_i(y_1, y_2, \ldots, y_n),$$

where

- U_1 is a quasi-random polynomial of $\mathbb{K}_{k-1}[X]$ such that $U_1(0) = \omega_1$,
- U_i is a constant polynomial defined as $U_i(x) = r_i \omega_i - \omega_1$, for $i = 2, 3, \ldots, n$, and

---

[1] Because the first term is constant and public, it is not included in the request.

– V_i is an n-variate polynomial defined as $V_i(y_1, y_2, \ldots, y_n) = y_i$, for $i = 1, 2, \ldots, n$.

In the set-up phase, each server S_j ($j \in \mathcal{I}_m$) receives from the sender $\mathcal{S}$ an n-tuple $\boldsymbol{u}_j = (U_1(j), r_2\omega_2 - \omega_1, r_3\omega_3 - \omega_1, \ldots, r_n\omega_n - \omega_1)$, but also shares, generated by Shamir's secret sharing scheme [10], of $r_2, r_3, \ldots, r_n$.

In the oblivious transfer phase, the receiver $\mathcal{R}$ selects the index $\sigma \in [n]$ of the secret she wishes to obtain, as well as a set $\mathcal{I}_k \subset \mathcal{I}_m$ of k servers' indices. Then, she prepares an n-tuple $\boldsymbol{z}_j = (1, Z_2(j), Z_3(j), \ldots, Z_n(j))$ where Z_i ($2 \leq i \leq n$) is a quasi-random polynomial of $\mathbb{K}_{k-1}[X]$ such that $Z_i(0) = \delta_\sigma^i$. When a server S_j ($S_j \in \mathcal{I}_k$) receives a request $\boldsymbol{z}_j$, it calculates $\boldsymbol{v}_j = \boldsymbol{z}_j$ and returns to $\mathcal{R}$ not only $\boldsymbol{u}_j \bullet \boldsymbol{v}_j$ but also its shares of $r_2, r_3, \ldots, r_n$. From the collected k responses, $\mathcal{R}$ interpolates a polynomial R and calculates $r_\sigma\omega_\sigma = R(0)$ if $\sigma \neq 1$ or $\omega_1 = R(0)$ if $\sigma = 1$. If the former case, $\mathcal{R}$ also calculates r_σ from the collected shares and with a simple division the chosen secret, ω_σ.

We note that (1) the masks r_i ($2 \leq i \leq n$) may be nil since they are selected in $\mathbb{K}$ and that (2) ω_1 is not masked.

Thus, if $n = 2$, each server S_j ($j \in \mathcal{I}_m$) receives a pair $\boldsymbol{u}_j = (U_1(j), r_2\omega_2 - \omega_1)$ in the set-up phase. It is clear that if $\mathcal{R}$ wishes to obtain ω_2 and if $r_2 = 0$, after collecting k shares, she will determine $r_2\omega_2 = R(0) = 0$ and will be unable to calculate the value of ω_2. Therefore, the correctness (security condition C_1) of the protocol is not guaranteed; it follows that multiplicative masks $r_2, r_3, \ldots, r_n$ need to be selected in $\mathbb{K}^*$ and not in $\mathbb{K}$.

In addition, not masking ω_1 may provide the servers with information on ω_1 like shown in the following example.

Example 2. In the prime finite field $\mathbb{K} = \mathbb{F}_{11}$, we assume that $n = 2$ and that the probability distributions of ω_1 and ω_2 are:

$$\begin{cases} p_{\omega_1}(0) = 0.5, p_{\omega_1}(1) = 0.5, p_{\omega_1}(i) = 0 \text{ if } i \neq 0 \text{ and } i \neq 1, \\ p_{\omega_2}(1) = 0.5, p_{\omega_2}(3) = 0.5, p_{\omega_2}(i) = 0 \text{ if } i \neq 1 \text{ and } i \neq 3. \end{cases}$$

If the value received by the server S_j ($j \in \mathcal{I}_m$) in the set-up phase for $U_2(j) = r_2\omega_2 - \omega_1$ is 0, S_j is able to infer that $\omega_1 \neq 0$, hence $\omega_1 = 1$, because $r_2\omega_2 = \omega_1$, $r_2 \neq 0$ ($r_2 \in \mathbb{K}^*$ like shown above), $\omega_2 \neq 0$ ($\omega_2 = 1$ or $\omega_2 = 3$), and $\mathbb{K}$ is a field and consequently an integral domain.

It follows that in the sub-protocol presented by Blundo et al., the secret ω_1 should be masked like other secrets $\omega_2, \omega_3, \ldots, \omega_n$ and that all masks should be selected in $\mathbb{K}^*$.

We observe that if the use of masks is a good technique to prevent the servers from learning linear combinations of secrets, it does not change the situation of a greedy receiver, since she can determine all the masks. Therefore, once the protocol has been executed, the cheating receiver who has determined a linear combination of masked secrets easily obtains a linear combination of secrets, and from there, possibly all secrets (see Lemma 1). However, an advantage of the masks is that the receiver cannot choose the coefficients of the linear combination of secrets she obtains by cheating. Indeed, each coefficient of the linear combination is the product of a coefficient chosen by the receiver with a mask, unknown from her at the time she prepares requests.

To conclude, the first improvement to Blundo et al.'s DOT protocol is insufficient to guarantee the sender's privacy. This is a contradiction with Blundo et al.'s claim ([3], Sect. 5, p. 350):

> "Notice that, in [8], for the case of two secrets, a proof that the Receiver can get *no more than a single* linear combination of the two secrets by running the sub-protocol described in Fig. 3 with k Servers was given. It is not difficult to show that the proof easily generalizes to our scheme for n secrets, i.e., after receiving information from k servers, the Receiver cannot learn more than a single linear combination of $\omega_1, \omega_2, \ldots, \omega_n$."

This is because, as stated by Lemma 1, the knowledge of a linear combination of secrets and of the probability distribution of the secrets may lead to the knowledge of all secrets.

5.2   Second Improvement

The major problem with the sub-protocol presented by Blundo et al. is that the receiver $\mathcal{R}$ is able to determine a linear combination of secrets, and then, depending on the probability distribution of secrets, the secrets themselves. However, if the secrets have a uniform distribution in the field $\mathbb{K}$, even if $\mathcal{R}$ (resp. a coalition of less than k servers) obtains a linear combination of secrets, she (resp. the coalition) cannot infer any of the secrets. So, the main idea underlying the second improvement is to transform a specific probability distribution into a uniform probability distribution. To this end, using the technique proposed by Naor and Pinkas [8], Blundo et al. have modified the sub-protocol so that it is executed twice: a first time on masks randomly selected in $\mathbb{K}$ (uniform distribution) and a second time on the products of the secrets and of the masks. To guarantee the consistency of receiver's requests, the same request sent by $\mathcal{R}$ to a server is used by the server for both the masks and the masked secrets.

The characteristics of the protocol are given in Annex A.3.

We observe that even if the protocol includes the technique suggested by Naor and Pinkas, the receiver may still obtain, not only a linear combination of secrets, but the secrets themselves (see example in Annex B).

In the demonstration proving that the protocol is secure, even with a greedy receiver (but with honest servers), Blundo et al. require an additional assumption: secrets cannot be identical. This assumption may be satisfied thanks to pads. For example, if q is a prime number such that $q \geq np$, the field $\mathbb{F}_p$ could be replaced with a field $\mathbb{F}_q$ and the pad $(i-1) \times p$ added to secret ω_i $(1 \leq i \leq n)$. We note that this additional assumption decreases the communication performance, since the new field has a cardinality larger than the original one.

However, even with this additional assumption, the claim on the security of the sender is incorrect (Condition (7) of Definition 2.2, p. 329 in [3], is not satisfied) against a greedy receiver. The case is illustrated with the same example (Annex B), because according to the probability distributions chosen in the example, the secrets are necessarily different.

This is actually due to the first improvement which is not taken into account in Blundo et al.'s demonstration. Indeed, Naor and Pinkas demonstrated that the receiver could obtain the system of equations:

$$\begin{cases} \alpha_1 c_1 \omega_1 + \alpha_2 c_2 \omega_2 = R^{(1)}(0) \\ \alpha_1 c_1 + \alpha_2 c_2 = R^{(2)}(0) \end{cases}$$

where coefficients α_1 and α_2 are chosen by the receiver.

It is clear that if $R^{(2)}(0) = 0$, the receiver can infer $c_1 = \dfrac{-\alpha_2}{\alpha_1} c_2$ which, reported in the first equation gives $\alpha_2 c_2(\omega_2 - \omega_1) = R^{(1)}(0)$. Then, if $R^1(0) = 0$, then the receiver can infer the linear combination $\omega_2 - \omega_1 = 0$, because $c_2 \in \mathbb{K}^*$ and α_2 can be chosen different from 0 by the receiver). This explains the additional assumption.

However, in Blundo et al.'s protocol, each secret value is masked according to the first improvement (see Sect. 5.1). Therefore, in the case $n = 2$, the system of equations that the receiver is able to obtain is

$$\begin{cases} \alpha_1 r_1^{(1)} c_1 \omega_1 + \alpha_2 r_2^{(1)} c_2 \omega_2 = R^{(1)}(0) \\ \alpha_1 r_1^{(2)} c_1 + \alpha_2 r_2^{(2)} c_2 = R^{(2)}(0) \end{cases}$$

Again, if we assume that $R^{(2)}(0) = 0$, the receiver can infer $c_1 = \dfrac{-\alpha_2 r_2^{(2)}}{\alpha_1 r_1^{(2)}} c_2$

which, reported in the first equation gives $\alpha_2 c_2(r_2^{(1)} \omega_2 - \dfrac{r_1^{(1)} r_2^{(2)}}{r_1^{(2)}} \omega_1) = R^{(1)}(0)$.

If $R^{(1)}(0) = 0$, then the receiver can infer the linear combination $r_2^{(1)} r_1^{(2)} \omega_2 - r_1^{(1)} r_2^{(2)} \omega_1 = 0$. The coefficients $r_j^{(i)}$ ($i = 1, 2, 1 \leq j \leq n$) being randomly selected in $\mathbb{K}^*$, there is no way to prevent the receiver from obtaining such a linear combination of the secrets.

However, it is easy to see that the first improvement is not useful when the second improvement is applied. Indeed, with the second improvement, servers do not receive linear combinations of secrets, but linear combination of masked secrets (which is the result of the first improvement) and linear combination of random masks. We conclude that only the second improvement of the protocol is necessary.

5.3 Third Improvement

Concerned with the degree of randomness necessary for the protocol, Blundo et al. suggest a simplification of the protocol to save a few random values ([3], Sect. 5, Remark p. 353):

"However, we can show that *the same* random values $a_1, a_2, \ldots, a_{k-1}$ can be used in both instances of *SubDot(.)* and the values $r_2^{(2)}, r_3^{(2)}, \ldots, r_n^{(2)}$ can be computed as a function of $r_2^{(1)}, r_3^{(1)}, \ldots, r_n^{(1)}$."

We show in the following example, that sharing polynomials with the same coefficients $a_1, a_2, \ldots, a_{k-1}$ make the protocol insecure, regarding the sender's privacy.

Example 3. In the prime finite field $\mathbb{K} = \mathbb{F}_5$, we assume that $n = 2$ and that the probability distributions of ω_1 and ω_2 are:

$$\begin{cases} p_{\omega_1}(1) = 0.5, p_{\omega_1}(2) = 0.5, p_{\omega_1}(i) = 0 \text{ if } i \neq 1 \text{ and } i \neq 2, \\ p_{\omega_2}(0) = 0.5, p_{\omega_2}(4) = 0.5, p_{\omega_2}(i) = 0 \text{ if } i \neq 1 \text{ and } i \neq 4. \end{cases}$$

Since the secrets are masked only once (see previous section), we can also assume that

$$U_1^{(1)}(x) = c_1\omega_1 + \sum_{i=1}^{k-1} a_i x^i,$$

$$U_1^{(2)}(x) = c_1 + \sum_{i=1}^{k-1} a_i x^i,$$

$$U_2^{(1)}(x) = c_2\omega_2 - c_1\omega_1,$$

and

$$U_2^{(2)}(x) = c_2 - c_1$$

where $a_1, a_2, \ldots, a_{k-1}$ are randomly selected in $\mathbb{K}$.

In the set-up phase, each server S_j ($j \in \mathcal{I}_m$) receives from the sender S the pair $\boldsymbol{u}_j^{(1)} = (U_1^{(1)}(j), U_2^{(1)}(j))$ (for the masked secrets) as well as the pair $\boldsymbol{u}_j^{(2)} = (U_1^{(2)}(j), U_2^{(2)}(j))$ (for the masks). The server S_j is able to calculate $d_j = U_1^{(1)}(j) - U_1^{(2)}(j) = c_1(\omega_1 - 1)$. We assume that $d_j \neq 0$. Therefore, $\omega_1 - 1 \neq 0$ and so, $\omega_1 = 2$, according to the probability distribution p_{ω_1}. Hence, $c_1 = d_j/(\omega_1 - 1) = d_j$. Moreover, since S_j holds $c_2 - c_1$, the value of c_2 can be determined: $c_2 = (c_2 - c_1) + c_1 = (c_2 - c_1) + d_j$. The server S_j has received $c_2\omega_2 - c_1\omega_1$ from the sender and is able to determine c_1, c_2 and ω_1; To calculate ω_2 is easy. It follows that, given the probability distribution p_{ω_1} described above and assuming that $d_j \neq 0$, every server S_j is able to infer ω_1 and ω_2 in the set-up phase and the sender's privacy is not guaranteed (security condition C_3 is not satisfied).

This weakness extends to a greedy receiver and security condition $C_{4.1}$ could not be satisfied with this improvement. Indeed, if in the oblivious phase the receiver sends the request $\boldsymbol{z}_i = (1, 0)$ to $k-1$ servers S_i ($i \in \mathcal{I}_{k-1} \subset \mathcal{I}_k, |\mathcal{I}_{k-1}| = k - 1$)

and $z_\ell = (1, 1)$ to the kth server S_ℓ ($\ell \in \mathcal{I}_k \setminus \mathcal{I}_{k-1}$), both secrets ω_1 and ω_2 can be determined thanks to the following method (we denote $P(x)$ the polynomial $\sum_{i=1}^{k-1} a_i x^i$):

- First, as soon as $\mathcal{R}$ has received from a server S_j ($j \in \mathcal{I}_{k-1}$) a response $(u_j^{(1)} \bullet v_j, u_j^{(2)} \bullet v_j)$, where $v_j = z_j$, she determines ω_1 with the technique described above. Thus, $\mathcal{R}$ receives $U_1^{(1)}(j) \times 1 + U_2^{(1)}(j) \times 0 = c_1\omega_1 + P(j)$ and $U_1^{(2)}(j) \times 1 + U_2^{(2)}(j) \times 0 = c_1 + P(j)$. She calculates $d_j = u_j^{(1)} \bullet v_j - u_j^{(2)} \bullet v_j = c_1(\omega_1 - 1)$. Because $d_j \neq 0$ and according to the probability distribution p_{ω_1}, $\mathcal{R}$ determines $\omega_1 = 2$. Hence, c_1 can be calculated too.
- Second, $\mathcal{R}$ determines $P(j)$ from the response of S_j: $P(j) = u_j^{(1)} \bullet v_j - c_1\omega_1$. The same operation can be executed from the responses of the other servers of $\mathcal{I}_{k-1}$, and $\mathcal{R}$ obtains $k-1$ values $P(j)$. The free coefficient of P is $P(0) = 0$. So, P may be written under the form $P = xP'$ where the degree of P' is at most $k-2$. With $k-1$ values $1/jP(j)$, the polynomial P' may be interpolated, which allows $\mathcal{R}$ to compute $P = xP'$.
- Finally, from the server S_ℓ, $\mathcal{R}$ obtains

$$(u_\ell^{(1)} \bullet v_\ell, u_\ell^{(2)} \bullet v_\ell) = (c_1\omega_1 + P(\ell) + c_2\omega_2 - c_1\omega_1, c_1 + P(\ell) + c_2 - c_1)$$
$$= (P(\ell) + c_2\omega_2, P(\ell) + c_2)$$

Since P has been computed in the second step, $\mathcal{R}$ is able to calculate c_2 from the second element of the pair and then the second secret, ω_2, from the first element of the pair.

This example shows that if the third improvement is applied, security condition $C_{4.1}$ is not satisfied either.

6   Conclusion

The main result of this paper is that when a party is able to obtain a linear combination of secrets, the sender's privacy (security conditions C_3 and $C_{4.1}$) may not be guaranteed for all secrets distributions. It follows that some weaknesses have been identified in the following polynomial interpolation-based DOT protocols:

- Naor and Pinkas's sparse polynomial interpolation-based protocol [8]: without the technique described in Sect. 4, p. 214, security conditions C_3 and $C_{4.1}$ are not guaranteed (in particular, Theorem 1 is incorrect). If the technique is applied, the size of the secrets space needs to be increased, and hence communication is less efficient (bigger shares need to be exchanged). The weakness is the same in Blundo et al.'s sparse polynomial interpolation-based protocol [2] which extends to n secrets Naor and Pinkas's protocol.

- Nikov et al.'s protocol [9] and Beimel et al.'s protocol [1]: for some values of the protocols' parameters, security condition C_3 is not guaranteed. However, this case is valid in regard to the security models presented by Nikov et al. and Beimel et al.: the protocols are considered as private even though each server holds the sender's secrets, assuming no server colludes with the receiver. On the other hand, Nikov et al.'s protocol [9] cannot guarantee security condition $C_{4.1}$, in spite of the claim of the designers.
- Blundo et al.'s protocol [3]: security condition $C_{4.1}$ is not guaranteed because of the combination of two techniques: the masking of secrets in the underlying sub-protocol and the parallel execution of the protocol on masked secrets and masks. If the masking of secrets in the underlying sub-protocol is removed, the protocol reaches the same level of security as Naor and Pinkas's protocol. In addition, the simplification suggested by Blundo et al. (reuse of the coefficients of the hiding polynomials) is a breach in the sender's security.

We also observe that the DOT protocol introduced by Cheong, Koshiba and Yoshiyama [5] is actually an application of the technique suggested by Naor and Pinkas to Nikov et al's DOT protocol; The level of security of the protocol is the same as in Naor and Pinkas's protocol.

A   Characteristics of Some DOT Protocols

A.1   Naor and Pinkas's DOT [8]

In the sparse polynomial interpolation-based DOT protocol introduced by Naor and Pinkas [8], the number of secrets is $n = 2$, the threshold parameter is k, the sender's privacy and strong privacy parameters are $\lambda_S = k - 1$ and $\lambda_C = 0$, the hiding parameter is $N = 2$ and the encoding parameter is $e = 2$. The encoding function is $E(s) = \left(1, \delta_s^2\right)$ and the polynomials U_i and V_i ($1 \leq i \leq N$) are:

- $U_1(x) = \omega_1 + \sum_{i=1}^{k-1} a_i x^i$, where coefficients a_i are randomly selected in $\mathbb{K}$, and $U_2(x) = \omega_2 - \omega_1$,
- $V_i(y_1, y_2) = y_i$ for $i = 1, 2$.

On the receiver's side, the number of contacted servers is $t = k$, the receiver's privacy parameter is $\lambda_R = k - 1$ and the first element of the encoding function being constant and public, it is not shared (i.e., $Z_1 = 1$) and is not included in the request transmitted by the receiver to the contacted servers.

A.2   Blundo Et Al.'s DOT [2]

The protocol introduced by Blundo, D'Arco, De Santis and Stinson [2] is an extension of Naor and Pinkas's sparse polynomial interpolation-based DOT protocol [8]. Only the following characteristics are different from those described in Appendix A.1.

- $n \geq 2$,
- $N = n$,
- $E(s) = \left(1, \delta_s^2, \delta_s^3, \ldots, \delta_s^n\right)$,
- $U_i(x) = \omega_i - \omega_1$ for $i = 2, 3, \ldots, N$,
- $V_i(y_1, y_2, \ldots, y_e) = y_i$ for $i = 1, 2, \ldots, N$.

A.3   Blundo Et Al.'s DOT [3]

The characteristics of the protocol introduced by Blundo, D'Arco, De Santis and Stinson [3] are similar to those of the protocol they presented in 2002 (see Appendix A.2). However, to improve the protocol, the secrets are masked twice:

- To prevent the servers from learning a linear combination of secrets, each secret ω_i $(2 \leq i \leq n)$ is multiplied by a mask r_i randomly selected in $\mathbb{K}$. Each mask is shared amongst the m servers involved in the protocol, thanks to Shamir's secret sharing schemes [10],
- To prevent the receiver from learning a linear combination of secrets, each secret ω_i $(1 \leq i \leq n)$ is masked with a mask c_i randomly selected in $\mathbb{K}^*$ and the receiver needs, with one request only, to collect shares of the chosen masked secret $c_\sigma \omega_\sigma$, but also of the corresponding mask c_σ.

More specifically, in the set-up phase, the sender $\mathcal{S}$ first selects masks c_i $(1 \leq i \leq n)$ in $\mathbb{K}^*$, which gives him two lists of secret values: $(c_1\omega_1, c_2\omega_2, \ldots, c_n\omega_n)$ and $(c_1, c_2, \ldots, c_n)$. Second, $\mathcal{S}$ selects random masks $r_i^{(1)}$ and $r_i^{(2)}$ $(2 \leq i \leq n)$ in $\mathbb{K}$ and builds two lists $L_1 = \left(c_1\omega_1, r_2^{(1)}c_2\omega_2, r_3^{(1)}c_3\omega_3, \ldots, r_n^{(1)}c_n\omega_n\right)$ and $L_2 = \left(c_1, r_2^{(2)}c_2, r_3^{(2)}c_3, \ldots, r_n^{(2)}c_n\right)$. Then, a set of N polynomials $U_i^{(1)}$ $(1 \leq i \leq N)$ is generated to hide the secrets values of L_1 and another set of of N polynomials $U_i^{(2)}$ $(1 \leq i \leq N)$ is generated to hide the secrets values of L_2:

- $U_1^{(1)}(x) = c_1\omega_1 + \sum_{i=1}^{k-1} a_i^{(1)} x^i$, where coefficients $a_i^{(1)}$ are randomly selected in $\mathbb{K}$, and for $i = 2, 3, \ldots, n$, $U_i^{(1)}(x) = r_i^{(1)}c_i\omega_i - c_1\omega_1$,
- $U_1^{(2)}(x) = c_1 + \sum_{i=1}^{k-1} a_i^{(2)} x^i$, where coefficients $a_i^{(2)}$ are randomly selected in $\mathbb{K}$, and for $i = 2, 3, \ldots, n$, $U_i^{(2)}(x) = r_i^{(2)}c_i - c_1$,

The e-variate polynomials V_i $(i = 1, 2, \ldots, N)$ are the same as those defined in Appendix A.2. Still in the set-up phase, each server S_j $(j \in \mathcal{I}_m)$ receives

$$u_j^{(1)} = \left(U_1^{(1)}(j), r_2^{(1)}c_2\omega_2 - c_1\omega_1, r_3^{(1)}c_3\omega_3 - c_1\omega_1, \ldots, r_n^{(1)}c_n\omega_n - c_1\omega_1\right)$$

and

$$u_j^{(2)} = \left(U_1^{(2)}(j), r_2^{(2)}c_2 - c_1, r_3^{(2)}c_3 - c_1\omega_1, \ldots, r_n^{(2)}c_n - c_1\right),$$

as well as the shares $[r_2^{(1)}]_j, [r_3^{(1)}]_j, \ldots, [r_n^{(1)}]_j$ and $[r_2^{(2)}]_j, [r_3^{(2)}]_j, \ldots, [r_n^{(2)}]_j$ (If $F_t^{(s)}$ is the hiding polynomial determined in Shamir's secret sharing scheme to share $r_t^{(s)}$, the share $F_t^{(s)}(j)$ allocated to server S_j is denoted $[r_t^{(s)}]_j$.)

In the oblivious phase, on reception of the request z_j, a server S_j $(j \in \mathcal{I})$ calculates $v_j = (V_1(z_j), V_2(z_j), \ldots, V_N(z_j))$ and returns $u_j^1 \cdot v_j$ and $u_j^2 \cdot v_j$, with the two sets of $n-1$ shares of $\left(r_2^{(1)}, r_3^{(1)}, \ldots, r_n^{(1)} \right)$ and $\left(r_2^{(2)}, r_3^{(2)}, \ldots, r_n^{(2)} \right)$ to the receiver. From the collected values, $\mathcal{R}$ interpolates two polynomials $R^{(1)}$ and $R^{(2)}$ and, if $\sigma = 1$, calculates $R^{(1)}(0) = c_\sigma \omega_\sigma$ and $R^{(2)}(0) = c_\sigma$. If $\sigma \neq 1$, $\mathcal{R}$ calculates $R^{(1)}(0) = c_\sigma r_\sigma^{(1)} \omega_\sigma$ and $R^{(2)}(0) = c_\sigma r_\sigma^{(2)}$ and also determines from the k collected shares $[r_\sigma^{(1)}]_j$ the value of $r_\sigma^{(1)}$ and similarly, from the k collected shares $[r_\sigma^{(2)}]_j$ the value of $r_\sigma^{(2)}$. Then, with simple division(s), $\mathcal{R}$ determines c_σ first and ω_σ second.

A.4   Nikov Et Al.'s DOT [9]

The sparse polynomial interpolation-based DOT protocol introduced by Nikov, Nikova, Preneel and Vandewalle [9] is characterized by the following parameters: the number of secrets $n \geq 2$, the threshold parameter k, the sender's privacy parameter $\lambda_S \leq k - 1$, the receiver's privacy parameter $\lambda_R \leq k - 1$, the hiding parameter $N = n$ and the encoding parameter $e = n$. The parameter λ_C is defined such that $\lambda_R + \lambda_C \leq k - 1$. In addition, the encoding function is $E(s) = \left(1, \delta_s^2, \delta_s^3, \ldots, \delta_s^n \right)$ and the polynomials U_i and V_i $(1 \leq i \leq N)$ are:

- $U_1(x) = \omega_1 + \sum_{\ell=1}^{k-1} a_{1,\ell} x^\ell$, where coefficients $a_{1,\ell}$ are randomly selected in $\mathbb{K}$, and for $i = 2, 3, \ldots, N$, $U_i(x) = \omega_i - \omega_1 + \sum_{\ell=1}^{\lambda_C} a_{i,\ell} x^\ell$, where coefficients $a_{i,\ell}$ are randomly selected in $\mathbb{K}$,
- $V_i(y_1, y_2, \ldots, y_e) = y_i$ for $i = 1, 2, \ldots, N$.

Like in Naor and Pinkas's and in Blundo et al.'s DOT protocols (see Appendices A.1 and A.2 above), on the receiver's side, the number of contacted servers is $t = k$ and the first element of the encoding function being constant and public, it is not shared (i.e., $Z_1 = 1$) and is not included in the request transmitted by the receiver to the contacted servers.

A.5   Beimel Et Al.'s DOT [1]

In [1], Beimel, Chee, Wang and Zhang propose a specific reduction from a DOT protocol to a polynomial interpolation-based information-theoretic private information retrieval protocol. The characteristics of the protocol are: the number of secrets $n \geq 2$, the threshold parameter k, the sender's privacy and strong privacy parameters $\lambda_S = \lambda_C \leq k - 1$, the receiver's privacy parameter $\lambda_R \leq k - 1$, the hiding parameter $N = n+1$ and the encoding parameter $e > 0$. The polynomials U_i and V_i $(1 \leq i \leq N)$ are:

- $U_1(x) = \sum_{i=0}^{k-1} a_{1,i} x^i$, where coefficients $a_{1,i}$ are randomly selected in $\mathbb{K}$, and for $i = 2, 3, \ldots, N$, the polynomial U_i is defined by $U_i(x) = (\omega_{i-1} - a_{1,0}) + \sum_{j=1}^{\lambda_C} a_{i,j} x^j$, where coefficients $a_{i,j}$ are randomly selected in $\mathbb{K}$,

– $V_1(y_1, y_2, \ldots, y_e) = 1$ and for $i = 2, 3, \ldots, N$, the polynomial V_i and the encoding function E must satisfy $V_i(E(\ell)) = \delta_\ell^{i-1}$ for $\ell \in [n]$.

On the receiver's side, the number of contacted servers is $t = k$. In addition, for efficiency purposes, each contacted server S_j ($j \in \mathcal{I}_t$) transforms the share $u_j \bullet v_j$ into a split s_j, which is sent back to the receiver. The receiver has just to calculate the sum $w_\sigma = \sum_{j \in \mathcal{I}_t} s_j$ to obtain the chosen secret.

B   Example of Insecurity in Blundo et al.'s DOT Protocol

—— Public Information ——

– Finite field $\mathbb{F}_{11}$
– Threshold $k = 3$
– Number of secrets $n = 2$
– $p_{w_1}(6) = 0.5$, $p_{w_1}(2) = 0.5$, $p_{w_1}(i) = 0$ if $i \neq 6$ and $i \neq 2$
– $p_{w_2}(1) = 0.5$, $p_{w_2}(3) = 0.5$, $p_{w_2}(i) = 0$ if $i \neq 1$ and $i \neq 3$

—— Set-up phase ——
Information private to the sender:

– $\omega_1 = 6$ and $\omega_2 = 1$

– $c_1 = 5$ and $c_2 = 7$

– $r_1^{(1)} = 1$ and $r_2^{(1)} = 2$

– $r_1^{(2)} = 4$ and $r_2^{(2)} = 5$

Intermediate calculus to prepare the sharing polynomials:

– $r_1^{(1)} \times c_1 \times \omega_1 = 8$
– $r_2^{(1)} \times c_2 \times \omega_2 = 3$
– $r_1^{(2)} \times c_1 = 9$
– $r_2^{(2)} \times c_2 = 2$
– Sharing polynomial $U_1^{(1)} = 8 + 2X + 9X^2$
– Sharing polynomial $U_1^{(2)} = 9 + X + 4X^2$
– S_1 receives $u_1^{(1)} = (8, 6)$ and $u_1^{(2)} = (3, 4)$
– S_2 receives $u_2^{(1)} = (4, 6)$ and $u_2^{(2)} = (5, 4)$
– S_3 receives $u_3^{(1)} = (7, 6)$ and $u_3^{(2)} = (4, 4)$

—— Transfer phase ——

– Request generated by the receiver: $z_j = (1, 6)$
– $v_j = z_j = (1, 6)$
– S_1 replies with $u_1^{(1)} \bullet v_1 = 0$ and $u_1^{(2)} \bullet v_1 = 5$
– S_2 replies with $u_2^{(1)} \bullet v_2 = 7$ and $u_2^{(2)} \bullet v_2 = 7$
– S_3 replies with $u_3^{(1)} \bullet v_3 = 10$ and $u_3^{(2)} \bullet v_3 = 6$

—— **The receiver tries to obtain all secrets** ——

- Interpolated polynomal from $(1,0)$, $(2,7)$, and $(3,10)$: $R^{(1)} = 2X + 9X^2$
- $r_2^{(1)} c_2 \omega_2 + r_1^{(1)} c_1 \omega_1 = 2 \times R^{(1)}(0) = 0$
- Interpolated polynomal from $(1,5)$, $(2,7)$, and $(3,6)$: $R^{(2)} = X + 4X^2$
- $r_2^{(2)} c_2 + r_1^{(2)} c_1 = 2 \times R^{(2)}(0) = 0$
- From the received mask shares, the receiver determines $r_1^{(1)} = 1$, $r_2^{(1)} = 2$, $r_1^{(2)} = 4$ and $r_2^{(2)} = 5$.

So, the receiver can infer the two equations:

$$\begin{cases} 2 \times c_2 \omega_2 + 1 \times c_1 \omega_1 = 0 \\ 5 \times c_2 + 4 \times c_1 = 0 \end{cases}$$

From the second equation, the receiver infers that $c_2 = 8 \times c_1$. Reporting the equality in the first equation, she obtains: $c_1 \times (5 \times \omega_2 + 1 \times \omega_1) = 0$. If $(\omega_1, \omega_2) =$

- $(6,1)$, then $5 \times \omega_2 + 1 \times \omega_1 = 0$,
- $(2,1)$, then $5 \times \omega_2 + 1 \times \omega_1 = 7$,
- $(6,3)$, then $5 \times \omega_2 + 1 \times \omega_1 = 10$,
- $(2,3)$, then $5 \times \omega_2 + 1 \times \omega_1 = 6$.

The only pair of secrets which satisfies the first equation is: $(6,1)$. The greedy receiver has obtained all secrets.

References

1. Beimel, A., Chee, Y.M., Wang, H., Zhang, L.F.: Communication-efficient distributed oblivious transfer. J. Comput. Syst. Sci. **78**(4), 1142–1157 (2012)
2. Blundo, C., D'Arco, P., De Santis, A., Stinson, D.R.: New results on unconditionally secure distributed oblivious transfer (extended abstract). In: Nyberg, K., Heys, H.M. (eds.) SAC 2002. LNCS, vol. 2595, pp. 291–309. Springer, Heidelberg (2003)
3. Blundo, C., D'Arco, P., De Santis, A., Stinson, D.R.: On unconditionally secure distributed oblivious transfer. J. Cryptol. **20**(3), 323–373 (2007)
4. Brassard, G., Crépeau, C., Robert, J.M.: All-or-nothing disclosure of secrets. In: Odlyzko, A.M. (ed.) CRYPTO 1986. LNCS, vol. 263, pp. 234–238. Springer, Heidelberg (1987)
5. Cheong, K.Y., Koshiba, T., Nishiyama, S.: Strengthening the security of distributed oblivious transfer. In: Boyd, C., González Nieto, J. (eds.) ACISP 2009. LNCS, vol. 5594, pp. 377–388. Springer, Heidelberg (2009)
6. Friedman, W.F.: The index of coincidence and its applications in cryptography. No. 22 in Riverbank Publications, Riverbank Laboratories, Geneva, IL, USA (1922)
7. Kasiski, F.W.: Die Geheimschriften und die Dechiffrir-Kunst. Mittler & Sohn, Berlin (1863)
8. Naor, M., Pinkas, B.: Distributed oblivious transfer. In: Okamoto, T. (ed.) ASIACRYPT 2000. LNCS, vol. 1976, pp. 205–219. Springer, Heidelberg (2000)
9. Nikov, V., Nikova, S., Preneel, B., Vandewalle, J.: On unconditionally secure distributed oblivious transfer. In: Menezes, A., Sarkar, P. (eds.) INDOCRYPT 2002. LNCS, vol. 2551, pp. 395–408. Springer, Heidelberg (2002)
10. Shamir, A.: How to share a secret. Commun. ACM **22**(11), 612–613 (1979)

Compact and Efficient UC Commitments Under Atomic-Exchanges

Ioana Boureanu[1]([⊠]) and Serge Vaudenay[2]

[1] Akamai Technologies Limited, London, UK
icarlson@akamai.com
[2] EPFL, Lausanne, Switzerland
serge.vaudenay@epfl.ch

Abstract. We devise a multiple (concurrent) commitment scheme operating on large messages. It uses an ideal global setup functionality in a minimalistic way. The commitment phase is non-interactive. It is presented in a modular way so that the internal building blocks could easily be replaced by others and/or isolated during the process of design and implementation. Our optimal instantiation is based on the decisional Diffie-Hellman (DDH) assumption and the (adversarially selected group) Diffie-Hellman knowledge (DHK) assumption which was proposed at CRYPTO 1991. It achieves UC security against static attacks in an efficient way. Indeed, it is computationally cheaper than Lindell's highly efficient UC commitment based on common reference strings and on DDH from EUROCRYPT 2011.

Keywords: Commitment · Universal composability

1 Introduction

A neat way to design a secure cryptographic protocol is to show that, even in adversarial environments, it emulates a target ideal functionality [1,3,21,25], i.e., a functionality modelling the corresponding primitive implemented by the protocol. One formalism that resides on this idea is the well-known framework of Canetti's, i.e., the universal composability (UC) [9]. This model is compelling because it comprises a composability proof, i.e., protocols proven secure in the UC-setting are guaranteed to remain secure if and when composed with themselves and/or other protocols in a parallel or sequential manner. In order to UC-realize any multiparty computation it suffices to UC-realize the functionality of (multiple) commitment [11]. Thus, commitments became an essential asset within UC-security.

Communication Models in UC. In the original UC papers [9], it was assumed that the channels were secure. However, this assumption was consequently [10] dropped; we will henceforth refer to these two models as the *secure-channel UC* and the *insecure-channel UC*, respectively. The latter means that in the case of honest real-world executions, one can imagine man-in-the-middle adversaries

© Springer International Publishing Switzerland 2015
J. Lee and J. Kim (Eds.): ICISC 2014, LNCS 8949, pp. 381–401, 2015.
DOI: 10.1007/978-3-319-15943-0_23

mounting attacks. To bypass this issue, most UC-secure constructions assume or intrinsically require authenticated channels. In this paper, we will place some focus onto which protocols of interest achieve UC-security solely if authenticated channels in the insecure-channel UC model are assumed, and which do so without this assumption.

Requirements for UC Commitments. It should be clear that it is not straightforward to UC-realize commitments. Beyond seeking for a protocol that is hiding and binding as in standard lines, we need the following properties. **(A)** Ideal adversaries should be able to commit reliably to values that they (may) ignore at the time at the commit. And, ideal adversaries should be able to open the simulated commitments to whatever value needed later. **(B)** The ideal adversary also needs to extract the message inside any commitment, particularly within those generated by the adversary. Both should be done without rewinding. Damgård et al., in [16], refer to the former requirement above as *equivocability* and to the latter as *extractability*. In fact, these requirements were first put forward in [11,17], and [16] formalized a scheme that would clearly exhibit these constraints (and meet them when properly implemented). Moreover, such a scheme had already been realized in [2] into a multi-commitment protocol. Nonetheless, authenticated channels are needed if insecure-channel UC model is assumed.

Unrestricted Communication & UC Commitments. Unfortunately, UC commitment cannot be realized in the standard, non-augmented, UC model. One way to achieve this UC-realization is to use setups [2,11,12,23,24], i.e., to work in the UC-hybrid model where all participants can interact with an ideal functionality whilst carrying out their part.

Efficiency of UC Commitments & UC Authenticated Channels. At EUROCRYPT 2011, Lindell proposed a highly efficient version of UC commitments, in [24], in the UC common reference string (CRS)-hybrid model, under the DDH assumption. Lindell's scheme required approximately 36 exponentiations for commitment and opening, if security against adaptive corruptions is offered. For protection against static corruptions only, 26 exponentiations are needed. Very recently, in [5], Blazy et al. proposed new UC-secure commitment protocols, making the ones by Lindell more efficient. In this line, they need 22 exponentiations in the static-corruption case and 26 exponentiations, in the adaptive corruption case.

Both Lindell's and Blazy's protocols need the extra assumption of authenticated channels, being cast in the insecure-channel UC model; this extra assumption is often the case, even if it is not always clearly stated in the papers. To see this, imagine the following setting. Let a sender S and a receiver R be both honest. Suppose the environment sends an input x to S, who will play the committer on x. Let $\mathcal{A}$ be a MiM adversary that picks x'. Imagine that $\mathcal{A}$ plays a sender session with R, committing on x', and a receiver session with S. At the end of the two openings, the honest receiver sends x' to the environment. The environment outputs 1 if $x = x'$. Clearly, this will happen in the above, real-world execution with a probability $\frac{1}{2}$, but in the ideal world with probability 1.

So, if no authentication is assumed, then this MiM creates the setting for two distinguishable, real and ideal worlds. The CRS setup cannot prevent it.

In this line, we propose a solution that bypasses the need for authenticated channels by using an unforgeable primitive. (Our proofs additionally rest on the soundness of a proof-of-knowledge employed in our construction). We need fewer exponentiations than in Lindell's case, and (with authenticated channels) the same number as in Blazy's case. But, with our protocol, 10 of the 22 exponentiations only need to be executed once, (even) in the case of multiple commitments. We use a different setup, yielding more lightweight building blocks, and a non-interactive commitment phase, to achieve UC-security over insecure channels in the presence of static adversaries.

Isolation as a setup assumption. Damgård *et al.* UC-realized multiple commitments [16] by using a setup assumption that relaxes the tamper-resistant hardware token to a functionality that models the partial isolation of a party, i.e., the restriction of *input and output* communication from that party. Damgård *et al.* offer in fact a general construction (rather than an instantiated protocol), relying on the following fact: if a functionality of isolated parties is available, then witness indistinguishable proofs of knowledge (WI-PoK) can be realized, which further provide a type of PKI that makes UC multiple commitment possible. (See [20] for details on PoK.) In this general setting, the UC-realization relies on the existence of one-way permutations and dense public key, IND-CPA secure cryptosystems with ciphertexts pseudorandom (which can be considered pretty heavy assumptions). In fact, the functionality of isolated parties had been used before, in order to realize specifically proofs of knowledge [15]. In [15], the authors motivated the isolation as a remedy to the fact that, in the PoK, the prover could run a man-in-the-middle attack between a helper and the verifier (resulting in the latter not being sure that a prover knows the due witness). This setting applies to the UC-insecurity cases as well, where the simulation fails in the case of simple relay attacks. Overall, we do find the idea behind the work in [16] convincing indeed, in that computation made in guaranteed isolation may alleviate fundamental shortcomings in UC simulators.

In [7], Boureanu *et al.* introduced atomic exchanges as a UC setup, being a somewhat similar alternative to the isolated parties of Damgård *et al.* The atomic exchange functionality has a different formulation to Damgård's isolation primitive. The main differences between the two functionalities can be summarized as follows. 1. The atomic notion requires isolation of a single message exchange, instead of an entire protocol session and it is used thus-wise. 2. If a responder R is releasing a response to an atomic query, then –in between the query and the response– R will have received no *incoming* messages from the environment (or from another party). Yet, R can leak as much as he likes to the environment (or to another party). At the same time, an R isolated à la Damgård *et al.* would have *both incoming and outgoing* communications blocked. 3. Atomicity implies full isolation on the incoming tape (i.e., there is no bit received by an atomically engaged R on its incoming tape). Isolation à la Damgård *et al.* can be partial, i.e., an isolated body can leak a fixed amount of bits. Linked to the requirements needed from UC commitments, the work in [7] formalizes input-aware equivocal commitment, which is a primitive given initially outside of the UC framework, encapsulating similar requirements to those above demanded from UC commitments. The authors also construct a single, bit-commitment protocol (i.e., not a multi-commitment and not working but on bits) emulating this primitive and then prove that the protocol is UC-secure if two atomic exchanges are granted and assuming secure channels. In this line, we will extend the work in [7], to multiple group-element commitments without secure channels and generalize the methodology therein. We will therefore employ some of the tools introduced in [7].

To meet the requirements (A)–(B), and achieve extraction and (strong) equivocability, the protocols use to public-private pairs of keys, $(\mathsf{pk}_X, \mathsf{sk}_X)$ and $(\mathsf{pk}_E, \mathsf{sk}_E)$, respectively. So, we use atomic exchanges in a minimalistic way to declare/register the public keys once for all. Then, these keys are used in multiple commitments.

There are cases where isolation in atomic exchanges make practical sense. E.g., by setting up a sharp time bound for the response and assuming that a responder communicating with a third party would necessarily produce a timeout [4]. We could use similar techniques as for distance-bounding [8,22]. Isolation is also real when a biometric passport is being scanned inside an isolated reader, or when a creditcard is being read in an ATM machine. It could also make sense in a voting booth (equipped with a Faraday cage), in an airplane, in a tunnel, etc. We could imagine hardware-oriented solutions such as a cell phone (responder) registering a key in a secure booth (sender) preventing external radio communications. The advantages of atomic exchanges over, e.g., tamper-hardware devices were discussed in [16].

Our Contribution. Our contribution is five-fold.

1. In this line of work, we further fine-tune restricted local computation, using atomic exchanges [7]. We use these exchanges judiciously.
2. We formalize a design-scheme C_{LCOM} that would achieve commitment in the UC setting. This is more precise/specified than the one in [11,16]. The blocks within C_{LCOM} are similar to those in [24], but the decommitment block is less heavy, i.e., ours is a witness indistinguishable proof of knowledge (PoK) and not a zero-knowledge proof of knowledge[1].
3. Linked to the above, we offer a different manner of obtaining extraction and strong equivocability: it is based on the Diffie-Hellman knowledge (DHK) assumption [14].
4. We advance a protocol UC-realizing $\mathcal{F}_{\mathsf{LCOM}}$ if a few atomic exchanges are possible at the setup phase. This protocol enjoys even more efficiency than the one in [24]. It is more concrete and it has a more judicious use of setups

---

[1] In [16], a witness indistinguishable PoK is used to create a "weak PKI" as part of a different block, i.e., the initialization/setup block. Our initialization/setup block herein is also more lightweight than the one in [16].

than its counterparts in [16]. We also show how to transform it into a protocol with other global setups such as a public directory or a CRS.
5. We also bypass the need of assuming authenticated channels (intrinsic to our predecessors [5,24]) by using a signature and a proof of knowledge, whose soundness deters MiM.

Structure. Section 2 introduces the hardness assumptions needed for special instances of our scheme. Section 3 presents atomic exchanges, i.e., the UC setups used herein. A commitment-scheme is put forward in Sect. 4. We then give the necessary requirements for this scheme to UC-realize (multi-)commitment. Section 5 offers a concrete, efficient protocol that implements the aforementioned compact scheme and UC-realizes commitment, with atomic exchanges used in a limited way. Section 6 details on the efficiency of our protocol(s) by comparison to existing ones. Appendix A discusses how to transform our protocol into one based on a global public-key registration with no further ideal functionality to be used between participants.

2   Hardness Assumptions

Definition 1 (DH Key Generator Gen). *A DH key is a tuple $K = (G, q, g)$ such that G is a group, q is a prime dividing the order of G, g is an element of G of order q. A DH key-generator is a ppt. algorithm Gen producing DH keys K such that $|K| = \mathsf{Poly}(\log q)$ and the operations (i.e., multiplication, comparison, membership checking in the group $\langle g \rangle$ generated by g) over their domain can be computed in time $\mathsf{Poly}(\log q)$. We say that (S, S') is a valid K-DH pair for g^σ if $S \in \langle g \rangle$ and $S' = S^\sigma$, where $\sigma \in \mathbb{Z}_q$.*

An example of a DH key is $(\mathbb{Z}_p^*, q, g)$ where p, q are primes and $p = 2q + 1$, $g \in \mathsf{QR}(p)$, $g \neq 1$.

In the descriptions below, we use an arbitrary ppt. algorithm $\mathcal{B}$ generating some coins ρ and states state. Such ρ and state will be used as auxiliary inputs to some other algorithms in the security games formalized below.

Definition 2 (ag-DDH$_{\mathsf{Gen}}$). *The ag-DDH$_{\mathsf{Gen}}$ assumption relative to a DH key generator Gen states that for any polynomially bounded algorithms $\mathcal{A}$ and $\mathcal{B}$ in the next game, the probability that $b = \bar{b}$ is $\frac{1}{2}$ but something negligible, i.e., $\Pr[b = \bar{b}] - \frac{1}{2}$ is negligible:*

1: $(\rho, \mathsf{state}) := \mathcal{B}(1^\lambda; r_{\mathcal{B}})$
2: $K := \mathsf{Gen}(1^\lambda; \rho), (G, q, g) = K$
3: pick $\alpha, \beta, \gamma \in_U \mathbb{Z}_q$
4: $A := g^\alpha; B := g^\beta; C_0 := g^\gamma; C_1 := g^{\alpha\beta}$
5: pick $b \in_U \{0, 1\}$
6: $\bar{b} := \mathcal{A}(1^\lambda, \mathsf{state}, A, B, C_b; r)$

The probability stands over the random coins $r_{\mathcal{B}}$, r, $b \in_U \{0, 1\}$ and $\alpha, \beta, \gamma \in_U \mathbb{Z}_q$. The probability is negligible in terms of $\log q$. The algorithms $\mathcal{A}$ and $\mathcal{B}$ are ppt. in terms of $\log q$.

In the above definition, "ag" stands for "adversarially-chosen group". This is a weaker assumption than the usual DDH assumption [19] (which is supposed to be hard for *all* generated groups).

We adopt the strengthening from [7] of the Diffie-Hellman knowledge (DHK0) assumption [14] (for a summary of the latter, refer to [19]).

Definition 3 (ag-DHK0$_{\mathsf{Gen}}$). *The* ag-DHK0$_{\mathsf{Gen}}$ *assumption relative to a DH key generator* Gen *states that for any polynomially bounded algorithms* $\mathcal{A}$ *and* $\mathcal{B}$, *there must exist a polynomially bounded algorithm* $\mathcal{E}$ *such that the following experiment yields 1 with negligible probability:*

1: $(\rho, \mathsf{state}) := \mathcal{B}(1^\lambda; r_\mathcal{B})$
2: $K := \mathsf{Gen}(1^\lambda; \rho)$, $(G, q, g) = K$
3: pick $\sigma \in_U \mathbb{Z}_q$
4: $(S, S') := \mathcal{A}(1^\lambda, \mathsf{state}, g^\sigma; r)$
5: if (S, S') *is not a valid K-DH pair for* g^σ, *then return 0*
6: $s := \mathcal{E}(1^\lambda, \mathsf{state}, g^\sigma, r)$
7: if $S = g^s$, *then return 0*
8: return 1

The probability stands over the random coins $r_\mathcal{B}$, r *and* $\sigma \in_U \mathbb{Z}_q$. *The probability is negligible in terms of* $\log q$. *The algorithms* $\mathcal{E}$ *and* $\mathcal{B}$ *are ppt. in terms of* $\log q$.

This assumption means that whatever the algorithm producing valid DH pairs (S, S') for a random g^σ with σ unknown, this algorithm must know the discrete logarithm s of their components except for some negligible cases.

What distinguishes these assumptions from the mainstream DDH and DHK0 assumptions [19] is that these should hold for all K selected by a $\mathcal{B}$ algorithm (even by a malicious one) and not only for some K which is selected by an honest participant. In fact, when it comes to selecting a DH key without a CRS in a two party protocol, the above assumption must hold for any maliciously selected K (since we ignore a priori which party is honest). Hence, the name we use: DH assumptions in an adversarially-chosen group. The latter assumption is a special case of the DH knowledge assumption required to hold in *any* group, introduced by Dent in [19]. Here, we do not require the assumption to hold in any group but rather in those groups G for which we can produce a seed for Gen.

In the next, for readability purposes, we will often omit the additional-input 1^λ from the inputs of the machines that require it, its presence being implicit.

3 UC Functionalities

3.1 The Atomic Setup Functionality

We start with the setup functionality we are going to use in our construction. This functionality is denoted $\mathcal{F}_{\mathsf{atomic}}$. Let *poly* be a polynomial. The $\mathcal{F}_{\mathsf{atomic}}$ ideal functionality involves some participants called *Caller* (C) and *Responder* (R). It works as follows (upon receipt of the messages below).

Ready(C, R, M) **message from** R. In this message, M denotes the description of the Turing machine run by R and the functionality parses the message, stores (C, R, M), and sends the message Ready(C) to the ideal adversary. Any other tuple starting with (C, R) is erased.[2]

Note that –by the above– R can resend this command to $\mathcal{F}_{atomic}$, possibly with a different M.

Cancel(C) **message from** R. This counts for an abortion from the atomic session. So, the functionality sends the message Cancelled(C) to the ideal adversary and any tuple starting with (C, R) is erased.

Atomic(R, c) **message from** C. The functionality verifies the existence of a tuple for the pair (C, R). If there is none, is aborts. Let (C, R, M) be the found tuple. The functionality runs $r = M(c)$ for no more than $poly(|c|)$ steps, then sends (response, C, R, r) to C and the ideal adversary, and (challenge-issued, C, R, c) to R and the ideal adversary. Finally, the tuple is erased.

Our objective is to employ $\mathcal{F}_{atomic}$ as little as possible. It is actually required only to set up public keys. So, we will use it in a key-setup/key-registration block, which is executed between each pair of participants who want to run a commitment protocol. This kind of block is bound to require a setup functionality. We could, for instance, rely instead on trusted third parties to whom we could register keys and obtain the public key of participants in a reliable way. In what immediately follows we describe the 2-party approach, without such PKI. However, a version based on a public directory is discussed in Appendix A.2.

3.2 The Commitment Functionality

We now continue with the functionality of commitment we would like to UC-realize. The (unusual) Init step denotes a part in which the parties involved register some data (e.g., public-private keys) that would be used in the remainder of the run of the protocol to carry out the final task.

The $\mathcal{F}_{\mathsf{LCOM}}$ ideal functionality works as follows (upon receipt of the messages below). It involves some participants called *Sender* (S) and *Receiver* (R).

Init(R) **message from** S. If R and S are already defined, abort. Otherwise, define (store) R and S, send an [initialized, R, S] message to R and to the ideal adversary.

Commit(sid, m) **message.** If this does not come from S, or S is undefined, or sid is not fresh, abort. Otherwise, store (sid, m, sealed) and send a [committed, sid] message to R and to the ideal adversary.

Open(sid) **message.** If this does not come from S, or S is undefined, or sid is new, abort. Otherwise, retrieve (sid, m, state). If state $\neq$ sealed, abort. Otherwise,

---

[2] We note that the Turing machine M is deterministic (or an equivalent one, a probabilistic one but with the necessary random coins hard-coded within).

send an [open, sid, m] message to R and to the ideal adversary[3], and replace state by opened in the (sid, m, state) entry.

We note that the above functionality is cast in the insecure-channel UC model. This is in the sense that the delayed outputs (i.e., having the functionality send the opening messages to the ideal adversary as well) would not be needed in the secure channels UC. However, they are needed in the insecure channel UC, since without them the ideal simulator would have problems simulating a real execution in which both parties are honest[4]. Unfortunately, in some cases [15,16] where insecure-channel UC is the underlying model, this delayed output is omitted (which would mean that the simulation of the honest, real-world case is impossible). However, in these very case, it can easily be fixed, because their settings rely on a step of a key-registration, and –in itself– this offers the means for authentication.

We will eventually UC-realize this functionality. However, we can easily (with a slightly more computationally expensive protocol) cast everything in terms of the standard multi-commitment functionality $\mathcal{F}_{\mathsf{MCOM}}$ (see Appendix A.2); the latter functionality can be seen, for instance, in [11].

Unlike $\mathcal{F}_{\mathsf{MCOM}}$ where there is no inner init-phase included and participants/roles are defined upon Commit, $\mathcal{F}_{\mathsf{LCOM}}$ allows multiple commitments from the same sender S to the same receiver R decided at its inner init-phase. In other words, $\mathcal{F}_{\mathsf{LCOM}}$ allows multiple commitments at a *link* level, i.e., *LCOM*. So, to UC-realize $\mathcal{F}_{\mathsf{MCOM}}$ with $\mathcal{F}_{\mathsf{LCOM}}$, we just need to integrate the LCOM Init phase in every Commit with a new S-R link.

4   Compact UC Commitments

4.1   A Compact Scheme for $\mathcal{F}_{\mathsf{LCOM}}$

In Fig. 1, we show a design of a UC commitment scheme based on several building blocks linked together.

These blocks are as follows: a parameter-generation procedure KeyGen yielding the secret-public key pairs $(\mathsf{sk}_E, \mathsf{pk}_E)$ and $(\mathsf{sk}_X, \mathsf{pk}_X)$; a Register block emulating key-registration; an unforgeable scheme $\mathsf{Comm}_{\mathsf{pk}_X}$ which is a commitment in standard lines extractable under sk_X; an interactive proof either of the message inside the commitment or of the knowledge of the secret key sk_E. Note that auth($\cdots$) is a shorthand to stress that the input are messages to be protected, either by some authenticated channel, or by means of a digital signature, with a key registered like for sk_X. All these will be explained formally in the sequel

---

[3] Sending to the ideal adversary is necessary for the simulation in the insecure-channel UC model because commitment protocols send the committed message in clear during opening and the ideal adversary must simulate such protocol when both participants are honest, although he cannot get the message by any other mean.

[4] It is often the case that, in the real-world execution, the committed input is eventually sent in clear, as part of the opening phase. To get a correct ideal world simulation, this delayed output from the ideal functionality is needed.

and an instantiation of each will be given (if not before, then in Sect. 5). We will show that, under the right assumptions, these methods can be implemented in a manner that is neither too expensive, nor does it involve many (atomic) exchanges.

Informal Explanations about the Scheme. Before everything, the participants generate their public and secret keys, e.g., pk_X and sk_X for S. Note that we do not assume a CRS to retrieve them from and –in general– we do not suppose necessarily the same domain for the keys of S and those of R.

Then, the sender essentially registers his public key pk_X to the receiver (while storing the associated secret key sk_X for himself). The receiver does the same for $(\mathsf{pk}_E, \mathsf{sk}_E)$, respectively. Further, based on some mechanism and on the setup functionality, each demonstrates[5] to the other that they hold the corresponding secret-key counterparts. To achieve this phase, we use the Register block. This phase, involving key generation (i.e., KeyGen) and key registration (i.e., Register), is called the *key-setup*.

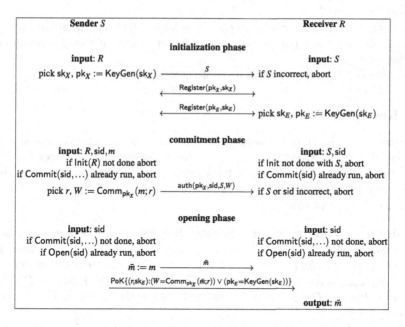

Fig. 1. A Compact Commitment-Scheme C_{LCOM} with Atomic Exchanges

Assume that the sender would like to commit to a message m. Assume that the message is embedded into some suitable domain (e.g., a domain where mathematical operations can be easily applied). The *commitment phase* proceeds as follows. Using his public key pk_X and some random coins r, the sender produces

---

[5] No WI-PoK, as in [16], will be used in this the implementation of this assertion.

W as the commitment to m using the block Comm. This block is an unforgeable commitment in itself. If it were not unforgeable, we would need to assume authenticated channels (like our predecessors [5,24]), so that a MiM were not able to perturb the honest transactions. I.e., $W = \mathsf{Comm}_X(m; r)$ should be bind S to m and hide m from R. But, to anticipate, if, e.g., an ideal adversary were able to know sk_X for S he could run $\mathsf{Extract}_{\mathsf{sk}_X}(\mathsf{Comm}_{\mathsf{pk}_X}(m; r))$ to obtain m. This would ensure extractability or requirement (B) on page x.

An essential block of the *opening phase* of this scheme is a *proof of knowledge*, denoted PoK. After sending $\overline{m}$, the sender practically uses this block to prove that either $\overline{m}$ is equal to m and r has been used in producing the commitment, or that he knows sk_E; as only R should know sk_E, this convinces R of the binding character of the commitment. But, obviously, for someone that knows sk_E this commitment becomes equivocal.

Then, for the ideal world to be indistinguishable from the real world, intuitively we need to make sure that the implementation of the blocks are such that their outputs look the same under some coins and an adaptively chosen respective counterpart of those. In the next sections, we will see a way in which this can be achieved.

Note that in order to realize $\mathcal{F}_{\mathsf{LCOM}}$, it is important that the sk and pk keys are fresh for every new pair (S, R) of participants and that Register is run only once for each key.[6]

We proceed with the formalization of these blocks.

4.2   Key Setup Block

We begin by the block of key-setup which includes key generation and key registration. Intuitively, KeyGen computes a public key pk out of a secret key sk. Then, the Register protocol is used for a prover to demonstrate that he holds sk to a verifier who has received pk from this prover. We are going to formalize the semantics of these blocks.

Definition 4 (The KeyGen and Register Blocks). *Let λ be a security parameter. The* KeyGen *block is a function from a domain D_{sk} to a domain D_{pk} (depending on λ). The* Register *block is a ppt. protocol involving a prover P, a verifier V, and an ideal functionality $\mathcal{F}$. The value* sk *is the input for P (which is denoted $P(\mathsf{sk})$). The value* $\mathsf{pk} = \mathsf{KeyGen}(1^\lambda, \mathsf{sk})$ *is the output of V (unless the protocol aborts).*

There must exist a polynomial time algorithm E such that for all ppt. adversary $\mathcal{A}$ and ppt. algorithm $\mathcal{B}$, in an experiment with V, $\mathcal{A}$, and $\mathcal{B}$ having access to $\mathcal{F}$ and V only interacting with $\mathcal{A}$, we have that $\mathsf{KeyGen}(1^\lambda, E(v)) = \mathsf{pk}$, except with negligible probability, where v denotes the view of $\mathcal{A}$ and pk is the output of V.

---

[6] In the C-at protocol to be defined (see Fig. 4), a Register block could be maliciously used as a $z \mapsto z^{\mathsf{sk}}$ oracle, allowing an adversary either to extract or to equivocate a commitment.

For every ppt. algorithm V^* interacting with $P(\mathsf{sk})$, with sk random, the following happens with negligible probability: V^* outputs s, $\mathsf{KeyGen}(1^\lambda, s) = \mathsf{KeyGen}(1^\lambda, \mathsf{sk})$, and P will have not aborted.

We say that $\mathsf{Register}$ is authenticating if there is no man-in-the-middle attack such that a honest verifier ends up with some pk such that $\mathsf{pk} \neq \mathsf{KeyGen}(1^\lambda, \mathsf{sk})$, where sk is the input of the honest prover.

This non-extractability property is cheaper than zero-knowledge. Note that it implies that KeyGen must be a one-way function.[7] In other words, over a domain $D_{\mathsf{pk}} \times D_{\mathsf{sk}}$ generated as per KeyGen it is computationally hard to retrieve the secret key $\mathsf{sk} \in D_{\mathsf{sk}}$, given the public key $\mathsf{pk} \in D_{\mathsf{pk}}$. In practice, the idea of such a non-extractability of the secret key sk out of the public data pk can rely on the hardness of some computational assumption.

Example 5. We now offer an example of this sort of key-setup. This example is part of the C-at protocol on Fig. 4, page xx. A key-pair $(\mathsf{pk}, \mathsf{sk})$, with pk generated by such an algorithm KeyGen can be given by $((\rho, g^x), (\rho, x))$, i.e., $\mathsf{pk} = (\rho, g^x)$, $\mathsf{sk} = (\rho, x)$, with ρ being some coins to generate $(G, q, g) = \mathsf{Gen}(\rho)$, and where G is a group, q is a prime dividing the order of G, g is an element of G of order q, and $x \in_U \mathbb{Z}_q$. One cannot obtain this sk out of this pk unless they break the $\mathsf{DL}_{\mathsf{Gen}}$ assumption (see Sect. 2).

We can define $\mathsf{Register}$ as follows (see Fig. 2): given $\mathsf{sk} = (\rho, x)$ and $\mathsf{pk} = (\rho, X)$, P sends ρ to V, V computes $(G, q, g) = \mathsf{Gen}(\rho)$, picks $\alpha \in_U \mathbb{Z}_q$, sends an atomic[8] $X_0 = g^\alpha$ to P. Then, P checks $X_0 \in G$ and sends back X and $X' = X_0^x$ to V. The latter finally checks that $X' = X^\alpha$. Finally, V sends α to P for checking that $X_0 = g^\alpha$.

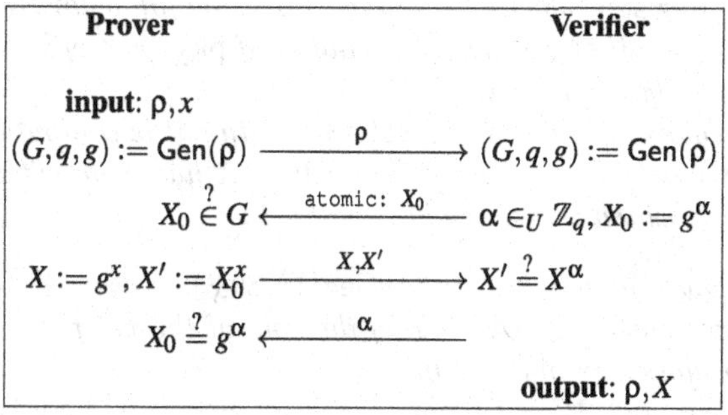

Fig. 2. A Register Protocol

---

[7] One-wayness here means for any ppt. algorithm $\mathcal{A}$ the following probability is negligible in λ: $\Pr_{r_\mathcal{A}, \mathsf{sk}}[\mathsf{Gen}(1^\lambda, \mathcal{A}(1^\lambda, \mathsf{pk}; r_\mathcal{A})) = \mathsf{pk} \mid \mathsf{pk} = \mathsf{Gen}(1^\lambda, \mathsf{sk})]$.

[8] V sending an atomic X_0 is a syntactic-sugar meaning that P sends a prior $\mathsf{Ready}(V, M)$ to $\mathcal{F}_{\mathsf{atomic}}$ where M is an algorithm to compute $M(X_0) = (X, X')$, then V sends $\mathsf{Atomic}(P, X_0)$ to $\mathcal{F}_{\mathsf{atomic}}$. (See [7].)

Lemma 6. *Under the* ag-DHK0$_{\mathsf{Gen}}$ *and* DL$_{\mathsf{Gen}}$ *assumptions, the protocol in Example 5 based on* $\mathcal{F}_{\mathsf{atomic}}$ *is a* Register *block with* KeyGen. *It is further authenticating.*

The idea of this protocol is that by preparing the atomic response, the prover provides an algorithm from which we can extract X based on the DHK0 assumption.

Proof. Based on the ag-DHK0$_{\mathsf{Gen}}$ assumption, the atomic response clearly leaks x. So, P's view can provide sk and the first requirement is satisfied.

Furthermore, based on the DL$_{\mathsf{Gen}}$ assumption, the protocol does not leak sk to V^*. This comes from that we could run V^* with a genuine ρ from the DL$_{\mathsf{Gen}}$ game, then continue with some dummy $\bar{X} = g^{\bar{x}}$ and $\bar{X}' = X_0^{\bar{x}}$ to get α (otherwise, P aborts). Then, he rewind to when X and X' are submitted to V^*. He gets a genuine X from the DL$_{\mathsf{Gen}}$ game and sets $X' = X^\alpha$. Clearly, this experiment cannot extract x under the DL$_{\mathsf{Gen}}$ assumption.

The authentication comes from that the atomic functionality authenticates X to the verifier. $\square$

We could also have a Register block based on a global CRS (à la [24]). The prover simply sends $\sigma = \mathsf{Enc}_{\mathsf{crs}}(\mathsf{sk})$ and $\mathsf{PoK}\{\mathsf{sk} : \sigma = \mathsf{Enc}_{\mathsf{crs}}(\mathsf{sk}) \wedge \mathsf{pk} = \mathsf{KeyGen}(\mathsf{sk})\}$.

4.3   The Extractable Commitment Block

We mention the requirements needed from the Comm block (and the Extract block) in the C_{LCOM} scheme; consider the notations therein.

Definition 7 (Extractable Commitment). *An extractable commitment for the* KeyGen *and* Register *blocks is defined by a set of algorithms* Comm *and* Extract *such that for all* $\mathsf{sk}_X \in D_{\mathsf{sk}}$, m, *and* r, *if* $\mathsf{pk}_X = \mathsf{KeyGen}(1^\lambda, \mathsf{sk}_X)$, *then* $\mathsf{Extract}_{\mathsf{sk}_X}(\mathsf{Comm}_{\mathsf{pk}_X}(m; r)) = m$.

Further, we require that an extractable commitment is computationally hiding with the Register *block. I.e., any ppt. algorithm* $\mathcal{A}$ *has a probability of winning the following game which is negligibly close to* $\frac{1}{2}$:

1: pick $\mathsf{sk}_X \in_U D_{\mathsf{sk}}$ *and set* $\mathsf{pk}_X := \mathsf{KeyGen}(1^\lambda, \mathsf{sk}_X)$
2: run the Register *block with* $\mathcal{A}$ *playing the role of the verifier*
3: $\mathcal{A}$ *selects two messages* m_0 *and* m_1
4: flip a coin b, *compute* $W = \mathsf{Comm}_{\mathsf{pk}_X}(m_b; r)$, *and run* $\mathcal{A}$ *on* W
5: $\mathcal{A}$ *outputs* b' *and wins if* $b' = b$

$\mathcal{A}$ *may use the functionality* $\mathcal{F}$ *coming from* Register *as per Definition 4.*

The reason why we introduced Register in the hiding notion is because we do not necessarily assume any zero-knowledge property on Register. So, some information may leak, but we want that it does not help to uncover the committed message.

4.4 The Equivocable Opening Block

Definition 8 (PoK Block). *Given the blocks* KeyGen *and* Comm *and an instance described by* (W, pk_E) *of an initialization and commitment phase, the* PoK *block is a witness indistinguishable proof of knowledge[9] from* S *to* R *for either* r *or* sk_E *such that* $W = \mathsf{Comm}_{\mathsf{pk}_X}(m; r)$ *or* $\mathsf{pk}_E = \mathsf{KeyGen}(\mathsf{sk}_E)$.

By *proof of knowledge*, we mean that the protocol is polynomially bounded, complete, and that there is an extractor who can compute a witness out of the view of a successful malicious prover. By *witness indistinguishable* (WI), we mean that the honest prover can use either r or sk_E as a witness to run his algorithm, and that the respective cases cannot be distinguished by a malicious verifier. (Again, see [20] for details on WI-PoK and PoK.) More concretely, and ppt. algorithm $\mathcal{A}$ has a probability of winning negligibly close to $\frac{1}{2}$ in the following game:

1: $\mathcal{A}$ selects an instance inst and two possible witnesses w_0 and w_1 for PoK
2: flip a coin b and set wit $= w_b$
3: run PoK with a prover for inst using wit as a witness and with $\mathcal{A}$ playing the role of the verifier
4: $\mathcal{A}$ outputs b' and wins if $b' = b$

$\mathcal{A}$ may use the functionality $\mathcal{F}$ coming from Register as per Definition 4.

4.5 UC Security of the Compact Scheme

Theorem 9. *Under the assumptions of Definition 4 (using a functionality $\mathcal{F}$), Definition 7, and Definition 8, in presence of a static adversary, the compact-scheme C_{LCOM} UC-realizes the $\mathcal{F}_{\mathsf{LCOM}}$ ideal functionality using $\mathcal{F}$ as a global setup.[10]*

In the insecure-channel UC model with authentication, the result holds when $\mathsf{auth}(\cdots)$ is just transmitting messages through the authenticated channel. In the insecure-channel UC model without authentication, the sender must register an additional (authenticated) key and auth simply appends a digital signature based on this key. So, we move the auth requirement to the initialization phase. If the Register block is authenticating, this is solved.

Proof (sketch). Let S (sender) and R (receiver) be two participants running one initialization $S_{\mathsf{init}}/R_{\mathsf{init}}$ and multiple commitments $S_{\mathsf{commit}}/R_{\mathsf{commit}}$ and $S_{\mathsf{open}}/R_{\mathsf{open}}$, upon activation by the environment. Note that S and R are paired by the unique $\mathcal{F}_{\mathsf{LCOM}}$ initialization.[11] In the ideal world, they run, if honest, the dummy_S

---

[9] See [20] for details on witness indistinguishable proofs of knowledge (WI-PoK).
[10] By *global setup*, we mean that the environment can access to it as well. This is also called GUC in the literature.
[11] So, proving GUC reduces to proving EUC: in a multiparty setting, the participant calling $\mathcal{F}_{\mathsf{LCOM}}$ with the identifier of another participant defines S and R. All other participants can be glued into the environment.

or dummy_R algorithms forwarding inputs/outputs between the environment and $\mathcal{F}_{\mathsf{LCOM}}$. Otherwise, they behave as instructed by the ideal adversary $\mathcal{I}$. While the ideal-world experiment is running, $\mathcal{I}$ runs an internal simulation of the real world experiment to make the interaction with the environment indistinguishable. So, $\mathcal{I}$ runs a simulation of the adversary $\mathcal{A}$, of the honest participants S or R supposed to run their specific algorithms, and of the setup functionality $\mathcal{F}$ (in due turns). He corrupts correspondingly to the real world the dummy S or R who then behave following the $\mathcal{A}$ simulation.

In what follows, we describe, depending on the corruption state, how the simulation of the honest participants is done. Our simulator will be straight-line, but *proving* (and only proving) that the simulation is indistinguishable may require rewinding, as allowed in the UC model.

Case where S and R are corrupted. There is no honest participant to simulate: $\mathcal{A}$ defines the behavior of S and R and the simulation is perfect. Actually, there is no interaction with $\mathcal{F}_{\mathsf{LCOM}}$ in this case.

Case where S is honest. R may be corrupted or not. If R is honest, its simulation is based on the normal algorithms R_{init}, R_{commit}, and R_{open}. Clearly, this simulation of R to $\mathcal{A}$ is perfect.

During initialization, the simulation of S is straightforward as it requires no communication with the environment: he runs the same algorithms S_{init} as in the real world. This simulation is perfect.

We note that while the honest S is simulated, even though R may be honest as well, his messages may be modified by $\mathcal{A}$. In any case, we consider the honest S interacting with some T where T is the complement of the simulation of S in $\mathcal{I}$. I.e., it includes the simulation of $\mathcal{A}$ and the one of R, no matter whether R is honest or not. Let sk_X be the secret key selected by the simulator of the honest S. Let pk_E be the public key registered to S. Based on the property of the Register block, $\mathcal{I}$ can extract sk_E corresponding to pk_E based on the view of T. (In Definition 4, T plays the role of $\mathcal{A}$ while the environment, the dummy honest participants, and $\mathcal{F}_{\mathsf{LCOM}}$ play the role of $\mathcal{B}$.)

During commitment, $\mathcal{I}$ simulates S running S_{commit} on some random message m.

During the opening, $\mathcal{F}_{\mathsf{LCOM}}$ tells $\mathcal{I}$ the value of $\bar{m}$ committed by the dummy S. Then, $\mathcal{I}$ simulates S equivocating the commitment to $\bar{m}$ by using sk_E in the $m \neq \bar{m}$ case: $\mathcal{I}$ makes S send $\bar{m}$ and run the PoK protocol with sk_E as a witness. In the $m = \bar{m}$ case, $\mathcal{I}$ simulates S normally: using S_{open}.

Indistinguishability. In general, to prove indistinguishability, we have to prove that all messages sent to the environment are indistinguishable in both worlds. There are two types of messages: the output from the dummy (honest) participants (in our case, there is only dummy_R, if honest, and during opening, which has content), and the messages from the corrupted ones, i.e., from $\mathcal{A}$. This reduces to proving that dummy_R, if honest, opens to a correct message, and that the simulation of honest participants is indistinguishable by $\mathcal{A}$ in both worlds.

Let us consider the honest R case. Clearly, dummy_R sends the outcome $\bar{m}$ to the environment, and it matches the input to dummy_S. In the real world, even though the adversary may corrupt the communication, we prove that R ending the opening on $\bar{m}$ while S began the commitment with a different message happens with negligible probability. For that, we assume that these messages are different. Thanks to the Register block and auth message, both S and R use the same pk_E and W. Since PoK is a sound proof of knowledge, from the prover (i.e., the entire experiment except the simulation for R), we extract a witness, possibly by rewinding. Since the commitment does not open to $\bar{m}$, this witness must be a secret key related to pk_E. Now, since sk_E is only used in Register, this shows that we can extract a preimage of KeyGen(sk_E) from the Register protocol. But this is excluded by Definition 4. So, the outcome $\bar{m}$ from a honest dummy_R matches the one of the real world experiment.

Then, we have to prove that the simulation of the interaction between S and R (when honest) makes the simulation of $\mathcal{A}$ behave in an indistinguishable way to the adversary in the real world. The case of a honest R is clear: the simulation in the ideal world behaves exactly like in the real world. As for S, the result is clear for $m = \bar{m}$ as they run exactly the same algorithms. It remains to consider the simulation of S in the $m \neq \bar{m}$ case.

Let Γ_0 be the ideal world experiment producing the output of the environment, in the $m \neq \bar{m}$ case. We note that sk_X is only used by Register during the initialization. So, we can use the hiding property of Comm to say that Γ_0 is indistinguishable to the game Γ_1 in which we run $S_{\text{commit}}(R, \text{sid}, \bar{m})$ for S instead of $S_{\text{commit}}(R, \text{sid}, m)$. Just as in Γ_0, this game Γ_1 is still using sk_E as a witness to run PoK. Due to the witness indistinguishable property, Γ_1 is indistinguishable to the game Γ_2 in which S uses r as a witness instead. This final game Γ_2 corresponds to the real world experiment. So, the real and ideal world experiments produce indistinguishable outcomes.

Case where S (but not R) is corrupted. During initialization, R is simulated by running the normal algorithm R_{init} interacting with $\mathcal{A}$ and $\mathcal{F}$. So, thanks to the property of the Register block $\mathcal{I}$ can extract sk_X based on his own view.

The simulation for the commitment phase starts normally by running the normal algorithm for R. After W is released, $\mathcal{I}$ computes Extract$_{sk_X}(W)$ to deduce the committed value m by $\mathcal{A}$. If extraction fails, m is set to a random message. Then, the ideal adversary $\mathcal{I}$ makes the corrupted dummy_S send a Commit(sid, m) message to $\mathcal{F}_{\text{LCOM}}$.

The simulation for the opening phase starts normally with R running the normal algorithm R_{open}. If R_{open} aborts, $\mathcal{I}$ aborts. If it succeeds and R_{open} outputs something, then the ideal adversary $\mathcal{I}$ makes dummy_S send an Open(sid) message to $\mathcal{F}_{\text{LCOM}}$.

Indistinguishability. Since R follows his algorithms, the simulation of the interaction (to $\mathcal{A}$) is perfect. We only have to prove that the outcome of dummy_R (which will be sent to the environment) matches the one by R. We observe that, due to the extractability of the commitment, it is perfectly binding. So, if R in the real world ends up with the opened commitment $\bar{m}$ and that $\mathsf{Extract}_{\mathsf{sk}_X}(W) \neq \bar{m}$, due to PoK being sound, we could extract (possibly by rewinding) a valid witness sk_E. Since R is honest and only uses sk_E for Register, the properties of Register make it impossible. So, this proves that $\mathsf{Extract}_{\mathsf{sk}_X}(W) \neq \bar{m}$ with negligible probability. So, we have $\bar{m} = m$ in the real world, which is also guaranteed by the simulation. $\qquad\square$

5   Instantiated Compact Scheme

Given a group $K = \mathsf{Gen}(1^\lambda, \rho)$, we define an injective function map from the set of possible values to commit to the group K. The function map, as well as its inverse, must be easy to compute. For instance, if $\langle g \rangle$ is the group of quadratic residues in $\mathbb{Z}_p^*$ and $p = 2q + 1$ is a strong prime, we can set the message space to $\{1, \ldots, N\}$ for $N < q$ and define $\mathsf{map}(m) = (\pm m) \mod p$, specifically the only one of the two values which is a quadratic residue.

In Fig. 4, on page xx, we present a protocol that implements the schema in Fig. 1. Then, we prove that this protocol is UC-secure with atomic as a setup, and under certain assumptions.

The KeyGen and Register blocks are as in Example 5. Based on $\mathsf{pk}_X = (\rho, X)$ and $\mathsf{sk}_X = (\rho, x)$, for $r \in \mathbb{Z}_q$, we have $\mathsf{Comm}_{\mathsf{pk}_X}(m; r) = (U, V)$ with $U = g^r$ and $V = \mathsf{map}(m)X^r$. This is the ElGamal encryption. We let $\mathsf{Extract}_{\mathsf{sk}_X}(U, V) = \mathsf{map}^{-1}(VU^{-x})$.

Lemma 10. *Under the* $\mathsf{ag\text{-}DDH}_{\mathsf{Gen}}$ *assumption, the above* Comm *and* Extract *algorithms define an extractable commitment in the sense of Definition 7, for* KeyGen *and* Register *from Example 5.*

Proof. To show that Comm is hiding, we consider the game in Definition 7: the adversary $\mathcal{A}$ receives ρ defining a group with a generator g, then sends some random X_0 in the group, receives X, X', sends α such that $X_0 = g^\alpha$ (otherwise, fail), sends some m_0 and m_1, receives (U, V) which is the ElGamal encryption of $\mathsf{map}(m_b)$ with key X, for some random b, and produces a bit b'. He wins if $b = b'$.

First, we play with $\mathcal{A}$ by submitting some $\bar{X} = g^{\bar{x}}$ for some random $\bar{x}$, with $\bar{X}' = X_0^{\bar{x}}$. Then we can get α and rewind, by submitting some external X and $X' = X^\alpha$. This reduces to the semantic security of the ElGamal encryption. We then use the standard result [6] that ElGamal encryption is IND-CPA secure under the $\mathsf{DDH}_{\mathsf{Gen}}$ assumption. $\qquad\square$

By using the standard construction [13] based on proofs of disjunctive statements [13,18], we construct a PoK for our instances. The protocol is depicted on Fig. 4 in which the prover uses r as a witness. To use $\mathsf{sk}_E = y$ as a witness (for equivocation), the computations of the prover are replaced by

$$b \in_U \mathbb{Z}_{q_2}^*, \; c_1 \in_U \{0, 1, \ldots, 2^n - 1\}, \; s_1 \in_U \mathbb{Z}_{q_1}^*$$
$$t_1 := U^{c_1} g_1^{s_1}, \; t_2 = \left(\frac{V}{\mathsf{map}(\bar{m})}\right)^{c_1} X^{s_1}, \; t_3 := Y^b$$
$$c_2 := c \oplus c_1, \; s_2 := (b - c_2 y) \mod q_2$$

We have the following result.

Lemma 11. *The 3-move protocol with the t, c, and s messages (in the opening phase) in Fig. 4 defines a Σ-protocol for $\{(r, \mathsf{sk}_E) : ((U, V) = \mathsf{Comm}_{\mathsf{pk}_X}(m; r)) \vee (\mathsf{pk}_E = \mathsf{KeyGen}(\mathsf{sk}_E))\}$. It is a PoK block in the sense of Definition 8, for KeyGen and Comm from above.*

Theorem 9 and Lemma 6–11 wrap up into the following result.

Theorem 12. *Under the $\mathsf{ag\text{-}DHK0}_{\mathsf{Gen}}$ and $\mathsf{ag\text{-}DDH}_{\mathsf{Gen}}$ assumptions, the $\mathsf{C\text{-}at}$ protocol on Fig. 4 UC-realizes $\mathcal{F}_{\mathsf{LCOM}}$ in the $\mathcal{F}_{\mathsf{atomic}}$-hybrid model considered, under a static adversary.*

In Appendix A, we discuss on possible extensions. I.e., relaxing the $\mathsf{ag\text{-}DHK0}_{\mathsf{Gen}}$ assumption, implementing the atomic exchanges, and making a PKI for multiple commitment.

6 Efficiency

To compare the efficiency of protocols, we count the number of exponentiations. There are some which must be done during the setup and which could be used for several commitments. There are some using small exponents (such as c_1 or c_2) which are faster than others. If we are not satisfied by the DHK0 assumption, we can use the ZK proof based on the DDH assumption as per Appendix A.1 (and if H_κ is say implemented via Pedersen commitment [27]). We compare the protocols of [24] and [5] with ours below.

Protocol	Setup	Fast	Regular
Lindell [24]		6	20
Blazy *et al.* [5]		2	20
our protocol with DHK0	10	4	8
our protocol with DDH	16	4	8

For 2-party protocols requiring many commitments, out protocol is thus at least twice faster than others.

The reduction in the number of exponentiations resides mainly on our use of the $\mathsf{ag\text{-}DHK0}_{\mathsf{Gen}}$ assumption. As aforementioned, it may be possible to select adversarial groups where the $\mathsf{ag\text{-}DHK0}_{\mathsf{Gen}}$ assumption may hold and then efficiently work in these groups. An example of this was given in Example 5. Also, to this end, the atomic exchanges are very limited within (and see Appendix A.2 for possible, efficient implementations through, e.g., distance-bounding [22]).

To achieve security, the previous protocols in [5,24] assumed authenticated channels, on top of the insecure-channel UC model. We can relax this assumption by using a signature, at the cost of a few more exponentiations. (E.g., 3 more regular ones for signature and verification, and 5 more during setup for registering verification key.)

All in all, in general, we yield a generally more efficient, very modular UC commitment protocol.

7   Conclusions

In this paper, we devised a design-scheme for multiple (concurrent) commitment-scheme operating on large messages. It uses the ideal setup functionality of atomic messages in a minimalistic way. We suggest how this functionality can be achieved in practice, and we claim that it is indeed lighter than other UC setups for commitments. Our scheme enjoys UC security under static attacks. It is presented in a modular way so that the internal building blocks could easily be replaced by others and/or isolated during the process of design and implementation. Our optimal proposed instantiation is based on the decisional Diffie-Hellman assumption and the adversarially selected group Diffie-Hellman knowledge assumption. This outperforms other efficient UC commitments [24] based on CRS and DDH. At the same time, it can be viewed as an alternative to the new protocol in [5], bypassing the need for authenticated channels, but keeping in place the same number of exponentiations with a more modular construction. However, our protocol can enjoy UC security *without needing to assume authentication* on top of the UC insecure channels, unlike [5,24]. If the adversarially selected group Diffie-Hellman knowledge assumption is dropped, another instantiation of ours performs still slightly better than existent efficient UC commitments.

A   Extensions

A.1   A Variant Based on ag-DDH$_{\mathsf{Gen}}$

We can drop the ag-DHK0$_{\mathsf{Gen}}$ assumption and solely rely on the ag-DDH$_{\mathsf{Gen}}$ one. For that, we construct a new Register protocol based on a zero-knowledge proof with the Schnorr Σ-protocol. See Fig. 3 on page xx. This would get us closer to [16], where a WI-PoK is used in the key-setup block.

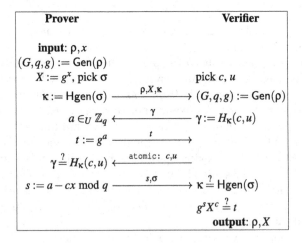

Fig. 3. A ZK Variant for the Register Protocol

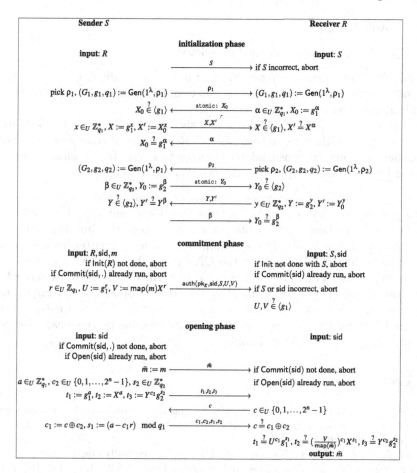

Fig. 4. C-at: A UC-Secure Commitment Protocol with Atomic Exchanges

Namely, we enrich the Σ-protocol with a trapdoor commitment Hgen on the challenge c, with the trapdoor σ released at the end. It is a trapdoor in the sense that for all γ and all c', $\mathsf{Equiv}_\sigma(\gamma, c')$ has the same distribution as u and $H_\kappa(c', \mathsf{Equiv}_\sigma(\gamma, c')) = \gamma$. This is quite a standard technique [26]. By making the challenge atomic, we obtain a ZK protocol in a regular sense. It is further straightforward to see that Register satisfies all requirements, based on the ag-DDH$_{\mathsf{Gen}}$ assumption. To make it authenticating, we can take advantage of the $\mathcal{F}_{\mathsf{atomic}}$ exchange to authenticate X at the same time as the response is sent.

In general we prefer to use the ag-DHK0$_{\mathsf{Gen}}$ to ascertain the private knowledge of sk. This may be more efficient in practice than a full implementation of, e.g., a WI-PoK. It essentially requires the selection of appropriate (and efficient) groups to work in, as done in Example 5.

A.2   Towards $\mathcal{F}_{\mathsf{MCOM}}$

The $\mathcal{F}_{\mathsf{MCOM}}$ functionality is defined as follows:

Commit(sid, R, m) **message from** S. If sid is not fresh, abort. Otherwise, store (sid, S, R, m, sealed) and send a [committed, sid, S] message to R and to the ideal adversary.

Open(sid) **message from** S. If sid is new or the record (sid, $S, ., ., .$) has no matching S, abort. Otherwise, retrieve (sid, S, R, m, state). If state $\neq$ sealed, abort. Otherwise, send an [open, sid, m] message to R and to the ideal adversary, and replace state by opened in the (sid, S, R, m, state) entry.

To realize this functionality, we use a similar assumption as in [16]: we assume that a participant plays the role of a trusted certificate authority (who is honest but curious), to whom participants register their keys sk_X and sk_E. The first time a participant is involved in a commitment, he must register his keys to the certificate authority (CA) and get the CA's public key at the same time. The CA would produce a certificate which could be verified with the CA's public key. Then, the Init phase between S and R would reduce to sending and verifying this certificate, without any ideal functionality. Due to the extraction nature of our Register block, all secret keys would become extractable by the ideal adversary and the UC security would still hold.

References

1. Backes, M., Pfitzmann, B., Waidner, M.: A general composition theorem for secure reactive systems. In: Naor, M. (ed.) TCC 2004. LNCS, vol. 2951, pp. 336–354. Springer, Heidelberg (2004)
2. Barak, B., Canetti, R., Nielsen, J.B., Pass, R.: Universally composable protocols with relaxed set-up assumptions. In: Proceedings of FOCS 2004, pp. 186–195. IEEE Computer Society, Washington, DC (2004)
3. Beaver, D.: Foundations of secure interactive computing. In: Feigenbaum, J. (ed.) Advances in Cryptology - CRYPTO 1991. LNCS, vol. 576, pp. 377–391. Springer, Heidelberg (1992)
4. Beth, T., Desmedt, Y.G.: Identification tokens – or: solving the chess grandmaster problem. In: Menezes, A., Vanstone, S.A. (eds.) Advances in Cryptology - CRYPTO 1990. LNCS, vol. 537, pp. 169–176. Springer, Heidelberg (1991)
5. Blazy, O., Chevalier, C., Pointcheval, D., Vergnaud, D.: Analysis and improvement of Lindell's UC-secure commitment schemes. In: Jacobson, M., Locasto, M., Mohassel, P., Safavi-Naini, R. (eds.) ACNS 2013. LNCS, vol. 7954, pp. 534–551. Springer, Heidelberg (2013)
6. Boneh, D.: The decision Diffie-Hellman problem. In: Buhler, J.P. (ed.) ANTS 1998. LNCS, vol. 1423, pp. 48–63. Springer, Heidelberg (1998)
7. Boureanu, I., Vaudenay, S.: Input-aware equivocable commitments and UC-secure commitments with atomic exchanges. In: Susilo, W., Reyhanitabar, R. (eds.) ProvSec 2013. LNCS, vol. 8209, pp. 121–138. Springer, Heidelberg (2013)
8. Brands, S., Chaum, D.: Distance bounding protocols. In: Helleseth, T. (ed.) EURO-CRYPT 1993. LNCS, vol. 765, pp. 344–359. Springer, Heidelberg (1994)
9. Canetti, R.: A unified framework for analyzing security of protocols. In: Electronic Colloquium on Computational Complexity (ECCC), vol. 8, no. 16 (2001)

10. Canetti, R., Dodis, Y., Pass, R., Walfish, S.: Universally composable security with global setup. Cryptology ePrint Archive, Report 2006/432 (2006). http://eprint.iacr.org/
11. Canetti, R., Lindell, Y., Ostrovsky, R., Sahai, A.: Universally composable two-party and multi-party secure computation. In: Procedings of STOC 2002, pp. 494–503 (2002)
12. Chandran, N., Goyal, V., Sahai, A.: New constructions for uc secure computation using tamper-proof hardware. In: Smart, N.P. (ed.) EUROCRYPT 2008. LNCS, vol. 4965, pp. 545–562. Springer, Heidelberg (2008)
13. Cramer, R., Damgård, I.B., Schoenmakers, B.: Proof of partial knowledge and simplified design of witness hiding protocols. In: Desmedt, Y.G. (ed.) CRYPTO 1994. LNCS, vol. 839, pp. 174–187. Springer, Heidelberg (1994)
14. Damgård, I.: Towards practical public key systems secure against chosen ciphertext attacks. In: Feigenbaum, J. (ed.) Advances in cryptology - CRYPTO 1991. LNCS, vol. 576, pp. 445–456. Springer, Heidelberg (1992)
15. Damgård, I., Nielsen, J.B., Wichs, D.: Isolated proofs of knowledge and isolated zero knowledge. In: Smart, N.P. (ed.) EUROCRYPT 2008. LNCS, vol. 4965, pp. 509–526. Springer, Heidelberg (2008)
16. Damgård, I., Nielsen, J.B., Wichs, D.: Universally composable multiparty computation with partially isolated parties. In: Reingold, O. (ed.) TCC 2009. LNCS, vol. 5444, pp. 315–331. Springer, Heidelberg (2009)
17. Damgård, I., Nielsen, J.B.: Perfect hiding and perfect binding universally composable commitment schemes with constant expansion factor. In: Yung, M. (ed.) CRYPTO 2002. LNCS, vol. 2442, pp. 581–596. Springer, Heidelberg (2002)
18. De Santis, A., Di Crescenzo, G., Persiano, G., Yung, M.: On monotone formula closure of SZK. In: Proceedings of SFCS 1994, pp. 454–465. IEEE Computer Society, Washington, DC (1994)
19. Dent, A.W.: The hardness of the DHK problem in the generic group model (2006). http://eprint.iacr.org/2006/156
20. Goldreich, O.: Foundations of Cryptography, vol. 1. Cambridge University Press, New York (2006)
21. Goldreich, O., Micali, S., Wigderson, A.: Proofs that yield nothing but their validity and a methodology of cryptographic protocol design. In: Proceedings of CSWF 1986, pp. 174–187, October 1986
22. Hancke, G.P.: Security of proximity identification systems. Ph.D. thesis, July 2009
23. Katz, J.: Universally composable multi-party computation using tamper-proof hardware. In: Naor, M. (ed.) EUROCRYPT 2007. LNCS, vol. 4515, pp. 115–128. Springer, Heidelberg (2007)
24. Lindell, Y.: Highly-efficient universally-composable commitments based on the DDH assumption. In: Paterson, K.G. (ed.) EUROCRYPT 2011. LNCS, vol. 6632, pp. 446–466. Springer, Heidelberg (2011)
25. Micali, S., Rogaway, P.: Secure computation. In: Feigenbaum, J. (ed.) Advances in Cryptology - CRYPTO 1991. LNCS, vol. 576, pp. 392–404. Springer, Heidelberg (1992)
26. Monnerat, J., Pasini, S., Vaudenay, S.: Efficient deniable authentication for signatures. In: Abdalla, M., Pointcheval, D., Fouque, P.-A., Vergnaud, D. (eds.) ACNS 2009. LNCS, vol. 5536, pp. 272–291. Springer, Heidelberg (2009)
27. Pedersen, T.P.: Non-interactive and information-theoretic secure verifiable secret sharing. In: Feigenbaum, J. (ed.) Advances in Cryptology - CRYPTO 1991. LNCS, vol. 576, pp. 129–140. Springer, Heidelberg (1992)

Issuer-Free Adaptive Oblivious Transfer with Access Policy

Vandana Guleria$^{(\boxtimes)}$ and Ratna Dutta

Department of Mathematics, Indian Institute of Technology Kharagpur,
Kharagpur 721302, India
vandana.math@gmail.com, ratna@maths.iitkgp.ernet.in

Abstract. Due to the frequent use of Internet in our daily life, *privacy* is a major issue in designing any cryptographic primitive. *Adaptive oblivious transfer with access policy* (AOT-AP) is a widely used primitive to create privacy preserving databases in which different messages have different access policies, allowing only those receivers who have the necessary permissions to access the databases. We provide the *first fully-simulatable* AOT-AP without the third party called issuer. To achieve our goal, we present a new ciphertext policy attribute based encryption (CP-ABE), which is a variant of Water's CP-ABE. The Boneh-Boyen signature is employed to control the malicious behavior of the parties, and proposed CP-ABE is used to encrypt each message of the database under some access policy. The proposed protocol is secure under q-Strong Diffie-Hellman and q-Decision Bilinear Diffie-Hellman Exponent assumptions in static corruption model in the presence of malicious adversary. Moreover, our AOT-AP is as efficient as the existing similar schemes.

Keywords: Oblivious transfer · Access policy · Attribute based encryption · Full simulation security model

1 Introduction

Adaptive oblivious transfer with access policy (AOT-AP) is a protocol run among a sender, an issuer and multiple receivers. The sender holds a database of N messages in which each message is associated with an access policy. The access policies could be rights, roles or attributes that a receiver should have in order to access the message. The receiver with an attribute set w interacts with the issuer to get attribute secret key ASK and recovers the message using ASK if w satisfies the access policy of the message. For instance, consider DNA databases containing information about each gene. Such databases are very costly, and thus receivers are charged per access to the database. The sender holds a database of DNA samples of different species and can charge different rates for different DNA species. The sender does not learn which DNA species are accessed by which receiver, and the receiver learns nothing about the DNA species for which it has not paid.

© Springer International Publishing Switzerland 2015
J. Lee and J. Kim (Eds.): ICISC 2014, LNCS 8949, pp. 402–418, 2015.
DOI: 10.1007/978-3-319-15943-0_24

The *first* adaptive oblivious transfer protocol was proposed by Naor and Pinkas [13]. In [13], the security of one party follows real/ideal world paradigm while the security of other party is supported by heuristic argument only. Such type of security model is called half-simulataion model. Camenisch *et al.* [5] introduced the first *fully-simulatable* adaptive oblivious transfer. The term fully-simulatable means that the security of both the parties follow real/ideal world paradigm. In literature, there is a wide variety of adaptive oblivious transfer [8–10,14]. The aforementioned adaptive oblivious transfer protocols do not put any restriction on the receivers. Coull *et al.* [7] presented the first AOT-AP in which access policies were graphs. Later, Camenisch *et al.* [4] gave an efficient construction of AOT-AP, but the access policies are of conjunction of attributes (e.g $a \wedge b$, where a, b are attributes). To cover disjunction of attributes, same message is encrypted multiple times. For instance, consider a message m with access policy $(a \wedge b) \vee (c \wedge d)$, a, b, c, d are attributes. To use [4] as a building block, the same message m is encrypted two times, once with access policy $a \wedge b$ and once with $c \wedge d$. Encryption of the same message multiple times under different access policies is called duplication of the message. To overcome this duplication, Zhang *et al.* [17] introduced the disjunctive property in AOT-AP.

Our Contribution. All the existing AOT-AP protocols assumed an issuer apart from a sender and multiple receivers. In these schemes, the issuer and a collection of receivers are restricted never to collude, otherwise, receivers can decrypt the entire ciphertext database by obtaining private keys for all the attributes in the universe of attributes, making these protocols insecure. From security point of view, designs without such restrictions are more desirable in practice. Our goal in this work is to design an issuer-free AOT-AP protocol, handing the role of the issuer by the sender. For this, we first propose a ciphertext policy attribute based encryption (CP-ABE) which is a variant of Water's CP-ABE [16] and may be of independent interest. In the proposed CP-ABE, simulation in security analysis is considerably different from that of Water's CP-ABE. The AOT-AP is a run between two parties – sender and receiver. The sender holds a database of messages, each message is encrypted by the sender under an access policy AP. Our protocol guarantees the following features: (i) only authorized receivers can correctly decrypt the ciphertext, (ii) the sender does not learn which message is recovered by which receiver, (iii) the sender is oblivious about the attribute set of the receiver and (iv) the receiver can only obtain a single message in each query. Moreover, the protocol achieves "AND($\wedge$)" and "OR($\vee$)" policies on each message without the duplication.

The proposed protocol completes in three phases, namely (a) initialization, (b) issue and (c) transfer. The sender holds a database of messages and publishes ciphertext database by encrypting each message of the database using Boneh-Boyen (BB) [3] signature and CP-ABE in the initialization phase. The receiver with an attribute set w communicates with the sender in the issue phase and obtains the attribute secret key ASK corresponding to w. The receiver interacts with the sender in each transfer phase to decrypt the allowed ciphertext and obtains the desired message. Proofs of knowledge are constructed to make sure that the sender and the receiver follow the protocol instructions and enable us to detect the malicious activities of the sender and the receiver.

The security of the proposed AOT-AP is analyzed in full-simulation security model which allows adversarial rewinding in which the simulator rewinds the adversary's state to previous computation state and starts the computation from there. The adversarial model adapted is static corruption model in which adversary pre-decides the corrupt party. During the protocol execution, the corrupt party remains corrupt and is handled by the adversary. The parties which are not corrupt are called honest parties and follow the protocol instructions. The proposed AOT-AP is secure assuming the hardness of q-Strong Diffie-Hellman (SDH) and q-Decision Bilinear Diffie-Hellman Exponent (DBDHE) problems in the presence of malicious adversary which can deviate from protocol specifications in static corruption model.

The efficiency is a major factor in designing any cryptographic protocol. The efficiency of the proposed AOT-AP is compared with [17], which is to the best of our knowledge, the only scheme available in literature with similar security notion. The AOT-AP of [17] is not issuer-free, and it has used BB signature [3], CP-ABE of [11] and covers disjunction of attributes in access policy. Our proposed AOT-AP is issuer-free, covers disjunction of attributes in access policy and is as efficient as [17].

2   Preliminaries

Throughout, we use ρ as the security parameter, $x \xleftarrow{\$} A$ means sample an element x uniformly at random from the set A, $y \leftarrow B$ indicates y is the output of algorithm B, $X \overset{c}{\approx} Y$ means X is computationally indistinguishable from Y, $[\ell]$ denotes $\{1, 2, \ldots, \ell\}$ and $\mathbb{N}$ the set of natural numbers. A function $f(n)$ is *negligible* if $f = o(n^{-c})$ for every fixed positive constant c.

2.1   Bilinear Pairing and Complexity Assumptions

Definition 1. *(Bilinear Pairing) Let $\mathbb{G}_1, \mathbb{G}_2$ and $\mathbb{G}_T$ be three multiplicative cyclic groups of prime order p and g_1, g_2 be generators of groups $\mathbb{G}_1$ and $\mathbb{G}_2$ respectively. Then the map $e : \mathbb{G}_1 \times \mathbb{G}_2 \rightarrow \mathbb{G}_T$ is bilinear if it satisfies the following conditions: (i) Bilinear – $e(x^a, y^b) = e(x, y)^{ab} \ \forall \ x \in \mathbb{G}_1, y \in \mathbb{G}_2, a, b \in \mathbb{Z}_p$. (ii) Non-Degenerate – $e(x, y)$ generates $\mathbb{G}_T$, $\ \forall \ x \in \mathbb{G}_1, y \in \mathbb{G}_2, x \neq 1, y \neq 1$. (iii) Computable – The pairing $e(x, y)$ is computable efficiently $\forall \ x \in \mathbb{G}_1, y \in \mathbb{G}_2$.*

Definition 2. *(q-SDH [3]) The q-Strong Diffie-Hellman (SDH) assumption in $\mathbb{G}$ states that for all probabilistic polynomial time (PPT) algorithm $\mathcal{A}$, with running time in ρ, the advantage $\mathsf{Adv}_{\mathbb{G}}^{q-SDH}(\mathcal{A}) = \Pr[\mathcal{A}(g, g^x, g^{x^2}, \ldots, g^{x^q}) = (c, g^{\frac{1}{x+c}})]$ is negligible in ρ, where $g \xleftarrow{\$} \mathbb{G}, x \xleftarrow{\$} \mathbb{Z}_p, c \in \mathbb{Z}_p$.*

Definition 3. *(q-DBDHE [15]) The q-Decision Bilinear Diffie-Hellman Exponent (DBDHE) assumption in $\mathbb{G}$ and $\mathbb{G}_T$ states that for all PPT algorithm $\mathcal{A}$,* with running time in ρ, the advantage $\mathsf{Adv}^{q-DBDHE}_{\mathbb{G},\mathbb{G}_T}(\mathcal{A}) = \Pr[\mathcal{A}(Y, e(g,g)^{\alpha^{q+1}s})]$ $-\Pr[\mathcal{A}(Y, Z)]$ is negligible in ρ, $Y = (g, g^s, g^\alpha, g^{\alpha^2}, \ldots, g^{\alpha^q}, g^{\alpha^{q+2}}, \ldots, g^{\alpha^{2q}})$, $g \xleftarrow{\$} \mathbb{G}, Z \xleftarrow{\$} \mathbb{G}_T, s, \alpha \xleftarrow{\$} \mathbb{Z}_p$.

BilinearSetup: The BilinearSetup is an algorithm which on input security parameter ρ generates params $= (p, \mathbb{G}, \mathbb{G}_T, e, g)$, where $e : \mathbb{G} \times \mathbb{G} \to \mathbb{G}_T$ is a symmetric bilinear pairing, g is a generator of a group $\mathbb{G}$ and p, the order of the groups $\mathbb{G}$ and $\mathbb{G}_T$, is prime, i.e. params $\leftarrow$ BilinearSetup(1^ρ).

2.2 Zero-Knowledge Proof of Knowledge

A zero-knowledge proof of knowledge [2] is an interactive protocol between a prover and a verifier. The notation of Camenisch and Stadler [6] is used in subsequent sections for the various zero-knowledge proofs of knowledge of discrete logarithms and proofs of validity of statements about discrete logarithms. For instance,

$$\mathsf{POK}\{(a, b, c, d) \mid y_1 = g^a h^b \wedge y_2 = g^c h^d\} \tag{1}$$

represents the zero-knowledge proof of knowledge of integers a, b, c and d such that $y_1 = g^a h^b$ and $y_2 = g^c h^d$ holds, where $a, b, c, d \in \mathbb{Z}_p, y_1, y_2, g, h \in \mathbb{G}$, where $\mathbb{G}$ is a cyclic group of prime order p with generator g. The quantities in the parenthesis a, b, c, d are secrets and are known to the prover only while all other parameters y_1, y_2, g, h are public. The prover interacts with the verifier and convinces the verifier that he knows a, b, c, d without revealing anything about a, b, c, d. The protocol should satisfy two properties. First, it should be *complete*, i.e., if the prover knows a, b, c and d such that $y_1 = g^a h^b$ and $y_2 = g^c h^d$ hold, then the verifier always accepts the proof. Second, it should be *sound*, i.e., if the prover does not know the secrets, then the verifier accepts the proof with negligible probability. The zero-knowledge proof of knowledge is said to be *perfect zero-knowledge* proof of knowledge if there exits an efficient simulator such that the probability distributions specified by the protocol with the verifier and with the simulator are the same. The protocol completes in three rounds. To verify pairing equation of the form $\mathsf{POK}\{(h) \mid H = e(g, h)\}$, we refer to [5].

2.3 Linear Secret Sharing Schemes (LSSS) [1]

Definition 4. *(Access Policy) Let* $\Omega = \{a_1, a_2, \ldots, a_m\}$ *be the universe of attributes and* $\mathcal{P}(\Omega)$ *be the collection of all subsets of* Ω. *An access policy (structure) is a collection* $\mathbb{A}$ *of non-empty subsets of* Ω, *i.e.,* $\mathbb{A} \subseteq \mathcal{P}(\Omega) \backslash \emptyset$. *The sets in* $\mathbb{A}$ *are called the authorized sets, and the sets not in* $\mathbb{A}$ *are called the unauthorized sets.*

A secret sharing scheme $\Pi_\mathbb{A}$ for the access policy $\mathbb{A}$ over Ω is called *linear* (in $\mathbb{Z}_p$) if it consists of two PPT algorithms– Distribute($\mathbb{M}, \eta, s$) and Reconstruct($\mathbb{M}, \eta, w$) which are described below, where $\mathbb{M}$ is a matrix with ℓ rows and t columns, called the share generating matrix for $\Pi_\mathbb{A}$, $\eta : [\ell] \to I_\Omega$ is the function which maps each row of $\mathbb{M}$ to an attribute index in $\mathbb{A}$, $s \in \mathbb{Z}_p$ is the secret to be shared, $w \in \mathbb{A}$ is the set of attributes and I_Ω is the index set of Ω.

- Distribute($\mathbb{M}, \eta, s$): This algorithm upon input $(\mathbb{M}, \eta, s)$, sets $v = (s, r_2, r_3, \ldots, r_t) \in \mathbb{Z}_p^t$, $r_2, r_3, \ldots, r_t \xleftarrow{\$} \mathbb{Z}_p$ and outputs a set $\{M_i \cdot v \mid i \in [\ell]\}$ of ℓ shares, where $M_i \in \mathbb{Z}_p^t$ is the i-th row of $\mathbb{M}$. The share $\lambda_i = M_i \cdot v$ belongs to the attribute $a_{\eta(i)}$.
- Reconstruct($\mathbb{M}, \eta, w$): This algorithm takes input $(\mathbb{M}, \eta, w)$. Let $I = \{i \in [\ell] \mid a_{\eta(i)} \in w\}$.
  1. Construct each row of matrix $\mathbb{F}$ by picking i-th row of $\mathbb{M}$, $\forall a_{\eta(i)} \in w$.
  2. Find the solution vector $\overrightarrow{x} = \{x_i \in \mathbb{Z}_p \mid i \in I\}$ such that $\sum_{a_{\eta(i)} \in w} \lambda_i x_i = s$ holds by solving system of equation $\mathbb{F}^T \overrightarrow{x} = e_1$, where $\mathbb{F}^T$ is the transpose of the matrix $\mathbb{F}$ of size $\nu \times t$, ν is the length of solution vector $\overrightarrow{x}$ which is equal to the number of attributes in w, e_1 is a vector of length t with 1 at first position and 0 elsewhere and $\{\lambda_i \in \mathbb{Z}_p \mid i \in I\}$ is a valid set of shares of the secret s generated by Distribute($\mathbb{M}, \eta, s$) algorithm. The algorithm outputs $\overrightarrow{x}$.

Theorem 1. ([12]) Let $(\mathbb{M}, \eta)$ be a LSSS access policy realizing an access policy $\mathbb{A}$ over universe of attributes Ω, where $\mathbb{M}$ is the $\ell \times t$ share generating matrix. Let $w \subset \Omega$. If $w \notin \mathbb{A}$, then there exists a PPT algorithm that outputs a vector $\overrightarrow{x} = (-1, x_2, x_3, \ldots, x_t) \in \mathbb{Z}_p^t$ such that $M_i \cdot \overrightarrow{x} = 0$ for each row i of $\mathbb{M}$ for which $\eta(i) \in I_\Omega$.

Converting Access Policy (AP) to LSSS Matrix: In our construction, we consider access policy as a binary access tree, where interior nodes are AND ($\wedge$) and OR($\vee$) gates and the leaf nodes correspond to attributes. Label the root node of the tree with the vector (1), a vector of length 1. Label each internal node with a vector determined by the vector assigned to its parent node recursively as discussed below. Maintain a counter c with initial value 1.

1. If the parent node is $\vee$ with a vector v, then label its children by v keeping c same.
2. If the parent node is $\wedge$ with a vector v, pad v if necessary with 0's at the end to make it of length c. Label one of its children with the vector $(v, 1)$ and other with the vector $(0, 0, \ldots, 0, -1)$, where $(0, 0, \ldots, 0)$ is zero-vector of length c. Note that $(v, 1)$ and $(0, 0, \ldots, 0, -1)$ sum to $(v, 0)$. Now increment the counter c by 1.

After labeling the entire tree, the vectors labeling the leaf nodes form the rows of LSSS matrix. If the vectors are of different length, pad the shorter ones with 0's at the end to make all the vectors of same length.

Example: Consider the access policy $\mathsf{AP} = (a_1 \wedge (a_4 \vee (a_2 \wedge a_3)))$. The root node, $\wedge$, is labeled with (1). Label the left child, corresponding to a_1, with $(1, 1)$ and right child, $\vee$, with $(0, -1)$ according to step 2. Now label the left child of $\vee$, a_4, with $(0, -1)$ and right child, $\wedge$, with $(0, -1)$ according to step 1. The left child of $\wedge$, a_2, is labeled with $(0, -1, 1)$ and right child, a_3, with $(0, 0, -1)$ according to step 2. This completes the labeling. The shorter vectors are padded with 0's at the end to make all vectors of length 3. The resulting LSSS matrix is

$$M = \begin{pmatrix} 1 & 1 & 0 \\ 0 & -1 & 1 \\ 0 & 0 & -1 \\ 0 & -1 & 0 \end{pmatrix},$$

where M_i, the i-th row M corresponds to the leaf attribute a_i, $i = 1, 2, 3, 4$. Let $s \in \mathbb{Z}_p$ be the secret. The shares $\{\lambda_i\}_{1 \le i \le 4}$ are generated using $\mathsf{Distribute}(M, \eta, s)$ as follows. Compute for each i, $\lambda_i = M_i \cdot v$, where $v = (s, y_2, y_3) \in \mathbb{Z}_p^3$, $y_2, y_3 \xleftarrow{\$} \mathbb{Z}_p$, $i = 1, 2, 3, 4$. Therefore $\{\lambda_1 = s + y_2, \lambda_2 = -y_2 + y_3, \lambda_3 = -y_3, \lambda_4 = -y_2\}$ is a valid set of shares. Suppose $w = \{a_1, a_2, a_4\}$ is the set of attributes. The secret s is recovered using $\mathsf{Reconstruct}(M, \eta, w)$ as discussed below. The matrix

$$\mathbb{F} = \begin{pmatrix} 1 & 1 & 0 \\ 0 & -1 & 1 \\ 0 & -1 & 0 \end{pmatrix},$$

The i-th row of matrix corresponds to $a_{\eta(i)}$, $i = 1, 2, 4$. Set $\overrightarrow{x} = (x_1, x_2, x_4)$, upon solving $\mathbb{F}^T \cdot \overrightarrow{x} = e_1$, we get $x_1 = 1, x_2 = 0, x_4 = 1$, where $e_1 = (1, 0, 0)$. The secret s is computed as $\sum_{a_{\eta(i)} \in w} \lambda_i x_i = \lambda_1 x_1 + \lambda_2 x_2 + \lambda_4 x_4 = \lambda_1 + \lambda_4 = s$.

2.4   Formal Model and Security Notion

An issuer-free adaptive oblivious transfer with access policy (AOT-AP) completes in three phases –(i) initialization, (ii) issue and (iii) transfer.

- **Initialization Phase**$(\rho, \mathsf{DB} = \{(m_i, \mathsf{AP}_i)\}_{i=1,2,\ldots,N})$. This phase invokes two PPT algorithms: InitDBSetup and InitDBVerify. A database DB has N messages, each message m_i is associated with access policy AP_i. In this phase, the database setup algorithm InitDBSetup with input security parameter ρ and DB generates a public/secret key pair $(\mathsf{pk}, \mathsf{sk})$ and encrypts each m_i to produce ciphertext ϕ_i with respect to AP_i. The sender runs this algorithm, publishes pk along with the generated ciphertext database $\mathsf{cDB} = \{(\phi_i, \mathsf{AP}_i)\}_{i=1,2,\ldots,N}$ and keeps sk secret to itself. Any receiver can verify the correctness of cDB by running the database verification algorithm InitDBVerify.
- **Issue Phase**$(\mathsf{pk}, \mathsf{sk}, w)$. This phase makes use of three PPT algorithms: IssAttRand, IssAttSk and IssAttSkExtract. A receiver with its attribute set $w \subseteq \Omega$, first runs the attribute randomization algorithm IssAttRand to randomize w and gives the randomized set w' to the sender, where Ω is the universe of attributes. The sender cannot guess w from w'. The sender then generates randomized attribute key ASK' for w' using the attribute secret key generation algorithm IssAttSk. Finally, the receiver extracts attribute secret key ASK for w on receiving ASK' from the sender through public channel using the attribute secret key extraction algorithm IssAttSkExtract.

- **Transfer Phase(pk, sk, cDB, w, ASK).** This phase calls three PPT algorithms: RequestTra, ResponseTra and CompleteTra. The receiver with input $(\text{pk}, \sigma_j, \phi_{\sigma_j}, \text{AP}_{\sigma_j}, w, \text{ASK})$ runs the request generation algorithm RequestTra to generate request Req_{σ_j}, where w satisfies the access policy AP_{σ_j}. Upon receiving Req_{σ_j} from the receiver, the sender with input $(\text{pk}, \text{sk}, \text{Req}_{\sigma_j})$ runs the response generation algorithm ResponseTra to generate response Res_{σ_j}. With input $(\text{Res}_{\sigma_j}, \phi_{\sigma_j})$, the receiver runs the algorithm CompleteTra to recover m_{σ_j}.

Security Model. The full-simulation security framework is adapted in this paper considering two worlds – *real world* and *ideal world*. In the real world, parties communicate with each other according to the real AOT-AP protocol Ψ in static corruption model in which some of the parties are corrupted by a real world adversary $\mathcal{A}$, and uncorrupted parties follow Ψ honestly. In the ideal world, parties and an ideal world adversary $\mathcal{A}'$ instead of communicating with each other directly, give their inputs to a incorruptible *trusted party*, called *ideal functionality* $\mathcal{F}$ and get back their respective outputs from $\mathcal{F}$. All the computation work is done by $\mathcal{F}$.

Definition 5. *The protocol Ψ securely implements the ideal functionality $\mathcal{F}$ if for any real world adversary $\mathcal{A}$ there exists an ideal world adversary $\mathcal{A}'$ such that for any environment machine $\mathcal{Z}$, $\text{REAL}_{\Psi,\mathcal{A},\mathcal{Z}} \overset{c}{\approx} \text{IDEAL}_{\mathcal{F},\mathcal{A}',\mathcal{Z}}$, where $\text{REAL}_{\Psi,\mathcal{A},\mathcal{Z}}$ is the output of $\mathcal{Z}$ after interacting in the real world with the parties and $\mathcal{A}$ and $\text{IDEAL}_{\mathcal{F},\mathcal{A}',\mathcal{Z}}$ is the output of the $\mathcal{Z}$ after interacting in the ideal world with the dummy parties and $\mathcal{A}'$.*

Real World: Let us briefly explain how the honest parties in the real world follow the AOT-AP protocol Ψ. The environment machine $\mathcal{Z}$ provides inputs to all parties and interacts freely with $\mathcal{A}$.

1. The sender S, upon receiving the message $(\text{initDB}, \text{DB} = \{(m_i, \text{AP}_i)\}_{i=1,2,\ldots,N})$ from $\mathcal{Z}$, runs InitDBSetup algorithm to generate a public/secret key pair (pk, sk) and ciphertext database $\text{cDB} = \{(\phi_i, \text{AP}_i)\}_{i=1,2,\ldots,N}$, where ϕ_i is the encryption of m_i under the access policy AP_i. The public key pk and cDB are made public by S.
2. Upon receiving the message $(\text{issue}, w \subseteq \Omega)$ from $\mathcal{Z}$, the receiver R engages in the issue phase with the sender S. After completion of the issue phase, R sends a bit $b = 1$ to $\mathcal{Z}$ indicating that R has obtained the attribute secret key ASK corresponding to attribute set $w \subseteq \Omega$. Otherwise, $b = 0$ is given to $\mathcal{Z}$ by R.
3. The receiver R, upon receiving the message $(\text{transfer}, \sigma_j \in [N])$ from $\mathcal{Z}$, checks whether w satisfies AP_{σ_j}. If not, abort the execution. Otherwise, R engages in transfer phase with the sender S and obtains m_{σ_j} if the protocol run is successful. Otherwise, R receives a null string $\perp$. At the end, R sends m_{σ_j} or $\perp$ to $\mathcal{Z}$.

Ideal World: In this world, all the parties interact with each other via $\mathcal{F}$. Upon receiving a message $(\text{initDB}, \text{DB} = \{(m_i, \text{AP}_i)\}_{i=1,2,\ldots,N})$ or $(\text{issue}, w \subseteq \Omega)$ or (transfer, $\sigma_j \in [N]$) from $\mathcal{Z}$, the honest parties passes it to $\mathcal{F}$, and forward their respective outputs from $\mathcal{F}$ to $\mathcal{Z}$. We briefly discuss below the behavior of $\mathcal{F}$. The ideal functionality $\mathcal{F}$ initially sets $\mathsf{DB} = \bot$ and an empty attribute set w_R for each receiver R.

1. Upon receiving the message $(\mathsf{initDB}, \mathsf{DB} = \{(m_i, \mathsf{AP}_i)\}_{i=1,2,...,N})$ from S, $\mathcal{F}$ sets $\mathsf{DB} = \{(m_i, \mathsf{AP}_i)\}_{i=1,2,...,N}$.
2. Upon receiving the message (issue, w) from R, $\mathcal{F}$ sends (issue) to S. The sender S returns a bit b to $\mathcal{F}$ in response to (issue). If $b = 1$, $\mathcal{F}$ updates $w_R = w$. Otherwise, $\mathcal{F}$ does nothing.
3. The ideal functionality $\mathcal{F}$, upon receiving the message $(\mathsf{transfer}, \sigma_j)$ from R, checks whether $\mathsf{DB} = \bot$. If yes, abort the execution. Otherwise, $\mathcal{F}$ sends $(\mathsf{transfer})$ to S. The sender S returns a bit b to $\mathcal{F}$. If $b = 1$, $\mathcal{F}$ checks if $\sigma_j \in [N]$ and w_R satisfies AP_{σ_j}. If not, $\mathcal{F}$ outputs $\bot$ to R. Otherwise, $\mathcal{F}$ returns m_{σ_j} to R.

3   The AOT-AP

Formally, the scheme is described below. We invoke algorithm BilinearSetup discussed in Sect. 2.1. Let $\Omega = \{a_1, a_2, \ldots, a_m\}$ be the universe of attributes.

- InitDBSetup($\rho, \mathsf{DB} = \{m_i, \mathsf{AP}_i\}_{i=1,2,...,N}, \Omega$): The database setup algorithm is run by the sender S. The algorithm first generates $\mathsf{params} = (p, \mathbb{G}, \mathbb{G}_T, e, g) \leftarrow$ BilinearSetup(1^ρ). It randomly chooses $c, x, \beta \xleftarrow{\$} \mathbb{Z}_p, h, h_1, h_2, \ldots, h_m, g_2 \xleftarrow{\$} \mathbb{G}$, sets $g_1 = g^\beta, g_3 = g^c, y = g^x, U = e(g_1, g_2), H = e(g, h)$. The public/secret key pair is $\mathsf{pk} = (\mathsf{params}, y, g_1, g_2, g_3, h_1, h_2, \ldots, h_m, U, H), \mathsf{sk} = (x, h, c, \beta)$. Generate the proof of knowledge

$$\psi = \mathsf{POK}\{(h, \beta, c) \mid H = e(g, h) \wedge g_1 = g^\beta \wedge g_3 = g^c\}.$$

The proof ψ is generated to convince the receiver R that the sender S knows the secrets h, c, β.

For $i = 1$ to N, the ciphertext ϕ_i is generated as follows.

1. Randomly take $r_i \xleftarrow{\$} \mathbb{Z}_p$ and generate BB signature [3] on r_i as $A_i = g^{\frac{1}{x+r_i}}$.
2. Compute $B_i = m_i \cdot e(A_i, h)$, where m_i is extracted from DB.
3. To encrypt B_i using our CP-ABE presented in Appendix A under the access policy AP_i associated with message m_i, the algorithm first converts access policy AP_i to a LSSS matrix $\mathbb{M}_i$ as discussed in Sect. 2.3, where $\mathbb{M}_i$ is the $n_i \times \theta_i$ matrix, n_i is the number of attributes in AP_i. The function η_i maps index of each row of $\mathbb{M}_i$ to an attribute index in AP_i. Pick $r_{i,2}, r_{i,3}, \ldots, r_{i,\theta_i} \xleftarrow{\$} \mathbb{Z}_p^*$, set $v_i = (r_i, r_{i,2}, r_{i,3}, \ldots, r_{i,\theta_i}) \in \mathbb{Z}_p^{\theta_i}$, compute $\mathbb{M}_i \cdot v_i = (\lambda_{i,1}, \lambda_{i,2}, \ldots, \lambda_{i,n_i}) \in \mathbb{Z}_p^{n_i}$ by invoking Distribute($\mathbb{M}_i, \eta_i, r_i$) algorithm described in Sect. 2.3 and set

$$c_i^{(1)} = B_i \cdot U^{r_i}, \ c_i^{(2)} = g^{r_i}, \ c_{i,\ell}^{(3)} = g_3^{\lambda_{i,\ell}} \cdot \left(g_1^{a_{\eta_i(\ell)}} \cdot h_{\eta_i(\ell)}\right)^{-r_i} \quad \forall a_{\eta_i(\ell)} \in \mathsf{AP}_i,$$

where $\ell = 1, 2, \ldots, n_i$. Set $c_i^{(3)} = \{c_{i,\ell}^{(3)}\}_{a_{\eta_i(\ell)} \in AP_i}$. The $(c_i^{(1)}, c_i^{(2)}, c_i^{(3)})$ is the encryption of B_i along with the description of $AP_i = (\mathbb{M}_i, \eta_i)$.

4. The ciphertext $\phi_i = (A_i, c_i^{(1)}, c_i^{(2)}, c_i^{(3)})$

The ciphertext database $cDB = \{(\phi_i, AP_i)\}_{i=1,2,\ldots,N}$. The algorithm outputs pk, sk, ψ, cDB to S. The sender S publishes pk, ψ, cDB by posting it on web and keeps sk secret to itself.

- InitDBVerify(pk, ψ, cDB): The receiver runs the database verification algorithm. The algorithm checks the correctness of ciphertext database $cDB = \{(\phi_i, AP_i)\}_{i=1,2,\ldots,N}$ by verifying for each $\phi_i = (A_i, c_i^{(1)}, c_i^{(2)}, c_i^{(3)})$, $AP_i = (\mathbb{M}_i, \eta_i)$, the following pairing equation

$$e(A_i, y \cdot c_i^{(2)}) = e(g, g), \quad i = 1, 2, \ldots, N.$$

The algorithm also verifies the proof ψ as discussed in Sect. 2.2. If all the verifications fail, the algorithm outputs $\perp$, otherwise, it moves to the issue phase.

- IssAttRand(pk, w): The receiver R runs the attribute randomization algorithm for attribute set $w \subseteq \Omega$ using $pk = (params, y, g_1, g_2, g_3, h_1, h_2, \ldots, h_m, U, H)$ by setting $w' = \{t_1, t_2, \ldots, t_m\}$, where $t_\ell = g_1^{d_\ell} \cdot h_\ell \cdot g^{z_\ell}$, $z_\ell \xleftarrow{\$} \mathbb{Z}_p^*$,

$$d_\ell = \begin{cases} a_\ell, & \text{if } a_\ell \in w \\ b_\ell, & \text{if } a_\ell \notin w \; b_\ell \xleftarrow{\$} \mathbb{Z}_p, \end{cases}$$

for $\ell = 1, 2, \ldots, m$ and $rv = \{z_1, z_2, \ldots, z_m\}$. The algorithm also generates proof of knowledge

$$\varphi = POK\{(d_1, d_2, \ldots, d_m, z_1, z_2, \ldots, z_m) \mid t_\ell = g_1^{d_\ell} \cdot h_\ell \cdot g^{z_\ell}\}.$$

The algorithm outputs $w' = \{t_1, t_2, \ldots, t_m\}, \varphi, rv$. The receiver R sends w', φ, to S and keeps rv secret.

- IssAttSk($pk, sk, w' = \{t_1, t_2, \ldots, t_m\}, \varphi$): The sender S runs the attribute secret key generation algorithm. The algorithm verifies the proof φ. If proof φ fails, the algorithm outputs $\perp$. Otherwise, it generates randomized attribute key ASK' for the receiver R using g_2^β extracted from $sk = (x, h, c, \beta)$. It chooses $s \xleftarrow{\$} \mathbb{Z}_p^*$ and sets $K_0 = g_2^\beta \cdot g_3^s$, $K_0' = g^s$, $K_\ell' = t_\ell^s$, for $\ell = 1, 2, \ldots, m,,$ $ASK' = (K_0, K_0', K_1', K_2', \ldots, K_m')$. The algorithm outputs ASK' to S. The sender S gives ASK' to R.

- IssAttSkExtract(pk, rv, ASK'): The receiver R runs the attribute secret key extraction algorithm. The algorithm first checks the correctness of $ASK' = (K_0, K_0', K_1', K_2', \ldots, K_m')$ by verifying the following pairing equations.

$$e(g, K_0) = e(g_1, g_2)e(K_0', g_3) \quad \text{and} \quad e(K_\ell', g) = e(t_\ell, K_0'), \quad \forall \ell = 1, 2, \ldots, m.$$

If the verification fails, outputs $\perp$, otherwise, the algorithm extracts attribute secret key ASK from $ASK' = (K_0, K_0', K_1', K_2', \ldots, K_m')$ as follows. It sets

$$K_0 = K_0, \quad K_0' = K_0', \quad K_\ell = \frac{K_\ell'}{(K_0')^{z_\ell}} \quad \text{if } a_\ell \in w, \; z_\ell \in rv, \; \forall \ell = 1, 2, \ldots, m.$$

The algorithm outputs $\mathsf{ASK} = (K_0, K_0', \{K_\ell\}_{a_\ell \in w})$ to R. The receiver R keeps ASK secret.

- $\mathsf{RequestTra}(\mathsf{pk}, \sigma_j, \phi_{\sigma_j}, \mathsf{ASK})$: The request generation algorithm is run by the receiver R with input σ_j. The algorithm parses ϕ_{σ_j} as $(A_{\sigma_j}, c_{\sigma_j}^{(1)}, c_{\sigma_j}^{(2)}, c_{\sigma_j}^{(3)})$, $\mathsf{AP}_{\sigma_j} = (\mathbb{M}_{\sigma_j}, \eta_{\sigma_j})$ and attribute secret key ASK as $(K_0, K_0', \{K_\ell\}_{a_\ell \in w})$. It chooses $v_{1,\sigma_j} \xleftarrow{\$} \mathbb{Z}_p^*$, sets $V_{\sigma_j} = A_{\sigma_j}^{v_{1,\sigma_j}} = g^{\frac{v_{1,\sigma_j}}{x + r_{\sigma_j}}}$, $X_{\sigma_j} = (c_{\sigma_j}^{(2)})^{v_{1,\sigma_j}} = g^{r_{\sigma_j} \cdot v_{1,\sigma_j}}$ and generates the proof π_{σ_j} as $\pi_{\sigma_j} = \mathsf{POK}\{(A_{\sigma_j}, v_{1,\sigma_j}) | e(V_{\sigma_j}, y) = e(A_{\sigma_j}, X_{\sigma_j}^{-1})$ $e(g, g)^{v_{1,\sigma_j}}\}$. The proof π_{σ_j} is generated to keep a check that σ_j is chosen from a valid set $\{1, 2, \ldots, N\}$. The algorithm sets $\mathsf{Req}_{\sigma_j} = (V_{\sigma_j}, X_{\sigma_j})$, $\mathsf{Pri}_{\sigma_j} = v_{1,\sigma_j}$ and outputs $\mathsf{Req}_{\sigma_j}, \mathsf{Pri}_{\sigma_j}, \pi_{\sigma_j}$ to R. The receiver R gives $\mathsf{Req}_{\sigma_j}, \pi_{\sigma_j}$ to S and keeps Pri_{σ_j} secret.

- $\mathsf{ResponseTra}(\mathsf{pk}, \mathsf{sk}, \mathsf{Req}_{\sigma_j}, \pi_{\sigma_j})$: The sender S runs the response generation algorithm in transfer phase with $\mathsf{Req}_{\sigma_j} = (V_{\sigma_j}, X_{\sigma_j})$ and π_{σ_j}. The algorithm first verifies the proof π_{σ_j} as discussed in Sect. 2.2. If the proof π_{σ_j} does not hold, the algorithm outputs $\perp$. Otherwise, it sets response $W_{\sigma_j} = e(V_{\sigma_j}, h)$ using secret h extracted from $\mathsf{sk} = (x, h, c, \beta)$ and generates proof δ_{σ_j} as follows. $\delta_{\sigma_j} = \mathsf{POK}\{(h) \mid H = e(g, h) \wedge W_{\sigma_j} = e(V_{\sigma_j}, h)\}$. The proof δ_{σ_j} is generated to convince the receiver R that the same secret is used to generate W_{σ_j} which was used in initialization phase to generate H. The algorithm sets $\mathsf{Res}_{\sigma_j} = W_{\sigma_j}$ and outputs $\mathsf{Res}_{\sigma_j}, \delta_{\sigma_j}$ to S. The sender S passes $\mathsf{Res}_{\sigma_j}, \delta_{\sigma_j}$ to R.

- $\mathsf{CompleteTra}(\mathsf{pk}, \mathsf{ASK}, \mathsf{Pri}_{\sigma_j}, \mathsf{Res}_{\sigma_j}, \delta_{\sigma_j}, \phi_{\sigma_j})$: This algorithm is run by the receiver R with $\mathsf{Res}_{\sigma_j} = W_{\sigma_j}$ and δ_{σ_j}. The algorithm checks the correctness of the proof δ_{σ_j} as discussed in Sect. 2.2. If δ_{σ_j} fails, the algorithm outputs $\perp$. Otherwise, it does the following to decrypt $\phi_{\sigma_j} = (A_{\sigma_j}, c_{\sigma_j}^{(1)}, c_{\sigma_j}^{(2)}, c_{\sigma_j}^{(3)})$ under $\mathsf{AP}_{\sigma_j} = (\mathbb{M}_{\sigma_j}, \eta_{\sigma_j})$ to extract m_{σ_j}.

1. Let $\{\lambda_{\sigma_j, \ell} \in \mathbb{Z}_p \mid a_{\eta_{\sigma_j}(\ell)} \in w\}$ be a valid set of shares of the secret exponent r_{σ_j} used to generate A_{σ_j} in the algorithm $\mathsf{InitDBSetup}$ using $\mathsf{Distribute}(\mathbb{M}_{\sigma_j}, \eta_{\sigma_j}, r_{\sigma_j})$ algorithm as discussed in Sect. 2.3.

2. The solution vector $\overrightarrow{x_{\sigma_j}} = \{x_\ell \in \mathbb{Z}_p \mid a_{\eta_{\sigma_j}(\ell)} \in w\}$ is computed satisfying $\sum_{a_{\eta_{\sigma_j}(\ell)} \in w} \lambda_{\sigma_j, \ell} x_\ell = r_{\sigma_j}$ using $\mathsf{Reconstruct}(\mathbb{M}_{\sigma_j}, \eta_{\sigma_j}, w)$ algorithm described in Sect. 2.3.

3. To recover m_{σ_j} from $c_{\sigma_j}^{(1)} = B_{\sigma_j} \cdot U^{r_{\sigma_j}}$, $c_{\sigma_j}^{(2)} = g^{r_{\sigma_j}}$,
$c_{\sigma_j}^{(3)} = \{c_{\sigma_j, \ell}^{(3)} = g_3^{\lambda_{\sigma_j, \ell}} \cdot \left(g_1^{a_{\eta_{\sigma_j}(\ell)}} \cdot h_{\eta_{\sigma_j}(\ell)}\right)^{-r_{\sigma_j}}\}_{a_{\eta_{\sigma_j}(\ell)} \in \mathsf{AP}_{\sigma_j}}$ using $\mathsf{ASK} = (K_0 = g_2^\beta g_3^s, K_0' = g^s, K_{\eta_{\sigma_j}(\ell)} = \left(g_1^{a_{\eta_{\sigma_j}(\ell)}} \cdot h_{\eta_{\sigma_j}(\ell)}\right)^s \; \forall \; a_{\eta_{\sigma_j}(\ell)} \in w_R)$, compute

$$\left. \begin{aligned} &\mathsf{val} = \frac{e(c_{\sigma_j}^{(2)}, K_0)}{\Pi_{a_{\eta_{\sigma_j}(\ell)} \in w}\left(e(c_{\sigma_j, \ell}^{(3)}, K_0')e(c_{\sigma_j}^{(2)}, K_{\eta_{\sigma_j}(\ell)})\right)^{x_\ell}} \\ &\frac{c_{\sigma_j}^{(1)}}{\mathsf{val} \cdot W_{\sigma_j}^{\frac{1}{v_{1,\sigma_j}}}} = m_{\sigma_j} \end{aligned} \right\} \tag{2}$$

4   Security Analysis

Theorem 2. *The adaptive oblivious transfer with access policy (AOT-AP) described in Sect. 2.4 securely implements the AOT-AP functionality assuming the hardness of the q-SDH and q-DBDHE problems, and the underlying POK is sound and perfect zero-knowledge.*

Proof 1. Consider a static adversary $\mathcal{A}$ interacting with AOT-AP protocol Ψ in a real world. An ideal world adversary $\mathcal{A}'$, also called simulator, interacting with the ideal functionality $\mathcal{F}$ is constructed in an ideal world. The task of environment machine $\mathcal{Z}$ to distinguish whether it is interacting with the real world or with the ideal world. Let $\mathsf{REAL}_{\Psi,\mathcal{A},\mathcal{Z}}$ and $\mathsf{IDEAL}_{\mathcal{F},\mathcal{A}',\mathcal{Z}}$ are as defined in Sect. 2.4. We will show that $\mathsf{REAL}_{\Psi,\mathcal{A},\mathcal{Z}} \overset{c}{\approx} \mathsf{IDEAL}_{\mathcal{F},\mathcal{A}',\mathcal{Z}}$ in each of the following cases: (a) simulation when R is corrupted and S is honest, (b) simulation when S is corrupted and R is honest. We do not discuss the trivial cases when both the parties are honest and when both the parties are corrupt.

The security proof is presented using sequence of hybrid games. Let $\Pr[\mathsf{Game}\ i]$ be the probability that $\mathcal{Z}$ distinguishes the transcript of $\mathsf{Game}\ i$ from the real execution.

(a) Simulation when the receiver R is corrupt and the sender S is honest. In this case, $\mathcal{A}$ corrupts R and gets all input from $\mathcal{Z}$. The ideal world adversary $\mathcal{A}'$ interacts with $\mathcal{F}$ as an ideal world receiver and with $\mathcal{A}$ as a real world sender. The adversary $\mathcal{A}'$ works as follows.

Game 0: This game corresponds to the real world in which R interacts with honest S. So, $\Pr[\mathsf{Game}\ 0] = 0$.

Game 1: This game is the same as the Game 0 except that $\mathcal{A}'$ extracts the attribute set w from $d_1, d_2, \ldots, d_m, z_1, z_2, \ldots, z_m$ which are extracted from the proof of knowledge $\varphi = \mathsf{POK}\{(d_1, d_2, \ldots, d_m, z_1, z_2, \ldots, z_m) \mid t_\ell = g_1^{d_\ell} \cdot h_\ell \cdot g^{z_\ell},$ where $d_\ell = a_\ell$, if $a_\ell \in w$, otherwise, $d_\ell = b_\ell\}$. The secrets are extracted from POK using adversarial rewinding. Initially, w is set to be empty. The adversary $\mathcal{A}'$ checks whether $d_\ell \in \Omega$. If yes, update $w = w \cup \{d_\ell\}$, otherwise, checks with the next value $d_{\ell+1}$, $\ell = 1, 2, \ldots, m$. The adversary $\mathcal{A}'$ simulates $\mathsf{ASK}' = (K_0, K_0', K_1', K_2', \ldots, K_m')$ exactly as in Game 0. The difference between Game 1 and Game 0 is negligible as the underlying proof of knowledge φ is sound. Therefore, there exists a negligible function $\epsilon_1(\rho)$ such that $|\Pr[\mathsf{Game}\ 1] - \Pr[\mathsf{Game}\ 0]| \leq \epsilon_1(\rho)$.

Game 2: This game is the same as the Game 1 except that $\mathcal{A}'$ extracts $(A_{\sigma_j}, v_{1,\sigma_j})$ from the proof $\pi_{\sigma_j} = \mathsf{POK}\{(A_{\sigma_j}, v_{1,\sigma_j}) \mid e(V_{\sigma_j}, y) = e(A_{\sigma_j}, X_{\sigma_j}^{-1})e(g, g)^{v_{1,\sigma_j}}\}$. If the extraction fails, Game 2 outputs a null string $\perp$. As the proof of knowledge is perfect zero-knowledge, the difference between Game 2 and Game 1 is negligible. Therefore, there exists a negligible function $\epsilon_2(\rho)$ such that $|\Pr[\mathsf{Game}\ 2] - \Pr[\mathsf{Game}\ 1]| \leq \epsilon_2(\rho)$.

Game 3: This game is the same as the Game 2 except that $\mathcal{A}'$ checks whether $A_{\sigma_j} = A_i$ for $i = 1, 2, \ldots, N$. If no matching found, then this means that

$\sigma_j \notin [N]$. This eventually means that $\mathcal{A}$ has constructed a forged BB signature $V_{\sigma_j}^{\frac{1}{v_{1,\sigma_j}}} = A_{\sigma_j}$ on random value r_{σ_j} which was used to encrypt m_{σ_j}. This is a contradiction to the assumption that the underlying BB signature is existentially unforgeable under the hardness of q-SDH problem. Therefore, there exists a negligible function $\epsilon_3(\rho)$ such that $|\Pr[\mathsf{Game}\ 3] - \Pr[\mathsf{Game}\ 2]| \leq \epsilon_3(\rho)$.

<u>Game 4</u>: Let σ_j be the matching index found in Game 3. The adversary $\mathcal{A}'$ interacts with $\mathcal{F}$ with the message $(\mathsf{transfer}, \sigma_j)$ to obtain m_{σ_j}. This game is the same as the Game 3 except that $\mathcal{A}'$ replaces the proof δ_{σ_j} with a simulated proof and simulates Res_{σ_j} in each transfer phase as

$$\mathsf{Res}_{\sigma_j} = W_{\sigma_j} = \left(\frac{c_{\sigma_j}^{(1)} \cdot \prod_{a_{\eta_{\sigma_j}}(\ell) \in w} \left(e\left(c_{\sigma_j,\ell}^{(3)}, K_0'\right) e\left(c_{\sigma_j}^{(2)}, K_{\eta_{\sigma_j}}(\ell)\right) \right)^{x_\ell}}{e(c_{\sigma_j}^{(2)}, K_0) \cdot m_{\sigma_j}} \right)^{v_{1,\sigma_j}},$$

where v_{1,σ_j} is extracted in Game 2 and w in Game 1 and $K_{\eta_{\sigma_j}}(\ell)$ is constructed from $K_{\eta_{\sigma_j}}'(\ell)$ using $z_{\eta_{\sigma_j}}(\ell)$ extracted in Game 1 $\forall a_{\eta_{\sigma_j}}(\ell) \in w$. The proof is simulated on a valid response. Due to perfect zero-knowledge, the difference between Game 4 and Game 3 is negligible. Therefore, there exists a negligible function $\epsilon_4(\rho)$ such that $|\Pr[\mathsf{Game}\ 4] - \Pr[\mathsf{Game}\ 3]| \leq \epsilon_4(\rho)$.

<u>Game 5</u>: This game is the same as the Game 4 except that $\mathcal{A}'$ replaces $c_{\sigma_j}^{(1)}$ by the random values in $\mathbb{G}_T$. In this case, the proof δ_{σ_j} is simulated on an invalid statement. The difference between Game 5 and Game 4 is negligible as the underlying CP-ABE is semantically secure assuming q-DBDHE assumption hold as discussed in Appendix A. Therefore, there exists a negligible function $\epsilon_5(\rho)$ such that $|\Pr[\mathsf{Game}\ 5] - \Pr[\mathsf{Game}\ 4]| \leq \epsilon_5(\rho)$.

Thus Game 5 is the ideal world interaction whereas Game 0 is the real world interaction. Now $|\Pr[\mathsf{Game}\ 5] - [\mathsf{Game}\ 0]| \leq |\Pr[\mathsf{Game}\ 5] - [\mathsf{Game}\ 4]| + |\Pr[\mathsf{Game}\ 4] - [\mathsf{Game}\ 3]| + |\Pr[\mathsf{Game}\ 3] - [\mathsf{Game}\ 2]| + |\Pr[\mathsf{Game}\ 2] - [\mathsf{Game}\ 1]| + |\Pr[\mathsf{Game}\ 1] - [\mathsf{Game}\ 0]| \leq \epsilon_6(\rho)$, where $\epsilon_6(\rho) = \epsilon_5(\rho) + \epsilon_4(\rho) + \epsilon_3(\rho) + \epsilon_2(\rho) + \epsilon_1(\rho)$ is a negligible function. Hence, $\mathsf{REAL}_{\Psi,\mathcal{A},\mathcal{Z}} \overset{c}{\approx} \mathsf{IDEAL}_{\mathcal{F},\mathcal{A}',\mathcal{Z}}$.

(b) Simulation when the sender S is corrupt and the receiver R is honest. In this case, S is corrupted by $\mathcal{A}$. The ideal world adversary $\mathcal{A}'$ communicates with $\mathcal{F}$ as an ideal world sender and with $\mathcal{A}$ as a real world receiver. The adversary $\mathcal{A}'$ works as follows.

<u>Game 0</u>: This game corresponds to the real world in which S interacts with honest R. So, $\Pr[\mathsf{Game}\ 0] = 0$.

<u>Game 1</u>: This game is the same as the Game 0 except that $\mathcal{A}'$ upon receiving $\mathsf{pk}, \psi, \mathsf{cDB}$, runs the knowledge extractor to extract h, c, β such that $H = e(g, h)$, $g_1 = g^\beta$ and $g_3 = g^c$ hold. If the extraction fails, $\mathcal{A}'$ aborts the execution. Otherwise, $\mathcal{A}'$ works exactly as in the previous game. The difference between Game 1 and Game 0 is negligible due to perfect zero-knowledge. Therefore, there exists a negligible function $\epsilon_1(\rho)$ such that $|\Pr[\mathsf{Game}\ 1] - \Pr[\mathsf{Game}\ 0]| \leq \epsilon_1(\rho)$.

Game 2: In this game, $\mathcal{A}'$ simulates t_ℓ by setting $t_\ell = g_1^{b_\ell} \cdot h_\ell \cdot g^{z_\ell}$, $b_\ell, z_\ell \xleftarrow{\$} \mathbb{Z}_p$ for $\ell = 1, 2, \ldots, m$ and simulates φ. During each transfer phase, the request $\mathsf{Req}_{\sigma_j} = (V_{\sigma_j}, X_{\sigma_j})$ is replaced by $\mathsf{Req}_1 = (V_1, X_1)$, where $V_1 = A_1^{v_{1,1}}$, $X_1 = (c_1^{(2)})^{v_{1,1}}$, where $A_1, c_1^{(2)}$ are extracted from $\phi_1 = (A_1, c_1^{(1)}, c_1^{(2)}, c_1^{(3)})$, $\mathsf{AP}_1 = (\mathbb{M}_1, \eta_1)$ and $v_{1,1} \xleftarrow{\$} \mathbb{Z}_p$. The proof $\pi_1 = \mathsf{POK}\{(A_1, v_{1,1}) \mid e(V_1, y) = e(A_1, X_1^{-1})e(g, g)^{v_{1,1}}\}$. Since Req_{σ_j} and Req_1, both are uniformly distributed, the difference between Game 2 and Game 1 is negligible due to perfect zero-knowledge. Therefore, there exists a negligible function $\epsilon_2(\rho)$ such that $|\Pr[\text{Game 2}] - \Pr[\text{Game 1}]| \leq \epsilon_2(\rho)$.

Thus Game 2 is the ideal world interaction whereas Game 0 is the real world interaction. Now $|\Pr[\text{Game 2}] - [\text{Game 0}]| \leq +|\Pr[\text{Game 2}] - [\text{Game 1}]| + |\Pr[\text{Game 1}] - [\text{Game 0}]| \leq \epsilon_3(\rho)$, where $\epsilon_3(\rho) = \epsilon_2(\rho) + \epsilon_1(\rho)$ is a negligible function. Hence, $\mathsf{REAL}_{\Psi, \mathcal{A}, \mathcal{Z}} \overset{c}{\approx} \mathsf{IDEAL}_{\mathcal{F}, \mathcal{A}', \mathcal{Z}}$.

Now, we show that the output of the real world receiver is the same as the output of the ideal world receiver.

In the real world, the receiver R decrypts $\phi_{\sigma_j} = (A_{\sigma_j}, c_{\sigma_j}^{(1)}, c_{\sigma_j}^{(2)}, c_{\sigma_j}^{(3)})$ under access policy $\mathsf{AP}_{\sigma_j} = (\mathbb{M}_{\sigma_j}, \eta_{\sigma_j})$, where

$$A_{\sigma_j} = g^{\frac{1}{x+r_{\sigma_j}}}, c_{\sigma_j}^{(1)} = m_{\sigma_j} \cdot e(A_{\sigma_j}, h) \cdot e(g_1, g_2)^{r_{\sigma_j}}, c_{\sigma_j}^{(2)} = g^{r_{\sigma_j}},$$

$$c_{\sigma_j}^{(3)} = \{c_{\sigma_j, \ell}^{(3)}\}_{a_{\eta_{\sigma_j}}(\ell) \in \mathsf{AP}_{\sigma_j}}, c_{\sigma_j, \ell}^{(3)} = g_3^{\lambda_{\sigma_j, \ell}} \cdot \left(g_1^{a_{\eta_{\sigma_j}}(\ell)} \cdot h_{\eta_{\sigma_j}}(\ell)\right)^{-r_{\sigma_j}} \forall a_{\eta_{\sigma_j}}(\ell) \in \mathsf{AP}_{\sigma_j}$$

using $\mathsf{ASK} = (K_0 = g_2^\beta \cdot g_3^s, K_0' = g^s, K_{\eta_{\sigma_j}}(\ell) = \left(g_1^{a_{\eta_{\sigma_j}}(\ell)} \cdot h_{\eta_{\sigma_j}}(\ell)\right)^s \forall a_{\eta_{\sigma_j}}(\ell) \in w_R)$ and response $\mathsf{Res}_{\sigma_j} = W_{\sigma_j} = e(V_{\sigma_j}, h)$ as

$$\frac{c_{\sigma_j}^{(1)} \cdot \prod_{a_{\eta_{\sigma_j}}(\ell) \in w} \left(e\left(c_{\sigma_j, \ell}^{(3)}, K_0'\right) e\left(c_{\sigma_j}^{(2)}, K_{\eta_{\sigma_j}}(\ell)\right)\right)^{x_\ell}}{e(c_{\sigma_j}^{(2)}, K_0) \cdot W_{\sigma_j}^{\frac{1}{v_{1,\sigma_j}}}} = m_{\sigma_j}, \text{ where } V_{\sigma_j} = A_{\sigma_j}^{v_{1,\sigma_j}}.$$

In the ideal world, $\mathcal{A}'$ decrypts $\phi_i = (A_i, c_i^{(1)}, c_i^{(2)}, c_i^{(3)})$, $\mathsf{AP}_i = (\mathbb{M}_i, \eta_i)$, using extracted secrets h and β in Game 1 as

$$\frac{c_i^{(1)}}{e(A_i, h)e(c_i^{(2)}, g_2^\beta)} = \frac{c_i^{(1)}}{e(A_i, h)e(g^{r_i}, g_2^\beta)} = \frac{m_i \cdot e(A_i, h) \cdot e(g_1, g_2)^{r_i}}{e(A_i, h) \cdot e(g_1, g_2)^{r_i}} = m_i,$$

as $g_1 = g^\beta$, where

$$A_i = g^{\frac{1}{x+r_i}}, c_i^{(1)} = m_i \cdot e(A_i, h) \cdot e(g_1, g_2)^{r_i}, c_i^{(2)} = g^{r_i},$$

$$c_i^{(3)} = \{c_{i,\ell}^{(3)}\}_{a_{\eta_i}(\ell) \in \mathsf{AP}_i}, c_{i,\ell}^{(3)} = g_3^{\lambda_{i,\ell}} \cdot \left(g_1^{a_{\eta_i}(\ell)} \cdot h_{\eta_i}(\ell)\right)^{-r_i} \forall a_{\eta_i}(\ell) \in \mathsf{AP}_i,$$

$\lambda_{i,\ell}$ are valid shares of a secret r_i, for $i = 1, 2, \ldots, N$. The adversary $\mathcal{A}'$ submits $(m_1, \mathsf{AP}_1), (m_2, \mathsf{AP}_2), \ldots, (m_N, \mathsf{AP}_N)$ to $\mathcal{F}$ and acts as the ideal world sender. The receiver R with message $(\mathsf{transfer}, \sigma_j)$ communicates with $\mathcal{F}$. The ideal functionality $\mathcal{F}$ checks whether w satisfies AP_{σ_j}. If not, $\mathcal{F}$ outputs $\perp$ to R. Otherwise, $\mathcal{F}$ returns m_{σ_j} to R.

5   Comparison

We compare our proposed protocol with the construction of Zhang *et al.* [17] which is, to the best of our knowledge, the only AOT-AP that realizes disjunction of attributes. Our AOT-AP is as efficient as [17] as illustrated in Tables 1 and 2, where EXP stands for exponentiations and PO for pairings. Both [17] and our AOT-AP use proof of knowledge POK, the cost of which are not exhibited in tables. The subtle differences between our scheme and [17] are listed below.

1. Zhang *et al.* [17] uses BB signature [3], CP-ABE of [11] and is secure assuming the hardness of q-SDH, q-Power Decisional Diffie-Hellman (PDDH) and q-DBDHE problems. In contrast to [17], our scheme couples BB signature [3] and a variant of CP-ABE [16]. The proposed scheme requires the hardness of q-SDH and q-DBDHE problems.
2. The scheme of [17] is run between a sender, an issuer and multiple receivers while our scheme is free from any trusted issuer.
3. In [17], the issuer is forbidden to collude with any receiver, otherwise the receiver may obtain the master secret key from the issuer making the scheme insecure. In this case, the AOT-AP of [17] is the same as AOT without access policy as the receiver can decrypt any ciphertext by interacting with the sender in the transfer phase. Our scheme does not impose these type of constraints on receivers as trusted issuer is no longer required in our construction.

Table 1. Comparison summary of computation cost, where n_i is the number of attributes in AP_i associated with m_i, and m is the total of attributes.

AOT-AP	Public Key pk Generation			Per Ciphertext Generation			Per Transfer Query		
	EXP in G	EXP in G_T	PO	EXP in G	EXP in G_T	PO	EXP in G	EXP in G_T	PO
[17]	$m+2$	1	2	$3n_i+2$	1	1	1	1	4
Ours	3	0	2	$3n_i+2$	1	1	2	1	5

Table 2. Comparison summary in terms of communication cost, where n_i is the number of attributes in AP_i associated with m_i, and m is the total of attributes.

AOT-AP	Public Key pk Size		Ciphertext ϕ_i Size		$(Req_{\sigma_j} + Res_{\sigma_j})$ Size		Assumptions
	G	G_T	G	G_T	G	G_T	
[17]	$m+4$	2	$2n_i+1$	1	1	1	q-SDH, q-PDDH, q-DBDHE
Ours	$m+5$	2	n_i+2	1	2	1	q-SDH, q-DBDHE

6   Conclusion

We have proposed the first adaptive oblivious transfer with access policy (AOT-AP) run between a sender and multiple receivers without any trusted issuer in full-simulation security model. For this, we have designed a CP-ABE based on [16] and provide a rigorous security analysis to prove its semantic security under q-DBDHE assumption. This CP-ABE has been used in our AOT-AP construction. The proposed AOT-AP has been proved to be secure assuming the hardness of q-SDH and q-DBDHE problems in the presence of malicious adversary. The protocol is as efficient as the exiting similar schemes. The adaptive oblivious transfer with hidden access policy (AOT-HAP) is an interesting area of research. How to use our AOT-AP to construct AOT-HAP is our future direction.

A   Our CP-ABE

We describe below our ciphertext policy attribute based encryption (CP-ABE) following [16] that is used as one of the basic building block in our AOT-AP construction. A CP-ABE invokes three randomized algorithm Setup, Encrypt, KeyGen and a deterministic algorithm Decrypt. The Setup, Encrypt, KeyGen procedures in our CP-ABE are different from that of [16]. Moreover, the simulation in the security reduction is also considerably different from that of [16].

- Setup($1^\rho, \Omega$): This randomized algorithm takes as input security parameter ρ and universe of attributes $\Omega = (a_1, a_2, \ldots, a_m)$, $a_i \in \mathbb{Z}_p, i = 1, 2, \ldots, m$. It first generates params $= (p, \mathbb{G}, \mathbb{G}_T, e, g) \leftarrow$ BilinearSetup(1^ρ), randomly takes $c, \alpha \xleftarrow{\$} \mathbb{Z}_p, g_2, h_1, h_2, \ldots, h_m \xleftarrow{\$} \mathbb{G}$ and sets $g_1 = g^\alpha$, $g_3 = g^c$, $U = e(g_1, g_2)$. The public and master secret key pair is PK $= (g_1, g_2, g_3, h_1, h_2, \ldots, h_m, U)$, MSK $= (g_2^\alpha, c)$.
- Encrypt(PK, m, AP): This randomized algorithm encrypts the message m under the access policy AP as follows.
    1. The algorithm converts AP to LSSS access structure $(\mathbb{M}, \eta)$ as discussed in Sect. 2.3, where $\mathbb{M}$ is $n \times \theta$ matrix, n is the number of attributes in AP, the function η maps index of each row of $\mathbb{M}$ to an attribute index in AP.
    2. Randomly choose $s, s_2, s_3, \ldots, s_\theta \xleftarrow{\$} \mathbb{Z}_p$ and set $v = (s, s_2, \ldots, s_\theta)$.
    3. Compute $\mathbb{M} \cdot v = (\lambda_1, \lambda_2, \ldots, \lambda_n) \in \mathbb{Z}_p^n$ using Distribute($\mathbb{M}, \eta, s$) algorithm as explained in Sect. 2.3.
    4. Set $C = m \cdot U^s$, $C' = g^s$, $C_i = g_3^{\lambda_i} \cdot \left(g_1^{a_{\eta(i)}} \cdot h_{\eta(i)}\right)^{-s}$, $\forall a_{\eta(i)} \in$ AP.
    5. The ciphertext CT $= (C, C', \{C_i\}_{a_{\eta(i)} \in \mathsf{AP}}, \mathbb{M}, \eta)$
- KeyGen(PK, MSK, w): This randomized algorithm using master secret key MSK $= (g_2^\alpha, c)$ generates attribute secret key ASK for the attribute set w. It picks $t \xleftarrow{\$} \mathbb{Z}_p$ and sets $K_0 = g_2^\alpha \cdot g_3^t$, $K_0' = g^t$, $K_x = (g_1^{a_x} \cdot h_x)^t$ $\forall a_x \in w$. The attribute secret key is ASK $= (K_0, K_0', \{K_x\}_{a_x \in w})$.
- Decrypt(CT, w, ASK): This deterministic algorithm recovers the message m from the ciphertext CT $= (C, C', \{C_i\}_{a_{\eta(i)} \in \mathsf{AP}}, \mathbb{M}, \eta)$ using attribute secret key ASK $= (K_0, K_0', \{K_x\}_{a_x \in w})$ as follows.

1. Let $\{\lambda_\ell \in \mathbb{Z}_p \mid a_{\eta(\ell)} \in w\}$ be a valid set of shares of the secret exponent s used to generate C in the algorithm Encrypt using Distribute$(\mathbb{M}, \eta, s)$ algorithm as discussed in Sect. 2.3.

2. The solution vector $\vec{x} = \{x_\ell \in \mathbb{Z}_p \mid a_{\eta(\ell)} \in w\}$ is computed satisfying $\sum_{a_{\eta(\ell)} \in w} \lambda_\ell x_\ell = s$ using Reconstruct$(\mathbb{M}, \eta, w)$ algorithm described in Sect. 2.3.

3. Compute

$$\left. \begin{array}{l} \mathsf{eval} = \dfrac{e(C', K_0)}{\prod_{a_{\eta(\ell)} \in w}(e(C_\ell, K_0')e(C', K_{\eta(\ell)}))^{x_\ell}} \\[2ex] \dfrac{C}{\mathsf{eval}} = m \end{array} \right\} \qquad (3)$$

Theorem 3. *The CP-ABE is semantically secure under the q-DBDHE assumption in the security model adapted in [16].*

Due to lack of space, proof of Theorem 3 will be given in full version.

References

1. Beimel, A.: Secure schemes for secret sharing and key distribution. Ph.D. thesis, Israel Institute of Technology, Technion, Haifa, Israel (1996)
2. Bellare, M., Goldreich, O.: On defining proofs of knowledge. In: Brickell, E.F. (ed.) CRYPTO 1992. LNCS, vol. 740, pp. 390–420. Springer, Heidelberg (1993)
3. Boneh, D., Boyen, X.: Short signatures without random oracles. In: Cachin, C., Camenisch, J.L. (eds.) EUROCRYPT 2004. LNCS, vol. 3027, pp. 56–73. Springer, Heidelberg (2004)
4. Camenisch, J., Dubovitskaya, M., Neven, G.: Oblivious transfer with access control. In: ACM 2009, pp. 131–140. ACM (2009)
5. Camenisch, J.L., Neven, G., Shelat, A.: Simulatable adaptive oblivious transfer. In: Naor, M. (ed.) EUROCRYPT 2007. LNCS, vol. 4515, pp. 573–590. Springer, Heidelberg (2007)
6. Camenisch, J.L., Stadler, M.A.: Efficient group signature schemes for large groups. In: Kaliski Jr., B.S. (ed.) CRYPTO 1997. LNCS, vol. 1294, pp. 410–424. Springer, Heidelberg (1997)
7. Coull, S., Green, M., Hohenberger, S.: Controlling access to an oblivious database using stateful anonymous credentials. In: Jarecki, S., Tsudik, G. (eds.) PKC 2009. LNCS, vol. 5443, pp. 501–520. Springer, Heidelberg (2009)
8. Green, M., Hohenberger, S.: Blind identity-based encryption and simulatable oblivious transfer. In: Kurosawa, K. (ed.) ASIACRYPT 2007. LNCS, vol. 4833, pp. 265–282. Springer, Heidelberg (2007)
9. Green, M., Hohenberger, S.: Universally composable adaptive oblivious transfer. In: Pieprzyk, J. (ed.) ASIACRYPT 2008. LNCS, vol. 5350, pp. 179–197. Springer, Heidelberg (2008)
10. Guleria, V., Dutta, R.: Efficient adaptive oblivious transfer in UC framework. In: Huang, X., Zhou, J. (eds.) ISPEC 2014. LNCS, vol. 8434, pp. 271–286. Springer, Heidelberg (2014)
11. Lewko, A., Okamoto, T., Sahai, A., Takashima, K., Waters, B.: Fully secure functional encryption: attribute-based encryption and (hierarchical) inner product encryption. In: Gilbert, H. (ed.) EUROCRYPT 2010. LNCS, vol. 6110, pp. 62–91. Springer, Heidelberg (2010)

12. Lewko, A., Waters, B.: Decentralizing attribute-based encryption. In: Paterson, K.G. (ed.) EUROCRYPT 2011. LNCS, vol. 6632, pp. 568–588. Springer, Heidelberg (2011)

13. Naor, M., Pinkas, B.: Oblivious transfer with adaptive queries. In: Wiener, M. (ed.) CRYPTO 1999. LNCS, vol. 1666, pp. 573–590. Springer, Heidelberg (1999)

14. Rial, A., Kohlweiss, M., Preneel, B.: Universally composable adaptive priced oblivious transfer. In: Shacham, H., Waters, B. (eds.) Pairing 2009. LNCS, vol. 5671, pp. 231–247. Springer, Heidelberg (2009)

15. Waters, B.: Efficient identity-based encryption without random oracles. In: Cramer, R. (ed.) EUROCRYPT 2005. LNCS, vol. 3494, pp. 114–127. Springer, Heidelberg (2005)

16. Waters, B.: Ciphertext-policy attribute-based encryption: an expressive, efficient, and provably secure realization. In: Catalano, D., Fazio, N., Gennaro, R., Nicolosi, A. (eds.) PKC 2011. LNCS, vol. 6571, pp. 53–70. Springer, Heidelberg (2011)

17. Zhang, Y., Au, M.H., Wong, D.S., Huang, Q., Mamoulis, N., Cheung, D.W., Yiu, S.-M.: Oblivious transfer with access control: realizing disjunction without duplication. In: Joye, M., Miyaji, A., Otsuka, A. (eds.) Pairing 2010. LNCS, vol. 6487, pp. 96–115. Springer, Heidelberg (2010)

Side-Channel Attacks

Memory Address Side-Channel Analysis on Exponentiation

Chien-Ning Chen[✉]

Physical Analysis and Cryptographic Engineering (PACE),
Nanyang Technological University, Singapore, Singapore
chienning@ntu.edu.sg

Abstract. Side-channel analysis aims at cryptography implementation by exploiting and analyzing side-channel information. Side-channel leakage of software implementation does not only depend on operators (instruction) and operands (value) but also on where operators and operands are called or stored in the memory. However, in contrast to the leakage of the operator and operand values, the exploitable leakage caused by the memory address is quite small. Side-channel analysis aiming at memory address usually needs a huge number of samples to eliminate the algorithmic noise. This paper presents a new attack method exploiting the leakage from consecutive addresses when accessing multiple-byte operands during evaluation of an exponentiation. By folding the observed side-channel leakage, one measurement is enough to perform statistical side-channel analysis and successfully reveal the secret key. Since only one measurement is sufficient, this attack even works in the presence of common side-channel countermeasures such as exponent randomization and message blinding.

Keywords: Address-bit SCA · Exponentiation · Horizontal side-channel analysis · Montgomery multiplication · Side-channel analysis

1 Introduction

As a part of public-key cryptosystems, computation of exponentiation suffers the threat of side-channel analysis (SCA) [13] which aims at cryptography implementation and exploits side-channel information. Many research results can be found in the literature, including SCAs on exponentiation and development of exponentiation algorithms as side-channel countermeasures. Timing attack [12] exploits the variance in time when the running time of exponentiation depends on its inputs (base number and exponent). Simple power analysis (SPA) aims at the computational sequence which usually depends on the exponent. Statistical power analysis, like differential power analysis (DPA) [13] and correlation power analysis (CPA) [1], aims at the difference in power consumption which is highly relative to the value of intermediate results. Side-channel countermeasures for exponentiation are usually developed by hiding and randomizing the computational sequence and the intermediate results, e.g., square-and-multiply-always exponentiation algorithm, exponent randomization, and message blinding [4,12].

© Springer International Publishing Switzerland 2015
J. Lee and J. Kim (Eds.): ICISC 2014, LNCS 8949, pp. 421–432, 2015.
DOI: 10.1007/978-3-319-15943-0_25

Most SCAs and countermeasures target the value of operands, but where the operands are stored is also exploitable side-channel information. The experiments by Messerges et al. [15] showed that the power consumption of a smart card depends on the activity on both data and address bus. An exponentiation consists of many multiplications, and the operands of each multiplication are determined by the exponent. Address-bit DPA in [7] averages over multiple power traces with different base numbers to eliminate the algorithmic noise (the part of power consumption depending on the value of operands) and determines the address of operands of each multiplication by the difference of means. Izumi et al. [9] point out Montgomery powering ladder [10] is vulnerable to SPA when the base number is fixed to zero. The value of the operands of all multiplications is identical, and the only difference is the location storing the operands. Localized electromagnetic analysis [6] recognizes the physical location storing each operand by comparing electromagnetic radiation on each location of the chip. After identifying the address or the physical location of operands of each multiplication, the secret exponent can be recovered.

A long-integer multiplication consists of many atomic operations (e.g., byte-wise multiplications), and each atomic operation accesses one or few pieces (e.g., one byte) of operands. Horizontal correlation analysis [3] computes the correlation factor on segments corresponding to the atomic operations, extracted from one execution curve. In contrast to [3] focusing on the value of operands, this paper focuses on the address. In software implementation, a long integer is stored in continuous memory space with consecutive addresses. The proposed method exploits the iterative structure of a long-integer multiplication and consecutively increasing address of memory access. In order to exploit leakage of addresses from all memory access, a power trace will be divided into small segments corresponding to each atomic operation. The address of operands is then determined by calculating the correlation coefficient between each segment of the power trace and the address of memory access in each atomic operation.

The experimental results show, when analyzing 512-bit exponentiation on the 8-bit AVR microcontroller, by fully exploiting the 64 consecutive memory addresses, one power trace is enough to identify the operands of each multiplication and recover the private exponent. Since the proposed address SCA requires only one power trace and does not need any knowledge about the base number, it can break countermeasures like exponent randomization and message blinding.

The remaining parts of this paper are organized as follows. Section 2 reviews exponentiation algorithms, horizontal correlation analysis and address-bit DPA. Section 3 presents the new memory-address SCA on exponentiation and also provides the experimental results, including insider attacks with the knowledge of memory address of operands, and a partial-insider attack without the knowledge of the address. Section 4 discusses countermeasures against the proposed attack. Section 5 concludes this paper.

2   Preliminaries and Background

2.1   Computation of Exponentiation

Exponentiation is a fundamental computation in many public-key cryptosystems. The performance of a public-key cryptosystem as well as its immunity against side-channel analysis highly depends on the underlying computation of exponentiation. The computation can be divided into two parts: the exponentiation algorithm on the top and the long-integer multiplication algorithm at the bottom. Figure 1 shows the binary square-and-multiply exponentiation algorithms, including both left-to-right (downward) and right-to-left (upward) versions.

Input: X, D = $(d_{n-1} \cdots d_0)_2$, M	Input: X, D = $(d_{n-1} \cdots d_0)_2$, M
Output: Y = X^D mod M	Output: Y = X^D mod M
01 Y = 1	01 Y = 1, S = X
02 for i = $n-1$ to 0 step -1	02 for i = 0 to $n-1$ step 1
03 Y = Y × Y mod M	03 if (d_i = 1) then
04 if (d_i = 1) then	04 Y = Y × S mod M
05 Y = Y × X mod M	05 S = S × S mod M
06 return Y	06 return Y
(A) left-to-right version.	(B) right-to-left version.

Fig. 1. Binary square-and-multiply exponentiation algorithms.

A modular exponentiation consists of many modular multiplications. Montgomery multiplication [16] is commonly used in modular arithmetic. It computes $\text{MontMul}(A, B) = (A \times B \times 2^{-kt} \bmod M)$ instead of $(A \times B \bmod M)$ to avoid modular operations (divisions). When employing Montgomery multiplication in a modular exponentiation, the base number X will be replaced by $X' = X \times 2^{kt} \bmod M$, and the final result can be retrieved by $Y = Y' \times 2^{-kt} \bmod M = \text{MontMul}(Y', 1)$. Figure 2 provides a typical implementation of Montgomery multiplication on a t-bit microcontroller, where A and B are the two operands, M is the modulus, $0 \leq A, B, M < 2^{kt}$, a_i is the i-th word of A in 2^t-ary representation, and $m' = (-m_0)^{-1} \bmod 2^t$.

The inputs and the result of a naïve implementation of Montgomery multiplication will satisfy $0 \leq A, B, C < M$. It needs to check if $C \geq M$ and optionally performs a subtraction $C - M$ before outputting the result. The optional subtraction might cause side-channel leakage. C. Walter [17] as well as G. Hachez and J.-J. Quisquater [5] proposed a technique to eliminate the check and the optional subtraction. In their methods, the parameters will satisfy $A, B, C < 2M$ and either $2M < 2^{(k'-1)t}$ or $M < 2^{(k'-1)t}$. However, in order to satisfy the new conditions, one additional byte is needed to store the inputs and result, which might cause extra costs in memory management.

```
Input: A, B, M
Output: C = MontMul(A,B) = A × B × 2^{-kt} mod M
01 C = 0
02 for i = 0 to k−1 step 1
03    m″ = ((c_0 + a_i × b_0) × m′) mod 2^t
04    C = (C + a_i × B + m″ × M)/2^t
05 if (C ≥ M) then C = C − M
06 output C
```

Fig. 2. Montgomery multiplication algorithm.

2.2 Software Implementation of Montgomery Multiplication and Horizontal Correlation Analysis

Referring to Fig. 2, a Montgomery multiplication MontMul(A, B) consists of k iterations. Each iteration (lines 03 and 04) is a small operation Comp[i], containing the evaluation of m'' and $C + a_i \times B + m'' \times M$. The computation $C + a_i \times B + m'' \times M$ is further divided into atomic operations comp[i, j] : $\mathtt{carry}_j + c_j + a_i \times b_j + m'' \times m_j$ when implementing on a microcontroller.

In a straightforward implementation, the operation Comp[i] of the iteration i will access the operand a_i from memory (also c_0, b_0, m'), compute m'', and then carry out the k atomic operations comp[i, j] from $j = 0$ to $k - 1$. Suppose the value a_i remains in a register, each of the atomic operation comp[i, j] will access the operands c_j, b_j, m_j, evaluate and store the result.

Horizontal correlation analysis [3] targets the k^2 atomic operations comp[i, j] $(i, j \in [0, k - 1])$ in one multiplication.[1] It computes the correlation factor on segments corresponding to the atomic operations, extracted from one power consumption trace, and identifies whether a multiplication is $A \times B$ or $A \times B'$.

2.3 Memory Address Side-Channel Analysis

The computation of exponentiation is a combination of multiplications. Side-channel analysis on exponentiation tries to identify those multiplications, e.g., whether each multiplication is $Y \times S$ or $S \times S$ in Fig. 1(B). Once all multiplications are identified, the private exponent can be recovered. Conventional side-channel analysis and also Horizontal correlation analysis in [3] aim at side-channel leakage from the value of operands, e.g., if the value $S \neq Y$, the two multiplications $Y \times S$ and $S \times S$ will cause different side-channel leakage. However, besides the value, the memory address of operands also causes side-channel leakage. Itoh et al. [7] proposed the address-bit DPA aiming at the memory address of operands in software implementation.

Itoh et al. assume the power consumption from the address depends on its Hamming weight. The address usually causes smaller difference in power consumption than the value. The address-bit DPA by Itoh et al. averages multiple

---

[1] Actually, the analysis in [3] targets $a_i \times b_j$ in a long-integer multiplication, but the same idea can be applied to Montgomery multiplication.

power traces with different inputs to eliminate the influence from the value. The averaged power trace will depend on the address only, i.e., if two multiplications are with the operands storing in the same address, the averaged power trace segment corresponding to them will be similar. By comparing each segment of the averaged power trace, the operands of each multiplication can be identified.

3   Memory Address SCA by Folding Power Trace

The proposed memory-address SCA fully exploits the leakage from every memory address appearing in one power trace. It assumes the power consumption from address is accordance with its Hamming weight, and the two operands A and A' to be distinguished are not stored with the offset equal to a multiple of a power of 2, i.e., $\mathsf{Addr}(\mathsf{a}_i) \neq \mathsf{Addr}(\mathsf{a}'_i) \pm m \times 2^l$, so the difference of the Hamming weight $\mathsf{HWAddr}(\mathsf{a}_i) - \mathsf{HWAddr}(\mathsf{a}'_i)$ is not a constant. When using the Montgomery multiplication in [5,17], this assumption holds because one additional byte is needed to store an operand, e.g., 65 bytes for 512-bit multiplication.

The proposed method needs only one power trace and assumes that the attacker can identify the iterative structure in the power trace. A power trace is firstly divided into segments corresponding to each Montgomery multiplication. When identifying the operands of a Montgomery multiplication, the corresponding segment of the power trace is further divided into smaller segments $\mathsf{Power}[i]$ or $\mathsf{power}[i, j]$ corresponding to the operation $\mathsf{Comp}[i]$ or $\mathsf{comp}[i, j]$, defined in Sect. 2.2. The idea is to calculate the Pearson correlation coefficient ρ between power consumption $\mathsf{Power}[i]$ and the Hamming weight of the address $\mathsf{HWAddr}(\mathsf{a}_i)$, where $\mathsf{Addr}(\mathsf{a}_i) = \mathsf{Addr}(\mathsf{a}_0) + i$. If $\mathsf{Comp}[i]$ accesses the operand a_i at the time t, there will be a higher coefficient $\rho[t]$.

Experimental results are provided. The experiments target 512-bit modular exponentiation, which is evaluated by the right-to-left exponentiation algorithm and executes on a modified Arduino Uno board with the 8-bit 16 MHz AVR microcontroller Atmega328p. The power consumption of the AVR microcontroller is measured by LeCroy WaveRunner 610Zi oscilloscope with AP033 active differential probe at the sampling rate 250 M/s. Figure 3 is the implementation of the atomic operation $\mathsf{comp}[i, j]$ $(j = 1 \sim 63)$ on the 8-bit AVR microcontroller, which needs 21 clock cycles (the instructions LDD, LD, ST, and MUL need 2 clock cycles). The first atomic operation $\mathsf{comp}[i, 0]$ in each $\mathsf{Comp}[i]$ is different from other atomic operations, because it also loads the operand a_i to the register r14 and evaluates m'' (storing in r15).

The proposed method and the experiments are divided into four parts. The first three parts show how to identify the operands A, B, and C of a Montgomery multiplication $\mathsf{C} = \mathrm{MontMul}(\mathsf{A}, \mathsf{B})$, with the insider knowledge about the memory layout (address of operands). The last part shows that the proposed memory-address SCA is still possible without the knowledge of the memory address.

```
01 LDD r0, Z+1     // r0 = c_j, Z → c_{j-1}
02 ADD r16, r0
03 ADC r17, r19    // r19 = 0
04 CLR r18         // r18:r17:r16 = carry + c_j
05 LD  r0, X+      // r0 = b_j, X → b_{j+1}
06 MUL r0, r14     // r14 = a_i
07 ADD r16, r0
08 ADC r17, r1
09 ADC r18, r19    // r18:r17:r16 = carry + c_j + a_i × b_j
10 LD  r0, Y+      // r0 = m_j, Y → m_{j+1}
11 MUL r0, r15     // r15 = m″
12 ADD r16, r0
13 ADC r17, r1
14 ADC r18, r19    // r18:r17:r16 = carry + c_j + a_i × b_j + m″ × m_j
15 ST  Z+, r16     // c_{j-1} = r16, Z → c_j, carry = r18:r17
```

Fig. 3. The atomic operation $\mathsf{comp}[i,j]$ ($j \in [1,63]$) on AVR microcontroller.

3.1 Analysis Targeting the Address of First Operand

The first analysis is to identify the address of the first operand in a Montgomery multiplication, i.e., to tell MontMul(A, B) from MontMul(A′, B).[2] Each byte (a_i or a_i') of the first operand (A or A′) is accessed once during comp[i, 0] of Comp[i]. The Pearson correlation coefficients ($\rho[t]$ and $\rho'[t]$) between power[i, 0] and the Hamming weight of address (HWAddr(a_i) and HWAddr(a_i')) are calculated over 64 samples ($i = 0 \sim 63$). The first operand can be identified by comparing the Pearson correlation coefficients $\rho[t]$ and $\rho'[t]$.

The results of the first 12 multiplications in one exponentiation are provided in Fig. 4, where the upper part is the Pearson correlation coefficient $\rho[t]$, the middle is $\rho'[t]$, and the bottom is the difference between two coefficients $\Delta\rho[t] = \rho[t] - \rho'[t]$. The thiner blue solid lines correspond to the computation with the operand A, and the red dotted lines correspond to A′.

The peak at $t_1 = 6 \sim 8$ corresponds to the instruction "LD r14, Z" which loads a_i or a_i' to the register r14 from the address storing in a pair of registers Z = r31:r30. The peak at $t_2 = 18 \sim 20$ corresponds to the instruction "PUSH r30" which treats the lower byte of the address as data and stores it to the memory (stack). This paper targets the power consumption at t_1 but ignores that at t_2 because analyzing the power consumption at t_2 is more like a conventional SCA targeting data rather than address.

The experimental result shows that the first operand can be identified by the difference of the correlation coefficients $\Delta\rho$. The first operand of the 2nd, 5th, 7th, and 11th multiplications is A′, and those multiplications are of higher correlation coefficient with HWAddr(a_i') at t_1. In contrast, the other multiplications are of higher correlation coefficient with HWAddr(a_i).

---

[2] This paper targets the right-to-left exponentiation algorithm, and the operands A and A′ are identical to S and Y in Fig. 1(B), storing in the addresses Addr(a_i) = 0x0344+i and Addr(a_i') = 0x0385 + i, respectively.

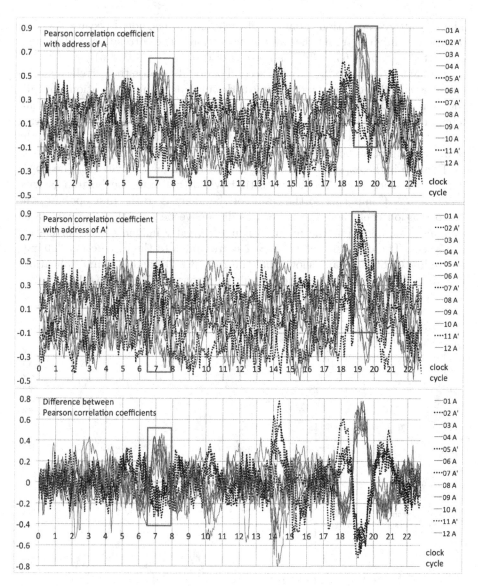

Fig. 4. Pearson correlation coefficient with HWAddr(a_i) and HWAddr(a_i').

3.2 Analysis Targeting the Address of Second Operand

The same idea can be applied to identify the second operand of a Montgomery multiplication, i.e., to tell MontMul(A, B) from MontMul(A, B′).[3] Each atomic operation comp$[i, j]$ accesses one byte (b_j or b_j') of the second operand (B or B′).

---

[3] In the second experiment, the two operands of the multiplication in line 04 of Fig. 1(B) are swapped, i.e., replacing $Y = Y \times S \bmod M$ by $Y = S \times Y \bmod M$.

The first atomic operation comp$[i, 0]$ of each Comp$[i]$ is ignored because its computation is different from other atomic operations. The correlation coefficient is calculated over $64 \times 63 = 4032$ samples ($i \in [0, 63]$ and $j \in [1, 63]$).

It might be easier to identify the second operand because the correlation coefficient is calculated over more samples. However, the implementation unwinds the loop containing comp$[i, j]$. The instructions of each comp$[i, j]$ locate at different memory address. The program counter is not identical when executing each comp$[i, j]$ and will greatly influence the correlation coefficient between the power consumption power$[i, j]$ and HWAddr(b_j) or HWAddr(b'_j).

Figure 5 is the experimental result of the first 12 multiplications. The upper part is the correlation coefficient with HWAddr(b_j), and the bottom is with HWAddr(b'_j). Comparing to the result of the analysis to the first operand, the 12 correlation coefficient traces are less dispersive because they are calculated over more samples, but the program counter greatly influences the correlation coefficient. The difference at $t = 5 \sim 7$ corresponds to the instruction "LD r0, X+" in line 05 of Fig. 3 and shows that the 2nd, 5th, 7th and 11th multiplications are MontMul(A, B') and the other 8 multiplications are MontMul(A, B).

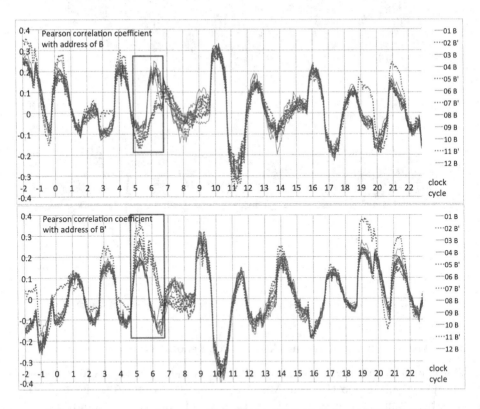

Fig. 5. Pearson correlation coefficient with HWAddr(b_j) and HWAddr(b'_j).

3.3 Analysis Targeting the Address Storing the Result

Storing operands to memory also reveals the address. Similar to the method identifying the second operand, the address storing the result can be identified by calculating the correlation coefficient between $power[i, j]$ and the address, i.e., $HWAddr(c_{j-1})$ or $HWAddr(c'_{j-1})$. The result is provided in Fig. 6, where the first 6 multiplications store the result to C and the others store to C'. The difference at $t_1 = 0 \sim 2$ corresponds to the instruction "LDD r0, Z+1" in line 01 of Fig. 3, and the difference at $t_2 = 19 \sim 21$ corresponds to the storing instruction "ST Z+, r16" in line 15 of Fig. 3.

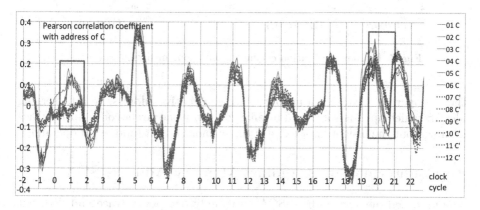

Fig. 6. Pearson correlation coefficient with $HWAddr(c_j)$.

3.4 Analysis Without the Knowledge of Address

The first three analyses and experiments show that if an attacker knows the address of operands, the inputs and result of a Montgomery multiplication C = MontMul(A, B) can be identified. However, the insider knowledge of memory address is not necessary, but only some partial-insider knowledges, like the length of operands and the iterative structure, are sufficient.

The Pearson correlation coefficient between the Hamming weight of two counting number sequences $HW(i)$ and $HW(i+k)$ is nonzero and depends on the offset k. When targeting the second operand, the attacker can randomly guess a memory address $Addr^*$ and calculate the Pearson correlation coefficient between $power[i, j]$ and $HW(Addr^* + j)$. Because of $Addr(b_j) = Addr(b_0) + j$, the result will depend on the offset $Addr(b_0) - Addr^*$.

Figure 7 is the experimental result of calculating the Pearson correlation coefficient between $power[i, j]$ and four incorrect guessing of $HWAddr(b_j)$. Even with the incorrect address of operand B, there is still significant difference in the correlation coefficient when accessing the second operand.

The experiments in this section show that on a microcontroller the address of memory access causes exploitable side-channel leakage. By exploiting the fact

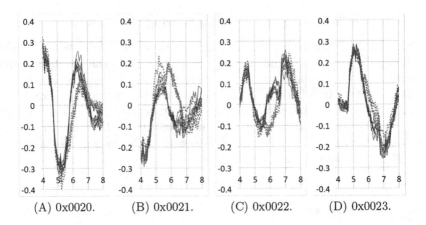

(A) 0x0020.   (B) 0x0021.   (C) 0x0022.   (D) 0x0023.

Fig. 7. Pearson correlation coefficient with four incorrect addresses.

that an operand is stored in memory with consecutive address, an attacker can identify which operands are used by analyzing only one power consumption trace even without the insider knowledge of the memory layout (address of operands).

4   Countermeasures Against Memory Address SCA

The proposed memory-address SCA needs only one power trace and does not need any knowledge of the message (base number). The DPA countermeasure, message blinding, only manipulates the value of the operands and does not change the result of the proposed method. Exponent randomization, e.g., replacing the exponent d by $d' = d + r\varphi$, changes the computational sequence, but the proposed method can recover the exponent d' used in one power trace. Countermeasures against the proposed memory-address SCA should target on address, and three potential countermeasures are proposed.

The proposed memory-address SCA is based on the assumption that the power consumption from the address is accordance with its Hamming weight. As described in [7], the straightforward countermeasure is to store variables in the memory address with the same Hamming weight, e.g., $\texttt{HWAddr}(s_j) = \texttt{HWAddr}(y_j)$ for the algorithm in Fig. 1(B), or with the offset equal to a multiple of a power of 2, e.g., $\texttt{Addr}(s_j) = \texttt{Addr}(y_j) \pm m \times 2^l$. The addresses might still cause slight difference in power consumption, which can be identified by more sophisticated power models, but those models usually need much more samples. Even the proposed method fully exploits the leakage in one power trace, one trace might be insufficient when employing those sophisticated power models against this countermeasure. Combining with countermeasures like exponent randomization to randomize the computational sequence can further prevent the proposed attack analyzing across multiple power traces.

Reducing the number of memory access to sensitive operands is also a countermeasure. A Montgomery multiplication $\texttt{C} = \text{MontMul}(\texttt{A}, \texttt{B})$ needs to load each byte of the first operand A only once but each byte of B multiple times. Assigning a sensitive operand as the first operand, or copying the second operand to a dedicated space prior to the computation instead of directly accessing it in each iteration will reduce the leakage. If where the result C is stored also depends on the exponent, the temporary result should be stored in a dedicated space instead of always stored in C directly. However, copying an operand also causes leakage about the address of the operand. This countermeasure can only reduce but not eliminate the leakage.

The third countermeasure is to randomize the memory address. However, existing methods of randomly switching the operands [8,14] might be insufficient to prevent the proposed memory address SCA. Randomly switching the operands prevents the original address-bit DPA to analyze across multiple power traces, but the proposed method needs only one power trace. The proposed method can target not only the address of memory reading but also writing, i.e., the switching can be identified. Once the operands and the result of all Montgomery multiplications are identified, the exponent can be recovered.

The memory address of an operand should be randomized but not only switched with other operands. An approach is to reserve twice space for each operand, e.g., 128 bytes for a 64-byte or 65-byte operand, and to decide consecutive space randomly within the reserved space each time storing the operand. This can be further improved by self-modifying code. Usually the memory copying is achieved by unwinding the loop as a subroutine containing multiple load and store instructions, e.g., "LD r0, X+" and "ST Y+ r0". The new subroutine for this countermeasure will copy an operand longer than the operands used in Montgomery multiplication. When copying an operand, the entry point of the subroutine will be decided randomly, and the instruction after finishing copying all bytes of the operand will be overwritten as a return instruction. Since the value of the program counter influences a lot when calculating the correlation coefficient, an unfixed program counter will increase the difficulty of identifying the operand especially both the address of the operand and the program counter are random and independent to each other.

5   Conclusions

This paper proposes a new method to perform memory address SCA on computation of exponentiation. Existing address-bit DPA needs multiple power consumption traces. The proposed method fully exploits the leakage from consecutive memory addresses, and only one power trace is enough to recover the private exponent. Existing countermeasures which randomize the computational sequence or randomly switch the operand might be insufficient to prevent the proposed attack.

Countermeasures against the proposed attack are also provided, which can be implemented on general purpose microcontrollers without modifying the hardware circuits. Analyzing the effect of the proposed countermeasures, especially randomizing both program counter and memory address, will be the future work.

Acknowledgments. The author wishes to thank Marc Stöttinger for his kindness to provide many useful discussions. He also likes to thank the anonymous referees for their helpful comments which improve both presentation and technical content.

References

1. Brier, E., Clavier, C., Olivier, F.: Correlation power analysis with a leakage model. In: Joye, M., Quisquater, J.-J. (eds.) CHES 2004. LNCS, vol. 3156, pp. 16–29. Springer, Heidelberg (2004)
2. Koç, Ç.K., Paar, C. (eds.): CHES 1999. LNCS, vol. 1717. Springer, Heidelberg (1999)
3. Clavier, C., Feix, B., Gagnerot, G., Roussellet, M., Verneuil, V.: Horizontal correlation analysis on exponentiation. In: Soriano, M., Qing, S., López, J. (eds.) ICICS 2010. LNCS, vol. 6476, pp. 46–61. Springer, Heidelberg (2010)
4. Coron, J.-S.: Resistance against differential power analysis for elliptic curvecryptosystems. In: Koç, Ç.K., Paar [2], pp. 292–302
5. Hachez, G., Quisquater, J.-J.: Montgomery exponentiation with no final subtractions: improved results. In: Paar, C., Koç, Ç.K. (eds.) CHES 2000. LNCS, vol. 1965, pp. 293–301. Springer, Heidelberg (2000)
6. Heyszl, J., Mangard, S., Heinz, B., Stumpf, F., Sigl, G.: Localized electromagnetic analysis of cryptographic implementations. In: Dunkelman, O. (ed.) CT-RSA 2012. LNCS, vol. 7178, pp. 231–244. Springer, Heidelberg (2012)
7. Itoh, K., Izu, T., Takenaka, M.: Address-bit differential power analysis of cryptographic schemes OK-ECDH and OK-ECDSA. In: Jr. et al. [11], pp. 129–143
8. Itoh, K., Izu, T., Takenaka, M.: A practical countermeasure against address-bit differential power analysis. In: Walter, C.D., Koç, Ç.K., Paar, C. (eds.) CHES 2003. LNCS, vol. 2779, pp. 382–396. Springer, Heidelberg (2003)
9. Izumi, M., Sakiyama, K., Ohta, K.: A new approach for implementing the MPL method toward higher SPA resistance. In: Proceedings of the The Forth International Conference on Availability, Reliability and Security, ARES 2009, March 16–19, 2009, Fukuoka, Japan, pp. 181–186. IEEE Computer Society (2009)
10. Joye, M., Yen, S.-M.Y.: The montgomery powering ladder. In: Jr., et al. [11], pp. 291–302
11. Kaliski Jr., B.S., Koç, Ç.K., Paar, C. (eds.): CHES 2002. LNCS, vol. 2523. Springer, Heidelberg (2003)
12. Kocher, P.C.: Timing attacks on implementations of Diffie-Hellman, RSA, DSS, and other systems. In: Koblitz, N. (ed.) CRYPTO 1996. LNCS, vol. 1109, pp. 104–113. Springer, Heidelberg (1996)
13. Kocher, P.C., Jaffe, J., Jun, B.: Differential power analysis. In: Wiener, M. (ed.) CRYPTO 1999. LNCS, vol. 1666, pp. 388–397. Springer, Heidelberg (1999)
14. Mamiya, H., Miyaji, A., Morimoto, H.: Secure elliptic curve exponentiation against RPA, ZRA, DPA, and SPA. IEICE Trans. 89-A(8), 2207–2215 (2006)
15. Messerges, T.S., Dabbish, E.A.: Investigations of power analysis attacks on smartcards. In: Guthery, S.B., Honeyman, P. (eds.) Proceedings of the 1st Workshop on Smartcard Technology, Smartcard 1999, Chicago, Illinois, USA, 10–11 May. USENIX Association (1999)
16. Montgomery, P.L.: Modular multiplication without trial division. Math. Comput. 44(170), 519–521 (1985)
17. Walter, C.D.: Montgomery's multiplication technique: How to make it smaller andfaster. In: Koç, Ç.K., Paar [2], pp. 80–93

Mutant Differential Fault Analysis of Trivium MDFA

Mohamed Saied Emam Mohamed[(✉)] and Johannes Buchmann

FB Informatik, TU Darmstadt, Hochschulstrasse 10, 64289 Darmstadt, Germany
{mohamed,buchmann}@cdc.informatik.tu-darmstadt.de

Abstract. In this paper we present improvements to the differential fault analysis (DFA) of the stream cipher Trivium proposed in the work of M. Hojsík and B. Rudolf. In particular, we optimize the algebraic representation of obtained DFA information applying the concept of Mutants, which represent low degree equations derived after processing of DFA information. As a result, we are able to minimize the number of fault injections necessary for retrieving the secret key. Therefore, we introduce a new algebraic framework that combines the power of different algebraic techniques for handling additional information received from a physical attack. Using this framework, we are able to recover the secret key by only an one-bit fault injection. In fact, this is the first attack on stream ciphers utilizing minimal amount of DFA information. We study the efficiency of our improved attack by comparing the size of gathered DFA information with previous attacks.

Keywords: Differential fault analysis · Algebraic cryptanalysis · Mutants · MDFA · Trivium · eStream

1 Introduction

Stream ciphers are encryption algorithms that encrypt plaintext digits one at a time. Trivium is a hardware-oriented synchronous stream cipher [5]. It was selected in phase three of the eSTREAM project [17]. Due to its simplicity and speed, it provides strong security services for many hardware applications, such as wireless connections and mobile telecommunication. In order to assess the security of these applications, one can use cryptanalytic methods. Trivium takes an 80-bit key and an 80-bit initial vector IV as inputs in order to generate up to 2^{64} key-stream bits. Trivium operates in two consecutive phases. In the initial phase Trivium iterates 1152 times before it actually starts to produce the key-stream bits of the second phase. The initial iterations are required in order to scramble the original vector to a random inner state.

The concept of differential fault analysis, firstly introduced for stream ciphers in [10], aims at generating additional information about the inner state of the cipher by inspecting and affecting its implementation. The so gathered additional information speeds up the process of key recovery. In this work, we are interested

© Springer International Publishing Switzerland 2015
J. Lee and J. Kim (Eds.): ICISC 2014, LNCS 8949, pp. 433–446, 2015.
DOI: 10.1007/978-3-319-15943-0_26

in DFA attacks on the stream cipher Trivium. As for other side-channel attacks, DFA consists of two stages, the online and the offline phase. In the online phase one induces a physical corruption to the cipher by injecting a fault to a random position in the internal state of the cipher. For instance, this is achieved using the technique proposed in [10]. An attacker needs to reset the cipher several times with the same secret information in order to inject more faults. As a consequence, with increasing number of injections one produces more information about the internal state that helps to recover the secret input.

The offline phase, however, is the process of analyzing the information gathered from the online phase. This part of the attack has a great impact on the practicability of the whole attack. To be more precise, the less information an attacker requires from the online part, the less assumptions we impose on the capabilities of the attacker and hence the success of the attack. So, the challenge here is to minimize the number of fault injection rounds.

Previous attacks aim at reducing the number of fault injections needed to find the secret key. The first DFA attack on Trivium was developed by M. Hojsík and B. Rudolf in [12]. The basic idea of this attack is to inject multiple one-bit faults into the inner state of Trivium. In this case, an attacker can generate, in addition to the system of equations that represent the inner state and key-stream bits, some lower degree equations deduced from the information obtained from the online phase. Classical linear algebra tools are used for the analysis of the information produced in the online part. Following this approach, the secret key can be recovered after approximately 43 fault injection rounds. In order to decrease the required fault injections, the authors introduced an improved DFA attack in [11]. This improvement is based on using the so-called floating representation of Trivium instead of the classical one. Applying this method, one needs approximately 3.2 fault injections on average and 800 proper and faulty key-stream bits to recover the inner state of Trivium at a certain time t, which subsequently allows to compute the secret key of the cipher.

Afterwards, in [13] an improvement to the Hojsík and Rudolf attack was presented using SAT-solver techniques instead of classical linear algebra. The idea of this approach consists in translating the additional DFA information together with the algebraic representation of Trivium into the satisfiability problem and then using a SAT technique to solve the underlying problem. This improvement enables the attacker to recover the secret key using two fault injections at a success rate of 100 %. In fact, this is the first attack combining differential fault analysis with an advanced algebraic technique.

In order to minimize the number of required fault injections, the mentioned attacks face the following problem: under the assumption that an attacker has a large number of key-stream bits before and after inserting faults, he is capable of using only a limited amount of this information. This is due to the fact that the degree of the additionally generated polynomial equations increases rapidly with increasing number of key-stream rounds. But the high degree equations built during the online phase are useless for an attack. As a consequence, this forces the adversary to carry out multiple fault injections. The challenge is, therefore, to derive more information (low degree equations) after each injection round and thus minimizing the number of required fault injections.

1.1 Our Contribution

After a careful analysis of the system of equations generated during the attack and the corresponding DFA information, we propose an improvement to the above two attacks. As a result, we present a more practical algebraic differential fault attack called Mutant DFA (MDFA). Specifically, instead of addressing the gathered DFA information with just one particular algebraic technique as suggested in [11,13], we combine several algebraic techniques. In this way we benefit from the advantages of each individual technique. Further, after studying the structure of the corresponding system of equations, we take advantage of Mutants to enrich the collected data after one injection. More specifically, we reduce the amount of DFA information required to solve the corresponding system of equations by enhancing the role of linear Mutants during the system generation stage. As a consequence, we efficiently derive new useful relations that were hidden. In addition to this, we even deduce more information about the system when using advanced algebraic techniques. For instance, we used an adapted version of MutantXL [7], a Gröbner basis technique, for exploring the polynomial ideal generated by the system of equations. This preprocessing step simplifies the corresponding satisfiability problem which subsequently speeds up SAT solver algorithms. Finally, we present a guessing strategy that deals with the high degree equations appearing during the attack in order to produce further Mutants. These improvements enable us to successfully find the key by injecting only a single bit fault into the inner state. Table 1 compares our results with other previous attacks on the selected eStream ciphers [17].

Table 1. Comparison of different attacks w.r.t required number of fault injections

Cipher	Attack	Key size	# Fault injections
MICKEY	DFA [1]	128	$2^{16.7}$
Grain	DFA [2]	80	$2^{8.5}$
Trivium	DFA [11]	80	3.2
Trivium	MDFA	80	1

1.2 Organization

This paper is organized as follows. In Sect. 2, we provide the relevant background of our attack. In Sect. 3, we explain how to generate the polynomial equation system that represents both the inner state of Trivium and the gathered DFA information. A detailed description of the attack and our improved differential fault analysis (MDFA) of Trivium is given in Sect. 4. Our experimental results are presented in Sect. 5. Finally, Sect. 6 concludes this paper.

2   Preliminaries

2.1   Algebraic Cryptanalysis

The discipline of algebraic cryptanalysis uses a range of algebraic tools and techniques to assess the security of cryptosystems, which are essential for trusted communications over open networks. Algebraic cryptanalysis is a young and largely heuristic discipline, and the exact complexity of algebraic attacks is often hard to measure. However, it has proven to be a remarkably successful practical method of attacking cryptosystems, both symmetric and asymmetric, and provides a strong measure for the overall security of a scheme.

The first step in algebraic cryptanalysis is to model a given cipher as a system of polynomial equations. The challenge is then to find a solution to the system, which corresponds to secret information used in the cipher (e.g. plaintext or secret key). In general, finding a solution to a set of polynomial equations is NP-hard. But equations generated by a cipher (from e.g. plaintext/ciphertext pairs) often have structural properties which may be exploited to find a solution significantly faster than a brute force search for the key.

There are many approaches in use today for algebraic cryptanalysis, such as linearization, Gröbner basis, and SAT-solver approaches. These approaches have many tunable parameters. Choosing the right technique and choosing the right parameters has a big impact on the attack performance, the running time and the memory consumption. Each of these techniques has the advantage on the others for certain cases. For example, when the system has many linear connections among large number of terms, a linearization technique performs better than others. One also observes, that Gröbner basis techniques operate more efficiently when the systems are dense or tend to have many solutions. Although having been used for several algebraic attacks, Gröbner basis algorithms yield a large number of new polynomials or, equivalently, huge matrices. This requires long computing time and large memory resources rendering these approaches inapplicable for real-world problems. However, Gröbner bases provide an implicit representation of all possible solutions instead of just a single (random) one. This perfectly complements solvers for the satisfiability problem that we present next.

In [7], Ding et al. present the so-called MutantXL algorithm (a Gröbner basis algorithm) which came with the concept of Mutants, certain low degree polynomials appearing during the matrix enlargement step of the XL algorithm. In this paper we utilize this concept in order to derive new low degree equations in the offline phase of the DFA attack as we will explain later. Involving this particular algorithm also helps to understand the structure of the system of equations.

In the last decade solving the satisfiability problem of Boolean logic (SAT) was heavily researched and SAT-solvers became one of the main approaches of algebraic cryptanalysis. In our setting a system of equations is translated into a set of clauses constituting an equivalent SAT instance, which is then given to a SAT solver (e.g. Mini-SAT2 [15]). Converting a SAT solution into a root of the corresponding algebraic problem is usually straightforward. A SAT problem is to decide whether a given logical formula is satisfiable, i.e. whether we can assign Boolean values to its variables such that the formula holds. A variant is to prove that such an assignment does not exist. We may assume that the formula is in conjunctive normal form (CNF): The formula consists of a set of clauses. Each clause consists of a set of literals that are connected by disjunctions and each literal is either a variable or a negated variable. Moreover, all clauses are assumed to be related by conjunctions. SAT solvers are usually based on the DPLL algorithm. This algorithm uses depth-first backtracking in order to search the space of all possible assignments of the decision variables. Advanced SAT solvers operate with various heuristics allowing for an improved search quality. For instance, they learn new clauses (conflict clauses) from wrong variable assignments in order to guide the further search. Courtois et al. [6] employed the SAT solver MiniSAT2 in conjunction with the slide attack to break 160 rounds of the block cipher Keeloq.

Recently there have been several works combining algebraic attacks with other methods of cryptanalysis. For example, [16] shows how to combine algebraic attack with side-channel attacks, and in [9] DES was attacked by combining algebraic cryptanalysis with differential attacks. In this paper we present a new framework, which integrates the power of several algebraic techniques to optimize differential fault analysis of the Trivium stream cipher. The key idea underlying our proposal, when handling DFA information, is to exploit the advantages of multiple algebraic techniques in order to extract more useful equations such that a solution to the secret key is efficiently obtained with less assumptions imposed on an attacker.

2.2   Differential Fault Analysis (DFA)

Differential fault analysis can be considered as a type of implementation attacks. The DFA attack is divided into two phases, the online and the offline phases. During the online phase of DFA an attacker investigates stream or block ciphers by the ability to insert faults to random places of the inner state of a cipher. There are different types of DFA, in this work we are interested in DFA attacks associated to the scenario, where the attacker is assumed to be capable of injecting a fault to the inner state of a cipher. This requires to permit the attacker to reset the cipher to its initial state using the same key and initial vector. Knowing the plaintext and both the correct and the faulty ciphertext generated after the fault injection, the attacker can deduce new relations that help at solving the underlying problem. In previous attack scenarios, the attacker is allowed to repeat the previous steps several times in order to succeed. Our attack, however, restricts the attacker to inject at most one fault and hence requires less assumptions as compared to previous proposals. The fault position can be determined following the approach provided in [11].

The offline phase, on the other hand, is the process of analysing the information gathered from the online phase. This part of the attack has a great impact on the practicability of the whole attack. More specifically, minimizing the amount of required DFA information entails a more practical attack. As a result, the challenge here is to minimize the number of fault injections.

2.3 Notation

Let $X := \{x_1, \ldots, x_n\}$ be a set of variables and

$$R = \mathbb{F}_2[x_1, \ldots, x_n]/\langle x_1^2 - x_1, \ldots, x_n^2 - x_n\rangle$$

be the Boolean polynomial ring in X with the terms of R ordered by a certain polynomial ordering. We represent an element of R by its minimal representative polynomial over $\mathbb{F}_2$, where the degree of each term w.r.t any variable is 0 or 1. Let p be a polynomial and T be a set of polynomials in R. We define the head term of $p \in R$, denoted by $\mathrm{HT}(p)$, as the largest term in p according to the order defined on R and the degree of p, denoted by $\deg(p)$, as the degree of $\mathrm{HT}(p)$. A row echelon form $\mathrm{RE}(T)$ is simply a basis for $\mathrm{span}(T)$ with pairwise distinct head terms (see [14] for definition). We define $\mathrm{V}(p)$ and $\mathrm{V}(T)$ as the set of all variables in p and T, respectively.

We define the ideal $I(T)$ of T as the set of all polynomials in R generated by T. A polynomial p in the ideal $I(T)$ is called Mutant if p is a low degree polynomial obtained from the reduction of higher degree ones in I(T). For example, let $p = f + g$ and $\deg(f) = \deg(g) = d$; p is Mutant if $\deg(p) < d$. In this paper, we restrict ourselves with Mutants which have degree ≤ 2.

Finally, we define the difference between two sets S_1 and S_2, denoted by $\mathrm{diff}(S1, S2)$, as the number of elements that exist in S_1 and do not exist in S_2.

3 Algebraic Representation

In this section, we revisit the algebraic description of both Trivium and DFA information introduced in [11]. First, we start with the algebraic representation of the Trivium stream cipher. Trivium builds a huge number of key-stream bits using an 80-bit secret key K and an 80-bit initial vector IV. It consists of three quadratic feedback shift registers X, Y, Z with lengths 93, 84, 111 respectively. These registers represent the 288-bits inner state of Trivium. The initial inner state of Trivium at time $t = 0$ is filled with K and IV as shown in Fig. 1. At time t_0 Trivium starts to produce key-stream bits.

In this paper we use the floating representation of Trivium according to [11]. Following this, the three shift registers X, Y, and Z are updated for $t \geq 1$ as follows:

$$x_j \leftarrow x_{j+1} \cdots \cdots \cdots x_{j+92} \leftarrow x_{j+93} = x_{j+68} + z_{j+65} + z_{j+110} + z_{j+109} \cdot z_{j+108} \quad (1.1)$$

$$y_j \leftarrow y_{j+1} \cdots \cdots \cdots y_{j+83} \leftarrow y_{j+84} = y_{j+77} + x_{j+65} + x_{j+92} + x_{j+90} \cdot x_{j+91} \quad (1.2)$$

$$z_j \leftarrow z_{j+1} \cdots \cdots \cdots z_{j+110} \leftarrow z_{j+111} = z_{j+86} + y_{j+68} + y_{j+83} + y_{j+81} \cdot y_{j+82} \quad (1.3)$$

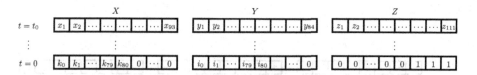

Fig. 1. Internal state of Trivium.

The output key-stream sequence o_j produced by Trivium is generated as follows

$$o_j = x_{j+65} + x_{j+92} + y_{j+68} + y_{j+83} + z_{j+65} + z_{j+110}, \quad j \geq 1. \tag{2}$$

Therefore, let t_0 denote the starting point as explained before. Further, denote by n the number of key-stream bits and let the inner state be represented as depicted in Fig. 1. By using the floating representation from (1.1)–(1.3) and (2), Algorithm 1 describes the procedure of generating a system of $4n$ polynomial equations (n linear and $3n$ quadratic). Solving this system requires to find the inner state of Trivium at time $t \geq t_0$ and then by clocking Trivium backwards, we get the secret key k. The best known algebraic attack on a scaled version of Trivium (called Bivium) was developed by Eibach et al. in [8] using SAT solvers and up to date there is no known algebraic attack better than the brute force on Trivium.

Algorithm 1. $T(o = (o_1, \ldots, o_n))$

$Sys \leftarrow \emptyset$
for $j = 1$ to n **do**
  $Sys \leftarrow Sys \cup x_{j+93} + x_{j+68} + z_{j+65} + z_{j+110} + z_{j+109} \cdot z_{j+108} = 0$
  $Sys \leftarrow Sys \cup y_{j+84} + y_{j+77} + x_{j+65} + x_{j+92} + x_{j+90} \cdot x_{j+91} = 0$
  $Sys \leftarrow Sys \cup z_{j+111} + z_{j+86} + y_{j+68} + y_{j+83} + y_{j+81} \cdot y_{j+82} = 0$
  $Sys \leftarrow Sys \cup o_j + x_{j+65} + x_{j+92} + y_{j+68} + y_{j+83} + z_{j+65} + z_{j+110} = 0$
end for
return Sys

As explained above, we assume that an attacker obtains from the online phase after inserting m fault injections the following DFA information:

- The sequence $(o_j)_{j=1}^n$ of the correct key-stream bits.
- The set of sequences $\{(o_j^k)_{j=1}^n\}_{k=1}^m$ of the faulty key-stream bits for each fault injection $k \in \{1, \ldots, m\}$.
- The set $\{l_k\}_{k=1}^m$ corresponds to the indices of the k fault injections carried out on the inner state of Trivium at time t_0.

The second step of the attack is the process of analyzing the gathered information. Intuitively, one has to carry out as many fault injections as required linear equations that are sufficient to recover all bit values of an inner state at time $t \geq t_0$. As in [11], we study the difference between the correct and the faulty

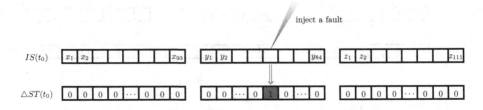

Fig. 2. Fault injection to the internal state of Trivium.

inner state at t_0 in order to generate a sequence of additional equations that we add to the algebraic representation of Trivium. In this case, the system of equations is enlarged without increasing the number of unknowns. In the beginning, the bit values of the inner state differences have zeros everywhere, except at the position of injection it has one. Figure 2 illustrates a potential attack, where the injection occurred at a random position of the second register Y.

As already explained above, each one-bit fault injection provides a sequence of faulty key-stream bits. Under the assumption that an attacker has also the proper sequence, he uses this information to build the sequence $(\Delta o_j)_{j=1}^n$ of key-stream bit differences. Using Eq. (2), we have for $j \geq 1$

$$\Delta o_j = \Delta x_{j+65} + \Delta x_{j+92} + \Delta y_{j+68} + \Delta y_{j+83} + \Delta z_{j+65} + \Delta z_{j+110}. \qquad (3)$$

Moreover, Eqs. (1.1)–(1.3) are used to deduce the sequences of equations $(\Delta x_j)_{j=94}^{n+93}$, $(\Delta y_j)_{j=85}^{n+84}$, and $(\Delta z_j)_{j=112}^{n+111}$ of inner state differences as in (4.1)–(4.3).

$$\Delta x_{j+93} = \Delta x_{j+68} + \Delta z_{j+65} + \Delta z_{j+110} + \Delta(z_{j+109} \cdot z_{j+108}) \qquad (4.1)$$
$$\Delta y_{j+84} = \Delta y_{j+77} + \Delta x_{j+65} + \Delta x_{j+92} + \Delta(x_{j+90} \cdot x_{j+91}) \qquad (4.2)$$
$$\Delta z_{j+111} = \Delta z_{j+86} + \Delta y_{j+68} + \Delta y_{j+83} + \Delta(y_{j+81} \cdot y_{j+82}) \qquad (4.3)$$

4   Generating Mutants

Now we are going to explain our improvements that aim at maximizing the amount of Mutants during the process of generating DFA equations. In previous attacks only the free Mutants obtained from DFA information and the deduced univariate equations were used to simplify the high degree equations. However, our approach also includes all new derived linear Mutants in order to provide more simplifications. This helps us to reduce the degrees of evaluated equations. Indeed, this helps to delay the appearance of high degree relations and enables us to generate further new Mutants.

To be more precise, our generator gets the set of equations T that establishes relations of the inner state and key-stream bits as depicted in (1.1)–(1.3) and (2). Furthermore, the generator is fed with a set of n key-stream bit differences $\{\Delta o_j\}_{j=1}^n$, which we use to build additional relations. As indicated in (3),

Table 2. Compare the size of generated linear mutants and total system

Generator	m	#Linears	# mutants
-	0	800	0
H-R [11]	1	992	192
Attack in [13]	1	994	194
our	1	1130	330

the polynomials represented by the sequence (Δo_j) are linear w.r.t the three inner state bit difference sequences (Δx_j), (Δy_j), and (Δz_j). These sequences as provided in (4.1)–(4.3) have a great impact on the procedure of generating new relations, since the degrees of the constructed polynomial equations rapidly increase. For example, assuming the last term of Eq. (4.1) $\Delta(z_{j+109} \cdot z_{j+108})$, it is algebraically equivalent to the two quadratic terms $(z_{j+109} \cdot \Delta z_{j+108}) + (\Delta z_{j+109} \cdot z_{j+108})$. Hence, when any of Δz_{j+108} or Δz_{j+109} equals to one, then z_{j+109} or z_{j+108} starts to appear, respectively. By time the degrees of such terms grow into the process of the system generator. Therefore, we give the expansion of these three chains more attention in order to generate many Mutants.

As shown in Fig. 2, the sequences (Δx_j), (Δy_j), and (Δz_j) start with constants (zeros everywhere and 1 only at the injection position). As j increased, the value "one" spreads to many positions of the three sequences. Afterwords, the variables express the Trivium inner state bit sequences (x_j), (y_j), and (z_j) are started to appear. In the early steps these linear terms transmit to (Δo_j) equations, which in turn leads to generating new linear Mutants. Thereafter, the relations become more complicated as j is incremented. We gathered all new deduced polynomials in M, the set of generated mutants.

In [11], the authors deal with the problem of building high degree relations in M by simplifying all constructed polynomial equations $H = T \cup M$ using any deduced univariate Mutants. Further, they used Gaussian elimination to evaluate the row echelon of H (see the notation in Sect. 2), which provides more univariates. In our approach, we use not only univariate Mutants but also we simplify H using new derived linear Mutants. The EQgenerator procedure constructs such equations as described in Algorithm 2. It takes as inputs m fault injection positions $(l_1, \ldots, l_m)$, the keystream vector Z before any fault injections and m keystream vectors $Z^{(1)}, \ldots, Z^{(m)}$ obtained after each one of the m fault injections, where each keystream vector $Z^{(j)} = (z_1^{(j)}, \cdots, z_n^{(j)})$, $1 \leq j \leq m$.

Table 2 illustrates the impact of giving Mutants a dominant role for building the system of equations. We compare our generator approach with the approaches used in the previous attacks. For this comparison, we assume an attacker has $n = 800$ proper and faulty key-stream bits. We denote the number of faults by m. We report the number of new derived linear equations (Mutants) and the total number of equations in the generated system. Clearly, the first attack generates only 192 mutants and the second one slightly improves it. Our generator produces 330 Mutants, which in turn improves the attack.

Algorithm 2. EQgenerator$(l_1, \ldots, l_m, o, o^{(1)}, \ldots, o^{(m)})$

$Sys \leftarrow \mathrm{T}(Z)$
$x \leftarrow [x_1, \ldots, x_{n+93}]$
$y \leftarrow [y_1, \ldots, y_{n+84}]$
$z \leftarrow [z_1, \ldots, z_{n+111}]$
$S \leftarrow \emptyset$
for $j = 1$ to m **do**
    $\Delta x \leftarrow [0, \ldots, 0]$ // length$(\Delta x) = n + 93$
    $\Delta y \leftarrow [0, \ldots, 0]$ // length$(\Delta y) = n + 84$
    $\Delta z \leftarrow [0, \ldots, 0]$ // length$(\Delta z) = n + 111$
    InjectFault$(\Delta x, \Delta y, \Delta z, l_j)$
    // Insert a one-bit fault to one of $\Delta x, \Delta y, \Delta z$ based on the value of l_j
    for $i = 1$ to n **do**
        $S_1 \leftarrow \emptyset$
        $dz \leftarrow o_i + o_i^{(j)}$
        $Sys \leftarrow \Delta x[i] + \Delta x[i + 27] + \Delta y[i] + \Delta y[i + 15] + \Delta z[i] + \Delta z[i + 45] + dz$ // (3)
        $\Delta x[i + 93] \leftarrow$ right hand side of (4.1)
        $\Delta y[i + 84] \leftarrow$ right hand side of (4.2)
        $\Delta z[i + 111] \leftarrow$ right hand side of (4.3)
        repeat
            $S_2 \leftarrow \emptyset$
            $S_2 \leftarrow$ ExtractMutant(Sys)
            $Sys \leftarrow$ Substitute(Sys, S_2)
            $S_1 \leftarrow S_1 \cup S_2$
        until $S_2 = \emptyset$
        $\Delta x, \Delta y, \Delta z, x, y, z \leftarrow$ Substitute$(\Delta x, \Delta y, \Delta z, x, y, z, S_1)$
        $S \leftarrow S \cup S_1$
    end for
end for
return $Sys \cup S$

In addition to that, we used a modified version of the MutantXL algorithm, in order to perform an intelligent exploration of the ideal generated by the set of equations H, where H is the set resulting from the process described above. This allows us to construct further additional Mutants. Specifically, we partition the set of equations H into subsets H_i, $i \in \{0, \ldots, 6\}$ based on the distance from the set of Mutants M. In this case, $H_i = \{p \in H \mid \mathrm{diff}(\mathrm{V}(p), \mathrm{V}(M)) = i\}$, see the notation in Sect. 2. In other words, H_0 is the set of all polynomials in H that relate only variables occurring in M, $\mathrm{V}(M)$. Thereby, H_1 is the set of all polynomials in H such that only one variable does not appeared in M, and so on. Our smart MutantXL aims to enlarge each subset H_i using elements from H_{i+1}. Without loss of generality, consider the subset H_1. Let p be a polynomial in H_1 and the variable v in $\mathrm{V}(p)$ is the different variable from $\mathrm{V}(M)$, i.e. $v \notin \mathrm{V}(M)$. If p is linear, then we use it to eliminate the variable v from the whole system. In case of p is quadratic, based on the structure of Trivium equations as in (1.1)–(1.3), only the head term $\mathrm{HT}(p)$ is quadratic and the remaining terms are linear. Let v

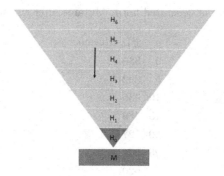

Fig. 3. Reducing polynomials from H_i to H_{i-1}, in order to derive additional mutants.

occur in HT(p) and HT(p) = $u \cdot v$ where $u \in$ V(M). If v does not appeared in the linear part of p, then we eliminate it by replacing p with $f = p + u \cdot p$. However, if v occurs in both linear and quadratic parts then we replace p with $f = u \cdot p$. Then p is transmitted from H_1 to H_0. Consequently, after performing the previous reduction procedure, all such polynomials are included in H_0. We perform the same reduction procedure on each subset H_i. Moreover, we use a linear algebra technique, namely Gaussian elimination, in order to derive more mutants. We repeat this procedure until we gathered all possible mutants. Finally, we include all new Mutants to M. Figure 3 illustrates the previous procedure.

In order to find the secret information of Trivium, we need to recover sequential 288 inner state bits $(x_j, \ldots, x_{j+92})$, $(y_j, \ldots, y_{j+83})$, and $(z_j, \ldots, z_{j+110})$ at certain $0 < j < N$ using only one-bit fault injection. The above procedure improved the algebraic representation of the system derived from the attack, however as we will show in the next section, we still have to gather more information to be able to solve the system. To be more precise, we need to derive a sufficient number of Mutants from the high degree relations in order to solve the system. It may be argued that the only way to do this is to guess some variables. The challenge here is to generate the required additional Mutants with fewer variables to guess.

We present the following smart guessing strategy for achieving the goal that has been mentioned. As we explained earlier, we are able to gather more mutants from the sequences described the inner state and key-stream bit differences as in (4.1)–(4.3) and (3). We noticed from the constructed chains (Δx_j), (Δy_j), and (Δz_j) for $0 \leq j \leq n$ that, each unsolved variable v constructed in these chains builds a tree for its relations with the consecutive constructed equations. The first level of this tree contains all linear relations with v, the second level all quadratic relations and so on. In order to deduce more hidden relations from those sequences, we select for our guessing approach some of these variables which have the biggest trees. In other words, we chose to guess the most frequent variables in the Δ chains. Table 3 explains the additional Mutants produced after guessing g variables.

Table 3. The size of generated linear Mutants after guessing g variables

g	#L. Mutants
0	330
5	392
10	436
15	489
20	527
25	576
30	620
35	649

5   Experimental Results

In this section, we present our experimental results which establish the performance of our improved DFA attack. Since we used SAT tools to solve the system obtained from the attack as explained in the previous section, we need to build CNF instances corresponding to our optimized algebraic systems of polynomial equations. We consider this as the final step of our attack. Since our system is represented by the algebraic normal form ANF, we used the ANF to CNF converter implemented in SAGE, a mathematical open source tool [18]. It uses two different techniques for converting ANF to CNF. The first one is based on looking at a form of a polynomial itself [3]: representing each monomial in CNF and then representing sums of monomials (polynomials) in CNF. The latter is a bottleneck for SAT, since XOR chains need exponentially large representation in CNF. To overcome this issue, one "cuts" a sum (a XOR chain) into several ones by introducing new variables; each sum is now of moderate size. One then represents each sum separately. This method performs better when the system is slightly dense, we call it the dense technique. The second method is based on considering the truth (value) table of a Boolean polynomial seen as a function (PolyBoRi's CNF converter [4]). We call it the sparse technique. We use a combination of the two methods based on the value of a sparsity parameter called sp. So, for example, if we set $sp = 3$, then each polynomial p in the system with $|V(p)| \leq 3$ will be translated to clauses using the sparse technique. Otherwise, the converters use the dense technique. As a result from the previous algebraic procedure, we optimize the representation of the satisfiabilty problem.

We used our C++ implementation to generate the optimized system of equations and the additional set of Mutants resulting from the input DFA information gathered in the online phase of the attack. Further, we use again SAGE and its Boolean polynomial ring to develop the smart version of MutantXL that we used in the attack. Finally, we use the SAT solver Minisat2 [15] to solve the system. The result is obtained as an average over 100 runs under a time limit 3600 s (one hour). We run all the experiments on a Sun X4440 server, with four "Quad-Core AMD Opteron™ Processor 8356" CPUs and 128 GB of RAM. Each CPU is running at 2.3 GHz.

Table 4. Results of our attack using only a one-bit fault injection

g	Time t (s)	Attack complexity C (s)
22	9248.13	$\sim 2^{35.17}$
23	4224.57	$\sim 2^{35.04}$
24	939.40	$\sim 2^{33.87}$
25	108.76	$\sim 2^{31.76}$
26	76.38	$\sim 2^{32.26}$
27	56.64	$\sim 2^{32.82}$
28	42.37	$\sim 2^{33.40}$
29	36.48	$\sim 2^{34.19}$
30	22.15	$\sim 2^{34.47}$
31	4.21	$\sim 2^{33.07}$
32	2.82	$\sim 2^{33.49}$
33	1.94	$\sim 2^{33.96}$
34	1.32	$\sim 2^{34.39}$
35	1.27	$\sim 2^{35.35}$

Table 4 reports our experiments. The number of guessed variables is denoted by g, the average time (in seconds) of the SAT-solver Minisat2 for solving one instance is denoted by t, and finally C is the total time complexity in seconds. In this scenario, we select g variables of the inner state sequences as explained in the previous section. We studied both the correct and the wrong guessing cases and took the average time. We found that at least 22 variables are needed to guess in order to solve the constructed system and guessing 25 bits gives us the lowest time complexity as explained in Table 4. Consequently, in order to recover the secret key of Trivium we require in (on average) about $2^{31.76}$ s using only one core. Since our generator can be used in parallel by dividing the 2^{25} possible cases on N cores and assuming we have a super computer with more than 1000 cores, then one can use our attack and recover the secret information in approximately 42 days.

6 Conclusion

In this paper, we presented an improvement of a differential fault attack (DFA) on the stream cipher Trivium. The main idea of the paper is to combine several algebraic tools to reveal the secret key by injecting only one single fault. First, we enhanced the role of linear Mutants (lower degree relations) during the step of processing the gathered DFA information. Secondly, we modified MutantXL in such a way that it generates additional sparse relations which in turn improves the CNF representation of the constructed system and speeds up the SAT-solver process. Finally, we presented a guessing strategy that deals with high degree relations appearing during the attack. Our attack methodology can be considered as a template for attacking other stream ciphers, such as MICKEY and Grain.

References

1. Banik, S., Maitra, S.: A differential fault attack on MICKEY 2.0. In: Bertoni, G., Coron, J.-S. (eds.) CHES 2013. LNCS, vol. 8086, pp. 215–232. Springer, Heidelberg (2013)
2. Banik, S., Maitra, S., Sarkar, S.: A differential fault attack on grain-128a using macs. IACR Cryptology ePrint Archive, 2012:349 (2012). informal publication
3. Bard, G.: Algebraic Cryptanalysis. Springer, New York (2009)
4. Brickenstein, M., Dreyer, A.: Polybori: A framework for Gröbner-basis computations with boolean polynomials. J. Symbolic Comput. **44**(9), 1326–1345 (2009)
5. Canniere, C.D., Preneel, B.: Trivium specifications. eSTREAM, ECRYPT Stream Cipher Project (2006)
6. Courtois, N.T., Bard, G.V., Wagner, D.: Algebraic and slide attacks on keeloq. In: Nyberg, K. (ed.) FSE 2008. LNCS, vol. 5086, pp. 97–115. Springer, Heidelberg (2008)
7. Ding, J., Buchmann, J., Mohamed, M.S.E., Moahmed, W.S.A., Weinmann, W.S.A.: MutantXL. In: Proceedings of the 1st international conference on Symbolic Computation and Cryptography (SCC 2008), Beijing, China, pp. 16–22, April 2008. LMIB
8. Eibach, T., Pilz, E., Völkel, G.: Attacking bivium using SAT solvers. In: Kleine Büning, H., Zhao, X. (eds.) SAT 2008. LNCS, vol. 4996, pp. 63–76. Springer, Heidelberg (2008)
9. Faugère, J.-C., Perret, L., Spaenlehauer, P.-J.: Algebraic-differential cryptanalysis of DES. In: Western European Workshop on Research in Cryptology - WEWoRC 2009, pp. 1–5 (2009)
10. Hoch, J.J., Shamir, A.: Fault analysis of stream ciphers. In: Joye, M., Quisquater, J.-J. (eds.) CHES 2004. LNCS, vol. 3156, pp. 240–253. Springer, Heidelberg (2004)
11. Hojsík, M., Rudolf, B.: Floating fault analysis of Trivium. In: Chowdhury, D.R., Rijmen, V., Das, A. (eds.) INDOCRYPT 2008. LNCS, vol. 5365, pp. 239–250. Springer, Heidelberg (2008)
12. Hojsík, M., Rudolf, B.: Differential fault analysis of Trivium. In: Nyberg, K. (ed.) FSE 2008. LNCS, vol. 5086, pp. 158–172. Springer, Heidelberg (2008)
13. Mohamed, M.S.E., Bulygin, S., Buchmann, J.: Using SAT solving to improve differential fault analysis of Trivium. In: Kim, T., Adeli, H., Robles, R.J., Balitanas, M. (eds.) ISA 2011. CCIS, vol. 200, pp. 62–71. Springer, Heidelberg (2011)
14. Mohamed, M.S.E., Cabarcas, D., Ding, J., Buchmann, J., Bulygin, S.: MXL₃: An efficient algorithm for computing Gröbner bases of zero-dimensional ideals. In: Lee, D., Hong, S. (eds.) ICISC 2009. LNCS, vol. 5984, pp. 87–100. Springer, Heidelberg (2010)
15. Niklas Een, N.S.: MinSat 2.0 - one of the best known SAT solvers (2008). http://minisat.se/MiniSat.html
16. Renauld, M., Standaert, F.-X.: Algebraic side-channel attacks. In: Bao, F., Yung, M., Lin, D., Jing, J. (eds.) Inscrypt 2009. LNCS, vol. 6151, pp. 393–410. Springer, Heidelberg (2010)
17. Robshaw, M.: The eSTREAM project. In: Robshaw, M., Billet, O. (eds.) New Stream Cipher Designs. LNCS, vol. 4986, pp. 1–6. Springer, Heidelberg (2008)
18. Stein, W., et al.: Sage Mathematics Software (Version x.y.z). The Sage Development Team, YYYY. http://www.sagemath.org

Author Index

Printed in the United States
By Bookmasters